Hometown Memories . . .

Penny Candy
and
Grandma's Porch Swing

Tales from the Good Old Days
in North Central Pennsylvania

A TREASURY OF 20TH CENTURY MEMORIES

Hometown Memories . . .

Penny Candy
and
Grandma's Porch Swing
Tales from the Good Old Days
in North Central Pennsylvania

A TREASURY OF 20TH CENTURY MEMORIES
Compiled and edited by Todd Blair and Karen Garvey

HOMETOWN MEMORIES, LLC
Hickory, North Carolina

Penny Candy and Grandma's Porch Swing

Publisher: Todd Blair
Lead Editor: Karen Garvey
Design and Graphic Arts Editor: Karen Garvey
Assistant Editors: Jodi Black, Greg Rutz, Monica Black, Heather Garvey, Megan Hice, Bob Lasley, Brianne Mai, Justin Shelton, and Tiffany Canaday

ISBN 978-0-9829681-6-1
Copyright © 2012

Published by

Hometown Memories, LLC
2359 Highway 70 SE, Suite 350
Hickory, NC 28602
(877) 491-8802

Printed in the United States of America

Acknowledgements

To those Northern Pennsylvania folks (and to those few who "ain't from around here") who took the trouble to write down your memories and mail them in to us, we offer our heartfelt thanks. And we're sure you're grateful to each other, because together, you have created a wonderful book.

To encourage participation, the publisher offered cash awards to the contributors of the most appealing stories. These awards were not based upon writing ability or historical knowledge, but rather upon subject matter and interest. The winners were: Sally Guiswite of Jersey Shore, PA; Mathilda Smith of Lewis Run, PA; Mary Arnold of Renovo, PA; Elizabeth A. Stine of Williamsport, PA; and Jane Kropinak of Punxsutawney, PA. We would also like to give honorable mention to the contributions from Kathy Rickard of Johnsonburg, PA; Ken Ostrum of Emporium, PA; M. Jane Pool of Beech Creek, PA; and George Shearer of Curwensville, PA (you'll find their names and page numbers in the table of contents). It was extremely difficult to choose these winners because every story in this book had its own special appeal.

Associate Editors

Raymond L. Allison
Pauline B. Bell
Ruth Berry
Nancy Brown
Rosanne Conaway
Shirley J. Confer
Peg Coulter
Ralph E. Crouse
Jay B. Decker
Marian Slawson Feness
Freda Foster
Georgeanne Freeburg
Frank H. Freezer
Barbara Long Glover
James Gotshall
Sally A. Guiswite
Carolyn A. Hanna
Darrell D. Harris

Lorrie Crawford Hartman
Leon E. Hillyard
Glenn C. Johnson
Betty Johnston
Floyd G. Jovenitti
Mary Marvin
Ron McGonigal
Lynn H. Ostrander
Ken Ostrum
Verna Paulhamus
M. Jane Pool
Mary Prince
Barbara A. Smith
Martha Snell
Pauline M. Steinbacher
Nancy A. Toles
Harry Wanamaker
Barbara L. Faque Sterling Wood
Dawn R. Zetto

INTRODUCTION

We know that most folks don't bother to read introductions. But we do hope you (at least eventually) get around to reading this one. Here's why:

First, the creation of these books is in its third generation after we took over the responsibilities of Hometown Memories Publishing from its founders, Bob Lasley and Sallie Holt. After forty-nine books, they said goodbye to enjoy retirement, and each other. Bob and Sallie had a passion for saving these wonderful old tales from the good old days that we can only hope to match. We would love to hear your thoughts on how we are doing.

Second—and far more important—is the who, what, where, when, why and how of this book. Until you're aware of these, you won't fully enjoy and appreciate it.

This is a very unusual kind of history book. It was actually written by 332 Pennsylvania old-timers and not-so-old-timers who remember what life was really like back in the earlier years of the 20th century in North Central Pennsylvania. These folks come from all walks of life, and by voluntarily sharing their memories (which often include their emotions, as well), they have captured the spirit and character of a time that will never be seen again.

Unlike most history books, this one was written from the viewpoint of people who actually experienced history. They're familiar with the tribulations of the Great Depression; the horrible taste of castor oil; "outdoor" plumbing; kerosene lamps; and countless other experiences unknown to today's generation.

We advertised all over North Central Pennsylvania to obtain these stories. We sought everyday folks, not experienced authors, and we asked them to simply jot down their memories. Our intention was by no means literary perfection. Most of these folks wrote the way they spoke, and that's exactly what we wanted. To preserve story authenticity, we tried to make only minimal changes to written contributions. We believe that an attempt at correction would damage the book's integrity.

We need to include a few disclaimers: first, many important names are missing in many stories. Several folks revealed the names of their teachers, neighbors, friends, even their pets and livestock, but the identities of parents or other important characters weren't given. Second, many contributors did not identify pictures or make corrections to their first draft copies. We're sure this resulted in many errors (and perhaps lost photographs) but we did the best we could. Third, each contributor accepts full responsibility for his or her submission and for our interpretation of requested changes. Fourth, because some of the submitted photographs were photocopied or "computer printed," their quality may be very poor. And finally, because there was never a charge, "fee," or any other obligation to contributors to have their material included in this book, we do not accept responsibility for any story or other material that was left out, either intentionally or accidentally.

We hope you enjoy this unique book as much as we enjoyed putting it together.

Todd Blair and Karen Garvey
August 2012

TABLE OF CONTENTS

The Table of Contents is listed in alphabetical order by the story contributor's last name.

To search for stories by the contributor's hometown or year of birth, see indexes beginning on page 387.

The Tales...

True stories intentionally left just as the contributor wrote them.

A Baker's Dozen
By June Elaine Woodling Houseknecht of
Muncy Pennsylvania
Born 1926

Audrey Wertman asked me to tell you what it was like growing up with 13 brothers and sisters, so here it goes! Maybe some of you can relate to this.

I have a picture, which was taken, at the Brick Church on mom and dad's 50th wedding anniversary. My dad was John Samuel Woodling and my mother was Edna Pauline Metzger. They married in 1923 and about every two years, another child was born. After nine girls and four boys, our family was complete. Dad used to say we were "a baker's dozen." I will name everyone for you, Wanda, June, Lois, Phyllis, Max, Ruth, Mary, Doris, Jack, Judy, Kenny, Ronnie, and Linda. I am next to the oldest and was born in 1926.

We lived in a railroad house in the country. The Bald Eagle Mountain was on one side of us and the Pennsylvania Railroad was on the other. We had no electricity, no running water in the house, no bathroom, no furnace, and no car. We had a long table that was as long as the kitchen; there was a bench on either side, which held more kids. Mom and dad sat on the ends with the baby in a highchair. We had a big kitchen stove and a Heatrola stove in the living room, the upstairs was not heated. We slept three to a bed by sleeping sideways, this kept us warmer. We had a mountain spring well across the dirt road and we had to carry all our water over to the house. If we had a dry summer, the well would go dry. Mom would put a big milk can and a dipper in our little wagon and we would have to pull it a half-mile up the road to a deeper well then fill it up and pull it back home. We had an outhouse and would use old Spiegel and Sears Roebuck catalogs for paper.

The bread man would bring our groceries along with the bread. The iceman would bring a big cube of ice and put it in our icebox. It melted very quickly in the summer and kept us busy emptying the run-off water. My sister and I would walk to a neighboring farm to get milk several times a week. I always hated these trips because they had a son, Junior Opp, who loved to tease us. Our milk would be in a cooler in the barn and Junior would be doing the milking and when he saw us, he would turn the udder our way and squirt milk all over us. They also had two Great Dane dogs that would come bounding out to meet us, and we were afraid of the dogs.

Mom had to do all the washing on a scrub board and rinse our clothes in a huge tub. It had a wringer on top, which we had to turn by hand. When I got a little older, we got a washer that had a big wheel to agitate the clothes when we would turn it. Before going to school, I would turn it as long as I could because I knew mom would have to

*John Samuel and Edna Pauline Metzger Woodling
and their 13 children*

do the rest of the laundry. The ironing was a big job. In those days everything had to be ironed, even the pillowcases, dad's big red and blue handkerchiefs, and the tea towels. The flat irons got hot on the kitchen stove. We had to use hot pads on the handle and keep changing the irons when they would cool off. If they were too hot, they would scorch the clothes and if they got cold, they wouldn't iron out the wrinkles. All the clothes were hung on the clothesline to dry. In the winter, they would freeze right fast to the lines.

We had to walk to the bus houses, and then ride the school buses to school. Sometimes

13

June and Wanda in 1926

War II and the service men needed the trains, planes, and buses. I went to work the day after I graduated in the office of Montgomery Mills. I made 36-cents an hour but I was able to save some money. I rode to and from work on a passenger train, which cost me 10-cents. When I got off at Montgomery, I would walk to the office. One morning when I got off the train a man grabbed me and was trying to hug and kiss me. I was fighting him off as it was dark and I couldn't see who it was. He had to hurry and get on the train as the conductor had called "All aboard!" and the train had started to move. I learned later that it was my uncle. He had enlisted in the Marines and was reporting for duty.

If we wanted to go on a trip, dad would get us a pass and we would ride for free. As we got older, we would walk to a farm and pick strawberries for a penny a box. A postage stamp cost three cents and a post card was one penny. On Saturday afternoons, we would walk to Muncy to go to the movies for 10-cents. We had a really big garden. Dad would dig and plant in it and us kids would pull the weeds. Mom would can the vegetables for us to eat in the winter.

At one of the alumna banquets they had printed in the paper, "Nine members of the Woodling Family had graduated from Montgomery Clinton High School." This set a record at the time. I'm not sure if it still does.

We had used coal oil lamps. After supper, we would clear the kitchen table off and we would do our homework. Everyone went to bed when our schoolwork was done so mom

they would get stuck in the snow and we would be late for school. We had to go to school at Montgomery even though it would have been closer to go to Muncy. I think it was because of the township.

My dad worked on the Pennsylvania Railroad all his life. Sometimes they would have to go far away and he would live in camp cars. They wouldn't get home for several weeks.

When I was in high school, we moved down to Muncy Railroad Station House. It was a big house with 15 rooms, long ago it was a hotel. When passengers got off the trains, they would stay at the hotel. This was much nicer for our large family. Now we had electricity and running water in the house. When the railroads started selling the houses mom and dad bought the house and put in a bathroom.

I graduated in 1943. We couldn't go on a class trip because it was during World

50th Wedding Anniversary
John Samuel and Edna Pauline Metzger Woodling
and their 13 children

and dad could blow out the lights. They would use flashlights to go upstairs.

I forgot to tell you when I was talking about the war, but us kids belonged to the Brick Church, so when the men and boys were drafted we mowed the church lawn.

We didn't have a phone but there was a railroad phone hanging on the wall. In case of an emergency, we could use the phone to call our neighbors. It had a handle on and we would crank it to ring a long and a short. They didn't have phone numbers at the time.

Wanda was the oldest girl and Max was the oldest boy. They were lucky as they got all the new clothes. When they grew out of their clothes, they were passed down to the younger children. If they were jeans mom would cut them up for patches.

One day our class had the assembly program. My teacher gave me a poem about Columbus Day. It had five verses, which I knew frontwards and backwards. When I went out on the stage, there sat Junior Opp laughing from ear to ear. He played an instrument. I couldn't think of a thing or hear the prompter. I finally thought of the title, Sail On, Sail on, Sail On and On. I said this three times turned and ran behind the curtain.

All in all, we had a happy home life and I wouldn't trade it for all the money in the world

Put Through the Wringer
By Sally A. Guiswite of Jersey Shore, Pennsylvania
Born 1937

As a child, I had a real desire to own my very own wringer washing machine. I was fascinated by this thing, which my mother got to replace the washboard she had used to get our clothes clean.

It was 1942 when I was five years old that we moved to Oakbourne Farms—my mom, dad, two brothers, and me. There was much work to be done, as it was both a large dairy and fruit farm.

My mother helped with both the animals and the fruit, so her time was important. This shiny metal machine was placed in the cellar to save her time with house chores. Each Monday, it was pulled close to the cement

water trough in the big room of the cellar. My mother would fill the tub part with hot water, using a bucket. The proper amount of soap powder was added. Our dirty clothes had already been carried to the cellar in a bushel basket and sorted into piles of all whites, colors, and work clothes. The white clothes were placed in the washer first, the machine was turned on and the swishing sound began.

While those washed, the rinse water was prepared. A square metal washtub was set upon an apple crate so it was beneath the wringer part of the machine. Cold water was bucketed into the tub, followed by something called "bluing." The rinse water turned a beautiful bright blue color. The bluing was meant to whiten the clothes more.

Now the fun began. The wringer was on a swivel, so my mother would position it to face the washtub. The agitator on the washer was stopped and the wringer turned on. She then picked up one piece of clothing at a time and aimed it toward the wringer. The wringer pulled the clothing between a set of rubber rollers, which wrung out most of the soapy water. When all that batch of clothes was in the rinse tub, a second color of clothes was added to the same water in the washing machine.

Now back to the rinse tub. Mom would splash the washed clothes up and down in the rinse tub numerous times. Then, the wringer was swung over to face an empty, cloth lined bushel basket. These whites were once again put through the wringer and ended up in the basket to be carried to the clothesline outside. This tedious process was repeated until all your week's clothing was washed.

One other step was needed when you had clothes that needed to be made stiff so they kept their shape while being worn. Remember the starched collars, aprons, blouses, doilies, curtains, etc.? This meant an extra but smaller bucket filled with warm water and cooked Argo starch. This required another trip through the wringer.

Mom usually got the clothes all washed and hung up before she had to go make a cooked dinner for Dad and any hired help. After that chore was finished, she would go back to the cellar to clean up. I would be allowed to carry the hose connected to the bottom of the washing machine over to the drain. Mom would remove a plug inside the machine and all the water would drain out.

She then would bucket the water from the tubs and place all to dry until next Monday.

As I got older, I realized why certain things were done on a particular day. That was because some jobs took all day.

I was eight when my five-year-old cousin, Patsy, came down with scarlet fever and was quarantined. Someone gave her a doll-sized washing machine to break her boredom. My aunt would give her small amounts of water to use in it. I remember watching my cousin crank the handle on top of that little machine to wash a piece of doll clothing. You could crank the wringer, but the clothes didn't go through it like they should, as it was too little. She loved it anyway, and so did I.

Now I really wanted one of my own, big or little. I didn't get scarlet fever and I never got a doll washing machine, but I did get to use my mother's and later, my own wringer washer.

As a teen, I was allowed to stay overnight with another cousin, Phyllis, who was a few years younger than me. Her mom had a similar machine and the next day was Monday. We were playing outside and came into the back porch while the machine was working. My aunt had to run inside to care for a younger son when my cousin decided to show me she could run her mom's washer. She picked up a piece of clothing to put through the wringer and turned to me in pride when her long hair got near the wringer. WOW! It pulled her hair so quickly that I thought her head would go through as well. I screamed for my aunt who came running. I was sure my cousin would be bald when she was finally freed from that big, bad, "hair raising" machine. We still laugh together about that day.

When I married in 1958, my grandmother gave me her old wringer washer, which was a white Maytag. We took it to Virginia in my husband's convertible. He rolled the top down, loaded the washer, and put the top back up. I enjoyed and appreciated that machine while raising my first three children when we still used cloth diapers.

I now have an automatic and can throw a load in any time while doing other things.

The old washboard and the wringer washer were both good inventions that served us well in their day.

Baby Sister and the Piglet
By Mathilda Jane Smith of Lewis Run, Pennsylvania
Born 1928

I am the youngest of six, born during the Depression. This is my oldest memory.

I was about two-and-a-half. My four-year-old brother came running home to get me. I was the nuisance—the pest—not often included in my siblings' activities. I remember how excited I was that he wanted me along.

We ran through the field to the neighboring farm, where Brother announced, "Well, here she is. You can have her, and give me my pig."

The farmer had newborn piglets and Brother wanted one, and was told if he didn't have money to buy, maybe he had something to trade. I was his trade for the pig.

Many years later, a man knocked at my door and asked if I was Matty who once lived in X town. When I said yes, he replied, "You were almost part of my family. Your brother tried to trade you for a pig."

At this time, we had a general store—old wooden floors and a potbelly stove. In the back was an area with a small last and hammers and supplies—soles and heels—where my dad repaired shoes. In the center was a barber chair where he cut hair for everyone in the area, and most exciting, besides food supplies, was a glass case with candy and cigarettes, accessible from the back. In the floor, right behind this treasure was a trap door to the basement. Because I was the youngest and least likely to receive too much punishment, I was the one selected to push up the door from the basement and secure some treats for the group.

Too many people could not pay their bills and we lost the store and moved to another area where my grandfather owned a small bungalow where we could live rent free. My mother got a job in a silk mill where she worked ten hours a day for twelve dollars a week. She wove silk neckties.

At four years old, I was accepted in a Catholic school. I walked every morning, and every morning the Sisters opened their back door and gave me a wonderful steamy bowl of oatmeal and dried my mittens and boots. I thought I was pretty special.

Biggest Little Town in the World
By Mary Arnold of Renovo, Pennsylvania
Born 1947

I am a "baby boomer." I was born in 1947 to wonderful parents in a very small town, Cross Fork, in Potter County in Pennsylvania. It was called the "Biggest Little Town in the World." This was due to big hunting and fishing seasons, which filled our little town, and many camps that many used for vacation about 9-10 months a year. My parents owned the local grocery store, bar, and five cabins for rent.

I have very fond memories of that time. I attended a one-room schoolhouse with 20-25 others. We learned from one another and were a very close family. We played "kick the can", built houses out of leaves and always participated in many programs put on for our parents. We picked leeks and were taught how to make Leek Soup. We formed just about anything you can imagine out of Plaster of Paris. Some of us walked home for lunch. Our teacher, Mrs. Ruth Jones, lived in the town so our parents always knew if we were in trouble.

Cross Fork School House

In the summer, we all met at the local swimming hole called the Whirlpool. We were there from the time we got up until bedtime. (In the summer, we had no bedtime). There were never any adults around to supervise. We usually packed a lunch. We were not allowed to swim until the "dog days" were over.

Some of the days, we would ride our bikes 8 miles to a park. We would eat our packed lunch, swim and head home. Other days we would walk 2-3 miles carrying our inner tubes and ride down the creek. We were always on the lookout for "mud puppies" or "water dogs "as they were called.

My family lived in our business so we had very little space for living quarters. We had a small "parlor" that was used only for guests. If the preacher came, we gathered in there where the bible was always on a stand. Every Wednesday the local doctor from a

bigger town 18 miles from us and his wife visited. The doctor caught up on his sleep in one of our cabins while his wife visited with Mom. There ended up being five of us kids. We had three very small bedrooms with bunk beds in two of the rooms. Our small black and white TV was in the kitchen and another in the bar for the Friday night fights (boxing). We watched very little TV as my mom had us always playing Scrabble, Go Fish, Chinese Checkers, Checkers, Old Maids, or just drawing. A lot of the local kids joined us every evening as we had a booth that held 6-8 of us in our kitchen. Mom joined in a lot with us if she was not running the "mangle" that ironed all the sheets from our five cabins. Every Friday night after we got our bath, all five of us had to line up for "Castor Oil." We got our bath in the kitchen sink until we were older. On Sunday, my grandparents and Mom and Dad's best friends came for dinner. We had an oak drop leaf table that we ate on every day.

Sometimes, the kids had to sit in the booth if we had too many people. The oak table is still being used today. My dad would gather up as many kids as he could to take to the Saturday night "drive in movie." It was about 1-1/2 hours from our home. We went about three times a year when it wasn't busy. Our big station wagon (with wood on the sides) held as many kids as it could. There were no seat belts. We also traveled this way once a year to Altoona to the Shrine Circus. We thought this was heaven.

In the winter, we all tried to build a fort out of snow that was huge in our driveway. This always made us laugh because our local constable sat in our driveway to catch people speeding. He had to find another spot. We didn't care for this man. In those days, we were taught to drive early. Most of the men worked away from our town so it was important that we all knew how to drive. I remember taking a lady in labor to the hospital 18 miles away when I was about 15. No one said a thing. Because we were sheltered a lot from the big

Mary's mom, grandparents, family friends, and Mary in 1952

cities, we were not exposed to a lot of crime or other negative things. The most trouble I got into was being caught smoking my mom's "Old Gold" cigarettes.

In a way, we had so many more advantages than most. We once had Gabby Hayes stop in our business because his brother had a camp in our area. It didn't take long to spread the word around on our "party line phones." Many of the kids in town came running. We also had Red Skelton come by.

My dad and my uncle called square dances on Saturday nights. Another reason why our town was called the "Biggest Little Town in the World:" The town would be packed. I was allowed to sit on the stage with the band until eleven o'clock. We had no fire trucks or ambulance service. Usually places burnt down or a sick person was taken in a vehicle. If someone died, my dad would have to haul the casket in the back of his "old power wagon" to the grave. This happened mostly in the winter. The power wagon named "Old Mary" was used every Saturday morning to feed the deer in the winter. As you can see, my growing up days were full of many good memories of the past. I think a lot of how fortunate I was to have led such a positive life with friends and family from our town as well as from the camps in our area.

Our parents instilled in us as we grew up working in the business that the customer was always right and that work never hurt anyone. Our business was very successful and all of us kids were exposed to so many good memories. My parents are both gone, but our little store and bar are still run by my brother and his family. I live and have always lived in the same area, as I wanted our daughter to be exposed to some of the great things I encountered. I am thankful that even with some major changes especially in technology, the "Biggest Little Town in the World" still survives!

Carefree Winter Days of Sledding
By Elizabeth A. Stine of Williamsport, Pennsylvania
Born 1935

Growing up in South Williamsport, Pennsylvania, the first snowfall of winter held fond memories for a young girl living in the 1940s. Fading into the recesses of my mind were my efforts of collecting scrap metal and scouring nearby fields for milkweed pods to be converted into parachutes for the war being fought overseas in Europe and the South Pacific. Within me, anticipation mounted to be the first on Winthrop Street to rush outside and be the first to wade through the virgin snow.

My mother was always one step ahead of me. She would have two snowsuits, complete with mittens and wool hats, ready and hanging from a pipe in front of our round, monstrous coal furnace. I dressed myself feverishly, rescued my Lightning sled from a corner in the basement, and ran outside to the cement sidewalk. I honed my sled's runners to a razor-sharp edge that gave me extra speed to race down our steep hill. The street was the center of our universe for all the kids living there during my younger years.

Rarely would a car venture an attempt to maneuver the unplowed street in order to avoid hitting us. Throwing all caution and safety to the wind hour after hour, time after time, we tirelessly sped down the hill. Not ever did we consider the possibility of being hurt or worse! Dragging our feet enabled us to come to a stop before approaching the intersection.

Only due to a lack of feeling in my arms and legs would I, in desperation, venture into the basement, to exchange very wet clothes for a dry, warm snowsuit. The call of the street once again would entice me to hurry outside until the call for lunch break.

Only as the light began to fade from the sky would we begrudgingly admit that our fun day had come to a close.

Many years have passed since those carefree days. Childhood friends matured and sadly passed away. Those wonderful memories remain within me. After all, wasn't it only yesterday?

Happy, Innocent School Days
By Jane Kropinak of Covode, Pennsylvania
Born 1922

I can just step out into my backyard and memories of the one-room schoolhouse come floating back into my mind. Those were innocent, happy days.

The schoolhouse was adjacent to the acre of ground that was in back of our house. I attended all eight grades in that school, but the oddest thing was how I got to go to school. I was five years old in June 1927, not old enough to go to school in September.

One nice September day, I was riding on my dad's lap on the mowing machine, the type that had to be pulled by a team of horses. The schoolteacher saw us out there, and she asked my dad if he would let me go to school, as she had no one in first grade.

You guessed it! I was off to school the next day. I didn't have to get special new clothes, as education was the priority, not your clothes. I was little and bashful, but I wasn't afraid. I had three older sisters going there also.

I sat on the first row, where the desks were the smallest. I still recall the reader with Dick and Jane and Spot.

The teacher's desk was up on a platform, and there were two big blackboards in back of her. In front of her were two long recitation benches, and when it was your turn for class, you went and sat on the benches. I always listened to the other classes and learned a lot.

During the first week of school every year, there was always one kid who acted up and deserved punishment. The teacher got out her paddle or leather strap and paddled the kid right then and there, in front of everyone. Everyone behaved after that. Of course, the teacher wouldn't be allowed to do that today.

At Christmas time, we pulled names from a hat, and we got a gift for that person. We also had what we called a program, with recitations, skits, songs, etc. My cousin, Jack and I always had to sing.

On Valentine's Day, there was a big, decorated box with a slit in the top. Everyone brought Valentine's to put in it. At a special time, the teacher opened the box and called out our names and we went up and got our Valentines.

I'll always remember those happy days of innocence of a one-room school.

Making Friends in a Snowstorm
By M. Jane Pool of Beech Creek, Pennsylvania
Born 1922

Since I was born in 1922, that makes me "going on 90" so I qualify to write about the "Good Old Days".

I lived on a farm when I was growing up. When I was a teenager, I had to get up daily at five in the morning to help milk. Then I fed the pigs, measured their food and kept records because I belonged to the FFA – Future Farmers of America. My dad said my sister and I joined just to "see" boys. From the pigpen, I went back to the barn and fed both the horses and cows. After eating a hearty breakfast, usually buckwheat cakes with liverwurst or eggs with bacon or ham, we walked a mile to Beech Creek to catch our school bus to Lock Haven High School.

On our farm we used horses, no tractors. When my dad planted corn and would cultivate it, I had to walk behind and uncover any that he covered with the dirt. I picked potatoes when Dad would dig them out of the ground and for each bushel we dumped in the wagon, I had a paper taped to the outside of the wagon and made tally marks so we knew how many bushels we had.

We grew a lot of our food. When the beans, like navy beans, were ready to harvest, our dad brought the stalks and all of the beans and dumped a huge pile on the barn floor. Then

Ruth Werts, Lois Werts, Eleanor Bechdel, and Jane Bechdel Pool in 1940

my siblings and I jumped on them to shake the beans loose.

Butchering was a special event we did each year. We killed about six hogs and cooked the liver and hearts, etc. in a huge black kettle with fire under it. We made our own liverwurst. Men cut up the hogs into pork chops, big pieces to roast, and Mother canned small pieces like she did when we killed cows and had steaks cut up. The women sat and cleaned intestines to put sausage into. This was a smelly job. We cured hams with salt and hung them in our meat house.

We had an icehouse with sawdust

Jane and her sisters sporting their brothers' or dad's bib overalls

that was filled with huge squares of ice cut from the creek in Beech Creek and covered with more sawdust. In the summer, we could uncover a block of ice and put it in a burlap bag to pound it on the concrete floor of the garage to get small pieces to put around the ice cream container to freeze ice cream. My mother made the best cooked custard that she put in the freezer to crank and make her ice cream.

We had a one-horse open sleigh and a big bob-sled that my dad would hitch to the horses. He would drive us to school in the deep snow. We would pick up any town kids who were walking.

Girls never wore slacks or jeans when I was a teenager. We wore dresses to school. We also wore ugly long, ribbed stockings. We would roll them down when we got to school. In high school, a girl got expelled for a week for wearing slacks for the first time. After school, we wore our dad's and brothers' bib overalls. We would cut off an old dress at the waist and wear the tops as a blouse.

We only had baths every Saturday. My sister and I both got behind the old black stove with a stool holding our basin of water. We used homemade soap, made with banner lye.

Seventy-seven years ago, when I was twelve years old, my parents, uncle, aunt, sister, and I attended the Pennsylvania Farm Show. On our way home from Harrisburg it started to snow, and within ten minutes, we could hardly see the road. Then our windshield wipers froze and wouldn't work. We went down a long steep hill and pulled off the road and stopped because we had no visibility. We thought we were near Spring Mills and Centre Hall. My dad and uncle walked back to the closest farmhouse, and the man, Mr. Smith, got his team of horses hitched up to his bobsled. He put straw in the bobsled, came for us, and took us to their house, where we stayed from Friday night until Monday morning. As we got settled in their warm home, a knock came at their door, and a man said his car was stuck in a ditch off the road. The three men took this man in the bobsled and brought his wife and old mother back to the Smith home. Soon after, three more knocks came, and there were three more trips in the bobsled to bring in more passengers. Now there were twenty-six people in the house. There were six girls, all twelve or thirteen years old, and we had to sleep in one bed for three nights. We had fun playing games and making pop-corn, fudge, and hot chocolate. None of us took baths, and we slept in our clothes. We slept horizontally and did more talking than sleeping. On Saturday, Mr. Smith killed several chickens, and the women helped clean and pluck their feathers. We had a delicious dinner of the chickens, mashed potatoes, canned corn and peas, and gravy. Mrs. Smith baked bread and sticky buns for us several times. Every year after this, the six girls from this event always met at The Grange Tent fair in Centre Hall.

Scooter, the Neighborhood Bandit
By George A. Shearer of Curwensville, Pennsylvania
Born 1949

When I was a young boy, my sister, Rosemary, said she was going over to town and buy a dog for $1.00. I figured she was going to buy a stuffed animal. She returned with a real dog—collie and beagle mixed. We kept him and named him Scooter. He was very playful and well-liked by the neighbors.

One Sunday I decided to walk to church. Shortly after I sat down, people started to laugh. I turned around to see what was so funny. Here comes Scooter, walking up to where I was sitting. He jumped up and sat beside me. We sat there for a while before leaving. Scooter and I walked home. I have to admit it was funny.

Little did I know, this was just a sample of things to come.

I remember walking home from school and stopping to talk to a neighbor. She seemed to be a little upset. She made an apple pie for supper and sat it out to cool. When she came out to get it, it was gone. I went home, about a half hour later here comes Scooter walking down the street with apple pie all over his face and mouth. I hurried up and cleaned him.

One day I was walking home and I stopped to talk to a neighbor. She said that she baked a loaf of bread for supper, set it out to cool. When she came out to get it, it was gone. I went home. Guess who was sitting in the front yard eating a loaf of homemade bread? Yes, it was Scooter, the neighborhood bandit. I checked the bread, it was still warm.

One of our neighbors lived down by the river. He had three horses and some chickens. We spent a lot of time down there. One day I stopped down to see the animals. The owner said that one of his chickens was missing. I helped him look for it. We never did find the chicken.

I went home to tell the family about the missing chicken. Scooter was sitting in the front yard with feathers all over his mouth. One thing for sure, Scooter liked good food— apple pie, homemade bread, and fresh chicken. My neighbors never did find out what Scooter did.

My Uncle Bruno lived near Pittsburgh and we decided to let him take Scooter home with him. It was ok, because we knew he would be well taken care of. The trip took about one hour and 45 minutes. Shortly after arriving at my uncle's home, Scooter took off. The neighborhood bandit was on his way home. Scooter made it about half the way. He was taken in by a lady. She probably had some food sitting out to cool. The lady took very good care of Scooter for about three weeks. My uncle placed a missing ad in the paper for three days. The lady called three days later and said that she has a dog that fits the description of the one in the paper. My uncle gave the lady $50 for taking care of Scooter.

Scooter was back home. Everybody was glad to see him, even the neighbors.

One day Scooter was in his doghouse when a thunderstorm hit. Lightning hit close to Scooter's house. It really scared him. We wrapped him in a blanket and took him in the house. He was ok. After this, we called him the "weather dog." When a storm was approaching, he would start to shake. One afternoon when I was sleeping on the sofa with my t-shirt hanging out, a thunderstorm hit. Scooter slipped his collar and ran in the house. He was very wet and muddy. Scooter jumped up on the sofa and ran his wet, muddy head up under my t-shirt. I jumped up and tried to take off my shirt, mud and water flew everywhere, what a mess. I cleaned everything, including Scooter.

We all had a good laugh and just chalked it up as one of Scooter's adventures. After what happened, we kept Scooter in the house. He lived a long life, and was well taken care of. We even made sure that Scooter got some apple pie, homemade bread, and some chicken.

A Time Cherished, a Time Happily Remembered
By Kathy Fowler Alaskey Rickard of Johnsonburg, Pennsylvania
Born 1949

Kickball, softball, hide and seek and sled

riding were just a few of the sports we enjoyed as children long before the age of Wii's and X-box. The weather often dictated which games we played—summer was always good for kickball, softball or swimming. Hide and seek was great anytime. Winter was a necessity for sled riding. We were never "bored". When we had free time, we filled it with creative times and made up our own games.

Kickball was one of the favorites. Two captains were chosen to pick teams. My athletic sister was usually chosen first. I knew I would be chosen last, or next to last. My chubbiness slowed me down and I just didn't hold the confidence she had in her strength. The best "field" to use was the old high school playground. Our "equipment" was dime-store balls, sometimes lacking air, rocks made great bases. We had great times on that field. When we tired of kickball, the playground offered swings with handles to push and we would soar higher and higher. Or, we could jump on the merry-go-round that would spin until we were all dizzy. Those who were skilled could jump on or off the merry-go-ground while it was spinning—a super feat! And yes, there were those sea saws, which we called teeter-totters. It took cooperation and trust for them. If your partner jumped off while you were in the air, you were sure to have a hard landing. Sometimes a friend would sit on the center and wave back and forth.

It seemed nothing to us to walk a mile or two along the main highway, Route 219, in the summer to get to our favorite swimming holes—Big Stony or Little Stony. We wore our suits under our clothes and carried our inner tubes on our backs. We'd near the spot with great anticipation, climb over the guardrail; walk down the hill and arrive at last, to a place hidden by trees and hills. You had to know where it was to find it. The water was always cold (no heaters or filters) but we didn't even think about it. To us it was the most refreshing place to be on a hot summer day, particularly when it was the reward for finished chores.

Hide and seek was especially fun in the fall. The town was our playground and it seemed there were millions of places to hide— old sheds, hidden doorways, and old cars. The "seeker" counted from 1 to 100, and we would scurry to find our safe spot. Hearts stopped when discovered and the race was on to beat

the seeker to the "safe place" where we yelled "free!" When the seeker exhausted places to search and no longer had any thoughts as to where anyone was, he would yell, "Ally, ally, in free" and everyone returned to the group, declared safe. We played amidst the smell of burning leaves that folks burned in the ditches throughout the town, fighting a never-ending battle with trees everywhere. There were no burning laws, or bans. This is how it was done back then. Sometimes we'd rake the leaves just to jump in them with no intent of ever burning them. Oh, to smell that fragrance again…

Sled riding was a great winter sport. Some of us were fortunate enough to have our own sled. I remember that my sister and I shared ours. It was beautifully varnished with red letters, claiming the name of Western Flyer. Everyone knew Western Flyers were made in two sizes—a long one which carried you fully and a shorter one that required you bending your knees to raise your legs in order to fit on the sled. Both had their advantages. The long sled was quite comfortable, but the shorter one allowed more flexibility as you rode down the hill, cinders under you sparking as you turned the front bar back and forth to guide your path. Someone would be at the bottom of the hill at the cross section of Buchanan and Kane Streets to watch for imposing cars—such as interference to our fun. If we could get away with it, we would turn into Mrs. Powell's hill and fly over the terraced lawn—a thrill in itself. The "big kids" went to Martin's Hill where they built a fire and spent many a good time. Sometimes we'd take a break and go home for a cup of hot chocolate (the REAL stuff, made with milk, sugar and Hershey's cocoa), and a sandwich or a piece of toast. Our mittens were speckled with ice, our bulky snow pants were soaked through, and our boots had to be tugged off so our feet could warm up. We wore rubber boots over our shoes—no Uggs or designer boots. We hung everything around our pot-bellied stove and waited until they seemed dry, then redress and head out again. I remind my children today, you can't appreciate the warmth until you've felt the cold. Somehow, that cold didn't seem so cold back then.

When we tired of organized games, we created our own. We spent hours by the Clarion River discovering flowers and rocks and bugs and fish. We climbed Locke's Hill and walked in the field that overlooked the town, feeling happy and free. Berry picking was always an option—blueberries on the cool hillside of Dahoga road and blackberries along the hill above.

It was a wonderful time and a truly blessed childhood. Wilcox was a town that understood the meaning of the phrase, "It takes a village to raise a child" long before the phrase was uttered. We believed we were safe and never even considered that we were not. We were expected to behave with respect towards everyone, because if we didn't a friend's parent did not hesitate to discipline us. Or, worse yet, if we really misbehaved, our parents would be informed and we were disciplined again at home. Funny, how our parents always seemed to know everything about us, back then. We were "everybody's kids."

We became strong physically and emotionally, building our confidence in what we did well and understanding too, what were our weaknesses. As we shared the teeter-totter, we learned that some efforts call for two to share the job. When we looked out for one another as we sledded down the hill, we understood the meaning of caring for others. We learned to compete and play fair and share. We learned to respect elders and each other, and to allow for differences—we weren't all the same, or gifted the same, but we each knew we had something to offer to the bunch. We learned forgiveness and tolerance. From this, we became leaders, team players, negotiators, caregivers and fixers. We chose careers as nurses, teachers, homemakers, engineers, mill workers, and mechanics. We became husbands and wives, fathers and mothers, and now grandparents. We learned to appreciate what God had given us, and our families and friends. It was a time cherished, a time happily remembered. Ahhhh, for the good ole days…

War Efforts Were Many
By Ken Ostrum of Emporium, Pennsylvania
Born 1932

I was born in 1932, during the Great Depression. Many men were not able to find a job in those lean days of the Depression. Not everyone was as fortunate or perhaps as ambitious as my father, J. Fred Ostrum, who was able to find some sort of work throughout his life. There was no unemployment compensation available at that time.

He was a lumberman, driving teams of horses from the time he was 11 or 12 years old, worked at local dynamite plants, a railroader, a forester, a lookout on the fire tower, a member of the Civilian Conservation Corps (CCC), delivered mail, drove a bread truck, worked on the highway with the Works Progress Administration (WPA)—all of this to support a wife and 7 children plus other relatives now and then. Finally, during WWII, he worked at Sylvania Electric Products, a Receiving Tube manufacturer that had found its birth in our hometown of Emporium, PA. His last job there was cleaning filament machines from which he retired in 1958 at the age of 75.

Hoboes: During the Depression, quite a few guys (at least I never saw a woman) would ride the rails and beg for food at people's homes; they were very common in our area. Someone observed, perhaps facetiously: "A **hobo** is a person who travels to find work. A **tramp** is a person who travels and won't work. A **bum** is a person who won't travel or work."

We didn't usually know any details about an individual's reasons for traveling around and begging. Reading about these people in later years, it turns out more than one quarter million teenagers also were living on the road in America in the Thirties; many crisscrossing the country by illegally hopping freight trains. These guys would show up mostly during the summer. They left the trains before they got into town, to evade rail police, and walked up and down the roads, stopping at any likely place to get a meal. They often marked homes with an "X" or other identifying means, to tell

Ken's father, J. Fred Ostrum with his horses

23

others where the good places were. I know we had a chalked "X" at the bottom of our steps on several occasions, since Mom was a soft touch. Sometimes they were given a meal and sent on their way, other times they would do a job and receive a meal as payment.

Summers During the Depression Meant Helping Our friends and Neighbors: During these lean times while growing up, besides doing our own small farm chores, we helped my Uncle Jim hay and pick up potatoes on his farm, all with no pay 'cause he was our uncle. We also helped our neighbors, the Hornung family.

The Hornungs would mow the hay using a horse-drawn mower. Timing was of the essence because you wanted to mow the hay, let it lay for a period of time to dry, and then gather it in. Sunshine and fair days were hoped for, to assure a dry crop. Stowing damp hay in the barn could lead to spontaneous combustion and a disaster.

In our more primitive time, a hay rake got everything going after the mowed hay

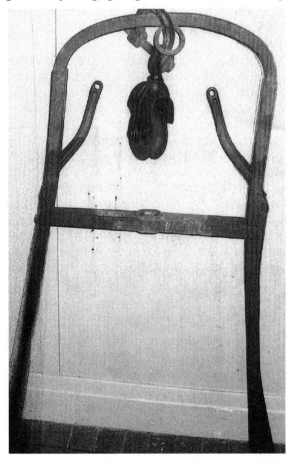

Hayfork

was dry. The rake driver sat on a horse-drawn contraption with perhaps fifty curved steel tines. Holding the lines in one hand and the dump lever handle in the other, he would rake hay until an acceptable amount was gathered and then he tripped the lever to leave the start of a windrow. Long windrows were created and then formed into haycocks to await the hayrack, a long, specially built wagon pulled by a large team of horses. A crew of four to six men, equipped with pitchforks, were needed. I was built rather slight so I would usually be the one to climb on board to help position the hay; that meant a lot of moving hay around but mostly I had fun jumping all over the load to make it compact. When the hayrack (wagon) was loaded to capacity, we headed for the barn.

A heavy rope, already assembled, hung from a pulley bolted to the highest beam outside the opening into the haymow; one end of the rope was tied to a huge two-tined fork that weighed probably 100 pounds or more; the other end was threaded through pulleys and hooked to a whiffletree on the opposite side of the barn which was then connected to the horse's harness. By the way, for those who are wondering, and I know you are, **whiffletree/whippletree** are the same thing; it depends on what area of the country you are in. Dad said **whiffletree**. Dad also told me the **reins** for a horse are those used with a riding horse whereas the ones used to drive a team were called **lines**.

Anyway, the big fork was dropped, free fall, about 20 feet to penetrate deep into the hay on the wagon. Pulling a cord would close the jaws to grab a huge fork-full of hay. Someone would walk the horse forward on the other side of the barn. The load was pulled high into the haymow where it was released by the man with the rope at the spot it was needed, until the mow was filled to capacity.

With hay in the mow, playing in the barn was a great way to end a day after helping them load hay. Sometimes we climbed up into the rafters to jump into the hay. It seemed innocent enough. We never thought about the fact we might land on the rafter supports hidden by the hay. We could have broken bones or even broken our backs if we should happen to hit one. One time, after delivering hay to the barn, I had a narrow escape.

To set the scene: We boys are playing a game of hide-and-seek at the barn. The owners are at lunch-break after we had delivered the loaded hay wagon from the fields and <u>before</u> it was unloaded. Being energy driven boys, we were bored and needed something to keep us busy, such as a game of Hide-and-Seek. After several "hiding" tries, I'm looking for a better place to hide from the guys. Suddenly the figurative lamp bulb went off in my head. "I know," I thought to my stupid self, "I'll hide in the wagon full of hay." Dumb idea! It would have been a good place except for the fact that just as I got into position in the wagon; the owners picked that very time to return from lunch to unload the wagon. They didn't have a clue I'm hiding in there and I didn't know they're back. When they dropped the huge 100 lb. hayfork from that height of about 20 feet, it missed me by inches. It really scared me; actually it scared the heck out of me! I was out of that wagon in a flash! The two owners' faces turned pale—then red—as they got mad! They chased me half way home and I didn't come back for quite a long time. That's the kind of thanks you get for helping out friends!

World War II Begins - Japan Attacks Pearl Harbor!! Horrible, everyone knew it was. Yet for me as a kid, "It was the best of times"; at least that's how I looked at it through my youthful eyes. For adults "it was the worst of times". The attack came December 7, 1941, a month shy of my 10th birthday. The war didn't mean that much to me then but within a couple years, it became very clear as to how it would affect my life. Life would change as I knew it. Between 1942 and 1945, all four of my brothers left for the service. The boys wrote home about their experiences and I was proud as a peacock. I had no concept of the dangers involved for all of them. Fortunately, all of them came home even though two of them went onto the beaches of France on D-Day.

I wished I could go to the service so I became a Boy Scout but then I had to wait until the war in Korea to serve my country.

The War Effort at Home: Adults were caught up in the rationing programs for shoes, gas, and various foods such as sugar, coffee, and meats of all kinds. "Meatless Tuesday" came to be the norm as Protestants joined Catholics in not eating meat on Fridays, which had been a Catholic tradition for many years. Victory gardens were promoted for all families but we already grew most of our own

food so not much changed for us on that front.

As a Boy Scout, I helped in the collection of newspapers and magazines. We rode in big trucks; people had their newspapers and magazines bundled and ready when we picked them up at their homes.

In addition to Boy Scouts, just plain kids, boys and girls, helped in the war effort. Scrap metal was vital to the cause. After the war began, no car manufacturers were allowed to make new cars; their factories had to be used for military production. Whatever car you had at the beginning of the war, you were stuck with for the duration.

The local movie theatre sponsored scrap drives by offering tickets to those who brought in a required number of pounds of scrap. One of the free movies for scrap was National Velvet. The movie starred Elizabeth Taylor and it was all about her adventures trying to win a horse race. Walking the railroad tracks was a good way to find rail spikes and discarded metal spike plates to turn in. The movie was standing room only for every night the film showed.

For other scrap material, we collected items we used at home. We saved tinfoil from discarded cigarette packs as well as chewing gum or candy tinfoil wrappers. We squeezed empty metal toothpaste tubes in the crack of a door to remove all the paste so the tubes could be recycled. Remember, there were no plastic items at that time.

People were asked to save tinfoil, tin, rubber bands, string and cord among other items. Oleo/margarine replaced butter (Mom still churned most of our butter for us but sometimes we bought oleo). The oleo was imitation butter so it was not allowed to be sold in the same color of butter. Oleo came in packages that looked like lard along with a yellow coloring packet that had to be mixed in, to make it look like butter.

Nylon stockings had just replaced silk hose for women and they become fashionable. Silk and nylon material was collected to make parachutes. Women painted their legs to look like they were wearing nylons; they even painted a dark stripe up the back of the bare leg to make it look like the seam of the nylons.

School kids went out to gather Pussy Willow (Milk Weed) pods. We spent hours picking the pods and putting them in burlap bags. The filling in the pods was used to make life jackets. They seemed to work as well as

Kapok from the Kapok trees, which we didn't have any of since they grow only in tropical countries.

Packaged cigarettes were hard to buy and were more expensive than "roll your own". So I helped my brothers, when they were home, by rolling cigarettes for them, using a little machine. I put thin, special paper in the rollers, added tobacco from a pouch and pulled the rollers across each other to form a cigarette. Then I licked it to seal the paper.

Anyone could save money for War Stamps that were traded in for a War Bond. I took small amounts of change to school where it was traded for War Stamps. After buying $16.75 worth of stamps, they were traded for a War Bond. After ten years, the bond would be worth $25.

When the Lions Roared
By Alice L. Wheeler of Mill Hall,
Pennsylvania
Born 1947

I was born and raised in Williamsport, Pennsylvania, Lycoming County. I am the middle daughter of John and Verna MacMillen's five children. Four of us are eleven months apart. Mom was having my baby sister, born on July 27, 1949, and my oldest brother (but I also have an older sister) was about to turn three years old on August 4, 1949. My younger brother and I were in between.

We were poor but didn't know it—the kind of poor where we wore socks on our hands as mittens. Most of the neighborhood kids were that kind of poor, too, so we didn't think much of it.

I do have some good memories. Remember the roller skates that needed a key? We wore the key on a shoestring around our necks. Well, my dad had an ingenious way of making those skates useable if the key was lost or the sidebars just didn't work. He would take the rubber tube from our bicycle tire, which of course was flat. He would cut it into strips and slide it over the skate and our shoes like a big rubber band. It always worked, and off we'd go, skating away. The bad thing was the uneven slate sidewalks. They were difficult to navigate. We'd always end up with brushed burned knees.

One memory that has stayed with me always occurred during the hot summer nights. Of course, our air conditioning was an opened window. If we were lucky, there would be a little breeze blowing through. On many hot summer nights for a few years with windows opened wide, it would always happen unexpectedly. There it was…the sound! It was loud and scary. All five of us kids would be awakened by it. That sound was "roaring lions". Honest!

We lived on Taylor Place, down from Avco. A railroad track was across the alley behind our house. At the end of those tracks was a place known as Woody's Garage. That's where the sound came from. It seems Woody's old friend Prince El Kigordo, a famous lion tamer, would come to visit every summer unannounced, with his many lions in a circus railroad car.

The lions made such a ruckus at night. We would be awakened by the sound of the roaring, jumping out of bed and running to our Dad's and Mom's bedroom. Dad would say, "Kids, go back to bed. It's just Prince El Kigordo in town to visit Woody!"

We would reluctantly return to our beds, whispering amongst ourselves. The next day, Dad would walk us up the tracks to Woody's and show us that the lions were in a railroad car and couldn't hurt us. So for a week in the summer, the lions didn't sleep through the night. And neither did we!

Our Country Christmas
By Elaine F. Harris of Oswayo, Pennsylvania
Born 1929

Our home was a small one, the next-to-last one on a dirt road. It was before electricity had come to our area. My parents shared the tiny six-room house, with no bath, with their five children, and we struggled to live together during those post-Depression years.

But Christmas was a joyous time! Each of we siblings were given one dollar with which we could buy gifts for our parents and each other. On the big shopping day, we wandered the aisles of the local Kresge store, carefully choosing just the right gift for each person. However, before the day ended, we children had burst from secrecy and divulged to each other the nature of our gifts.

When the last week before Christmas arrived, all at once exciting, special activities began. Mom began to make candies – potato candy, spread with peanut butter, rolled and cut into pinwheels, and dates coated with powdered sugar, with a walnut enfolded in the center. A large pail of hard candy had been ordered from the *Sears* catalog, and it stood ready, along with nuts to crack.

We older girls then bundled up on a mild day, to climb the hill behind the house, carrying a rope and a saw with which to cut and then drag a lacy hemlock tree from the wooded valley over the hill. Often we gathered princess pine (ground pine) as well, to make a wreath from a wire coat hanger.

As soon as Dad had arrived home from work in the oil fields, and had milked the family cow, he would nail two boards together to use for a tree stand, using cords to keep the tree steady by the wall. Out came our much-used store of ornaments and icicles. We added paper ornaments, which we had made at school, and popcorn ropes, which we had strung that afternoon. It was such a delight to see, and to dream of Christmas morning.

And Christmas morning did come! Some gifts were left unwrapped, while others were wrapped in previously used gift-wrap and some in new tissue with lots of Christmas stickers to keep them wrapped. One by one, gifts were unwrapped to make the event as long as possible. Much pleasure was ours all day. Not only to enjoy our gifts of sleds, new mittens and caps, red plaid fabric, topped with pattern and thread (for a new jumper, soon to be sewn), but…Christmas was the only day in the year when we were allowed to eat as much as we wished! And we did that.

Many trips were made to the buffet in the dining room to enjoy the many dainties spread across it. Mom's best dishes held these treats. I especially recall a green glass candy dish with a lid. Inside was chocolate fudge filled with hickory nuts from our large tree in the pasture.

We never thought of ourselves as being poor, but thoroughly enjoyed what we had and thanked God for it.

Ironing Boards and Yellow Spots
By Lois Bamonte of Williamsport,
Pennsylvania
Born 1926

My sister and I were country kids during the Depression, and everyone in our village loved Mr. Crossly, our rural mail carrier. On Mother's pie baking day, she would place a piece of pie on a saucer with a fork and we kids would put it in the mailbox. She always reminded us to put the flag up so he would know there was something in the box. What fun we had, watching him eat his pie! (We were behind the curtains.) He would put the flag down and drive away with a smile on his face. I'm eighty-five years old and I still remember Mr. Crossly—especially that smile!

Things I remember: Mother heating irons on her kitchen cook stove, wrapping them in towels to warm our beds in the winter.

Mother had an ironing board with no legs, okay for ironing flat pieces, but when it came to Daddy's shirts, she had to extend the board from the table. No matter what we were doing, we had to stop to sit on the ironing board. Since there were two of us, we had to take turns. How I hated sitting on the ironing board—but Daddy had some beautifully ironed shirts.

Daddy raised chickens and when they laid lots of eggs, we kids would take one egg each to the store. The lady who owned the store gave us candy in exchange for the eggs. We were using the barter system and didn't even realize it. Most candy was two pieces for a penny, so we each got two pieces of candy. What a thrill for us!

Mother used to make us snow ice cream.

Lois and her sister
All grown up in the 1950s

She would give us a pan and tell us, "Don't get the snow where the yellow spots are." It was quite a while before we realized that the neighborhood dogs were the reason for the yellow spots.

Mother played Santa Claus at our school Christmas parties. It was years before we learned that *she* was our Santa Claus. Imagine what she thought when we always declared that we had been good little girls. She must have been chuckling under her whiskers.

On the way home from Grandma's, we decided to play follow the leader. My sister was the leader, and suddenly she said, "Close your eyes!" I pinched my eyes shut and found—to my dismay—she had spotted a dollar bill in the grass and was afraid I would see it before she did. Needless to say, we each got fifty cents, a good amount of money to us.

Our Sunday school class was having a summer picnic halfway up the mountain in a nice open spot. My playmate, Bob, coerced his mother to let him take his wagon to the picnic. She was not keen on him taking his wagon, but he pestered her until she finally agreed to let him take it. While playing a game, I stepped in a hole and sprained my ankle. So, I got to ride home in the wagon.

I treasure every memory, and sometimes it's hard to realize I'm this old…but I had so much fun I didn't realize I was growing old. I'm still enjoying my life—going to McDonalds every day with a childhood friend. We call it our "therapy" session. We're both widows and enjoy the kids and the people who come to McDonalds. So fortunate to have reached this age: still healthy and going strong! Enjoying every day of life.

Buses and Trains
By Betty McKinney Koser of Montoursville, Pennsylvania
Born 1928

When I was six or seven, my dad would take me to Williamsport with him. We would go to the A&P on Market Street to get a roast or some piece of meat for Sunday dinner. He was to take me to the five-and-dime store on Pine Street, to get me a hat for Easter. We got a light green sailor style hat (which my mom didn't like). It looked nice because I had

long curls. Then we stopped at 21st Century Bakery and got a dozen molasses cookies to take home! We would stop at the Old Corner Hotel to get something to eat, but he wanted something to drink. Then he took me to the bus stop at Market Square and put me on the bus with the carrying bag. He told the bus driver to drop me off at Loyalsock Avenue. He went off to visit friends at the hotel. I got home before dark. My mom would be watching for me to get off the bus.

In 1946 my sister, Martha, and I worked at Warshaw's Silk Mill. We worked eight hours each day, on Saturday we would work overtime. We would get home about 3:15. We would wash up and change clothes to catch the four o'clock passenger train. The Reading Railroad ran past our house so we knew the schedule. We would ride to Williamsport station and get off to walk over to town. It was a short ways. We would shop, then go to a movie. We would get something to eat before we got the bus to come home. If it was dark, we would run down the middle of the street and hope no train was passing then.

We had to go to Sunset Park on Lycoming Creek to go roller-skating (1940). My friend and I took the bus on Broad Street to Market Square, then transfer to another bus to go to Lycoming Creek. We usually skated til it started to get dark, then we would ride the bus to Market Square and get the bus to Montoursville. This time it was later than usual by the time we got to Market Square. The last bus already left for Montoursville, so we had no other alternative than to start walking. This was about 10:30 at night. We had to go down Golden Strip. At that time, it was mostly fields instead of buildings. We were scared, but we went. A couple of cars stopped and asked if we wanted to ride, but we refused. We got home late and we both got in trouble for staying too long. We didn't get to go skating for quite a while.

In about 1945, we had a path down past the airport, which took us down to Mill Street. There was a golf course down there, privately owned, and tennis courts. A friend from our street was caretaker (Carl Kaufman) and then Bill Koser would help him out. Bill had a Model A, so he would take some other guys up to Third Street (Golden Strip) to get watermelon and whatever fruit we could get for the money we had. We all chipped in. We would stop at our house and get a butcher knife so we could cut the watermelon. Then we would go to the golf course and have a watermelon party.

Bob and Dean McNett had a park over in Montgomery in 1950-51. Bill Koser (by now he was my husband) would take a farm truck and put seats in the back. We would have picnic baskets and whatever else we wanted to drink. We couldn't afford to buy too much eats over there. We would eat while we watched the entertainment. They had Roy Acuff and his players. They came in by airplane and landed it at the Montoursville Airport. Gene Autry and his group came in. Hank Snow, Jim and Jane would come in from State College. I can't remember who all came. There were different entertainers each week. It was a good afternoon of entertainment. We had my parents, his parents, sisters and brother. We went several times a season.

Two guys from our street had cars with musical horns. One night they decided to go to each end of Broad Street and come up the street. One came from the East and the other one from the West, blowing their horns. It sounded nice, but the Police Chief didn't go for it.

Great Memories of the Hunting Camp
By Donna J. Jones of Pottstown,
Pennsylvania
Born 1948

To many of you, forty years seems like an eternity. To us, it seems like yesterday. My husband belonged to a hunting camp west of Coudersport. The year was 1970. Back then, few "families' would spend a weekend together there. This was a man's haven to go hunting and to get away. Our family broke the rule.

It was summer and the weather was warm. Rich asked if we would like to go to Potter County and spend a weekend at the cabin. WOW! This was exciting. I'd never been that far away from home before. After hunting season, one of the members would remove the fuses from the electric box and take them home. So before we went anywhere, we had to retrieve the fuses so we would have electricity.

We left early Friday evening. After two-hundred and forty miles, and six hours of driving, we arrived at 1:30 Saturday morning. Well, we did not exactly arrive at the camp then, but in the vicinity of the camp. Rich had only ben to the camp twice before in the previous years. He knew the cabin was between Hebron and Coneville. We drove back and forth between these two points for at least fifteen minutes. Our patience was wearing thin, but our daughter managed to stay asleep in the back seat. Finally, we got the spotlight out and shined it down every driveway to our left until we saw the driveway. Here at last! We toted our suitcases in, and as I got our daughter ready for bed, Rich primed the pump and turned the water on. We did, however, stay up for a little while since we were too excited to sleep.

When morning arrived, we made breakfast with food we packed into a cooler. The morning menu consisted of eggs, bacon, toast, and juice. Those old cast iron pans were supposed to be the best things ever invented for making breakfast, but I didn't have such luck. The eggs stuck like glue.

Naturally, when it was time to clean up, I washed all the dishes, including the cast iron frying pan. I added extra dish detergent and scrubbed that pan with an SOS pad. At least it was clean. But come hunting season, they didn't see the pan as being clean. Jack, the head cook, took one look at that pan and screamed, "Who has been washing these pans"? Needless to say, a few extra words were added, and he was not a happy camper. My husband sat there, acting as innocent as could be. But when he got home, I got a lesson on how to clean cast iron pans with oil and using salt as an abrasive.

We went there many times during the next seventeen years. Our family grew with three more children as we continued to create new memories. We would visit the old Oswayo General Store to buy a snack. It gave us a sense of going back in time, seeing the Post Office in the front corner of the store and the old stove in the rear. Our children learned how to shoot (and respect) a gun. Their first experience was shooting soda cans in a small stream of water that ran in front of the cabin. Just about every night, we would spot deer, counting almost one hundred deer in an evening. There were times we would have to stop the car to let the deer cross the road. You may take this for granted, but we enjoyed the excitement and emotions that came from our children.

One evening, we had all the children tucked into bed. We, ourselves, went into our room, tossed and turned for probably one hour or more, but could not fall asleep. My husband looked at me and said, "Let's go to the cabin". I thought he was crazy, and our gas tank was almost empty. You must understand, back in those days we did not have gas stations that were open twenty-four hours. I called several gas stations until I found one that was going to be open until 11:00. We only had about twenty minutes. While he went for gas, I quickly packed a few things to get us through the weekend. When he returned home, we carried the children out, one by one, and lay them down in the back of our station wagon. We arrived at the cabin just in time to make breakfast. As we prepared the food and set the table, we opened the oven to take out the cast iron pans that were stored in there. EEEEEEEK! Lying in the oven was a dead rat. Needless to say, I never used that oven after that.

We shared many fun times with family and friends – laughing, playing games, target shooting, cooking on the campfire – but as we all know, all good things come to an end. All of the original cabin members are no longer with us, and the hunting club has been dissolved. The old cabin has since been knocked down and replaced with a permanent residence.

But time marches on. In 1989, after a two-year search, we bought our own cabin, which we named 'Little Green Acre'. By now, we have seven grandchildren. When our oldest grandson turned twelve years old, he went deer hunting with my husband for the first time. He had practiced a few times, shooting targets and clay birds at the gun club, but by no means had he practiced on a regular basis. Monday morning they went into the woods. By 10:00 that morning, Billy had shot his first buck, an 8" spike. That was his first and only time deer hunting with Pop Pop.

As old age creeps up on us, we have talked about selling the place. Our granddaughter says we would be selling all of her memories. Is that a guilt trip or what? Good times, love, and fun were all shared by our family and friends. There are many stories to tell, but for now, we will continue to enjoy and share our times together for as long as we are able.

Two Narrow Escapes
By Dorothy A. Phillips of Curwensville,
Pennsylvania
Born 1925

My husband, Hugh, grew up in Grampian, Pennsylvania. Twice in his life, he was nearly killed by trains. The first time was when he was a toddler, and the second time he was a grown man.

Hugh's family lived beside the railroad tracks in Grampian. It was August 1923 when his first near-death experience occurred. His mother, Mrs. Phillips, was working in the kitchen of their home, canning plums, when Hugh wondered out of the house. He was fifteen months old at the time. His mother realized he was gone and started to look for him, but she couldn't find him anywhere in the house. She walked out to the end of their lot to look over the embankment, but he was not there. She went into an outhouse and looked for Hugh behind the door, thinking he might be hiding there, but he was not. She looked up toward the railroad tracks, which ran past the upper end of their lot, a distance of about 200 feet, and she saw his head showing above the weeds. These weeds were what had kept her from seeing Hugh when she first came out of the house.

Just as Mrs. Phillips saw Hugh's head, she heard the train whistle. She started to run, crying out as she was running that her baby was on the tracks. The next-door neighbors heard her as she passed by their house, and they started following her towards the tracks.

Grandmom, Janet Phillips (Mum) with her son, Hugh in 1924

Hughie Phillips in 1926

Just as Mrs. Phillips reached the railway crossing, the train drew even with her. She could see Hugh standing right in the middle of the train tracks, about fifty feet away from her. She could do nothing but watch the train rushing towards her son. If he had turned and seen his mother standing there, he might have started to walk towards her, stepping over the tracks and being cut to pieces. Instead, he looked at the train coming toward him, and he sat down right there in the middle of the railway.

The train rushed over Hugh. Mrs. Phillips ran toward the place where she had last seen her child and looked under the train for him. There he was, with his back toward her. As she looked, he got knocked down, as if something had hit him. She covered her face with her hands, thinking, "My God, he is killed". She looked again, and after what seemed like an eternity, she saw him moving. She started jumping and yelling, with her arms waving over her head. The baggage man was standing at the open door of the baggage coach. He noticed her and signaled the conductor. With a hiss of steam, the train stopped. Mrs. Phillips reached around the wheel of the coach and lifted Hugh out. She pulled him from under the last wheels of the first passenger coach. The engine, tender, baggage coach, and most of the first passenger coach had passed over him.

Mrs. Phillips told me that her memory of what happened after pulling Hugh out from under the train was very faint. Someone took him from her arms and carried him into a neighbor's house. They began to baptize him in the bathroom, because they thought he was surely dying after such an experience. Hugh was crying at the top of his lungs. The water

and the crowd of strangers around him scared him more than the train, because he was too young to realize what had happened. Mrs. Phillips remembers the conductor of the train saying he was sorrier for the mother than the child, and she remembers he was writing something in a book. She kept crying for her baby, so at last someone put Hugh in her arms and half carried and half led her home, helping to take the weight of him from her arms as she could hardly walk herself.

Hugh escaped with only seven strokes across his head. The ones on top were the deepest and took the longest to heal. The railway company sent their doctor to examine him. The family had their own doctor look at him as well.

When Hugh was forty-six years old, he had his second brush with death when his car was hit by a Penn Central freight train as he was coming home from work. He was not injured this time, but his car was totaled. It was a narrow escape. I lost Hugh in May of 2011. We had been married for sixty-seven years.

Hughie and Dot Phillips on their 40th Anniversary

The St. Patrick's Day Flood of 1936
By Priscilla Barrett of Lock Haven,
Pennsylvania
Born 1927

On March 17, 1936, just a month before my sister was five years old; we had the big flood that I will never forget. It was known as the St. Patrick's Flood or the '36 Flood.

The winter had been a long and anxious one with very deep snow and lots of ice on the river. For about one month that winter, we were completely snowed in. Myself and my brother had many experiences in getting to school. First, our father attempted to haul us on a toboggan, but it was too much of a pull, so we had to walk or wade the rest of the way. Only about half of my brother stuck out for he was down almost as much as up. Next, we tried to go to the bus on "Zippy," our pony, and that was just fine until the wind came and drifted the lane shut. Then our father had to take us on the tractor through the field or wherever he could get through.

Now on February 14th of that year we got 100 peeps, hoping to have an early spring start. Dad built a large brooder pen that stood on high legs and we kept them in our house.

In late February, the days began to warm up and then came the thaw and rain that started the river to raise and the ice began to crack and heave up, with all the snow on the mountains to melt and run into the river. We then knew from past experience what to expect, so we moved everything. Just to be safe we came down to Pine for our grandfather's. We moved down there three times. First for the ice floods (each a week apart) and then for a water flood that came just high enough to run into the cellar windows and fill it.

The ice was all gone now but it kept right on raining and raining. We knew then it was going to be very bad. We were getting tired of leaving the house by that time and moving the little chicks with us, so my father took the pens all apart and moved it upstairs into our bedroom. He filled all the feeder pans and water pan and left them there.

They had moved our cattle, pony, tractor, and wagon out to Lew Wilson's barn during the third flood.

Just before March 17, my dad took the car out across the railroad and left it near the hickory tree. At about 8:30 we were ready and knew we would have to leave the house. It was pitch dark and just pouring. My Uncle Kenny stood on the railroad hill and pointed a flashlight in towards the house, while my dad made trips by the boat to get us all out. He had put on a flashlight between his knees. He took my grandmother and my sister first and they got into the car and waited while he came back for me and my brother. By this time, corn shucks were floating down across the lane and bumping the boat. He had to push them away with the oar. A neighbor had helped at the house and was closing the shutters on all the windows while my dad was doing his second trip. Then he came back for my mother and the neighbor.

Now boating in the daylight is not bad, but at night, when it's pitch dark and raining along with floating things bumping the boat, it is something you never forget! The weight of two people in one end of the boat plus the suitcases caused the rainwater in the boat to come to that end—so all things in the suitcases were soaked.

All night long, you could hear the seagulls squealing and the water roaring under the iron railroad bridge. You could hear the fire siren at Avis and see floodlights flashing in that direction.

The next morning my dad and mom went to see what things looked like. While we were watching we saw our big garage and machine shop raise up and float away like a duck, then it cracked against the trees. We could see that the water was almost at the upstairs windows on the house. Then my mom noticed that the big barn looked queer. It was twisting around and raising up. It was terrible. I can remember my mom screaming the whole time. She looked away and started to run. She never looked back until the water was almost gone and back in its banks (about 2 days later). We were afraid we wouldn't see the house.

We lost everything—all the buildings had floated away. The hay, oats, wheat, and straw were in the barn. The new corncrib with $100 worth of corn, a new chicken house with 37 laying hens, 2 pig pens, the coal house and coal, the toilet and playhouse that my dad had made for us. Besides all this loss our two milk cows at Lew Wilson's got into the dry feed and foundered. Both cows died.

We had sold three young calves before the first flood came so we could take care of the rest better. So now, all we had was the house, one cow, the pony, and our little chickens. For several days, my mom was right down in bed. Words can't describe how terrible it was.

That awful roar for 2 nights and 2 days with barns, garage houses, etc. floating past all the time, as well cattle, some alive and many dead.

We stayed down at my grandfather's during the flood and afterwards until Easter Sunday. My dad's folks had a very comfortable home and we were thankful to be safe and have a warm dry place to stay.

During that time, we only went to the

house long enough to build fires and try to clean out some mud. It looked like we'd never get the mud out. I can still remember the smell. It certainly didn't look like home.

The water had been about 4 inches deep in the upstairs bedroom over the kitchen part of the house. Such a mess. The house didn't dry out very fast because the walls were 1 foot thick of brick. One end of the back porch had washed away and two big windows were smashed out.

You could never imagine how terrible everything looked between McElhattan and Lock Haven, you just couldn't believe what you saw, yet you knew it was real. Some people lost everything.

The three farms just above us lost 104 hogs, 40 cattle, and 3 horses along with their buildings. One of those families was trapped on their barn roof screaming for help from 2 am until 8 am the next morning. Their screams could not be heard because of the roaring of the water and the screaming of the seagulls. The people were Gaylord Confer, his wife Fanny, her father, and Danny Wolfe who was helping them with the cattle on the barn floor when they were trapped and had to go up through the roof and hang on. Fanny said that all night things kept bumping against the barn then daylight came and they could see buildings hit the iron bridge and smash up.

Our barn had floated down through the field in front of the Pine Church and smashed up down in the swamp. Later my dad tried to salvage the good timber and enough lumber to fix some kind of shelter for the cow, calf, and pony. The Red Cross was very helpful. They allowed us enough money to get a flock of 30 laying hens and four pigs, as well as feed for everything. They also gave us tools and materials needed to build a chicken house and a pigpen.

Because of the severe winter and past flood experience, we had pickled our meat from our butchering in barrels that sat upstairs in our little back hall. So thank goodness we had our meat. When it was ready to be smoked, we had no smokehouse so we took it to a neighbor at McElhattan and they smoked it for us.

We had to tear off every bit of wallpaper on the first floor. It looked like a barn.

Later when the walls dried out, a neighbor helped my mother paper the whole house with paper that was picked up after the flood. Huge bundles of paper floated out of the Swartz wallpaper store in Lock Haven and the bundles were tied so tight it didn't wet through. The neighbor had enough to paper her house too.

Slowly, very slowly, things got back to normal. Myself and my brother finished our school term with a last day picnic at Woolrich Park and by this time we had a nice garden started and did what everyone else had to do, we began making plans for a fresh start.

Annie's House on Skids
By Judith Garrison of Avis, Pennsylvania
Born 1938

Being born in the late 1930s in the last house on what is now called Beagle Road, I tend to have a strong feeling for the east end of the valley as well as the whole Nitany Valley I truly love in the spring and fall, especially to drive the whole length of the valley with my eyes closed at certain times just to remember what it used to look like.

My dad and mom purchased the old East End schoolhouse, now owned by the Richard Garbricks, and this was our home for nine years. The road was not paved at the time, as back then, if you didn't have the funds to do something, you did not beg, borrow or steal the funds to get it. I lucked out with my

Judith's mom, Ott Kramer and Annie Burrell

33

grandparents, the Courters, on one side of us, and my other grandparents, the George Stovers, on the same side on what is now called the East End Mountain Road.

I started to school when first and second grades were at the old Mackeyville School, taught by Miriam Hayes and Elizabeth Taylor. Although it was my first year in school, the war was going on overseas and my dad had been drafted. In some ways, it was a lonely time, but in others, it was a wonderful time to show your appreciation to the Lord and valley people. Every family was touched with someone being in the service. Fathers, sons, uncles, cousins, and everyone shared their concern with each other. If one person would receive a letter in the valley, it was shared by way of mouth, at one of the stores, Post Office, etc. Even the mailman would wait to have the letter read sometimes, so that he could pass on the information.

Annie Burrell's new house

Only two telephones were in the end of the valley at this time, and they were battery powered ones you cranked. One telephone was owned by Harry Karstter and the other was owned by Billy Berry. Gas was rationed, and when families could not get to church, church was brought to them by caring preachers and good men. We would go from house to house, singing a few songs and many prayers for the safety of our loved ones. Oh, there were air raid sirens, blackouts, women folding bandages for the Red Cross, gathering milkweed pods to send by train for the purpose of making parachutes, etc.

We listened to the news and prayed again for the safety of our loved ones by kerosene lights. We were actually glad when we hadn't heard from my dad in months, when we finally heard he had been wounded in the Battle of the Bulge, and was in England in a hospital, safe from the war zone, and he would soon be coming home.

We moved to a seventy-acre farm on Beagle Road about 1947, across the road from what was then a general store run by the Carl Bower family. Carl had no use of his legs, so he was always on crutches and had a Packard car made especially for him.

This was the little town of Rote, named for a preacher by the name of Daniel Rote who was there in the 1800s. At that time, only a few houses were there. About five on the left, and the church township building, and about five on the right until you got further out Beagle Road.

This farm had a well and cistern for water. We had to pump the water up with a wheel with chains on by turning the handle before we got a better one. We pumped by hand water for a herd of about ten cattle, pigs, chickens, and of course, our own use. No one was happier when we at last had a spigot coming up that we could turn on in the house and the watering trough at the barn.

My Grandmother Courter was a sewing woman, and made a lot of my clothes from the pretty colored feedbags that farmers got grain in. The pretty bags usually meant new aprons for them, also.

About 1950 or 51, we got enough equipment and stock together and were offered a chance to move to a 500-acre farm just up from the crossroads on Auction Road now. What a step up for us, although we still farmed on the thirds, so the landlord got what you call a third of the profit from the crops. We said goodbye to the old farmhouse at Rote, where the silo we had built by Raymond Orner and others, to a much bigger place. We now had spring water that ran from up near I 80 that wasn't there then.

We didn't know at the time, until it happened that an old well from the home of Daniel Hastings, the first governor of Pennsylvania existed until one of the young cattle fell into it. We felt so badly this happened we were not real happy to see the sign acknowledging him way down by what used to be the Ax Factory Hollow near the dam.

There were many good times on this farm, and we had many visitors from all over.

Our outhouse was uphill from our twelve-room house and, in winter, it was miserable to get to. We often wished we had six rooms and a bath instead of twelve rooms and a path.

I had been driving something ever since I was able to sit on my dad's lap and steer a wheel. My granddad had me driving the tractor when I wasn't able to sit on the seat to reach the pedals. I would steer carefully as straight on the row so the wagon was centered and the hay loader would pick up the hay and bring it up into the wagon where it was caught and stacked until ready to go into the barn. We then backed the wagon onto the barn floor, and a team of horses were hitched to long ropes attached to a huge hayfork where one man set the fork and then the fork was drawn up over the haymow, and at the right time, a rope was pulled to release the fork full of hay.

It took a lot of manpower for these chores back then, and a lot of food for all who would come and help for haymaking, combining, etc. Friends were made and cherished for a lifetime.

Now, all of the valley is getting populated so much I just close my eyes and think of the good old and bad days, and always of the wonderful people that helped to raise a little girl whose dad was overseas. Although I was an only child, I had huge families looking out for my welfare, and one another.

Yes, I can remember the little stores, the two in Rote and two in Salona. Charlie Herr ran the one in Salona and I could always count on him for a piece of candy, a bottle of pop when we would go for a little can of kerosene for our canning stove and lamps.

The other store was owned by the Tate family, and run by Nestlerodes. We would often go there for cheese and cold meats.

There was also a little store across from the Lamar Township (Salona School) that was run by Mrs. Howdy Herr, who made homemade chili and sold it for lunch in her little store when we were lucky enough to have enough money to buy our lunch on Fridays.

There was another little store on close to the intersection of Beagle Road and Auction Road on 477 run by the Rossmans. They sold gas, and kerosene, too, for a long time until too old to pump it any more.

The Bower store did more business, as I think folks felt sorry for Carl, who would come out, pump gas, check oil, and do your windshield until he was no longer able.

I remember a very older lady by the name of Annie Burrell that, due to an unhappy love life, moved into an old, fallen-down house beyond the end of the valley where Beagle Road goes around and meets East End Mountain Road. I guess some of her relatives lived in Salona at this time, and were the owners of the property. She barely had enough to eat, clothes to wear, and the old house was not very warm at all. Most of the families at that time in the end of the valley would take her things, and now and again, she would come around with berries to trade for food or money. When the farmers butchered, they would always remember Annie with a pan of pawn-hass or scrapple as it is called today, sausage, and other meat. I don't think I will ever forget taking her a pan of scrapple and her licking the pan after putting it over into something so we could bring home the pan.

When she got so she could no longer walk over the mountain into town, which is only about four miles into Castanea, all the neighbors became concerned about Annie. The old tumbled down house was no longer safe, and the roof had been patched so many times we were afraid for anyone to go up on it safely. Well, this is when all the neighbors got together and donated material, time and energy and made her a safe and warm little house. Due to it being on some property that we thought that the house may be taken away from her and she could lose the little, her neighbors put it on skids so that we could move it quickly if needed. My mother and I were the ones to take Annie away so the friends could move all her things that was worth moving into the new little house. However, she trusted me and Mom more than most, and due to the October weather being a little chilly, when she stepped inside and felt the warmth and saw the good food on her old stove, she adapted very well. I still have a glass pitcher she gave me years ago, and a picture of the new little house and Annie. It is one of the stories from my growing up with neighbors that were truly good neighbors, and just downright good and Godly people.

Closing my eyes may not be the best way of looking back sometimes, but the memories are still there, and some of the generations of the older ones come to view. What a shame that sometimes when things get bigger, they are not always better.

Young and Foolish
By Clyde R. Johnson of Port Allegany,
Pennsylvania
Born 1940

I was like any red-blooded American boy that grew up in the 40s; I loved hunting and guns. I was 12 years old and running the family farm on my own. How many kids could do that today? I was exceptionally strong—even at the age of 12—because of wrestling with bulls, calves, and heifers. The farm work, such as lifting 100-pound bags of cattle-feed, also contributed to my strength. I was skinny but strong. One day, when the farm chores were done I decided to go hunting. I dressed up in red hunting gear, took my hunting knife, and a .30-30 caliber rifle. I went up on the hill above our farm for about two hours, but I never saw anything to hunt. I decided to go home and get some work done. I ate my second big meal of the day and didn't feel like working afterwards, so I went back out to hunt. This time, all I wore was a red shirt and hat, because the temperature had risen from the 30s to the 50s. It was December in Pennsylvania. My brother had taken the 30-30 rifle and the hunting knife while I was eating; all I had to hunt with was a .20 gauge shotgun and two pumpkin-ball slugs. I walked back into the woods a few hundred yards, taking the bottom trail, when lo and behold; a huge buck appeared on the trail above. I nervously pulled up and shot at him. He dropped. It was the first time I had ever shot that gun. I walked up the hill, hanging onto trees, because the hill was a steep, vertical incline and very slippery with ice and snow. When I got to the buck, he was standing up, so I grabbed him by the antlers and threw him back to the ground. I tried to finish him off with the remaining pumpkin ball, but I missed because he jumped up as I fired. I threw him down again and tried to kill him with the butt of the shotgun and a stone; neither worked, so I decided to lead him back home. It was hard to hang onto the gun and the buck, because we were going straight down and slipping. I vowed to myself that I wouldn't let him get away, because he was my first deer. I eventually had to leave the gun at the edge of the woods and concentrate on steering my deer. We were probably 300 yards from the house. He was finally leading pretty well, but once we got to a woven wire fence, I tried to lift it and push him underneath; he had

made up his own mind, and we went over the top of the fence instead. I vowed to myself that I would never tell anyone about this, because no one would have believed me anyway. When I started across the road with the buck, a car and a truck were stopped at the stop sign. The drivers were friends of our family and in later years, I worked with both of them at the town factory. So naturally, they blabbed the story to everyone. I continued leading the deer down the road and turned into our driveway. Grandpa was swirling chickens through the air to make them dizzy, so he could behead them with a hatchet. He saw me and belted, "Are you crazy?" "You could get killed!" He killed the deer with his chicken hatchet. Before we dressed him out, he had weighed 226 pounds. He was a monster of a deer for these parts. From that time forward, everyone called me "bring 'em back alive Clyde."

A Boy and His Alpha Shepherd
My dog was like Lassie in the sense, that he was a guardian angel for us kids. He was born around 1950 and died in the early 70s. He was a pure white German shepherd with a white cross on his tail, and he weighed about 80 pounds. He was smart beyond belief and understood almost everything we said to him. Whenever he did something wrong and got scolded by dad, he would climb the barn ladder and hide in the haymow. He used to sleep under the covers with us until he heard my mother coming down the hall and then he would leap onto the floor, as quiet as a mouse. Whenever we had ice cream mother would always say, "Don't give Rover any", so of course we would sneak him a bowl, and he would lick it clean. I believe mother knew what we were doing though.

He "adopted" my oldest brother first and then the rest of us. I remember that when we wanted to go ice-skating, he would herd us away from the ice; we weren't allowed on it until he went out and checked it, to let us know it was safe. Rover was the king of the neighborhood, from the highway to the town. For some reason, all the other dogs knew he was the king and never bothered him. Whenever my brother would ride his bicycle to town—three miles away—without Rover, the dogs along the way always chased him, but when he rode with Rover, all was quiet. Rover would often sit outside of the movie theater until my brother came out of it, if Rover went searching for a female dog, then my brother would leave him, and dad would have to go get him in the morning.

When I went to the movies with him, I was never afraid. Occasionally, I would go to a horror movie, and afterwards, the panthers would be hollering in the distance; I was never afraid to ride home in the dark with Rover. If I went to the movies without him though, my bike pedals were going full speed the whole way home. I remember him catching huge snakes in the hayfield. He would shake them around until they died, and then our little dog would proudly carry them around as if she had killed them. He kept the woodchuck population down as well. He guarded us as if we were his children. Once, we went ice-skating, and Rover checked the ice for us as always; while we were skating, I accidentally drifted from the thick ice to the thin ice and fell through. Rover was instantly there to pull me out, before the water froze over my head. When my brother left for the military, Rover became our dog. He never let us out of his sight. No matter what we did or where we went, Rover went with us.

He stayed with us when we went camping and would guard the door to our tent. He slept inside of it with us and never moved from the entrance. If we heard someone stealing corn, we would let him outside and he quickly resolved the issue. Rover had a female friend on the way to town, and would sometimes run away from home to find her. Dad decided to chain him to the chicken coop to keep him from running off, and lo and behold, Rover took the chicken coop with him when he left. Onetime, the neighbor boy came over to our farm crying. He was having issues with a mean bull. The bull would chase him into the river, every time he tried to herd their cows back home. I told him I would go with him and we would bring Rover with us. That mean bull had the surprise of his life. Rover latched onto the bull's rear leg and broke it in two; the bull had to be butchered.

The neighbors had 14 kids and lived in a nearby shack. They had a huge bobcat as a pet. He weighed at least 20 pounds. He would come over to our farm and sit on our windowsills. Dad told Rover to leave the bobcat alone and Rover did. That cat thought that he was the king instead of Rover. One day, dad was butchering a cow in the barn when the cat snuck in and jumped on top of the meat. Dad threw him out and plugged the hole

he had used to sneak in the barn. Somehow, the bobcat got back in and jumped all over the meat again, so dad picked him up to throw him out again; as he did, the cat scratched him up very badly. The next morning, dad's arm was blue and swollen so we took him to the town hospital, and of course, Rover came with us. They managed to save his arm, and we came home the next day. As we arrived, the bobcat was lounging on our windowsill. Dad opened the car door and told Rover, "Go get him." The cat flew off the windowsill at the mere sight of Rover and headed for the hill never to be seen again.

I had cousins that lived in Buffalo and when they came to visit, they would bring their dog, Ricky. He was the meanest, most vicious, dog on the Earth. If you even blinked, he would tear you apart. They often brought him to our farm, but dad had told Rover to leave him alone on the first encounter. Ricky thought he was king, just like that bobcat had. One day, he killed a couple of dad's prized housecats, so dad told Rover, "Go get him", and that was the end of Ricky. Rover wasn't afraid of bears, panthers, or anything, except minks, which he stayed far away from.

I used to have a crush on the neighbor girl. One day, an older, larger guy came to claim her. He threw me down and was beating on me, when Rover saw him. Rover raced over and latched onto his leg just as he had with that old bull. That was the last time I ever saw the bully; I got the girl too. Later in life—when he was very old—he was chasing a female German shepherd, and three young male German shepherds attacked him; they almost killed him. We poured peroxide on his wounds until he healed. Years later, he became senile and dangerous, so sadly, we had to put him down.

Burnt Tires for Light
By Harry R. Litz of Beech Creek,
Pennsylvania
Born 1947

The year is 1959, I'm 12 years of age and we are in the middle of winter. Back then, we played outside after school, on the weekend, into the night, ice-skating on the canal. Our parents never had to worry they knew where we were. We didn't have computers, cell phones, or video games, but we did have a lot of friends to enjoy the winter season. I can remember we would collect a lot of firewood and old tires to burn for heat and light to skate by. Life back then was simple and carefree. Just around midnight on weekends, we would hear our parents yelling for us and we knew we had to go home. Some of our friends would stop in on their way home to get some hot cocoa and homemade cookies my mother baked. When I bumped into some of those old friends, our thoughts would go back to those good old days. I wish our children had those days to enjoy and to have friends that will be friends for a lifetime.

Wet, Cold, Red Cheeks, and Starving
By Betty Plotts of Port Allegany,
Pennsylvania
Born 1934

Hi! I don't know about you, but the older I get at 77, the more I realize just how much fun I had growing up. I grew up in Coudersport, Pennsylvania in Potter County. When I was a kid, you looked forward to all four seasons because they all had that special something you looked forward to, but for now let me talk about winter.

I can't remember the snow being too deep or the weather being too cold. It just meant another fun day on a snowy hill with your two-runner sled with its long towrope along with several other kids all falling down and trying to stay out of the way of another flying sled. Such fun! By the time you toted your sled along with your soggy wet snowsuit, you were winded and you had to sit for a minute at the top of the hill and catch your breath. You didn't sit for more than a minute before you were ready to do it again and again and yeah, again. Without a watch, (what kid would have a watch?) I managed to get home by six o'clock for supper, wet, cold, red cheeked and starving but already knowing what I would be doing tomorrow and already knowing tomorrow it would be as much fun as it was today. Then, oh yes my day isn't over yet because at seven there would be ice-skating on Othmer's pond. Now it was just a pond, but a huge one that Mr. Othmer would allow lights to be strung across. There was a small building where Bucky Shreaves faithfully would build a fire in a small wood stove so we

could go in and get warm from time to time. Oh, how I remember the 10 or 12 of us hand in hand doing crack the whip and watching someone go flying across the ice, such fun and such laughter! We were getting great exercise, we just didn't know it, and by the way did I mention bruises were plentiful in January and February? Bucky would tell everyone at nine o'clock the little shack would be closing so it was time to take off my skates and head for home. Sometimes I would have sparkly snowflakes drifting softly around my head and would be thinking, isn't it wonderful that there isn't a worry anywhere in the world tonight. I knew there would be hot cocoa not made from a packet but made from cocoa powder, sugar and vanilla simmering on the stove, a warm bed and mom and dad waiting at home. Now I ask you, does life get any better for a kid than that?

Sandblasted and Pin Striped
By Douglas Tressler of Bellefonte,
Pennsylvania
Born 1962

I remember in the early 1970s when my little sister's birthday came around. She wanted a bicycle real bad and my parents did not have the money. My buddies and I came up with a great idea; we wanted to build my sister a bicycle out of other bicycles. We had some old bicycles and used the good parts off of them. First, we had the frame sandblasted and painted and then pin striped it. Then I went and bought her a new seat, basket, bell, mirror, tires, and rims. It took my friends and I about a week to finish. The hardest thing about the whole process was keeping my little sister from finding out. The day of her birthday, she was so surprised. Just seeing a smile on her face was well worth all the work my friends and I did. I really liked growing up in the 1960s and the 1970s. We didn't have computers and video games, we had to go outside and find something to do. We also had a little store in the alley where I used to live. A husband and wife ran it, it was called Alice's. I wish things were like when I grew up. It was so simple back then, I miss the good old days. I grew up on 310 East Lamb Street and I raised my family on 829 West Lamb Street, kind of funny. I know I'm not 60, but I thought you would enjoy my story!

Blowing Bubbles Through a Spool
By Martha Snell of Williamsport,
Pennsylvania
Born 1934

I was born February 5, 1934 in Proctor on Hoppestown Road. A midwife delivered me. I had five sisters, one was a year and a half older than me and the other four were younger than me. We were all delivered by a midwife except the youngest.

We lived on Hoppestown Road, about three miles above Proctor, and I still live on Hoppestown Road today. Back then, there was no electricity, no telephone, and we heated the house with wood. We carried the water from a spring and cooked on a cook stove.

When I was about nine years old, my mother became ill and my dad basically raised us. He was a good dad and a hard worker. He walked to work about four miles and he worked on a sawmill. I remember his pay was about $28 a week. We never went hungry; he taught me how to bake bread. I wasn't very old, but I remember I had to get up on a kitchen chair to mix it. We helped take care of the garden and he taught us how to can stuff. We washed clothes on a washboard, hung them on a clothesline, heated the iron on the cook stove, and ironed the clothes.

We always had enough to eat, not always meat, but lots of vegetables and fruit. We baked pancakes in the morning and had eggs with them. We had an outhouse; I can remember using a Sears and Roebuck catalog for toilet tissue if we ran out.

We were happy kids, we were outside a lot during nice weather, playing hop scotch,

Pricilla, Genevieve, Catherine, Martha, and Myrtle

climbing trees, walking on stilts, picking berries, and fruit. One time my dad caught us, he wasn't happy about it, but we were up on the house roof blowing bubbles through a spool.

As we got older, we used to walk to the community hall, about two and a half miles, to go to square dances. We went swimming quite often, we had to walk about a mile, and we enjoyed it. We went to Barbours to school, where you could go until eighth grade. The school building is still there. One thing I will say is we didn't get a lot of new clothes or a new pair of shoes when school started, we never were on welfare or got food stamps, but we survived. We are all alive still except our oldest sister. I must say I really enjoy reading The Good Old Days Magazine.

Catherine, Genevieve, their dad, Priscilla, Martha, and Martha's sisters

Skinner with his Jackknife
By Ernest C. Butler of Emporium,
Pennsylvania
Born 1939

The Pennsylvania Railroad had a main line on the Northern Region known as the Buffalo Division, which ran from Harrisburg, Pennsylvania to Buffalo, New York. It had a six mile long grade at three percent that started at mile post 113, reached its apex at mile post 107.2 at Keating Summit, Pennsylvania and went downhill at the same three percent angle to mile post 101. During the steam engine era, which ended with the introduction of diesel engines in that area about 1953, the freight trains needed helper engines to assist that were based in Emporium, Pennsylvania. Each steam engine needed a fireman and an engineer because the steamers only pushed forward. There was a wye at Keating Summit, so the helpers could be turned to push either north from Emporium JN, or south from North Relay NR. There was a small manned control tower at Keating Summit called KS. The helpers would disconnect from the train they were assisting and wait for the next assignment, or travel on into JN and finish their days work there and "tie up".

My father was a trackman, or "gandy dancer" for the railroad as was my mother's brother. My dad's brother was a top official out of Buffalo that rarely came in that area. Through the years, many of my family members worked for the railroad including myself, as a signal tower operator or telegrapher.

While I was still a young lad, my first love was the railroad. I absolutely loved the hustle and bustle of all the workers and the railroad lingo, which I pretty much understood. My life's dream was to work for the Pennsy! As I was growing up many people were seriously injured or killed trying to hop aboard a slow moving train in the slowest assent of its uphill climb. Therefore, the employees would chase us away from the property with threats of bodily harm if they caught us.

One man in particular named Skinner, he was an engineer for one of the Emporium helpers, had threatened to cut off my pecker if he ever caught me on the property. On one of my trips to KS I asked who was on the helpers today, and they weren't quite sure but didn't think it was Skinner, whom I was deathly afraid of. To make a long story short, the helpers showed up and guess who was on duty, Skinner! Short, fat, nine year old me took off with Skinner right behind me. Well I'll just outrun him I thought, but I didn't. He caught me, took out his jackknife, opened my pants, had my pride and joy in his hands and I was begging, crying, praying, promising, and vowing this was my last time I would ever be on railroad property and then he let me go. It took me years to realize he was just trying to save me from harm.

For the Love of Hedges
By Shirley L. Johnson of Houtzdale,
Pennsylvania
Born 1949

During the spring of 1990, only two months after my mother died, a stray gray-striped kitten came into my life. Men were crushing cars in a junkyard about a mile up the road and this kitten's mother must have deserted her car-home because he was living in the hedges among three houses. Junkyard cats are usually very mean and untouchable. The neighbor's children must have been petting this kitten because he was very friendly and let one know that he was grateful for attention with loud purring and persistent rubbing of his head on my legs. The cute rolling around and exposing his underside caught ones attention as well.

A young couple had been painting outside with white paint and the kitten had put his front paws right in the tray and tried to drink. One could not help but laugh at his antics. Just a few dishes of milk and a few visits into my home convinced the kitten and myself that he was mine, he was sent to me, and that is why his name became Hedges.

Hedges always wanted to be the center of attention. He liked to play and bite my hands; he even stood up on his hind legs and boxed. He would expose his underside to get his belly rubbed, sometimes he would just lay there and enjoy it and sometimes he would act disturbed and give little love bites, but he never broke the skin. When I was looking at a newspaper or reading a book he would lay right on the top of it to let me know I was not paying enough attention to him, just like a male! Hedges liked to look out windows, and he was smart because he knew the seasons. He was the boss of the house and could look out almost any window he wanted. Hedges was fascinated by baby robins, the rain, the snow, or anything moving, especially other cats. One would not think that he was fixed. When I knitted or crocheted the moving yarn fascinated him, and we danced one stitch forward and two stitches back. When I left for work I would say, "Be a good boy, don't break anything!" and when I returned home, he was always glad to see me and I was glad to see him.

My friend Helen told me I should get a Benson to go with Hedges, but when I tried to

Hedges

adopt another kitten Hedges was so jealous he would not eat for three days. I thought if I got a little Benson, it would have to be a canine, so there was no competition.

Hedges, did you know how important you were to me? How appropriate your name was! You hedged loneliness from me. You have lessened my grief and multiplied my joy. You were entertaining when you wanted to play. You were always there waiting for me to come. You were more faithful and loving than a lot of people I knew. You shared my friends and you consoled me by sitting on my lap, purring and letting me hug you often. You would follow me from one room to another, watching my every move. Oh, what love you showed me! Our love for each other outlasted your nine lives and my one. May we meet again in Heaven someday.

Back When Kids Were Kept in Line
By Betty J. Hazel of Williamsport,
Pennsylvania
Born 1944

I would like to share my memories about the good old days. I was one of ten children born to Alice and Forrest Peterson. I was born in Wellsville, New York. My mom told me I looked like a little bird when I was born. She said I didn't walk until I was about two years old, I always wanted to be carried all the time. Of the ten of us, I have one sister who is my oldest sibling who lives in Elkland, Pennsylvania and three brothers whom all live here in Williamsport.

Growing up as we were in our younger days, we didn't have much, but we had each other. We would make our own entertainment by putting on plays for our parents or singsongs, all my brothers could play any instrument,

which they still do today. My oldest brother, William, and my younger brother, John, play at different clubs around town. My middle brother was on a championship basketball team in the 1960s in high school.

The kids today don't know how good they have it and they want everything. We were happy with our gifts that we got for Christmas and a game of bingo or checkers to share. Hand me downs were a must for us. Food was something we didn't have much of but we never complained because we knew our folks did the best they could. My mother did day work for different households and would make sure we had something, but we were never on welfare. We didn't dare talk back to our parents like some kids do today or we would get backhanded. We were taught to respect our parents and our elders by saying yes ma'am and yes sir.

I quit school in the second half of the 11th grade to go to work and have been working ever since. I started working for my aunt after school before I quit school. Then she told me about a job at the old Carroll House downtown. Her older daughter was working there and was going to retire so I went and applied for the job. I was 17 years old and you had to be 18 years old. I told them I would be 18 in a couple of weeks, so they hired me in 1963 and I worked there for 10 years. I was married in 1965 and had a daughter. When I had my daughter I took a leave for about eight months then went back to work for a few

Betty's mom, Alice m. Peterson

41

Betty's husband, James Hazel, Jr.

more years. They were going to cut my hours as the store traffic was slowing down, but I told them I had to work full time, because I had a daughter to take care of. I left there and went to Buckeye Pretzel Company, but only worked there for a few months. I saw an ad in the paper for a housekeeper in a nursing home. I went and applied and was hired the next day and am still there after 38 years almost 39 years come June. I work at the Williamsport

Betty and her daughter, Tina

Home, I started there in June 1973 then I had my second daughter in 1979.

I have two older grandchildren and two younger grandchildren. They all live in Virginia and North Carolina. I only see them in the summer, usually in August when we have our Sunday school reunion with all the churches. They keep in touch by phone. My oldest daughter was in the Army and traveled the world and ended up in Virginia. When my youngest daughter graduated from high school, she wanted to be near her sister who was like a second mom to her, so she went to be with her.

I didn't say much about my husband, we used to be the best dancers in town in our younger days. He was in a singing group and they called themselves the temptations, not the famous group seen on television but they sang in a lot of towns. We don't get around much anymore as he has a problem walking well.

That's about it for now. I could probably write a whole book just about the Williamsport Home, I have been there so long and met a lot of residents and co-workers along the way.

We lost a lot of friends along the way and most of the elders are gone now they kept the kids in line back when.

A Coalminer's Son
By Glenn C. Johnson of Madera, Pennsylvania
Born 1926

My dad was born in 1894 to an immigrant Norwegian family. I recall him telling me that his father took him in the coalmines at age 13 and that he was so small his dinner bucket would drag on the ground. Coal cars were allotted, if you would bring your sons along you would get a bigger allotment. My dad and mother had very little schooling because my dad had to go into the coalmines and my mother was the oldest in a family of seven. My mother had to take over the family after her mother died at a young age.

I was born in 1926 just in time to experience the good and the bad of the depression. There was good because it made us appreciate everything we had and bonded us together closer as a closer. I remember the

42

house where we lived in a small village on the outskirts of a small mining town. It had a wooden shingle roof that caught fire several times from sparks, and there was no way to call the fire company. There was a chicken coop and an outside toilet at the rear of the lot. The kitchen had my mother's dream, a coal fired cook stove, with a big oven, a warming oven above and chrome bars across the front. Our living room had a "warm morning" coal stove and the bedrooms were unheated. In the hall, there was what we called a "Slop Jar" which we used as a toilet during the night. During the day, we would grab an old Sears and Roebuck catalog and run up the yard to a cold seat in the outhouse. One job I always hated was to clean out the chicken coop. I had to shovel the droppings off the floor and put it in the garden. However, having chickens provided us with eggs and a good Sunday dinner once in a while.

My dad would do carpentry work when it was available, but very seldom received any money. He would come home with a few chickens, eggs, and sometimes a sewing machine or a deer rifle, money was scarce for everyone. I remember my dad got a pretty big job to build a summer camp for a local dentist, but he didn't get any money, instead he let his wages ride on deposits so his kids could get free dental service. My brother said later in life that we were poor but we didn't know we were, everyone was in the same boat. With a lot of hard work from my dad and mother, we survived to find things getting better in the late 1930s. Speaking of hard work, I remember my dad going up on the hill behind us and digging a shaft to get enough coal out for the winter in a bucket then taking it home in a wheel barrel.

I had hand me down clothes until I was 12 or so. What wasn't used my mother sewed, she was a good seamstress. My first store bought clothes I remember were a suit, white shirt, and tie. My mother gave up a lot so her boys could have a white shirt and suit for church.

Saturday night was the time to do the shopping and for us kids the movies, 11-cents gave us about two hours of entertainment. We didn't have a car and I remember holding dad's hand and walking home half asleep and my mother carrying her shopping basket with whatever groceries we could afford. We had no scheduled recreation; we had to provide it ourselves. I remember our baseball team; a neighbor called us "The ragged-ass nine".

If you had a glove, ball, or bat you were automatically on the team.

Our first car that I remember was a huge four door Studebaker with windows and a soft top. After it stopped, running us kids played in it. The next car was a 1932 Dodge Coupe with a rumble seat and later a 1934 Terraplane with suicide doors that opened the opposite way. Gasoline was six gallons for a dollar and kerosene was 10-cents a gallon. When we were old enough my brother and I would each put up a quarter and buy three gallons of gasoline. We would go to a local state park where we had a boat stashed away.

My first job was selling "White Cloverine Salve", we didn't get money only prizes, I got my first wristwatch this way. My next job was selling the "Grit" a weekly newspaper published in Williamsport, Pennsylvania. It sold for five cents a copy and I got two cents for delivering it. I built my route to about 60 customers and made a $1.20 per week, which made me feel very independent. I couldn't participate in sports in high school because I always had a part time job after school and on Saturdays for $7 a week. I joined the Four H Club and grew sweet corn, which I sold for 20-cents a dozen.

We kept busy and had what we thought, was a good and full life. It was the worst of times but I think many times it was also the best of times.

The Painful Laundry Lesson
By Joyce S. Kuntz of St. Marys,
Pennsylvania
Born 1926

My story dates back to 1939 when I was finished with grade school at thirteen and about to enter high school.

It was late summer and I guess my mother decided it was time to teach me more than just doing dishes and odd jobs. We went down to the basement where an older wringer washer stood; it was electrified. We had a mobile set of laundry tubs with two compartments; one side was filled, from a hose, with clear warm water, and the other side with cold water with liquid bluing added.

The trick was to swing the wringer in position to lift the soapy washed clothes through the wringer into the clean warm water

Joyce Smith Kuntz 1939-40

on one side of the laundry tub. The soap used in the washing machine was a bar of Fels-Naptha soap, which my mother shaved into the hot water in the washing machine.

So after she demonstrated how, I was then supposed to lift the rinsed clothes, swirled around by hand, swing the wringer into another position, and feed clothes into the bluing water, this made white clothes whiter and colored clothes brighter. Then the final step was to take the clothes, put them in the wringer again on their way to the clothesbasket on the floor.

My mother left me to go to the second floor to remake beds.

So I, bored I'm sure, tackled my new job. I finished stage number one and was performing the second stage, into the bluing. I had medium length blonde hair and was leaning into my task when all of a sudden I felt the top of my hair being tugged into the wringer.

I'm yelling, my mother is not hearing me, and when my scalp reached the guts of the wringer and pulling hard, I had presence enough of mind to grasp above my head and try to feel for the reverse handle on the wringer.

As I could feel the pressure letting go, and what was left of my hair being slowly released, my mother appeared, got all excited, and I'm shaken and moaning about the loss of my hair.

Needless to say, I had a headache for a few days, and a bald spot on the top of my head.

I can't recall if my mother ever again asked me to do the laundry.

My Grandmother
By Anonymous of Williamsport,
Pennsylvania
Born 1947

Williamsport, Pennsylvania was a good, clean, friendly town when I was growing up. People seemed to do more things for their neighbors and were part of their lives.

My grandmother passed away when I was just nine years old, but I remember so much about her.

My grandparents lived in Newberry and not too far away from the railroad yards. My grandfather worked on the Reading Railroad until he retired.

Back then, we had what they called hobos who came into town as stowaways on the railroad cars and they left the same way. My grandmother would answer her doorbell and there would be a hobo standing there. She asked them to go around to the back of the house and wait on the porch steps. She would take them out a drink and sometimes a snack to hold them over until she could either warm something up or cook them something to eat. She kept a special set of dishes and silverware just for them to eat from so they would feel special. She had a heart of gold. Wintertime it was a hot meal and summer time usually a sandwich or two and soup and always a dessert of some kind. Plus a sandwich or two and or sometimes just buttered bread in a plastic sandwich bag to take along with them when they left. Another thing I remember well was they always rang the porch doorbell when they were finished with their meal and thanked my grandmother for her thoughtfulness.

What was really funny, about an hour or so after they left my grandmother's house, she would send one of us kids out front to wash a yellow mark off the front steps. Sometimes you really had to look hard for it, up between the steps a yellow X showed the next hobo coming to town where to find a good meal. I am sure they passed the word around anyways.

My grandmother was the type of person who never turned anyone away from her doorstep, especially if they were hungry.

Growing Up on the Move
By Ida E. Norris of Curwensville, Pennsylvania
Born 1920

I was born to Asbury and Artensa "Swatsworth" McKee on December 7th, 1920. I am the youngest of six children, Edward Lee, Lavoine Joe, Howard Clark, Annie Zoe, Elden Emory, and Ida Elizabeth.

My home was about a mile below Olanta, Pennsylvania along the Little Clearfield Creek Road. I walked up the hill and through the field to the Evergreen School, an old one-room country school with eight grades in one building and one teacher. At that time, my first grade teacher was Eldon Bloom. My second grade teacher was Floyd Knobbs.

Sometime during that year, my parents moved to Franklin, Pennsylvania at the suggestion of my brother, Howard. He was able to get some carpenter work for Dad. That did not last long, work slowed so my parents moved back to Mother's childhood home which had been vacant for some time. Dad repaired the house and we lived there for several years. I went to another country school, Mt. Calm, until after eighth grade.

After I took the eighth grade county exam, I was ready to go to high school. Then I went to live with Aunt Martha Wallace, Mother's sister, in Clearfield. I lived there for a year or so when Dad decided to move to a farm below Clearfield, near what is now the Truck Stop Restaurant. I went from there to high school, riding with a neighbor each morning when he delivered cans of fresh milk to the dairy in Clearfield. For some reason, Dad decided to move to Hyde City, also near Clearfield. While living there, I graduated from Clearfield High School in 1938.

After graduation, I baby sat the children of Violet Carter for a while. Olen and I were married at the Methodist Parsonage in Curwensville, Pennsylvania on July 14th, 1940, by the Rev. L. Vance Greene with Mrs. Marie Shaffer and Miss Olive Snyder as witnesses. Olen and I had four children: Ruth Ann (Norris) Mitchell born February 10th, 1941; Olen James Norris Jr. born July 22nd, 1942; Lavoine Alan Norris born November 5th, 1946; and Dennis Eugene Norris born March 4th, 1954. As of this time, there have been two deaths in my family, my husband Olen on March 14th, 1987 and my son Lavoine on June 3rd, 2001.

Dairy Farm Memories
By Ellen Trebik Wiker of Lancaster, Pennsylvania
Born 1932

My parents were Tony and Laura Trebik. I was one of five kids, Pete, Eva, me, Betty and John deceased. We lived on a six hundred acre farm two miles outside of Ellisburg. We went to a one-room school in Ellisburg until seventh grade then we went to Genesee High School.

Miss Kathryn Cooney was our teacher from first through sixth grade. Bill Collar used to come early Monday morning and start the fire in a big stove and kept it burning all week. We got water from Fred Costell's store for drinking. We had outside toilets, one for girls and one for boys. We went to church and Sunday school in Ellisburg. Robert Shannon was the minister. We had Christmas plays at Christmas time. We got a box of candy, nuts, and an orange. I remember when john was little; he had to recite a poem at Christmas. I told old Shep on Christmas Eve that he had to sleep in bed with me because he might bark at Santa Claus and chase him up the Christmas tree.

Charlie Haskell was our neighbor; he helped my dad a lot. We made maple syrup, raised chickens, and had a dairy farm. We lived two miles from the main road on a dirt road. Wintertime was brutal. The milk man used to take us to school if my dad couldn't

The farm in 1951

get out and if the milk man couldn't get up, my dad used to take us in a horse and sled with the milk cans and us all bundled up to stay warm. We walked home from school in the winter and summer.

We had a pony and Charlie used to take him over the winter because he took the lids off the milk cans and drank the milk.

We didn't participate in school activities because we had chores to do at nighttime.

In the summer, we went about a mile and a half through the pasture to a watering trough to pump water for the cows and at nighttime to bring them home to be milked.

Pete, Eva, and I graduated from Genesee High School.

In 1952, dad sold the farm to Ivan Smoker and we moved to Union City, Pennsylvania on a small farm.

We married and moved our separate ways. I live in Lancaster, Pennsylvania and love it. No dairy farm.

We go back when they have the school reunions but even that is getting smaller.

The farm in 2003 after the tornado went through

The Patch Kids
By Jay B. Decker of Cogan Station,
Pennsylvania
Born 1940

The Patch is a section of Williamsport that is a remnant of a bygone era of lumbering. Today a highway has taken a large portion of it but when I lived there as a young boy it contained a dozen or so houses with lots of kids. It's isolated from the rest of town by an elevated railroad with one street that goes under a stone overpass and that is the only way into the Patch. That isolation made it a unique place to grow up with fields, gardens, woods, ponds, and many other rural things that most kids don't have in a town setting.

In the late forties, the victory garden idea was still going strong and the river bottom soil in the Patch was ideal for it. Many people from other parts of town would rent plots, spending evenings after supper tending their vegetables. Nearby at the edge of the gardens high weeds bordered the deep woods that ran to the riverbank. All though the summer, we would hide in the weeds watching the progress of the vegetables. We were like highwaymen waiting for the exact right moment to strike.

I can still remember the odor of damp earth and sweaty sneakers as we crawled along, single file, through the rows of plantings. It would be dark and the only sound would be the buzzing of a mosquito next to your ear. We didn't consider ourselves thieves. We were simple sharing the harvest of gardens that were, after all, in our domain. Under the only streetlight in the Patch, we would later sit and share our loot munching away and swatting bugs until we were called home for bedtime.

Even though nearly everyone had gotten some form of inside plumbing by then there were many outhouses still in use in the Patch. It was an unwritten rule that kids could use any of them if they were in the area and had to go. Mr. Mancy had an outhouse for when he drank too much and his wife would get mad at him and yell if he just went behind a tree. Chubby Hansel had an outhouse. She weighted about three hundred pounds and a trip to her upstairs bathroom was often too much effort for her. She had the finest outhouse in the world, too. It was made of concrete from floor to roof. The story was that she had made friends with W.P.A. workers that were building a culvert under the railroad during the depression and she had traded pies made from her pear tree in exchange for them making her an outhouse. When they ordered concrete for the culvert, they made sure there was enough to make Chubby's outhouse too. The pies must have been pretty good because they didn't just make a plain box. Inside it had a baffle wall and two seats with little windows up high enough so no one could see in. The roof was peaked with a little chimney at the top that emitted a bad smell.

Mr. Hansel had a garden behind the outhouse and he would prop his wheelbarrow against the back wall when he wasn't using it. It made a great makeshift ladder for us to get on top of the outhouse roof. It was our favorite place to play war or cowboys and Indians, pretending we were on a stone ledge ready to carry out an ambush.

One year, just before the 4th of July, my father returned from down south with a box of fireworks. I was fascinated with them and particularly the little cherry looking things. They even had a green stem on them that I guess was the fuse. My dad noticed my interest and sternly warned me not to touch them, which made them even more special and I knew I was going to take some of them at the first opportunity.

No one thought anything of it when I went into my grandfather's outhouse one day soon after that, but I didn't have to use it. I was after some of the barnburner matches that he kept there for lighting his pipe. We were never allowed to carry matches so when we needed them for something special we would "borrow" them from grandpap's outhouse. They were particularly neat because you could light them by striking them on any rough surface.

I took our secret path through the woods along the railroad bank where I met up with my best friend Fred and his buddy Jim. We continued to a small run that widened out to a stagnant pond everyone called the "gut" behind Chubby's house. A little scratched from the wild raspberries, but unnoticed, we crawled up the bank of the gut until we could peer over the rhubarb leaves at the end of the yard. About twenty-five yards away between the house and garden sat the outhouse with a maple tree off to the side that blocked any one inside from seeing us as we sprinted to the back of the outhouse. Reaching the concrete wall, we stood with our backs to it soaking up its coolness through our damp polo shirts. Just then, a shrill call came from three houses away, "Jaiimm!" It was Jim's mother calling him.

He looked at us briefly before dashing for the gut and only then did he answer with an "I'm coming, Mom."

A slam that nearly scared us to death announced that somebody had just come out though Chubby's back screen door. As soon as we heard the top step groan, we knew Chubby was on her way to the outhouse. Without a word, we moved over to where the wheelbarrow was leaning on the wall and slithered up over it and onto the roof. Sitting on the back sloped part of the roof, still out of sight of the house I reached in my pocket and took out one of the cherry bombs. Beneath us, we could hear Chubby go in and with a rustling of clothes, she settled herself down.

As if we had planned and rehearsed it, Fred struck a match on the roof, lit the fuse and I reached up and dropped the cherry bomb down the little chimney. Neither the why of it nor the results of what might happen entered my mind. It was such a purely natural act, at the time, that it seemed for an instant as if that was the end of it. The explosion was not only loud enough to shock us out of our wits; we could feel it reverberate through the concrete roof. I felt as though my heart had jumped into my throat and my toes and fingers tingled. We stared open mouthed at each other for a second or two while a wispy puff of white smoke drifted lazily out of the little chimney.

Chubby burst out through the outhouse door, her mouth was wide open letting forth with a high pitched scream that hurt my ears nearly as bad as the fireworks. She ran with little baby steps, hobbled by her pink underpants that were still down around her ankles. She flailed her arms in an effort to gain momentum and with her dress only half way down her legs we could see her thighs were jiggling out of step with the rest of her legs.

The shock of what we had done hit us suddenly and we stood and ran off the back of the roof with such abandonment that our feet were still moving in the air causing us to stumble and fall when we hit the ground. We scrambled to our feet and raced for the safety of the bank where we half crawled through the under growth along the gut. Struggling through the vines and brambles, we made our way to a tree house we had built above the edge of the gut far from any house. Scurrying up into it we sat in silent terror, the only sound was our heavy breathing. I looked at Fred and he had that blank wide-eyed look that kids get when they are really scared. His cheeks were slack and his mouth was slightly ajar. As I watched him, the corners of his mouth began to curl into a faint smile. Without realizing it, I also began to grin. From his throat came a bubbly giggle and I felt something vibrating up into my throat too. Suddenly the laughter burst from us with a roar, spending all our breath and causing us to roll on the floor gasping for air. We laughed so hard that my ribs hurt and tears flowed down my cheeks as we hung onto each other to keep from falling out of the tree house.

Eventually we calmed down enough to try to plan our lie. The lingering giddiness kept us from forming a really good story so we finally decided to fall back on the universal plan that kids use when in trouble; we were going to play dumb and deny knowing anything about it.

Three rhythmic blasts from a car horn was my signal to head home for supper. I knew from experience not to ignore that signal so I ran for home planning my alibi as I went. To my surprise, not a word about Chubby was said during or after the meal. Later I walked to the streetlight where Fred was waiting. He asked if my mom had said anything and then said that he had not heard a word from his family either.

When Jim joined us later his eyes were wide and he asked us what had happened because there had been a real ruckus over at the Hansel place. Fred and I giggled and shoved each other until he insisted we tell him. After we told him the whole story, his eyes were even bigger and he kept saying how much trouble we were in. we were feeling pretty confident that if there was going to be trouble it would have happened to us by now so we decided to walk by the Hansel's house and see what was what. We sauntered down the dirt street hands stuffed deep in our pockets trying to look casual but probably looking as guilty as could be. Trying not to be obvious as we passed, we sneaked looks while pretended to wipe our noses on our sleeves. There didn't seem to be anyone around until a voice dripping with sweetness said from the porch, "Hi there boys."

Chubby had been sitting on her specially made swing behind one of those colored bamboo strip curtains. She asked what we were up to wandering around when it was nearly dark. She was being so nice that I was starting to feel badly about what we had done to her except she was being a little too nice. She called us over to talk a bit so we wandered over to the steps and plopped ourselves down mumbling something about the weather, the damned mosquitoes this year, etc.

Then without warning, she dropped the bomb on us. "You know, somebody pulled a real mean trick on me today." We stared and waited as she went on, "Somebody scared me so bad in my own outhouse that I couldn't make it up my own back steps. Poor Mr. Hansel tried to help me and hurt his back something awful. I just know he won't be able to do his gardening this summer."

We sincerely said how sorry we were to hear that and shook our heads at how anybody could be so mean as all that. She said that it was especially terrible that they would be going without fresh vegetables all summer since Mr. Hansel wouldn't be able to weed and hoe. After some more small talk, we made our way back to the streetlight. Jim looked at us with his most serious expression and said, "You guys know what you have to do now, right?"

We did and later that night a large paper bag filled with fresh picked vegetables was left on the Hansel's front porch. All though the summer other garden produce would find its way to their porch. Not once did it occur to us to offer to work Mr. Hansel's garden for him. We did what any Patch kid would have done and I think Robin Hood would have understood.

School Days
By Vivian A. Steinbacher Eck of
Williamsport, Pennsylvania
Born 1935

I started first grade in 1942. At that time, there were no kindergarten classes. Since I was from a Catholic family who belonged to Immaculate Conception Church, I attended our parochial school. There was no bus transportation for me because I lived on a farm, which was located in Bastress Township. The students who lived in Collomsville, Oval, and Ecktown were provided bus transportation by the church.

I had a sister that was five years older than me who also attended the same school. Each day we walked two and a half miles to school. If the weather was good, no deep snow, we walked over the mountain and saved ourselves a half mile. It took us about one hour to complete the trip.

We didn't think this was a hardship and if we were lucky enough to have a car stop and offer a ride, we gratefully took it, even if we didn't know who was driving. My parents were never afraid that we were going to be abducted, nor ever warned us about strangers.

There was no fancy playground equipment, but we played old fashion games, such as Red Rover, jump rope, and baseball games. Oh, yes, our bathroom facilities were outdoor privies.

Vivian holding Tom (nephew)
1942

When you managed to get to the seventh and eighth grades, your room was in the basement next to the furnace room, which was fueled by burning wood. Of course, the boys kept the fire going. Also, the seating was four across for each grade with no aisle between the seventh and eighth grades. Therefore, if the person on the inside had to go to the blackboard, everyone in that row had to get up to let them out.

In that time, there were no snow days. We started school the week after Labor Day and ended the first week of May because most of us were needed at home to work on the farms.

On the first Friday of each month, we had a special Mass at our church and after we were able to buy a tin cup of coffee from the "Cook Sister" to drink with our breakfast. Everyone looked forward to this special treat.

After I graduated from eighth grade, I began high school at St. Mary's High School in Williamsport. As there was at that time a private bus service to the city from our area I used it for transportation. As it stopped on Mulberry Street, I ran from there to St. Boniface Church on Washington Blvd. in order to get to Mass at eight o'clock in the morning. I didn't want to be late because that was one of the requirements, along with many others, to be exempted from taking any finals, which I managed through my four years at St. Marys.

My parents paid twenty-five dollars a year for me to attend that school. At Immaculate Conception, there was no tuition as we were members of that church.

I enjoyed all twelve years of my education and never expected anyone to make excuses for me. I was responsible and I worked to do my best.

In My Father's House
By Barbara L. Faque Stirling Wood of
Muncy, Pennsylvania
Born 1932

I have lived forty years at 10 Bruner Street, in the rural town of Muncy, Pennsylvania, near the Susquehanna River, in my Father's house. Let me tell you about my Father and his house when he was a little boy. His name is Harland Dimm Fague.

He and his mother, Emma Dimm Fague, and his father, John Wilson Fague, moved into this house in 1905 when he was five years old with Esther, his big sister, six years older than he. They came from Op, Pennsylvania where the family ran its country post office and store. His father weighed in the lumber. He was kicked by a horse while unloading some and his kidneys were injured; thus, their decision to move to town.

Little Harland was a toe head and a bright, curious boy. I imagine him getting about in this house. Especially do I think of him on those wooden stairs to the second floor that became narrow on the inner side when they turned.

Barbara's father, Harland Dimm Fague with his sister,
Esther M. Fague

49

The house is a clapboard, wooden, white painted house with an "L" shaped front porch and a small back porch. Its porch roofs have always been painted forest green underneath and their floors are grey. It wouldn't look right if it wasn't that. There is a back pantry with built in white painted, wooden cupboards. Here canning could be stored and a pull out flour bin was a definite need for making bread. In this room, a well with a hand pump brought needed water up into a zinc dry sink for the family's use. The outhouse, always a necessity, was built over a pit in the backyard but chamber pots were used inside on cold nights or for emergencies. I think back to the years when Father was a child in this house. It was from 1905 until 1921, the year he graduated from Muncy High School. The jelly closet was upstairs in the room where indoor plumbing was finally installed, about 1945. There was a parlor stove and a cooking stove to keep the house warm. The parlor and the dining room could be made into one big room, as you could push the room divider, wooden doors, apart. The family pride and joy was a pump organ which Harland's mother played when the "Women's Home and Foreign Missionary Society" met there in 1910, when Harland was seven. Each one had a bed upstairs.

The cousins, Roy, Lena, and Helen lived in town and the families visited back and forth frequently. When you saw the horse and buggy tied up outside, then you knew Aunt Mary, Uncle Clarence and Cousin Emma from Milton had come.

The backyard had a barn just like the other

Barbara's father's house, his mother is standing in front 1916

houses on the street, big enough for the buggy, a horse, and some hay. It stayed up until it was no longer used and started to lean. So it was torn down in about 1940. The family also had their own chickens for fresh eggs. The garden path runs down the middle of the back yard from the back porch to the alley. On the one side would be the potato patch and on the other, a vegetable garden. A grape arbor and apple tree also provided family fruit.

At the end of the block was Glade Run, which made a fun place for little children to wade and cool off. The Lutheran Church had rebuilt out of the flood district of town by March 1, 1908 and could be walked to on Sundays for Sunday school and church. Every summer, there was the Hoffman Reunion at Trout Pond Park, like an all day family picnic.

When Harland was sixteen years old, his father died; his father had worked as a night watchman for a local industry. He had been in declining health since their move. Harland's mother, to make ends meet, took in boarders, female students at the Muncy Normal Teacher Training School. The old, oak boarding table now had all its leaves in use and filled the whole dining room. Harland was relocated to sleep in the attic so his bedroom could be rented out.

By this time, he was considering what his future studies could be. The new Lutheran minister, Rev. B.F. Bieber, became like a father to Harland. He encouraged him to attend Susquehanna Lutheran College in Selinsgrove and then go on to seminary to become a minister.

Aunt Mary Bieber's mantle clock still needs winding every week and the days are now quieter in this old house but I know and feel that this is my Father's house.

The Neighborhood
By Ronald F. Calkins of Muncy,
Pennsylvania
Born 1929

The half-mile square Williamsport neighborhood where I was born and raised was an area where any active boy would like to be born. It was bound on the north by High Street, the south by West Fourth Street, the east by Stevens Street and the west by Dewey Avenue and Arch Street. It had Lycoming Creek flowing through it for swimming, fishing, ice skating, and playing along. In addition, it had Bowman Field Minor League Baseball Park, Memorial Park Playground, a roller skating rink, two sandlot baseball fields, and a tennis court. Along with all the recreational opportunities, it also had an elementary school, two churches, an aircraft engine manufacturing plant, two silk mills, a soft drink bottling plant, and a grain storage warehouse. With the tree-lined streets, the neat homes, and the well kept yards, it was an ideal place to grow up in.

Our little neighborhood had many small businesses to take care of the residents needs. They included six Mom and Pop grocery stores, a meat market, ice cream parlor, steak house, bar, funeral parlor, bank, post office, used furniture and used book store, drugstore, lumber yard, and two auto repair garages, one that sold gas. My father had a general repair shop where he repaired locks, guns, bicycles, lawn mowers, and many other things too numerous to mention.

I was born in 1929 and raised during the worst financial depression in our country's history and the worst war in the history of the world, World War II. Despite the National and International troubles that occurred during those sixteen years from 1929 to 1945, I only have fond memories of growing up in the neighborhood.

Some of the residents of the neighborhood went on to become involved in well known events of the 20th century. They include the founder of Little League Baseball, a World War II hero, a Pennsylvania State Senator, a musician, and an average working man.

June 6th, 1939, when I had just turned ten years old, the first Little League game was played on one of the sandlot fields outside of Bowman Field. I saw that game and many of the first Little League games. Carl Stotz, the founder of Little League, conceived the idea while playing ball with his two nephews in his backyard. As time went on Carl and his associates had a field built that was called the Original Little League Field. The first twelve State, National and World Series games were played on that field. Little League baseball that is played by millions of children around the world and the Little League World Series, shown on TV all over the world each August, started there in our neighborhood.

Al Yearick who was the first Little Leaguer to sign a Minor League Baseball contract and

The entrance to The Carl E. Stotz Field

Ed Younken who pitched the first no-hitter in Little League history were both residents of the neighborhood. The fact that the first Little League game field and the first Little League World Series field are located in the neighborhood is due to Carl Stotz and his wife along with his associates and their wives. They had a vision and with great leadership made it come true.

Joe Lockard, another resident, is listed in World War II history books as one of the two soldiers that were manning a radar station on Oahu Island in the Hawaiian Islands on December 7th, 1941. They informed their superior there were planes approaching Oahu from the north. He told them that they were probably some of our B-17 bombers coming in from the States and ignored their warning. The result was the surprise attack on Pearl Harbor that caused us to become involved in World War II. Joe was awarded the Distinguished Service Medal by our government and also was called a "Hero of Pearl Harbor" by the Associated Press.

Dick Confair was the owner of Confair Bottling Company that had its bottling plant located in the neighborhood. He lived next door to the plant. Active in politics, he became a Pennsylvania State Senator. Despite having great opposition from big city lawmakers, he was able to get the interstate highway Route 80, then known as the "Keystone Shortway", built in north-central Pennsylvania. Route 80 now runs from New York City to San Francisco. The Pennsylvania section of Route 80 is named after him due to his efforts.

Dan Eddinger, a boyhood friend of mine, went on to become an accomplished musician and played for well known orchestras that backed up some popular singers including

Frank Sinatra.

My involvement in well known events of the 20th century began from 1947 to 1951 as an employee of Harder Sporting Goods Company, a supplier of equipment for Little League teams in the Williamsport area. I helped outfit Little League players in the first State and National Series games that led to the Little League World Series that is shown on TV all over the world every summer.

In 1961, while employed by M.W. Kellogg Power Piping, I was part of a team that bent pipe to make piping assemblies for Con-Edison's first nuclear power plant in the New York City area.

As a material control coordinator for Litton Corporation, I had to get material sent in to manufacture the "Cooker Tube" which was one of the first electron tubes used in microwave ovens that are found in millions of homes around the world today. While I was employed by Litton in 1967, the first commercial Litton Microwave Oven using the tubes we were making was offered for sale to the public.

Starting in 1974, I had to get material sent in to make electric motors for the Alaska Pipeline while employed by U.S. Electrical Motors in their production and material control department.

I think the involvement by people of our neighborhood in well known State, National, and International events of the 20th Century is quite remarkable. All this participation in our country's history came from residents of a half mile square neighborhood located in a beautiful rural area of Pennsylvania on the West Branch of the Susquehanna River.

The Raft
By Melvin D. Woodring of Osceola Mills, Pennsylvania
Born 1943

It was February 1956, hunting season was over, the holidays a distant memory, and when you are thirteen with an active imaginative mind the next adventure is just around the corner. The fuel that fed this mind was found in the school library. Not seeking academic excellence, but searching for heroes the likes of Huck Finn, Tom Sawyer, Davy Crocket, and anyone who could brave the unknown frontiers of history and be victorious. Add

to this a twenty-three inch black and white television that teamed with western heroes who were six foot tall and bulletproof. Good and evil was clearly defined then. There was no shading of either entity. You would have been judged extremely weird to have elected to be anything but upright and virtuous. To that, add the Christian values that is still prevalent in our little community of Scotch Hollow and you have the foundation of an admirable person.

Scotch Hollow was in fact a little village, but no one called it a village, it was always, the "Hollow" or properly Scotch Hollow. We were three miles from town, had a graveled dirt road through it, and almost all nineteen houses that were there faced the road on one side or the other. At the end of the road was the community church, a simple white building, which is still there today. Of course, the road didn't end, it continued on for another two or three hundred yards, formed a T intersection, and from that point, it was hard paved road. There was no city water or sewage, electricity had only been available for the last twenty or twenty-five years. Telephones were rapidly being installed; there were about a dozen houses that now had them. All on party lines of course. For those who don't know what a party line is, it is where more than one person shares a telephone line into their house. Each person would have a distinct ring on their phone for their incoming calls, one long two short or some combination. It was not uncommon for someone on the line to pick on your ring and hear everything that was said, all by mistake of course. People got very good at detecting when a third party was listening in. I still have a phobia about talking on a phone, but I'm almost over it. Still nothing beats face to face communication.

All this said, by today's standards this was a pretty boring life, but in fact, it was just the contrary. Very little inhibited a kid from searching out their own entertainment or adventures, with parental restriction and common sense the exception of course, but even these was debatable when you're thirteen.

It was after all February, the slow boring time of winter. I left the house searching for something to do. I walked up the old railroad tracks, which was just in front of the house where it crossed the road and traveled to the tipple where the rail cars were loaded with coal. The tracks had been inactive for several years now. The easy reached coal having been extracted, and until bigger and more powerful equipment came along, it would remain the same way.

I traveled a short distance then turned to climb the huge spoil pile that was parallel to the railroad tracks for a quarter of a mile. This area had once been a slow sloping hillside, but had been opened mined, or stripped as the locals called it. The spoil pile was the results of the earth being removed over the vein of coal they were trying to reach, the results being huge piles of earth that resembled miniature mountains. To a thirteen year old, they were mountains, full of adventure. When I reached the top, I looked down into the cut that was made when they removed the coal; this had been abandoned and was no longer active. There had been no effort to reclaim the land. Reclamation laws were very lax then. The results of which was ruined trout streams, fresh water and land that would have devastating results down to the Chesapeake Bay from here in central Pennsylvania. Men were ignorant, thinking it would clean itself up with time, others just greedy, in the majority I expect was a combination of the both. Right now, these things were not firm convictions that needed to be corrected, for right now in this imaginative mind the seed of a new adventure was beginning to sprout. As I stood looking down into the cut, which was about three hundred yards long, I saw a road leading into the cut for a hundred yards abruptly ending at the beginning of the water that formed the rest of the cut. The water was filled with muddy runoff and alkaline that stained it a light red. This was all frozen solid, a good six inches thick and as smooth as glass with a light covering of snow on it. Funny what the eye can see but the mind will interpret when you wish it to do so. I saw a fresh clean body of water and on it a splendid watercraft. A raft in fact, on it a fine cabin and a white four cornered sail. I would of course be the pilot of this craft, transporting people from one end to the other. I would be the envy of every kid around. I, in no way, had the muscle or resources by myself to bring this to fruition. I would need help! Enter select members of the Scotch Hollow Gang, Jim Butterbaugh, Blaine Patterson, my brother Dean and myself. With these guys, I had muscle, tools, additional engineering and

most importantly, enthusiasm, fanned by an imitative mind.

If the gang were to play a part in this plan, they had to be committed to the end results. To get this was like building a fire. You start with some tinder, place a match to it, it would ignite a larger piece of wood and it in turn do the same until they collectively would be creating a working fire. It didn't take long to assemble the four guys, and not much longer to ignite their imagination. Now remember there weren't any video games, computers, or other electronic devices in 1956, you had to manufacture your own entertainment. None of us would have volunteered to do what we were about to do, that would be hard work. When you are excited with the potential end results and you are having fun with what you are doing, then it's not hard work. A fact many adults should keep in mind. Soon a hodge podge of tools, nails, hammers, and saws were assembled with each guy drawing from their family supply and possessions. We were particularity enthralled with the two man cross cut saw. Once used to cut mine timbers, but now pretty much inactive. With a little coordination between two guys, you could cut a ten-inch log in two real quick. Chain saws were not even a thought in our neck of the woods yet, and even if they were available, you wouldn't dare think of touching one. That would be way too expensive to commandeer for any kid's project.

On one side of the cut was a high wall, which was twenty to thirty feet high and was straight up and down, the opposite a very steep sloop making the spoil pile side. On the high wall side, the timber had been removed and pushed aside so the area could be minded. From this supply came our logs for the raft. We soon had enough eight and ten-inch logs cut to assemble the floor of the raft. It would measure eight by four feet, never mind there be no room for the cabin or passengers for that matter, an engineering over site that would be worked out at a later date. The four of us rolled and tumbled those logs to the bottom of the cut. We assembled the logs on the ice, because once it was together we wouldn't be able to move it. It would just be too heavy. We nailed it together with lumber and an assortment of nails we took from someone's supply. Almost everyone had lumber put somewhere, because there was always something to be built or repaired. Our parents came through the Great Depression and you didn't throw anything away that had a possible future use. Finally, there it sat on the ice, a thing of beauty that would be the envy of everyone and anyone that would lay eyes on it. All we had to do was be patient until the sun melted the ice.

In time the sun did its job and there it was floating on the water just as proud as any naval craft ever manufactured. We soon gathered for the maiden cruise. No waiting for warmer weather, the excitement was too great. We were dressed in wool hunting clothes, this was standard for the time, and we wore them all winter, along with rubber boots of some kind. We soon deducted that two guys was all that was going to get to test float the raft. Another engineering flaw that was soon lost in the excitement of the moment. Jim and I climbed aboard and Blaine shoved us out into the water. We only went about twenty feet when we realized that if you didn't stand just in the right spot the raft would plane to the right or the left, and that side would slide perilously. All this happened in seconds or so it seemed. When we finally got it stabilized, it just started to sink, first in the front then the back, in a back and forth motion. It wouldn't support the weight. When it was about ten inches under water, Blaine, realizing the danger, started to pull the rope we had attached. Why we attached a rope, I don't remember now, but I still remember his arms moving like a pistol engine. The raft came to the surface and reached shore in a blink of an eye. It would be the quickest departure in the history of boating. Why we didn't fall into the water, I can only attribute to the Good Lord looking over the stupid. With those wool cloths and rubber boots, we would have sunk like a rock and our swimming skills were not the best at this point of our life.

We walked away that day laughing and slapping each other on the back for the daring and heroics of the day. Not thinking that logs sitting on the ice as it melted would suck up the water and lose their ability to float well. Nobody ever told their parents, God's way of protecting their sanity. I don't know whatever happened to that raft, it just disappeared. God's providence again I think.

We would build another raft. Having learned from past mistakes we would replace the wooden logs with steel barrels, with much better results. Failures are often times the

foundation for success. These adventures would be a natural classroom that would teach us skills, mold our adult lives, and give us memories that we shall never forget.

Military Service Versus Farm Chores
By Leon E. Hillyard of Eldred, Pennsylvania
Born 1944

The subject of party lines caught my eye and I can remember vividly what our party line number was, 26R3. I can also remember the woman who managed to listen in on every conversation on it. I suppose every party line had at least one of those folks on it. She would listen right through the conversation of the other folks until someone would say, "Ok, (name deleted) hang up."

We got our first television in the late 50s and we were all full of anticipation as Dad worked to get it hooked up to the outside antenna. I recall the first image and that image's voice as the set was turned on. There she was in all her glory, Kate Smith, singing her heart out doing her rendition of "God Bless America."

After the initial thrill of having a television wore off, the only thing of note involved the wind blowing the antenna around and losing the picture. I can hear Dad yelling as I was outside and he was inside telling me which way to turn the antenna until we got the picture back. I could never figure out why Dad didn't get around to fixing the antenna so it wouldn't turn.

I never really considered who my favorite teacher was but now that I am older and often think how it was back then, it would have to be my senior industrial arts teacher, Ralph Jordan, a most talented man in the art of woodcrafts and metal craft. He was an ex-marine and we all know what that means, he was tough. The toughness didn't really bother me, as my Dad was as tough as they come and a disciplinarian of the highest degree so I figured I was used to a tough task master who taught discipline and respect. We don't see much of that anymore and I personally believe that is why we have so many troubled youth.

It had been years since I had seen Mr. Jordan but we somehow ran into each other at the local barbershop and got into conversation. He trilled me when I realized he actually remembered me. We ran into each other often after that and that event was the forum for a lot of good talks and I began to realize Mr. Jordan's toughness was hiding his inner feelings and the toughness disappeared.

On one of those gabfests, I approached him with the subject of his making me an apparatus that I could display my collection of all 50 of the new state quarters in. he said he would and when I asked him how much the undertaking would cost, he said nothing, then said "I always thought I was too tough on you guys in shop and this will be a small way to make up for that." I told him he had nothing as far as I was concerned to atone for but he wouldn't budge on the issue.

At our next haircut time, he presented me with the completed case. It was so precisely built, compete with a wooden frame and Plexiglas side so you could see both sides of the coin; I was amazed. I still look at it from time to time and recall that gentleman not as a tough ex-marine but as a generous humanitarian who left a lasting impression on my life. I am honored to know him.

A good family friend of mine came by one early August day and asked me to go berry picking with him. I was ready to go but the only hitch was he needed a pail to put them it. He had already spied the very shiny and very new 14-quart stainless steel milk pail hanging on the back porch. I knew it I took it and something bad happened to it, I'd be in for far more than a lecture.

I finally gave in, grabbed the pail and hung it over one of the handlebars of the rickety cobbled up bike and then got up on the handlebars with one foot dangling on either side of the front wheel. Off we went up the blacktop road until we came to the bottom of a long steep hill. We got off and walked the bike to the top where we mounted again and set out on a dirt road that ran along the top of the ridge. The blackberries were so thick and the plants were so profuse, it only took a short while to completely fill the pail so we mounted the bike and peddled out the dirt road to the main highway at the top of the hill.

I didn't know it then but we were about to experience a ride, with me sitting on the handlebars like a roosted chicken, that could still give me nightmares. After catching his breath, my companion said, "Let's go." We

certainly did. We hadn't gone far before we picked up enough speed that the wind made my eyes water uncontrollably so I shut them. That may have been a small measure of a blessing just as my pal leaned forward as yelled something about riding the brakes and for all intents and purposes, they were, well, gone. That registered immediately and the fear set in.

I will never know how we ever made it but we got to the bottom with only a handful of berries left in the pail and about an inch of juice. Years later, we met each other at the local barbershop and we began talking about that adventure. I could tell the others there didn't believe a word of it but we chatted on. I finally asked him what he would have done had we come up behind a car on the hill and us with no brakes. He looked at me as serious as a heart attack and said, "We'd of had to pass them."

Living on a small rural Pennsylvania farm and being the oldest of five kids, I guess it was logical that I was the chosen one to do lots of chores there. I started at a very early age and continued on until I graduated at the age of seventeen and joined the Air Force and the chores got handed to my brother because our other siblings, all girls, weren't capable of doing most of the harder jobs on the farm. I was however, accused of joining the military for no other reason than to get off the farm and leave all those chores behind. That wasn't true but looking back it wasn't a bad move though.

Farm chores can't be mistaken for joyous labor in most cases. They included shoveling and spreading manure, throwing hay down from the mow and feeding the livestock that hay, knocking potato bugs off the potato plants into a bucket with an inch or two of kerosene in it and then turning the bucket into an inferno sending the bugs wherever dead potato bugs go, seemingly constantly being in the garden pulling weeds on the three acre family garden, and many more task that I really didn't find myself missing much when I left home.

The most dreaded farm activity in my mind was de-horning the young stock when the weather got cold enough. Dad didn't even try to make that chore any less appealing for me and said it was necessary while I felt it was simply a bloodbath. He was also my mentor in the fine art of picking rocks out of the garden when he plowed each spring. I am sure those rocks grew anew every spring and were possibly the most prolific thing the old farm produced. Pick rocks? I am willing to bet if I had a dollar bill for every load I put in the old stone boat, I could have retired much earlier than I did. I may have been the champion rock picker in the state of Pennsylvania or maybe even the entire northeast U.S.

Another story while on the farm, and one completely true, was about Dad and his dearest and most beloved farm inhabitant, his loyal work horse Queenie. She was the horsepower that allowed Dad to raise nearly everything we needed and feed the family and a lot of neighbors too with the surplus he always grew. After Queenie was gone, Dad had to downsize the garden and resort to doing what he could with a gut busting rot tiller until he finally got a big orange Allis-Chalmers 17 diesel tractor. He was happy with the tractor but still missed Queenie and every time something broke on the mechanical beast, Dad would always say he never had that problem with old Queenie. She, unlike the tractor, would obey Dad's every command and was willing to pull her guts out working for him or rather working with him.

Dad bought her when I was very young but I recall many times, as he repeated the ordeal that he and Queenie endured in becoming a team. He went to an auction some twenty-five miles from home and as soon as he saw Queenie he decided he wanted that horse and none other. He bought her a hay wagon complete with the hayrack and just about

Leon's dad, Ernest Hillyard in 1990

every horse drawn implement known to man that he thought he might need.

With all those implements loaded on the wagon, Dad and his new found companion set out on that twenty-five mile trip back home. As I look back, it must have been quite an ordeal. Stopping for only rests, they traveled those twenty-five miles or so. I sadly can't remember how long Dad said that trip was in duration but I do know there are few men or horses that would undertake such a task and even less who could endure it if they did try it.

I joined the Air Force at the age of seventeen and after I had been in for several months, I got a letter from Mom, while I knew would eventually come, I wasn't really prepared for. Old Queenie's teeth were gone and she couldn't eat right and there was nothing to be done and she had to be put down. I don't know and never asked who had to do that regrettable job but I always believed it was not Dad based on the feeling s I knew he had for the horse being so strong. It's just another unexplainable case of the bond that occurs between man and beast. Reading that letter was one of the saddest things I ever had to do and I know the situation had to be one of the most traumatic for Dad, short of losing a beloved family member.

I was apprehensive in my ability to capture long past childhood memories. Once I commenced however, I feel that I could write 400 pages of those dearest memories as this attempt has open the flood gates of years past. I am confident that the good old days were indeed, the good old days.

Leon E. Hillyard in 1968

Favorite Teacher
By Vivian P. Miller of Mill Hall,
Pennsylvania
Born 1923

I was six years old when I started school in Clarence, Pennsylvania (Centre County). In third grade, I had what they called rheumatism. I couldn't walk, to go to school or anywhere. That was in 1929.

I had a wonderful teacher. Her name was Miss Hubler. Every day after she taught school, she came to our house and gave me my lessons, etc. for hours. I passed to the fourth grade, even after missing three months of school that year.

She was crippled and had one shoe built higher than the other, but she walked to our house anyway. I got better that year.

In sixth and ninth grade, I got it again. Both times I missed at least three months of school, but none of the sixth and ninth grade teachers came to the house. They sent my homework home with my sister. I don't remember them as I do Miss Hubler. If not for her, I might not have been able to finish school.

In 1941, at age 17, I graduated from Snow Show High School. I am now 88 years young.

Remember When
By Raymond L. Allison of Montoursville,
Pennsylvania
Born 1928

There were five theaters in Williamsport and one in Montoursville and Muncy. We had a choice of what you would like to see from a western to a musical to drama to cartoons. And the tickets did not cost much. When you left the theater, you always wanted to get a snack at places like Hurr's Dairy on 4th Street. They had the best ice cream that came to a peak in the cone. From there it was a short walk to Ways Garden where you could sit on a bench and enjoy your ice cream.

Another thing to do was go dancing at the Canoe Club to the music from a jukebox. This was just across the Maynard Street Bridge to South Side. In the summer, it was crowded and when you were on the dance floor, you could be dancing with two partners at a time. A good way to make friends.

Then there was the circus that came in July to Maynard Street Bethlehem Steel lot. A very good show under the big top. Maynard Street was filled with vendors of all kinds. How many of you remember the ice cream stand on Lycoming Creek Road that was the shape of a milk shake cup with a straw in the top of it? It was called the Hi-Ho and next to it was a burger stand.

Remember the Wil-Mount barbecue at 3rd Street and Country Club Lane? What is better than a pork barbecue and a hot chocolate on a cold night?

We lived in a double house with no furnace or hot water. There were five children, plus our parents. The house was heated with a coal stove in the kitchen and a stove in the dining room. A register in the floor above the dining room helped to heat the rooms upstairs. You took a Saturday night bath by taking a pan of hot water upstairs in the middle room and closed the door to bathe yourself.

Monday was laundry day. Dad would put a double copper broiler on the stove Sunday night and fill it with water so there would be hot water for Mother in the morning to do the wash in the wringer washer. The clothes were hung on lines in the backyard to dry. If it was winter, all the clothes would freeze, so when they were brought inside, we had to put them close to the stoves to thaw out.

When we lived in Williamsport, Pennsylvania, we had a four-stall garage behind our double house. My dad's brother lived in one side of the house and we lived in the other side.

My dad was in the grocery business and in 1925; he opened up a store in the garage in one of the stalls. It was heated by a small, pot-bellied, coal stove. The store had only the basic groceries. Then, in 1936, we had a flood and had to move to higher ground. We stayed there til the water went down. This took weeks, as Williamsport was completely flooded. When the water went down, we had to work to get the store in shape for business. In 1938 dad took two more stalls and it stayed that way til 1963.

In 1946, we had another flood. We stayed in the house, as the water only came up a few steps to the second floor—not like the 1936 flood, when the water was two steps from the second floor. Each flood made a lot of clean-up work.

All of the men in the family were in the Navy. Two were in World War II, one in

Korean War, and two in the Naval Reserve.

I hope this brought back some memories for you as it has for me.

The Icebox
By Dolores P. (Amon) Taylor of Clearfield, Pennsylvania
Born 1930

I had a great childhood and, now at age 82, I can look back and reflect on things that I pull out of my memory and share the most important incidents to me of my early childhood.

Looking back, I realize life was good. We've come a long way, from when I was age five.

My mother gave me small jobs, or responsibilities. This particular job was to watch for the ice truck, which came several times a week. I'd take the cardboard sign off the side of the brown icebox, which was probably about 45 inches high and 30 inches wide, and maybe 30 inches in depth. The sign was black, about 16 inches square. To start at the top, numbers in white told the iceman how many pounds or blocks of ice were needed. Numbers started at 25, turn the sign around to 50, turn again to 75, and last was 100. Sitting on the window seat in our living room, I waited patiently for the sound of the ice truck.

When the ice truck came, I hung the 50 number at the top. That was what we usually got, depending on the weather. The driver would grab a 25-pound block with a large, split, circular hook and carry it around to the back door, where I was waiting. He'd take it in, put it in the left side of the icebox, which sat in a corner in the dining room, then go back to the truck for the other 25-pound block, and place that block on another shelf, and we were good for several days.

The inside of the icebox was white and shiny, and I'm guessing was some kind of insulation material. The dictionary wasn't much help with definitions. The inside, on the left, had two, long, vertical shelves for the ice blocks and on the right side were two top shelves to hold the milk and food that needed to be kept cold. All across the bottom was a tray to catch the water as the ice melted. That was another job for me, to empty the trays before they overflowed. I soon learned to

check it often. Water on the rug wasn't much appreciated. I knew I would be facing the corner in the living room for a while, while my mother went on with her housekeeping, which could take her to the attic or basement. That corner got pretty lonely. Good thing I knew some songs and poems to help me pass the time.

Times were changing and new appliances, refrigerators by name, began appearing in storerooms and were advertised in papers and circulars. What a wonderful idea! The wall telephone lines were buzzing, as housewives declared with approval, "What will they think of next?"

My parents gave in and soon the icebox was replaced by a gleaming white refrigerator and sat in that corner of the dining room.

For my parents it was a step up from living on the farm and keeping food cold in the spring house which was usually built in a dugout over a little, running water creek. We had relatives living in the country, and there were many things to explore and learn when we visited.

Riding the Train
By Mary Jane Wright of Kersey, Pennsylvania
Born 1936

My favorite memory from the good old days was walking from Fillmore Avenue in Ridgway, Pennsylvania at the age of nine and ten years old to N. Broad Street, a good mile into town from my home. My mom would give me money for a ticket on the train from the Pennsylvania Railroad station to St. Mary's, Pennsylvania, and a nine-mile trip to visit cousins in the summer. This railroad station still stands today in the town of Ridgway. It needs lots of work from not being used for many years. Looks hopeful. I feel that would be great.

On my train ride to St. Mary's, we would stop in Daguscahonda for water for the steam engine. Then on to meet my cousins in St. Mary's at their train station, which is no longer there. It is a parking lot. So glad our station still stands in Ridgway, Pennsylvania. Before getting back on the train for my trip back home. I would stop at Joe Demetries for my ten-cent Mexican Mountain, an ice cream

Mary's brother, Paul and Mary

treat. Then back home to Ridgway. The train ride was so neat and holds a special place in my childhood memories. Wish I could remember the price of my train ticket at that time. Being 75 years old now, I really don't remember.

Also, how my friends and I would climb up a huge, huge hill to pick "Huckelberrys." It was called Elephant's Head. It kind of was shaped like that. Very steep and very high. At that time we would pick berries all day, then walk into our town of Ridgway about a mile from home and sell them to the "Bogert" and "Salberg" hotel restaurant and also the "Penny's Restaurant," which was next door to the train station. We would get 25 cents a quart at the time. They made them into homemade pies to sell at their restaurants. That is how we earned spending money for our treats.

Also loved ice-skating with my friends on Elk Creek, not far from home. Someone always had a nice big bonfire that kept us warm here and there.

I loved playing marbles down on our corner. The roads were not paved. We would make a circle in the dirt and play for hours. Of course, I had a favorite "shooter" I used most of the time. Collecting them all in a well-used wicker basket.

Walking on homemade, wooden stilts was lots of fun too. It was quite a challenge. We also liked to play "Kick the Can," "Release," "Mother May I," and of course baseball and making forts in the winter and having snowball fights.

Taking walks, my little brother and mom and me, to see Aunt Ann, mom's sister. Having no car, we had to walk wherever we wanted to go. On our way back home, we would be so tired. My mom was a single mom who did without so much just to raise us. She was an angel in disguise.

Also loved singing all the old songs together with my mom. I keep most of them in my heart today. That will always be a special time for me to remember.

I think way back when life was simple and to be able to have such good memories, we have a lot to be thankful for.

Another little tidbit I would like to mention was we were always taught to be thankful for what someone gives you. No matter how small it would be. My mom's theory was even if it's a ten-cent hanky. These you could buy at McCory's Five & Dime.

Trout Fishing with Grandpa
By Marcia A. Hoffman of Endicott, New York
Born 1943

I was raised in Roulette, Potter County, Pennsylvania. It is a small town about ten miles west of Coudersport, the county seat. State Route 6 ran thru the middle of town. There was one traffic light in the middle of town. It had been a very busy logging town in the 1800 and early 1900 years. My father's grocery store, the only one, was on that Main Street. To the north of town on the mountain where I hiked many times was a large boulder with a dinner plate size hole in it. It was said to be where the Indian ground their grains. East, West, and South of town were beautiful mountains. I climbed them all with my father. My hometown had a Catholic Church, a Methodist Church, and a Baptist Church. There were two gas stations, a drive-in movie, and three cemeteries.

Winter in Roulette was great. Although I wasn't much for ice-skating on the pond, I did like shoveling and cleaning the driveway and walk. We made snowmen, snow angles, and played Duck, Duck, Goose. The most fun was sled riding in a cow pasture with a barbwire fence at the bottom of the hill. One of my next door neighbor's children, "Little Brother" as I called him, died because he didn't get off his sled before the fence. He was around eight or nine years old. After that, no one could sled on that hill. It was too bad as it was a very good hill to ride on. We had named it "Old Baldy."

When there was bad weather, it was bad. I remember one year having to walk to the bus stop up the street in five to eight inches of blowing "raining" down snow. There was no shelter while we waited for the bus to take us to the high school in the next town west of Roulette (Port Allegany). My parents couldn't take me to school either. As I look back on that stormy day, I know that current schools today would have called school closed that day. We didn't think anything of having to go out in the storm. Most of our snow came from Lake Erie direction and could drop feet of snow in some of the storms and sometimes more.

There was no swimming pool in our town. There was one in Coudersport at the high school and one in Port Allegany at the high school there. But we made the best of Fishing Creek that ran near town. It had some very good fishing holes that made for good swimming. One time my family was swimming in one of these fishing holes, which were fairly large. I was small, maybe seven or eight years old. I didn't know how to swim yet. My father was trying to teach me to swim and playing with me in the water. At one point, I found myself under the water and not coming up. I became very scared and almost drowned. My father saved me. From then on, I never liked to swim where I couldn't put my feet on the bottom. These fishing holes had undercurrents in them, so it wasn't safe unless you knew where those currents were. It wasn't until the summer of my graduation from high school that I decided that I should take swimming lessons to know what I should be doing in the water to keep me from drowning. My high school gave lessons. It took all I could muster to learn, even more to do one of the requirements to pass the test. I had to jump off the highest diving board into deep water, of course. To this day, some 51 years later, I still feel and see that jump. Oh! By the way, I did pass the test.

For first and second grades, I went to a small, red brick schoolhouse. I remember it as a relatively new building compared to most of the buildings in town. I believe it was a library at some time after it was a school. It was close to my home, maybe about two or three blocks. I walked to school every day

in the sun, rain, and snow. Deep snow never closed school. The school classmates I started school with were the classmates I had all thru elementary and high school. It was where I learned reading, writing, and arithmetic. For grades three thru sixth, I went to the high school, which was across town. I still walked to school, but, on nice days, I would put on my roller skates to go to school. The high school was also the same one most of my family members before me went to school.

I remember older classmates telling me that I didn't want to get into Miss Razey's classes because she was really strict. Well, wouldn't you know it, I did! You didn't have a choice in those days of teachers. Miss Razey was, I think, the town spinster. She painted outside of her house, made repairs, went fishing, and was good at it also. She was also a very good cook. I believe I have one of her recipes. There wasn't anything she couldn't do. At the end of the school year, I passed into the next grade level. I found that she wasn't as bad as the kids made her out to be.

My most favorite teacher was Mrs. Hancock. She was my homeroom teacher and taught me other subjects. She would read us stories if we were all good at some point during the day. I loved that, as my mother read stories to my sister and me at home.

Recess time was one hour, so town kids could go home for lunch. We played baseball, jumped rope with rhymes, ran around every day, except rainy and very cold winter days. We also could spend time in homeroom before classes would start again. A typical class day was 8 a.m. to 4 p.m.

I had chores from a very young age. My father, who was a photographer, took a picture of me standing on a chair at the kitchen sink, helping my mother with dinner dishes. I remember in a small room off the kitchen was a wringer washer. I would have to sort the clothes and then help put them in the washer. When the washer was done, mother would put the clothes through the wringer into the rinse water basin; put them back through the wringer when rinsed, and into the clothes basket. I had to be very careful not to get my hands into the wringer.

When I was tall enough to reach the outdoor clothes lines, I would have to take the clothes basket out to hang clothes on the lines. They would be there all day as my mother worked as a clerk in our grocery store in town. When I came home from school, I was expected to take the clothes down and fold them. I remember in winter months the clothes would freeze stiff as a board, but some would get dry. The "boards," I had to take down, bring in, and hang on a wooden hanger in front of the heating stove to finish drying. Boy, do I love that smell of the clothes dried outside.

Other chores were to keep our bedroom cleaned, as well as the playroom. We always had to pick up toys, books, and put them into their proper places. We had to help my mother with setting the table for meals and washing dinner afterwards. When old enough we sweep and mopped the floors, dusted the furniture, and ironed our dresses. Although my sister and I fought sometimes about whose turn it was to do certain work, it was good training for later in our lives.

My favorite pet was a cat. My father always had one or two around. The first one I can remember, I was around three or four years of age, was black and white with four white feet. She loved to be outside when it was warm. My family owned an empty lot in the back of our house. It grew up with tall grasses in the summer. My cat loved to go out in the lot, hide, sleep, and try to catch whatever was in the grasses. She was so funny. My sister and I would play hide and seek with her.

She had a funny name. At the time, there was a popular song called, "Petunia in the Onion Patch," or maybe it wasn't a children's song. Anyway, we named our black and white cat "Petunia." She would sleep under the song bird's cage that was my mother's pet. Petunia was trained to never mind "Tweety Bird." If Petunia didn't she would get smacked with a newspaper. Petunia died at a very old age.

Family was very important to my mother and father. Family came first in everything not only for us, but we respected other people's family time also. We did a lot together. We would get together with my aunts, uncles, grandparents, and cousins to catch up on what was going on in their lives. All of the family would gather in the living room or outside after dinner in a circle. One aunt or my grandfather would start, "Do you remember when …?" and a story would ensue with many different points of views of the same story. Most of the time it would end up with laughter producing tears. If the family was at our house, one of the aunts would ask mother to play the piano. Mother had taught herself to play and played hymns for church. So she would sit down and start playing hymns. One of the aunts would hear her favorite song and start to sing along. Before you knew it, we were all singing like a choir with all female parts. We would sing all night or until someone said, they were hungry. We all would have supper then.

One of my favorite memories is when my grandfather picked me up very early to go trout fishing in the Allegany River, which ran thru the valley. I was young enough to not have to have a fishing license. He taught me how to throw the line into the water, pull the line a little at a time, and then to reel the line back. He also would not put the worm on the hook for me. We fished all day, walking down the sides of the river. When I did catch a Rainbow Trout, I was so excited. The trout had to be at least eight inches long to keep it. The limit was eight fish. We had fun all day together. Come to the end of the afternoon, we counted our fish. My grandfather was a very good fisherman so I didn't expect to have more fish than him. But when we counted the fish, I had eight nice Rainbow Trout to take home for dinner. So when we returned home, grandfather said I wasn't finished. It wasn't just the fishing, but I had to clean the fish. He proceeded to teach me how to clean the fish. Boy that was a good supper. I never let my grandfather forget that I had more fish than he did the first time I went fishing.

Another time when I was a young lady, I asked my grandfather how he met my grandmother. The only part of the story I can remember is, he would hitch up the horse and sleigh, go across the bridge to pick her up for a ride in the country. I would love to go back to write down all the stories that were told. I heard them so much that at that time I figured I never would forget them. Well, I have forgotten a lot of them.

Other times, my sister and I would ask my father to bring out the slide projector and show us our favorite group of family pictures or flowers and scenes he had taken. Mother would sometimes make popcorn to eat. We did this so much that my sister and I could tell who it was, when and where it was taken. I have those pictures today. The funny part is that now I don't know a lot of them either.

These are only a small part of my memories of "the good old days." It was a time for family, a time to grow, and a time that was filled with love of family, extended family, and the community. How I wish that it was that way again.

Chickens and Strawberries
By Frank H. Freezer of Montoursville, Pennsylvania
Born 1927

I was born April 26, 1927 in a farmhouse, one mile from Warrensville, Pennsylvania. The seventh child of a family of 11 children, six boys and five girls.

I do not recall too much til the age of six when I started to school. We had to walk one

Leon E. Hillyard in 1968

Frank H. Freezer in 1932

mile to a one-room schoolhouse. The school consisted of grade one through eight with usually around 30 pupils. One teacher taught all eight grades with all of the subjects—reading, writing, arithmetic, geography, history, health, English, and spelling.

There was a large, coal-fired furnace in one corner of the room for heat in the wintertime, which did not do a very good job on some of the cold days.

School took in at nine a.m. We had a 15-minute recess in the morning, one hour for lunch from 12 to 1 p.m., and a 15-minute recess in the afternoon. School let out at 4 p.m. and then it was the one-mile walk back home. We went from the day after Labor Day til the end of April. We went 160 days at that time. We did not have any snow days off as

they do now when it snows. It was quite cold in the wintertime and we had to wade through some deep snow at times. There was usually four of us going to school, so the older ones would go ahead of the smaller ones to make a path.

My dad raised chickens, around 3,000 or 4,000 each year, and sold eggs for most of the income from the farm. As we got old enough, we had to help feed and water all of the chickens, morning and night. My dad raised corn, wheat, oats, buckwheat, and hay. The corn would be cut by hand while the leaves were still green and put in shocks. Later on in the fall, my dad would husk the ears of corn

*Frank H. Freezer in 1951 by a
F-80 with 500 pounds of bombs under the wings*

all day long. Us boys had to hurry home from school and bag up the corn and haul it into the barn and store it on the second floor of the barn to dry, as we did not have a corncrib as some farmers did.

The wheat and oats would be cut with a binder, pulled by horses, which tied it in sheaves. It was then put in shocks of eight or ten sheaves, later to be hauled into the barn and stored til someone that went around threshing would come and thresh for us.

The hay would be mowed down and left to cure. It would then be raked up with what they called a dump rake. Then put in piles. We then had to load it on a wagon, hauled to the barn to be used for feed for the horses and cows.

We also raised about three acres of strawberries for several years. As they ripened, we would be up by 5 a.m. to pick berries. Some would be taken to Williamsport, Pennsylvania to a grocery store to be sold. Some would be taken to Montoursville, Pennsylvania to be sold from door-to-door for 15 cents per quart or two for 25 cents.

We also raised tomatoes for Chef-Boy-Ardee. When ripe, were picked and hauled to Milton, Pennsylvania to their cannery.

As the family members got older, they would get other jobs away from home. So my dad sold the farm in 1946.

My mother and father both died at the age of 81 in 1973 and 1974, only nine months apart.

Of the six boys, five of us served our country in the military.   Three sisters and three brothers have died, leaving three boys and two girls. My two older brothers are now 91 and 89.

I have been to several other countries and it is my opinion that we live in the greatest country in the world.

The Hawk Run Years
By Shirley Melius of Philipsburg,
Pennsylvania
Born 1943

At the end of my sixth grade of school, we moved from Morrisdale to Hawk Run, where I met some great neighbors and friends. We had quite a few kids in our family, so it seemed the neighbors would assemble at our house to play ball, kick the can, sled ride, hide and seek, or just pass the time away on the porch swing.

Wintertime:

Sled riding was one of the big wintertime pleasures. One of our neighbors would tie our sleds to his Jeep and pull us up the road, past the Episcopal Church, through the pines, and back home. I don't know if anyone else ever did this—I never did—but one boy (name omitted to protect the guilty) would hitch a ride on moving cars going down our street by holding on to the back bumper with his gloves and sliding the whole way down, letting go at the bottom of the street.

Most winters the snow would arrive in November and stay until May. We would build igloos, snowmen, and have snowball battles.

Summertime:

We did have a little watering hole in Hawk Run, but mostly on real hot days, we would walk to the Morrisdale Reservoir taking the track route. Quite a few kids gathered there. It had a pier with a little deck on top about six feet or so out of the water. One hot day I mustered up the courage to walk out on the pier and climb up on the deck, but lo and behold, some boy pushed me off and on that day I learned to doggie paddle to shore.

Outings:

On Wednesday nights, they held dances at the Saint Agnes Social Center in Morrisdale. We would walk from Hawk Run through ParDee, stopping to pick up a couple of friends there, and go to the dance. We would walk back the same way in the dark, scared but giggling the whole way home. Every time a car would pass us, which was few and far between, we would hide behind bushes until the car went and then continue our journey home.

Trips to Philipsburg:

I must have been in high school when I was allowed to venture into Philipsburg. My girlfriend and I would pick and sell berries (all kinds) or collect pop bottles. I believe we got two cents a bottle. Catch the last bus home, which stopped at Passmore Hotel, which is now Philipsburg Towers.

The Outhouse:

For the first two years at Hawk Run, we had an outhouse and then the landlord put in a commode. One day my brother got mad at me and threw my new doll (12 inches with little, red pajamas on) which was bought from the blanket man who traveled from house to house selling various items, in the outhouse. My sister and I fished it out and hosed it off a few times. Funny, I don't remember what happened to her after that, the doll that is. Maybe that was when we started playing with cutouts. We would make furniture out of matchboxes and other odds and ends we would gather from around the house.

Bare Necessities:

What we would have given for yard sales back then. We usually got a skirt and shoes when school started, and then maybe something at Christmas time. I would wait until my older sister left for school and then borrow one of her blouses or sweaters, then rush home before her to put it back before she got home.

We had a wringer wash machine. When we got home from school we had to help drain the water from the machine, clean the machine, take the clothes off the line outside, and then dish up the lima beans and homemade bread, each of us fighting over the crust.

On Sundays, my dad and I would stay home and make dinner while my mother went to church with the other kids. Dad would fire up the kitchen coal stove while I made the cake. He knew just how hot it had to be to put that cake in. We also made taffy and fudge.

The Weekly Bath:

The weekly bath consisted of putting a big tub in the kitchen, heating water on the coal stove, and inserting the smallest child first. Privacy was curtains between the kitchen and living room and also kept the kitchen warm. In between baths, we would take a basin and sponge up to our bedroom.

River Quicksand
By Ruth Garvey King of Williamsport,
Pennsylvania
Born 1944

I was the youngest of the three "Garvey" girls that were raised in downtown Williamsport, Pennsylvania (West Street to be exact). I remember the early days in the 50s and 60s. My sisters and I would go downtown either early Friday evening or Saturday afternoons. What really sticks in my mind the most is the Christmas season. The entire town and all the stores would be beautifully decorated. L.L. Stearns & Sons was one of the most popular stores in town

then, especially for us kids. On the third floor is where we would go to see Santa, talk to him and tell him what we wanted for Christmas. My request as a little girl was always a doll baby. Santa always listened to me and, sure enough, on Christmas morning there would be a beautiful doll under the tree. I remember one year my doll had blonde, soft hair with pretty blue eyes and a blue dress. She had a blue ribbon tied around her hair and a tiny comb and brush and mirror came along with her. I became the best hair stylist there ever was, in fact, I even cut her hair and then cried because it never grew back. Under the tree there was always a new pair of nice, warm, flannel pajamas that I would wear Christmas night and there were always a few other little toys for me. My older sisters always would get what they ask for, I remember my oldest sister asked for a new pocketbook and my other sister asked for a nurse's watch. Now back to L.L. Stearns & Sons, also on the third floor where Santa was there was a train that would give us all rides all around the floor. At that time, it seemed like a big train and a long ride. Oh how joyous! On the first floor of that store, there was a big bell that hung from the ceiling that had a child hanging onto it. It would go back and forth as if it were ringing. (Later in years, I remember seeing that bell at the Lycoming Mall in Muncy being used as a decoration. I haven't seen it in the last couple of years so evidently it was sold or stored away.)

We'd all walk through all the downtown stores with amazement at all the bright decorations. People would be scrambling around preparing for the holiday. I will never forget the five and ten cent stores (there were two of them). One was Woolworth five and ten and S.S. Kresge's. I loved walking through them and looking at all the items they had for sale from candy and notions in the front. (I remember every year buying my dear mother "Evening in Paris" cologne in the little blue bottle for Christmas. Her love and expression each year made me feel like I gave her gold!) In the back of the store there were little, live turtles for ten cents. We would buy them and bring them home. Our parents would buy us the little, plastic bowls with the tiny plastic palm tree up the middle. However, we'd take them out of the bowl to play with them and forget to put them back. Days later, my mother would find them all dried up under a chair or couch. We'd be sad and promise that next time we wouldn't be so careless.

They always had birds in cages and we'd go by them quickly, as I was afraid of birds and was afraid one would get out and get in my hair. Oh, the fun days of growing up.

Growing up on West Street in downtown Williamsport, I was told quite frankly by my parents not to go near the river at the Susquehanna River (which was at the foot of my street). My parents told stories about people, including children that had drowned in the river. There were whirlpools that would get a hold of you and just pull you right under, they said. I was in eighth grade in 1958 and old enough to know better, but one day one of my friends (Theresa) came to spend the day with me. Both my parents were working at the time. Always being inquisitive about the "river," both of us decided to go for a walk and we went to the river, which was only about one block away. We ventured up one side of the dike and down the other until we actually got close to the water, when all of a sudden we started to get stuck in the soft, sticky mud. It was pulling at our feet like quicksand. My friend and I started to scream and were holding onto each other. Somehow we managed to get out of it and we started to run home so we could clean up before my parents came home. As we were running, my friend tripped and fell over the railroad tracks that run alongside of the river. She was crying all the way home to my house and while she was cleaning up she was crying harder and harder saying her wrist hurt her. We called her dad to come get her. He took her to the hospital and found out her wrist was broken. We told a little white lie to our parents, how she fell while we were playing. That was 54 years ago and to this day, when I see my friend, we still get a good laugh out of thinking we were going down in quicksand. It wasn't funny then, but is now.

I was in the fourth grade at St. Joseph's Parochial school. We were always saving our pennies and bringing them in to be sent to the missions for the poor children that needed food and clothing. One day, one of my classmates named Pauline brought a cardboard box with a little, brown and white puppy in it. Her parents said she could bring it and sell chances for five cents each and all the money would go to the missions. Let me back up just a little and tell you that my dad never wanted us to have a dog. So, now, you have an idea as to where this story is going. I had five cents that day so I could buy a pack of crackers for morning snack at school. Instead, I took just one five-cent chance and, you guessed it, I won the puppy. I was so happy and immediately in love with that little, brown and white, furry puppy. I carried the box home and, when I arrived, my mother was in our backyard hanging up clothes. She thought it belonged to my friend who had walked home with me. She said it was up to my father if I could keep it or not. My oldest sister, Dot, and her boyfriend, Steve, came home. They took me to where my dad worked and we called for him to come out. I know now my father had to see the love and anxiety on my face, and he said I could keep him, but I had to promise that I would take care of him and feed him every day and that he would make a doghouse for the backyard. My dad made the best doghouse an animal could ever want. I named him "Teddy" because he was soft and cuddly like a little teddy bear. My Teddy lived ten years and gave me much happiness. He got cancer and while I was on my honeymoon in 1965, my parents had him put down. He was my first dog and I will always have a soft spot in my heart for him.

A Stroll Through Williamsport
By Joan M. Miller of Williamsport,
Pennsylvania
Born 1936

I was born in July of 1936, which is the same year of a huge flood that occurred on March 17 and 18 here in Williamsport. This flood was known as the St. Patrick's Day

Joan's parents, Nellie Culp-Hess and Fred Hess

65

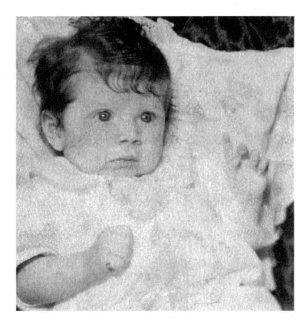

Joan M. Miller in 1936

Flood, which crested at 33.9 feet.

I grew up here in Williamsport in a family of 13 people. My dad, Fred Hess, was a loving, caring man who drove a coal truck for a living. My mom, Nellie Culp-Hess, was an amazing woman who taught me so much about a family and taking care of my home. She was the smartest woman I had ever known, even though she had only gone to school through first grade. She had stayed home at an early age to help my grandmother when my grandfather became ill and passed away.

My earliest childhood memory seems to be the knowledge that I was part of a very large family. At that time, I was one of ten children and there was a lot of laughing, singing, and dancing going on in our home. I remember dancing on the tops of my dad's shoes and loving every minute of it. We learned to love all kinds of music from waltzes to polka. Yes, our family was large, but at our house, there was always room for one more and everyone was welcomed. By the time I was nearly four years old, the family was completed by one more addition, and, in 1940, I got a sidekick, my little sister, Sandy.

World War II lasted from 1939 to 1945 and I remember getting little, silk flags with three stars on each of them to represent our three brothers and three brother-in-laws, who were in the Service fighting for our country. We were introduced to new concepts like air raids, pulling down the blinds and turning out all the lights, collecting stamps for gas and sugar and collecting tin cans to buy savings bonds to help our troops. All six members of our family came home from the ware safe and sound. Praise the Lord!

We didn't have TV's in those days, but we would listen to Gabriel Heatter on the radio, giving us the latest news. Our favorite show was Fibber Magee and Molly. Oh, how we would laugh as we would lay on the floor in front of the radio in the dark.

There was always a good smell coming from our house. Mom was always baking bread, pies, or sticky buns, but she was a woman of many talents. We would walk down to Kaplan's Barrels and pick out white and printed flower bags, from which mom would make marvelous school clothes. Since mom left school so early, she didn't read, so my dad would read the Bible to her each morning before he went to work and they would both pray for all of us.

As for the rest of the town in those years, let me take you on a stroll on a sunny, Sunday afternoon in the 1940s.

Let's start on Third Street and work our way through town. Up that way, about five blocks in the Third Street underpass. This memorable "dip" in the road was always a signal to us sleeping children that we were almost home from a car trip. The B & E Cleaners and the Nabisco Cookie Shop was in this area. Here they had boxes and boxes of cookies and you could buy a whole bag of them for only 25 cents.

Joan and her side-kick, Sandy

The Cadillac showroom, which was run by one of my dad's friends, was a little farther up the street. Then there was the City Bus garage, the Weis grocery store, JPM Sylvani's Furniture Store, and, oh yes, a shoe repair shop which is pretty obsolete nowadays. Whenever we got a new pair of shoes, Mom would send us to the shoe repair store to have them attach a 25-cent-piece to the heels. These were called taps, and saved them from wear and tear.

Up ahead was the Busy Bee Restaurant where you could get a hot dog and a plate of beans for 50 cents and down the alley right next to it, taking us to 4th Street, was the O.K. Barber Shop. My dad would go in there for a haircut and when we needed one, they would put a board across the arms of the chair for us to get a trim, bangs and all.

Across the street over there to the left was the James V. Brown Library, where we used to get books and gramophone records to play on the phonograph and sing and dance to them. Next is the Lake to Sea bus terminal, where we would get a real Coke mixed at the soda fountain. Kelchner's Candy Store is where you could get candy, stamps, or send a package all in one place.

Reliable Furniture, Dixie Grogan's Hardware (you could get anything and everything there), a flower store over there. My sister, Ann, worked in the Day & Night Restaurant just there. Here in the center of it all was Market Square. The Grower's Market was always a great place to get fresh produce, meat, homemade furniture, candy, pies, and maybe a doily or two—just about anything homemade.

We've seen many a parade come through town right here, between Third and Fourth Streets in this area, and we even had a P.T. Barnum Circus in a different part of town.

The Carroll House and LL Stearns & Sons were great places to shop (and window shop on Sunday afternoons), especially at Christmas time when the stores were decorated so beautifully! There was nothing like walking store-to-store through the snow.

On Pine Street to our left was the Karlton Theater. Here, the Bowery Boys might be showing this week and over there is the Rialto Theatre. "Duel in the Sun" with Gregory Peck may be showing there.

Right here was the Woolworth's five-and-dime store, where you can get your photo taken, your fortune read, and they'll guess your weight all in one visit.

As we now continue up 4th Street, the Capital Theatre was right here, and my mom may have said that Dan Daly is singing and dancing this week. The Keystone Theatre was right here and was the place to be to watch those western flicks. You could ride the seats and dodge the bullets like you're a part of the movie and with every movie ticket, you'd get a glossy photo of Roy Rogers or Gene Autry!

On the corner of Hepburn and 4th Streets, there is our own Williamsport Sun-Gazette, which was founded back in 1801 when Thomas Jefferson was President. It still stands strong today as the publisher of our daily newspaper.

A few blocks north on Hepburn Street where it meets Market Street is Brandon Park. I have been to many community shows there in the band shell and this is a great place for a picnic or playtime.

A couple of blocks up the street sat the Park Hotel, which was in front of the railway station. It was from this station that I saw my brothers off to war. The Park Hotel flourished, but was later changed over to the Park Home for the elderly and it is now used as office space for doctors and such.

A block from here is the Historical Museum. Did you know that Williamsport was a thriving, lumbering town? Here at the museum you can learn all about the lumbering days and see many exhibits about the Indians who were here long before we were. It's worth the visit! As we walk farther up West 4th Street, you can see all of these beautiful homes that used to belong to the lumber barons of Millionaire Row. The carriage houses in the back of each home were normally where the staff lived above the garage for the carriages. Today, at Christmas time, people can tour Millionaire's Row and take in all the beautiful decorations and nostalgia of the good ole days.

Williamsport was and is the home of Little League Baseball thanks to its founder, Carl E. Stotz in 1939. Every year since then we have a big parade and get to see teams from all over the world compete for the championship. It's during the games that we are visited by people from all over the world who come to root for their children and their teams. Little League originated up the street at Memorial Park.

Memorial Park was at one time a place where you could paddle a canoe. It was also once an amusement park and a zoo.

Eventually, Bowman Field came to be and, on Saturdays, my dad used to take us on the bus to see the Tigers play baseball. The section that was once a Henry's BBQ here in the park and miniature golf is now a public pool.

Joan, Sandy, and friends
in Lycoming Creek

The Green Convertible with a Plaid Top
By Carol Confer of Houston, Texas
Born 1933

My parents had ten kids, two boys and three girls older than me, two boys and two girls younger than me. We were all born on a farm. I was born in a farmhouse in Washingtonsville, Pennsylvania. The thing I remember is what the house looked like and my older sister sitting on a railing at the top of the stairs, singing a song about a robin. At the age of about three-and-a-half or four, we moved to a farm at Turbotville, Pennsylvania, like the one before. That farm was the one before we had no running water or electricity. My brother and me two years younger than me would go to the movies in town one-and-a-half or two miles from the farm. Most times, we had to walk to and from town after dark. We had to pass a cemetery, and we'd run like mad past it. I was about eight years old; he would be six years old. But he was bigger than me.

We had the wringer washer, outhouse, chamber pot at the top of the stairs. I was in the outhouse doing my business at a very young age when the workmen came to replace it with a new one. They just pushed it over and there I sat. One of the guys even buttoned up my underwear. As I got older, my mom would remind me of that. I do remember!

Bath time for us was Saturday night. We took our bath in a large galvanized tub behind the big, black, iron, kitchen stove. In the summer, we had to wash our feet every night in a bucket out on the porch. First one in line got the clean water. We were always barefooted. When I had the measles, I had to stay in a dark, back room til I was over it because the light would hurt my eyes.

I went to school in town by bus. My first grade teacher, Ms. Belva Crumis did not want me to write with my left hand so I struggled writing with both hands. Of course, now I am left-handed. I still remember her name. Another girl, Betty Weaver and I were fighting on the bus and the bus driver stopped the bus and made us walk home. Her dad, George Weaver was the bus driver. We were about eight years old.

As kids on a farm, we would hide in the cornfield and roll dry corn silk in the husk and smoke it. What a terrible taste! Living on a farm with lots of kids was fun. The lane going back to the house was lined with maple trees. My dad would tap the trees with a plug in the trunk and buckets hanging on the stake. When I was little I wondered why were these

Carol Confer's family

68

George, Carol, Joyce, Nancy, and Dick

buckets hanging on a tree trunk? Our dad would go to the feed store and get feed for the hogs. We girls went along because the feed came in printed cotton bags. So we picked the bags, as we like to sew our own clothes. We made homemade ice cream for everyone's birthday. With 12 family members, we had six birthdays in September.

I was about 11 years old when we moved into a big, brick house on the Loyalsock Creek. I was told it was at one time a stagecoach stop. It had running water, electricity, one and a half bath. It had six fireplaces, three in bedrooms upstairs, and three downstairs. We never used them while I lived there. The garret (attic) was completely floored. We also had a bedroom up there. Sometimes my brothers would have their friends spend the night. They would sleep up there.

We also went to a one-room school, first thru eighth grade. My first job was planting potatoes for a nearby farmer. My dad took my brother and me to spend the day planting. The farmer made a trench and we would drop the potatoes in and step on them to push them into the dirt. We were paid by a check! We were about 10 and 12 years old.

We would help dad hoe the corn while it grew. The field was by the main road, Route 87. As the cars drove by, they would honk their horns. We girls always wore our bathing suits, living by a creek; we did a lot of swimming. So with people blowing their horns at us, my dad says, "Ok, girls, go put some clothes on!"

Our friends were from town, Montoursville. They spent a lot of time on our farm. We cooked hot dogs by the creek very often, played hide and seek in the barn. Most of the town kids were boys.

My oldest two sisters were married when we moved to the Loyalsock. One brother-in-law, Charlie Green was in the Army. Another brother-in-law, Bill Ball was in the Navy. After they were discharged, my oldest brother, Lynn Confer was in the Marines and the next oldest, Don Confer was in the Army. So we had six kids living in the brick farmhouse.

My sister, Faye Confer two years older, had a job, as a young teen, in Loyalsockville (we called it Slabtown, I think because there was a sawmill there years ago). Anyhow, she was a telephone operator. She made 30 cents an hour. We were about the first people in the area to get a phone. Our number was 10R13.

We were young teens, along with a few other girls from town would rent a cabin up the creek. There would be about five or six of us. We were in a cabin in Forksville. We went to the only store there to stock up. One of the girls put a watermelon under her shirt, pretending she was pregnant, then she dropped it on the porch, watermelon everywhere. We cooked spaghetti and dropped it into the sink while straining. So, of course, we were not going to eat it, so we hung it on a clothesline to dry. The next day it broke into tiny pieces.

My sister, Faye Confer had a green convertible with a plaid top. She and I drove it to Virginia to see our brother in the Army. On the way home we ran into a telephone pole after dark. Smashed her car near Fredericksburg, Maryland. I remember sleeping on a hard, wooden bench in the police station while waiting for our brother-in-law, Charlie Green in town to come get us.

Another time we wanted to go to Virginia,

Don and Carol Confer in Virginia

but no car. She and I stood out on Route 87 with our suitcase, hitchhiking. A local guy picked us up. He was going to Florida, so he dropped us off in Virginia. Our plan was to drive our brother's car home, but he, instead, put us on a bus to Williamsport, Pennsylvania, back home. We did a lot of square dancing at the local fire hall in the winter. We all had our chores to do on the farm. We still had a wringer washer and a big, black, cook stove. A furnace used wood or coal.

Memories of Cameron County
By Shirley Wiggins of Lancaster,
Pennsylvania
Born 1931

I have so many good memories of growing up in Cameron County, as I lived in many places in Cameron County. I spent my first seven years in the town of Emporium and started first grade in the West Ward School. This, at one time, was the old high school before the new high school building was built.

We had an iceman who delivered ice for the iceboxes. At that time, most homes had an icebox. The ice was carried by trucks and was in 25- or 50-pound blocks, and these would be put in a special door in the icebox and it would cool the food in the other compartments of the icebox. Under the icebox, a pan was placed to get the drips from the ice as it melted. These drip pans had to be emptied daily. My mother had to be extra careful as we lived in a second floor apartment over an elderly lady and she would have felt the overflow or at least had a watermarked ceiling.

The iceman always had chunks of ice for the children as we followed the truck.

We moved from Emporium to Portage Road. While living there, we went to Plank Road Hollow School. My sister, Pat, and I were in the same room, as the first and second grades were in the same room. I was the older of the two, so I was, and rightfully so, supposed to keep an eye on her. One day I got on the bus to go home and Pat wasn't there, but I was too shy or afraid to say she wasn't on the bus. We started home, one of the older children asked me where my sister was, and I said I didn't know and she might still be at school. They told the bus driver and he turned the bus around and went back to the school

where Pat was still waiting. Not too happy and quite frightened.

While we lived there, we had some favorite swimming holes. My favorite one was a place near an old bridge, near a family named Johnson. I couldn't swim, but the water wasn't very deep, and I could touch bottom so I wasn't afraid to jump from a spot of the bridge to the water below and walk out of the water.

This got me into another situation at a later date when I was visiting my cousin in Driftwood and we went swimming in the Castle Garden swimming hole. I saw kids jumping from a diving board into the water. I then asked my cousin if I could jump in too. He said I could if I wanted too. I jumped, but I couldn't touch the bottom as I could at the old swimming hole. I sunk. My cousin yelled for me to swim and, upon my second resurfacing, I yelled that I couldn't swim. One of the bystanders jumped in and pulled me out. I woke up lying on the shoreline. So much for my showing off.

We then moved to a farm where the Emporium Country club is now located. We moved from a house that had hot and cold running water, an indoor bathroom to an old farmhouse with no electric, no phones, no running water, and an outhouse.

Water was carried into the house in buckets and set on a wooden stand. Water was then dipped out of the buckets for all our daily use. Hands were washed in a basin that sat on another stand. Dishes were washed by hand in a dishpan at a dry sink and rinsed in hot water in another pan. Water was heated on a coal stove. Our heat was the kitchen stove and a coal stove in the living room. The bedrooms were unheated. Think of that, on a cold, winter day. I often do.

Our lifestyle changed for all of us, especially my mother, when every day was a challenge, and especially wash days. On those days, she had to carry the water from a spring located behind a springhouse that was about 200 feet from the house. She then had to heat the water in a boiler on the stove. While the water was heating, clothes were separated into piles by color and materials.

Next, she then had to transfer the water into three washtubs, one was used for washing the clothes and the wash water was usually quite hot, the other two tubs were used for rinsing the clothes and were much cooler or cold. The third tub was cold and had often had bluing added to further whiten the whites and refresh the other clothing. These tubs were set on sturdy benches.

The boiler was filled again, in preparation for the boiling the white clothes. All clothes were scrubbed on a washboard and then fed through hand-operated wringer from the washtub, to rinse tub one, and rinse tub two, and then into a basket to be hung on the clothesline.

The white clothes, sheets, and pillowcases were washed first and transferred to the boiler, in which the water was now boiling. This boiling was to make them white. No housewife wanted to have "Tattletale Gray" wash. Items that needed to be starched were dipped in starch to be ironed the next day.

All clothes were then hung on wash lines, even the hanging of wash was done in a special way with whites first and then down to the colored clothing and heavier items. Lines often sagged under the heavy loads and often needed to be supported by clothes props. After the wash was dry, things that had been starched and needed to be ironed were dampened or sprinkled, rolled, and put in baskets, to be ironed the next day. Other ironing was just put in a basket to be ironed. Warm days were a delight for the hanging of wash, but rainy days and winter days made washdays an extra hard job.

On rainy days, empty rooms or an attic was put to use. The winter meant clothes froze on the line and were brought into the house like stiff boards and draped over any available support until dry from the heat in the house.

Ironing day was another challenge for her. Two or three irons were placed and heated on a coal stove. One iron would be removed from the hot stove when it was hot enough to be used for ironing. She would iron with this hot iron until it became too cool. She would then place the cooler iron back on the stove, picking up another hot iron, and repeating these steps until she was done ironing.

My sister and I learned how to iron by ironing handkerchiefs and pillowcases.

We had our milk delivered by a milkman. He placed the milk bottles in a wooden box at the end of our driveway near the road.

The springhouse is where we kept food items cold. A springhouse is a little house built over a spring. The cold, running water didn't freeze in the winter, so items were kept cold without freezing. The water was cold in the summer and kept our food cold. An early geo-thermal system.

One interesting thing about the springhouse, there was a stone we used to step down to the area where we put the food items to cool. It was an old tombstone inscribed with the name of Mary Strawbridge. Where it came from, we never found out the story behind it.

Living on the farm was fun for us children. We had a lot of space to roam, woods to explore, and nearby brooks to fish, and abundant areas of huckleberries and blackberries to pick. We had lots of hills to sled on. We had dangers too, as there were many rattlesnakes and copperheads in that area. We learned quickly the warning signs of nearby snakes by sight, odor, and sound. On this property, there was one of the oldest, if not the oldest, barn in Cameron County. I remember at one time, men came to hunt rattlesnakes in this barn.

There was a swamp by the driveway and occasionally we would see deer just standing in the water for a couple of days, and then leave. My mother said that they had been bitten by a snake and that was their way of drawing out the poison.

One job my sister and I had was cleaning the outhouse. We scrubbed the seats and floors with hot soapy water, and then we had to rinse it with two rinses of cold water. Oh, the joys of being a girl.

While living there, we went to a one-room school in the town of Cameron. There was no inside water or restrooms. We used an outhouse. We had a coal stove for heat. The teacher and older boys kept the stove going so we would be warm in the wintertime. Students carried the water needed for the day in a bucket from neighbors living nearby. Our teacher, Mrs. Morgan, saw the need for something hot for lunch, so each week a designated pupil would bring either sugar or cocoa to be made for the lunch period. Many of the older children helped the teacher with the smaller children, especially at lunchtime.

Mr. Rod Shadman told me the school used to be an old Catholic Church and that there were four babies buried there. This building still stands. It is a hunting camp now. There was an area behind the schoolhouse after we crossed a brook there was a grave of a Civil War Veteran and is decorated every year.

The Cameron School was closed and we were all sent to Sterling Run School. This was a two-room school with no running water or indoor plumbing. One room the grades were from first to fourth and the other was fifth to eighth. There were Boys' and Girls' outhouses. My youngest brother started first grade there and after a short period of attending school, he wouldn't go to school. My mother checked into this, as he was really afraid of something at school. She and the teacher found a wasp's nest in the boy's outhouse. It was removed and he liked going to school.

We lived there during World War II. We lived miles from town and only had kerosene lights. One night there was a knock on our door telling us there was a blackout and our kerosene lights could be seen.

In school, we had stamp day where we bought a War Savings Stamp at the cost of ten cents a stamp. Every class strived to get a 100 percent every stamp day.

We collected foil from cigarette packages, grease, newspapers. We had Ration Stamp Books for obtaining rationed items such as sugar, gasoline, and many other scarce items.

We then moved back to Emporium to another house with no plumbing or bathroom. We stayed there a very short time, as the well water wasn't fit to drink. We moved from there to a house on Second Street and for the first time in many years had running water, an indoor bathroom. Oh! What heaven that was.

Alas! That didn't last too long as we moved again to Driftwood to a house with no plumbing or indoor bathroom. Driftwood was a town filled with so much history. There was a monument depicting the Bucktails Regiment leaving the area to fight in the Civil War.

Driftwood was at one time a bustling community and played an important part in Cameron County history.

I still miss Cameron County, the mountains and their beauty every season of the year, especially the fall.

Love and the Lord
By Joy Strauser Spare Himes of Brookville,
Pennsylvania
Born 1934

My hometown of Heathville, Pennsylvania will always be etched in my memory. The town had 17 homes, one Evangelical United

Joy and Sport

Brethren Church, one post office, and a one-room schoolhouse. I started first grade, but the teacher, Miss Steiner, was mean to me. My neighbor told my mom to keep me home. The next year I went to a man teacher, Franklin Mowrey, and I sat still then. So see I quit school in first grade. My brother took us to school in a six-seated, black hack, drawn by a horse to Heathville School. Next school was Conifer, a four-room school, six grades in three rooms downstairs and seventh and eighth grades upstairs. I'll never forget those wide, steep stairs—I had a habit of running up and down the stairs. Well, once I caught my heel and slid down on my bottom end. That didn't feel very good. My favorite teacher in third and fourth grade was Miss Lulu Burns. She smelled so good and let us girls put make-up on her and us. Oh, Friday was the best day for singing and saying poems. Miss Burns had me say "The Village Blacksmith," my favorite poem. Oh yes, we had the big outhouse there at the school, just like we had at home. We also had softball games, the girls and boys together.

On May 28, 1934, I was born near New Bethlehem, Pennsylvania. After I was born, my parents took me to my Aunt Allie's house in Summerville, where I stayed until I was nine days old, then I went to live with my Aunt Clara, my dad's sister. My cousin, Gene, was 13 years old, and took me on his bicycle in a basket to my Aunt Clara's house, which was approximately two to three miles from Summerville to Heathville. This was told by mom Aunt Clara to me.

My dad did not want a girl, so when I heard they were having another child; I prayed that it wouldn't be a girl. God answered my prayers and I had six brothers, Don, Bob, Ron,

Dick, Fred, and Russ. I was the only girl and weighed three pounds (premature) when I was born, but my Aunt Clara kept me by the wood cook stove to keep warm and there were many prayers said for me. My mom (Aunt Clara) took me to see my two brothers because they lived with Grandpa and Grandma Strauser and we could play together. I was six years old when Grandma Strauser died. When we went there, I slept in the next room to her and she had a death rattle, and that scared me. In 1945, Grandpa Strauser died and my cousins, Gene and Bill, came home from the US Service to be pallbearers for the funeral in Summerville.

For only six years the Strauser Homestead was owned by someone other than a Strauser—and today the road is called Strauser Road. Grandpa David Strauser was a blacksmith, putting shoes on neighbors' horses, which were used for farming and traveling, cause not many people had cars in the 1900s.

This, today, is the house where my mom was born and nine of her sisters and brothers, the flu went thru and only four children lived. The house has been remodeled and got water when Clara got money from grandpa's estate. Clara Strauser Spare and Frank Spare moved to the farm after about six years of marriage.

Summer was chore time. Mine was weeding the onions and the carrots, watching the cows from getting into the cornfield. I studied my homework then. Pap didn't believe in putting up fences.

My job was watching the hen sitting on

Joy and Wayne Himes in 1955

eggs. I tied her leg with a twine to the wood crate and put 12 eggs in with straw and put her under the apple tree in the front yard. I had a rope swing there for swinging.

Another job was helping make hay—we had a horse and wagon. My brother mowed the hay and raked it in rows and took forks and lifted the hay on the wagon. My job was to tramp it down. One time, when it got as high as the back brace, around six feet high, the horse gave a leap and I fell off the back of the wagon and the fork stuck in the ground. My guardian angel was watching me—nothing broke, but my bottom was sore for a while.

All farm work was done with horses. Then, to get the hay into the barn, the hay wagon was backed into the barn, but needed to be put up into the haymow and a hay fork was put into a bunch of hay, closed it, and a rope was attached to a horse and the horse pulled the fork and hay up into the haymow and someone would be in the mow to take the fork out of the hay and let it come back to the wagon. Meantime, the horse and rope were at the road and I pulled the rope back to the wagon, while my brother brought the horse back to hook up and pull another load up. Wow, time consuming and little rope pieces pricked my hands.

My brother, Albert Spare had a big, old Mercury car. In 1950 I was in seventh grade, my brother's wife died and he moved in with us with his children, Walter, 8, Harold, 4, Gary, 2, and Birdie, three months. Well, I got a babysitting job then.

Sometime in the early 1940s, a gas well was drilled and we got gas heat in the house and a gas cook stove. In 1942, we got electricity. I was so happy, now I could see to read and get homework done and listen to the radio. Evenings I listened to "Hour of Decision" with Billy Graham and "Night Sounds." And, while mom milked eight cows, I cooked the supper for the family, but mom always had the potatoes pared, so I watched that nothing burned and listened to the radio, "Just Plain Bill" and "Portia Faces Life," a radio soap opera of that time.

One job that bothered me was holding the chicken legs while my Pap cut off their heads with a hatchet. I would jerk back and he would miss and holler at me to keep them still. We had chickens to butcher for Thanksgiving, we never had a turkey.

A good time of summer was the youth of

Wayne and Joy's family in 1970

our church had class meetings; we met three times once a month in three homes. One was mine. We had Bible devotions and a good snack, then the ones from Heathville walked up the hill to take Shirley home then they four or five went home to Heathville. Life was centered around the church for mom and me. We walked to and from church every Sunday and sometimes Wednesday to Bible Study in the summer and two weeks of Revival. If it rained, someone brought us home in a car.

The big highlight was the Christmas Eve program we put on. All the youth, me being the tallest, had the Mother part. We practiced from October so we knew our parts well. Three small towns around attended the program and the church was full.

Living in the time of the outhouse, chamber pot, no phone, only sponge baths in a basin wasn't that bad. We did with what we had and was happy. One thing we had was LOVE for each other, plenty of food and friends.

I had a pet Collie dog named Shep. He was good to chase cows for me.

I had an electric 45 record player and had Western records of Jim Reeves, Patsy Kline, and Hawkshaw Hawkins, and Slim Bryant— the Wheeling West Virginia gangs in the summer. Brother Albert took us to Alcola Park to see them sing on Sunday afternoon. He had a car then in 1950.

In summertime, we did have a swimming hole down below the barn in the Red Bank Creek. All five of us went swimming, more wading in the water and catching crawfish.

One thing I remember once a summer day we got a man visitor who walked up the railroad track and in the road and stopped for a sandwich. Mom said he was a bum, but she always gave him something to eat.

From 1950 to 1953, I attended high school in Brookville. Shirley and I ran to the bus to Heathville. We wore skirts and blouses and black and white saddle shoes. I only had one pair of shoes a year. Doris and I rode with Clair to Brookville YMCA and took Hawaiian guitar lessons for two years. We once played in the assembly program in the auditorium in 11th grade.

I would run over to Heathville to Doris and Dick and Don and Raymond's home in 15 minutes. Dick played the piano and we all sang in the summer time once a week. I would get the mail at the post office.

Some Friday nights a bunch of us would walk up Heathville Hill to Ohl to Heckman's warehouse and sit on bales of hay and watch a projected little movie. We also walked up the hill to Shirley's and they had a 17-inch screen TV.

On March 20, 1955, I met the love of my life, Wayne L. Himes on a blind date on the first day of spring. We were married on November 19, 1955 and moved to a farm near Brookville on October 19, 1959 with five small children—David, three, Gail, 18 months, Paul, three months old, Susan born 1961, and Lisa Born 1968. I finally got a clothes dryer and had a telephone—and still have the same number for 53 years. My life always has been blessed by the LORD with five children, 21 foster children from 1974 to 1985, and 22 grandchildren, and 21 great-grandchildren,

Wayne and Joy Himes with their 5 children

and two more expecting in 2012. Our three daughters are nurses, two sons work in the gas fields as supervisors. Five granddaughters are nurses and one grandson, Ken, is an orthopedic surgeon in Harrisburg, Pennsylvania and the twin brothers, Wayne is a chemical engineer in Greensburg, Pennsylvania.

Mountain Beach in the 30s
By Sarah Hays Bubb Bruch of Muncy,
Pennsylvania
Born 1925

I have very fond memories of Mountain Beach in both summer and winter. In the early 30s and forward, most of my sports activities were focused there.

Mountain Beach, now an apartment complex, had a lovely sandy beach on the south that one could reach by a wooden walkway on the extreme east side of the property. A deep round diving pond on the northeast corner; had Hart Bugbee, a handsome young Southside native, doing miraculous dives for my young admiration. A raft in the middle of the big pond gave a resting place for young swimmers.

The refreshment stand was at the northeast side of the long boardwalk stretching all the way west to the highway toward the south.

In the winter, a large main pond was frozen for ice-skating. I loved it, and remember I had brown figure skates. (I was only six or so, and they didn't make any white ones in my small size).

I remember Laurie and Charlie Maynard, and they were fine skaters, twirling and spinning and showing off their talents to the Strauss Waltz strains. All had a great time.

Ah! Sweet memories…

Gramma's Music of the Night
By Joy M. Grafius of Williamsport,
Pennsylvania
Born 1924

Since I was the oldest of three sisters, my mother dropped me off at her mother's to be of some help to her while she took my two sisters with her to visit her sisters in town.

I loved watching Gramma kneading dough for bread in her pantry on her pullout worktable in the Hoosier cupboard. The smell of homemade bread coming from the old black kitchen stove and later, her fresh hot corn bread, was pure heaven. This same stove was also used to heat the irons, with clip-on handles, for ironing. The ironing board was a large 2" x 10" x 6-foot plank covered with a large blanket and fastened underneath with pins. It lay across the backs of two chairs.

On washday, the stove held two large oval copper containers of water heating to be poured into the washtubs sitting on a big bench on the porch. One was for washing clothes with Fels Naptha or Octagon soap and washboard, the other was for rinsing. Water was obtained from the well off the porch, 3 foot square with a round lid in the middle that could be removed to put the bucket down to the water and bring up on a rope.

On the other end of the house about 25 feet away was a covered spring with cool clearer water. Inside the kitchen next to the door was a small table with a bucket of water for drinking, with a blue and white enameled dipper next to it.

Down the front yard path and across a small dirt road was the outhouse with two accommodating seat holes and the Sears catalog and a bag of lime in the corner.

I loved sitting on the porch swing with Gramma after the day's work was done. She would name clouds as buttermilk, mare's tail, cotton puffs, etc. As the sun set all the lightning bugs came out and the yard and fields looked like a fairyland. Then the cicadas (Katy Dids) and frogs croaking in the small stream across the road made our music of the night.

The small dirt cellar had a stream running through it. Several large flat rocks held crocks of butter or milk that came from farms nearby. Half a dozen shelves against the walls held shiny glass jars of canned fruits and vegetables, and in season, canned venison.

Memorial Park
On the west side of our city is Memorial Park and Bowman Field Baseball stadium.

In the middle of Memorial Park was a large enclosed pavilion that was used for many large functions and had a dance floor and stage for the many big bands traveling the country: Glenn Miller, Tommy Dorsey, Louie Prima, etc. were here. I danced to them.

Dancing was the rage in our town. We had Handy Haven, Mountain Beach, Canoe Club, Trout Pond, HyWy at the YWCA, Park

Ballroom, and many more. That's where our young people went to release all that energy.

These places are all gone now and big bands are a lovely memory—how sad!

One-Room Schools
By Mary Lee Harris of Montoursville,
Pennsylvania
Born 1945

I attended two of the one room schools in Lycoming County—Steam Mill School, which was on Quenashuckney Rd. and Pine Run School. At first, each school had all eight grades and then, later on Steam Mill had first thru fourth grades and Pine Run had fifth thru eighth grade. When it was time for your grade to have its class you went to the front of the room, where there were long benches to sit on and that was where you had your class. The other grades were to read or work on assignments while you had your class. (One of the things that I remember very well is that the children were well behaved and listened to the teachers. They did not chatter and act up while other classes were going on).

I remember how the chicken feed that Dad bought came in cloth bags that were printed with flowers and such. My mother would wash the bags three or four times to get all the feed out of the material, and then she would make skirts and blouses for my sister and I to wear. (The girls all wore skirts and dresses— no slacks).

We had to walk over half a mile from our house to the bus stop every morning and every afternoon. I remember one winter it had snowed several feet over night. When we left our house to go to the bus, I went first because I was the oldest in sixth grade, next came my little brother who was in the first grade, and then, my little sister who was in the fourth grade. I broke the path and they followed me. You see, back then we still went to school when there was bad weather. Not like today, where if there are more than a couple of inches of snow it is "No School".

Oh yes, and if someone did not behave at school the teacher could give you a spanking right there in front of God and everybody. You know what, it hurt like the dickens, but you learned from the first one and never wanted another. And when you got home, it usually meant another one at home. We lived

thru them and learned a lot more than children now days do.

There was no indoor plumbing at these schools. If you needed to relieve yourself, you went to the outhouse. Someone had the chore each day to pump several buckets of water and bring inside for washing our hand and such.

Usually one of the older boys that lived close to the school would come early and take care of the fire in the big old furnace that sat in the corner of the room. We had grates laid on top of the furnace and we would bring a potato or some homemade soup for our lunch and heat it on the top of the furnace. (No cafeteria!) Back then, we didn't think much about it. That's just the way it was.
What I wouldn't give to go back to those "good old days", the simpler life without all the headaches of today.

Was It "Snake-Oil" For The Beauty Queen?
By Clara M. Gerber of Williamsport,
Pennsylvania
Born 1918

Just past 1st Street, on Maynard, was a big field known as Rundios. This is where the circus came every year. This was a big event. You have to remember, this was in the late 20s or early thirties. Most people didn't even have radio.

Well anyway, my aunt would take her children and me over to watch the circus set up. This was so interesting and exciting to watch the "big-top" to go up. It was a busy time getting ready for the afternoon performance.

One thing that fascinated me, was watching the cooks flip pancakes. This went on and on. You can imagine, until all the workers and circus people were fed.

Following this, which was a show in itself, we went home for lunch and came back in the afternoon to see the parade. I think all the performers, all the workers, and all the animals were in the parade. Clowns walked along the sides-sometimes performing for us. There always was a man selling balloons. Also, sometimes, a man had little yellow birds on a string. I didn't have any money to purchase those things, but the excitement of it all was enough for us kids. I think my

Aunt Mary enjoyed it as much as we did. We never even gave it a thought about going to the show. None of us could have afforded it anyway. It was a happy day for us kids, what a day!

Sometime after the circus had been in town, we heard that a Medicine-Show was coming. This was new to us. We didn't know quite what to expect. Maybe my grandmother had some idea, I certainly didn't.

Well, the first night my grandmother grabbed a folding chair and we walked over, (one block). There was quite a crowd—a good turn-out.

They had a band that played lively music and two fellows on stage that told jokes. Then, the Dr. came out giving a big talk on "snake oil". Then, the entertainers walked among the audience selling their wonderful "snake-oil". It was amazing how the crowd grabbed it up, considering it was hard times. There was more music, but I can't remember if anyone sang. I think this entertainment would be called a Minstrel Show. After the first night, we were hooked, and so were a lot of other people. I can't remember if it was one or two weeks, but whatever, we were there every night.

The show followed the same pattern each night, but advertised different products.

One night this woman with gorgeous red hair down to her ankles strutted on stage. Of course, this night they sold hair tonic. Another night, the Dr. held up a tape worm he had taken from a man. It looked like a 3 ft. long noodle to me. (I bet the younger generation never heard of a tape worm), I'm wondering if there really is such a thing.

The last night was a Beauty Contest. There were six girls on stage from the audience. They were judged by crowd clapping. A beautiful redhead won the prize, but for the life of me, I can't remember what it was. I hope, "not snake-oil"! Those were the days!

Some Roads May Be Rocky, but Rocks Brought Me Happiness
By Mary Skiba Siders of Riverside, California
Born 1930

In the 1930s, I grew up in the little town of Johnsonburg, Pa. Elk County, population, 5,000. It was a hilly region, so you either went up town or up home.

The main industry was the paper mill, (NY & Pa. Co.) located on the shore of the Clarion River. You either lived in "West End", "East End" (Decker Town) in town, or the Avenues, or Clarion Heights. Our home was on Blaine Avenue (#235) in the Clarion Heights section. Our house was on a hill, the second to the last on the left side, to be exact. There were no houses across the street from our house, only a hilly area with some grass, and then a lot of trees.

I enjoyed going "into the woods", where there were rocks and trees to climb, and as kids we had names for many of the rocks. There was the "Frog" rock, which you needed a running start to get to the top, and if you had leather soles shoes, it was a slippery climb. It was worth it, because you could slide right down like it was a sliding board.

Further up the hill was the "Picnic Rock". It was flat on top and we enjoyed many picnics of peanut butter and jelly sandwiches and cool-aid out of a pint jar. It had several large steps that made it possible for us to reach the top. I loved to sit at the edge with my legs dangling over the side and have a panoramic view of our little town. From my vantage point, I could see the B&O Railroad Station at the lower end of Blaine Ave. and the Paper Mill with its tall chimney and white smoke floating to the sky. I could see "The Flat" with the Clarion River flowing south, the Pennsylvania Railroad Station on the opposite side of the river, and the town with Route 219 passing through town. The trucks and cars looked so small from where I sat.

I could spot the Community Building and playground (compliment of the Paper Mill) where I spent many childhood hours on the swings, rings, teeter-totters, slides and large sand box. That side of town was also on a hill.

My most favorite time of year was the fall. I could sit on the picnic rock and never tire of looking at the hill across the river with the leaves of gold, red, and yellow and some evergreen trees mixed in. It was a sight to behold. To this day, I can still close my eyes and see that beautiful sight.

But, closer to home was the most famous rock of all, "The Duck Rock". It was shaped like a duck floating on water. It wasn't easy to climb, but the boys had cables to help them reach the top. Many times a group of us would gather wood and build a fire behind the duck rock and roast potatoes that were "donated" (borrowed) from someone's garden. Butter and a saltshaker appeared like magic. The potato skins were burnt black and the potato, most likely a little raw in the center, but they were "Oh-So Good!"

Its memories like these that put a smile on my face now that I've reached my "Golden Years". It was fun being a kid in those "Good Old Days."

The Ice Man, the Sheenie and the Huckster
By Jack R. Jones of Hughesville, Pennsylvania

During my youth in the 40s, 50s, and 60s, I have fond memories of these men traveling through the neighborhood and down our street. I can hear younger people are asking, "What are they?"

Let me just tell you: During the days before refrigerators, the Ice Box was commonplace and the state of the art way to keep perishables. The Ice Box looked much like a small refrigerator with a small compartment at the top with a tray beneath to catch the water from the melting blocks of ice, which were about the size of an automobile battery. Usually an Ice Box would hold two blocks. The Ice Man would canvas the neighborhood finding out who might be potential customers. He would give them a two-sided card approximately the size of an 8 ½" X 11" sheet of writing paper. On one side, it was green and on the other side, it was red. When a family needed ice, they would place the card in either the front door or window with the red side out facing the street, which told the Ice Man to stop and deliver ice. If no ice was required, the green side facing out meant go - no ice was required today.

The Ice Man would drive slowly up and down the streets of town only stopping in response to the card's color. Our family moved three times on the same street. In the fall of 1953 with my help, my mom started a home delivered bakery, which afforded us the necessary monies to purchase full-sized appliances, which included an electric refrigerator.

The Sheenie was a junk dealer who rode through the neighborhood in a pickup truck blowing a raspy horn usually on a Saturday morning. When folks had miscellaneous scrap, usually metal, they would walk into the street and hail him. He would take a look at what you had and quote you a price, load your junk and drive on down the street. I suppose he'd sell it to a large scrap dealer (Much like Staiman's or Mid-State Trading does for junk cars in Williamsport, PA).

Lastly comes the Huckster. He was a produce vendor driving a 40s or 50s vintage station wagon with specially constructed horizontal windows which would open up to allow the stay-at-home moms in the neighborhood to buy all of their vegetable needs without leaving home. Remember not many families had multiple cars yet and when Dad was at work, the only way Mom could get out to shop was using public transportation buses, which meant she'd have to lug large sacks of groceries home from the nearest bus stop.

Quarantined
Until the late 1950s, I can remember that when one family member contracted a communicable disease like chickenpox, measles, or mumps it was a major public health threat. A placard was given to the head of the household to be placed in the window of the front door stating that this house was Quarantined and no one was permitted to enter or exit this home until clearance was given by the proper public health official. As with most illnesses, schoolchildren were a hot bed for spreading sickness. Usually when one child would contract something it would spread through the entire family, hence every family member was restricted to the home. I don't remember quarantines after about the mid to late 50s when immunizations for many things like the Saulk Polio vaccine were discovered.

Hard Work has Made Me Live to be 89
By Helen Tucker of Williamsport, Pennsylvania
Born 1923

I am 89 years old. I can remember living in Allenwood, PA, on a farm owned by the McCormick's. My father and mother had seven children and I was the oldest. What I can remember is taking turns every three nights to take our baths in a round washing tub, sitting on two chairs, and the hot water in another tub on the stove. When it wasn't our turn we hand-washed.

Going to school, we walked two miles, through big snowstorms and all. Being the oldest I carried a 2-quart tin pail with chocolate milk in it and a potato for each of us. We were in a one-room school. There was a round furnace and we would put the potatoes around the edge of it. They were delicious baked potatoes.

After we got home then we milked the cows. It was hard work, which is why I have lived to be 89.

Growing Up in Northern Pennsylvania in the 1950s
By Michael L. Myers of Elizabethtown, Pennsylvania
Born 1947

I had the privilege of growing up in northern Pennsylvania, Lycoming County to be specific, in the 1950s. Some of my fondest memories took place on my Grandad Myers's farm.

My grandfather's farm was much like it had been in the late 1800s except that he no longer worked with horses. There was electricity in the house and the farm buildings, but there was no running water, no telephone, and we used the outhouse.

I would often spend a week with my grandparents. On Monday morning, my grandmother would set a match to the waste paper that had accumulated under the large copper kettle in the out kitchen. This "recycled" paper would then heat water that she would use to do her wash in the old wringer washer. She would dip water from the big kettle to the washer. For those really dirty clothes, she would use lye soap that she had made and the washboard.

After my grandfather came in from doing the early morning chores, we would sit down to a breakfast of eggs, fried potatoes, and thick slices of homemade bread smeared generously with homemade jelly. I would often have the privilege of going up to the jelly cupboard to pick the jelly. My grandfather would always pour his coffee out into the saucer to let it cool and then pour it back into the cup. I think that is what the saucers were made for because they always held the whole cup's worth of coffee.

In the summer months, I would help with bringing in the hay or run the clover seeder or when I was younger, help Grandma in the garden or feed the chickens.

During supper, you could hear the milk separator running in the out kitchen. When the hand-milked liquid was fully separated, the cream would be put in a large can that was kept in the springhouse. The remainder, or skim milk, would be fed to the hogs with a little saved to put in an old frying pan that was laid on the ground for the swarm of wild cats that would come out from under the out kitchen. There was no use trying to pet them.

If it was Saturday night, I would take my weekly bath in a washtub either in the out kitchen or sometimes outside behind the house. We would then get dressed in our Sunday clothes and go over to town where all the local farmers would come. My grandmother had one of those fox stoles that was kept together by the fox's mechanical jaws. If we didn't happen to go to town, we would sit on the front porch and just wait. Someone always would come by to visit. And we were ready.

My grandmother went to the grocery store about once a month. She would spend $3.00 to buy coffee, sugar, and a bag of those green, pink, and yellow mints. They raised everything else they needed.

I would sometimes see my grandfather catch and chop the head off an unsuspecting rooster. The spectacle of the headless rooster running around the yard was something to see. It was a little scary. My grandmother would then scald the chicken and clean it. She would sometimes carefully lay out the internal parts of the chicken and tell me what they were. I had a very early biology lesson.

At the end of one of these chore-filled days, it would be bedtime. My grandmother would unwind that hair bun revealing a ponytail that reached down below her waist. The "thunder mugs" would be located under the bed and we would all say good night. It was a very satisfying day. And 60 years later, these are very satisfying memories.

From a School House to a Mansion
By Judy Schell of Clearfield, Pennsylvania

Just a few years before my birth, the site of that event had been a one-room schoolhouse. Both my father and his father had gone to school there. The "midwife" was my maternal grandmother. She was not inexperienced, however, as she had delivered many babies for other family friends and neighbors. Quite different from modern birthing centers!

This one room school was the Pine Grove School, located in Lawrence Township, Clearfield County, Pennsylvania. Its coordinating church, Pine Grove Bethel Presbyterian, is still in existence today.

My parents bought this school building in 1939, after it had been vacated as a teaching facility when the new grade school with individual classrooms was built in Glen Richey, Pa. With much hard work, they transformed it into a home. After digging out one-half of the basement to install a coal furnace and coal bin (the schoolhouse had been heated with a single pot-bellied stove), they built two bedrooms, a living room, a kitchen, and a space for a bathroom. Money was tight, and I remember Dad often reminiscing about the decrepit furnace he salvaged somewhere by his father, saying, "I suppose we can make it work, if that's the best we have."

I don't know when electricity was installed, but I can remember living without running water. My father had hand dug and stoned lined a well a ways down a hill near a little creek. The well was only about six feet deep, and although the water was laden with iron, it never went dry. We did have drains into a cesspool, allowing for kitchen sink. Mother and Dad carried water by buckets for cooking and drinking. The night before "wash day" they would carry a large metal boiler full to be heated on the coal fired cook stove. My mother was fortunate to have an electric wringer washer. Of course, no running water meant no inside toilet facilities. We had a very elite outhouse, though—a "three-seater" left from the schoolhouse days.

When Dad received notice of his draft into the U.S. Navy during World War II, he and my uncle dug feverishly down the hill, which was through woods, to lay pipe to get water into the house for my mother. My brother was six years old, I was four, and my sister was born six weeks after Dad left. He was home on "boot leave" at the time of her birth, which also took place in the converted schoolhouse. At least Grandma had running water this time. We now had a bathroom sink and a flush toilet. It was June 1944.

The winter of 1944-45 was extremely severe. Our precious water line froze, and once again, we were without running water.

My grandfather brought us water in milk cans from his adjacent dairy farm. I don't know the details of how my mother managed, but we all survived.

One vivid memory I do have of the unrelenting winter was a major snowstorm while my brother in first grade, was in school. In those days, school wasn't canceled or dismissed early because of bad weather. We lived about three miles from Glen Ritchie. This day the snow fell so rapidly that the school bus was not able to get through to our house. The bus driver was able to get down the main road to town however, so he took my brother to our mother's parents, who lived in town. This was good, except we had no telephone for anyone to let my mother know. She was frantic! Eventually, a boy in high school, who lived on another country lane about a half mile through the woods from us, came to our door. He was cold and covered with snow, which had continued to fall. He had walked home, and at the request of the bus driver, had come to let my mother know where my brother was. I'm glad I was only a child during "The Greatest Generation."

My parents prospered well in later years. Two upstairs bedrooms had been built after Dad's return from the war, and later that house was remodeled with carpeting, paneling, a built-in kitchen, and electric heat. There was no resemblance to the old school house. Mother and Dad lived there until they died; Mother in 1989 and Dad in 2002. The one room country schoolhouse had become their mansion.

1948 Was a Magical Year for Me
By Ralph E. Crouse of Renovo, Pennsylvania
Born 1937

Living in the small town of Renovo, PA, located in North Central PA, between the Allegheny Mountains and along the Susquehanna River, 1948 was a magical year for me because I was waiting for the Christmas holidays to be here.

I have three sisters and a little brother that love Christmas, just like me. Their names were Rosemary, Sarah, Regina and brother, George, who is six years younger than me, and my sisters were all older than me. In those days, there were only a few presents under our tree, not quite like today. We all saved our

Grandpa Crouse holding Ralph, Jr. with Sara, Rosemary, and Regina

of kitchen glasses, usually very decorative with flowers. They came in a set of eight and came in a wire basket. Dad always got red or blue work handkerchiefs. The girls got some kind of jewelry from J.J. Newberry's. My brother, I forget, probably some kind of squirt gun. My nickels did all of this.

We all shopped in Renovo; no need to shop any other place. At that time, we had a 5 & 10 cent store, shoe store, variety store, furniture store, jewelry store, clothing store, and hardware store, plus other places to shop. Our town was self-sustaining with two or three bakeries and multiple small grocery stores.

Christmas, to the Crouse family, meant so much to all of us. Dad would bring home a forest-cut yellow pine tree, usually tied to the front fender of his '37 Buick. The tree was probably borrowed from the Commonwealth, somewhere on his way home from work at CT

Ralph in front of the 1937 Buick

money so we could each buy a single present for everyone in our family.

I was a Buffalo nickel saver; you older people know what I'm talking about. I had a daily paper route in Drury's Run and delivered The Sunday Patriot in South Renovo. My tips amounted to a lot of nickels! With the money I saved over the summer months, I could buy each one of my siblings a single present, and one for Mom and Dad. Mom usually got a set

tower in Keating. We always put the tree up on Christmas Eve.

He also never forgot to bring two live Rhode Island Red chickens home for our Christmas dinner. These he would be head and I was the lucky one to help him pluck them after a bucket hot water bath, in the basement. I didn't mind this at all. Mom, of course, got to singe them on the gas stove, before stuffing and roasting them. We all looked forward to a great dinner.

I remember what struck me the most about our tree; my sisters took great pride in hanging

Regina, Sarah, Rosemary, Geroge, and Ralph

81

*Ralph Crouse with the Remington .22 in 1941
in front of his first car a Pontiac*

the lead-like icicles one at a time and placing Angel Hair all over the tree. We had about 1 dozen "bubble lights" mixed with the regular lights and red cellophane lighted wreaths in most of our windows. If there were too many holes in the tree, Dad would bore a hole in the trunk and insert an extra limb to fill it in.

Up until Christmas, we would sled-ride down the 8th Street bridge approach, mostly on the sidewalk. No need to worry about traffic-not many cars in town using the slippery roads.

I hoped for a "Red Rider" BB Gun that year, but I was really surprised when my dad bought me a single shot Remington .22 instead. He said if I was about to learn to shoot, I should learn with the real thing instead of a BB gun. The understanding was to only shoot it at camp with his supervision. I even got to shoot it at Hall's Run Park on Christmas Day; he was a super dad! All of us got great presents and we appreciated them.

The American Flyer train was especially fun to play with. It was set up on a 4x6 plywood platform and ran from morning to bedtime; fake smoke streaming from its stack. Our Christmases were not rushed. The holidays were not stretched out and none of the holidays started three months before they came. I think that is why we truly enjoyed every minute of them.

My memories are still strong. I love to think back over my younger years and I was truly lucky to be born in the 30s. I only hope I continue to remember the memorable time with family and friends.

Having my new Remington .22 was my best Christmas present ever, especially

knowing it came from my dad, but the super present I was not aware of, at that time, was just being born in Williamsport Hospital in December 1948. I would not get to meet her for 20 more years and she became my beautiful and loving wife, Betsy.

Daisies Became Eggs and Buttercups Became Butter
By Mary Marvin of Bolivar, New York
Born 1934

I grew up in McKean County, Pennsylvania, on a farm in Pierce Brook, near the village of Smethport, which is the county seat of McKean County.

When I was in grade school, I went to school in Farmers Valley, a place that back then was built around the Quaker State Refinery. Farmers Valley had an old fashioned grocery store, a feed store, a car repair shop, a restaurant called The Dairy Bar that made wonderful ice cream tubbers, a church, and an elementary school.

The school was so close to the refinery that when the kids went outside for recess, they came back in dirty from the black smoke that settled on everything in Farmers Valley.

Hickory nut trees grew on the playground of the school, so lots of kids went home from school with hickory nuts in their lunch pails in the fall. Sometimes the boys would fill their pockets with them, and then, they would spill out in class. If that happened, the nuts would be confiscated by the teacher.

I was six years old when we moved to the farm. My parents had bought it for $1,700. The farm was run down and needed a lot of work, but my parents were young and proud to have land and a big house where they could raise their five children. Also, there was a barn in fairly good shape, and a chicken house and a milk house. And best of all, there was many acres of land, some of it tillable and some of it wooded.

When we first came to the farm, one of my grandfathers lived with us. He was a teamster, and so he tilled the land with a team of horses. One day the horses ran away while they were hitched to the drag that my grandfather was using, dragging him for quite a distance. Then, although my grandfather argued against it, my parents decided to get rid of the horses.

My dad then devised his version of a tractor by taking the doors and roof off an old car and putting chains on the tires. He called it the "Jitney." It did the job until he was finally able to purchase an Allis Chalmers tractor.

Eventually the farm prospered, but as the children were growing up there wasn't much money for toys. We did have one bicycle that we all shared.

Since I was one of the girls, memories still linger of playing house on the front porch of the old farm house with my two sisters. We practiced being mothers by taking care of our rag dolls, and we practiced being housewives by "cooking" with our little plastic dishes. What did we cook? Well, we used our imaginations so that the daisies became eggs, and buttercup flowers became butter. The mud puddles in the driveway that eventually dried down to a hard crust became our fudge. Dust was flour. And the most wonderful food of all was real, because right beside our front porch there was an early transparent apple tree. Apples fell from the tree in late July and early August, and we pretended to cook with them as we ate them.

On winter evenings, we all gathered around the radio to listen to our favorite shows. In our imagination, we could picture what the people speaking in those show looked like.

Popcorn was popped in a large cast iron frying pan that we shook over the burner of the stove. The popcorn was topped with fresh butter churned from cream from our own cows. Some evenings as we ate the popcorn, Grandma read stories to us from chapter books that she got on loan from the library in Bradford, Pa. where she lived. Other evenings we might all help cut and sew carpet rags that my mother then crocheted into throw rugs.

We always ate well, because we had large vegetable gardens and animals that were raised for meat, like chickens and pigs.

We wore dresses made from printed feed sacks and had never heard of designer jeans or Nike sneakers. But, we had love, good food, two parents, and grandparents who loved us.

My hair is gray now, and wrinkles appear here and there, but whenever I think of those days long ago, with my family and wonderful farm family neighbors, and school chums, I smile and feel blessed to have lived in Pennsylvania many years ago when life seemed to go at a slower pace. I appreciate what I have now, but I appreciate even more what I had then.

"Thanksgiving Day"
By Edna M. Burge of Morrisdale,
Pennsylvania
Born 1930

I remember "Thanksgiving Day". It was a day that we gave thanks to God for the plentiful harvest that He bestowed upon us. The gardens were put to sleep for the next spring and the cellar was full of canned vegetables. The potato bins were full and the wooden fruit boxes were stored nearby. The smell of sauerkraut filled the cellar and Grandmother had just covered it with clean cloth, weighed down with a large plate topped with a large polished stone. Everything smelled so good. We were thankful for the plentiful year. The sauerkraut would be ready for the celebrated "New Year".

I remember "Thanksgiving Day" because it was another big eventful day in our live. It was also what we called "The Butcher Day."

All the other goodies would not have much meaning if we had not a supply of meat for the winter months.

I remember three big tri-pods in the yard. There was a large copper kettle hanging by chains from each tri-pod. They all had a purpose. Firewood was set under each kettle, ready to start a fire. One kettle (the largest one) would be boiling hot and ready to scald skin on the pigs. The other kettle fires would be started later than needed.

The men began to work toward getting the pigs ready for the butchering task, while the women worked on getting the Red rooster that they had butchered for "Thanksgiving Day", but that was a small task compared to the things that the butcher day commanded for the women to do.

I remember the old plank bottom chair located close to the back door with a wooden bucket filled with water close by. A smooth oak board about ten inches wide was in the wooden bucket, along with a blunt scraper nearby. This is where Grandmother would do her work for the day. The other women would have the pots and pans ready as needed along with all the utensils that the men would need as the butchering task proceeded.

I think I was six years old and with all the other children, we were told, "You children get an apple and go sit out of the way." It wasn't long until we heard the men making noises that told us that the pigs were ready for the hot water bath. The men used a special gun to kill the pigs, usually two were butchered. They hooked up the old gray horse to haul the pigs into the work place of butchering.

The pigs were in place near a trough, and it was filled with scalding hot water. The men were strong and slowly moved the pigs into the scalding hot water. There were several scraping bells that were used to take the hair off the skin of the pigs.

After they were cleaned, a pulley on the tri-pod that had a kettle on it was used to pull the pig up to start cutting it up. The knives were sharpened by Grandfather the previous week and could split a hair.

They would have a large wooden tub to catch the intestines of the pig for they had many uses as the butchering continued. Several buckets of cold water would be used for the items they saved. The heart, liver, sweet meats, the tongue, and other small pieces of inside meats were put in one bucket. The next thing that almost turned our stomach, the intestines were cut in about three foot lengths. The inside matter was squeezed into a bucket to be thrown on the old garden for fertilizer.

Now we come to the purpose of the old plank chair and the wooden buckets located at the back door. The men would bring in the pieces of the intestines to be scraped, cleaned, and to be used for casings for the sausage that was to be smoked in the smokehouse. This was Grandmother's job, and she sat there scraping and singing that old song, "The Old Rugged Cross".

The men used one of the copper kettles to cook the special meats they had saved and it would be used later to make, what we call "liverwurst", which would be used on pancakes. The broth would be used to make "pudding meat" also used for the breakfast meals. This would all be in place about noon on "Thanksgiving Day" when we heard the old cowbell ring loud and clear, dinner is served. We all dropped everything, we were starved, especially all the men who had been up and working since 5:00 AM.

We all left our chores and gathered around the table set and fit for a king. Grandfather folded his rough stained hands and said, "Let us Pray", and thank God for the bountiful year of harvest. Help us to share with others if there is a need and remember to always be thankful for all the blessings we have in this life, Amen."

The meal was over and the women had a big task ahead of them. As soon as the meat was cut up for sausage, the grinding began, then the filling of the casings that Grandmother had cleaned and prepared. The hams were trimmed, the shoulders prepared and the bacon sides were trimmed and made ready to soak in the brine that gave them a special taste as they hung in the old smoke house where Grandfather had smoldering hickory wood making an aroma that made you hungry just to smell it.

Although the sausage was ground and packed into the casings, the remainder would be canned by Grandmother to put on the shelves along side of the canned vegetables. The same would be done with liverwurst.

We can't forget the shelves of peaches, pears, apples, that Grandfather had prepared long before "Thanksgiving Day".

A lot of work not mentioned, was done before and after "Thanksgiving Day" as there was an invitation to come back to Grandma and Grandpa's house next Saturday for a big breakfast of Sausage and Pancakes.

With thankful hearts for a bountiful year of yester year, we will probably never see such a Thanksgiving Day again. Our memories linger on, even when we fry sausage for our pancakes, but the taste will never be the same. In those days shopping for groceries was never needed and our "Thanksgiving Day" was a thankful day and a time to thank God for all His blessings showered on our family.

This article has been written by Edna Burge who is 82 years old and remembers the old paths we trod years ago. We thank God for His Blessings.

North Fork, My Home Town
By Jeanne Sherman of Harrison Valley,
Pennsylvania
Born 1950

My name is Jeanne Snyder Sherman. I am from Potter County, Pa. and would like to share some stories of my past as well as some my parents, (Richard and Ardath Anthony Snyder) and Grandmother (Martha Hammond Anthony) often spoke of.

My grandmother's grandmother was one of the first settlers to come in from the New England states. She told of hauling a stone boat with a team of oxen. The milk cow was milked in the AM and the milk was anchored to the stone boat while they traveled. In the evening there would be butter floating on top of the milk.

They settled near Brookfield, Pa. Eventually, my grandmother's father became choir director and organist in the church there.

As my grandmother raised her family of five boys and two girls in the town of North

Jeanne with her Grandmother Pickering

Fork, they were given their springtime dose of castor oil. Their father (who later died when the baby was 2) would line them up with castor in one hand and a stick in the other. If the participants were reluctant to take the medicine, a tap on the head and a prompt "open up" was immediately rendered.

North Fork had a one-room schoolhouse and the school board would hire a teacher, but would board the teacher with whoever had students attending the school. My mother told that her teacher would sleep with her. The schoolhouse had no water or plumbing. There were two separate outhouses, one for girls and one for boys. The room was heated with a pot-bellied stove that my uncle would fire up in the AM. There was a bucket for water and a ladle to drink from. A couple of students were sent to the nearest house to "fetch" the water. (It happened to be Richard Snyder's grandmother's house.) She would meet them at the well and offer each hauler one of her famous sugar cookies with a raisin in the middle. They were about 5 inches in diameter. Needless to say, everyone wanted to go for water.

Years passed and the teenage girl who slept with her teacher married the guy with the sugar cookies Gramma. They lived in the house where the girl had grown up. They had married during WWII and her brother was stationed in England in the Air Force. There was no indoor plumbing yet, but a party-line telephone had been installed up the North Fork. The uncle would call occasionally to speak to his mother. Rings on the telephone were long rings and short rings. Maybe your ring was two longs and a short. Everyone soon learned who was getting the call. When they heard my grandmother's ring, they would all pick up and listen to hear from the boy "across the pond". This split the signal till my grandmother could hardly hear and she would have to ask them all to hang up so she could hear.

My grandmother Snyder (Pickering) was one of the first to get indoor plumbing. However, on Friday nights, she and her husband would like to watch the Friday night fights on the one channel of television. They didn't want to be bothered by a pesky two or 3 year old, who was homesick for Mom and Dad and always had to go to the bathroom. (Maybe, she was a brat!) They would put the chamber pot under the bed and told me if I had to go, "use this". I still can remember the smell of that room, however, when my gramma came up stairs and got in bed with me, all was right with the world

In the morning, I could hear robins sing outside the window. To this day when I hear robins, I think of those days and long for the peace I had then.

As my parent's family bloomed into two girls and a boy, my mother would sew clothes for her girls. She only had a treadle sewing machine, but was able to make her own patterns from brown paper bags and use cloth from feed sacks.

My Grandmother Pickering's husband raised chickens. I'm not 100% positive, but maybe he even "fought" with his Banty roosters. I was never allowed to be in on anything like that anyway.

Well, chickens had to be fed and they would go to the feed store in Westfield, Pa., back the truck up to the loading deck and throw on colorful print bags of chicken meal. The prints were always very small and mostly of flowers. They would dump out the chicken feed into the covered drum, wash the bag and viola', turn the cloth into dresses. We wore a lot of "feed sack" clothing.

As we grew, my mother would take her brood from North Fork to the grocery store in Westfield for groceries. Often, my Grandmother Pickering would ride along, as she didn't drive. Watching for rattlesnakes was not a priority on our list of fun things to do on shopping day. We were more interested in the gumball machine at Fitzwater's Grocery. However, one summer day, as we passed by the Rumsey house in lower North Fork, we saw a large snake crossing the road. My mother intent on causing bodily harm to the snake; drove over it, backing up and going forward many times. She stopped once and my grandma opened the car door and started to step out. My mother yelled at her to get back in the car before she got bit. Eventually, the snake crawled to the nearest house and was finished off by the man who lived there. They cut the rattlers from the snake and kept them in a metal band-aid box to show anyone who came to our house to visit. What a conversation starter. When we moved to Blossburg, the band-aid box went too.

Still in elementary school, our father's work took him to Blossburg, Pa. and in a few years to Covington. I remember snooping through my mother's dresser and finding this extra-large mechanical pencil. On the outside was written, "Merry Christmas". I asked if I could use it, and was promptly told, "No!" The reason it seems, that was the only gift my father had received for Christmas one year when he was a child. It was the first time I realized how poor people must have been during the depression.

We would take trips back to North Fork all the time. We were allowed to stay weeks at a time if we wanted. Grace and Bennie Truax owned the North Fork store. If my grandmother's didn't have any money, they would send us to the store with a couple of eggs to buy penny candy. The eggs weren't enough to get money to put in the coke machine. That needed a quarter. That quarter would release the mechanics and the bottle

William "Bill" Anthony

that was kept in very cold water, would slide out and over to the hole where you could raise it out of. As soon as a bottle was out, the metal would click back together until another quarter came along.

My father always had stories of his Uncle Tom Snyder who ran the milk run from all the little farmers in North Fork, down to Westfield. Milk was strained into heavy metal milk cans and covered with a heavy metal lid that fit down inside, and then loaded by hand onto a truck. All the boys in town would ask to go with Tom, as he owned the corner store (where the Cowansque High School is) and his wife would get them candy. For fun, Tom would give the boys eggs to take to the store. However, upon lifting and dragging the boys over the side of the truck (they always rode in the back) the eggs would "accidently" become broken in their pockets. Mrs. Tom would have to clean them up, wipe their tears and give out candy anyway.

When Hillary Clinton said, "It takes a town to raise a child," I think of North Fork because after my mother's father died, the whole town looked after her five brothers. They fished up and down the creek, helped with farm chores here and there, and just enjoyed life.

Another Day, Another Time
By Dorothy J. Britton of Smethport, Pennsylvania
Born 1936

How times have changed in the 75 years I have lived (I/E—no e-mail, no phones as a child,) I was born in the country, miles from town. Seems like now, looking back, I realize how self-reliant folks had to be. As a child, though, none of this affected me. My early memories were for the most part self-reliant. We had our own chickens for eggs and meat;

cattle for our own milk and butter, our garden for potatoes and all vegetables, a springhouse to keep milk, butter, eggs, Mother would pick berries for jelly, and can some for pies.

Later on in summer, hay was cut using our faithful horse. Hay was pitched on the large hay wagon. I was put on top with strict orders to stay there, reason being there were a lot of rattlesnakes where we lived. My dad pitched the hay by hand on the wagon and Mother in her long dress would tramp the hay down. Back to the barn, a long hay tongue would pull with the aid of a horse into the haymow for winter.

Saturday was a big day back then. My folks would take all the extra eggs and butter from the springhouse. We had a small car with a rumble seat where the goods to be sold in town were put. It was 12 miles to town and what fun it was to go to town.

My dad trapped then, so well treated furs were sold for extra money. The furs were sold, after a bit of haggling, to a man who had a clothing store with a large back room for furs.

At the store, only necessities were bought. Flour, sugar, and salt was very important and kept in tight containers. The local stores were a great wonder to me. Flour and sugar were sold in brightly covered print cotton bags. These bags were treasures. Once empty, they were used for everything, curtains, dishtowels, even clothing. Nothing was ever wasted in those days.

After shopping and selling of goods were finished, then came my turn. I would get a small bag of penny candy, a great treasure for me, sometimes a coloring book, crayons and a storybook. I surely felt well off in those days. My early memories were of the large horse, who helped us to live in those days. I and our old farm dog would set by the fence and watch the horses eat their hay and an apple or so that I would give them. I loved the gentleness of those huge horses, the calmness as they ate, their large brown eyes watching the tiny girl and old dog that seemed enthralled by them. Those times, I can still remember now, in my later years. The peace of those quiet days long gone now, I fear.

A few years later, the farm was sold and we moved to town. I missed the old farm home a lot at Easter back then. At the local 5&10 Store, baby chicks were sold. My dad bought some and made a small pen for them so the little chickens became my friends. I made pets of them.

At that time war had come in Europe. From time to time, the air raid siren would go off. The factory's cut off their lights. All lights in town had to be turned off until an all-clear siren would later go off. I did not like town much and wanted to go back to the farm with the horses and peace I loved as a child. It was not to be, though.

During the 2nd War, families were greatly affected. Lots of things were rationed. We were given tokens then, similar to bingo chips now. You used these chips for sugar, pepper, spices, and gas, which were rationed then.

I was in first grade of school then. I did like things about school though. I loved to learn to read and write. The world opened up to me then. Still though, the war made no more sense than now.

In school the smell of the oiled wood floors, the chalkboards, and when good you were allowed to clean the chalkboards for the next day. In school we were asked to bring in clean, crushed tin cans. My dad would crush them with a big hammer and I took my share to school.

In town near us; a man allotted out spaces for gardens. Most folks had to grow food. They were called "Victory Gardens." Once in town we had electricity. We would hear of the war, but on Saturday night Mother would make a pan of homemade fudge or popcorn. We would listen to a country music station. I remember one Saturday night my folks ran outside to look in the night sky. I was scared to death because of the war, but it was a beautiful display of the Northern Lights. They were so clear then, no interference from all the modern things of today.

My dad still hunted, trapped, and fished. He had a trap line behind our house. He left before light to check his traps. I loved to tag along, much to his dismay. Occasionally though, I was allowed to go along. I was told firmly to keep behind him, and no talking for even then, there were dishonest folks around. One time he told me, in later years, early one AM he saw a man helping himself to my dad's furs. He always carried an old 22-rifle. He asked the trap robber if he really wished to steal from his traps. He never saw that man back there again.

My dad always tended his hides carefully. He would turn the hides on a shaped board to dry. In our cellar he had a jar of foul smelling bait he used in the traps. Mother sure hated the smell of the bait. I still have my dad's old 22-rifle. It is quite valuable. I have been offered a lot for it, as they are no longer made. He had the gun from his own youth and it shall be passed to a family member of my own.

Ginseng was highly prized then, and was dug and dried. Things then were delivered by old freight trains in our town. Trains then used coal and huffed and puffed spilling black smoke with whistles blowing as they neared town. Mother tried to never have washing out then, as the black coal smoke would not be appreciated on the wash. When the war ended the trains had camp cars. Some prisoners of war were brought through town. They were well treated, fed and clothed. They worked on the Railroad, in CC Camps, or wherever needed. I was firmly told to never, ever go near those trains.

I had a bicycle then, and was allowed to ride to school. Those years were a lot different, once in town. Every Sunday night though, Mother would find me hiding, as she had a bottle of cod-liver oil. A spoonful had to be taken since I did get sick once in a while. For a cold, I was put to bed beneath homemade quilts and a large white china cup of hot water with a bit of whiskey was given to "sweat out the cold." It did work though.

When someone passed away, then they were laid out at homes. A large wreath was hung on the door to show a death had occurred in the family. To this day, I do not like wreaths of any kind.

Even in town, things had not changed a lot. Folks still had gardens, and canned and preserved their own foods. Even today as I grow older, I still do the same things that were done as a child.

People today seem to have GIVEN AWAY THEIR POWER by getting most things from stores, etc. We give our power away by buying things we could easily do or make ourselves. Not in my early years though, we were for the most part self-reliant and proud to be so.

Finally the war ended, the schools were let out, whistles blew everywhere and modern times were then upon us, some good, some not so good. Seems that time and the modern ways have not taught us much.

It is good to be able to share memories of those days long gone, while most youth of today, as a rule, do not care to hear, read, or experience them for themselves. What it is to be self-reliant. Some people still though, care to preserve the old ways, hear the old true stories from those who have lived them. So much progress is indeed good, but things of the past should be preserved for those now so they can appreciate the things and ways of today.

I have so much enjoyed sharing a few treasured memories of my life in those early years, and hope those who may read these memories can relate in a small way and enjoy reading them. I hope there are elders around to record or tape their memories, old songs, or music of yesteryear for all too soon, I fear they shall be gone.

Road Trip with the Agriculture Class to California and Canada in 41
By Alice H. Fox of Jersey Shore,
Pennsylvania
Born 1923

I'm 88. Many memories come back at this age. The first part was told to me when I was born at Hyner, Pennsylvania, on the banks of the west branch of the Susquehanna. The only way to get to our house was over the river by boat or ice, no bridge then. A relative, Alice L. Heisey from Elizabethtown came by train to stay with Mother. The river was covered with ice (it was March 1st.) so she followed my father across the river on the ice. That week the ice "went out" on the river. I was born a little later.

When I was one year old they moved from there to the town of Jersey Shore a farm downriver about ½ mile from town. It was situated in a small cup-shaped valley in the hills. The closest neighbor was across on another hill. If they wanted one of my older sisters, Barbara to come and help around the house they hung a white sheet out their bedroom window and she would walk over through the woods.

We didn't have a phone, electricity, or indoor plumbing. There was no car, just a horse and buggy to go. I was 7th of 9 children. In summer time, the woods and fields were our playground. We went barefoot from spring to fall. It wasn't all play as we were given work to do in the garden and helping Mother in the house and helping our father when and where we were needed. There were horses, cows, and calves and chickens. When the little "peeps" (baby chicks) came in the spring it was fun to play with them. I would place them on my shoulder and they would "snuggle" under my hair. One grew up to be a big black and white barred rock rooster and he would follow me around and wanted to keep riding on my shoulder. They had "Free Range" and their own chicken house but he wanted to come in our house also. That was not permitted.

I would also sit out in the pasture with the young cows (calves) and one day petting one while sitting on the ground in front of him, he jumped over me without touching me. He was feeling frisky! When it was time for me to go to school we had 1 ¼ mile to reach the 1 room school (Vilas Park). The number attending with one teacher went from 20 to 40 students over the various years.

The teacher called the classes up front to recite their lessons. After lunch (we carried our own) she had 1st-2nd grade come up to the front then sent them home as they were finished for the day. Many of them lived close to the school.

I didn't mind walking home alone through the woods but one chilly early winter day it was wet and the ground was starting to freeze. I knew it was against the rules but I had my first pair of new school shoes on and didn't want to get them muddy so I took them off to carry them. There was a run (water way) to cross then a stretch of narrow road where the water came off the bank and made it very muddy. By the time I passed these areas and

The Agriculture Class as they prepared to start the 33 day western trip

the rest of the road was not so muddy, I put my shoes on again as my feet were numb from the cold. I never told anyone but the next week I became ill with pains throughout all the joints in my body and ran a high fever. After a month of this the doctor was called and came to look at me. He gave me a "fever medicine" and said I had "acute rheumatism." I was home in bed that winter.

The next year I started again in 1st grade to our little country school, graduating from there when I reached 8th grade. In the meantime we had moved to another farm closer to town and I only had a short distance to walk to high school. This was in the 30s and 40s period during the Depression and I had to decide what course to enroll in. Secretary or College Prep were not for me so I decided to take Home Economics about cooking and sewing. Those classes were down in the basement of the school and at the other end of the basement was the Agriculture department. We had some of our classes together and I think if the principal had someone he didn't know where to place, he sent them there. When I came to my sophomore year I had Study Halls that "fit" the time when the Agriculture Class was in class. I knew the Agri. teacher and asked if I could take his class also—He said "yes." I went to the principal, I.V. Grugan. He became upset at my request and said "Girls do not take Agriculture." I told him the Agri. Teacher, Edwin Rice said it was OK with him and I had the time to carry both. He gave in and I took 3 years of Agri. along with my Home Economics class.

This Agri. class was working toward a summer trip by raising truck crops and anything else to have enough to take a trip to California, Canada, and back.

Crossing the river to Hyner

Our summers were busy raising and selling produce. They had a 4-ton stake body Ford truck we used and each person going on the trip supplied canned food. We had potatoes we had raised in potato boxes along the inside of the truck, there were also canned food, the members supplied in the box. The boys sat on the boxes covered with their clothes and sleeping bags. A stove was put together with a stovepipe and mounted in a holder underneath the truck on one side. We cooked breakfast and we cooked our evening meals at our camping area and bought our noon meal. We each supplied a certain amount of money and after graduation in the spring we left for the west.

All of us were poor but we didn't know it. The boys slept under the stars or "whatever." Marion Rice, the teacher's daughter, was going to college and had never been on any of her father's school trips so she went along, too. We slept in the back of the truck under a canvas cover. One night we were driving in West Virginia and a sudden shower soaked all the boys in back. They slept in the truck that night and Marion and I slept in the doorway of the gas station and we were awakened by the owner's dog when he came to open in the morning. In Yellowstone Park the bears came to hunt for food and caused a big blockage at the restroom doors by the boys seeking shelter from them.

The year of our 33-day summer trip was the summer of '41. When Pearl Harbor was bombed that December our world changed. I had been at home helping on the farm. There were more girls than boys so I did a lot of the work "outside" which I enjoyed. They were calling up all able-bodied young men. Many occupations were looking for girls to fill in. Defense plants needed welders. The "Cow Tester" farmers had lost their young men so the state college was giving short courses to fill in. My sister, who had worked her way to become a teacher, loaned me the money and after taking the class I had a job in Berks County to go around to 16 farms, taking milk samples and testing the milk and doing the bookwork. I enjoyed the people and the work but the war was still on and after two years there I thought of joining the "Waves." My numbers said "no" but then the Gov. came out with the Nurses' Cadet Corps where you could get training as a nurse "at the school of your choice." I couldn't pass that so off to

university of PA in Philadelphia for 3 years of strict training I went. I graduated in 47 as a registered nurse after passing my state board examination.

Beech Grove Schoolhouse
By Virginia A. English of Benton,
Pennsylvania
Born 1937

Going to a One-Room School: When Grandma Ginny was a girl, she started first grade in a one-room schoolhouse. A one-room school is just that: a building with one room, usually the shape of a rectangle. In the center of the room was a potbellied stove (A metal stove that burned wood. It had a pipe, which went through the roof and allowed the smoke to go outside.). At the front of the room was a slate blackboard the entire width of the room. The teacher could have the whole class working at the blackboard at the same time, doing math problems or whatever she wanted them to do. The classes were small, compared to the classes now. The whole school might have only 20 to 30 children. In front of the blackboard was the teacher's desk, facing the classroom. In front of the teacher's desk, facing the teacher's desk was a long bench where the students sat during their class time. Each class took turns sitting on the bench in front of the teacher. While each class had their turn, the other students could do their homework or listen to the subjects being taught to the class on the bench.

The students' desks faced the teacher's desk. Near the front, nearest the teacher but behind the class bench, were the first graders' desks. Behind the first graders were the second graders and in sequence the other grades up to eighth grade. Anyone wanting to go to high school had to go to another school.

The desks had a top that lifted up so books and pencils could be kept inside. They were made of wood and some parts, like the hinges, were made of metal. The front of a desk had a folding seat that gave the person in front of the desk a place to sit and the desk behind provided a place for the student to sit. The desks had to be lined up in a row because of this. Some desks still had a round opening in the upper right corner of the writing surface. This hole was used to hold a bottle of ink in the olden days. Grandma Ginny used a pencil.

There were no closets. Coats and scarves were hung on hooks along the wall. The tall, large windows allowed sunlight into the room. There were electric lights hanging from the ceiling. The bulbs were covered with large, white globes. The school did not have running water (in modern homes and buildings there are pipes, which bring water from a well or city water. The pipes are behind the walls and carry water to the kitchen, bathrooms and outdoor spigots.). A bucket of drinking water was placed on a table in the back of the room. Everyone drank from the same long handled ladle or dipper.

Since there was no running water in the school, there could not be an indoor bathroom, There were two outdoor toilets—one for boys and one for girls.

There was a bell tower on the peak of the roof (A bell tower is a little roof over a bell on top of a building. In some countries, such as Austria, there are some very fancy bell towers.). It held the bell that was rung at the beginning of school and to call the students in from recess.

Bordering the school property were large sugar maple trees. In the spring there would be icicles hanging on the ends of the branches of the trees. The children loved the icicles, they were very sweet. The icicles were frozen sap from the tree. It's the same sweet sap that makes maple syrup when the sap is boiled down (Sap is gathered from the maple trees and boiled to take the water or moisture out of the sap. This makes it into syrup. In the olden days, the sap was collected in metal buckets with a lid on but the modern method is to have the sap flow through plastic tubing into a large vat).

One teacher taught all the classes. The older boys carried the bucket of drinking water into the school. They also carried the wood for the stove. In the winter when it was very cold, the potbellied stove provided the only heat in the school. A student was warm on one side toward the stove and cold on the other side of their body.

Some of the classes the first graders had were Reading, Writing, Arithmetic, Art and Music. There was no kindergarten in rural schools. Some schools in the city had kindergarten.

The students carried their lunches in lunch boxes as there was no kitchen.

This school was in Beech Grove, about 25 miles north of Williamsport, Pennsylvania, in the mountains. Beech Grove was named for the many beech trees that grew in the area. There were many one-room schools in the country because there were fewer school buses and the larger schools were too far away.

Some of the things the school did not have was a gymnasium, a telephone, or an office because the teacher did everything. There were no ballpoint pens, computers, typewriters, electronic games, skateboards, snowboards, or television.

Going to a one-room school was a unique situation compared to schools of today.

As a child growing up, our family did not have a lot of money. My father worked as a laborer for Bethlehem Steel as a wire winder. He was a good worker and found work to do when other workers were on strike. (There is one building in Williamsport, PA, about three stories high that, when being built, he took wheelbarrow loads of cement to the top floor for the bricklayers.) There were no "elevators" or devices for such heavy work.

When we lived in Beech Grove, some of the things I remember include a special treat was taking spoons along on a ride and stopping at a store for ice cream. We must have taken a knife along to cut pint containers in half, so each person received a 1/2 pint of ice cream for a treat.

The Sleigh ride: In the mountains there were many times when the snow was very high, making high banks of snow on the back roads, almost like a tunnel. A neighbor gave us a horse and sleigh ride. The two large horses were impatient to get going, throwing their heads back with manes flying and stomping their feet. We slid past glistening fields of fresh snow and through the woods with tree branches laden with snow. The branches hung so low you could reach out and touch them, sending sparkling snow into the moonlight. When the horses breathed in the cold, crisp air, it came out their nostrils like steam because it was so cold. With every step the horses took, you could hear the sleigh bells jingle. Snuggled under heavy wool blankets, it was a magical ride. Sometimes when someone does something special for you, you remember it forever.

After two years at Beech Grove, we moved to Cogan Station, 5 miles north of Williamsport, PA. I graduated from the Williamsport High School in 1954. Because we lived in the country, I could not have a job during my high school years to save money for nurse's training. After high school, I worked at the Home Dairy Cafeteria to earn money to go to nursing school. I started nursing school the fall of 1955. The Director of Nurses told me that if I stayed out of school for a year, I would probably not go the following year, but I did. She underestimated my spunkiness. As an adult, I was always a little ashamed of being spunky, but it has paid off in my life. (I did not know about scholarships!!) The total amount of money needed was $350, which included a semester at Lycoming College. The initial amount needed was $5 registration and $170 down payment. I earned $28 a week, well, $23.11 clear a week.

Not too long ago I started to laugh out loud. I was paying bills and came across one for $23.11. It brought back memories. I had an old car to go to work and spent $1.00 for gas a week. I did not spend any other money until I had the $ 170 needed, then I went out and bought 2—$3.00 pair of shoes. One of my co-workers said, "It's good to see you buy something, Ginny". It never occurred to me that anyone noticed that I did not spend money. About that old car, I had: it had such "bald" tires the strands holding the tires together would show. The tires would not "blow out" but would just go "psssst" slowly and I would have a flat.

Tales of a Rail Fan
By Robert Ginter of Bellefonte, Pennsylvania
Born 1953

I write a humor column for our local National Model Railroad Association group. Here are some selections I think you'll enjoy:
You Too Can Be a Big Time Rail Fan! Do you remember when you went from a guy who likes trains to being a serious rail fan? I do. It was May 5, 1976.

My grandparents lived in Confer's Development in Milesburg just across the Penn Central (Pennsylvania Railroad) Bald Eagle secondary main in the late 1970s. My dad worked nights at Penn State so on occasion I did his banking at the Milesburg branch on my way to mow their lawn. A special offer that spring day was a Kodak 110 camera with a flashcube and 12-exposure film with a $500 deposit. Way outta my league.

Lehigh Valley F7B #6112

I did his banking and started over the bridge above the tracks (always checking both ways for headlights) when I saw something on the one siding near Miles tower. It was a Lehigh Valley F7B. Man, that shouldn't be here! ConRail was a couple days old, (I knew so little I thought it meant Congressional Railroad.) So I did think a few things might pass by, but not this. I knew I needed a picture.

At that time I subscribed to RMC (mostly Eastern stuff then), read MR at Bald Eagle High School library, bought 2 or 3 TRAINS a year and never heard of RAILFAN. So, I think I'll get a picture and send it in and be just like those guys. A 110 is as good as a 35 mm with Kodachrome, right?

Zoom to Pap's. That Pontiac 400 cubic inch engine was handy, but geez, gas at $0.45 a gallon? The crooks!

"Pap, I need $500!"

"Well, boy, gonna go buy your own car? Let's get my coat..."

"No, I need $500 cash RIGHT NOW!"

"Huh?"

"Don't worry, I'll pay you back tomorrow, I need $500 ten minutes ago!"

Pap was known to keep money laying around, like Bob Hartle keeps big green in his wallet. (Of course, not as much as Rich Steiner.) He dug around, gave me $500 and zoom back to the bank.

"I wanna deposit this and gimme a camera!" "Weren't you just here?" "Camera, now!"

The only cameras we ever had were a 126 only Mom knew how to use and a smelly Polaroid I actually got working in the 90s. Zoom, back to the tracks. Pull up to Miles tower and two guys are welding underneath the "F".

"As soon as this is fixed the next west bound takes this junk to Altoona."

Yeooww! Read the directions. Open back, drop in film, snap shut, advance, done.

Shoot, I took three pics. It took a month to take all twelve. Nowadays, I really let it fly. In a week in Kansas in 2001, I took 545 slides and over 100 prints. Kodak and Mystic Photo love me. But the day it all started was the day the brakes froze up on Lehigh Valley F7B.#6112.

Mahaffey Branch 1976: In the spring of 1976, I started working the first of 14 summers for the Pennsylvania State Parks. I began at Curwensville State Park, whose entrance road is only about 300 yards from Steve Clark's house, Division II member and May host.

From the beach, the relocated tracks to Mahaffey are clearly seen. Near the boat area turnoff, you can still see a gully that had been the New York Central line.

Being from Bellefonte where SW1's and SW9's were the rule, "big" units like U23B's U25B's, GP35's, and GP40's (rare) were a treat. I could use the lifeguard's binoculars to see across the lake. Sometimes, strange units showed up; only once did I see an FP7A, no pure F7's came by. An Alco C425 set outlawed at Clearfield Cheese near Irwin Park once. With my handy 110 camera, I took two pictures.

I soon purchased a scanner and moved into the big time! Two ConRail channels, the Bellefonte Central channel, and the local Curwensville cops. Yep, four channels, Radio Shack's big one.

EMD's were preferred power, mostly due to shorter wheelbase, about 81/2' vs. GE's 10+'. Easier on the mine switches. Since it had been Penn Central only months earlier, track was horrendous.

Scanner conversations tended to be formal, no one knew if ConRail was taping them looking to get rid of people. One memorable evening an empty coal train tried to go west against traffic. He was held two or three times, becoming agitated even over the radio. He had two ex-P.C. GP38-2's, very modern power for the neighborhood, 8088 and 8080. He argued back and forth with the dispatcher. The dispatcher finally had enough of him, told him to leave the siding and go west. The engineer angrily "thanked" him. I heard him from Irwin Park throttle way up then shut down. Then,

"Engine 8088 to dispatcher Clearfield"

"Now what, engine 8088??"

"I just derailed my unit in the switch"

"You *#@^ dumb *^# bleeping bleep!!!"

All talk by all trains ceased. The engineer wound out his unit and probably went into wheel slip in the switch. He derailed. The dispatcher sent the yard truck and traffic was done for the night

Today R. J. Corman trains serve the area. One mine is not far from Bill Drummond's house. It is still four-axle territory, only after trains return to Clearfield yard do six axle power take them to the Buffalo Line. Trains are infrequent.

How Did They Get Here? Like a lot of rail fans and model railroaders, I enjoy going to train meets more than hobby shops and mail order. Sometimes you see stuff you didn't know you needed. At a certain point though, some meets are too far gas wise and time wise, unless...

In the late 1970s, a nice train meet was held at the Geeseytown (Altoona area) Fire Hall. One time, just when exiting, we all heard some ungodly racket outside, loud and near. "Jerry" went out and hanging above the hall were two bundled up guys in an open experimental type, homemade helicopter! Yeah, you can't make this stuff up.

A guy throws down a note on a rock, "Is this the Train Meet?" We all indicated yes, and they landed on the lawn. It had been too far to drive from Cleveland so they flew. Me, no, I don't think so! I'll stick to cars.

We're Going Out Now! I was a substitute teacher for 26 years. In the mid-70s, I worked a lot in Bald Eagle Area Elementary Schools. I was a road sub to Pine Glen, Port Matilda and Clarence. Clarence 5th grade was best. The room overlooked Conrails, ex-PC, exx. NYC Beech Creek to Clearfield line, cut back to end at Clarence.

I had a lesson going on when I heard

Alco Locomotive C425

distant horns. "Stop, get your coats on! We're going out now!" I remember some teacher gave me a hard time, probably the de facto principal. Sure enough, here comes locos with a refractory delivery. Conrail. Four axles only. No SD's to that area!!

Those kids are adults now. The Clarence school closed, was used for storage and eventually sold by the district to the municipality. Conrail tore up the line Christmas Day 1994. I took a photo of a Southern hopper at the refractory in 1993. It might have been the last car. It sat there for weeks. Very little evidence of any trains remains. (Some rail fans in the 80s did travel from Orviston to Clarence.) The Snow Shoe Rails to Trails group took over the R-O-W. It's perhaps the finest R.T.T. in Pennsylvania.

Bad Influence? Nah, Not Me. Do people even know you're into trains? Within two minutes of meeting me, they know.

In 1986, Mom and Dad were northbound on the interstate to Denver. Dad was in "his" lane. The far left on a 6 — 8 lane road. The one he used to pass starships. Very near an exit, they see it... a CF7, and Dad knows what this is. He goes from his lane across the highway through traffic, up the ramp and zoom to where the CF is parked. That's the day Mom's hair turned white. Eight pics later, he's satisfied.

My brother-in-law often shops at the surplus store in Bellwood. When he took my little feller nephew along they had a routine. Stop for cheap roller dogs in Tyrone and eat them at the station while waiting for one train. Old Rod is as interested in watching trains as watching haircuts. Young Rodney is getting to be train nuts thanks to Uncle Bob. One day I'm at their house as they return. Yes, they saw a train. Rodney seems overjoyed at what

Moshannon on the way to Clarence, PA
8135—GP-38-2

they saw. Rod is definitely confused. "Look, I don't know much but, "Where's the flat cars!!?? Rodney: "We got a roadrailer!" You have learned well, young Skywalker.

A few years later, I'm at their house again. I say to Rodney: "What do you want for your birthday?"

"CP AC4400CW"

I know what he wants, his mother surely doesn't. If he would have spoken Greek, she would have got more. This was Klingon. By now, Rodney gets RMC and TRP. He's a Canadian Pacific fan. He wants Athearn's new model of a General Electric AC4400CW. A large wide nosed, six axle, alternating current, heavy freight engine. A small tear comes to my eye. My work here is done. Another model train nut is born.

Sometimes Things Spiral Out Of Control: In the 1980s and 1990s I substitute taught A LOT at the Philipsburg Senior High School, 90-95 days a year sometimes. The school is less than a mile from the Chester Hill Conrail railroad grade crossing, used to access Power Coal Company.

One nice day with the windows open, we heard the train going to the mine. I remarked that to me it sounded like an odd horn, probably being one chime not working, and I wondered what loco was pulling it. Being 10th or 11th graders, a couple said right away they were going student driving next period (always out to Chester Hill and Osceola Mills) and would watch for the train for me... at a price. I said no way money, but I could find something for them if they succeeded. Wotta mistake!

In the school's administration's continuing effort to tick off students, one bright guy suggested changing chocolate milk for kids to only Fridays, with a double standard of teachers getting it every day. Well, of course, those kids got the loco numbers, GP38's, GP38-2's ruled Clearfield with very little else, and I paid off by buying both driver and passenger chocolate milk.

It didn't spread like a rumor, it spread like wildfire! We had to make rules! Only morning drivers could "win". You can't fool Mr. Ginter with fake numbers; 692, 88 and 1102 would not be right, but 8081, 8088 and 7960 would be correct.

Driver's Ed teachers noticed right away.

"My kids always Stop, Look & Listen, even with no lights flashing."

"Huh?"

"Yeah, the other day "Joe" pulls up to the crossing and stops, no lights going. He shuts off the engine, on the road, and both he and the passenger put down the windows."

"What are we doing?"

"Quiet! We're listening for horns."

"What about drivers behind you?"

"Screw 'em!"

One day one kid bangs on the door, "I need to see you now!" The morning crew caught the train and one unit was "3400", a GP40-2 off its regular piggyback duties. It caused great excitement among the crowd. I made the mistake of buying him a double. Eventually the powers that be had enough, especially with Driver's Ed teachers saying kids were driving 5 mph near crossings and 105 mph to get to the next one. For a few months, I had several hundred eyes rail fanning for me.

I Remember These
By Glenn Owen Confer of Mill Hall, Pennsylvania
Born 1957

I remember outhouses and chamber pots when we lived in our old house before my dad added on to our house. The only toilet was our outhouse. I hated using it in the winter. As a little kid, I used the chamber pot. We didn't have an inside bathroom until my dad added on to our house in the early 1960s. I was born in 1957 and I was the youngest kid.

I remember we had a party line phone. A lot of people don't know what a party lines was. It was when you shared phone lines with one or two other people in your town. You had to wait until the other people were done talking. You had to know if your phone had 2, 3, 4, or 5 rings. Ours was 3-rings. Most people had party lines to save money on your phone bill. It was a pain in the butt!

We had a little girl in our town. If her mother didn't let her answer the phone, she would pick up the phone and the person would have to call back. A lot of people didn't like party lines. You could also listen in on other calls, so they went to private line phones, which most people have today.

My dad and our family in our town fixed their own cars because it was expensive to take them to a garage. Most of my relatives worked on their own cars. We were self-reliant in our town. We built our own homes in Drake Town. We had a lot of old cars to use for parts.

We all processed our own game. I use to trap and made some money, but it was hard work. I remember going hunting at our camp in the Beech Mountains. It was very cold and there was a lot of snow. We use to go there on the Fourth of July and there was still snow out there. We all did a lot of fishing, mostly for trout. I almost lived at Bald Eagle Creek in the summer.

My mom used a wringer washer up until 1972 when she had her own washer and dryer. We sold our home when they put in the new highway. We put a trailer in our back yard.

We watched Chiller Theater on Saturday night at midnight. Sometimes I watched it at my cousin's house beside our home. She would walk me home, because I was afraid to walk home after watching the movie.

When I was still in school, we had a large storm. It buried a tractor-trailer under interstate 80 in Lamar. Everything was closed for days. I really liked it, because I didn't have to go to school. I remember we had all snow, all winter most of the time.

I had a lot of pets, mostly cats and dogs. I remember them to this day. We had a cat that liked to eat potato slices when my mom or dad peeled potatoes. I also had a dog that would smile and show his teeth like a person when you would tell him he was a good dog.

I was always picking up snakes or other critters. My mom would tell me to put them down and let them alone. Our trips to Beech Creek Mountain on the Forth also included softball. Sometimes they would hit the ball under our porch. The ball went behind a log, but the log moved! It was a very, very, very, large rattlesnake. They killed it, brought it from under the porch. It was about 10 ft. long and it was about 4 or 5 inches in diameter. It was the largest snake I've ever seen, to this day. One of my relatives has a picture of it.

We had a lot of swimming holes in Bald Eagle Creek and the Susquehanna River at the Railroad Bridge in Farrandsville. I practically lived in the Bald Eagle Creek all summer fishing and spearing fish with wooden sticks or poles.

My dad had 23 brothers and sisters in his family. They owned two farms and rented two other farms. They didn't have a lot of transportation so they would live at the two farms. They used to make a lot of "moonshine" and homemade beer. Also, they didn't have to worry about anyone stealing anything from their farm, because they had the best guard dogs, about 300 guineas, and at night if they heard a noise they didn't recognize, they would all start squawking and wake everyone up.

My other grandfather spoke Dutch. They learned English when they went to school. That is why, when you try to talk to Amish kids, they won't talk back. They can't speak English until they go to school.

My grandfather's dad had a sawmill up-stream from the covered bridge in Loganton. They used a water wheel to pull the logs into the mill and had a steam engine that ran the saw. They also had a sawmill in New Jersey.

I had a lot of memorable people in my life. My mother and her family are very close. We all lived next door in Drake Town. When my grandfather got older, he had trouble trying to hold the razor when shaving, so I would shave him. He liked that very much.

Writing this letter, I'm in tears thinking of my grandfather. I miss him as he died in 1970 and my grandmother died the next year. My father died in 1980 and my mother died in 1997. I miss them very much.

My mother always bought Wolfgang Candy before Christmas and Easter. I love peanut butter and chocolate very much. She would always try to hide them from me, so one year before Christmas I found them. I had to come up with a plan to eat them without my mother knowing, so I made a hole in the side of the box. I made it look like a mouse got into them. When she got them out for Christmas, she thought they would not be any good. She was going to throw them out. I wouldn't let her. I let her know it was me. She was very

upset. I never heard the end to that for years after.

I remember the milkman would come early in the morning. We only got milk from him a short time because my father worked at the Sealtest Milk Plant in Mill Hall across from Bengies, now Grant Millers car lot. There is a bag company in there now. We always had lots of milk. We had our own pasteurizing machine at home. He was the Forman and had the keys to the plant. They used to hold milk there from the farmers that used milk cans before the farmers converted to bulk tanks. They moved the milk plant to New York

I remember when me and my dad went to the milk plant at night to get milk for home. There was a very large holding tank in there. It must have held thousands of gallons of milk. We would take a stainless steel dipper and test the milk in it. My special memory is going up the ladder in front of the holding tank. Up at the top there was a porthole widow where you could look into the milk tank. My dad would turn on the lights so you could see inside. There was a large propeller that would turn slow so the milk would not have the cream on top. It was on a timer and would rotate real slow. Sometimes the tank was almost full, then, sometimes it was half-full, so we didn't need a milkman, but my neighbors did. I remember that much.

I told you we would always go to our camp to see all of my mother's family, the Geyers. Also, we would go to my dad's family, the Confers. We had so many relatives we would have two reunions. For my dad's family, some couldn't make it to Saturday's so they would go on Sunday. We weren't as close a family as my mother's because most of us lived in the same town. I remember my mother would cook a large meal on Sundays and bake cakes and pies.

I remember when we use to go to town to go shopping. I remember some of the brick streets and the trolley tracks that went down Main Street and some of the side streets. Then, we would go to the Texas Lunch and get Texas Hot-dogs and I always got chocolate milk and a soda. We knew Pete and Nick very well because my mother's brother worked there. His name was Lewis Geyer. Also, something a lot of people didn't know about him, he would take an order at a full table without writing it down. He would remember the whole order.

Also, he knew Pete and Nick's ingredients for their sauce used on their Texas Hot-dogs. He would not tell my mother or anyone else. Pete and Nick trusted him with the ingredients. He would make the sauce sometimes. He was the only employee that ever worked there that knew the ingredients.

I also remember Hogan Boulevard. Much has changed in my life. I am 55 and I have a lot of picture of the Boulevard as it changed over the years.

Bobbing for Chickens
By Geraldine Starr of Jersey Shore, Pennsylvania

Outhouses, I never want to see one again. When I was 11 years old, we lived in an old farmhouse without plumbing. We raised a few chickens and one day a hen fell down the hole in the outhouse. Because I was so skinny, my dad held me by the feet and I had to go down the hole to get the chicken.

Sayings and Quotes
By Ernest T. McKay of Mansfield, Pennsylvania
Born 1908

Here are a few of my dad, Ernest T. McKay sayings and quotes.
A cold wet May is a barn full of hay. A dry hot June will sing another tune.
Paint in the fall, might as well not paint at all.
Clear as a bell. And colder than hell.
My dad would always say how to look for a good horse, "4 white socks and a white nose, might as well knock him in the head and feed him to the crows."
What a tangled web you weave, when you first practice to deceive.
My dad always had a lot of riddles too. I remember this one.
Mary had a little lamb, the butcher killed it dead. Now Mary takes her lamb to school between two hunks of bread.
Thunder showers in the fall, no winter at all.
Once a job is begun, don't you leave it till it's done, rather its large or rather it's small. Do it right or not at all. Labor it, if it may be, do it right or leave it be.

Three Loaves of Bread for a Quarter
By Ida M. Condon of Lock Haven, Pennsylvania
Born 1927

Living in Vilas Park, Jersey Shore, Pa. where the people were friendly and helpful to others was a real joy. Where almost everyone had a garden in the summer and canned what they grew.

We went to a one-room schoolhouse. Everyone walked to school. The ones that lived close could go home for lunch; the rest had to carry their lunch.

In winter when the snow was pretty deep my brother Ernest, would go to our neighbor and put a little guy, Seth, on his shoulders and carry him to school with some of us following him to school.

We had some very nice teachers. There is one still living. She is Barbara Heisey Miller. She lives in Jersey Shore, Pa. with her two sisters, Harriet and Alice. She was a great teacher and everyone liked her. She is a great young lady at the age of 101.

You could buy three loaves of bread for 25 cents and 5 gallons of gas for a dollar.

My grandfather, Finny Maggs made homemade ice cream. He would sell it for 5 cents a cone. He drove a horse and wagon. When my brother was old enough, he would take the horse and wagon with the ice cream. Everyone would listen for the bells on the horse, then, they knew they would soon get some ice cream.

Those were the days when there was no TV's or computers.

Escape From the Castle
By Kathleen L. Fullmer of Williamsport, Pennsylvania
Born 1923

My family moved to the Williamsport area in the mid-1930s because of the shirt factory. The shirt factory later became the Weldon Pajama factory. My sister, brother, and I were all preteens when we moved here. We had neighbors, Jimmy, Dale, and Bobby, who were also preteens. They could not wait to take us to Links Castle, which was beyond Rural Avenue. It had been vacant for years. It had been invaded by a lot of kids, even though it was guarded by a lady said to have "a shotgun that fired rock salt".

Most of the furniture that remained in the castle was covered up. There was a large, mounted black bear standing on his back legs. He had been mounted with his front paws stretched out. The bear was standing on a platform that was on wheels. He had been used as a coat rack.

Jimmy had a secret window that he used to get into the castle without being seen. The house had an old dirt cellar where Jimmy had buried a lunch box filled with his "treasures". After he had buried it, he tried to leave the house, only to find the lady with the gun and a friend were visiting in the room where his escape window was located. He couldn't get to the window without being seen. After waiting a long time, Jimmy came up with an escape plan. He got behind the bear, gave it a big push, and sent it sailing across the room. The ladies screamed and ran out of the house. Jimmy went to his window and got out.

Several years later, a doctor bought the property and demolished the castle to build a new house. It broke our hearts to see the old castle go.

Moss Rooms and Rattlesnakes
By Linda Kopchik of Morrisdale,
Pennsylvania
Born 1947

When I was a child growing up in (Shiloh) Woodland, Pennsylvania, I went to the barn with my dad and watched him milk the cows. I liked it when he would squirt some milk into the cat's mouth. Dad would kill chickens for us to eat, and after he chopped their heads off, they would flop all over the yard.

We had no bathroom in the house, so we had to go to an outside toilet. We had a chamber pot to use at night, unless we wanted to take a flashlight and go to the outhouse. We boiled water on a coal stove to bathe with in a basin of water.

I can remember my dad saying that he bought a ton of coal in 1937 for $1.50. Our parents worked very hard for all they got back then.

I had friends who would come to visit. We played house in the woods. We used green moss to separate the rooms. We also played hopscotch, jump rope, and lots of board games. We didn't have video games, like kids do today.

Once in fifth grade, I got a good paddling from my teacher for crawling through to the next room. We did respect our elders, though!

My brothers, sisters, and I would go to the stripping cuts and pick blueberries. My mom would make some yummy desserts. Once we went to the river, because we wanted to see in the cabins. My sister got on her tiptoes to look in the window. She looked down, and she was standing on a rattlesnake! Luckily, it didn't bite her, and she is still living today.

I can still see my grandfather sitting in his rocking chair, listening to the radio. He loved the ballgames. My family always went visiting friends and relatives every weekend. Those were the good old days!

The Legend of the Scythe-Man
By David Johnson of Smethport,
Pennsylvania
Born 1949

Clermont in the mid-1960s was a far cry from the boomtown it had been in the 1880s. Still, with 150 residents, we kids had no problem making our own fun.

One night, Don Himes, Jay Confer, and I took our sisters, Dot, Beth, and Marlene snipe hunting. We trekked to the old Erlandson farm, now owned by Bob Clark's family. This was about a mile from town. Fog usually enveloped the pasture, and this night was no exception. We left our sisters holding a bag, assuring them we'd chase the snipes to them.

We started to walk along Route 146 toward Clermont. At the baseball field, we agreed to take a shortcut across the diamond, up the hill by the old ball field, then down to the fire hall in the middle of town. We cut across the baseball diamond. To our left was the expanse of left field. Small pine trees formed a fence. Beyond them was a strip mine, perhaps fifty feet deep.

Suddenly, a large dark shadow loomed over the four-foot trees, rising from the mine below. It towered over us, and then stopped. There was no mistaking it. It was the Grim Reaper, scythe and all.

The three of us ran back to the highway and raced to town nonstop. As we reached Tom Walker's garage, we finally paused to catch our collective breaths.

The next day, I shared this story with Jim Kane. He and I hiked over to the strip mine behind the ball field. Something had slid down the shale slope, leaving an easy-to-detect avalanche. As we stood there, we heard metal hammering. Legend had it that there was a mineshaft under the ball field. We were certain something was in it.

The next few days our attention shifted to the Erlandson farmhouse. It had long been vacant, but every night now, a light appeared in the cellar. Finally, we organized a posse, armed to the tooth, to enter the house. It was, of course, deserted. But hanging on a hook over the toilet was a pair of hip-high fishing boots – and a scythe!

Ice Cream and Screams, a Young Girls Dreams
By Irene G. Turnbaugh of Bellwood,
Pennsylvania
Born 1931

Homemade ice cream means more to me than just the good sweet taste. I had six siblings, and of course, each one had a birthday, plus Mom and Dad. My Dad worked for an ice plant (made block ice for refrigerators, etc.) Every birthday we had a homemade ice cream party. No gift, just a big freezer of ice cream and a birthday cake with the appropriate number of candles. The flavor was determined by the birthday girl or boy, as well as a choice of cake to each one's liking. It was so thrilling to see Dad bring home a big block of ice and get out the arm churning ice cream freezer. Each child's excitement led to the other. Eyes were wide and bellies were tasting the ice cream before it was even mixed. I don't believe we ever missed one birthday, and that would be a lot of birthdays. In later years, we promoted to an electric freezer, but it sure was fun, each one taking our turn in turning the mixture in the good old days. To this day, I really enjoy the idea of homemade ice cream and I know it is because of the happy birthday parties we each enjoyed as a kid.

I am very afraid of snakes. When I was pretty young, my older sister and I went to pick some blackberries on a hill behind our home. I was so afraid I would see a snake and I was over cautious, I'm sure. I was wearing an old pair of sneakers and they had long shoestrings.

We both had our buckets pretty full of nice blackberries and I happened to look down and see my feet. I saw the shoestring on my one foot and thought it was a snake. I screamed and upset my bucket of berries and my sister was so overtaken with my scream and commotion, she upset her bucket of berries too! She never let me forget that time and I'm not sure we went for blackberries again together. We both lost out on a nice berry pie that Mom would have made for us.

Summers with Baseball's Greats
By Tom Woodring of South Williamsport,
Pennsylvania
Born 1949

When I was ten years old, my parents, Melvin and Kathryn Henne Woodring, better known as Woody and Kay, took over the concession stand at Bowman Field in Williamsport, PA. The year was 1959. Bowman Field was the home of the class AA baseball team, the Williamsport Grays. They were a Philadelphia Phillies farm team, which lasted for a few years. Later, they became a New York Mets farm team, known as the Williamsport Mets.

During that first summer, I spent most of my time watching the baseball games instead of helping in the concession stand. I believe my parents understood the need for a ten year old boy to take the summer off and watch the players as they played the great sport of baseball. During the second year, I started to sell soda, popcorn, peanuts, and Cracker Jacks to the patrons in the stands. By the third year, I was twelve and able to start working the concession stand with my parents and my older brother, Lee.

Many times before the game would start and the concession stand would get busy, my brother and I would go out to shag balls

The Williamsport Grays
1960

99

during batting practice with the baseball players. It was during that summer, and the eight summers that followed, that I remember meeting some of the baseball greats. I met Bobby Wine, who went on to play for the Philadelphia Phillies. I met Ron Swoboda, who played for the Mets. I also met Ted Savage, Tony Curry, and Rich Allen, who all went on to play for the Phillies. Curt Simmons also went on to play professionally, as well as Bob Gonkoski, who went on to pitch. Then there was Hank McGraw and Duffy Dyer. Nolan Ryan also made an appearance, pitching for two days before heading to New York to pitch for the New York Mets.

Even though it was batting practice, the players took their time to mentor the young boys who came to watch them practice. In my opinion, it is why they are considered some of "The Baseball Greats". They did this because of their love of the game.

If I had to choose a favorite memory, I would have to say all of them. Each one holds a special place in my heart.

Pictures in the Outhouse
By Iva McCoy of Muncy, Pennsylvania
Born 1927

I was born in 1927, number 11 of 12 children, 8 boys and 4 girls. Seven of my brothers fought in World War II. I lived on a farm where we had no electricity and that meant we had an outhouse (a necessity). I liked it to look nice, so I put pictures on the walls that I got from calendars.

My dad farmed with horses and never owned a tractor. Everything we ate was raised on the farm except sugar and coffee.

The Outhouse

Dad took grain to the mill in town and had it ground into flour. Mother baked our bread and churned our butter. She even made her own yeast! I'm not sure how she did that, but it worked. She took eggs to the store and traded them for groceries. She churned butter and once a week a man (called a huxter) came and bought it. He delivered to the stores in town.

We had a shed that we put ice in. The men cut big chunks of ice in the winter and put them in this building and covered it with sawdust. It kept many months. In the hot summer, we would make ice cream.

I went to a one-room school. Eight grades were taught there by one teacher. Once we finished eighth grade we weren't required to go to school anymore. I wanted to go to high school, but we had no bus service, and living two miles from school was a big problem. I found a family in town to live with. I worked

The school that Iva attended for her first 8 years

for my board. I wasn't encouraged to go to school. Girls were supposed to marry and have babies. My eighth grade teacher did tell me I should go to school somehow. I cleaned house and babysat for the extra money.

The games we played were Annie Over, Hide and Seek, Marbles and lots of ball. All of the electronic things were not around yet.

One day in elementary school the teacher said that we would be able someday to turn a button and we could see a picture. I thought that would never happen and now here we are with TV and lots of other things.

The highlight of the week was going to town on Saturday night when we wore our best clothes. Everyone went to town on Saturday night. We got to visit our friends and went to the movies for 11 cents. We didn't have a lot of money, but neither did anyone.

I did finish high school and enjoyed every day of school and I did get married at age 21 and had six children.

The house where Iva was born and lived in most of her life

Fun at a Two-Room School
By Barbara Steinruck of Williamsport,
Pennsylvania
Born 1947

I went to grade school in Ogdensburg, Pennsylvania from 1954-1959, and it was a privilege to go there. It had the distinction of **not** being a one-room schoolhouse but a two-room schoolhouse. In one room were grades one through three, and in the second room were grades four through six. The seventh through twelfth grade students were bused all the way down to the big town of Canton.

The "little" room was where grades one, two, and three were. These grades were taught by a lady named Miss Stokes. The basic subjects of reading, writing, and 'rithmetic were taught. Miss Stokes had the honor of teaching everyone how to print and write in cursive. At the end of each school year, someone got the award for best penmanship. I got that award one year. Miss Stokes also taught arithmetic, but I don't think I paid a lot of attention to that subject. That was for boys!

In the "big" room, which was for grades four, five, and six, we had more to learn.

There was history, geography, and music in addition to the basic subjects. The teacher in this classroom was Mrs. Hutchinson. She made us all work hard, especially the girls. She made us understand that arithmetic was also for girls. When it came to simple algebra, the girls outdid the boys. Mrs. Hutchinson also knew the value of learning music and how it all tied into arithmetic. Music was a lot of fun for all of us, and we laughed a lot during that time.

When it was recess, we could go out to play on the monkey bars or go play baseball on the other side of the outhouse. The monkey bars were metal, and they were cold. There was also a big, long slide. We had to slide down very carefully, because girls wore dresses or skirts. It was tricky to slide down and not let your dress blow up in your face.

The baseball diamond was a big field, and it seemed like the distance between third base and home plate was longer than the distance between the second and third bases. Everyone played baseball, regardless of age, whether you were any good or not. It was a fun sport, because it was a big, long field. Everyone tried to hit the ball down into the woods, but no one was ever able to do it, not even when my older brother was in school there.

The outhouse was sectioned off. One side was for girls, and the other side was for boys. If we were lucky, we had toilet paper. Sometimes we had to resort to the old *Sears, Roebuck Catalog*.

We all had to bring our lunch to school. Some people carried lunch boxes and some people carried lunch bags. We would compare our lunch boxes with others. Some of the lunch boxes were Howdy Doody, Mickey Mouse, and Popeye. The one thing I remember is in the fall, everyone had at least one apple in their lunch. A peanut butter sandwich was pretty common back then.

Transportation getting to Ogdensburg was an adventure. Back then, buses did not run all over picking up the students. My siblings and I were lucky enough to be transported by station wagon. A neighbor drove down to the end of our lane to pick us up. By the time we got to school, there were at least seven kids in the car. Sometimes we would walk down the lane to the "hard" road, and sometimes we rode down on the tractor. In the wintertime, we might ride the snowmobile. It was always fun getting to school.

The Milkman
By Margaret Plotts of Muncy, Pennsylvania
Born 1939

The "milkman" is a long ago, but not forgotten creature. I remember his bringing us milk in all kinds of weather in a milk wagon drawn by a horse from Hurr's Dairy barn! He would jump down from the box-in wagon that contained everyone's bottled milk on his route and bring the bottles to our steps and put them in the icebox.

I would run out to see him and help bring in the milk. Sometimes I would get to talk to the horse and pet it while the milkman would talk to my parents. He became a close friend of the family and later his wife was one of my mother's friends in a retirement home.

One day our milkman lost the opportunity to deliver milk with his wagon and horse anymore. My parents, brother, and I were sitting on our back porch, when suddenly there were a lot of flames and smoke shooting up in the sky down by the Hurr's barn where the horses were kept and the wagons were stored. My father took off like a sheet of lightning, running down the railroad tracks toward the fire. He worked there since he was sixteen years old and, so he knew that something was very wrong and he needed to go help. The smoke was coming from the hay barn where the horses were kept and from the garage where the wagons were kept.

My mother, brother, and I ran to the front of the house where we saw several horses running wild down the street. I was so scared, I ran up on our front porch to watch the bedlam, people trying to catch the horses, people running to help with the rescue of the other horses in the barn and to get the wagons out. Fire sirens were blowing and fire engines were coming from all over. It took a long time for the fire to get under control and get the horses out of the barn. The rescue of the horses was not totally successful.

After that fire, there were no more horses drawing wagons filled with bottled milk to be delivered to the people. The milkman had lost his means of delivery, but that didn't stop the milkman from delivering, for it was soon afterwards that our milkman came in a green and white truck filled with bottled milk to deliver once again our milk to our house. He probably enjoyed the new way of travel. It was safer, warmer, and he didn't have to deal with the horses and we didn't have to watch our step anymore when crossing the street, if you know what I mean.

I am not quite certain when the milkman stopped delivery at our doorstep, but I know that he was one of my favorite people to watch for, especially during the summer when I was not in school. Today I buy my milk at the grocery store, but in the "good old days", it was the milkman who provided that personal touch to the milk bottle.

Frozen Ears and Dog Bites
By Helen McKay of Mansfield, Pennsylvania
Born 1920

When I was about 8 years old I went to town with my mom with a horse and wagon and got caught in a rain storm. A farmer came out and told us to put the horses in the barn till it quit raining.

My dad would cultivate the corn with a one horse cultivator and I would walk behind him and move the stones off the corn plants and I was about 9 years old then.

I always did my homework by the oil lamp. We had no electricity and always walked to school every day, about 1 and ½ miles no matter what the weather was. There was a boy that would walk farther and get there early and start the fire and have the school warm when we got there. I remember he froze his ears one very cold morning walking to school.

When I was about 13-14, I milked 19 cows all by hand because a storm was coming in and my Mom and Dad and a hired hand worked until dark to get the hay in the barn before the storm.

When I was younger, my cousin and I were out playing and my dad and uncle were butchering a couple hogs. They worked a good part of the day dressing them out and had them hanging to cool on a homemade hoist. They went in the house to rest and my cousin and I thought it would be fun to jump up and down on the planks that the hoist was resting on and the pigs came down in the dirt. We took off and hid in the barn and they never found out how the pigs really got on the ground.

When I was just a toddler I was sitting on the kitchen floor eating crackers and chicken broth and a big St. Bernard dog came right through the screen door and bit me on the head and ear. My grandmother cleaned it out and put salve and dressing on it each day. When I would see her coming I would run and hide because it hurt when she had to change the dressing.

I and a friend of mine went out to the woods and dug up some little pine trees and planted them in my yard. They all died but one and that one is still in the yard where we planted it years ago. It has grown 75-80 feet high now.

My mom remembers mail getting delivered by horse and buggy.

My dad built a stone float just the size for my pony to pull and he would put a bushel of potatoes on it and it would take them to the field for him to plant.

When I was little I had to turn the grindstone wheel while my dad sharpened the mowing machine blades for cutting the hay.

Never got electricity at the farm till 1940 and my mother-in-law said she did not realize how dirty the house was. I would take the oil lamp to the barn and hang it up so we could see to milk the cows.

At 10-12 years old my neighbor and I went in the woods looking for hickory nuts and pretty fall leaves. We was looking for quite some time, and when we came out the folks in the house wanted to know if we saw the bear and we said, No! We never went back in the woods again.

When our first child was born on November 23rd, we had such a terrible storm. It had snowed so much when my husband took me to the hospital. Our daughter was born and he went back home and was snowed in for at least three weeks. I stayed at the hospital for 10 days, and then stayed with friends until my husband was able to get out and bring me and the baby home.

Brickley's–What a Place
By Carolyn A. Hanna of McElhattan,
Pennsylvania
Born 1943

Being a resident of McElhattan all my life, I often think of a special place called Brickley's Ice Cream Place in Lock Haven, Pennsylvania. Now, there was the best ice cream a person could ever eat. This was before all the Dairy Queens and Tastee Freezes that are around now.

Our family wasn't rich by far, but when Dad pulled into Brickley's, my brother and I got very excited because we knew we were in for a special treat indeed. To think you could even sit in a booth and be served as though you were royalty. Why, we even got a glass of good, cold water to drink, and it tasted almost as good as the ice cream on a hot summer day. Maybe it did not mean much to kids who had everything, but to us poorer country kids, it was a treat we just did not get every day.

Dad worked for New York Central Railroad and in those days, when work was slow and Dad got laid off awhile, there was no unemployment to fall back on. We had a big garden, all dug by hand. Mom would do a lot of canning so we could make it through the winters. There was no waste allowed in our home.

Mom and Dad would get a dozen or two dozen peeps, and we would raise our own chickens. We'd have our own eggs then. We also had a pig or two and several turkeys. Dad would hunt for a deer. In those days there didn't seem to be a large slaughter of deer as there is now. You were permitted to get one deer and that was it. Dad felt totally blessed when he was able to supply our family with meat for the winter, because the canning and meat came in handy when he was laid off and there wasn't any money coming in.

Before we owned our own freezer, Dad and Mom would rent one at the Lock Haven freezer plant, now the Lucky Seven. Back then, we could rent a big drawer, where we stored our meet and venison. At that time, we only had a very small freezer on top of our refrigerator, so this came in handy.

We made do with what we had and enjoyed life so very much. The feed sacks that the pig's food came in where made out of pretty cotton material back then. Mom would wash the feed sacks in her wringer washer and take them to a friend of hers who liked to sew. The friend made several skirts for me to wear to school when the weather was warmer. I was thrilled to wear such pretty skirts, and most people never knew where they had come from.

We had good Christian parents who went to Sunday school and church every single Sunday. My brother and I were in children's day programs and Bible school and all sorts of things where we learned about Jesus Christ.

Sunday afternoons were spent quietly.

Dad would take us on walks in the woods to look for lady slippers. Later in the season, we would pick teaberries, huckleberries, and ground berries, too. We learned about all the different trees, birds, and animals we saw in the woods. We didn't need fancy things to entertain us. We communicated with our family and loved ones.

Once in a while, we got another real treat when we were taken to see a Shirley Temple movie. The movies then were in black and white, of course. The theater usually showed the movie twice, and we would plead with Mom and Dad to sit through it again, because we were fascinated with such good entertainment. Usually, Mom and Dad would agree, but there were times when the answer was no. We were disappointed, but there was no screaming, crying, or back talking. We would put our heads down and walk out to the car in silence. If we misbehaved, we knew a smack on our behinds was coming, along with a stern look from Mom, so we straightened up in a hurry. Mom was the one who did the correcting. Dad was meek and mild, but he loved us very much all the same and wanted us to listen when we were told something.

Today I have a nice home out on the side of a mountain here in McElhattan, where wild animals come into my yard, and most of the time it is peaceful and quiet. I can't help but think of the times when life seemed to go so much slower, the air seemed fresher, and people seemed more satisfied and content with what they had. Life was enjoying what you had, visiting with family and sitting on the porch, a trip to Brickley's, or going to a movie now and then. We worked in our gardens, took walks in the woods and enjoyed all the good things in life that God gave us. We didn't have to be entertained. We were content to enjoy the quiet things in life. We were thankful for what we had. Life was so wonderful back then and so different from today. I am glad I had a part in it. I will never forget it.

Childhood Memories, Looking Back
By Linda "Hock" Avery of Cogan Station,
Pennsylvania
Born 1945

I'm 66 years old, so I have many memorable times. My first memory comes to mind living on Walnut Street, 300 Block

across from Wentzler's Garage. I remember the 1946 flood with water coming down the street. My parents took me to the second floor while we watched the water going down the street before the Dike was built.

I started first grade at age 5 and walked all the way to Washington School by myself where Kohl's store is now. Next to our house on Walnut Street back then, was Weis Market. There was a small walkway between the side of our house and Weis Market and large icicles would go crashing off our roof. I could see the ladies in the bathroom putting lipstick on and combing their hair, and when the icicles fell, they would yell saying, "Oh, What was that?"

Later we moved to Cherry Street to Live, where I'd sled ride for hours on Louisa Street. They closed the street off. They had put little black round "flame smudge pots" that produced a black smoke that must have been

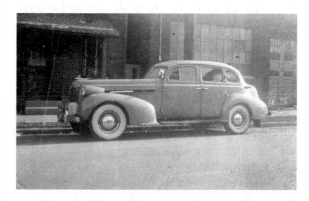

Dad's car in 1947

kerosene. I'd walk at night to Hoover's Store on High Street to get penny candy and usually bobby pins along with Green-Wave Set. My mom always set my hair. It would be so stiff. I'd always see cars and taxicabs with chains on going by, for the snow was very deep back in 1958.

Places I'd go also would be to the Armory on Penn Street to ice skate. They flooded the field for us kids. Every Friday night was a trip to the Williamsport downtown with my dad. We had to always wear dresses and little Patent-leather shoes (never sneakers). We'd go to the Brozman's to shop, Woolworths and Glick Shoes. We'd always look at our feet in the shoe x-ray machine. None worried or thought of radiation then. Then, we went to Woolworths and Kresge's to take pictures in the photo booth.

Sometimes we bought "Evening in Paris" in beautiful blue bottles. It smelled like vanilla to me. Then, to the L.L. Stearns Department Store so Dad could pay on our bill, and then after that, up to the other end of town to Dickey Grugan's Hardware. We would love to watch the cop direct traffic. He'd be in the middle of Market and Third. He had a little booth he'd go in.

Years later, I moved to Baldwin Street and loved the Park dances at the tennis court. I'd walk to the high school on Third Street every day, no matter how cold and how deep the snow was. I never remember any snow days off; we always had school.

I have always kept my memories in my mind and think that the 40, 50, and 60s in Williamsport, PA were the best years of my growing up days.

A Century Past & a Lifetime of Memories
By Meda E. Stroble of Montoursville,
Pennsylvania
Born 1911

I don't know what time of day Columbus discovered America. I've been told very early on the 12th day of October 1911 the stork delivered a little red haired baby to the home of Mr. and Mrs. Robert Bryan of Montoursville, Pa., later known as Meda Elizabeth, known as me. My 18 year old brother was not happy with my arrival, as I cried most of the time, but they kept me. By the time I was three years old I had learned a lot of things. I could get around on my own. Mother asked Hazel, my older sister, to go on an errand to grandmother's house, which was not far away. Of course, I was told I could not go. When Mom was not looking, I took off as fast as my legs would go. Mom saw me and she sure could run. She caught me and I learned what a spanking was, at least I remember it for it was the only spanking I got.

I guess I was like most average kids. Time passed and the next thing I learned about was school. At 6 years old, I was allowed to go. I still remember my first teacher. I was her pet. After 50 years, I met her again. She told me what a good little girl I was and that I always had a ribbon in my hair. It was a one room school, of course. I fell in love with a nice boy that lasted for many years. They are

happy memories of my school days at 15 year. It was my last year in school. Our teacher, a Miss Snider was a very good teacher. She lived with her uncle and grandmother near the school. Her grandmother, an old lady in her 90s got very ill and Elsie could not get there early in the morning.

Everyone had the old crank phones. She would call me to go to the school house and ring the bell. The key to the school would be in a mail box on my way. I'd hurry off from home, get the key and go to the school house, unlock the door, and ring the bell. The kids came at 9 o'clock. I'd ring the bell to start school. I would tell the kids, "I'm teacher till Miss Snyder comes". First, it was Bible reading and then the Lord's Prayer. School started with first grade. A little first grader had problems with his numbers and I figured out a way to help him, so I won that round. Elsie would try to get there before the noon hour. I had 25 scholars. One day one of the big boys tried my patience. He made a big paper wad and shot it at the ceiling. It cracked pretty loud, of course, the kids laughed. I knew they were thinking what I'd do. I called the boy out and told him I saw what he did. There were to be no more paper wads and I'd forget about it and no telling the teacher. The other kids were not to tell, so it would be forgotten. There was no more trouble with that boy or any of the others. That was an experience I'll never forget.

During my early years, I saw my first car, a Ford sedan. It belonged to our neighbor. He had always driven horses and when it went too fast he would yell, "Whoa!" His wife was a very stout woman. She always rode in the back seat. Of course, us kids thought that was funny.

I was milking a cow when my sister said an airplane was coming. I jumped off the milk stool and ran outside to see. Sure enough, it was an airplane, a two winged affair. What a thrill that was!

My brother served in the First World War. While he was gone, I was very ill with an infection and almost lost my life. Our good old family Dr. Born saved my life. I wrote my brother a little letter after the war was over. When he came home, he brought me the letter, about 2 by 4 inches. He was in Germany on guard duty for some time after the war was over. When he came home, he brought me the letter, a precious treasure. Today his uniform is in a Historical Museum and my little letter is back in the pocket after nearly 100 years, "Praise the Lord."

I lived through what was called the "Flapper Stage", bobbed hair and short skirts. I got a cute letter like a Valentine and it had a verse. ("You bob your hair and wear short skirts. You think you look quite dapper. You haven't sense enough to know. You are just a foolish flapper.")

My first perm I got, I thought they were going to electrocute me. Somehow, I lived with the hair-do.

I know how it was to live through the washboard days. We had a hand washer. It helped a little with hand power. It had a wringer. One day my mother and I was making homemade noodles. I thought it would be a good idea to run the dough through the wringer. It didn't work! We forgot to flour the rolls.

Our father was a farmer, so we girls had to help with all the work on the farm such as hay making, grain shocking, corn cutting and husking, and we helped with the threshing. The farm work was hard. The thing I hated about the farm, it was close to the Allegheny Mountains with lots of snakes of all kinds. Being afraid of snakes, we met up with lots of rattlesnakes and they about scared me out of my mind. Later, Dad bought me a gun that I learned to shoot. I'd shoot every snake I saw. Now, it is illegal to kill them. I'm glad I don't work on the farm anymore. I still hate snakes!

In the year 1939, we got electric service in our community. We had the house wired and soon we were getting all kinds of electric fixtures.

My father had died and he left me the farm. I got married in 1940 and the first addition was a new bathroom. I helped my husband dig the septic hole. The biggest hole I ever helped dig!

I was also in the chicken business, requiring lots of work along with remodeling the big farm house. I took off a day and went fishing with my cousin. We fished in a creek with a large swimming hole and it was deep. I was a small person, (five foot two, about 100 lbs.), of course, I fell in the hole. I sure did some struggling to get out. My cousin laughed herself out. She told me how funny I looked, just like a drowned rat.

Life was good to me and I ended up in the antique business. I remodeled a chicken house into an antique place and did a lot of the carpenter work myself.

Along with everything else, my husband and I were Harmony singers. I played the piano and guitar. We did lots of public singing. Life was enjoyable until my Earl was stricken with Leukemia. We had 54 years of married life. Now I'm alone, still in the big farmhouse with my two lovely cats. I celebrated my 100 year Birthday Anniversary October 12, 2011. I planned on writing a book, but I guess it is too late for that, as I have several health problems.

Talking and Teaching
By Winifred A. Doan of Knoxville,
Pennsylvania
Born 1929

My school days started in 1935. I lived with my family on a farm between Nelson and Elkland. There were no buses, so I walked two miles to a two-story white building in the town of Nelson. I did this until my family moved into town. We lived on Depot Street. The schoolhouse was on a lot by the Cowanesque River. It had four classrooms with three classes in each room, except for seventh and eighth grades. The school had no indoor plumbing. The toilets were on each side of the building, with a wooden fence around them. There was no cafeteria so I carried my lunch to school. Lunchtime was a fun time to play outside. If the weather was good, the games were kick-the-can, softball, and roller-skating. In the winter, we would ice skate. There were four teachers for the eleven grades. The classroom teachers also taught the special classes of art, music, and gym.

My sixth-grade teacher told me not to sing so loud because I could not carry a tune in a bushel basket. This kept me from singing for the rest of my life. I still had a deep appreciation of music, however.

I remember a couple of times when I was punished for talking. Once was when a teacher put some kind of tape across my mouth. It hurt when the tape was taken off. The next time, I was asked to make a fist, and the teacher hit my knuckles with the edge of a ruler. The worst punishment for talking when I shouldn't was when I called a classmate a "skinned chicken" because she had no hair. The teacher came with her cane, placed the

Winifred A. Doan in 1931

hook around my neck, and took me upstairs to the high school room. She made me sit in a chair and tell the older kids what I had done.

In spite of my talking when I should have kept quiet, I loved learning. I skipped second and fifth grades and completed my eleven grades in nine years.

In high school, my social life was to get together with my friends. The seventh and eighth grade teacher operated the projector in the movie theater in Elkland. He would take us kids with him on Saturday nights. I think tickets were a quarter. We had a party once a month at the school. Our favorite game was spin the bottle. Many Saturdays, we would make a picnic and spend the afternoon in the Savey's Woods. Our favorite swimming hole was on the other side of the town, across the river on the Kelts farm.

Every day after school, I would work at Swan's store until six o'clock. When I got home, I had to change my dress, which was made out of material that came from feedbags. We didn't wear blue jeans back then. Once I finished changing, I helped get supper. My first job was to mix the oleo with the yellow coloring. This was needed to put on our potatoes or pancakes. I was shown how to properly set the table. After supper

was done, and if time permitted, I could listen to the radio. My favorite program was *Inner Sanctum*. If the nights were really cold, I took a bottle of hot water to bed with me.

On Saturday nights, it was bath time in the big laundry tub. We filled this with water heated on the wood stove. Since I was the middle child, I got to use the water second.

The toilet was an outhouse that was outdoors, with the *Sears, Roebuck Catalog* for toilet paper. We had a telephone that was on the party line. This means that several people were on the same line. Our ring was one long and two shorts. The only "iPad" I had was the strainer pads from the milk house sewn together. We used these washed milk pads for dishcloths, quilts, washcloths, sanitary pads, and more.

I met my husband on Memorial Day, 1945. We were married on October 19, 1945. After raising four children on a farm, I finished my education at Mansfield University in 1964. I taught school for Northern Tioga for thirty-one years. I am now retired and enjoying seven grandchildren and five great-grandkids. I love the casino, traveling, crafts, and reading. In spite of what some people would call hardships, I became my own person.

At War With a Wringer Washer
By Carolina F. Edwards of Avis,
Pennsylvania
Born 1937

Way back when (my daughter calls them the "olden days"), our family of seven kids and two parents had what we thought of as pretty normal lives. Both my parents worked in the shoe factories. Our friends and neighbors lived like we did. Everyone did their part. Each Sunday, we went to church, then played checkers or Monopoly or listened to the radio. Sunday was sort of our resting day. On the weekdays, our lives started again. We kids went to school, and Mom and Dad went to work. We would all eat our supper together and then listen to special radio programs: *The Lone Ranger*, *The Shadow*, and *Inner Sanctum*.

Our weekends started on Friday nights. As soon as I got home from school, I had to strip all the beds in the bedrooms. I got home the earliest, so by the time the other kids got home, everything was off the beds. We

107

females got to change the linens in the four bedrooms. That wasn't a job for the males in the family. They would help my dad.

On Saturday mornings at seven o'clock, my mother had already started the laundry set up for the wringer washer, with Dad's help. They put two metal tubs on wooden boxes or boards across the bathtub, with the bathtub full of water. Our bathroom was only eight feet by ten feet, but Mother had a system that fit all the tubs and the wringer washer in so that the wringers could swivel a full three-hundred and sixty degrees, because she used it three or four times per load of laundry.

My mother believed in clean clothes! We bought our Clorox from the store on the corner. We'd take our empty gallon jug to the storeowner, and he would fill it in his basement for thirty-five cents. Believe me, that was strong bleach. If you spilled some on yourself, it would burn if you didn't get it washed off right away.

No one can imagine the amount of dirty clothes that the family went through in one week. Most of what we wore was handmade or hand-me-downs. Each load was washed for thirty to thirty-five minutes, and then went through the rinse water twice. We had to wash all the sheets, pillowcases, towels and washcloths, white shirts, white blouses, and three loads of T-shirts, underwear, and white socks. Then all of that had to be put through the wringer into the two rinse waters, and then put through the wringer again before being hung out on the lines to dry. After the whites came two loads of light colored clothes, then one load of dark socks and dark clothes, and two loads of overalls, dungarees, and jeans. The last batch was any of the rugs that needed it and washable rags. Lunch was in between loads.

That wringer washer and I were always at war! I can't remember how many times my fingers got caught in the wringer. I was always in a hurry to get everything done, so I unfortunately made the clothes too thick to go through the wringers. I would have to reverse it and try and try again.

After the washing was finished, the washer, two tubs, and bathtub had to be emptied so the floor could be scrubbed with a brush and Fels Naptha soap. During the time the laundry was being done, the boys had moved the furniture in the living room so it could be swept and mopped. Our house had linoleum floors,

which all needed to be swept and mopped. There wasn't any carpeting, except for the hand-loomed rugs my mother had made. Our home was heated by coal so the floors turned gritty fast. After the mopping, only the kitchen was left to be cleaned.

My mother would give the three youngest children a treat, but only after all the work was done. When I finished the bathroom, I would change my clothes. My mother would give me one dollar. Since the movie theaters changed their prices at five o'clock, I had the job of running downtown to one of the theaters to buy movie tickets. We always decided earlier what we wanted to see, so I would buy one adult ticket at thirty-six cents for my sister and two kids' tickets at fourteen cents each for my brother and me. I would wait at the theater for them to arrive. We would then watch two movies, newsreels, cartoons, and even coming attractions. Don't forget we still had thirty-six cents left to buy goodies. We would end up buying a large box of popcorn for twenty-five cents to split between us, and two boxes of long-lasting candy, like Jujubes, Juicy Fruit, Good 'n Plenty, or Sugar Daddies for five cents each. We still had a penny left over. We always took turns in keeping that penny. You could get a lot of candy for a penny in those "olden days".

My Hometown of Coudersport
By William M. Morey of Galeton, Pennsylvania
Born 1937

I was brought up in the small town of Coudersport, Pennsylvania. It was actually the county seat. My family was living on Hill Street, where we moved in 1944 the year my youngest brother was born. My family consisted of eight children and Mom and Dad. This was in the World War II era and things were still tough. Even though we had a large family, we always had food on the table and clothes on our backs. We had one cow, some chickens and a pig, which my father would butcher in the late fall.

The one and only railroad train, the C and PA, ran up through the center of town, on West Street. This was directly below where we lived on Hill Street. Back in those days, it was the good old steam-driven locomotive. In the winter, it would have a train car with a snowplow in the front. The train ran from Coudersport almost to Ulysses. It used to run to Port Allegany, PA, but the flood of 1942 washed out a lot of the track and the crossings, so that section was abandoned.

There was a small restaurant on Main Street, owned by Grandma Oneil. A person could get a generous piece of apple pie and a cup of coffee for twenty-five cents there. In those days, twenty-five cents was hard to come by, for a kid. Across the street there was a soda shop called the Olympic. You could get an ice cream cone for a nickel or a double-dip for ten cents there. They also had sundaes, malts, banana splits, and other fountain goodies.

There were three five and ten cent stores in Coudersport. We could go in them and get penny candy or nickel candy bars. It was always nice to shop there at Christmas time, as they had small, inexpensive items to buy.

The Chamber of Commerce always put up the Christmas lighting on Main Street and on the courthouse square. Ed Fisher, a good neighbor and friend, would bring Christmas trees from his tree farm to be put up around the square.

In the wintertime, we enjoyed ice-skating at Othmers Pond across town. They had a shed with a wood stove in it for warmth. Some years a civic organization would make an ice rink on the courthouse square for everyone

Bill's neighbor, Paul, Bill, and his youngest brother, Ron

to enjoy. In the summer, there was the community swimming pool, or we had a few swimming holes in the river. We always had summer chores to do, too, like mowing lawns, tending the garden, looking after livestock, and playing games.

Our town also had a Western Auto Store, where I bought my first bicycle. The owner let me buy it on time. After a few weeks, I had it paid off and was able to take my new Western Flyer home. There was a JC Penny Store in town, too. This is where our parents bought our clothes at the time. I don't know why, but everything was $1.98, $2.98, etc. It seems like everything ended in ninety-eight cents. Montgomery Ward and Sears catalogs were used to order a lot of merchandise, especially for Christmas gifts. We always had a nice Christmas.

The Waltons had the Baldwin sisters. Our town had the Stocumn sisters. Kate was a retired schoolteacher, and Flora was a retired clerk. Kate had taught in some of the one-room schools in the area, while Flora had worked in the drug store. We did odd jobs for them, running errands, mowing their lawn, and keeping their walkways shoveled in the winter.

There were two outhouses in our neighborhood, but they were only being used to store garden tools and other things. However, one was used as a private smoking area for "Granny". She would go in it and enjoy her corncob pipe and tobacco. We could see the smoke coming from the outhouse through the cracks and partially open door. We never tipped the outhouses as a Halloween prank.

My brothers, sisters, and I would walk the six blocks to school every day. The school had no cafeteria, so we had to go back home for lunch and then back to school. School started at nine o'clock and let out at three-thirty. In the winter, we could ride our sleds and use the snow scooters we would build.

My first sweetheart was in the second grade. I didn't have another real sweetheart until my eleventh and twelfth grade years, but I didn't marry them. It was several years later that I married. My high school girlfriend and I would go to the Saturday night square dances and to the movies. She eventually moved out of town after she graduated from high school.

My family was the descendants of the fourth settlers of Potter County. The Peets came up from Elizabethtown, New Jersey in 1811 and settled here. My brothers, sisters, and I only had one grandparent living when we were growing up. She was my father's mother, and she was a direct descendant of the Peet family. She lived with another son and his family, and we would go visit Grandma on occasion. We had several aunts and uncles to visit, too. Aunt Katie had her share of tragedy. She and her husband lost at least three youngsters through death and had their homes destroyed by fires a couple of times. Through it all, she was fun going and great to be around.

Bill's 1953 Chevy and his nephew, Wes

At home, we had a party line, meaning we had to share a phone line with the Stocumn ladies. They had 6-J for a phone number and we were 6-M. It wasn't too inconvenient most of the time. We probably used the line more than they did. Back in those days we had the telephone operators, who would say, "Number, please"? They would connect your call for you and even get the time of day if you asked.

When I got older, we would pick green beans with the migrant workers who would come up from down South. They would stay in migrant camps furnished by the farmers. Later on, we would pick potatoes by the bushel for the potato farmers. We didn't earn a lot, but it gave us money for the weekend movies. We also earned extra money by setting pins by hand in the local bowling alley. A paper route added to our resources, too.

The movie theater was ten cents for kids under twelve and twenty cents for adults. We always enjoyed the movie with some candy and a box of popcorn from Popcorn Joe's concession stand. John and Doris Rigas owned the theater, and they come into Coudersport in the early 1950s. I wasn't aware of it at the time, but John Rigas started the Adelphia TV, Co., which over time grew into a large corporation. He did a lot of very good things for the community as well as for a lot of people.

Our neighbor and friend, Ed Fisher, would take a few of the neighborhood boys and drive us up to his farmland. He had potatoes and pine trees planted there. We would pull the wild mustard seed plants out of the potato patches, as well as pull weeds out of the pine seedling plots. We had to be careful not to pull up too many seedlings. One afternoon we were working in the seedlings, when one of the boys heard a strange noise. He yelled, "Quick, duck down! It's a swarm of bees passing through". We all hit the dirt and they passed over. I didn't see them or where they went. All's well that ends well, though.

Later, around 1955, I bought my first car. It was a used 1953 Chevy. It was a basic, standard shift, six-cylinder. That was followed by a 1956 four-door hard top. I wish I had that beauty today!

We can't forget the good Lord in all of this. I am thankful every day for His goodness and mercy. My family started out going to Sunday school at the Presbyterian Church. We went to vacation Bible school at the Missionary Alliance. Later, we were members of the Methodist Church as well as the Free Will Baptist Church. God has been good.

My Dad, the Greatest Man I Ever Knew
By Marie Yoas of Sigel, Pennsylvania
Born 1932

The Depression years was slowly coming to a close, and we didn't have any money, but lots of love and we worked together. In 1934-35, Dad purchased the old Miller homestead for $2500, containing about 70 acres. In winter, Old Man Winter would paint beautiful pictures on the windows, no two alike. About age 6 or 7 I would sit in my brother's little rocker and watch for gorgeous snowflakes falling softly to the ground.

In summer months, we had a big garden

and canned everything we could. Pickles were often times put in a crock with grape leaves. We would pack cucumber sandwiches and after the dew was off the berry bushes, walk a half mile and pick berries all day. We would can all we wanted and would sell cleaned berries for 10 cent a quart. Cabbage and carrots would be buried in sand mounds covered with straw. When we wanted to use some, we would dig the frozen dirt and straw off, get what we wanted and cover them back up till next time.

John M. Miller and his son, Harry Miller

Mother made lots of butter, which we used freely. Sometimes we would sell butter and deliver it for 10 cent a pound. We added lard or butter for all our cooking and baking. Grandma Harvey made raisin cookies, going door to door to sell them for 10 cent a dozen.

Mother made my clothes from sacks. She always got 2 or 3 bags of the same design so there would be enough of the same to make clothes.

On my 6th birthday, a couple farm neighbor kids came over. How well I remember the excitement this was. I received a pencil, an eraser, a nickel and a big little book.

We had an old Edison record player that played real thick records. One time I told Dad

Marie Miller (Yoas) in 1934

I wanted to buy the ever popular record, 12th Street Rag. Dad went to the record player, opened the door and pulled out the record. That same song had been popular 25 years before.

When I was about 5, my sister and I went to Bradford where Dad shantied all week, and came home on weekends. The oatmeal had condensed milk on it, making it oh so good. I also remember at night, Dad standing over the coal/wood stove frying potatoes and carrots together. What wonderful memories!

Our house was an old farm house with cracks so big around the windows, the snow would blow in. Jack Frost painted such lovely designs on the windows on cold frosty days. We had gas stoves (2 small) to heat our home. We had gas jet lights, which the mantles on them were very fragile. In the summer months, the "miller moths" would knock holes in these by flying into the flame.

Out toothpaste was soda. Early every day we washed our hands and face with cold water right from the spring. At the old spring house behind the door hung a dipper. We all drank from the same one. We did the same by dipping butter-milk from the crocks.

I can remember when we had lots of snow. Dad would hook up the Belgian horses to the big wooden bob-sled, and we would go many miles to get limestone rock to build a lime kiln. Dad made one every year, as getting lime then was not readily accessible.

The crib we all slept in as children was very narrow. I remember sticking my feet through the rails and against the walls, pushing myself away from the wall. This crib that held my brother 91 years ago still remains in the attic on the family homestead.

I don't recall having many toys at all. Dad would take an empty wooden thread spool and cut notches around both ends. He put a rubber band through the hole and matchsticks at both ends and wound it up. I really thought this was great. I do recall having a wind-up little train that went round and round on a track.

Also, I had a set of Diana Quintuplet dolls. Dad always managed to keep us entertained. Somehow, he did a trick with a string around his leg. He never gave away the secret and to this day, I don't know how he did it. He would also put two ends of string in his mouth, and when he took the string out, the ends would be tied together.

We had a home toboggan; a sheet of tin turned up at one end with two holes in it to put a rope through. This really wasn't a very safe toy and could have caused a tragedy.

When I was about 4 years old, my sister took me to the roller rink to roller skate. Nothing fancy back then, just skates that clamped to our shoes. My brother bought me little wooden skies at about the same age. They were 2 little long slats of wood turned up on one end with a leather strap to stick your foot through. He always bought me a bicycle, which he rode more than I did. I recall going around and around the house. Although only one car a day on our road, but I couldn't ride my bike on the road much.

About the age of 12, I was allowed to deliver butter on the dirt road when Dad worked in Bradford. He brought home a rubber ball bigger than a grapefruit with a twinkle ball inside. Every time you bounced it, the ball would twinkle. Guess mother knew where I was. We all learned to play checkers as soon as we were big enough.

My father-in-law said when they were a kid in school of course they had to carry their lunch from home. Then they decided that all the kids that lived in town had to go home for lunch. He had a long walk through town and up a hill. He said he would just get in the door, Grandma would shove a sandwich in his mouth at the door and he would have to turn and leave again to get back to school on time. He use to smoke terrible cigars which about drove you out of the car with the windows up.

I was always a tender hearted animal lover, so we had dogs, cattle, horses, coons, mice, birds and much more. In the summer, it was always fun in haying season to find a baby mouse out in the field. We would put it in an oatmeal (round) box and punch holes in the lid, but at the end of the day, we had to give them back their freedom.

Dad got up early one morning and discovered a rat in the bird cage. After eating the bird, it could not get back out. Dad took rat and cage to the watering trough and drowned it. Dad had another bird before the day was over. When old Teddy, my dog got real sick, Dad had me another dog before Teddy left us.

I was very young when Dad came home from coon hunting, and sound asleep when he bought the littlest coon I ever saw and put it in my bed. I had to feed it with a teaspoon. We kept her for about 8 or 9 years. Another time it was a baby deer he brought home and put in my bed. We bottle fed it and it just hung around the farm. Once a day she would come up on the back porch for her slice of bread. We had a big black dog, which she didn't like and would stomp him. Later someone shot her in the back leg. After that, she gave birth to a cute little fawn.

The greatest man I ever knew was my father, Harry Miller 6'6" tall and extremely handsome. He was stern with his ways, but always had time for us no matter how busy he was. He always took me everywhere he went but work, and even sometimes then. No matter how dirty my little face was from being out, he still took me. We ate meals together, praying before each. We went to church together, everything was done as a family, there were no secrets kept from us kids. On Sundays after church, aunts, uncles, and cousins would come for Sunday dinner. Then, we would gather around the piano, which Mom played and would sing hymns. Nothing more was done on Sundays than absolutely necessary.

My father loved and respected his parents, John and Anna Beer Miller very much. They were extremely devout Christians. When Grandma Miller was leaving this world, she began to sing hymns. This was told to us many times.

Many years went by and Dad loved his fat, fat meat. The guy at the meat market told Dad that fat meat will kill you some day. When Dad passed and the guy came to the funeral home, he said, "I told that old man that fat would kill him." Dad was 96 and 1/2 years old.

Another great man, "Hank" Beer was the neighbor that worked for us. He worked for $1 a day and he got his meals. If he worked ½ day for us, he would walk somewhere else for the other half. I can still picture him walking over the hill, winter and summer. In late October or November, we would all take the lantern and go to the barn after supper to husk corn. This seemed more like fun than work. This gentleman only had one tooth above and

Henry "Hank" Beer

below. He drank his coffee from a saucer. He never owned any type of vehicle or had any electric in his house.

At age 6 or 7 Mom and dad bought their first gas refrigerator. It remained in the Miller homestead until 1991, but was still in working condition, some 52 years old. They also bought Mom a player piano and Dad a 1939/40 John Deer- B tractor. Our lives had improved tremendously.

When I was 15, Mom passed away so I had to do many things I had eluded in the past. We had cows that needed to be milked morning and evening. We had a cream separator that separated the cream from the milk. We had an oval churn about 2' tall with a paddle inside that went around when you cranked the handle. After the butter would form, we would retrieve the butter from what is now called buttermilk. You would put the butter in a wood butter bowl and use a wooden paddle to work out the milk. The butter would be rinsed several times and reworked. Then, a little salt would be worked in. The butter was put into a round 1# butter print with a leaf design on an oblong butter print. The buttermilk was kept in a crock in the water trough that ran from the spring. A dipper hung beside the springhouse door on a nail and was used by all of us to drink buttermilk or water from the spring

I went to a 6 room school about 1 ½ miles from our house. There was grades 1-2-3 in the first room on 1st floor. The second room was grades 4-5-6, and the third room was grades 7 & 8. There was a set of wide wooden stairs going to the second floor. Everyone in grade school played ball at recess and I still have a piece of gravel in my left knee from a fall. That was some 70 years ago.

My favorite teacher was Lucille Shawkey, who was a great inspiration to anyone that had the privilege to be one of her students.

I never got any spankings at school, but my one teacher hit me over the head with a geography book because I was having study hall, but was not studying the subject she taught. Back then spankings were discipline, not child abuse. Parents also gave you another spanking when you got home if you got one in school. Parents always knew what was happening in school.

I walked all twelve years to the same school and graduated at age 17. My sister graduated at 16.

We never had snow days. To keep up the road maintenance, it belonged to whoever lived on the road. Sometimes when the snow was too deep for me to make tracks, Mom and Dad would walk ahead of me. Also, sometimes Dad would plow the road with the Belgian horse with a makeshift plow. In springtime the roads would be muddy and greasy with big ruts in them. Dad pulled out many old vehicles with the team.

We were not supposed to run in school, but of course, we did and a boy and I collided. The teacher caught us and made the boy apologize. We had wood seats that attached to the front of your desk for the next student. One of the boys stuck a pin through the toe of his shoe and stuck it through the crack, poking the girl in front of him. The old coal stove would be "banked" overnight. The person beside the stove sweated, and the other side of the room froze.

Darning Needles and Lightning Balls
By Shirley J. Confer of Williamsport, Pennsylvania
Born 1936

My grandmother came from rich farm people. Her father owned three farms, where he raised peaches. They wore rich beaver coats and hats and wanted for nothing. One of their children became a schoolteacher, and another one was a dentist when he grew up. Another son was locked up in an insane asylum because he stole chickens. When he stood in front of the judge, he threatened to kill him, so the judge ordered him to be put in the insane asylum. There he stayed until many years later, when a new judge came to the bench and let him out, saying, "You never belonged there anyway". My grandmother caught the fancy of a man driving a surrey with fringe on top. They married and had nine children. His name was Lenord, and he was a tall, dark haired man with some Indian blood in him.

Virginia (Ginny), Jerome, Joan, and Shirley

Lenord's father-in-law set him up on one of the family farms, thinking Lenord could make a good living there for his family. However, Lenord had wanderlust and was always looking for something else. He walked away from the farm. Over the years, his father-in-law set him up twice again, and twice again, Lenord walked away, each time leaving more children behind. Eventually Lenord and my grandmother had nine children. They were poor – dirt poor. What a come down for my grandmother from her childhood.

My grandparent's first child was my mother, Lorrain. She came into the world a pampered child. She wore rabbit skin coats and hats, white stockings and patent leather shoes, which her grandmother bought for her.

Times were getting bad. A lot of the men went to the lumber camps, where they ate, slept, and worked. They seldom went home. This probably accounts for some of Lenord's absences.

My mother describes a Christmas when her mother was standing by a window, looking out with tears running down her cheeks. She was so sad because she had hoped her more well off relatives would have provided some Christmas gifts for her children. They had sent some used toys and cast-off clothing and shoes. She wept, "They at least could have provided a doll for the baby".

As the oldest child, a lot of the worry and work of raising nine children fell to my mother. Water needed to be carried into the house for everything. Washing had to be done on a scrub board, and chamber pots had to be emptied. Children needed to be dressed, clothing needed to be made, and hand-me-downs had to be cut down to fit younger children.

The family lived in a house a few fields from the peach orchards. One evening they were sitting on the front porch, watching it rain. They noticed smoke in the air, and after a bit they could see flames shooting up. Lorrain shouted, "That is over on Grandpa's farm"! Her brother, Merrill was just coming into the barnyard with a load of hay, so they unhitched the wagon and the men hurried over to the fire on the tractor to help. The women and children walked over. They saw the barn full of hay blazing furiously. Little could be done to save it. Great-grandfather kept running back into the barn. Other men were trying to stop him, but he would not be stopped. Later they found out that he had all his money hidden in that barn in tin cans. He kept running in to try to rescue it. My mother said she picked up quarters in the soot for many weeks after the fire.

The years marched on, and Mother's family grew poorer. They were now living on string beans from their garden and the few berries they managed to pick. My mother, Lorrain took the wagon and went to her grandfather's farm with her sister, Katherin. She asked her grandfather for something to eat. She knew better than to ask her grandmother, because her grandmother would say, "Do with what you have or do without". Her grandfather gave her some wizened up potatoes and some apples that were not good enough to sell.

One day the milkman came by and told Lorrain to get a bucket or pan. He said, "I will give you some of your grandfather's milk, and he will never know the difference". They were then able to count on this milk.

Another day, a man who owed Lorrain's father for some work stopped by the house.

Lorrain stepped up to him and asked for the wages. He told her he only had a quarter, and she spoke up, "Well, give it to me". She quickly gave the quarter to her brother. Lorrain told him to catch a ride with the mail truck and go to the store to buy some dried beans. Lorrain was a smart child, though she was only able to reach her sixth year of school.

There was talk of work in Ralston. Mining was going on there and lots of lumbering was being done as well. The family moved there to get what work they could. Lenord worked at cutting down trees. Lorrain was sent to a camp to help prepare food for the loggers and to do kitchen duty. She was thirteen and was used to hard work. Soon, however, they decided to move to town for better opportunities. They lived in Newberry. Things were touch and go, but they survived.

My mother was fifteen when she met my father, Art. She got pregnant, and they lived with Lorrain's mom and dad. Art worked when he could.

When Lorrain turned sixteen, she got a job in the rubber factory, making strippers. She walked to work, crossing a swinging bridge. Her mother, Lula, was also pregnant. Then the whole family got the measles. While everyone was sick, Art was the only one bringing home a paycheck. Lula and Lorrain had their babies within days of each other, but Lula's baby, Pearl died. Even though Lorrain had the measles, too, her child survived. In later years, they found out the baby, Ginny had very bad vision. When she was a child, she wore glasses with lenses as thick as soda

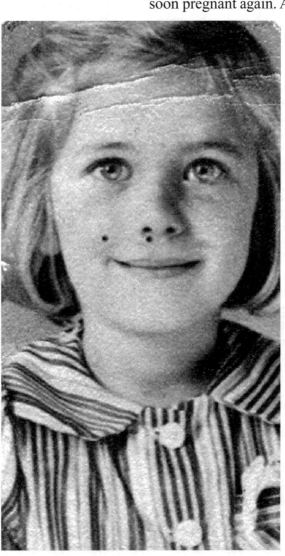

Shirley Bassett (Confer) in 1st grade

bottle bottoms.

Lorrain's brother, Merrill decided he would get married. When Art heard that, he told Lorrain, "If he is getting married, I guess we can, too". Lenord drove the four of them to a justice of the peace, who refused to perform the service for Lorrain and Art, because Art did not have parental consent. Lenord suggested they drive to Towanda, where Art could lie about his age. This was acceptable to everyone. Then they were on their own. Merrill and his wife, and Art and Lorrain decided it would be better if they all lived together. At this time, Lula and Lenord decided to return to the country, leaving the house to the two young couples.

Times were still rough, but the guys were able to get jobs in the steel mill. Lorrain was soon pregnant again. After their son was born, she went back to work at the rubber factory. Unfortunately, the men got laid off. They were supposed to watch the children but they mostly played cards all day. One day Lorrain decided to walk home for lunch, only to find the baby in a sopping wet diaper, which she had to change. She was also furious to find that the men had charged cupcakes to her store bill, which she had to pay for.

There were bread lines, but the men refused to stand in them. After working their jobs and tending to the house and kids, the women would go stand in these lines. Lorrain was handed a jar of peanut butter and told; "Now this is just for the kids. No one else is supposed to touch it".

Things in the city were too difficult so my parents decided

to move back to the country. They could live in an old house on one of Great-grandpa's farms. Half the roof was gone, but Grandpa had some old tarpaper that he let them have. There were huge cracks in the sides of the house where the wind blew in. Grandma gave them some old window blinds that were real tough, which they nailed to the walls. An old cook stove was the only source of heat in the house. They sewed quilts out of old coats and tied the three layers together with yarn. Lorrain had one baking pan, which she used for baking bread. She used coffee cans to bake bread. She would stand by the table, kneading the bread over and over, with a strip of flypaper hanging over her head in warm weather to catch the flies that had drifted in.

There was still no work to be had, because the Depression was in full swing. Art would do a full day of work haying and come home with a bucket of eggs as payment. Merrill and Art had an offer of some farm work. Merrill said, "I don't think I can do a day's work with nothing to eat". Art told him that if he could get through the morning, they would be given a full meal at noon. So off they went, in Merrill's old car, with his tires stuffed with rags to keep them inflated. They got through the morning's work. When dinner was served, it was codfish gravy, something Merrill hated.

I was born in 1936, during the winter. Mom and I were in the hospital for three days after I was born. There was a big snowstorm while we were there. No cars could get through to pick us up. Dad approached a neighbor who had a horse and sleigh and told him about the problem. The neighbor agreed to come for us, so I was brought home from the hospital in a horse and sleigh. I was my parents' fourth child and their third daughter.

When I was about five years old, Mom was teaching me to sew. She had given me a piece of material and a huge darning needle. She got up to see to something on the stove. I laid my needle and material down in the rocking chair. Mom hurried back and sat down. Then she jumped up with a yelp. The needle had gone into her hip, and she had to get a pair of pliers to use to pull it out.

When I was growing up, all the water had to be carried from a spring out by the side of the house. There was a tin water bucket that always sat on the counter by the sink. It had a dipper that hung on the side of the bucket. Everyone in the house drank out of the same

dipper. I was always afraid of that spring. It had a roof over it, and there was almost always a snake in there, trying to keep cool.

We had an outside toilet, of course. Yes, last year's *Sears, Roebuck Catalog* was always sitting close by. This was another place snakes liked to try to keep cool. I remember Mom walking to the outhouse one night. She gave one of her shrieks, because she had stepped on a snake. Boy, could she shriek!

We used oil lamps for light in the house and lanterns if we were outside. I remember a small child's lamp we had. It had a circle on the base where you would stick your finger, to help keep it balanced. It was just right for a child to carry to bed, where we huddled down under our homemade quilts.

By now, President Roosevelt was putting men to work on the roads. Dad came home one night with a story for us. He said he had sat down by the side of the road to eat lunch. He felt something moving underneath him. When he got up, he saw he had been sitting on a black snake that was all coiled up.

Mom had something to do one day, so she sent me to school with the other kids. The teacher must have resented being used as a babysitter. Someone whistled, and she blamed me. She told me to come up front to get my knuckles cracked with a ruler. My brother jumped up and said, "She can't even whistle. If you are going to hit someone, hit me".

Mom would wash clothes on a metal washboard in a tin tub. One day she was washing clothes during a storm, when suddenly the stove lid blew off and a lightning ball came out of the stove. It passed across her tub and went out the screen door. In warm weather, Mom would do the washing out in the yard. The grass was all stubble, like a hay field. We had a clothesline. Once it was full, Mom would lay the laundry on the grassy stubble to dry.

Once in a great while, we would walk over to Grandma's house. We had to go through the cow pasture. Mom would say the bull was ugly, and we needed to watch out for him. I would shiver in my shoes. At Grandma's, I remember two elderly people sitting side by side in rocking chairs. They had pennies stacked up on the wainscoting. I was amazed that they had money to pile up that way. I looked over at them, and their four eyes were looking at me. They were afraid I might take something, I guess.

Television Days
By Christine Taft of Lawrenceville,
Pennsylvania
Born 1945

There were a lot of things I experienced as a youngster, but probably the one that my children thought was the funniest was about getting our first television. My children take television for granted because it's just always been there for them.

I remember how excited I was when my parents first purchased a television. There was no cable only antenna and they had to be turned in the right direction to get a picture. It took about three people to get the antenna turned in the right direction, one to watch the television for the best picture, one to relay the message to the person outdoors turning the antenna. The reception wasn't the best, but we really thought it was great!

There were only two television stations that we could watch, Elmira and Binghamton. The pictures were only black and white there was no color. Sometimes late at night my mother would watch a movie on a Buffalo station that would come in late at night. Television reception was always better in the winter when the leaves were off the trees.

Later when I was a teenager television was much better, I always watched Dick Clark's American Bandstand after school. I think what was really amazing was watching the television coverage of the assassination of President John F. Kennedy. My entire family watched television for days. I will never forget that important historical event.

Handful of Watermelon and Candy
By Rosemary McKinney of Montoursville,
Pennsylvania
Born 1936

Back in the 1940s, I lived on Fifth Street in Williamsport between Elmiria and Lycoming Street. The railroad cars would back in alongside a loading platform and men would work on this platform with hand trucks to unload the freight. Well it often happened that they would drop a carton of candy and it would break open and they would call us kids over to get a huge treat of candy. The same thing would happen when they unloaded watermelons and dropped them and cracked them open and we got a treat of watermelon. Now that I think back, I think they were deliberately dropping things so all us kids would get a treat!

Also in the 1940s we had horse drawn wagons hauling ice. Everyone would put a sign in their windows for five cents up to 25 cents indicating the size block of ice you wanted for your icebox and they would chip it off for you. This had to keep your food cold so you weren't allowed to chip of any for a cold drink.

We kids used to have ballgames in the evenings on the corner and some old lady then didn't like it so she would always call the police. Well they would always turn on their sirens a couple of blocks away so we could all scatter and no one was ever there when they got there. We didn't have any ball fields and there wasn't much traffic back then so I guess the police were doing us a favor.

Baiting the Cows
By Donna Erway McCaslin of Ulysses,
Pennsylvania
Born 1925

A memory I have from my childhood is when my sister Rita and two of my brothers, Gene and Pret, baited the cows. This meant that in late spring when the grass got high enough, after the first cutting of hay, it was our job to tend the cows in the field.

We four older kids had to hurry home right after school and change into "everyday clothes". We would go outside just as mother was opening the gate for the herd to come across the main road and into the field to start eating the tender grass. This was important because eating the new grass increased the butterfat content in the milk, which raised the value of the milk when it was sold.

Each of us would take our stations on the four sides of the field. We were to keep the cows from going into the corn or oat fields. The cows had to eat just the grass where we were guarding. Sometimes the cows were really hungry and behaved themselves and then there were those times they were just wanderlust! They would break away from us and a bunch of them would head for the cornfield. We would have a terrible time getting them back where they belonged. We would have to run up to the cornfield and surround them and chase them back to the grassy field and hope they would all follow! Sometimes we would have to get mother to help us, and we would take the whole herd back across the road to the barnyard.

At suppertime when we would tell dad about our troubles that day with the cows, he had no sympathy for us. He would tell us that if we had been watching the cows instead of playing they would not have gotten away from us. Sometimes that was true, I may have been looking for pretty pebbles, but most often the cows were just being cows, with a mind of their own.

USS Newman K Perry
By James K. Williams of Coudersport, Pennsylvania
Born 1942

In the early 1960s, while on board the USS Newman K Perry DD883 we experienced a rather difficult time. We were scheduled to go to the Mediterranean Sea for a six-month cruise. I worked as a radioman in communications. One of our operations was involving five other ships and also the USS Shangrila aircraft carrier to carry out sea going operations. The carrier had a set course and it was up to the squadron to keep clear while conducting maneuvers. All ships were supposed to turn right and pull away from the carrier. They made a grave mistake and turned left, all at the same time steering into the path of the carrier. We were the closest ship and had nowhere to go. If we slowed down, the ship behind us would hit us. If we sped up, the carrier would cut us in half. So we collided with the carrier approximately 100 feet from her bow. I had been working all day and I was on watch that evening until midnight. I started reading a western paperback to unwind a bit. The ships PA speaker was at a short distance from me and I could faintly hear voices from the bridge even when the lever wasn't activated. I could hear yelling and such just before we hit the carrier. The ship hit the carrier and we rolled over 90 degrees dumping out sailors still asleep. As I was quickly getting dressed, the general alarm sounded and everyone scrambled to their respective stations. I made sure everyone was out of the sleeping quarters; all were present and accounted for except two sailors up forward. One fellow was coming out of the forward most scuttle hatch as the carrier scraped by just feet from him. The other sailor was coming up the paint locker ladder as he was pinned in the wreckage. The ship's bow was bent over like a nail from the forward gun mount to the bow tip. The sailor at the scuttle was injured and made it ok. The sailor at the paint locker didn't make it. We were able to make headway back to Naples, Italy to the dry dock at five knots per hour. This was my personal account of that night.

Outdoor Trips with Mrs. A
By D. LaVerne Zilcosky Sober of Greensburg, Pennsylvania
Born 1931

Miss Trambley taught the 6th grade at Johnsonburg West End Elementary School and was a very good teacher, but what I most remember were her planned outside field trips. I can't imagine that anything similar could be done today. The 5th and 6th grade students were invited to participate and many did. The years were 1941-1942 during the war years. No cars were being produced, my family did not own one at the time, and so we did a lot of walking.

The first trip I remember was a train ride, which was my first ever; to St. Marys, Pennsylvania where we attended a movie there called *Sleepy Time Gal* and then rode the train home. I have no idea what we did for lunch, so I guess it didn't matter. It was fun.

Another adventure was a trek from Johnsonburg to Ridgeway by way of the less traveled Montmorenci road, about seven or more miles. A couple of my good friends that went to the First Avenue School were able to come along and we had a great time skipping along and enjoying the sights along the way. I don't know if we had anything to eat or drink during the trip, so I guess it wasn't important. When we got to Ridgway, we ate our lunch and rode the train home.

In the winter, we walked to Bloomies, a roadside restaurant, and went ice-skating on a small pond that was frozen over. We had ice skates that clipped onto our boots, like the old time roller skates, and after a fun afternoon, we walked home. We didn't even have bicycles. I got my first bike after the war.

During that time, Miss Trambley got married and became Mrs. Abplanalp. She lived about a block from our house so after the wedding ceremony, the bride and groom were there before the evening reception, and some of us kids in the neighborhood gathered with cans filled with stones that we shook to make noise to serenade the bride and groom. After a while, the groom came out and threw a big handful of change to the kids, so we happily gathered what we could and then went home. The following year I went off to Junior High so, I don't know if the new Mrs. A continued her fun adventures.

Audrey

Learning How to Milk a Cow
By Audrey Zilker of Fillmore, New York
Born 1932

I'm Audrey Jones Zilker. I lived on Silver Creek road in Johnsonburg, PA with my grandparents, Albert and Katie Gaker. On one side of the road were small farms and houses; on the other side was the paper mill wood yard. They stored the wood shipped in from Canada in the wood yard. There were train tracks that the Dinky would pull cars of wood to the paper mill for processing. They also had stackers that would run the wood up on a conveyer belt and drop it in the piles. Sometimes they would work at night and I would go to sleep, hearing the click, click of the belt and the thump of the wood hitting the pile below. I miss that sound.

I went the first nine years of school to Rolfe School. Then years 10 through 12 I went to the public school in town. One of my best school friends is Louise Dauber Webster. We met in 1st grade and have been friends ever since. I introduced her to her husband, Clyde, and they live in the same town as I do.

I had a good childhood and have a lot of good memories. I remember that we had an outhouse behind the barn, we used until I was nine years old and then we got an indoor bathroom. I was the first one to use the bathtub, which was pure pleasure. My grandmother made butter, homemade bread, and we had canned blackberries and blueberries that

we picked. We also had our own milk and chickens. The first time grandpa tried to teach me how to milk was a big disaster. I had long fingernails, which was not good. The cow kicked the bucket and then put her foot in it. Guess what, I didn't have to milk anymore. While I was in grade school, my grandmother made all my clothes. Back then, the cow feed came in beautiful flowered materials; she made me skirts from it. She also made quilts from the same material. I have quite a few of her quilts, and I am still using them today.

Today I have two children, one girl and one boy, two grandchildren, one girl and one boy, and seven great grandchildren, five girls and two boys.

Nursing School Strictness
By Barbara Leavy Spotts of Hughesville, Pennsylvania
Born 1929

I went to the Transeau Grade School on the corner of 1st and Park Avenues. All students went home for lunch because no food was served at school. In 1935 when I was in 1st grade, we received an eight-ounce bottle of milk at mid-morning to nourish the children who came without breakfast.

I walked to school in the alleys from 4th

119

avenue between Park and High Streets because it was shorter. There were many potholes with mud in them. I was a curious one and wanted to see what was in the puddles. They were always deeper than I thought and I would get my feet and stockings wet from stomping and splashing in them. The stockings were long, made of cotton, and fell down when active. Galoshes were worn over my shoes but this did not keep them dry. Going home at lunchtime the stockings needed changing and my shoes would be dried in the oven before returning to school.

When I walked the street to school there were some wonderful bushes along the way with white berries that when picked and stomped on would pop to my delight. The old woman who lived in the house with these bushes would watch my friends and I make this mess and we would run away when she opened her door to yell at us. In those days, we had one pair of shoes for school and one pair for church. I had one dressy dress for church and three dresses for school. The school dresses were worn two days in a row before being washed.

I met my only love before grade school. Our fathers were veterans from World War I and they both worked at the Post Office. They would take their beagle dogs walking in the woods and take Ray and myself with them. Then we met again in high school, our senior year, in Problems of Democracy class. He was quite a kidder with a big line about his many girlfriends. This was in 1947. I went to nurses training at the Williamsport Hospital and Ray went in the Marine Corp a year later.

Nursing school was just like the strictness of the Corp, students signed in and out, they wanted to know where we were at all times. We had food and shoe stamps to hand in to the hospital. They told us when and what to wear as far as uniforms, our hair and our nails. It was three years of training and no sick time. If we got sick and issued a day, we had to make it up before we could graduate. In the summer we worked on the wards, we could sign up for two weeks of vacation, taking it when they could spare us. We worked many split shifts, 7 a.m. to 11 a.m. and 7 p.m. to 11 p.m. our work included giving baths to patients each morning and putting them to bed each evening. We went to Dickenson Seminary, now Lycoming College, for the first six months of training, this was a probationary period. After successfully completing the probation the next two and a half years we were taught by our doctors and graduate nurses at the hospital.

In 1950, I graduated and took the Registered Nursing exams in Harrisburg. December 24th Ray and I were married and lived in Morehead City, North Carolina until he was discharged from the Marine Corp. we came home to Williamsport to live.

The Corralling of a Heifer
By Lynn H. Ostrander of Bradford,
Pennsylvania
Born 1923

A little, story and a half house in Liberty Township, McKean County, Pennsylvania was the site of my birth on July 5, 1923. There was a living-dining-kitchen room, a small bedroom, and a pantry downstairs. Upstairs there was a bedroom and an attic. An old black iron wood stove that had been converted to natural gas supplied heat and cooking. Plumbing was a water pail on a shelf in the main room and a washbasin on another nearby shelf. In cold weather, a spring not far from the door supplied us with water. In hot weather, we carried or hauled water from other springs. The toilet facilities consisted of a three holer out behind the house. Sixteen by twenty-two is the best I can come up with as the size of the house. I did a lot of figuring as I worked on a replica for my model railroad. For lighting, we had two down hanging mantle gas lamps and two oil lamps. We did have a lighted tree for Christmas. A tree was cut the day before so it would be fresh, candles were carefully arranged on the tree, and lit one time, on Christmas morning.

Dad worked for a natural gas lease and we were fortunate because he had work all through the depression. He kept four or five cows, which he milked in the morning before he went to work, and again when he came home at night. Dad raised a pig and some chickens and for a while, we had some geese. In the summer, he had a large garden. One winter night dad set moms wash bench in the living-dining-kitchen room, he then carried in a quarter of beef and laid it on the bench. He used his axe to cut up that quarter of beef. His brother came to butcher the pig and the whole valley rang with its squeals as he killed it.

Entertainment was reading or playing games. Mom bought a wind up record player. She had some classic recordings, but most were popular songs of the day. My older brother and I scoured the countryside for old buggy parts from which we made a skeleton buggy that we could pull up the hill and ride down. Out in the country there was not much traffic so we felt safe riding on the dirt road. In the winter, we rode on sleds and played fox and geese. The schoolhouse was not far from our house. It was one room and open to grades 1st thru 8th. There were only 13 kids so some grades did not have any pupils.

Sundays were for going to church and in the afternoon, we often went to grandpas house. There we feasted on apples from his orchard and popcorn that he had grown in his garden. One of the favorite stories told at such times was the corralling of a heifer that had been allowed to run wild. It seemed that all the kids in the neighborhood had joined the chase but finally she was herded into the barn and locked into a stanchel. Grandpa had gone to the house but two of his boys stayed with the heifer. One dared the other to ride her, so he climbed up above her and dropped on to her back. Braww she said, broke out of the stanchel, jumped through he feed door, ran out the main door, and down across the field with her tail waving in the air. Hearing the commotion grandpa came to the door asking what was going on. "Oh this heifer has gotten out!"

The Celery Farm
By Betty Mengee of Wellsboro, Pennsylvania
Born 1928

My story begins in 1928 when I was born; I was one of 10 children. My parents owned a small farm; my dad had a few cattle, a couple of horses, some chickens, and some pigs. The depression came along in 1929 and times got pretty hard to support our large family. I was number 10, with seven more to come later, the youngest a boy in 1942.

My dad would go to the junk pile in Wellsboro, where he often would find outdated cereal and even candy. He would bring them home to us children and we were happy to have them. This was the first time I ever saw small boxes of cereal, if it was stale we didn't notice. I often wondered in later

Curtis L. Van Order and baby Ralph in 1943

years why the merchants didn't realize that there were so many folks who would make use of those things. We ate a lot of shredded wheat at that time for breakfast; it was packed in layers with three biscuits to a layer, with printed cardboard between the layers. We would color the pictures and then we made use of them by cutting them out to fit our shoes, which usually had holes in the soles, they wore quite well for weeks. Nothing went to waste in those days. That's why we senior citizens still make use of many things that the younger folks wouldn't think of.

My dad also had a celery farm there in the valley. The soil was called muck, derived from many years of trees that had deteriorated. It was so rich and loamy and you could grow anything. It is still there but not used anymore for crops, it has been turned into a bird sanctuary. I feel so sad every time we pass by because my memory still sees the beauty of growing things, now it's just swale and flooded.

My dad would start his greenhouse early in March; he had beds of soil in there where he prepared it for the tiny little seeds, celery, tomatoes, lettuce, cabbage, and many others. A fire had to be tended night and day during the cold weather. Then when the plants outgrew the beds in the green house, they were planted outside in hot beds; they still had to be protected from the frost at night. He covered the beds with window sash and sometimes warm covers. Then when the plants were about three to four inches tall by about early June then they got planted in long rows down on the muck. They needed lots of care even then, side dressed with fertilizer and

121

the weeds needed to be kept out. As the plants grew to maturity, they needed to have boards placed alongside of them and fastened with wires, which allowed the celery to bleach out white, which was desirable to sell. When the time was just right, then the boards came off the stalks and were pulled out. The leaves and roots were trimmed off then taken to the washhouse where it was washed and tied into bunches of four to six stalks.

My dad would ship it by truck to New York, Baltimore, and Philadelphia. Then when the crop was out, he would take a few crates in his old Chevy truck and get a couple of we older children to go along. We would go to small towns and peddle it up and down the streets, the ladies were happy to get it for four stalks for a quarter but I didn't enjoy that at all. My dad worked very hard for his 72 years. We all survived very well. The great depression didn't hit us so hard because my dad was able with the good Lords help to keep going. I'm sure we children did not thank him near enough. He was special to us all the time.

The Curtains' Torture
By Barbara J. Natalie of State College, Pennsylvania
Born 1941

From the time my parents purchased their house in 1940 until after my father died and my mother became too old to shovel coal, our house had a coal furnace. Coal is a dirty fuel that leaves a grunge residue on walls, furniture, and draperies. Heating with coal required a top-to-bottom house cleaning twice a year. Walls and ceilings had to be washed, upholstery cleaned, carpets beaten, and window dressings laundered.

In those days, irons didn't have settings for fragile materials. They were designed to produce a high temperature for ironing what most people wore--cotton. In fact, most irons came with instructions that the user "should always place the iron on an insulated surface to prevent fires." Delicate fabrics, like curtains, linen tablecloths, and woolen blankets, had to be stretched taut to retain their shape and dry without wrinkles.

On any given day in the spring and fall, Mother would ask me to go to the attic and bring down the curtain stretcher. It was at that

precise moment I knew I needed a place to hide the following day. Using that piece of equipment was agony. I was the only family member at home during the day that was skinny enough and strong enough to climb the ladder and hoist myself the rest of the way through the opening in the ceiling to the attic.

The Maid of Honor collapsible stretcher, purchased from Sears & Roebuck, was easy to find; its box was eight feet long. Inside were all of the pieces to assemble the 5x8 foot stretcher. The stretcher was made of a lightweight wood, presumably because the manufacturer didn't believe most women could handle the contraption otherwise. I'd drag the box across the floor and feed it down through the opening in the ceiling into my mother's arms. If I'd been paying more attention, I would have seen that Mother had already washed the lace curtains and had them rolled up, saturated with starch. This wasn't ordinary starch; it was a thick glue-like substance with a consistency resembling wallpaper paste that stuck to your skin and stiffened flimsy materials. "You'll be helping me stretch curtains tomorrow," Mother said. "But..." "There'll be no ifs, ands, or buts about it, missy. You'll be right here to help," she'd say, bouncing her pointed finger at me. I knew what arguing would get me, so I helped prepare for the next day by spreading two old bed sheets on the living room floor, one on top of the other, to sop up any starch that dropped off the curtains. Mother pulled the pieces out of the box and we assembled the stretcher on top of the sheets, adjusting the wing nuts and clamps to fit the size curtains we had. We were ready for tomorrow's torture.

Next day, I rolled my sleeves above the elbows and stood on a chair to begin pinning the curtain to the stretcher's frame. Mother pinned the top of one side while I did the other, and the rest of the job stretching and securing all four sides of the curtain to pins was mine. Starch covered my hands and forearms from contact with the curtains. Each pin, made of brass to prevent rust while the curtain dried, was permanently embedded in the framework. The pins were an inch apart around the perimeter of the frame and stuck out about an inch. Regardless of how careful I was, the pins would prick my fingers and some blood would get on the curtains, much to Mother's chagrin. It was always the thumbs that went first. I'd just stick the injured finger in my mouth, starch and all, until the bleeding stopped, then start pinning again. Days later, when all of the curtains were dry, they did look clean and crisp. The pins also produced a pretty, scalloped edge one or two inches apart on the curtains' border, depending on how many pins were used in the stretching process. It was a job well done, at least for the next six months.

The Class of 1930
By Mary Ann Fees Johnston of Kane,
Pennsylvania
Born 1912

I am submitting a writing done by my mother, which describes her days at Kane High School in Kane, Pennsylvania. The writing was part of a journal that my mother left for her children. Mary Ann Fees Johnston was born in Kane in 1912 and throughout her life was in contact with her very dear friends from the 1930 graduating class.

One of the best parts of growing up in Kane were the days spent at Kane High School. We did graduate in 1930, but many of our friendships started in grade school around 1918 or before that. Once we arrived at Kane High School there was a camaraderie among us that firmed up and grew stronger as the days, weeks, and months passed, and suddenly we were seniors. Although we were naturally into competitions, scholastic, musical, and sports, we were never rivals. The 30-ers moved as one. Through the four high school years, we consistently raised money, which took us to Washington, an event that is forever preserved in my mind by the incomparable picture on my home's walls to this very day.

We split naturally into interest groups, dramatics, band, orchestra, choruses, clubs, and course selections. My most meaningful activities were basketball, chorus, and working on the school newspaper, and eventually qualifying as a staff member of the outstanding yearbook, the *Hurri-Kane*.

Someone has said that school isn't real life. It's a period of years during which we learn skills and then we go into the real world to put those skills into the business of living. Even though learning was polished and perfected by

us, along the way ties were formed and made firm, and friendships and mutual respects became evident. We were the typically young; we still had the simple honesty that had not learned to choose associates for advantage or prestige or for any reason but liking and caring for one another. Love, concern, and tolerance all showed there in Kane High School in the 30s, and continued up through the 80s.

At reunion times, everyone faces up to the fact that there were ever choices and every other ways to go. There were other people to become involved with or places to live. In 1930, most of us had our courses plotted by our parents' circumstances and in so many cases by the Great Depression. It was hard for even the most affluent to come up with tuition and housing fees, and it was not uncommon for classmates' families' mortgaged homes to pay tuition for Penn State. One of us borrowed money from our Latin teacher. I was in my second year at Allegheny when the banks closed. It was frightening for my mother to tell that they had, it was frightening for me to hear that they had. The customs and conditions of our times saw most of the girls getting married at once and making a career of raising families.

I look at my 1930 yearbook picture; I was so young, so vulnerable, and so striving for dignity. I was wearing the suggested white blouse with its face-framing collar, my brown eyes very serious. I don't know that girl anymore. I often long to visit with her for a time to hear again her dreams discussed, and to reconsider her hopes. I kind of liked her. I would want to tell her about some of the good things that have come my way, confide some of the disappointments, and show her some of my modest accomplishments.

Time, 58 years of it, has passed. We are most surely strangers to those people we were back then, but most of my classmates and I are still drawn to the mystique of our similar roots, to our hometown, to our school, and to each other. I was never an officer of the Class of 1930, but at this point in time, I am lovingly called "30-ers Girl Friday".

I have consistently collected through the years an ever-changing list of addresses and in many cases the addresses too of children I could contact in emergencies. Birthdays of each and every class member are on file, as well as many of their mates. A card goes out with my love and that of the Class on each one's special day.

The year 1980 saw us "revving up" for the 50th reunion. Preparations for this day went back about three years when I started collecting all 30-ers social security numbers. I needed them to order wonderful gold social security cards for each classmate to celebrate our golden reunion, my gift to each in recognition of 50 plus years and loyalty and friendship shared between us.

One grandson, Alec, contributed his artwork with drawings of "flappers" and "sheiks" of the 20s. Another, Bob, remembering how much I love music in my home and how I associate people with certain tunes, sad, nostalgic, happy, and some just for remembering, brought Peter, Paul, and Mary's album called, Reunion. It said clearly what the Class of 1930 has been about for so many years. It says, "We're a song that must be sung together."

Finally, every decoration was in place, every question had been answered, every travel plan was completed and there we were assembled on Kane Country Club's steps. The bearded young photographer was taking our picture almost 50 years to the day later than our class picture was taken on the Washington trip. There were smiles on our faces by then, but a little while before there had been tears when classmates carried classmates up the stairs in wheelchairs.

The Class of 1930 is not entirely self-serving. When Kane's new hospital called for help, I sent the word to 30-ers. The checks came in to the amount of over $1,400. I was disappointed, I wanted more. Then word got around and when the class treasurer gave me the check to present to the hospital's administrator on the night of our reunion dinner, the amount was $1,930 from the Class of 1930. Again, there were tears. We also support the tiny Friends Library. A memorial book is placed on its shelves for every classmate that has to leave us, plus we have made several donations through the years to its modest budget. I always purchase at least a dozen of their wonderful calendars for New Year's greetings.

Many of Kane's graduating classes faced reunion time with apprehension and misgivings. They realized that the loss of members brought increasing dread of get-togethers. In Kane a very special lady, Miss Helen Curtis Davis, dealt with this situation in a wonderful fashion. Hers was the force behind a new venture. Through perusals of class records at Kane High School, she made lists of classes out of school since the turn of the century. She asked each of these classes who were past their 50th reunion to return to Kane on Reunion weekend to attend a dinner at the school. Thus the Emeritus Dinner was born to coincide with all other homecomings on the fourth weekend in June. The success of this occasion is increasingly obvious. Well over 200 people gather, seated by classes. They move about before and after dinner to greet those they knew as seniors when they were freshmen and freshmen when they were seniors.

Usually the Class of 1930 has an additional get-together on Emeritus Day. We early on discovered there was not enough time at the dinner for visiting. The last several years' luncheons have been at Lovely Ludlow Manor, thus I get back to my other hometown. Ludlow Manor is right across the valley from our house and farm. We are almost always joined at both get-togethers by one or all of our mentors from those long-gone days, Miss Allio, our 9th grade English teacher, Miss Bollinger, 9th grade Latin, and Mr. and Mrs. Rickert. When I taught I was inspired by them and found myself using their methods. The English classes studied The Ancient Mariner, The Lady of the Lake, and Dickens' Great Expectations. There was also emphasis on grammar, spelling, and writing of book reports. Latin emphasized not only language study, but also a large portion of Roman history. The Rickerts came to Kane High School in 1926, the same year the Class of 1930 arrived. My name then was Mary Ann Fees. I still remember and treasure Mr. Rickert's signing of my Hurri-Kane the year we graduated. He wrote, "Give to every man his dues, but save the Fees for me!"

Through the years people have asked me what sort of friend this person or that person has been. I am thereupon reminded of Willie, a character in the Family television show. Willie said, "It's not important what kind of friend each of mine has been to me, it's important what kind of friend I've been to him." The 30-ers still claim their places as my best friends. It's 1988 by now, and just lately one of them wrote to say that the ties kept firm by the classmates make these growing older years a delight. Strong foundations were laid way back when, so you and you are still saying, "Happy Birthday", "Merry Christmas", "Have a good New Year", "Get Well Soon", Take Care of Yourself", and so, so often, "I love you."

My family and I talk at times about "the hereafter" and what it will be like. I of course cling to the assurance that the ancient Greeks gave. We will see our loved ones in their own forms as Ulysses saw his loved mother and many of his warriors. Then of course we ponder on how we will be seen, at what age, and if I am to go to that place in my 70s, how will my mother recognize me since when she last saw me I was 20. I read somewhere that in Heaven each of us will be at the age when "We were most our true selves". So I will be like I was in Kane High School, like we all were then in the Class of 1930.

Eileen's mother, Kathryn Joyce Marjorie Larger and a cousin in 1927

Smoke Run
By Eileen Scramuzzo of Chicago, Illinois
Born 1924

In 1932, it was quite common for families to send their children with relatives that would temporarily care for them until things got better. In Detroit, better never came. By the time I was eight years old I had been in several homes of friends and relatives, but times were tough for everyone and I never felt I belonged. My mother's long illness and no work for my dad made me a fortunate person to go to another home. I carefully clutched my paper shopping bag with all my worldly possessions and after many hours of traveling, I watched the flat roads of Michigan become a beautiful patchwork quilt of the green mountains of Pennsylvania. The amber and red foliage that decorated the roadway was the most beautiful scene I had ever witnessed. My dad had a Ford V8 that had been borrowed from his brother who was lucky enough to still be employed by the Ford Motor Company. Gas money was somehow obtained and we were on our way to a strange mountain village called Smoke Run. A deer peaked out to see this strange vehicle on the road as not many cars were around in those days. I inhaled the aroma of fresh fields of clover, hay, and wonderful scent of pine trees that were new to me, but also a good sign that this time things would be different. My dad told me the history, as he knew Smoke

Run to be a coal mining town with a mixture of nationalities from Croatia, Poland, Wales, and Ukraine, with a few Germans thrown in. Everyone somehow understood each other, and the only foreigner would probably be me, from the big city of Detroit.

In a field close to our destination, an elderly woman paused, being very curious to see a stranger in a car to be passing her farm. She was small and deeply suntanned, dressed from head to toe in black with a babushka on her head as she held an axe in her hand, chopping wood. She waved a toothless grin and went right back to cutting her firewood. Her smile and friendly wave was another good sign for me. A huge oak tree hid the tiny house that had been built by my great grandfather, long deceased and to me it looked like something out of a Charles Dickens fairytale. My Aunt Annie and daughters Madeline and Bernice greeted me warmly as my dad made a hasty goodbye. I worried if he had enough money for gas to get back to Detroit. A kiss goodbye and I walked through a looking glass and entered a world of love and kindness I had never known before.

All water was obtained from the well that was also built by my great grandfather and told in time of draught; neighbors often came to their house for water. Butter and small items were lowered into the well to keep cool, as there was no refrigeration. Because of this,

125

food was bought daily from the Cloverleaf store, which was an exciting adventure. I thought it was better than the JL Hudson, a large department store in Detroit. Barrels of grain, farm machinery and miscellaneous items I never did figure out what they were stood in front of the store. On Saturday after our bath in a wooden tub, we did our shopping. Gossip was no more than, "Guess who's pregnant?" and the usual reply, "No, not again." The mixture of languages, crying babies, women buying yard goods as boxes of produce were hauled out to waiting wagons and carts. Penny candy held the attention of kids all ages and the best thing about it all was I thought it was free. No money was ever exchanged and all you had to do was yell to Taft or Foster Williams to put it on the book and walkout. I knew I was going to like it here.

My aunt Annie was a fabulous cook and admitted to that as she always replied, "All I need is something to cook." Her house was sparsely furnished and spotless. We had no household chores and she said she could do it faster and better than the three of us put together. This was probably correct. We did have duties, such as keeping the coal bucket filled. We would carry the coal bucket to the trains coming from the mines and pick up all that was dropped from the moving cars. With a full bucket, we would take it home for the cool evenings as we looked forward to listening to *Lone Ranger, Fibber McGee,* and *Molly.*

Eileen's father, Elmer Burchill

Now and then, we had a bonfire with singing and dancing for that was free, and we took full advantage of that. In our leisure, which we had a lot of; our noses would lead us to fields of wild strawberries. We ate more than we took home but were rewarded with strawberry pie, to this day cannot be duplicated.

A summer adventure was to gather all of the shoes in the house and walk three miles to Madera, another small village, to the shoemaker. With shoelaces tied and slung over our shoulders, we would get shoes from everyone in the house and take them to get half soled and heels with medal taps for the girls so they would last all winter. The smell of leather and glue were as great as the taps on our shoes. The hot breath of July's heat made us stop in a forest of pine trees and eat our lunch. We repeated the trip the following week except we wore the repaired shoes home so we could tap dance on the cement road and dance like Shirley Temple. All of those shoes together cost about two dollars and fifty cents, a great deal of money in those days.

When we were close to home, we neared Burchells dry goods store, which was also a post office. We stopped for mail, but none ever came. I did not mind anymore as I felt I had found my home. We passed Lloyd's barbershop that was a peaceful retreat for the men that worked in the mines for a well-deserved glass of beer. My aunt also loved the white and pink lozenge candy that could be purchased there when we

126

were lucky enough to get a nickel for a very generous snack that was lovingly doled out.

The road to the house was in full view of the Croatian club, where we spent our Saturday and Sunday. We fussed for hours fixing each other's hair and hand sewed our broom-skirt skirts from material that sold for 59 cents a yard. Our neighbor friend would join us after she filled her front teeth that had many cavities with melted paraffin wax. I thought she was very beautiful. We all wanted to look like Lana Turner with our purple lipstick and saddle shoes as we danced the night away until we were totally exhausted. The men stayed in the bar, the young men our age never danced; they sat on the bench near the huge stove and watched the girls. The older women, most of them widows, all dressed in black, sat back and watched the boys that watched the girls that loved to be watched. The polka and newest jitterbug steps kept the laughter and screams going all evening. Life was great, but that too, was about to change.

December 7, 1941 the heavy fog dampened our hair as we hid our boots at end of the road, as we didn't want to go to the dance with our legs spattered with mud from the unpaved road. We put on our saddle shoes as usual and entered the club. The beer barrel polka screamed out until the sudden silence stunned me and everyone else. The jukebox was turned off and the radio from the bar announced that the United States had been attacked in Pearl Harbor. Panic and shock overtook everyone. This mass confusion was beyond our comprehension. I had never heard of Pearl Harbor.

The bartender Grouchy Mike stood on the bar and asked for silence and self-composure. Some children started to cry as they felt unknown emotions emitting from their mothers and neighbors. Grouchy Mike wiped his face and called out. "We are at war; the school bus will be here at 6 a.m. to take anyone over 18 or men without dependents to Altoona, the closest recruiting station."

I did not pick up my boots that night as I got my saddle shoes ankle deep with mud. I didn't care. I knew my life as I had known it would never be the same and it was not. Many of our boys never came back. But they were first to help to defend our wonderful but not perfect United States of America. They had high ideas, ideals and never ending loyalty to family and to the greatest country in the

Walter "Sonny" Joyce in 1930

world. I am so proud of the young men I grew up with in Smoke Run.

It had been 20 odd years since I had been to my old hometown and the beautiful mountains of Pennsylvania. The spectacular view of the changing colors of October took my breath away. I had almost forgotten. I took this trip because I wanted to see it, at least one more time. The place that made a child at last believe in people and a good life was after all, possible.

After World War II, job opportunities were limited to the coal mines. Needless to say, most of the young people left town and I was among them. I made my new life in Chicago. A lifetime had passed all too soon and now I was newly retired and my thoughts and heart needed to make this sentimental journey. Family and friends had long gone, relocated, or passed on in my little town of Smoke Run. I'm sure you have never heard of it, yet I will never forget it. The crisp fall air and overwhelming scent of pine trees made me stop at the side of the road to get a better view of the fields of wheat and corn. Even though darkness was coming, the view was like a patchwork quilt. A sense of déjà vu overtook me as I wandered knee deep in Tiger Lily's that nodded and seemed to point me to the small white church I had attended in my youth. I was saddened to read the sign at the entrance that stated the church was closing due to poor attendance. A kind old gentleman in bib overalls said that I could enter as he was just cleaning up for the auction to be held the next morning. I trembled as I walked across

127

the threshold. I headed for the huge ledger that held signatures of friends and neighbors since the opening in 1924. I turned down the worn yellow pages and choked back the tears as my family name appeared. The kind old gent coughed delicately to indicate he was ready to lock up. A smile came easily as I glanced at the gold stars hanging from the handrails as they had always been for the children with perfect attendance. Everything was the same, the ten pews, the stained glass window, and the hymnbooks, worn out with time but unchanged. The kind caretaker who was trying to close handed me a hymnbook as a remembrance. I walked to my car and put the precious book beside me. The fog rolled in as I said my last goodbye. The church and steeple disappeared in the darkness but will forever remain in my memory.

My Street
By Fred J. Guarino of Curwensville,
Pennsylvania
Born 1920

I grew up during the 20s and the early 30s in Clearfield, Pennsylvania. Clearfield was a small town on the West Branch Susquehanna River. I lived on Reed Street and it was two blocks long. The county jail was on one end of the street and Kurtz Bros. was on the other end. Kurtz Bros. was a printer and paper converter where I spent all my working years. Reed Street was a busy little place. It had six apartment buildings, two hotels, a rooming house, a Coca-Cola bottling plant, a dairy that made great ice cream, three taverns, The Elks Club, a mom and pop store, my Dad's barber shop, and a railroad station with eight or 10 trains passing through each day.

Now I know that seems like a lot to fit onto two blocks, but five of the apartment buildings had a business on their ground floors. The actual business district of the city was three blocks away, but it seemed that Reed Street was the hub of the community. There was always something going on, and many great people lived there. Well, today it is a little different. The jail is still there and Kurtz Bros. is still going strong. The Elks Club and a restaurant named St. Charles are also still around. The railroad station has become

a Laundromat. The Grice Gun Shop is a new addition, and is the largest gun dealer in our state. Well, that is my story and I'm sticking with it.

Fifth Grade with the Big Kids
By Bruce Shaw of West Decatur,
Pennsylvania
Born 1942

I entered first grade in the fall of 1947, at the age of five. There was no kindergarten at the time. My school was a one-story, two-room, brick, building that was located in the center of town. It was adjacent to the Methodist church in the village of Wallaceton, in Clearfield County, Pennsylvania. The population served by the school included approximately 351 people from Wallaceton, plus an additional 250–300 people from neighboring towns. Grades one through four were taught in one room and grades five through six were taught in the other room. We didn't change rooms for different classes and we had only one teacher for every subject. There was no gym, cafeteria, auditorium, or any other supporting amenity. Each classroom was furnished with the teacher's desk and chair, a coat closet, the students' desks, a couple of tables, and a wall-to-wall, slate, blackboard.

Students brought bag lunches, and ate them at the tables or at the desks. Water was supplied by a shallow well with a concrete top, which was located in the playground. Heat was provided by a large, coal-fired, gravity furnace. The heat would waft up through a large floor-register within each room. The register was a popular place for drying gloves, coats, and socks during the abundant snowfalls. Naturally, these registers were the warmest places to huddle after recess or lunch. Our teacher, Mrs. Brown, taught all four grades in the first room. We had time to study, complete homework, take naps, and goof-off while other grades were in session with her. Grades one–three passed uneventfully, but entering grade four was a big deal.

The next year I would pass to room two, where the "big kids" were. The first few months were fairly routine and seemed to fly by. Then, one day in December, our lives were abruptly changed. It was a cold day with a lot of snow. Just before recess, one of the students noticed smoke coming through the floor, from the basement. With no delay, Mrs. Brown directed each class to rise, walk single-file to the coat closet, retrieve their boots and coats, and proceed directly to the main exit. Simultaneously, grades five and six were going through the same drill. Once outside, we all stood across the street—against the church—and watched as the smoke and flames became more intense. Our town had no city water, thus, there were no fire hydrants. Water was trucked in by fire trucks and a passing steam locomotive that was travelling on the New York Central tracks.

The locomotive was stopped near the school and it provided extra water from its tender. Our school was destroyed that day. Following the Christmas break, we were all bussed to a vacant one-room school in a nearby community; classes were continued to the end of their scheduled terms. Needless to say, passing on to grade five didn't put me with the "big kids", but rather, at yet another school. Many fifth graders in another community school jointures were becoming the norm.

The Siegfried Line Invasion
By Doreen Jo Cherry of Ridgway,
Pennsylvania
Born 1952

With an American Infantry Division in Germany on September 21, 1944, tales of heroism are a dime a dozen. This particular division blazed the way for one of the most formidable military endeavors into the Siegfried Line. Every enlisted member and officer that served in this section of Germany during WWII knew about the 10 men who paved the way for our troops. The names of these 10 men aren't common knowledge, but all 10 men deserve credit for the first cracks in the Siegfried Wall. This Pennsylvania division was assigned the job of being the first to advance on the Siegfried Line. Their commanding officer ordered two patrols to start the advance. The first two patrols crossed from the Luxembourg side the Our River into Germany on September 11, 1944.

One patrol scouted the land and returned with reports. The second patrol remained behind to guard the bridge over the Our River.

The next day the entire division moved across the bridge. The tanks were ordered to lead the way, but their forward progress was halted by a cunningly placed cement roadblock. Someone had to clear that roadblock or the division would never make it across the Siegfried Line. Lieutenant George Reuter—of Rathway, New Jersey—volunteered for the task with nine of his soldiers. One of the nine soldiers, Sergeant Rudy N. Loverkovich—of Detroit Michigan—conveyed this story:

"We each took 50 pounds of dynamite on our backs and went to it. We couldn't carry our rifles, because it was all we could do to carry the dynamite; what good would rifles be anyway, when one shot would blast us to hell. We carried the stuff seven-tenths of a mile, without drawing any fire, but 200 yards from the road, we began catching hell. The Germans opened on us with sniper and machinegun fire. Lt. Reuter called for artillery, but the gunfire continued until we reached the roadblocks and set the charges. We got away, and just about the time the blast went off, the Germans got their 88's to work on us; we caught more hell all the way back. We made it though. I still say it's a miracle that any of us got back. It was our 'Lucky Day'. Not one of us got hit."

The charges that those brave soldiers set destroyed the roadblock and opened up a direct route to the perimeter of the Siegfried Line. At dusk on the same day, two full battalions

Dorik M. Metelski during WWII

were across the Our River. Soon afterward, the entire division was across with all of its tanks, weaponry, and other equipment. They chiseled away at one of the toughest parts of the Siegfried Line. A French reporter visited with some of the soldiers after they made it through the Siegfired Line and secured the general area. He watched them practice with artillery and talked with them.

Some of the soldiers that were present on that day were: Privates Walter Rodell of Philadelphia, Charles Tramontana of New Jersey, and George Proud of Pennsylvania; Corporals John Podolski and Fred Cope of New Jersey; Sergeant George Teetcalfe; Master Sergeant Dorik M. Metelski of Pennsylvania; First Lieutenants Robert W. Dale Jr of Pennsylvania and James O'Meara of Maryland; Captain John A. McKinley of Pennsylvania, and Lieutenant Colonel Carl L. Peterson of Pennsylvania.

A Childhood in Woolrich
By Jane O. Naval of Lock Haven,
Pennsylvania
Born 1920

In 1920, Woolrich was a small town of about 100 houses, a church, and the Woolrich Woolen Mill. It was located in a small valley in Clinton County, Pennsylvania. Almost every house had at least one person working in the woolen mill. The Chatham Run tributary meandered through the middle of town and provided water. It also served as a place for us children to play during the summer or ice skate in the winter. I was born in my parent's bedroom, in a house that was across the street from the mill. Our family consisted of mother, father, four boys, and five girls. I was their fifth child. Our house was two-stories, had a woodworking room in part of the attic, four bedrooms, and a balcony. The balcony was later enclosed to make a fifth bedroom. On the first floor, there was a kitchen, a pantry, a large dining room, and two connecting living rooms. At first, we used an outhouse, but then dad installed interior toilets on each floor. We kept the outhouse for several years and used it while working or playing outside.

Baths were taken every Saturday night in a kitchen washtub, into which, mother poured heated water. When dad installed the toilets, he also had a bathtub put in the upstairs bathroom, so we washed there. Our barn with its attached woodshed was close to Chatham Run. In our large backyard, there were several sheds and fruit trees. One shed held ice packed in sawdust, because we didn't have an electric freezer. We had no phone or radio when I was very young, but eventually a phone station was built, and phones were installed in houses. An operator at the station would ring our house when a call came for one of us. The phones were on a party line, so neighbors' phones rang at the same time. Each house had its own number and duration of ring, but anyone could lift their phone and listen to the conversation; some people did!

Father was a supervisor at the mill and mother was busy with cooking, cleaning, gardening, sewing, laundry, and raising nine children. As we grew, we helped by washing dishes, hanging laundry, weeding the garden, taking the cow to and from the pasture, making beds, dusting, and more. Our clothes were mostly handmade and they were given to younger siblings once outgrown. One of our aunts was good at sewing and she made many of our clothes. Mother had a wringer washer, where she washed only our dark clothes. Then she'd hang them to dry. We girls helped bring them inside and fold them, but we were too young to iron. Every Sunday evening, father took our whites to the woolen mill in a wagon. A worker there would put them through a special washer that was reserved for the families of administrators. Mondays—at 10:00 a.m.—we girls pulled the wagonload of laundry home, and helped mother hang them on the clothesline.

A garden was necessary for such a large family, and dad dug one by hand. We children planted the vegetables. There was a small orchard in the backyard containing apple, pear, peach, and cherry trees. Dad would put a stepladder up for us to pick the ripe fruit. Our older, taller brothers could use the apple picker—a wire basket on a long pole—to reach the highest apples and peaches. Our cow supplied us with milk and butter. The Chickens gave us eggs and meat; they had a coop near the barn. The cow had to be lead to a pasture—about a mile over a hill—every morning, and then brought back in the evening. We usually found her waiting at the gate. Every Friday, however, it seemed like she would hide somewhere; we had to go looking for her, thereby delaying our fun night. After the cow died, milk was delivered to the house every morning. The bottles were left on the front porch early in the morning. Mother washed the empty bottles and returned them to the porch for the milkman. Mother baked bread every Monday and pies four or five days a week.

On Saturdays, she made a couple of cakes for the family and all of our friends. Her stove was heated by coal, and there was a woodstove in the "out-kitchen"; it was used in the summer so that the house wouldn't overheat. The "out-kitchen" was a large shed, attached to the back of the house; it contained the stove, a box of wood, a table, and a sink. The guys fished and hunted. Mother cooked the fish and canned the venison. Thanksgiving and Christmas turkeys had to be eaten carefully, for fear of biting a piece of shot. I remember helping mother clean the turkey. It would be dipped in hot water, to make it easier to pluck out the feathers. We helped mother in the morning, but after lunch, we could play. We'd give each other rides in our homemade wooden wagon, coast down our hill, and parade up and down the sidewalk, with our dolls in the wagon. We weren't allowed to leave the sidewalk. Sometimes five or six of us would parade, waving our little U.S. flags. We had very few toys, and most of those were homemade, so we made up games.

If we found a dead bird, we'd put it in an old shoebox, dig a hole, and bury it. We'd all say something about the bird as we buried it. Tag was one of our favorite games, and our huge lawn with the barn, coop, sheds, and trees, provided ample hiding places for tag, as well as, hide-and-seek. When we played tag, we picked the largest apple tree and tried to touch it before the leader touched it. We chalked a hopscotch board on the sidewalk as well as a circle for playing marbles. There were many trees to climb. We also sang and played *Here We Go Round the Mulberry Bush*. On hot days, we played in Chatham Run. Once the community pool was built in the late 1920s, we swam there instead. All of us learned to swim in the community pool. On rainy days, we girls would get catalogs and cut some people out of them. Then we'd cut out dresses to put on our new paper dolls. It was always a lot of fun! We kept our cutouts in a box for when we had to play inside. We loved winter because it would snow from November to March. We'd ride down small hills on our wooden sleds, with two or three of us per sled. Sometimes the mill would close one of its roads so children could sled on it. Making snow houses and snowmen were other enjoyable activities.

Only our brothers could ice-skate, because they were bigger and could fasten the skates to their shoes. Our shoes were too small; the skates would fall off when we tried to fasten them. The boys mostly skated at the Woolrich dam. There were bonfires and hotdog roasts on the side of the dam. If the weather was too cold, we all played inside. We occasionally played hide-and-seek in the dark, in our two living rooms. We would also play dominos, checkers, and card games. We made up a game called Crazy House. It involved a blanket and two little chairs, set about a foot apart from one another. One girl would be blindfolded, and then a blanket was laid across the two chairs. Two other girls sat on the blanketed chairs, stretching the blanket taut across the space between the chairs. The blindfolded sister would be placed on the blanket. Then the two seated girls would stand up, sending the blindfolded child to the floor. In another part of the game, the blindfolded child had to crawl around chairs, which were placed randomly around the room. Whether it was winter or summer, inside or out, we never lacked for fun and games! Other forms of entertainment were few. There were no dances or movies, but occasionally special dinners were held at church.

During the holidays, there were special programs at the fellowship hall—a large building in the Woolrich City Park. Fellowship hall was a two-story building with a kitchen and stage on the first floor. A men's organization used the second floor for meetings; the first floor was used for social events such as plays, programs, and suppers. At Christmas there was always a special program put on by the children. Afterwards, Mr. W.F. Rich gave each of us an orange and the mill gave us a box of candy. Family time was on Sunday afternoons. Dad and mom would fill the car with us kids; they removed the two folding seats in the back, and laid a board across the empty space, for more seating. Dad would drive us around the county, and we'd end in Jersey Shore to get ice cream. Mother would have baked a cake earlier. Sometimes we made our own ice cream. In the summer, dad drove us to town.

While he and mother shopped for groceries, we children were each given a nickel, to spend at the five and 10 cent store. That nickel sure gave us a lot of choices!

Sunday mornings were for church and Sunday school. Woolrich only had one church—a Methodist church. Our parents were strict about attendance; if we didn't go on Sunday, then we weren't allowed to play. When one of her children became ill, mother's first recourse was castor oil. She'd send for our grandmother who was a heavyset woman; Grammy Shaffer put us on her lap, put her legs around ours, and held our arms down. Mother then forced our mouths open and poured castor oil down our throats. The oil was followed by a glass of orange juice—to take away the taste—but it didn't really help. If the castor oil didn't work, sometimes the doctor would be called. He drove from Jersey Shore, about eight miles away, to take care of our family. He delivered mother's first eight children at home. Only our youngest brother, Dick, was born in a hospital. Mother's third child—our brother Bob—died of pneumonia at age 19. I was also ill with pneumonia, but obviously, I recovered. My siblings were sent to stay with relatives until I recovered.

Father sent my three surviving brothers to college. They all became surveyors and had good jobs. One of them also had a farm. My oldest sister went to work in the woolen mill right after high school. The rest of us sisters continued our education. Two of us became secretaries, one became a nurse, and I earned a teaching degree. During WWII, two of my brothers and one of my sisters enlisted. My sister became a secretary in the Women's Army Corp, and both of my brothers joined the navy, one as an officer. Teaching was always something I had wanted to do. As a child, I played "teacher" in my room, giving assignments to my "students"; I would write out the work, then check and grade the papers.

I taught sixth grade for 42 years and I loved it. Every day, when my students went outside for recess, I played ball with them. After retiring at age 62, I volunteered at the same school, every day for 28 years. Would I want to change anything in my life? No! We had good times growing up together. We never knew there was a depression or that we were poor; dad worked, we had plenty to eat, and lots of places to play. As an adult, I married my first and only love, and had the job of my dreams. At age 92, the last surviving sibling, I look back over my life with happiness.

Bradford's Three Musketeers
By Patrick Buccolini of Bradford, Pennsylvania
Born 1941

Looking back to the late 40s and early 50s, I stop and think of how simple life was back then. I lived in the small town of Bradford, Pennsylvania, the home of Zippo Manufacturing Company and the township of Foster Brook. In 1930 mom and dad immigrated from Sarano, Italy to Bradford, Pennsylvania where they raised a family of seven—two boys and five girls. Their house was next to the B&O Railroad tracks. They had a fenced in area for their pig, goat, and multiple chickens. Dad always had a big garden. Growing up in Foster Brook was a good thing. I had two good friends, and we were all the same age. Their names were Walt and Duane, but Duane was called Swede. The summers were the best, because we had no school. All we did was kick around and have fun. I remember going to their houses on a nice sunny day and yelling out, "Hey Walt", or "Hey Swede, come out and play!" There were no phone calls, just a walk down the street to their houses and shouting.

We would get together with other neighborhood kids. We all shared a small wooded area where we played softball. We just made it work. We spent many hours there. Then I'd see my mom walking up the street looking for me, with a switch in her hand. It seemed like Walt, Swede, and I were always together; everything we did, we did together.

Bradford's Three Musketeers
Pat, Walt, and "Swede"

132

When I got my first bike, I paid $5.00 for it. We would tear our bikes down and rebuild them. I remember all three of our bikes were painted red, white, and blue. When we wore hats, they were identical. When one of us had foxtails on our handlebars, we all had them! After a while, people started calling us the three musketeers. As we got older, we had a baseball field across from the railroad tracks. The field had a backstop and it was called Kendall Field, after a nearby oil refinery. The play wasn't organized; we just got two teams together and played ball. I remember having a model plane with a gas engine in it. One day, it flew right into the backstop and that was the end of the model plane.   Walt's dad always chewed tobacco. One day, he let us try a chew. To this day, I don't think any of us would chew tobacco. We did get a hold of a pack of cigarettes, but I don't remember paying for them. We got into a ditch that was overgrown with weeds and tall grasses, next to the railroad tracks. We each smoked one. I have never smoked another cigarette since that time. Mrs. Carlson—Swede's mom— always seemed to be baking pie, but I don't recall ever getting any; maybe that is why my favorite dessert is apple pie. As time went by, we had a BB gun, and now I wonder how we survived those years. We would take a shotgun shell, put it in the crotch of a tree, and try to shoot the primer; we never did manage to hit it. Then we took the bbs and the powder out of the shell. We placed the empty shell into a vice, in Walter's garage; we then hit it with a nail and hammer. The primer would ricochet all around the inside of the garage. It wasn't very smart of us, but luckily, we survived it.

One night, we made up a fake skunk, tied a string to it, and dragged it across the road while we hid in the trees. Cars would stop for fear of hitting it. One driver even got out of his car. That's when we ran like heck. It was simple but fun. As we entered our teens, we became anxious to drive a car. We started by driving our family cars up and down our driveways. One day, Walt's parents weren't home, and he was driving in the driveway; he took out the wooden steps at the back of his house. Yes, those were the simple days. We had lots of fun, and fortunately, never got into deep trouble.

Later in life, we all kept in touch. We all got married after high school. Walt married Kay and they had two children. I married Bonnie, my high school sweetheart, and we had two children as well. Swede married Sheila and they had two children as well. Swede passed away at an early age. I think of him often, because I have a picture of the neighborhood's three musketeers. Walt and I run into each other once in a while, and reminisce about the good old days. It was definitely a more simple time.

Stuck in the Elevator at Carrol House
By Jean Shink of Cogan Station, Pennsylvania
Born 1941

When I was young, we were so excited to go to the Keystone Theater in Williamsport to see western movies. We thought Roy Rogers and Gene Autry were great.

There were four department stores: The Carrol House, Sears, Penny's, and Stearns. Some time ago, they all closed up.

When I was in high school, I ran the elevator at the Carrol House. One day the elevator got stuck between floors and the lights went out. I was so glad when it started again. There were two women on it and they were really upset.

I can remember we had a wringer washer and a big tub to rinse the clothes in. We hung them out winter and summer and they really smelled good.

I'll never forget the day I wore a new dress that my mom had made. I was so proud of it. I wasn't looking where I was going and fell in the mud puddle just when the principal drove by. I had to stand in the bathroom next to the radiator to get dry. The kids thought I was funny but I didn't.

We had a garage next to the house. My dad backed a big state body truck into it and knocked it down. The neighbors all thought he was mad.

Life is so different today.

The Dinkey Train
By Donald Speaker of Ridgeway, Pennsylvania
Born 1934

While growing up our family lived in northern Pennsylvania in the little town of Johnsonburg. The "burg" as it was called was also known as "paper city" because of the paper mill, which was the main industry there.

The mill owned and managed a huge wood yard from which the hardwood small logs came from to produce the cellulose fiber for the high quality paper they manufactured.

Since the wood storage yard was about one mile from the actual plant the small wood logs were hauled to the plant in open cars on a narrow gauge railroad and pulled by a small steam-powered locomotive called "the Dinkey Train."

These cars were unloaded at the mill and the "Dinkey" would return to the wood yard to be reloaded. This work was all done by hand for years.

While in the Army stationed in Alaska in the early 50s I received our local "once a week" and once it reported big news. The paper stated that a local resident's auto was struck by the "Dinkey" at the one street crossing.

My fellow GIs read this and several laughed and stated, "They can't even spell donkey right," and wondered why there were donkeys running loose in our little town.

I'll never forget that funny experience of trying to explain what a "Dinkey" was.

The Dinkey Train is now long ago past history but it will always be a hometown memory from my "Good Old Growing-Up Days."

A Real American Hero
By Shirley A. Carey of Morris Run,
Pennsylvania
Born 1936

My fondest memories include when I was 11 years old. My parents owned a large pond on their property in the middle of our town. People were warned not to go near there nor go swimming in the pond. One hot summer day a group of people decided to go swimming.

There were two girls in an inner tube and neither one could swim. They floated out to the deepest part of the pond, which was over 12 feet deep. The one girl lost the tube and got frantic and grabbed the other girl. Both went under.

They were going down for the third time when my brother-in-law came along. He saw what was going on and jumped in and brought both girls up at the same time. He was home on a weekend pass from the Air Force. If it wasn't for his being there and quick action these girls wouldn't have survived.

If you go swimming and don't know how to swim stay off inner tubes as they're dangerous and stay out of water 'till you have someone around you that can swim or there's a lifeguard!

My brother-in-law was in the German war. He dropped bombs from planes. He brought many gifts home to my sister, made from parts of planes, like necklaces, bracelets, and earrings. One thing in particular he brought home was a beautiful picture frame with a large bullet shell on each side. After the war was over, he married my sister. They grew up as childhood sweethearts.

In 1972, they lost everything they owned to a flood. They had just enough time to get themselves out. This took a toll on their lives to relocate to another town. They ended up divorcing.

My brother-in-law is now deceased. To me he is an American hero. These girls wouldn't have survived if it weren't for him. He lost his shoes and wallet in the pond.

Thank God for this wonderful ending. Today I am 75 years old and still can see these two girls walking by my parents' house with their lips purple. I think of this often.

Riding Bikes into the Quarry Swimhole
By John H. Phillips of Hughesville,
Pennsylvania
Born 1946

There are a few things I remember from my childhood.

Castor oil and Father John's, every day I had to take a tablespoon of each one. One at night and one in the morning. "YUK." Father John's was the better tasting of the two though. Saturday night baths. We had an old copper tub and Mom filled it up with warm water and that was our bath in the winter. The creek and soap was the summer baths then.

This Mom told me: She used to make me shirts out of feedbags. I guess it had to be true cause Gram agreed with her.

My chores were to keep the woodpile back of the stove stocked and take ashes out. I remember Mom talking on the old party lines to the ladies on the line at the same time and griping about some they didn't want to hear what was said.

I remember the Saturday matinees at the Capitol Theater. I think it was a dime to get in and a nickel for popcorn. Try that now. We moved to Miami when I was about 12 years old. And after school, a few of us would go to a rock quarry. Maul and Oolite was the name of the company that dug those quarries and left large holes that filled up with water. They had about 6 feet or higher banks that we would ride our bikes off into the water then drag the bikes back up and swim for a while. Well the "very last time" we rode our bikes off the banks we were side by side as usual peddling as fast as we could to be the first to hit the water when there was about maybe 10 or so snakes all right off the bank in the water swimming. Too late to stop. I know we were screaming and hit the water scared stiff. You never saw boys move so fast as we did getting up that bank. By the time we all got up the snakes were gone and it took us an hour or so to be brave enough to retrieve our bikes. We kept swimming in those holes but never rode a bike in them again.

Mischief, well there was an incident at Roosevelt back in the early 60s that three of us did that is better left alone. Let's just say that the whole school was brought to the auditorium.

Judy's dad, Harold Rupert, her mom, Minnie May, her sister, Elizabeth "Lib", and their dog, Lassie

the radio.

In the winter, if it wasn't too cold we went ice-skating on the old pond. One time my sister and my aunt fell in when the ice broke. I never learned to skate on skates but I had fun anyway. We rode bikes and played hide-and-seek.

Those were the days. We didn't have or need the toys that kids have today to be happy. We made our own fun. My grandfather

Going to My Grandfather's House
By Judy M. Cain of Beech Creek,
Pennsylvania
Born 1943

When I was growing up, we always went to my grandfather's for Sunday lunch. We went every Sunday, rain or shine, winter and summer. They always had a big meal with lots of home-baked items. The best was my aunt's home-baked bread. I can still sometimes dream about its taste and smell.

On summer days, we would head to the creek to swim until almost dark. They then would call us in. We would then eat a small supper and dessert and then we were allowed to play near the house until time to go home. My grandfather was the first in my family to get a black and white TV set. It was a real treat to watch the programs that we used to hear on

Judy Rupert Cain age 6 or 7 with her pet chicken

Grandpa Joshua Rupert and Aunt Edna Rupert

passed away in 1963, and then my aunt sold the house. It's all gone now but the memories of all the fun we had. I have lived in Beech Creek all my life except for a couple of years. My growing up years were happy years I treasure forever.

A Rowboat Trip Down the Susquehanna River
By Verna Paulhamus of Williamsport, Pennsylvania
Born 1923

Starting during the 30s my father along with my help would build flat bottom boats for cabin owners up the Loyalsuck Valley and in the Williamsport area and when the snow melted in around May we (my dad and I) would pack our overnight supplies and when Friday classes were over we would start our yearly (sometimes more than one trip in a year) adventure. But one in particular I will never forget.

Well, we were on our way Friday p.m. after floating along shore a couple of miles. I always sat in the bow of the boat. As usual, I always had my eye peeled for fish or whatever took my eye. This time I spotted something that looked like a man's plaid shirt. I called my dad to pull into shore and after poking at the object, we were sure it was a body.

We tied the boat to a tree and went up the bank to a farm and phoned the city police. They along with the page undertaker, horse-drawn hearse, and couple of planks got into the water and got the body on a plank under the water. We were lifting it out of the water and the air hit the face and head. I couldn't believe my eyes, the man's skin seemed

to disappear and all that was left was his eyebrows and hair. A sight I'll never forget. The undertaker went through his pockets and found his wallet. The man worked in the woods logging in Clearfield, PA, about 100 miles to the north and disappeared into the water before we found him in the spring.

After things quieted down and they took the body to their business, we pushed off a half mile down river and camped on Canfield's Island for the night. The island was widely known for its Indian artifacts and many people dig for these things. Next morning at sunrise we were up and going camping just north of Harrisburg, which was our destination tomorrow. Well, our last day of leisurely floating down the river but something new happens every day.

We pushed into the island at Harrisburg where people keep boats for their own use. Well, since we were early no one greeted us but a cute little nine year old boy. He was happy to see us and when my dad asked him if he knew anyone who might want to buy a brand new rowboat, the little guy popped up and told my dad he would like to have a boat. Dad asked him if his dad would let him have one, BOY!! He took off to bring his dad. Of course, his dad didn't know what was going on, But Dad explained that when we took these river trips we always got rid of the boat and we usually took the train home or my mother came for us in the car.

The boy's dad asked his son where he would get the money and would he take care of it. To both questions "Oh, Yes!" but he said, "Dad, all I have is my Boy Scout knife." My dad said, "Son, let me see that knife." He said, "Son, the boat is yours."

A great end of a great interesting trip. One last thing, I was in my teens at the time and to this day, I still have that knife. And I am now 88 years old.

I Guess You Don't Fool the Teachers
By Linford Frey, Jr. of Muncy, Pennsylvania
Born 1932

Back in the days when we had outhouses and chamber pots, each bedroom had a chamber pot under the bed. We called them thunder mugs (for obvious reasons).

Saturday night when we were small if our

136

parents went out they would get us soft drinks and potato chips and our aunt would babysit. The big thing was we would listen to the Hit Parade. I think that was what it was called.

Back in those days my parents said if you get a spanking in school when you get home you will get another one (today the parents would sue the teacher).

During WWII, most things were rationed and everybody had what was called a Victory Garden. Most people raised their own vegetables. My mother would take part of our sugar ration every month and put it in a lard can and keep it in the attic until spring so she would have sugar for canning.

When I was young, every Monday was washday and Monday after school, my job was to empty the wringer washer and carry the water out to the garden. Also, there were all kinds of stories about people getting their fingers or even their arms in the wringer.

Every Saturday afternoon our theater had a matinee, the price 15 cents. The man who owned the theater had a box with compartments and each compartment had an envelope with a coin in it. As you entered the theater, you could choose an envelope and you could get a penny or any coin up to a dollar. If you won the dollar, he would announce you as the winner before the show (this was a big deal).

During the 30s and 40s, almost nobody had any money. If you were lucky, in the spring you would get a pair of sneakers and by the end of the summer, you would have to put tire tape (we called it) on them to hold them together. If somebody was lucky enough to get a baseball for Christmas, we would play with it until we knocked the cover off and then wrapped it with tire tape. After school, every day we would play whatever sport was in season. Our obesity rate was very low.

When I was in high school one afternoon, my friend and I hooked school and went hunting. The next morning we went into the school office and said we were ill yesterday. The secretary gave us a blue slip, which told our homeroom teacher we were ill. When we handed them to our teacher, he looked at my friend who got hit in the eye with a branch while hunting and had a bloodshot eye, and said, "What's the matter Burkholder, powder burns?" (I guess you don't fool the teachers).

Our refrigerator was an icebox on the back porch. We had a hole drilled in the floor and

Linford Frey, Jr. in 1935

had a hose fastened to the ice box to drain the melted ice. On hot summer days, we would look forward to see the ice delivery truck so we could get a piece of ice to suck on. We would get a 10-pound piece of ice for the icebox.

We would get 2 quarts of milk delivered every other day. In those days, milk was pasteurized and the cream would come to the top in the bottle. My mother would take half the cream from each bottle and make whipped cream to put on her homemade gingerbread.

Great Aunt Winnie
By Bob Johnston of Lutherville, Maryland
Born 1936

If they ever get around to drawing up a job description for great aunts, I have many suggestions. Winnie was as ideal a great aunt as any niece or nephew could ever hope for. Her unique gift to those she touched was to make each person feel very special. This was particularly so with her flock of great-nieces and nephews. My cousin, Rosie, often relates how she was Winnie's favorite. Her sister, Kathy, argues that she was definitely Winnie's favorite, and so on down the family line. Incidentally, I *know* that I was Winnie's favorite. How she pulled this off, how she truly loved and expressed love to so many people, is the fascinating story of Winnie I. Johnston.

Winnie lived her whole life in Bradford, Pennsylvania, where just about the entire population of 19,746 people knew her. Her brother—my grandfather—Bobo started a ladies department store in the early 1900s that thrived during the oil boom days. Winnie worked fulltime in his store as a saleslady and was quite successful. She lived with and cared for her mother, until grandma's death in the early 1940s; thereafter, she lived alone. Winnie filled her rich and active life with work, church, many friends, and a large extended family. The latter centered primarily on Bubo's family, consisting of his four children and then their families; this is where I came in, among 11 nieces and nephews. When I think about Winnie, I am flooded, mainly with the memory of her remarkably positive spirit; a combination of joie de vivre, vitality, selfless giving, and her extraordinary capacity to tap into her fun loving inner child. Memories of events that demonstrated her spirit trickle back to me in two streams: The times that I spent with Winnie alone and the times that I shared Winnie with a group of close-knit cousins. My affair with Winnie spanned approximately a quarter of a century and encompassed my entire childhood. My earliest recollection of her is stimulated by an often-seen photograph of Winnie and me. I was bedecked in a gray flannel blazer and short pants. Winnie wore her Easter finery. Her shiny white hair peaked out of a large plumed Easter hat. The most striking feature of the photo is her face. I don't think it aged at all during the subsequent years that were her sixth and seventh decades. Winnie's face can most aptly be described as full, in every sense of the word. Her face was full of life, full of sparkle, and full of vitality. It was one of those faces that didn't know how to scowl. It was poised to smile at the slightest provocation. It had a certain Santa Claus ambience to it, but it was totally devoid of any coarseness. Ample fat stores highlighted her rosy cheeks. There was sufficient relaxation of the muscle tone around her eyes and wide lips, to invoke a sense of softness, without the slightest suggestion of droopiness. Winnie didn't fuss much about her face. She didn't have to. She did pinch rouge onto her cheeks and run a powder puff briskly over her face, which often would leave small clumps of powder on her nose or ears; details didn't really matter with Winnie.

Her real facial beauty came from the fact that, all of her features harmoniously meshed in an effortless manner, to fold into a large smile and a hearty laugh. That was Winnie's trademark and part of her appealing beauty that never changed. In that photo, I was cradling a large loaf of Lorenz's bread under my right arm. It had a tunnel burrowed through its center; I had devoured the soft, succulent, core of the loaf, much to my total and absolute pleasure; no doubt, to Winnie's delight as well. That's the way I remember it starting with Winnie and me. We peaked early, and it only got better from that point. During my early grade school years, I frequently stopped at the store on Main Street to catch a ride home with my father. Immediately upon entering, I would be greeted by Winnie. She was always characteristically standing behind the jewelry counter, with its glass-enclosed shelves of beads, earrings, necklaces, etc. No matter how busy she was, she would always make a great fuss and greet me with cheery enthusiasm, "Well now, look who's here!" It was as if she hadn't seen me for many weeks. There was nothing subtle about Winnie as she went about her activities in that store.

She was hearty and healthy. Her medium sized frame handled the stress of being on her feet all day, and her adequate stores of fat protected her from the ravages of the bitter cold winters. She usually dressed in something bright, most notably pink, with a colorful accessory or two; a necklace of big beads, a fancy colorful pin, a lacey neckerchief and some dangly earrings; the larger the better. Her perfume was fresh and sweet; it made me think of Juicy Fruit gum. Her voice, somewhat uncontrolled, carried a great distance throughout the store. The intermittent bursts of reverberating, hearty laughter became part of the territory. No one seemed to mind at all. It was Winnie's way, and that's the way the Johnston Store was; so be it. She invariably chatted with me and showed me the new arrivals in the jewelry line. More often than not, she took a break and bought me ice cream or some other suitable treat. On special occasions, I escorted her home, a two mile walk that wound through most of the downtown business district. We took frequent pleasure stops along the way.

First, we would go to Hatch's Emporium.

There were endless tables of novelties, toys, tricks, and a gigantic rack of comic books. "Hi Hatchy", she would say. "Hi Win", he would respond, "Got your boyfriend along with you today, huh?" Lots of laughing and chattering would go on while I was looking for my treat among the many treasures. I never even suspected that the balding, grey haired, somewhat overweight, Mr. Hatch could have been a romantic interest of Winnie's. He seemed so much older than she did. With my new edition of Captain Marvel, we soon ambled on, covering the three blocks to the head of Main Street. We chatted amiably, while we window-shopped. We were frequently interrupted by many of Winnie's friends though. She greeted them all enthusiastically and introduced me with some pride. "Well now, is that Bob's boy", they would ask, "Hasn't he grown!" "Look at all those curls, would you?" "You two make a handsome couple." Winnie would break into gales of laughter; I always wanted to move along. We soon reached Allegretta's Candy and Ice Cream Parlor. It was quite dark inside for an ice cream shop, but Winnie brightened it.

Joe appeared from behind the marble-top counter and without a word, he poured two large lemon blends. Winnie mused, "Ah, that's very good Joe. You sure pour a great drink. Uh, huh, that's right, you sure do." I inspected the display of chocolates. Joe was no dummy. He had Clark bars, Milky Ways, and other candy bars without their wrappers and charged five cents more for each one. Winnie didn't even seem to care. We soon were on our way and took a left on Washington Street, where the Army-Navy Store loomed large. It was jam packed with all kinds of military surplus items that kept my eyelids at full alert. The sleepy proprietor awoke fully when Winnie walked in; they had been grade school friends. He went into his backroom cache and returned with an astonishing assortment of treasures: a German armband, a Purple Heart medal, a shiny eagle insignia, and others. Winnie placed my selection in my sweaty little palm, and we were off on the final leg of our journey, well fed and well satisfied.

Sometime around third grade, Winnie and I went into business together. She was the supplier, and I was the salesman. From the store's supply of merchandise, she smuggled pins, beads, buttons, bolts of ribbon and lace, a few hats and numerous other excess articles, which I took home and displayed on my bookshelves. My parents' bargain-hunting dinner guests then received a gracious personal invitation to my store after their coffee. The prices were right, and I made 100% profit. My supplier required no cut of my profits and became a prized customer upon her visits to our home. My father—who was the store bookkeeper and accountant—initially got a kick out of the arrangement, but later appeared somewhat shocked at the quantity and quality of my merchandise. I think Winnie received a few gentle suggestions to discontinue our partnership, but she remained true to our arrangement. It was one of my most successful financial endeavors ever.

Throughout my school years, our ventures together continued; changing only in nature but not in quality. I lived some distance from town, so I occasionally spent a night at Winnie's, when transportation from a high school dance was lacking. No matter what time I got there, Winnie always waited for me. If I was obviously tired from the late hour, she limited the chatter and directed me to my quarters. On these occasions, she moved into the guest room and gave me her upstairs front bedroom. It housed an enormous brass bed with a two foot pile of down comforters, four fluffy down pillows, clean sheets, three of the latest life magazines, a box of Ritz crackers, and the piece de resistance: an entire quart of Canada Dry Ginger Ale! It was all just for me. I thought I had died and gone to heaven.

It seems like we always went to Winnie's for Sunday "Chickie", as she called it. There was a seven or eight year span of Sundays—during my grade school and early high school days—that featured Winnie treating all of her great nieces and nephews to a sumptuous chicken feast. Adults weren't necessary; this was the kids' day. During those years, there were 11 cousins that attended the festivities at one time or another. There was a hardcore nucleus of about six cousins, separated in age, at most, by five years. They attended regularly for the entire duration of Winnie's feasts. I was the oldest of the clique, having edged out Rosie by four days. Winnie's Sunday dinners were something very special. There were other family gatherings for Christmas, Thanksgiving, and Easter at my grandparent's—Minga and Bobo—house. Those dinners were delicious and the company was fun, but they just weren't Winnie dinners. Going to Winnie's house was like going to a three-ring circus for the first time. Going to Minga and Bobo's was like sitting through Fantasia for the second time; it was enjoyable, but lacking in certain elements of warmth and excitement.

Winnie tolerated her festivals well. I'm not so sure, how the house fared though. It certainly was a lively house, with Winnie and all the rest of us kids storming through it every Sunday. When I see that house now, it looks sleepy and somber, its yellow exterior appearing shades darker than ever before. We got to know each nook and cranny of that house. From the unfinished mud flooring in the basement—where we once thought Winnie had been done in and buried by the visiting "Uncle Frank"—to the magical attic, full of intrigue and undiscovered treasures. Even the small, front yard attested to Winnie's vitality. Her crocuses were the talk of the town each spring, as they once again—weeks ahead of any others—pushed through the seven months' worth of snow that shrouded them. One of the few times that Winnie ever got mad was when someone stepped on her beloved crocuses. We often admired them from the front porch, while rocking hypnotically in one of the two wicker chairs or the long swing.

Playing Army and Being a Boy
By J. Milton Rogers of Williamsport, Pennsylvania
Born 1938

My name is John Milton Rogers, most commonly known as Milt. I was born at 7:25 a.m. on December 12, 1938, at 1026 Meade Street, Williamsport, Pennsylvania. My parent's names were Harry L. and Catherine J. Dincher Rogers. At a very early age, I moved with my parents into my grandparent's house, on 1159 Almond Street. We then moved to 329 Hughes Street, which is currently the entrance to Bishop Neuman's auditorium. When I was in sixth grade, we moved back to my grandparent's house where my sister lives to this day. I attended St. Boniface School, St. Mary's School, and St. Boniface Church. I grew up in East End, therefore my memories are primarily of that area, particularly, Dutch Hill. Some of my early childhood memories were rather unpleasant. I broke my left elbow

when I was eight years old, and it has been a lifelong injury.

Growing up in the 50s was wonderful. My brother Steve and I, went to Wilson's and Lenny's Army Surplus Store with our friends. We bought haversacks, pistol belts, machetes, canteens, and ammo belts. We played army a lot. I still have some of the things we bought hanging in my basement. It's ironic after playing army so much, that I would end up joining The United States Naval Reserve. I served two years as a radio operator on the destroyer, U.S.S. Noa. I have many fond memories of the skating pond at the Penn Street armory. I was not a very accomplished skater, but I could stand up and go forward. The only ice skates I ever owned were old, oversized, hockey skates given to me by a neighbor. I still had a lot of fun standing by the burning barrel to keep warm.

I smoked cigarettes and drank wine with my brother and friends. It caused more than a little consternation for my parents. After I grew up, my father told me, "I knew what you were doing, but I didn't know when, because I did the same thing as a kid." It was all a part of growing up, I guess. We kept things hidden in Grampian Hills, which made for many interesting hikes. As a child, I remember our parents taking the seven of us to Mayor Williamson's "Community Sings". It was hosted at the band shell in Brandon Park. We also spent many days playing in that park. We would coast wagons, tricycles, scooters, or anything with wheels down the sloping sidewalks. I didn't realize then, that someday I would be a participant in Mayor Campana's "Community Sings"; I have been one for the past two years. I had one experience that I don't remember telling my parents about. I climbed up the side of the quarry on Freedom Road, because I was trying to show off to a girlfriend. A couple of friends scaled it with me. As we got about halfway up, we decided we probably weren't going to make it to the top and needed to go back down. Seeing that it was impossible to go back down, we somehow made it to the top without a rescue squad. I counted my blessings that day.

Compared to modern times those days were more relaxed, even though we had The Korean War, we didn't have the violence and drug issues that are prevalent today. I took many hikes up Almond Street to Grampian Hills with a .22 caliber rifle hanging on my shoulder, a belt full of ammunition, and a bunch of cans to shoot. When I became 17, I also carried a pistol to shoot the cans. I had a permit for it, but I think that nowadays this would be a questionable behavior. Many days, we played sandlot football on the Sheridan School grounds, part of which is now occupied by buildings. It was on these school grounds, that I broke my left arm again, but this time it happened in a bicycle wreck. I had to spend another six weeks in a cast. There was an old, mysterious, abandoned, and haunted slaughterhouse on Almond Street; we somehow, survived the exploration of it.

We knew we heard the footsteps of invisible creatures, in the weeds, behind the slaughterhouse. They were probably just pheasants or opossums though. My friend Jack Love lived on Sheridan Street; we would go over to Nippenose Valley where I now reside and then out to Lochabar on our bicycles. We would stay a few days in a little red hut, along the run that branched off from Antes Creek. I was only 13 or 14, and Jack was probably 15. The property was a chicken farm owned by his Aunt Cleo Barclay. We had our clothes and food packed on our bicycles. We pushed our bikes up and over the mountain. These were the days before high-speed bicycles.

I have multitudes of memories that other people probably share with me; experiences of our childhoods. I feel fortunate. So far, I have lived to be 73, I have a wonderful wife, I'm retired in good health, I have four great children and four lovely grandchildren, and I have been blessed with the gift of music. I played in bands: "The Continentals" and "Airborne"; I am still musically active. I thank our great God for his many blessings, and our savior Jesus Christ for his endless mercy.

Christmas Anticipation
By Ruth Berry of Loganton, Pennsylvania
Born 1944

Christmas in the 50s, was always a time that our farm family of eight enjoyed. My older sister, Louise, decorated each present creatively. Every year, mother would say, "The gifts are too pretty to open." On Christmas morning, dad and mom insisted that we eat a hearty breakfast. We rushed through the meal, because dishes had to be washed before we

Christmas at the Smith Farmhouse

could open presents. Then and only then, did dad open the living room door. There we saw the tree, dressed in all its glory and surrounded by gifts. One by one, the gifts were opened and displayed. The anticipation alone was worth the wait!

Dancing with Vicki
By Darlene Dutton of Philipsburg,
Pennsylvania
Born 1952

I grew up in Philipsburg in the 50s. At the time, the coalmines were where most of the Philipsburg men worked. When they came home from work all you could see was the whites of their eyes; they were so black from the coal. Of course, much later on in life, they developed black lung from the fine coal dust. Fridays and Saturdays were the big nights in Philipsburg. Everyone you knew was shopping. I remember walking past the Western Auto store and there was a wonderful smell that seemed to be all over the town. We went a little ways further, past Brown's Boot Shop, where most people bought their

141

shoes and boots. I remember when you went inside of Brown's there was always someone to check your shoe size. You would put your foot on a metal pad and the person would move a metal slide and read you your shoe size. Nowadays, you have to try on your own shoes, maybe 10 pairs, before you find the one or two that fit right.

Next to Brown's Boot Shop was the bakery. We stopped in the bakery and then went down the street, and the pleasant smell kept getting stronger. One of the stores, called The Peanut Shop, was roasting peanuts on the sidewalk. They had a peanut roaster with a handle on the side, which was used to turn the peanuts. People just had to stop to get a bag of warm roasted peanuts. A large bag cost maybe $0.10 and was big enough for at least four people. Next was the Ibberson's Drug Store; then we crossed the street and the Nickel and Dime Store was on the corner. There was two-way traffic on Front Street at that time. I didn't care much when they changed it to a one-way with two lanes. I remember the Grant's Department Store. It had two floors and sold everything. At Easter, you could go to Grant's and see chicken eggs in the back of the store under warm lights. You could dye them different colors: pink, blue, purple, and yellow. They also had turtles, very small turtles.

There was Ziff's Store, a little more expensive, but they sold brand name clothes and you could join their club. They sold real silk stockings, not nylon ones. Then there was Cowdricks Drug Store; they had a snack bar, pharmacy, and anything else you could want. You could have a sandwich and coffee while you waited on your medication, or just for the fun of it, a chocolate, malted milkshake or coke. You could get anything you wanted. It was always packed for breakfast. I remember a little woman with short hair and glasses that took your order. She was maybe five feet tall, but she sure was a good and friendly waitress. I never knew her name. I was only four years old. Later, when I was 13, she still worked there. Behind Cowdricks was a lot with houses lined up in rows; it was on Second Street. Chuckie Dixon lived there with his mom. Everyone liked Chuckie, because he was Philipsburg's happy person. He was short, heavyset, and wore thick glasses.

At the end of the road was the A&R Department Store. It was like a Macy's,

expensive but beautiful clothing. It sold perfume such as Chanel No. 5 and Coty makeup powder. The Passmore Hotel was across the street from the A&R. When you entered the hotel, you were in a beautiful lobby and off to your left there was a restaurant. There was a bar to your right, and the stairs to the rooms were straight ahead of you. If you just wanted to have a drink, there was a side door that took you out onto a patio; I think it overlooked Spruce Street. The Philips Hotel was on Presqueisle Street. I always called it Main Street, because you took a left from Front Street to get to it. I never got a chance to go in that hotel, but I saw pictures and it looked fabulous. Across from the Philips was a soda shop. My brother's girlfriend took my sister and me in there, because we were pretty young.

It was packed with teenagers. There was a jukebox playing, a long bar, and red barstools that swiveled. The teenage girls were dancing with their boyfriends. The store sold cherry and chocolate flavored cokes and milkshakes. I loved watching people and I still do. The boys had Elvis hairstyles, with a small patch of hair over their foreheads and a D.A. in the back. It was called a D.A., because it looked like a duck's ass. Main Street was packed with modified cars, 1967 GTOs, with the tops down, and boys yelling at the girls. The girls wore hip huggers, which are now called low riders. Shirts were called body suits. You would put one on, and it snapped together between your legs, over your panties; that way, you didn't have to keep tucking your shirt in. We had to wear dresses until about 1965 or 66; the girls at the Sixth Street Junior High School went on strike. They had a sit-down about wearing pants to school. The girls that had to walk were freezing on the way to school. We didn't have pantyhose; we had to wear a garter belt and four stretch straps with clips—two on the back and two on the front.

Dianne Ross, The Monkeys, and Davy Jones were big hits; they were always on the teen magazines. Elvis was too, of course. The twist was popular; everyone did the twist. My youngest brother came home from a school dance and showed me how to do the twist. When I started seventh grade, my brother Leonard, was in ninth grade. People always asked us if we were twins. They wanted to know why I wasn't in the same grade if we were twins. We used to call our school principal, Muddy Lucas. I still can't remember his first name, because the teachers required us to call him Mr. Lucas. Whenever the guys at school were pissed off at each other they would use their fists to solve their problems. They would meet up at the school and end up with black eyes, busted lips, and bleeding knuckles; after the fight, they were friends again. My brother's school picture was nice, but it could have been better without the black eye. We girls just pulled hair.

When I was in first grade, my school was North Lincoln Hill. I only had to walk a block to school. My teacher's name was Mrs. Warring. One day, we had a test on a book titled *Run Dick Run*. I was wearing a red velvet dress with ruffles on the back. I thought the test went well, but Mrs. Warring was mad because I missed one question. The question was, "What did Susan play with?" The answer choices were a ball, a bunny, or a doll. I knew the answer, but for some reason I circled a ball and got it wrong she had played with a bunny. Mrs. Warring pulled me out from my desk, took me over to the stool, pulled my red velvet dress and slip up, and gave me the spanking of my life. It took me 23 years before I was comfortable touching anything that even felt like velvet. I hated velvet, all because of my first grade teacher. The school had a man to fire the furnace and fill it with coal. One night he had the furnace very hot and it caught the school on fire; it burnt to the ground.

Ponytails were very popular with the girls and so were poodle skirts. I loved the poodle skirts, because they made you look awesome when you danced. My sister and I loved to dance, because on Saturday mornings American Bandstand was on, with Dick Clark as the host. The teenagers would wait for hours outside of the studio to see if they could get on the show. Vicki and I watched them dance, so we learned to dance just like the kids on television. My mother heard of a dance contest in Chester Hill and she entered us in it; we were the only preteens. We were the best dancers though, and won a shiny silver dollar for first place. Anytime afterwards, if our mother knew about dances she entered us in them. We didn't win the first contest just because we were younger; it really was because we were good. As we got older, there were street dances on Main Street. When we got up enough nerve, we danced the night away. Most of the teenagers would stop dancing to watch Vicki and I dance.

Our outhouse was built at the end of the yard, because the smell was so bad in the summer. Try walking through snow just to go pee. There was a board across the inside of the outhouse, with two holes cut into it for sitting. If you looked down the holes, you could see maybe 30 feet into the ground. I'm not sure how far it was, but if you fell in, you couldn't climb out. I don't remember ever having toilet paper. If you were a toddler in a big family, at night you would use a chamber pot inside the house. Can you imagine running to the outhouse at 2:00 a.m. because one of your kids had to pee? You would be up all night, running kids to the outhouse. Everyone had clotheslines attached to metal poles for drying their clothes. My grandson asked me once, "Grandma why are the clothes hanging outside?" He didn't know what a clothesline was for, because his mother uses a dryer. We used to have a wringer washer. You filled it with water from your sink and there was a rinse tub behind the washer. If you wanted your whites, whiter, then you had a second tub with (Blue La France) in the water. It turned the water blue. One day my mother was out hanging clothes so I thought I would rinse the other clothes for her and put them through the wringer.

The wringer was rolling and it clamped so tightly that the clothes came out flat. The socks were rolling in great but I didn't let go of them in time and my hand got caught in the wringers. It rolled my hand through and then my arm, almost up to my elbow. My mother heard me screaming for help, and she got there just in time; otherwise, my elbow would've been crushed. On the side of the wringer rollers was a clamp and she popped it off, so that the rollers could come apart enough for me to get my arm out. I couldn't believe the pressure that the rollers had, on that washer. I never helped again.

If you ever lived in Curtis Park then you were wealthy; people with a lot of money, beautiful homes, and cars. I heard about 20 years ago—and again more recently—that no black Americans are allowed to live or buy a home in Curtis Park. I hear that it is still on the books that way, and thought people should know, because that just isn't right. I wish a family or a few families, would buy all of Curtis Park, and turn it into a real community; not the one they want you to think they are right now. I hold onto my pleasant memories of dancing with Vicki and spending Fridays and Saturdays on the town.

Virginia and her younger brother, Ron in 1942

Great-Aunt Maggie
By Marybeth Carpenter of Cogan Station, Pennsylvania
Born 1954

My Father's aunt, Maggie Jones, was born in England. It was said that she suffered from what they called, "milk leg" and the doctors in England advised her family to come to the United States. They felt the weather in the United States would be better for her condition. They settled in Gearhartville, Pennsylvania. Maggie's Father owned the general store and post office in Gearhartville. Maggie's one leg was so much shorter than the other that she had to wear a special shoe with a seven-inch cork sole to allow her to walk evenly. Her husband was a mine inspector. One day, just as he and another man were going into the mines, there was an explosion. Maggie's husband was killed instantly while the man entering the mine just behind him only singed his beard. Maggie was left alone to raise their children. In those days, there were not many opportunities for women. Many of the coal miners could not read or write, since Maggie was able to read and write; the miners would go to her to order items from catalogues for them. They would pay Maggie to place the orders and help them with any correspondence. Eventually Maggie became the postmaster. Maggie was also quite a seamstress. She made and sold beautiful quilts to earn money to support herself and her children. We are fortunate enough to have inherited one of Maggie's quilts that she had given to another of my Father's aunts. It is a lone star design in red, white, and blue patches.

A Busy Farm Life
By Virginia M. Houseknecht of Trout Run, Pennsylvania
Born 1932

I was born on June 20, 1932 in a farmhouse on Bush Hill. I was the ninth of eleven children, five girls and six boys, born to Harry and Florence Freezer. The nearest town was the small village of Warrensville, Pennsylvania that was about a mile away.

My earliest memory is the 1936 flood in Williamsport, Pennsylvania. Dad took the older boys in to help get our neighbor's aunt out of her flooded home.

Most of the months, September to the end of April, we spent our days going to a one room school. Our teacher not only taught about thirty pupils eight different subjects, but also was responsible for keeping the fire going in the furnace, which sat in the back of the room. She arrived about seven o'clock in order to get it warm when school took in at nine o'clock. We children took turns carrying drinking water from a private home next door. Having eight grades in one room was a great advantage as the younger ones would listen and learn from the older children.

Our summer months were spent working on the farm. Dad raised thousands of chickens each year, getting them as peeps, and when they were big enough separating the roosters to sell them to a local grocery store. The hens were used to produce eggs, which were also sold to the same grocery store. We weighed each egg to determine size like small, medium, or large.

We raised corn, wheat, oats, and hay. No chemicals were used so we had to pull weeds by hand out of the rows and rows of corn. We also planted pumpkins between the stocks of corn. Wheat and oats were cut with a binder, shocked, and later hauled into the barn to wait

144

until a neighbor with a thrashing machine came, as we couldn't afford one. Dad also raised potatoes. We were paid one penny per hundred for picking potato bugs off the plants by knocking them into a can of kerosene. Yes, we had to count every one of those bugs. A penny was worth a lot more in those days.

We carried our drinking water from a spring about a fourth of a mile away. We had a dug well, but it wasn't good for drinking.

Making hay was a lot of work; mow it down, when it dried, rake it up, pile it in piles called doodling, fork it onto a wagon pulled by two horses, take it to the barn, and using a hayfork and a horse pull the hay up into the haymow. I usually got to lead the horse to pull the hay into the mow.

For several years, Dad raised strawberries and I was told more than once how my Mother picked strawberries the day I was born. My

Virginia's brothers Harry, Howard, Carl, Frank, and Grant in 1934

Mother was special with the patience of Job, hardworking, and a great love for the Lord and her family.

Saturday nights were special. Dad would go to Kurtz's a small general store in Warrensville, and get pints of ice cream. The younger ones, my brother, sister, and I, would get half pints. The older ones got a whole pint, eating them out of the cardboard carton.

I hope this little story doesn't give anyone the wrong idea. My childhood was some of the best years of my life. I was never bored; none of us ever got into serious trouble. Five

Mom, Dad, Rachel, Esther, Margaret, Harry, Howdy, Carl, Frank, Grant, Virginia, Ronald, and Ellen in 1961

of my brothers served in the military.

I thank God every day for the life and the family He gave me.

The Icebox
By Lois E. Romanak of Renovo, Pennsylvania
Born 1921

An icebox was an important piece of furniture for most families. It stood about five feet high with two compartments. The top portion had a hinged lid that lifted up and was insulated to keep the ice from melting too quickly. It had a little cup hung on the side to hold the money for the cost of the day's delivery. The residents had a foot square card with numbers on it to indicate what size block of ice they wanted which was displayed in their window.

The bottom portion of the icebox was also insulated and was used for keeping food cold. Such food was generally eggs, milk, bacon, fresh fruits, and vegetables. There was a tube down the back of the icebox that carried away the melted ice water. Some people had a hole in the back porch floor to drain the water because that is where the icebox would sit. If not that, a pan was underneath to catch the water and had to be emptied frequently.

In my days, the iceman would come into the area with his horse and wagon, park at the curb, check the window cards, and start sawing. After cutting a block, he would grab it with his ice tongs and take it to the rear of a resident's house. When the children of the neighborhood knew he was there, they gathered around to scoop up the ice chips made by the saw. As long as they didn't get in his way, he didn't mind. It was a real treat on a hot day and none ever got sick from dirty hands.

It was a far cry from refrigeration, as we know it today.

A 1940s Christmas
By Pete Bennett of Stevensville, Ontario
Born in 1939

Usually it's what's under the tree on Christmas morning that stays with us in the form of memories as the years go by. Not so for me though. It was what was under the tree on Christmas Eve, that I recall.

It was December 24, 1948, when I was just 9 years old, that I got my electric train. It was an American Flyer made by the A. C. Gilbert Company, it smoked and made the choo choo sound. I also recall getting my first bicycle around that same period of time, maybe 1946. The bike was a Schwinn, was blue and had one of those fancy horns that were mounted between the crossbars. Also, a bell adorned the handlebars and a light was mounted on the front fender.

Why December 24th you might ask. Well, at our house, it was a family tradition to open our gifts on Christmas Eve. That is, if we went to Christmas Eve services at church first. Oh yes, the requirement also was, that we had to behave too. That, for me, was always the hardest part. I was always a little hyper, especially at Christmas time. Perhaps a better word is, excited.

I never recall thinking it was strange that Santa always came to our house, every year, while we were in church. I guess I just took it for granted that by "doing the right thing" and for going to church, we were rewarded.

I still recall the engine of that train, it was the model of a Pennsylvania Railroad engine of the type used at that very time, had 6 drive wheels and the number 316 on it. There were 5 cars and a "little red caboose." Why I recall so well, is because, I still have the train in our attic and I still set it up occasionally at Christmas time just to re-live the thrill of the first sight I ever had of it. My mother had told me to take good care of it because the $53.00 that she had paid for it was a lot of money for a struggling family to spend on a toy!

Now maybe you may feel that my mother

shouldn't have told me how much she had paid for it, but I'm glad she did. It made me value it even more and made me feel I had a good reason to treasure it for a lifetime. I have! Recently I passed it on to my son so that he can show it to his grandson on Christmas.

Christmas in the forties, I will always recall as happy times, but not because they were always easy. Youth was so blissful. The only real obligation we really had was behaving in church. Yes, in church, where for several years was required to recite Clement C. Moore's poem, "The Night before Christmas." Now, looking back, I often wonder why they had me recite a poem not of a religious nature. Do you think it might have been part of their strategy to get me to behave? (It's a l-o-n-g poem.) Maybe you would like to read it to your child, this Christmas season, as my mother once read it to me. It' not television, but oh the memories it made! I still feel excited each time I hear those words—Happy Christmas to all and to all a good night, my good friends, is my wish to you this Christmas Season 1996. The same one I might have wished you fifty years ago. Now, let's get home and open those presents!!!

Pennsylvania Towns

Much has been written about Pennsylvania towns, but not much by me. So, I got out my handy PA map, compliments of Governor Ridge and found a lot of nice towns that I am recommending that you might consider visiting this fall. Now you won't possibly be able to visit them all, but the ones you do visit I am sure you will find the colors of leaves will be fabulous, maybe even breathtaking. Autumn is my favorite time of year. Enjoy your trip!

Did you know that you don't have to go to Russia to visit Moscow. There's one right here in Pennsylvania and that's not all, Athens and Rome are here too. We don't have a New York City, but we do have a York. Just for fun, I call it Old York! Other well-known places include Akron, Bangor, California, Dover, Columbus, Dallas, Denver, Egypt, Geneva, Berlin, Wyoming, Oklahoma, Fayetteville, Georgetown and Nazareth. Nazareth is where they make those wonderful Martin Guitars. If you want to go to the beach, you can go to Jersey Shore. Our Oakland's football team is the Pitt Panthers. Our Etna has no volcano! Are there dikes in Holland, PA. Do they have races at Camptown? You don't need to take a cruise to our Kingston and there is no Wabash River near our Indiana.

For your next Holiday, try visiting Hollidaysburg. Everyone is at Home in Home, PA, there's also a Homer City. Must be where the pigeons return to. No, that would be the town of Pigeon up near Lake City, which, by the way, has no lake! What do they use for money in Wampum? King of Prussia is just a place and not a person with a crown. I'll tell you there is no lack of harmony in Harmony, PA and that they truly value there freedom in Freedom. Liberty has liberty and Oil City has oil, at least in the name.

Do you think there is a Ford dealership in Ford City? Does it cost anything to dock in Freeport? What do they grow in Garden City? Hope it's not near Weedville! Is everyone considered a Turkey that lives in Turkey City? What can the news media dig up in Clintonville? Do they allow wooden horses in Troy? I'll tell you there is nothing dull in Sharpsburg! I'd like to say "hello" to every lover in Lover. Are the rocks in Moon, PA called moon rocks?

Does Library, PA have one? Is Hatboro a town of hats? We all know where Grant, PA is in Elk County because I wrote about it. Of course, it was named after the famous Civil War General U. S. Grant who visited there while he was President. Speaking of Presidents, there is a town in Clinton County named Clinton. Don't suppose he ever visited there though. He might have been at Slickville, I think. Another town is Green Tree, near Pittsburgh and also a Cherry Tree in central PA. Also, there is Fairhope and Fairchance. Wonder why no fat chance. There's a Smithport and a Smethport! How about Polk, Plumville or Cross Forks. I always wondered what a Shamokin Dam would look like.

Ever hear of DuBois, Chicora, Galeton, Johnsonburg, Snow Shoe or Mansfield? Are they happy in Jollytown? How's the view in Fairview? Fair! There's also a Rochester, a McVeytown and a Mount Union. Some places named for women are Sharon, Hazen, Ashley, Lilly and Jeanette. Men's names include Milton, Jerome, Chester, Lincoln, Glen Lyon, Glen Hope and Glen Campbell. Animal names are, Red Lion, Whitehorse, Buck Run, Beaver and Buffalo Run. There's also a Trainer and a Sandpatch, PA. A Bath, PA is also on the map. Also, there's a Pocahontas and a Hooker!

Now you may think I'm running out of names! I'm not. Our Austin is not the capital of Texas. Did you know that Port Allegany is the first port of call on the Allegany River. Right up by the headwaters, how about Sergeant for a name, Betula or Huntley. Did you know that since 1992, Rathburn is a town within a city? Saint Marys of course. Carman is a beautiful name. How about Renovo and Daguscahonda (means water that flows up). The name Vowinckle always got me. And there's Rasselas, Dahoga and Hutchins.

I remember one time a guy from Ridgway got in pretty big trouble down in Pittsburgh. The Pittsburgh Press ran a story about it and they identified him as being "from Ridgway, a small town about 10 miles south of Wilcox". One time a map didn't seem to help! I have not yet mentioned Sterling Run. I don't know if there's any silver there, but I recall the run used to be orange. Hope it's better today. There's a Trade City in Indiana County, Emporium, is the "center of trade" in Cameron County and Driftwood is still floating in the stream.

Then there is Sinnemahoning, my old hometown. It lost out on becoming a Cameron County borough because there were only two required to fulfill the legal ruling at the time. Emporium and Driftwood were already chosen.

I don't know how many towns I've named in this article, but it's quite a few. I think I've visited most of them. If your town didn't get mentioned, don't write an angry letter to the editor, because she just may ask me to write another article and mention the rest of the towns. That would be torture!

Well you know how it is, when I finally get to Sinnemahoning I must pause so, until next time...

Memories at the time of Brother Jacob's Funeral
By Mary Heisey Singley of Jersey Shore, Pennsylvania

Jacob was my brother, my older brother. First came Pauline, then Barbara, then Jacob, Irvin, myself, Jay, Alice, Ruth, and Harriet.

How did the Heiseys get to Jersey Shore?
When Jacob started school, we lived in Hyner in Clinton County. He and brother Irvin and our two older sisters, Pauline and Barbara, rowed a boat across the Susquehanna River to get to and from school. One day as

Virginia's brothers Harry, Howard, Carl, Frank, and Grant in 1934

they came out of school, they heard the ice upstream begin to break. They could hear the sound of it cracking. They knew they had to get home quickly so they got in the boat and started rowing as hard as they could. Mother also heard the sound of the ice breaking. She quickly got baby Jay and myself and ran down to the bank of the river on our side. She called encouragement and direction to her children in the boat as she silently, yet urgently prayed for their safety. Barbara recalls they landed up-river, but thankfully landed safely. After that, our mother said to our father, "We're moving." That's when we began to get ready to move to Jersey Shore.

We came to Jersey Shore in the summer of 1923 and moved into the old house on the farm back in the hollow. At the time of moving Dad loaded our household goods on our largest wagon. He hitched up the horses, and put Pauline in charge of driving up the old mountain road. She was fourteen years old. She drove down the other side through Waterville and along Pine Creek to Jersey Shore. Barbara was plenty worried about Pauline and the wagon, but Pauline made it. She was a good driver.

Jacob never allowed us to play in the barn when we were young. A boy had been hurt in the haymow and Jacob didn't want that to happen again.

Jacob was a senior in high school the year I was a freshman. I loved school that year. Jacob was handsome, had a good sense of humor and was like by the girls and they were

very nice to me. One day Mother asked me to get Jacob's blue corduroy pants for her to wash. In the small watch pocket, I found four or five folded notes from girls. One of them said, "You are so cute." Another one was, "I like the way you comb your hair." Very carefully, I refolded them and placed them in a drawer with his socks. When I returned to school as a sophomore, I wondered what happened to all those nice people.

Jacob was a farmer. I became a teacher. Teaching in those days also meant heating the room with the potbelly stove and keeping the building clean. When school was out it was fun to get away. Two friends and I planned a trip to Florida. One of the girls' father said we could use his car but we needed a driver. Jacob agreed to drive and we had a wonderful time. We stopped overnight for $.50 a night for each person. For that, we also got a good breakfast of eggs, toast, pancakes, cereal and fruit. We got rooms right on the beach at Miami for $1.00 a night a person. We returned

Heisey young folks and cousins at Jacob's high school graduation in 1933

home the way we had come. Sometimes the places we stayed made homemade ice cream. Jacob would say at breakfast, "If you have ice cream I could eat that," and sometimes he would get it.

Later when I had earned a little money, I gave Jacob my October pay to help buy a car. Often he drove me to school and would start the stove fire. One time with some friends, we took a trip to Niagara Falls.

Our sister Alice went to nursing school in the 1940s and returned home with a friend named Perry. Perry was from a farm in New Jersey. Jacob and Perry married at a Presbyterian Church near Perry's home in November 1953. Raymond and I and the girls lived in New Jersey about forty-five minutes north of Kingston. I asked Jacob and our parents to come to stay before the wedding for breakfast. It took Jacob's wedding to get them to come to New Jersey.

Jacob milked cows and could hardly leave the cows alone while he got married so he convinced our brother Jay to stay home to milk the cows. Jay would have been Jacob's best man, so brother-in-law Raymond agreed to be Jacob's attendant.

These things and more I remember about my brother Jacob. Jacob was kind and gentle, thoughtful and caring to his family and friends. He worked hard and provided well. We all loved him and will miss him.

Jacob H. "Jake" Heisey
1915 - 2004

How a Family Wedding Made Local History

By Stacey Turner of Cambridge Springs,
Pennsylvania
Born 1987

Some of us have less of her than others. Some of us have memories stretching back to Christmases with oranges in our stockings, and others—we just have pictures of her delicate hands holding red and blue balloons at a family reunion at the Woodland Park. We hold onto those pictures like they are the most beautiful of portraits, even though they are merely hands with balloons, and seemingly nothing more. Some of us remember dressing her up like the Easter bunny, caking her face with makeup and whiskers and dressing her red hair with a set of bunny ears; some of us only recall the pictures and the story, accented

by laughter. Some of us remember caring for her in that corner room of her house in Bigler where she died in May of 1990; some of us only have the chalky vanilla taste of Ensure in our mouths from when she snuck sips to us from the tiny plastic straw peeking from the aluminum can on her bed table. We remember her life and her death as our mother or our grandmother, whether through memories or pictures or stories or some blending of each, but some sections of that catalogue of experiences predate all of us. They aren't our stories to tell.

But there is one. On a June evening in 1956, she made history—family history, local history. She married a young man who was born and raised in the small town of Egypt, neighboring her hometown of Woodland in Clearfield County. The ceremony was called "impressive" by the reporter who printed the story in The Progress the following day when he slated the headline "Old Fashioned Wedding Draws Large Crowd" across the front page of the local paper. For most families, a wedding tale between two parents or grandparents would be shared through a series of photographs in an old album and stories with smiles and romance. For our family, however, we have historical archives and newspaper clippings to complement the pictures hanging in our homes and the dress we can view at our historical society. It wasn't because they were local celebrities, but because they were average people of meager means who wanted to share their love, their marriage, with anyone who wanted to witness. And so they did. And many came.

Phoebe Marie Rowles married George Edwin Graham on the steps of the Clearfield County Courthouse on June 7th, 1956 in front of a crowd that was reported to have "jammed the plaza and the street in front of the courthouse" with friends, family members, acquaintances and, to a greater extent, complete strangers. Earlier that week, a ribbon stretched from the courthouse to County National Bank on Main Street, and when Burgess D.L. Mohney cut it, the weeklong Old Fashioned Days celebration in downtown Clearfield commenced. From parades to concerts, street dances to bargains and shopping in the 82 local shops and retailers, the excitement lined the streets for a week that was aimed at celebrating an earlier era. The matriarch of our family entered that celebration in 1956 in a beautiful, old-fashioned wedding dress with a veil of antique lace and a small bouquet of flowers in her hand. She joined in marriage our father and grandfather, who fashioned himself in a cut-away outfit from the 1890 era. For most of the spectators, it was an element of the festival and an aesthetic spectacle garnering excitement for the street dance that would take place in the following hours. For her, it was the most important day of her life.

Given away by her father, Andrew Rowles, Rev. Hubert A. Boles united the couple as the songs "I Love You Truly" and "Ave Maria" sung by her Aunt Kate echoed in the streets. Hordes of Clearfield merchants loaded them with gifts to start their new lives together in their house in Woodland. From a pitcher with drinking glasses to waffle irons and wall décor from Sherwin-Williams Paint Co., their wedding day was commemorated not just by traditional gifts from friends and family, but gifts given from the businesses that had supported the community they each had been home to. They were honored with a crowd that, when perusing the pictures of the event from the newspaper, would have been likely to follow a celebrity. Instead, it was for them—all of the people in Jack Zipf's photographs smiling and cheering and providing love and support to the soon-to-be-wedded couple.

The list of gifts, the description of her gown, her honey-mooning plans of going deer-spotting with her new husband—these topics of conversation were not just talk of those who had attended her wedding, but they were printed in the newspaper on display for the entire Clearfield circulation area. It was an event that was talked about, written about, and remembered by the most distant of strangers in her community, allowing her special day to transcend the traditional excitement that a wedding would render. For us, it is a family tale, more than an archive in the local historical society. It gives greater history and meaning to the pictures we own and cherish of the couple we loved so dearly sitting in the back of the car, preparing to depart their illustrious event. They weren't just beginning their lives together—they were making history.

When George Edwin Graham, known to us as "Pap Ed" or "Dad," died in 2004, our family created a collage of newspaper clippings and pictures of the wedding that we displayed in the area just beyond his casket in the local funeral home. For each family that

passed to give their condolences, a friend or stranger would stop and reminisce about the wedding that made local history—whether they were in attendance themselves or had received the story from a family member who spoke of the event with great pleasure. The fascination with the event never died, even in the decades after Phoebe and Ed had left us, and it would have been of no less importance to them, were they still here today. One doesn't forget a wedding with no guest list, a wedding open to the world and on display in front of an entire town. One doesn't forget a dress like that or an exchange of vows that requires a microphone so it can be heard over the bustling noise of an evening city landscape. One doesn't forget the climactic event of the first day of Old Fashioned Days when the entire town had the opportunity to partake in an old-fashioned wedding on the steps of their very own courthouse. Luckily, for our family, its unforgettable legacy lives on not just as an event that characterized the city, but an event that was the cornerstone of the family we know today.

Fresh Maple Syrup
By Judy Niles of Port Allegany, Pennsylvania
Born 1949

At sixty two years in northwestern Pennsylvania, looking back is something I do daily. My best childhood memories are from my father, Norman "Roe" Niles. Watching and helping my father make maple syrup each year is something I'll never forget. Dumping sap buckets and sneaking a sip of the sweet fluid on the way back to the outside fire; he boiled the syrup there. He had a way to purify the syrup when it got to the right temperature. He would crack an egg in the syrup. It would attract all the impurities from the beautiful golden syrup. When he scooped it out we would eat the egg. It was a taste I'll never forget. He would also have us kids get a bowl of nice, clean, fluffy, snow; then he would pour some hot syrup on it, and we'd have homemade maple taffy. Making maple syrup is a hard job, but it's well worth it, and if you include your children, it's an experience they'll never forget.

Dirty Rex
By Jean L. Booth of Muncy, Pennsylvania
Born 1929

In response to a request for memories, I am submitting this true, but unique story about an outhouse. It is as vivid in my mind as it was when it happened, 55 years ago. My husband and I were a young couple with two small children. We lived in the country with no conveniences, except for an outhouse and a spring. Late one brisk night, our outdoor, crippled, black dog, Rex, was barking incessantly; I sympathetically put him in the outhouse, because it was warmer. The next morning our first grader had to visit the outhouse before walking to school. He ran terrified to the house, screaming that something was in the outhouse. Upon my investigation, I found that Rex had fallen down backwards, through one of the holes. His bulky head, shoulders, and front paws were above the board and he was peering at us pathetically. I frantically used an iron bar to pry up the seat and pull this heavy animal, now completely filthy, out of the hole by his collar and chain. The ultimate insult, was anchoring him to a stake, carrying buckets of water from the spring, and scrubbing him down with a broom and homemade soap and Ivory flakes, all the while seething, because my husband went to work early and was unaware of my predicament with "his bird dog".

Jean's son, Jeffrey Booth and Rex (Bird Dog) in 1955

The Creek
By Leon Tillotson of Roaring Branch, Pennsylvania
Born 1919

My name is Leon Tillotson; I am 92 years of age. I have memories of old times from many years ago. I remember Fairbanks and Anderson, Bill Branns, Harmen's Market, and Lundy's Market. Along the main creek, there were four little buildings where the butchers would butcher their hogs. My father helped them on Saturdays. I also remember The Belmar in Canton, which made all kinds of clothes hangers. They also made all kinds of wooden toys; some had wooden wheels, which turned. If the toys were broken, they were thrown down the creek. I can remember my mother making my clothes. We had one pair of shoes to last us one year.

Someone's Been Eating My Sausage Patties
By Jane F. Grassi of Bradford, Pennsylvania
Born 1932

I was born on March 1, 1932, so you can see that I've reached the four score mark. I now live next door to the three-room house that I was born in, which my father built in 1930. I have lived on our road longer than anyone else has. My youngest son and his wife now live in the original house; it now has nine rooms, including the bathrooms. The wintery day that I was born, the family doctor was met by three buffalo running down the road. Even though Doctor Robbins thought that they were horses, she was still a little addled to see them. Her fee for birthing was $25.00 and an additional $5.00 for her registered nurse. It seems a pretty good deal, even considering inflation. I remember very well the wood and coal stoves, the outhouses, and the outdoor hand pump for water. This area is noted for normally hard winters and wild animals.

Our kitchen woodstove had a reservoir on the side, which was used to heat water for bathing in a washtub, washing dishes, or doing laundry. We did have electricity, but no gas or direct water supply to the house. We also had a telephone, but it was a party line, so we couldn't gossip about the neighbors! Our entertainment was usually listening to the radio shows, "Amos and Andy" or "Fibber

151

McGee and Molly". During the summertime, we often swam in the creek across the road. We would dam it up and then dive into it from a large flat rock that was nearby. Winter brought sledding with the neighborhood kids, at our house, because we had the best hill. These were some memorable times for my brother, sister, and me. Living in the country, we rode the bus about 12 or 13 miles to and from school.

We had very little money growing up during the depression years, but my father would take any job available, to make sure we were kept warm and fed. Each fall, he would butcher a pig that we had raised during the year. We didn't have a milkman back then, because we had a cow named Minnie, and her calf named Polly, for our milk. Dinner was together as a family, when my father got home from work. Meals were homemade and home baked; my mother was a good cook. Our family car was a black 1935 Chevrolet; we had it throughout the 40s. About 1947, my dad said that he was getting a new car. We were all excited, until he brought home a MAROON 1935 Chevrolet! In 1950 or 1951, he did upgrade to a 1947 Chevrolet. I then learned to drive, because it wasn't a stick shift like the other cars.   One   night,   hearing noises outside, my father looked out and saw a bear sitting down. It was eating from a brown crock-type of bowl that was filled with sausage patties packed in grease, as a preservative. This bowl had been stored in an icebox on the back porch. The bear had the ingenuity to open the icebox and help himself. He licked the bowl clean and left everything else intact. This is one of many incidents of bears visiting our rural Pennsylvania home.

Artisans, Peddlers & 'Bos' the 30s'
By Floyd G. Jovenitti of Saint Marys, Pennsylvania
Born 1925

As a child, I can remember the photographer who came to our home. He traveled with a horse and buggy. The buggy carried his equipment, and the horse was used in taking pictures of youngsters sitting in the saddle. My sister had her picture taken astride the saddle. I still have the photo of me sitting at the wheel of my toy pedal car. It is appropriately tinted and framed in a large,

gold, oval, glass frame. We also had the knife and scissor sharpener who called on us in the spring and fall. He would setup his grindstone, with its foot pedal, on our porch. Papa was a tailor; he needed very sharp scissors to cut the cloth used in making suits.

How about the 'Umbrella Man'? A song was written about him in the late 30s'. He carried a suitcase filled with umbrella ribs, waterproof cloths, and small tools. He worked at our kitchen table, making repairs, as we watched in awe!!

We called our 'peddler' Choo Choo, because he traveled by rail, in boxcars. He carried two suitcases. One was filled with second hand clothes; the other held kitchen utensils and various tools. Choo Choo was a natural salesman. He was soft spoken, with the demeanor of a cleric. He had watery blue eyes and a well-trimmed 'goatee'. He traveled the B&O rail line from DuBois to Rasselas.

If The Lord has a place at his table for compassionate people then mama is truly sitting at the 'head table'. Mama never turned a 'Bo' away. We had special cups, dishes, and silverware for the hobos. In the summer, they ate on the porch, and in the winter, they sat in the pantry, by the old potbellied stove. They left our home with sandwiches and milk. Our 'Bos' were not derelicts. Some of them were well educated and just out looking for work. We lived across the street from the B&O passenger station, which made our home an easy stop.

Basement Bear
By Arlene Eck of South Williamsport, Pennsylvania
Born 1925

Although I spent 20 years in New England, I consider my hometown to be South Williamsport. We have lived here for 66 years. My husband, Gene, is a native son; he was born on Howard Street in South Williamsport. We lived in a duplex house on Main Street. It was owned by Gene's uncles and the rent was $25.00 a month. Gene had been in the air force for two and a half years so we had little savings. I had worked and bought savings bonds, which we used to pay for all of our furniture, except for the stove. For a wedding gift, we had received a Cory coffee maker,

152

which had two burners, similar to a hot plate. I cooked our meals on it, until we were able to buy a kitchen stove. Our icebox was given to us by Gene's parents. We had an iceman deliver the ice when we put a card in the living-room window, stating how much ice we needed. We also had milk delivered by horse and wagon.

B-24 Plane Crew in 1944

Our washing machine was another thing that Gene's parents gave to us. It was a wringer washer, but instead of an agitator, it had three cups that went around, and then up and down, to thoroughly clean the clothes. It made a clumping sound. The boys next door in the other apartment used to hear it, and their mother told them that we had a bear who stomped around our cellar. For entertainment, we had a very small radio, on a small bench, in the living room. I used the lower part of the bench for a bookcase. We didn't have a clothes dryer, so we had to hang everything in the backyard on a clothesline. We had lines in the cellar for rainy days. Water was heated in a "Bucket-a-Day" coal-fed heater. Since I was the first one to wake up, I had cold water to wash my face and hands. I'd then go to the cellar and light the water heater. Our furnace was also coal powered.

In the spring and fall, we had wood delivered and dumped in the backyard; we took it to the cellar and piled it neatly, so that it was convenient to get to for burning. Since we didn't own a car, we walked or took the bus. The city has changed a lot since we've lived here. There used to be many stores and theaters. There were no one-way streets as there are now. The Market Street Bridge has been replaced twice since the 40s. It is now called the Carl Stotz Bridge, in honor of the man who started the little league ballgames. The baseball games for young boys are so popular, that another ball field has been added to the first field. There is a museum on route 15.

Gene and I met through "Our Sunday Visitor", a church paper. His sister sent her name, address, and hobbies to the paper. I like to write, so I answered her pen pal advertisement. After receiving many letters, Evy gave her brother, Gene, my name and address. He had graduated in 1942 and was working, but was drafted into the air force. We wrote each other for two and a half years before we ever met one another. He was stationed in many places in the country, and then sent to England with a crew. His plane was shot down on its 13th mission. The crew got a new plane and completed 30 plus missions, enough to be sent home to America. Gene eventually was sent to Westover Field A.F.B. in Massachusetts. In March of 1945,

Arlene LaPah in 1945

153

he surprised me with a visit to Lebanon, New Hampshire; I was living there with two girlfriends, and working at The Woolen Mill on the Mascoma River. We were married in 1946 and have 11 children.

Gene and Arlene's sister, Evy in 1945

Single Chamber Schoolhouse
By Blanche Chamberlin of Brookville, Pennsylvania
Born 1928

I was born a coal miner's daughter on June 28, 1928. I attended a one-room school for eight years, where the teacher wore the hat of janitor, nurse, or anything else we needed. We started our day with bible reading and flag salute. Our teacher taught seven subjects: reading, writing, English, math, history, geography, and music. We also had recess, which was our gym class. The teacher usually played ball and other games with us.

Most of us walked at least a mile to school, and we never had snow days for bad weather. We had a large potbellied stove in the center of the room. A metal skirt, covered with asbestos, kept us from getting too close to the stove. We each carried our own lunch, and we also had our own tin cup for water. We had a large crock filled with water that we carried in from a nearby water source. If we were good, we got to take turns getting the water. Usually, two of us could go, and always during school. We used outside toilets.

In the front of the room, we had a recitation bench, and as she called each subject, we recited from that bench. There was a chalkboard for math, or for whatever we needed. A rule at my house was, if I got paddled in school, I got paddled at home. The teacher was always right. We had our fun times though. Valentine's Day was a big event. We had a heart trimmed box, and we took valentines for whoever we liked. We liked almost everyone. Most of us couldn't buy valentines so we made them. Most of us were poor, as far as money was concerned. We really didn't know it though, because we were all the same.

At Christmas time, we traded names before our vacation started. We exchanged gifts for the name we had. We had a price range, so no one got more than anyone else. On the last day of school, we had a big picnic. Our moms brought food and we partied. We got our report cards, telling us we could move to the next grade, when the New Year started.

I had four different teachers over those eight years. We didn't always get the same teacher; sometimes they were moved, to another one-room school, in the surrounding area. We averaged 30 or 40 students to one school.

The Price of a Memory
By Herbert A. Schueltz of Bradford, Pennsylvania
Born 1928

In response to your Hometown Memories booklet request, I have been thinking of my memories, specifically those of my youth in a small town in western Pennsylvania. Since I was born in 1928, I have a long lifetime of memories of a time that is quite different from today. I remember Burma Shave signs along the highways. I remember Reader's Digest magazine cost $0.15 a copy and had no advertisements. I remember that candy bars cost $0.05. I remember the penny candy in the display case, at the neighborhood grocery store. The local newspaper cost $0.03. If you were from the city (Pittsburgh in this case), it cost $0.04. I delivered 26 papers each day (six days) and then went over the route on Saturday mornings, to collect money. I got $2.00 a week. Several families paid the $0.24 weekly charge and would let me keep the penny change from a quarter; that was an extra candy bar.   I remember S&H green stamps. I remember half soles and rubber heels came together in a package, to repair worn out shoes. I remember opening cans with a key attached to the can top. I remember the newsboys folding newspapers into a square or lengthwise. Movie tickets cost $0.10 for kids or $0.25 for adults, age 15 or older. The price increased by a penny once World War II started. I remember walking home from school for lunch. There were many one-room schools and school buses didn't exist. Cigarettes cost $0.10 a pack. I didn't smoke, but my father did. Wings brand of cigarettes had a small card included that displayed an airplane. As prices went up, packs of cigarettes sold in machines for $0.20, had the correct change with one, two, or three pennies packed along the inside of the cellophane.

I remember horning bees; neighborhood kids welcomed back newlyweds from their honeymoons by banging on pots and pans. They got candy treats in exchange. Dad said he gave out nickels in 1924. I remember slices of rubber inner tubes (before tubeless tires) used to make guns that also fired the slices. I remember making money during the summer, by mowing lawns, and during the winter by shoveling sidewalks. I made $0.25 or $0.35 per house and did all the work with a push mower or shovel, no motors. I remember when my older sister bought a new car in 1946. It was a Chevrolet and it cost her $1,750.00.

In general, gasoline was $0.19 or $0.20 per gallon. The cheapest I ever saw gasoline sold for was seven gallons for $1.00, but I only saw that once. I remember my single-speed bicycle that had a coaster brake. It had cost $17.00. I remember using a telephone. A woman always answered the line and said, "Number please?" Party lines were disappearing at the time. Party line phone numbers were usually three numbers followed by a letter. I remember having to drain the alcohol out of the car's radiator. It had been added in the autumn to prevent the engine cooling system from freezing during the winter. If it wasn't drained, the alcohol would boil out during the spring and the ride ended; it had to be replaced with water. The Prestone brand of antifreeze ended this problem. Mail was delivered twice a day, except on Saturdays when it was delivered only once. Man, I really tried, but I thought I would never grow up; or maybe those days, prices, and so forth, should have lasted longer.

Life in Youngdale
By Phillip Yothers Sr. of Bellefonte, Pennsylvania
Born 1931

Here are some of the things I remember from a long time ago. I was raised in Youngdale. My dad built the house that I was raised in. We went to a one-room school near Pine Station. I remember the coal stove in the rear of the building; there was an outhouse as well. I had two teachers: Mrs. Mary Gardner, who lived in Pine, and Mrs. Ethel Rich. There was a small store up from the school, where we went on recess, to get penny candy. That building is now someone's home. It's next to the Simcox place.

I remember Mr. Shoemakers' mansion; above his home, he had animals in cages. There was a Boy Scout dam, and there were cabins in that area. There was also a house, with two beautiful dams, and lots of fish in them. Where I lived, we had to carry water. We got our water from the overflow pipe of the water tower, which was used to fill the tanks of the steam engines. There was also the swimming hole that we went to almost every day.

We had no electricity so we used kerosene lamps. We used a kerosene stove that had three burners for cooking. My mother had an oven that she sat on the burners, for baking. We also had a wringer washer that needed to be cranked. We listened to stories on the radio: The Lone Ranger, The Fat Man, Inner Sanctum, The Shadow, and The Green Hornet. We used a wind up record player for music.

The car my dad had was one that needed to be cranked; you had to be careful, because if the crank kicked back it could break your arm. His car had a rumble seat. We had an outhouse as well. When the hole got full, dad dug another one, moved the outhouse to the new hole, and tied it down.

The snow back then, was much worse than now. One year, it was so bad, that the National Guard had to take food out on the mountain to the Simcox family. We had an icebox and the iceman came around once or twice a week; the kids liked it when he chipped ice and gave it to them.

During the war, you had to get food stamps for different things, such as meat stamps. I forget just how they worked, but I think they went by points. Then there were the mock air raids, where you needed to keep the lights off at night; there were air raid wardens that checked on this.

These are just some of the things I remember. I am sure, that as I think about it, I will remember more.

American Lover
By Elke Burrows of Eldred, Pennsylvania
Born 1940

I grew up in a small village in Germany on the Rhein River, and even though it has been many years since I came to The United States, in 1961, I still have very clear memories of what life was like in Germany, during World War II. Our house was the last four-apartment house on the edge of town. Food was rationed, and only the landowning farmers were allowed in the fields. My father and some other men from my neighborhood would go out at night; they scavenged for potatoes, cabbage, turnips, and anything else they could find to feed their families. My mother always had a meal on the

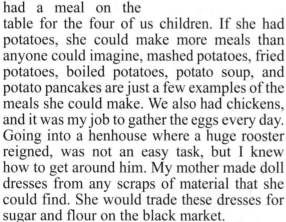

Elke's brother is on the right side with an American soldier

table for the four of us children. If she had potatoes, she could make more meals than anyone could imagine, mashed potatoes, fried potatoes, boiled potatoes, potato soup, and potato pancakes are just a few examples of the meals she could make. We also had chickens, and it was my job to gather the eggs every day. Going into a henhouse where a huge rooster reigned, was not an easy task, but I knew how to get around him. My mother made doll dresses from any scraps of material that she could find. She would trade these dresses for sugar and flour on the black market.

Things changed for the better when the American soldiers entered our village and setup their headquarters outside of our house. When they saw the 30 or 40 scrawny kids hanging around, they made sure that when their meal truck came, the food was shared with us. To this day, I can taste the first spoonfuls of peanut butter and chocolate

syrup that they shared with us. They were truly angels in disguise; we had never eaten that well! My father would play his accordion at night, and the soldiers would dance with the older girls in our village. I wish that my father would have gotten the names and addresses of all the soldiers we met, because in 1958, I married an American soldier; three years later, we moved to The United States. I would have loved to have been able to find some of those soldiers who were so kind to me when I was a child. Their kindness came at a time when it was needed the most.

When I was growing up, Christmas was always an exciting time. We always got presents that were made by my parents, a new dollhouse for the girls, and a rocking

horse for my baby brother. My brother wanted to trade his rocking horse for the dollhouse. One year, my mother had a large piece of chocolate. It was 24 small squares on a sheet, a piece for each of us. My brother ate all of his before the night was over and wanted to borrow some of ours, thinking that my mother would get more the next day; that wasn't likely to

happen, considering that she had traded the only piece of jewelry she owned, a brooch, for the chocolate that he had already eaten. We never knew that fact until many years later though. That Christmas, of 1947, was one that I'll never forget. December sixth was also an anticipated day for us children. That's when Benzenickel (St. Nick) came. He came in the evening; we were excited and frightened all at the same time. He brought apples and cookies for the good kids and coal for the naughty kids. The one year that I remember the most, is when my brother hid in the coat closet, my sister hid in the box that held wood for the stove, and my oldest sister hid outside of the window, hanging from the eaves. Thank goodness, that St. Nick never looked behind the curtains, because she probably would have fallen two stories to the ground.

Bath time on Saturdays was fun for me. A huge tub was brought in and put between two chairs. Since I was the youngest, I got to bathe first. My mother would just add more hot water into the tub after each kid was done. School wasn't my favorite place. I preferred to go with my friends, Ursula and Rita, to the woods, to gather wood for my mother, so that she wouldn't have to buy a bundle for 50 pfennigs. Money was extremely scarce in our home, and I liked to help out as much as I could. Stealing pears, apples, and cherries from trees that were owned by the state, and lined the Rhein River, was always fun; getting caught by the forester, however, was not fun. Two of my friends and I had to clean the courthouse every Saturday for three months after getting caught. All in all, my childhood was a very happy and carefree time for me, even though I grew up during WWII, and life wasn't always easy. We never realized just how poor we were, because everyone else was in the same boat.

Coming to The United States, was a very exciting experience for me, but it involved some major culture shock as well. Wooden houses, big cars, and stores that stayed open late, were all new things to me. I thought that even the doorknobs were strange. Before I got used to my American way of life, I often wished that I could swim back to Germany. After being here for a year, having a one-year-old son, and another on the way, I realized that swimming back to Germany was impossible. Things became much better after I learned to speak English and made some new friends. I met people who helped me so much back then, and they are still friends to this day. After moving a few times, we finally settled in Eldred, Pennsylvania in 1967. It is such a great town to raise kids in, and it reminded me so much of my hometown in Germany, where neighbors looked out for one another. The feeling was the same here in Eldred as it

was there. This made life so much easier for me, being in a town so similar to the one in which I had my childhood. Having lived here for 45 years, I wouldn't want to live anywhere else. To me, America is my home, and having visited Germany more than 20 times in the 45 years since I left, I realized that I would never want to live there again. I found Americans to be very friendly, and I am proud to say that I am one of them, as I got my citizenship in 1968. I got divorced in 1970 and could have taken my children back to Germany to live, but I know that I made the right choice, raising them in The United States, the freest country in the world. God bless America!

Corduroy Pants
By Otto Bud Burrows of Westfield, Pennsylvania
Born 1928

In July of 1928, I was born into a poor family, on a very small farm, in a village known as Happy Town, Pennsylvania. I started school at Lyman Run Country School. It was a one-room schoolhouse. I walked 1.25 miles to school. In the wintertime, we had to split and carry firewood into the building, for an extra-large wood stove. We used outhouses to relieve ourselves; they were doubled with girls on one side and boys on the other. During the summers, when we had no school, porcupines would come chew at the wood and put holes in the outhouses. At the age of eight, I had to milk one cow by hand, and carry in firewood.

Every Friday night we could look forward to our regular does of castor oil which we washed down with black coffee, or possibly an orange if we had one. After our weekly medication, we would listen to Tom Mix and his Ralston Straight Shooters. We also listened to the Amos & Andy show. Sometimes we listened to Little Jimmy, who ended his program with, "Now I lay me down to sleep."

Party lines were controlled by a central telephone operator. Grandmother lived in the area near the operator. I was mad one day, so I got a chair and started ringing the phone. My grandmother came out and told me I better get off the phone; it was all taken care of when my parents came in the house. Spankings in school, on my part, were plentiful; if I got one in school, I got two when I got home.

Elke's dad is on the right, her uncle is in the uniform children are Inge, Marie, Rud and Elke

Saturday night baths were taken in a regular washtub, with water heated from a cook stove. My mother had a gas wringer washer with an exhaust hose. We would run out the door anytime she used a scrub board. Most of my clothes were homemade. My shirts were made from G.L.F. feed bags. We wore short pants, until knickers came along. Most knickers were corduroy, and when you walked they would say, "rip-rip-rip." In 1937, our farmhouse burned, and my first pair of long pants were inside. I was determined to go in the burning house to get them, but four men from The C.C.C. Camp restrained me. I got away from four of them, so they got a fifth man and held me down. We moved to Galeton, Pennsylvania. It had the only theatre in the world, where you went down stairs, in order to get upstairs to the balcony.

I would like to tell you a lot more, but I am 84 years old, and I'm getting tired. I do, however, want to thank god, for allowing me to submit my early history. Good luck, and may God bless.

Life in Houtzdale
By Grace Landes of Clearfield, Pennsylvania
Born 1934

As a child, growing up on a farm, in the small community of Sanborn, eight miles from Houtzdale, Pennsylvania, I well remember the "good old days". We didn't have indoor plumbing or electricity. Instead of a house with a bathroom, we had a home with a path, which lead to an outhouse that was wallpapered and kept clean. Buckets of water were carried from our spring to the kitchen for drinking and cooking. A small enameled ladle hung on the bucket and was used for dipping water; a tin cup beside the bucket was used for drinking the water. A stream of fresh water ran through our springhouse where milk and cream, from our cows, was kept cold. The milk was for drinking and cooking; the cream was churned into butter. The shelves in our cellar were always full of canned vegetables from our garden and fruit and jelly from our trees. The shelves also held apple butter, which was made outdoors in the fall, in a large black kettle. During the week of Thanksgiving, we butchered our pigs and the meat was either canned or preserved to prevent it from

spoiling. The chickens supplied us with eggs and sometimes a delightful chicken dinner.

Those noisy gasoline washers always let everyone know when it was washday. We heated water in a boiler to wash the clothes and filled a large tub with water to rinse them. They were put through the wringer after they were washed and again after they were rinsed; they were then hung on the clothesline to dry. The clothes that needed to be ironed were sprinkled with water and tightly rolled; they were then placed in the clothesbasket to be ironed the next day. We had three irons, which could be attached to a wooden handle, and were kept hot on our kitchen stove. When one iron cooled, it was replaced with a hot one from the stove. In 1940, I started first grade at the new two-room school in Sanborn. Mrs. Lillian Zimmerman taught grades one through four. Miss Ann Hutchinson taught grades five through eight. The school didn't have indoor plumbing, and each teacher had to fire a huge heating stove. The boys were responsible for carrying in the wood and coal. Two girls, one on each end of a broom handle, would walk nearly a mile to bring back a bucket of water. The water was then placed in a cooler for drinking.

I learned so much during those grade school years. We were taught reading, writing, arithmetic, spelling, English, history, and geography. We walked to school and waded through snow in the winter. The teachers lived in Houtzdale, but they couldn't make it to school at times because of the snowdrifts; we wouldn't have school until a bulldozer could open the roads. In the late 1940s, I remember seeing poles that were set in the ground with wires strung, for electricity. Before too long, we had bright lights, indoor plumbing, and a four-party telephone line. As I look back at those "good old days", I realize how poor we were, but we actually never knew it. We never locked our door at night, and everybody helped each other.

All the kids played well together. They played games such as, tag, Annie Annie over, hide-and-seek, softball, and tree climbing. We were very thankful! We never went to bed hungry. We always knew we were loved. We had the very best parents, pastors, and Sunday school teachers in our little country church, which we attended faithfully. Although I never missed what I didn't have, I am much more appreciative of the conveniences and advanced technology that I now enjoy. I truly thank God for the "good old days" and what they have meant to me.

Quarantined, Coal Yoil, Gram's Sewing
By Norma L. Flook of Jersey Shore, Pennsylvania
Born 1938

There were no vaccines available in 1946 for childhood diseases. Polio, chickenpox, mumps, and measles were commonplace and highly contagious. If your family contracted any of these diseases, the state health officer would come to your home, and post a large orange or yellow quarantine sign on the front of your house. It was always next to the front door, and it meant, no one could enter or leave.

There was one case of polio in our neighborhood, a young boy surviving in an iron lung to help him breathe; naturally, everyone was scared. Myself and four siblings walked several blocks to and from school; we even walked home for lunch. There would be small groups of kids in front of us and behind us, making the same trek. Whenever we spotted a quarantine sign on a house, we wouldn't go near it, otherwise we might catch something. Everyone would cross the street, and walk down the other side. We believed if they opened their door, the germs would float out.

Needless to say, our family came down with the chickenpox, and was quarantined. I was pretty sick and missed my friends at school. One day, I waited at the living room window with the curtains pulled back. I wanted to see the neighborhood kids go by and wave to my friends, but as they neared my home, the whole pack crossed the street. MY HOUSE, THEY SHUNNED MY HOUSE! I was so humiliated and angry. I swore I would never speak to any of them again. We all pulled through just fine of course. That summer our town had a bad flood, and we had to move out of harm's way; at the same time, my family came down with the German measles. We were quarantined again, this time, at my aunt's house. God bless her, for housing five sick kids.

Coal Yoil
In 1946, my mother cooked on a three-burner coal oil stove, and it was my chore to go the two blocks, to the mom & pop market for fuel. I carried a glass, gallon, jug with a cork stopper and a finger handle. It was very heavy for an eight year old. I set it down a lot to rest my fingers. I couldn't pronounce coal oil; I always said it "coal yoil" and the storeowner would repeatedly ask me what I wanted. I would have to say it again and again, and he would laugh each time I said it. Any other customers in the store, within earshot, would laugh as well.

We would go outside the store, where a 50-gallon barrel, sat on the sidewalk next to the storefront. It had a crank handle to pump out the fuel, and fill up my jug. Again, he would ask, "Now what did you say you wanted?", and I would tell him, "I need a gallon of coal yoil." He would then give me a big belly laugh. When I got home, I told mom, "I'm not going over there again, because he laughs at me all the time, and gets me to say coal yoil." Mother said, "The next time we need fuel, you ask for a gallon of kerosene."

Gram's Sewing
My Grandmother bought a Treadle Singer sewing machine in 1937, for 80 dollars; that was a lot of money back then. They were farmers, and made payment of two dollars a week. The sales slip and payment agreement are still in one of the machine drawers, in an envelope bearing a three-cent stamp. One of the questions on the application form, was, "are you a negro?" I don't know why they asked it. It was just a sign of the times.

Gram would make dresses for my two sisters and I out of feedbags. Chicken mash, corn, and other grains would come into the feed store, in brightly colored cotton bags. Once emptied, the bags were sold for garment making. I remember seeing piles of clean, neatly folded, printed goods, on the shelf to choose from. Sometimes you could buy the dirty ones cheaper, if you were willing to open the seams and wash them yourself. Several times, I went to the feed store with Gram, to pick out the material for a new dress. She also sewed them into aprons, pillowslips, and kitchen t-towels.

That old Treadle was singing all the time. One year, about 1946 or 47, our doll babies disappeared. Gram was sewing new clothes for our dolls for Christmas. What we didn't know, was mom had taken the dolls to a lady in town. She repainted their faces so they looked like new, and added new wigs.

My brunette doll now had long blonde curls, and my sister's doll was a red head. With the new clothes, matching coat, and bonnet, we never recognized them as our old dolls. They were just beautiful. I still sew on that Treadle machine I inherited in 1963, when Gram passed away. I've had it 48 years, and it still works great.

June Rovenolt Kline at age 1

Turbotville Times
By June Rovenolt Kline of Turbotville, Pennsylvania
Born 1939

I am a daughter of the late Alfred Sr. and Edith Rovenolt, of Turbotville. We lived on a dairy farm at the edge of town, right next to the school. I have three sisters: Dorothy, Margaret, and Loretta. I also have one brother. While growing up, we had lots of ponies. At one time, there were 40 plus ponies, and also four workhorses. They were also a hobby of my dad's. My mother helped with milking the cows and she had a garden. She also had chickens, and she would sell the eggs. She was a very good cook and seamstress; she made many clothes for us girls. She did a lot of canning as well. We had to use an outhouse, until about 1945, when we got a bathroom in the house. While growing up, we often asked for bicycles, because all of our friends had them. Dad always said, "No, because they have to wear their legs out to give their behinds a ride." He reminded us that we had ponies and they didn't. We reminded him, "We have to fork pony manure every Saturday." The four of us girls, helped with the fieldwork, baling hay, bindering the wheat and oats, and also

June's parents, Alfred and Edith Rovenolt in 1964

working the ground for planting during the spring.

I remember as a kid, we were not allowed to have sandals, because we lived on a farm. When we were sent out to the store for bread, we wore our "homemade sandals", which were made from movie posters and yarn. They were worn, till we got back home. In the winter, after a snowstorm, dad would hitch a team of horses to the bobsled and go through town. It didn't take long to get the sled full of riders. We lived within the Turbotvilleboro Line, so we got our newspaper delivered to the house. The carrier was Birdie Craven for many years; he was a classmate of mine. We had a field that flooded over; whenever it froze, we were joined by many kids from the town that wanted to ice skate. I recall, when I was about six years old, my sister Dorothy and I, were riding our ponies around town. Down where the lumberyard was, there were always huge water puddles after it rained. We thought it was cool to hear the plopping noise when the horses walked through the puddles; one day, I changed my mind after my Sandy laid down in the biggest puddle. Boy, was I mad. Dorothy took Sandy by the reins and led him home, with me hanging onto the saddle and crying the whole way. In 1953, mom and dad had bought a new car. We were having a tornado storm, and dad parked the car out in the front yard, away from the trees. Then he had second thoughts and moved it to behind the school. Only about a half hour later, part of our house roof landed nearly where the car had been previously parked.

When Bloomsburg had a centennial celebration, dad loaded one of his old carriages, and Nancy, our donkey, into the truck to go to the parade. Mother, Edith drove the donkey, while my sister and I rode in the back; we cranked an old Victrola that was playing "Pittsburg Pennsylvania". Turbotville had a Sesquicential Celebration

June holding her youngest sister, Loretta with Margaret driving Sandy

in 2009, so we girls put a float together that emphasized the ponies and the dairy. We peddled bottled milk in town. We had several grandchildren and great-grandchildren on the float. In 1957, there was a big fire at the Somers & Smith Grocery Store in Turbotville. This store supplied many residents of the town and the surrounding community. During the depression, people stood two and three deep in line to get certain limited items. In June of 1958, I married Bill Betz. We had four children: Cheryl, Bill Junior, Dawn, and Shane. In 1969, he had nearly lost several fingers when he got caught in a combine belt. In 1970, while working at a food plant he was burned on both legs from scalding water, when a pot filled with hot water, dumped onto the floor; he slipped and fell into it as he was trying to avoid it. In 1971, unfortunately, the kids and I lost him in a farm accident. He suffocated in a corn silo, while trying to break lose frozen corn. The kids were, 11, 10, eight and a half, and 14 months in age. It took rescue workers one and a half hours to get him out of the silo.

About one and a half years later, I lost my mother due to heart complications. She had been in a Philadelphia hospital in 1965 for heart surgery. While she was there, dad was with her most of the time; the wheat and oats still had to be harvested though. Several farmers from the area got together and harvested it all in one day. Dad didn't know it was done, until he came home several days later. After my husband's death, I decided to build a house, as we had planned to do the following year. My parents didn't want to see me out in the

country alone with the kids, so I built a house about one block from them. My oldest son helped my father with feeding calves and ponies. He also mowed the lawn for my mother. While they were visiting my sister in New Jersey, on a weekend, Billy was supposed to feed the animals for my father and check on the furnace for my mother. He thought the fire was out, so he did as he had seen my mother do to start the fire, but it burned out onto his face and arms. The doctors thought that he might need skin grafts, but fortunately, he didn't. Just recently, in October of 2011, he got pinned between a livestock trailer and a post, in the process of loading a bull onto the trailer. He broke his arm, still loaded the bull on the trailer, and then went to the emergency room. He ended up having surgery; a plate and six pins were placed in his upper arm. He has 150 dairy cows, 75 of them are for milking.

Shane and his boys, Tim and Zachary, really helped a lot; so did the Amish boy who had been milking for two years. Shane's girlfriend went to milk every morning before she left for work. Don Gresh and several other farmer friends helped to see that the silo got filled. One day, when Dorothy and I were

June checking over the float before the Sesquicentennial Parade in 2009

doing flowers at the cemetery, I had taken Zachary, who was about nine years old at the time, with me. He questioned various names on the headstones and after I explained things to him, he said, "My gram is going to live till she's 130." My sister said, "She'll be a dried up prune." He responded by saying, "Oh no, I'll put lots of water on her." The good lord only gives us what he thinks we can handle.

Growing Up
By Gene O. Harlan of White Pine,
Pennsylvania
Born 1951

My life started in March of 1951. I was born on a fourth generation family farm. I was just one generation away from a very primitive pioneer lifestyle. We had cars by this time, so I can only take the means of transportation for granted. Electricity was also a luxury, and telephones were in use. The first telephone number I can remember was ME4-2131. These numbers were identified by rings called longs and shorts. Each party line had sequences of them.

So I am growing up with no worries, the way it was, was all we knew. We used an outdoor privy, and running water was not installed until about 1960. Our bathing ritual was every Saturday night, whether we needed one or not. We would heat the water on the kitchen's wood stove; then pour it into a galvanized washtub to scrub up. I was the youngest, so my turn came first. The older ones got to stay up later, and it just didn't seem fair to me.

Since there were three boys and no girls, we all had to take turns at drying those darn dishes for mother. "Why me??", "It's his turn!!", "Do I have to??", "There isn't that many mom, you can do it, please!!", "Get out there and help your mother!!" Dear old mom - what a cook - we didn't have much, but we never went hungry. We cut our eyeteeth on venison, and grew up on it. We always had to at least try the food on the table. We didn't have to eat something that might make us gag or get sick though.

We seldom ever got candy or soda pop, because we just couldn't afford it; it wasn't necessary anyway. The store in White Pine was real handy, since we had to go up to our mailbox anyway. Gas was around 20 cents a gallon. I recall getting a five gallon can, for our tractors, for one dollar. Occasionally we would sneak some penny candy. *Don't let dad see that!!* The ride home was so fast, with my mouth stuffed full of the things, that dad didn't approve of. We never got in trouble for it, so I guess he never knew, or maybe he really didn't mind after all.

My school years started at Oregon Hill, in a one room, six grades school. For two and a half years, I got to experience this kind of education. In my third year, they transferred us to Wellsboro, in the basement of the old Grant Street elementary school. From there I went through the four-school system. I had to try to follow in the shadow of my two older brothers. The three of us graduated from Wellsboro High School. It was impossible for us to play hooky; dad was paid, to take us to meet, the big bus at English Center.

Farm life was a lot more simple back then; you got to do things that you really liked to do. We entertained ourselves being outdoors, and doing outdoor things that boys did. Our playtime would be making dams in the stream, or tunnels in the haymow, after the invention of balers. Toys were very few, and usually, hand me downs. I never had a new toy of my own. We occasionally would play "catty-on-the-bounce" ball, but it was not fun for me. I always had to chase the ball and never got to hit it, because I was the youngest.

My dad had the farm in the soil bank, for a number of years, until farming picked up for us in the early 60s. At this time, some of our modern conveniences appeared: a furnace, a television, the pond, house water, an indoor bathroom, and kitchen cabinets. These conveniences, along with the landscaping of the yard, made us more modern than we ever dreamed. What a change everywhere, inside and out, we thought we were rich. After the modern age of farming emerged, I was fortunate enough to experience the operation of many machines, some of which I taught myself; some were taught to me. The basics today never seem to stray very far from my initial experiences.

Dad never had much time for laziness or relaxation when he was in his prime years. I think all of us became accustomed to work for that reason, and to this day, I have no regrets with the cycle of my life. Even though we have evolved into a modern lifestyle, I still think of our old things, like listening to Gunsmoke or Lum and Abner on the radio. Those little things, I accredit to the creation of our imaginations. A lot of wonders of the little boy in me have been answered, but new ones never cease to emerge into a curious mind. Someday, maybe they will all be fully answered, but I doubt it. This little bit of information, may never have been preserved, if it weren't for the invention of this personal computer I am using. Sho is fun fer an ole country boy like me.

A Tribute to Mr. Wayne Chamberlain
By Myles E. Casey Jones of Kane,
Pennsylvania
Born 1931

I grew up in a very small unique town, and went to a very unique grade school, that had a very unique man as the principal. When I say unique, I mean special and one of a kind. I want to relate the story of the "Patrol Boys" of Lincoln grade school in Sheffield, Pennsylvania. I will recall it, as well as an 80-year-old mind can. I would like to tell the story before my mind starts to forget the things that impressed me the most.

The "Patrol Boys" were started by Mr. Wayne Chamberlain, and were one of a kind. A fifth grade boy could watch and learn, as the sixth through eighth grade boys, would perform their duties. The boys had to have passing grades to be eligible for membership. They also had to be in good standing with their peers and the teachers. The boys had to march, as a group, into every classroom. Each boy had to tell the class why he should be a "Patrol Boy". Once each boy gave his little speech, the class would vote on them. I think the teacher had to vote as well.

As I recall, only the eighth graders could become captains and lieutenants. We had two captains and quite a few lieutenants; there was one lieutenant for each station. These officers were elected by the students. I think whoever had the most votes became captains and lieutenants. I can't remember anyone not becoming a patrol boy if he wanted to be one.

There were seven or eight stations as I recall. The first station was in front of The Lincoln School. The second was at the railroad crossing. The third was somewhere in front of the old White Lunch, or in that area. This crossing was for the kids coming from Mill Street, and those that had to cross the bridge. There was also a station at the other side of the bridge, because after crossing it, you had to cross over a street to get to school. Then going west, I think we had two more stations. Most of the kids living west of the school didn't have to cross route six, but they still had to cross the side streets.

The Patrol Boys had to be at school before everyone else. The captains would line them all up in front of the school, according to what station they had. The stations were assigned ahead of time, at meetings the officers would attend. When the sound of a bugle would come from the second floor window, all the boys would march off to their stations. Usually, the boys were assigned to a station in their own neighborhood, because they knew the names of the other kids. They could turn them in for any wrong doings, such as snowballs or teasing the girls. After a while, the bugle would blow again, at this time all boys had to be on station.

Each station had a lieutenant, and he had a whistle that was made from two pieces of bamboo. The pieces were about five to seven inches in length; they were attached together and covered with a varnish like substance. Mr. Chamberlain handcrafted all of them. Each whistle was made to produce a different pitch. They could be heard from station to station, and each station was identified by its own unique sound. Mr. Chamberlain held practice with the whistles so that we could identify each station. Once the second bugle blow sounded, each lieutenant would blow his whistle. The captain stationed at the crossing in front of the school would then know that all stations were manned properly.

Each patrol boy wore his white belt with his AAA badge on it. The captain badge was red, and the lieutenant badge was blue. The school bell would ring, and we knew that we had a certain amount of time to get to class. When the second bell rang, you better hurry, or you would be late. After the second bell had rung, the patrol boys would start to march back to the building. Everything was in reverse order. We had to carry poles with red flags on them, and stand them all in the corner of the entranceway. The teacher would let The Patrol Boys leave the classroom early, so that when school ended, they would be ready to perform their duties all over again.

I am sure as people read this article they will remember a lot more about Lincoln School, like the drum and bugle corps started by Wayne Chamberlain. They were so wonderful and successful. That would be another story though; one that I wish someone would write about someday. I graduated from Lincoln School in 1945. I remember all of my teachers, how lucky I was to have them, and how lucky I was to grow up around people like Mr. Wayne Chamberlain.

While talking with a few people and trying to remember things about The Patrol Boys, I came across a lady friend of mine. She told me she had been a patrol person for Mr. Chamberlain during those same years. I have not yet, been able to confirm that girls were part of the patrol. If anyone can help on this matter please feel free. I started digging through my box of memories the other day, and sure enough, I found my patrol badge. "It is red". I don't think we were allowed to keep them when we graduated.

Ladder Climbing Dog
By Evelyn M. Gibson of Hinckley, Ohio
Born 1938

Dad, mom, my younger sister Pat, and I lived on a small dairy farm in Potter County. I would like to share some of the things I remember about life on a farm in the "good old days" while I was growing up in the 40s and 50s. Our dad owned and drove the school bus all through the years that we went to school. As soon as we got home each day, Pat and I had a small snack, changed out of our school clothes, and carried wood in for the kitchen and living room stoves. Those

Pat, Dad "Red", Mom "Rolla", Evelyn, and Shep
1947

Evelyn's dad, "Red" McCloskey in 1951

stoves were the only heat sources we had in our house. We helped set the table, so that we could eat supper by five o'clock every day. After supper, dad and mom went to the barn to feed and milk the cows. Pat and I cleared the table, washed and dried the dishes, and put them in the cupboard. After we finished the dishes, we went to the barn. Our best job there, was teaching the calves to drink from a pail. The calves would suck our fingers, then we placed them down into the milk to get them to drink it from the pail; we fed milk to the barn cats as well.

As we grew older, my sister and I helped carry the pails full of milk, from the milking machine to the milk house. We poured the milk into a strainer that sat on top of a 10-gallon milk can. The big milk cans were kept cold in a large milk cooler that was filled with water and powered by an electric motor. A milk truck came every morning to take our milk cans to Abbott's Dairy, to be sold. I met my husband when his family, from Ohio, came to our farm for milk. They vacationed at their camp, near our farm, every summer. When we were done at the barn, the rest of the evening was spent listening to the radio. Edgar Bergen and Charlie McCarthy, Amos n' Andy, and The Shadow are just a few of the programs that were our favorites. We also spent time doing homework from school, jigsaw puzzles, playing checkers, or playing card games. Everyone went to bed by nine o'clock at night, because we had to eat breakfast and get ready for school early the next day. Dad had to do the milking before breakfast, and then be ready to drive the school bus in the morning.

Before we had electricity, we heated our water on the kitchen stove, in a big container called a boiler. The stove also had a built in reservoir where our water was heated. At that time, we didn't have a bathroom with a bathtub, so we used a big, round, metal washtub for our baths. During warm weather, we bathed in a room off of the kitchen. When the weather was colder, we took our baths in the kitchen with the washtub in front of the open oven door. Water wasn't plentiful, so we took baths once a week on Saturday nights. My sister and I used the same water and took turns being the first to bathe. The second person would add more hot water to the washtub. The other days of the week, we took sponge baths. We washed our hair in the kitchen sink using a pitcher to pour water over our heads. Sunday was a day of rest during the 40s and 50s. All stores were closed. After milking was finished on Sunday morning, there was no work done

Evelyn in 1951

on the farm, until the cows were milked again in the evening. During the winter months, we would visit relatives or neighbors, or someone would visit us. On other Sundays, we would listen to the radio, read, or take a nap in the afternoon. Dad was a baseball fan. During summer, we would attend the baseball games of our hometown team. Sometimes we would go to the away games as well.

On the way home, we would stop at a food stand where they served foot-long hotdogs with chili on top. Dessert was a soft serve ice cream cone, what a treat that was! Mom had a day off from cooking. We got home in time to do the evening milking after a relaxing afternoon. My uncle had a green two-passenger coupe with a rumble seat in the back. He would take my sister and me for a ride in the summer. What fun it was to ride in that rumble seat, and sing as the wind blew our hair! I remember that he had a dog who

would sit on the running board of that car for the short ride from his house to our house. My uncle would hold Jack's collar with one hand and steer the car with the other hand. I never saw another dog who would sit on a running board and ride. Spring and summer are busy times on a farm. Dad would hire one or two men to help during those times. The fields had to be plowed, oats and corn had to be planted and then harvested, and hay had to be cut and placed into the haymow. Dad had a team of horses that he used to plow, plant, and harvest the crops. All that work was done at a slow pace. I saw the evolution of horses being replaced by tractors, bailers being used to bale hay, and combines being used to harvest oats. Farmers could get things done much faster with this new equipment. Dad had a team of horses for many years. One of the most memorable experiences he had with a team was when he used the horses to pull the electric line for the Tri-County Rural Electric Company, to bring electricity to the valley. He was proud to have the opportunity to use his horses to help.

Eventually, the horses weren't used and they were sold when I was about 12 years old. All of us loved those horses and didn't want to let them leave. I cried so much, that dad promised me he would buy a two-wheel bicycle if it would make me feel better. I had that bike for many years. One day, while I was at my aunt and uncle's house, their chickens got into the basement through an open door. My aunt asked me to chase them out of the basement and close the door. As I started to chase them out, the old white rooster decided that he didn't want me chasing his hens. He turned around and chased me! I ran, screaming, for the basement stairs as he flew and landed on my back, spurs and all! My aunt was so upset; she ran outside, grabbed a wooden clothesline pole, and took off after that rooster. She caught up with him and hit him with the pole. He ended up in the stew pot that night. I was about nine years old when this happened, and I was quite shaken by the experience. I learned to <u>never</u> upset a rooster!

Our dog, Daisy, liked to climb ladders. She first started climbing ladders to get up to the haymow in the barn. One day, dad was repairing the roof on grandma's next-door house. Daisy climbed the ladder and sat the roof to see what was going on. The one thing she couldn't do was come back down a

Daisy the ladder climbing dog in 1954

ladder. Our home was a two-story house with a big wraparound porch. The porch was our favorite place to relax at the end of the day. The main road went by about 100 feet from our porch. Friends and neighbors would stop by and talk when they were out for a drive. We loved to sit there on hot summer nights, especially during a thunderstorm. We could see lightning flash and hear the thunder echo up through the valley. We had a good life, living on the farm, even though farming was hard work. We always felt safe and loved. Mom was there when we came home from school. Supper was on the stove. Dad drove the school bus and worked on the farm, so he was usually around. We had time to talk and do things together. Sadly, dad passed away at the age of 48. Soon afterwards, mom sold the cattle and equipment, but remained on the farm. She remarried and lived there until our stepfather passed away. The farm was sold in the 80s, and mom moved into town. The new owners of the property built a house up the road. Someone else lived in our house until just a few years ago, when the house was torn down after a small fire, what a shock it was, to see that vacant spot where the house had been! The house is gone, but the memories remain forever.

To Grandmother's House
By James H. Surfield of South Williamsport, Pennsylvania
Born 1946

When I was growing up in Williamsport, I did something every Saturday that no parent would ever let their child do in today's times. From the time I was seven years old, I would walk from my house in the 1200 block of West Third Street, down through the center of town, to my grandmother's house in the 800 block of East Third Street. It would usually take about an hour to complete this journey. The only fear I had, was seeing a dog on the loose or that it would start raining before I arrived. My sole purpose was to visit my grandmother and help her in any way that I could. My grandfather had passed away before I was born so she lived by herself. She had arthritis really bad, so I was the one to mop her floors with my grandfather's long-johns (obviously he didn't need them any more), dig her garden, plant her garden, trim the fruit trees, and pick any fruit as it ripened. For having such a small property, she utilized every square inch. She had one oxhart cherry tree (which the birds got the majority of), two sour cherry trees, two clingstone peach trees, one freestone peach tree, three quince trees, and a duchess pear tree. She also had concord grapes, red grapes, and white grapes. She would sell her fruit to help make her ends meet, and I was happy that I was able to help get that accomplished.

She was very proud of her quinces and would get her picture in the paper showing how large they would grow for her. I learned a lot from my grandmother. I learned how to prune fruit trees, how to prune grapevines, and to put a potato over the cut end, so that the vine wouldn't bleed. I learned how to plant just about anything in the garden, and that the wood ashes I carried out, all winter long, and dumped in the garden, really made things grow. I learned how to save and dry some of the items from the garden, such as beans, to be able to use as seed for the following year. She would pay me at the end of each day. It started at a nickel and by the time I was 16, I was getting paid a quarter.

Sometimes I would go with my grandmother to the rummage sale, which was held in a large hall type of building; it used to be where the parking deck is currently, next to the old jail. At the end of the day, an older gentleman would pull up with his horse-drawn wagon, and take what remained after the sale. Unlike today's garage sales, the only items that were for sale were clothing items. I would see this same gentlemen on my weekly walk to my grandmother's house. He would be traveling down East Third Street, with his horse and wagon, calling out, "ragsie ags".

I was never sure whether he was trying to buy or sell rags, but I saw him often. At the end of the day, I was grateful that I didn't have to walk home. My uncle worked for a local undertaker in the east end of town; he stopped every day after work to check on my grandmother before he went home to the west end of town. I would get a ride back with him. He would also match what my grandmother gave me, as far as pay, and if I was really lucky, we wouldn't go straight home; we'd make a stop at the Eagles instead.

He would have some liquid refreshment and buy me a coke and chips or peanuts; he would always shove the remaining change over to me. I grew up with my mother raising the four of us by herself. She worked three jobs in an effort to make ends meet. We never went hungry, but we didn't have any extra spending money to buy clothes from a store. My mother made the clothes that we wore to school. Since she worked three jobs, she wasn't home on Saturdays, and that is why I had to walk to my grandmother's house. I saved my nickels, dimes, and quarters; by the time I was 12, I bought my own bicycle and I would ride it back and forth to my grandmother's house.

A Little Hickory Tea
By Robert (Buzz) Reynolds of Watsontown, Pennsylvania
Born 1936

Being raised on a farm, and a lifetime in Delaware Township, outside Watsontown, was where the experience of my life began, the farm, church, and then the school, all in that order. I still reside within a mile of each. All three still stand in good order, even the one-room school, which is well over 100 years old; it is still in good shape. I see it every day, and being born in 1936, I've been around for a while. My father was a strict man, but mother wasn't quite as strict. With eight kids, five boys and three girls, to feed and clothe, there was no time for nonsense. My dad was a no-nonsense kind of guy. With 15 kids in his family, dad was just like his own parents. If he told you once to do your chores, then they best be done. A reminder was unpleasant. That was the fetching up that we had. I liked the first day of school; it was fun. From that point on, all I wanted to do was have fun, but my teacher had other ideas. After a few days, me and my two of my new friends decided it would be fun to put some minnows, from the Delaware Run, in the drinking water; just to see what the girls would do when a minnow would come out of the spigot into their cup; after all, nothing would be wrong with that; everyone liked fish.

Imagine our surprise, when the teacher got thirsty first. A minnow came out in his cup. The teacher was a big man; the kind you would fear. It didn't take long to find out who had done the caper. My friends and I were the ones who had filled the cooler that day. I tried to convince the teacher that the minnows must have pumped up from the well that we got the drinking water from, but he didn't believe that story. I couldn't imagine why not. Without showing any anger on his face, he said that he would give us a dose of hickory tea. Wow, I thought that would be good, because I had never had any tea before, of any kind. Then I saw it; out from under the desk, where he sat, the teacher pulled a board, about four inches wide and two and a half feet long, with a cut out handle, and holes in the wide flat part; what's that, I found myself wondering. It wasn't long before I found out. My friends and I got our first taste of hickory tea in the front corner of that one-room school. It consisted of an order to "Assume the position, bend over, grab your ankles, and don't straighten up, until I tell you." The whole class got to see it. The hickory board landed on our butts, one after the other, until the teacher felt we had enough, about three whacks each. I knew I had, had enough; my friends probably felt the same way. I react very quickly to pain, so I didn't put any more minnows in the water cooler. I learned a lot from that experience. I guess teachers, can't do that anymore. I didn't think so at the time, but it did me well. I didn't like school after that though. I certainly wasn't about to run home and tell my parents either, or I would have had more "tea" to deal with. I stayed on the straight and narrow after that.

At recess, my friends and I would whittle sticks to see who could cut a stick the fastest. We also played flip the knife; with the blade of our pocketknives open, we would flip them to see who could stick one into the ground more often. That isn't allowed anymore, because you can't have weapons at school. We also used to draw a circle on the back of the outhouse and try to throw our knives and have

167

them stick in the circle. It was fun at the time, but we didn't want to get caught by the teacher; he would be mad that we damaged the wood and we would get more "tea". In the evenings, after supper, the chores, and homework was done, the whole family would gather around the old Philco battery-powered radio.

Robert "Buzz" Reynolds in front of The Delaware Run School

We used coal-oil lamps that were turned down low. Everyone was quiet, and shadows would move across the wall whenever one of us shifted about. We all listened to the programs on the radio: Tom Mix, Red Ryder, and The Lone Ranger and Tonto. They were all westerns, and my favorite was The Lone Ranger. I always loved the music and still do to this day. We also listened to mysteries: The Squeaky Door, The Shadow, and the Grand Ole Opry. By nine o'clock at night, it was off to bed for us. They were good old days and family time.

Farm chores had to be done every day. We had to milk cows by hand. There was nothing like the cow who would be bothered by flies; she would swish her tail and smack you up along the side of your head. It knocked your hat off and into the manure every time. The stables had to be cleaned with a pitchfork, and the manure had to be loaded onto a manure spreader. There was not much fun in that. We fed the chickens and slopped the hogs. Cleaning the pigpen was the same amount of fun as cleaning the stables. I did like plowing the fields though. A strange thing happened one day while plowing; dad had an old John Deere tractor with steel wheels on the back a narrow front end, and rubber tires with about four or five inches of space between them. You would come to the end of the field, look back to the trailer-type trip plows, pull the trip rope, and the plows would rise up out of the ground; then you turned the corner and went back to the other furrow. Well, our field had pine trees at the end of it, and they were about five or six inches in width. As I came to the end of

the field, I looked back to grasp the trip rope and turn the corner. I couldn't turn the corner, however, and the tractor was acting funny. It was only a matter of seconds, before I looked back to the front, to find that the front end of the tractor was higher than I was, while I was seated on it.

Here's what happened. I got too close to the end of the field to trip the plows, and the front wheels centered a pine tree. They bent the tree enough that the front end of the tractor ran up the tree. I was scared to death, until I got the tractor stopped. The front was very high; it was like being on a rearing horse. At 15 years of age, I knew I couldn't climb down and go tell my dad, and I was afraid; good luck was with me; I was able to back the tractor up to come down the tree and get myself out of that predicament. I never told my dad after that. I made sure that I had plenty of room when I pulled the trip rope. I sure didn't have fun that day. Around our farmhouse, we had a barn, a pigpen, a smokehouse for smoking meat, a chicken coop, a woodshed, and an outhouse. We didn't get indoor plumbing until about 1950. The outhouse was an uncomfortable, but necessary place that we all visited on a regular basis. I did notice, that zero degree weather, prompted you to get your business done as soon as possible. You forgot about browsing through the Sears & Roebuck Catalog. When we planted a garden, we dug up the ground with a spade. We used a hand rake and a hoe to clear around the plants. We grew our own vegetables. Garden work didn't agree with me, so I got out of doing it as often as I could; the veggies tasted really good though.

We raised and butchered all of our meat. Butchering day was a favorite day for me; keeping a wood fire blazing under the cast-iron kettle, cooking the meat to make scrapple and pudding meat, and sampling the meat out of the cooking kettle with a splash of salt. My

God, it was delicious! Rendering lard and eating cracklins with salt. Nothing compares to it. My mom canned pork tenderloin, and smoked ham and bacon, the old-fashioned way. If you haven't ever had home canned beef and mashed potatoes and gravy, done the old-fashioned way, I can accurately say that you have missed out on one of the finer things in life. The same goes for canned pork tenderloin. You don't see this type of butchering done today. I expect that perhaps the Amish still do it though. My mother used to make dresses for my sisters and shirts for us boys. They were made from feedbags, which dad had purchased to feed the cattle. Some of the feedbags were flowered for our sisters, but the plain colored ones were used for our shirts. Mother worked hard at this; she did lots of sewing. You had to save a nickel anywhere you could; we were always proud of our new shirts.

Dad would take us to the movies on Saturdays, in Milton, Pennsylvania. We went to the old Legionnaire Theater. Mom would go up the street to the Capital Theater. The Legionnaire was mostly western shows, and it was a kind of rough and ready place. It cost adults $0.50, children 12–15 cost $0.25, and anyone under 12 years of age got in free. Popcorn cost $0.05. The Capital Theater had romance movies. Mom preferred those over our cowboys hopping, hollering, and shooting stuff. We would pile into the 1935, two-door, Ford sedan, and to Milton we went. We didn't make many trips to town, because it was too expensive. I remember one of the favorite sayings when you stopped for gas. It was "Gimme a buck's worth." That was a pretty high price back then; you only got four gallons for a buck. In the new days, you get one gallon for four bucks. I have fond memories of the town of Milton, Pennsylvania. It seemed that everybody went to Milton on Saturday night. The streets would be full of people that were shopping or visiting each other. The smell of chocolate and fresh roasted peanuts came from the Woolworth Department Store. The smell of chocolate, fresh roasted peanuts, and freshly popped corn, drifting on a cool night breeze, is something of the good old days that I'll never forget. It is all gone forever. It is very sad, I must say.

Martha Marty's Large Emporium of Stories
By Martha T. Ryan of Emporium,
Pennsylvania
Born 1924

William Lewis and Elida Spangler Thomas were my grandparents. William moved from upper Oxford, Chester County, Pennsylvania around the 1870s, at the age of 17, to make his home in Cameron County. He worked for Mr. Whittemore at a lumberyard in West Creek, and on his 180 plus acre farm on Whittemore Hill. Mr. Whittemore was one of the first settlers in Cameron County, hence the name for the area. On May 15, 1896, for the consideration of $624.03, Mr. Whittemore sold the 180 plus acre farm, which was known as Parcel Four, to my grandfather, thus establishing what became known as "The Thomas Farm". We have William to thank for our heritage, which resulted in being designated a Pennsylvania Century Farm. On October 29, 1914, William purchased an additional 62 plus acres of land that was known as the Seaver Place or Parcel Five from a man named Raymond Ostrum. William was responsible for the clearing of the land; he established an apple orchard of about 60 trees, developed one of the most prolific fresh water springs in the county, and built a springhouse. The springhouse was kept cool, even on the hottest of summer days, by the water that was piped directly from the spring through concrete storage cells, for each day of milking, in large lidded containers. (I can remember skimming off the top layers of rich cream that we used to make our ice cream and whipped cream; it was yummy and we didn't even get fat.) When William and Elida married on February 2, 1882, they made their home in the family homestead, which was situated on Parcel Four. Elida's sister, Augustus Spangler, was the wife of Samuel Parks, who was one of the oldest Civil War Veterans living in Pennsylvania. Upon his death on September 23, 1915, William was interred on a plot of land on the Parcel Four, thus establishing the "Family Cemetery".

My dad made his home on the family farm, on Whittemore Hill, for his entire life. On July 6, 1910, he purchased additional acreage, known as Parcels one, two, and three or also known as "Parks Place", which was originally owned by Uncle Sam Parks. He inherited Parcels four and five from William, making

169

the total acreage of the farm 268.98. Dad was a rangy, big man; he was six feet tall, and weighed 200 pounds. He was a hardworking and reliable citizen; honest as the day is long, his handshake was good as a contract. He was a multifaceted and intelligent individual, not just a farmer. Over the years, he owned and operated a coalmine, a sand pit, built the first fire tower on Whittemore Hill, built the road leading to Bryan Hill, and more. He was a man of advanced ideas, being the first in the neighborhood to install a gas-fired electrical generator; he was the first to have electric lights and running water in his house.

My mother originally came from Jersey Shore to work for Grandma Thomas, as a caretaker and housekeeper. When she was no longer needed, she prepared to go back home. Dad begged her to stay, but she told him she wouldn't unless he married her. She was sitting on a barrel at the train station when dad came down and proposed to her. Even though mom was a small lady, five feet tall and weighing only 100 pounds, she was a hard worker. She too, was multifaceted. She raised a family of 12, was an excellent cook, fed the farm hands (her favorite saying was "If you can't work, you can't eat, if you can't eat you can't stay around here"), boarded and fed the schoolteachers, and boarded and fed 20–25 hunters, during deer and bear seasons. She also preserved every harvest, raised the chickens, milked the cows, sewed lots of clothes, and more. My parents raised a family of 12, all born on the farm. I am the eighth child. My siblings were: Oliver, Mackey, Elyda, Beulah May, William Jerome, Leon Rex, Fennii Augustus, Helen Mary, Jackson, Junior, Harry Dalton, and the twins Mabel Pauline and Howard Paul.

We didn't have much money but we were always well cared for, we had food in our mouths, clothes on our backs, handmade or hand-me-downs, and a roof over our heads. We learned to appreciate what was important in life. We all had chores to do. Dad always said, "Hard work never hurt anyone." All of our meat, dairy products, and fresh vegetables came from the farm; very few things were store bought. My parents took weekly trips into the town to buy groceries that we couldn't produce and food for the animals. They used chickens, eggs, and vegetables to barter for what we needed. Our occasional treat would be one stick of gum, never a pack.

Mom administered the discipline. We girls were sent to cut willow branches, and if they weren't ample enough, we had to go cut more. The boys were the ones that got whipped. I can't remember dad ever raising a hand to any one of us. I grew up during the era of World War II, when gasoline, tires, sugar, meat, silk, shoes, nylon, and many other items were rationed. The Great Depression that started with the stock market crash, on October 29, 1929, known as Black Tuesday, ended with the onset of the war in 1939. Franklin   D. Roosevelt was President of The United States during these times. He served four terms and led us through The Great Depression and WWII. Roosevelt initiated his "New Deal" and setup the Agricultural Adjustment Administration to support farm prices, he setup the Civilian Conservation Corps to employ young men, and he established the Works Projects Administration to provide jobs for laborers. He also setup the Social Security Act that provided unemployment compensation and disability for the elderly. Sylvania Electric Products was the primary employer in Emporium. The company put a lot of effort towards winning the war, so much so, that a grateful government bestowed upon it the Army-Navy E Award, the highest award given to any industry. There was an article in Collier's Magazine entitled "Girls Town" that featured Emporium; 20 girls for every man were employed by Sylvania, because only the females had the patience, or the skill with their fingers, for the work required in the manufacture of radio tubes. Cameron County's flashflood of 1942 happened during my childhood as well. Fourth Street was like a river.

Traveling salesmen, such as the Fuller Brush Man, delivered household items to your door. Doctors still made house calls. Normal School was established in an effort to train high school graduates as teachers. It tried to establish standards of teaching or "norms". Students only had to attend two years of Norm Schooling to be certified as a grade school teacher. There were saddle shoes, jukeboxes, Brownie Box cameras, Burma Shave road signs, cork popguns, drive-in movies and restaurants, carhops, erector sets, S&H green stamps, reel-to-reel tapes, tinker toys, pickup sticks, Lincoln Logs, jacks, hula-hoops, jitterbug dancing, nickel and dime stores, and gas was $0.09 a gallon. We did not have televisions, penicillin, polio vaccines, frozen foods, Xerox, plastic, birth control, radar, laser beams, ballpoint pens, dishwashers, clothes dryers, air conditioning, spaceships, daycare centers, nursing homes, VCRs, typewriters, or computers. We made do with what we had, but we survived pretty well.

From 1930–1938, I attended grade school in a one-room schoolhouse on Whittemore Hill. In those eight years, I only had three teachers, all of whom acquired their room and board from my parents. You can bet that if we got in trouble at school we got it again at home, because the teacher came home with us. We didn't have snow days and we always walked to school no matter what. Our education was of the highest caliber that it could be. It was accomplished in that one room where every pupil could hear the lessons of the other grades. A long bench stood in front of the teacher's desk, where one grade at a time sat for their lessons. The remaining seven grades sat at a typical desk, studying, until it was their turn to be called up front. The school had a big woodstove that stood in the right front corner. There was a round metal cover encircling it to help retain the heat. Families took turns keeping the fire burning and making sure it was stoked up overnight. There were two cloakrooms, but no bathrooms. We had one outhouse for boys and one outhouse for girls. A Sears catalog was used as toilet paper.

If we needed to use the outhouse while class was in session we had to raise our hand and indicate our reason for going by raising one finger for urine or two fingers for solid waste; that way the teacher was aware of how long we would be outside. We didn't tarry in the winter or we would have frozen our butts off! Our outhouses usually had a trapdoor on the back for easier cleaning. After I finished the eighth grade, the school was closed down. I was the smartest and dumbest kid in the eighth grade; I was the only student in that grade; I didn't get a graduation ceremony. After the school was closed, the grade school students were bused to Plank Road Hollow School. I remember my sister, Beulah, used her purple car with a big wooden "School Bus" sign mounted on the front bumper. In 1938, I went directly into the Emporium High School, which was located on East Fourth Street. It was a three-story building with individual rooms for each subject and teacher. The building is still there, but it is a church now. My first days of high school were a nightmare. Coming from a one-room schoolhouse to an environment of individual rooms and various teachers was hard for me. We had very little time between classes in which to find our lockers and report to the next class. I was constantly in fear of losing my way or being late.

I was literally a stranger, because most of the other kids had been together since the first grade; they had already formed cliques, which kind of left us "country hicks" out of them. Eventually, I made friends that have lasted throughout the years. I chose the commercial curriculum all throughout high school. I took bookkeeping, typing, and shorthand as my favored subjects. My worst subject was history, because I could never remember the names and dates. I believe that if it weren't for the fact that my history teacher (a female) took a liking to me, I would have flunked. My favorite teacher was Mr. Patterson, who taught in a manner that prepared me for a job in the outside world. When he realized one of the students didn't like having anyone looking over her shoulder, he moved her up to the front, beside his desk. As it turned out, her first job was typing up check vouchers for employees, who were leaving on business trips, while they stood looking over her shoulder. Whenever Mr. Patterson typed, he made music with the keys, easily recognizable tunes. He had a crippled foot from polio, but the disability didn't hamper him in any manner. He was a great dancer and attended all the school functions. During my free periods, I worked in the school office for the principal. One of the pieces of advice he gave me was, "You can't always do the jobs you like to do. You learn more doing jobs that you don't like to do." Our senior class trip was to Washington D.C. We took in all the sights, movies, and stage shows. We went during the period when the theaters had a live program on stage along with the regular movie.

The Corner Drugstore
By Virginia Bell Lesher of Coalport,
Pennsylvania
Born 1938

The building still stands at the corner of Main and Spruce streets in Coalport, but that is all that remains of the bygone era of the corner drugstore and the soda fountain. It was

Tom Bell in the Corner Drug Store

first established as McCartney's Drug Store in 1885, in a small coal town, in southern Clearfield County; the first prescription filled, was for a pint of whiskey. The drugstore saw many changes in the pharmaceutical profession over the years, but it remained a profitable business for 115 years. It changed ownership only three times within that period. Charles Eckbert purchased the business in 1924, and it became known as Eckbert's Drug Store. Then in 1947, Tom Bell came back to his hometown and purchased the business; he changed the name to Bell's Drug Store. When Tom died in 1971, his daughter became the pharmacist-owner, and the store remained as Bell's Drug Store until it closed in 2001.

Originally, there weren't many drugs to choose from; more were compounded by the pharmacist from a prescription written according to the wishes, whims, and intellect of the local physician. Pills were hand rolled, suppositories were made with the aid of a mold, ointments were mixed with a spatula on a tile, and cough syrups were mixed and flavored to suit the taste buds of the patient. Penicillin, which ushered in the "antibiotic age", wasn't even discovered until 1928. Today, most medications are manufactured in large quantities by a pharmaceutical company, stocked by a pharmacy, and dispensed in a smaller quantity by a pharmacist, according to the prescription from a doctor. In the early years of Bell's Drug Store, a local doctor had a special stomach remedy; the pharmacist at the time kindly referred to it as Mrs. Sutter's Powders. It was a combination of six different powdered drugs that were divided into dose portions, placed on individual medicinal papers, wrapped, folded, and dispensed in a small box of 24 doses, with directions to

dissolve the powder in a glass of water and drink it four times a day. The process to fill the prescription took several hours. Can you imagine doing that today when large pharmacies fill more prescriptions in one day, than the corner drugstore ever filled in a matter of weeks?

The prescription end of the drug store was only a small portion of the business. Over-the-counter medicines, gift items, cosmetics, and tobacco were also sold; the biggest attraction was the soda fountain. Originally, the serving area at the soda fountain was a long marble counter with high stools in front and several small tables; each table had four, high-backed, wire chairs. In later years, the small tables were replaced with other tables and comfortable booths. The fountain area, behind the counter, remained the same with three sinks, to hand wash the beautiful sundae dishes and soda glasses; and freezers that held a variety of flavored ice cream, refrigeration for milk products, and the tasty soda flavors and toppings. The most important pieces of equipment on the fountain were the soda arms. They weren't arms as a person has, but two tall, fancy water spigots with a handgrip on the top of each. One spigot was used for just plain, cold water, but the other one gave out the magic carbonated water, that produced the fizz and bubbles in the fountain drinks and ice cream sodas. The name "soda jerk" was coined from the manner in which the clerk jerked the handles forward to get a full stream of water, or jerked them backwards to produce a thin, more forceful stream. The fountain itself was a maze of refrigeration, but in the store's basement was a motor, a compressor, and a large tank of carbon dioxide, which were all connected to the waterline to produce the magic bubbles. The water had to be kept under pressure and very cold to maintain the fizz, or else the drinks would be flat and taste bad.

Early in the 1800s, soda water was flavored, bottled, and sold as a soft drink by such companies as Coca-Cola, Pepsi, Hires, and Canada Dry. Soda fountains in drug stores increased in popularity when these companies sold just the flavored syrups to individual stores. The Hershey Company made chocolate syrup and toppings for milkshakes and sundaes. With the increased demand, other companies began to manufacture high quality fountain syrups and many toppings of other flavors included marshmallow, butterscotch, and various fruit flavors. The availability and variety of syrups and toppings paved the way for a more interesting and tasty menu; the corner drug store soda fountain became a great hangout and fascination to young and old folks alike. As a teenager in the 1920s, Tom Bell began to work as a soda jerk at Eckbert's Drug Store. His job was to make all of the tasty concoctions at the soda fountain. Other fellows found it an interesting place to take a date, to share a soda or sundae, or maybe just to flirt with the gorgeous young girl behind the counter. High school girls often brought their brown bag lunches to the store and bought a drink, or more often, a delicious sundae was their lunch. Youngsters were more devilish and were known to push the syrup pumps when nobody was looking. One such youngster thought it was fun to watch the soda jerk put a dab of eight different syrup flavors into his drink. He ordered it often and told his friends. The drink became known as a "Trip around the Fountain". The fun of making the extra work for the clerk was gone when the syrups were combined and placed into one pump, but the popularity of the drink remained until the close of business.

Bell's Drug Store

Tom Bell's love for his job at Eckbert's Drug Store was the main factor in him choosing pharmaceuticals as a career. In 1929, after completing three years of pharmaceutical education, he got married. He then worked for a number of retail drug chains and started raising a family. Just before the start of World War II, he bought his first drug store with a soda fountain, in Gallitzin, Pennsylvania. His expertise as a soda fountain manager was more profitable than his pharmacy license was. During the war, sugar was rationed, and it was very difficult to buy syrups and toppings. Tom experimented with other available foods, and created new and more interesting fountain specialties. Fruit cocktail sundae was a seasonal specialty, which was made with fresh oranges, bananas, and cherries. Another creation that really caught on was a sundae with a peanut butter topping. Peanut butter sundaes are still popular in that area, but his recipe remains a secret to this day. The Tom Mix Cooler became a popular summer drink at Bell's Drug Store. A combination of ice, ice cream, flavored syrup, and soda water placed in a blender, and served in a tall soda glass, with whipped cream and a cherry, made a delightful, very cold drink. Banana split sundaes were always popular. Tom's always had three scoops of ice cream on top of a split banana, in a special elongated dish. The ice cream was usually topped with chocolate syrup, marshmallow, walnuts pineapple, and cherry topping, plus whipped cream and a cherry, which made for a beautiful and delicious tasting treat.

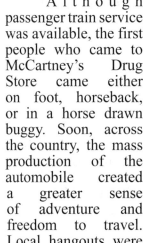

Although passenger train service was available, the first people who came to McCartney's Drug Store came either on foot, horseback, or in a horse drawn buggy. Soon, across the country, the mass production of the automobile created a greater sense of adventure and freedom to travel. Local hangouts were passed by, as people ventured to the cities where there was more variety of everything. Merchandising changed drastically. Serve yourself came into vogue and bigger became better. Small "Mom and Pop" stores began to fail. Less than 100 years after the opening of McCartney's Drug Store, we moved into the space age, when men walked on the moon. The age of the corner drug store and soda fountain is gone. My, how quickly the times have changed!

In the early 40s, I remember milk being delivered to the porch of our house in the wee hours of the morning. I don't remember actually seeing a truck or a man; my bedroom was close to the road, and I could hear the truck coming, stopping, and then after a short pause, I could hear the slight clank of the glass milk bottles as they were set upon

173

the porch. Each evening, before bedtime, my mother would set empty, clean, quart-sized, glass milk bottles on the front porch with an order note and money stuck in a bottle. The milkman would then leave the full milk bottles on the porch and be on his way long before daylight. In the wintertime, on an exceptionally cold morning, it was comical to retrieve the milk from the porch. The frozen cream on top of the milk would push the little cardboard cap up about an inch or two above the neck of the bottle. The bottle had a funny new hat, until it started to melt. The cat was always on hand to catch the drippings. If the bottles had been sealed as they are today, they would have burst. 70 years later, that little milk farm is still in operation. Their milkman still brings milk, butter, eggs, and even ice cream to the front porch of my daughter's house. Not much has changed except for the packaging. She puts an order note and money, in an insulated cooler on her front porch. The milkman comes around noon, once a week, and puts her order in the cooler. Everything is packaged in cardboard containers, and everyone is wide-awake when the milkman comes.

In early 1900, the first large coalmine operation was opened in downtown Coalport. It was owned by the Imperial Coal Company, and it was always known as the Sunshine Mine. A large coal tipple, cleaning plant, railroad tracks, coal cars, and company houses made up the complex that was nearly in the center of the town. Behind the tipple, the drift mouth or small cave-like opening into the surrounding hill was the entrance to the mine. There was no shaft entrance as there is in the very deep mines. The men rode into the mine on little motorized coal cars and spent at least eight hours a day underground, digging out their livelihood with only a pick and a shovel, in a tunnel that was only as high as the vein of coal. The underground tunnels followed the vein of coal under the hills around Coalport to a distance of ten miles or more. The mines in our area were all "B" vein of coal, which was the deepest we had and averaged about 24 inches in height. The "A" vein of coal is the deepest type of coal vein, but it has never been mined in this area, because it is said to be 10 feet below the level of the creek that runs through the town. As the men picked the coal, it was loaded onto the little coal cars and brought out of the mine to the tipple, where it was cleaned, graded, and loaded onto large Pennsylvania railroad cars, for shipment all over the country.

In 1931, it was reported that 380 men had dug 210,308 tons of coal for the Imperial Coal Company at the Sunshine Mine. I wasn't a coal miner's daughter, nor did I ever enter the mine. As a youngster, I was intrigued to watch very tired, very dirty, black-faced coal miners, with a large, empty lunch pail under their arm, as they slowly walked down the hill from the mine, past our corner drug store, up the alley, and into the basement of a local saloon, where showers were located for the miners. It was amazing that they came out white and mostly clean. Next to the drug store was the company store. It was owned and operated by the Imperial Coal Company. It was strongly encouraged that the miners frequented the store for all of their general merchandise needs, and they were allowed to purchase items on credit. To me, the store was more interesting than the mine.

If You Can't Catch Em, Shoot Em
By Dominick "Chiz" Mazzante of
Williamsport, Pennsylvania
Born 1923

When I was a young boy approximately 13 years old, I took the city bus from Market Square to Newberry. A larger lady boarded the bus in front of me. She was carrying a box filled with peeps. She paid her fair and proceeded to find a seat amongst a full bus.

Somehow, the box that she was carrying broke open and the peeps got out and started running around the bus. As the lady started bending over to try and gather the peeps, she passed gas several times, sounding like gunshots going off, to which the bus driver turned around and said, "Hey lady, if you can't catch Em, shoot Em!"

Everyone on the bus laughed and he got fined.

Our School Was Better, Back Then
By Dorothy L. Knarr of Antes Fort,
Pennsylvania
Born 1920

School was so different back in my school days. The school bell rang and everyone went to their room and sat in the seat that was assigned you. The teacher said, "Good morning", scholars responded with the same, then, the class was called to order. We were told to stand to attention, we saluted and recited the "Flag Salute", followed with the reading of several Bible verses read by the teacher and everyone said the "Lord's Prayer" then, classes started.

After graduation from grade school, we started to High School in Jersey Shore, which was about three miles from where we lived in Antes Fort. We walked both ways because there was no school bus from our town of Antes Fort. All 4 years, we walked both ways.

Sometimes the "island" that we lived on would be flooded and we would have to wait for a truck to come along and we'd stand on the running boards to cross over the water. There was no school bus available for us all 4 years. Sometimes there would be 4-6 of us girls. One of the girls was "Prince Farrington's daughter, Gladys. Sometimes she'd have a $20.00 bill and she'd take us to a movie at the Victoria Theater, then, to the "Villa" next door for an ice cream cone and start walking home after school to Antes Fort.

I think our school was better back then, than now. Course, I could be wrong, but I'm 91 years old, seems all they do now is push buttons!

The "Secret Five"
By Peg Coulter of Kane, Pennsylvania
Born 1922

My mother was the first liberal woman I knew. She was for the "rights of women" and all girls should be educated. She wished to send my sister and me to finishing school, but the Depression changed that. She did make me take Elocution lessons from a local lady. Every week after school, I would hike up the hill and learn monologues. Sadie Hawkins was my favorite, complete with costume— then, I would get stuck performing at PTA meetings, etc. At my performance in church I caught some boys laughing like crazy, so that was the end of my acting career.

When I finished Jr. High school age, my friends became the "Secret Five". We were an active group with Cheerleading, Band, choir, plays, and our friendship lasted forever. So, the Secret Five went off to colleges, but June and I had to wait a year before we were age 18 to enter Nurse's training. So, I worked in Woolworth and made $10.00 a week.

The war in Europe was taking our boys and we were restless. Telegrams started to arrive from the State Department. Rations were put into effect limiting gasoline, nylons, and sugar. Our group found college friends and husbands and moved away, but we managed to keep in touch. Years later, we started meeting on Nancy's back porch for picnics with our husbands every summer.

In 1997, the Woolworth legacy ended and we discussed our great memories. We all worked there during high school. Helen remarked how enriched we were after 8 hours a day earning $1.80. We were enriched, not by money, but in experience. She worked in the stationery cards, nails, bolts, and cosmetics selling "tangerine lip stick." Joyce worked in the candy department weighing on a scale, chocolate bonbons, nonpareils, and filling Easter baskets. Nancy sold bobby pins and curlers. After closing at 9 PM Saturday night, our dates would be waiting outside and off we would go to get a hamburger and a coke, and jitterbug to music on the jukebox. Curfew was 12 midnight and the town clock over the courthouse would chime. We were learning our work ethic in 1940.

We ended our picnic at Nancy's with a champagne toast to Woolworth's. All my friends have passed away.

Truck Patch Gardens and Rubber Band Guns
By Mary Fischer of Williamsport,
Pennsylvania
Born 1937

My childhood memories began when I was approximately five years old. Prior to that, we lived in upper Fairfield. My father was a logger in and around that area. My mother died seven days after my birth. I was one of eight siblings. It was a very traumatic time for my father and my siblings.

175

When I was four or five years old, we moved to a small village in Columbia County. Dad had gotten a job at what was then the largest employer in the area, Magee Carpet Company.

The house we rented had no running water or indoor bathrooms. We used an outhouse and on Saturday nights, we took our baths in a wooden tub. Because I was the youngest, I got to go first. Of course, there was no changing the water. Winter and summer, we brushed our teeth with baking soda at the outside pump.

We had quite a large garden, commonly referred to as a truck patch in those days. I remember that the children were responsible for the weeding, and in the fall at harvest time, there was the preserving. Everything was "put up" in jars, as there wasn't any freezer.

There were also fun times. Homemade ice cream was a popular treat.

My closest siblings are two brothers. How they liked to get after me with their rubber band guns when our parents weren't home. The guns were made from old tire inner tubes.

Chamber Buckets and Banty Hens
By Nancy Hess of Muncy, Pennsylvania
Born 1945

As young children, my sisters, brothers, and I would stay with my grandparents on the farm and help them through the summer months and on weekends during the school year.

I remember the old hand water pumps on the back porch that we used to wash dishes and for cooking and cleaning. We would bathe in a big, round tub, and then it was off to bed at 9:00 pm, to be back up again at 4:30 am. The only heat that they used was an old cook stove that looked like it was made of cast iron.

The grandparents had an old "chamber bucket" that sat on the stair steps, with a roll of toilet paper to be used during the night only, and Grandpap would take it out and empty it in the old outhouse on his way to the barn to milk the cows. Oh yes, not to mention the old *Sears, Roebuck Catalogs* and corncobs we had to use when we were out of toilet paper. I'm sure you remember.

The big barn is gone now, but we sure had a lot of fun jumping down the hayloft. Grandpap would take us out in the fields on a wagon with our buckets to pick all types of berries: raspberries, strawberries, blueberries,

An old wind-up clock

cranberries, etc. Then we would help Grammy make jams and jellies. Paraffin was used to melt and pour over the top of the jars to seal them.

The old farmhouse and wagon barn are still standing just outside of Hughesville, Pennsylvania on Route 405 Highway. The land on which the farmhouse and wagon barn stand is now a mobile home park, and the fields are all built up with new homes.

I remember having rheumatic fever at the age of seven and being confined at home all summer that year and half of the new school term. My parents let me have a black and white speckled banty hen that I kept in a box during the night. During the day, she would follow me all over, so I made a leash out of yarn and we would go for walks. When I had to return to school, she had to go back to the farm and eventually she passed on, because

The chamber bucket that set on stair steps at night

176

she would not eat or drink through the week without me.

To this day, I still have the old chamber bucket and an old wind up clock that my grandparents used to keep time.

Those Dirty Rats
By John Hammond of Williamsport,
Pennsylvania
Born 1939

I grew up in the 1940s and 50s with a group of kids my age who closely resembled the gang in the old TV shows "The Little Rascals" or "Spanky and Our Gang." We had one fat kid, one black kid, one who was not too bright, and one who was tall and skinny and couldn't keep his hair-lick down. We all had nicknames: Butch, Spike, Benny, Cris Bolt, Kubla, and Tiny (me—although I was the biggest of the bunch).

We never had a fight with another group of guys, but we did hang out on the steps in front of the Milton YMCA and pretended to be the defenders of Milton turf from rival towns like Danville.

The local police chief, who was known as Honest John, viewed us with great suspicion and blamed us for most of the town vandalism. This was not true and we did not steal.

There was little entertainment in those days except the movies or swimming in the river. We all came from poor families and often took up a group collection of change to buy 1 or 2 dollars of gas so we could cruise around the streets of Milton and Lewisburg.

One of our gang lived very close to a "dump" (now called landfills) there were many of them in those years and they were smelly, rat infested, and totally exposed. As we were riding around one evening without any money and very little gas, the kid who lived near the dump mentioned that the rats were getting bad. Someone else said we should get our 22 rifle and shoot some, which we did. This proved to be so much fun that we did it several times again. We would tape a flashlight to the barrel of the 22 rifle and hunt at night when the rats came out. One evening we had finished a late baseball game and someone suggested we go shoot rats. The problem was; we had no ammunition and no money. Someone else said we could use the baseball bats to kill rats. The technique was simple: hold the flashlight in one hand and the

John "Tiny" Hammond in 1956

club in the other. So, we engaged in clubbing rats.

We did this a number of times and late one evening as we had most of the gang in an old sedan the Police Chief pulled us over. He asked our names and asked where we were going so late. We said just cruising. Then he saw some of the bats and clubs on the floor of the back seat. He made us open the trunk and saw more clubs and old shoes we wore. He demanded to know where we had a gang fight or where we were going to have one! We replied that this did not happen and was not going to happen. His reply was, "What are all the clubs for?" We tried to explain to him the art of rat clubbing at the dump. By the look on his face and the way he shook his head, I'm sure he didn't believe us. We gave up trying to convince him and took his advice to go straight home. That ended the rat clubbing.

The Nicest Christmases We Ever Experienced.
By Judith E. Hudson of Kane, Pennsylvania
Born 1949

In 1956, when I was six and my brother, Wayne was seven; my parents were carless, so as a family, our family walked everywhere. We lived in Kane, Pennsylvania.

The night before Christmas (the 24ᵗʰ), was the day my family opened their gifts.

This particular Christmas we were invited to our cousin's house for a family Christmas party. I remember my mother baking a cake with red candy hearts and silver bead decorations on her cake. It was the beginning of a beautiful Christmas.

During past Christmases, I often wondered how Santa would be able to come, as all we had were stovepipes. Mother and Dad told me not to worry. Santa would come while we were at the Christmas party because they would leave the door unlocked so he could get in.

It was dark when we left the house, but it was a beautiful night. No snow was falling at the time of our journey and the sky was filled with stars. It was about one mile for our journey. Wayne and I were bundled up for winter and the long walk.

About two blocks before we arrived at our destination, I proceeded to fall into a 2 or 3 foot deep hole beside the sidewalk because it was so dark and there were few if any streetlights to mark our way. I wasn't scared at all, and remember looking up at the stars. I didn't even try to get out of the hole. I can remember my parents lifting me out of this huge trench or hole beside the sidewalk.

As we arrived at our destination, I remember all of us, including all of my cousins around the same age really played hard. We were not a quiet, peaceful bunch whenever we got together.

Later on that night after all of us had eaten and after we sang Christmas songs, my folks decided to come home to see if Santa had made it to our house. I was afraid he wouldn't come or else I was afraid I'd receive a lump of coal. Coal gifts were a sign that you had been naughty.

My parents, brother, and I started to walk home, but since our arrival time at our cousins' house, there had been an ice storm, so we couldn't walk up the hill from my cousin's place. We went back and one of my uncles who lived in Bradford, Pennsylvania, drove us home. My uncle and family were going home to their house also at that time.

As we entered the house, I saw Santa had been there. He had brought me a set of miniature doll dishes with miniature pots and pans, silverware and plates, cups and saucers all placed neatly inside of a blue wooden

cabinet, which also had cup hangers on the top shelf. The bottom had pull out drawers filled with tiny silverware. I remember also, there was a note from Santa clipped to the tree saying Wayne and I had been good children and we received gifts, therefore, rather than coal. Wayne, my brother's gift was a wood cabinet with a tool-belt filled with tools for little hands. I remember I said, "Santa is really real." Both Wayne and I shouted, "Thank you Santa." I couldn't figure out how the gifts got there while we were away at the family party, so that helped my belief in Santa to grow.

Years later, after I was grown, I questioned the folks. I found out, not only had my dad constructed the cupboards and painted them a sky-blue, but he left the party for a while and with the help of a relative he got a ride to the house, arranged the gifts, pinned the note on the tree, ate the goodies left for Santa and returned to the party. We were so busy being busy he wasn't even missed while he was arranging everything under the tree. But, to make a long story short, with a lot of planning our folks gave us one of the nicest Christmases we ever experienced.

Homemade Bread, Not "Botten"
By Patricia P. Ulrich of Allenwood,
Pennsylvania
Born 1931

I was born in 1931 and started school at age five at the "Pleasant Green" one-room school. It was one of five one-room schools in Washington Township, Lycoming County, Pennsylvania. There were four rows of double seats, six in each row beginning in the front with "class performance seats" and desks attached behind so that when our class was called, we would move to the front seat. The teacher's desk was in front and center. The wall behind the teacher's desk was lined with blackboards, and topped with rolled up maps. We had one rolled up black rubber map of the outlined United States. We could fill in the states names and capitols with chalk. When finished, it could be washed off and someone else could fill it in.

There were two in my class, myself and another girl when I was in second grade. There was none in 1ˢᵗ grade, two in 2ⁿᵈ, two in 3rd, one in 4th, two in 5th, three in 6th, 3 in 7th, and three in 8th grade, making a total of 16 students.

My father, Lemuel Pauling was one of the five men on the school board and he was Treasurer. The others were Thomas Waring, President, Brady Russell, Secretary, and Ralph Baker and George Hain. I remember the teacher was paid $100.00 per month. Her duties included firing the pot-bellied stove in the center of the room, which included carrying coal in and ashes out, keeping the school clean, cleaning the girls and boys (separate) outhouse toilets, carrying drinking water for the students from a neighbor down the road, and of course, teaching eight grades, except in this case, only seven (there was none in 1st grade). Students were assigned simple tasks like clapping erasers, leading the singing, passing out books, paper, and pencils.

Our class being the youngest, would be called first, moving to the front seat, be instructed and given assignments and then return to our seats. Then the other classes would come forward in succession up to the 8th grade and then we would begin all over again, rotating from English, Arithmetic, spelling, Geography, and History. Once weekly, we had Penmanship, Music, and Health etc.

When the bell rang pulled by a rope to the bell tower, there would be roll call, Pledge of Allegiance to the Flag, the teacher would read a passage of scripture and we prayed "The Lord's Prayer." Then we would sing a song usually "America", or "America the Beautiful", the" Star Spangled Banner" or something else before we all settled down to work.

Earlier grades would be sitting just behind the "performance seats" and often would listen and absorb the lessons being taught to the older classes so that by the time I reached 7th grade, I took the 8th grade exam, passed it and skipped 8th and continued on to 9th grade at Montgomery High School.

Once a year all five schools participated in "County Institute." It was held in in the Elimsport United Methodist Church. The county Education Superintendent came and all students were prepared to demonstrate how much they had learned in English, Math, etc. There was always a spelldown in which all students participated.

I don't remember many discipline problems. I walked about ½ mile to school

that began at 9:00 AM and dismissed at 4:00 PM. There were two 15-minute recesses and 1 hour for lunch. In the winter when we had snow, (I seem to remember every year having lots of snow) we would chug down our lunch, grab our sleds, run up Rt. 44 to the top of the hill and sled ride down. The snow would be packed down by the few cars that traveled there so that we often could turn the corner at the township road and slide on another ¼ mile. There were no snowplows then, so the road remained snow covered all winter.

1936 was still depression era and no one had much money. I remember every mother made homemade bread and you were really something if you ever had a sandwich made of "botten" bread. You got new shoes to start to school and hoped your feet didn't grow too much before spring. You went barefoot all summer. Not much emphasis was placed on style. You wore whatever hand-me downs you could get. We had snowsuits we hated to wear except when the sled riding was good. Some of the students had more than a mile to walk and it was often pitch dark by the time they got home.

Then of course, there were the chores to do. Almost everybody lived on farms so there were chickens to feed, eggs to gather, pigs to slop, and cows to milk, buckets to wash and horses to feed and then supper. Occasionally there was still time to listen to radio. There was Fibber McGee, Molly, Amos and Andy, Inner Sanctum, The Green Hornet, Jack Armstrong, the All American Boy, Ma Perkins, and the Lone Ranger. At five or six years old, I was sent to bed early and didn't get to listen too much.

The social highlight of the month was the PTA meeting. Besides church, it was about the only time the community got together. Everyone came—folks who never had any children, folks whose children were raised and gone, new families with babies— everyone. The school kids would prepare a little entertainment and holidays were observed. Halloween parties when everyone would dress up, and Christmas and Easter, I also remember box socials when the girls would fix a lunch in a very fancy box and the boys were expected to buy them. The fun was that the fellows never knew which box was which, and would sometimes spend a lot for a special girl's box only to find it was someone else's box. Mostly, everyone had a good time.

Farm Girl Marries Love of Her Life
By Imogene Winnie of Mansfield,
Pennsylvania
Born 1927

I was born and raised as a farm girl. My parents had a dairy farm. When I arrived, I had two brothers and one sister waiting to no doubt spoil me. Two years later a baby brother arrived, so I was no longer the youngest. To this day, I call him my baby brother. We were all born at home. The past few years, I was given a copy of my great-grandmother's diary from the year I was born, and she stayed at our home and helped out at that time. Also written in it, she told of a neighbor lady who came in and cared for me, bathing and dressing me.

When growing up on the farm, we had pet cats, dogs, and lambs. We made pets of farm animals, too. The cows were all named.

As the years went by and we all got older, we helped out with chores and such like. Mother did all the baking, cooking, washing ironing,

Imogene's mom, Evina Morgan

etc. in the home, in addition to working outside on the farm. She helped with barn chores and in the fields. We had no modern machinery. Horses were used. Cows were milked by hand.

There wasn't any electric, until the early thirties, when the electric company put the electric through the countryside. When the house was wired, I remember the first light in the house was in the kitchen, overhead in the ceiling. My, what a big difference that was compared to the kerosene lights we had been using all the years! So many changes to more modern things came then.

Mother cooked, baked, and heated water on the old-fashioned cook stove. There was always a fire in the stove year around, even in summer time. The stove had a reservoir on one end where water was kept hot. I must say that Mother was a wonderful cook and baker. She always baked bread, pies, cookies, and cakes.

For washdays, the copper boiler was used to heat water. Laundry was done once a week and year around hung outside to dry, and in winter, the frozen things were brought inside to air dry on a rack behind the cook stove. Before electric, the washing was done in the Maytag washing machine run by a gasoline motor and after we had electric, we had an electric wringer washer. One time my younger brother got his finger caught in the gears on top of the tub, and so a quick trip to the doctor was made. To this day, one of his fingers where the nail is shows what happened that time. Ironing was done with irons heated on the stove.

Weekly bath time was usually on Saturday night for everyone. Water was heated on the stove. The washtub was brought into the kitchen, and we all had our turn using the tub.

After electric came to the home, we soon had a bathroom in the house. The pitcher pump was replaced by an electric pump. The pantry was torn up and the bathroom was installed. No more chamber pots and no more outhouse. That was such a wonderful blessing. We didn't have to empty pots each day or run outside to the privy. And no more using an old *Sears Catalog* either.

Once I started school, it was a one-room school with eight grades in it. This had outhouses, one for boys and one for girls. Older students carried water from a spring. There was a woodshed, too. This school

Imogene's dad, Ray Morgan

was heated by a big stove. When there was a lot of snow, we got to school by horses and bobsleds.

My first year turned out not so great, and I didn't go back until the next year. The teacher pounded his thumb when putting a nail in the wall at noontime and took his disposition out on some of us students. One of the older girls took me to a neighbor's home, and my parents were called. The next year I had a nice teacher, and he became my favorite.

Once we completed eight grades in school, children took an eighth grade exam. If we passed it, we went on to high school in town by bus.

Telephones in the homes were wall phones and party lines. This was neat as everyone if

Francis, Richard, Wilber, Imogene, Ray, and Evina

wanted to could listen in and hear the news of families. So many shorts and longs was each one's ring. Also, so many short rings were for an emergency in the neighborhood.

We very seldom went to the doctor, only when we really had to. Our doctor was Mom. I remember if we were barefooted and stepped on a nail, the turpentine bottle came out and turpentine was poured on our foot. Good Samaritan Salve was a good drawing thing, too.

We could always find something to do to entertain ourselves. Games played were Old Maid and dominos. Mother played the old pump organ and later the piano and we

*Wallace Winnie, Jr. and Imogene Winnie
1981*

had fun singing together. We always had our birthday celebration. Christmas was great but simple. I had one doll. We didn't get a lot at Christmas like children do these days, but we were happy with a coloring book and crayons or books to read.

In the winter, there was always a lot of snow, so we rode downhill and shared a sled. Roads used to be drifted.

I had neighbor friends. When we went to play with the neighbor kids, a note was sent to the mother that we could only stay thirty minutes. We didn't get to go often, either.

I used to stay a while at my aunt and uncle's house. One time, I turned the handle on the cream separator and couldn't turn it off and the cream ran out. And this was what my aunt used to churn butter. I was scared to tell her. Well, when she learned what I did, needless to say, I was punished and sent to bed for a while in the middle of the day. I only turned the knob to see what would happen, just a curious little girl.

I remember World War II. When Pearl Harbor happened, we learned of it when the radio was turned on for the evening news. My brother was drafted and was in the Army. He served time overseas and was in the Battle of the Bulge. I have ration books from when sugar and other things were rationed.

My first love was a blind date, and this turned out to be my only love, because I married this lovely young man. We shared over forty years together, and then I lost the love of my life when he became suddenly ill and passed away. It will be twenty-one years this year since he passed away.

I have lots of memories, especially my Dad and how he worked so hard on the farm.

Ghost Stories, Milkweed Pods, and Training Dogs
By David L. C. Albert of Trout Run, Pennsylvania
Born 1941

My name is David LC Albert. All important people have two middle initials, and I am the exception to the rule. The L. and C. are my grandfathers' first names, Lloyd and Charles. I live in Calvert, about eighteen miles north of Williamsport, Pennsylvania, with Marian, my wife of fifty years. We have three children and nine grandchildren. We can look out our windows and see our two sons' houses.

We live on the farm my great-grandfather, David, bought in 1882. The adjoining farm is the homestead farm bought in 1856 and is still in our family. I have lived in Calvert all of my life of seventy years.

When I was growing up there was a country store on the corner not far from our house, it was owned by Harry Carr. At the age of four or five, I would go to the store with a nickel and the store owner, an old man, sixty-five when I was born, would greet me with, "What do you want"? After a while, I got used to him.

At the age of eleven, in the summer time, I would go to the store in the evenings, sit on the porch with the store owner and another old neighbor, Buff Ely, and listen to ghost stories. Buff, who lived about a mile from the store, would come with his lantern and would walk home in the dark. He said one night as he walked home, he saw a horse and wagon with a lantern, flying through the air. I don't know the exact distance from that porch to our front door, but I do know I hold the land speed record for that distance!

School Days
I attended a one room school house for eight years. I could walk to school from home. It was about one-fourth of a mile. One year in the fall, I picked milkweed pods on the way to school each day and put them in my desk. When school was over for the year, we had to clean out our desks. As I removed the milkweed pods, seeds went all over the school. The teacher made me clean all of them up.

Another day when school was over, I had a new bike. As I came out of the school, a neighbor boy took my bike and was going down the road. I heard him yell back, "Share and share alike; thanks for letting me ride your bike".

My favorite teacher was Mrs. Esther Grimes. She came to teach at Beech Valley School when I started school. She was my teacher all eight years I attended this one room school. She taught me much more than what was in the books, like how to have respect for others and how to help others. She taught at the school for twenty years, until it closed in 1968.

Tales My Grandfather Used to Tell
My grandfather, Charles Albert told of the neighbor man who wanted to buy a dress for his wife. He went to a store down the road and said he wanted to buy a dress. The store owner said, "What size"? The man said he didn't know, but looking around the store, he saw a pickle barrel and told the store owner to try a dress on the barrel, and if it fit the barrel, it would fit his wife.

I would ride with my grandfather as he hauled manure up the hill above our house. Part way up the hill, he would stop the horses to let them rest, and they would fart. He would say, "A farting horse will never tire, and a farting man is the man to hire".

Mischief We Got Into
Living in the country, we had to create our own entertainment. Two neighbor boys and I decided to do something about neighborhood dogs that chased cars. We put the sprayer

pump and gas engine that one of the boys' dads had in the back of my dad's old pickup truck. I drove the truck, and they rode in the back. As we would approach a home where we knew a dog would come out, they would start up the engine and build up pressure. Then they would wash the dog. We cured many neighborhood dogs from chasing cars, at least for that summer. The best part of this entertainment was when a neighbor boy saw us coming and stepped out from behind a tree by the road and threw a bucket of water at us. To say the least, he got back a lot more than a bucket full!

Katherine and her brother, George Moore

We Had Music and Dancing!
By Katherine Moore Nittinger of
Williamsport, Pennsylvania
Born 1935

I grew up in the yellow brick house my (omitted) built on Third Street at the end of Tinsman Avenue. Aunt Tommy and Uncle Walt lived on Tinsman Avenue. I spent a lot of time there. I had my own crib and later my own bed at their house. Uncle Walt had a bike shed, so I had cars, trikes, and my first two-wheeler by the time I was four. I also had a black and white scooter with a fold down seat. There were few sidewalks and not very much traffic, so we rode in the streets.

Third Street was very different then, in the thirties and early forties. The houses were

Katherine "Tootie" and Gene Landon
1939

big and most had porches, shade trees, and gardens. The street was two lanes, the trolley didn't run anymore, but the tracks were still there. Bus fare to Williamsport was ten cents, five cents to Montoursville. I remember when they cut down the trees and covered over the tracks to make the street wider. I cried.

I was the youngest of five. The twins, Betty and Ann, were thirteen, George was eight, and Polly was seven when I was born in 1935. It was a big house with five bedrooms, but I had to share a bed with Polly. She'd tell me sad, scary stories, so I'd end up with the twins.

We had a big front porch with honeysuckle growing up the west side. How sweet it smelled in the morning. Mom and I both liked summer storms and would head for the glider on the porch when the rains came.

In the kitchen, Mom cooked on a big black gas stove with burners on one side and a coal stove on the other. My brother used to make lead soldiers on the lid of the coal side. On cold mornings, we would get dressed in front of that warm stove. Mom did a lot of cooking, canning, and baking with that old stove. The icebox was on the enclosed back porch. I remember getting ice chips off the back of the ice truck. I was about eight when we got a "Frigidaire".

The laundry was done in an "Easy" washer. It had three "bells" that agitated and a wringer. The men's pants and jeans and the buttons on shirts had to be put through the wringer just so, so nothing would break. The wash was done out there in warm weather and then hung on the line to dry. In freezing weather, the washer and double tubs were rolled into the kitchen to be used. How the windows used to steam up! A wooden rack that folded down from the wall was used to hang ironing or finish drying clothes that were hung out.

We had music. There was an upright piano just inside the dining room. Mom played ragtime, pop, and played just about anything from *The White Cliffs of Dover* to Chopin. In the living room, there was a small pump organ and a grand piano. My sister, Ann played both. Dad played the violin. He was a big man and had been a bare fisted prizefighter in his youth. He was a gentle man, however.

My parents liked to dance. Mom would roll up the rugs and everyone would dance through the house. On the back porch, the double tubs held beer and soft drinks. Music was played on the Victrola. We had to lift the arm to put the needle on the record. My father taught me to dance.

Polly, George, Ann, and Tootie
1944

We played games, read, danced, roller-skated, and went for long walks, and played jacks and marbles. There was always something to do. On Sunday evenings, Dad would settle down with a book while Mom and her friends played cards. My friend, Kenny Entz and I would sit in the dark in the kitchen with our eyes glued to the lighted dial on the radio, listening to *Inner Sanctum* and *Only the Shadow Knows*.

We had rose bushes and a large vegetable garden with asparagus and rhubarb growing along the fence. A grape arbor ran along the back of the garden. It was a nice, cool place to hang out and daydream on a hot summer day. An old apple tree grew beside the garage. It was great for climbing and provided apples for pies and applesauce. Haug's parsley fields were behind the garage. I smoked my first and last corn silk behind that garage. Was I ever sick!

The house next door was Welker's Boarding House. Several of the Williamsport Grays Baseball Team players and their families lived there. Pudding Maxie, whose dad was the pitcher and Jane were my early ball playing buddies. We did get in trouble once when Jane and I made Pudding help us throw stones through a large number of garage windows. I was the youngest, but we were all three guilty. It was a barn that had been converted into a six-car garage for the boarding house. There were a lot of windows, and we broke them all.

My sister, Betty, was a big baseball fan. I can still recall the day she stood me behind the door in the dining room and dressed me in my official Williamsport Grays Baseball uniform. I was about five and thought I was big stuff. I wore that suit to all the games.

Bubb's Gas Station was about a block up the street. I loved to go there to "shop". For five cents, I could get an ice cold soft drink from the big, red Coca Cola cooler. Chunks of ice floating in ice cold water kept the bottles cold. There was Coca Cola in those curvy bottles, chocolate Yoo-Hoo, Orange Crush, root beer, and ginger ale, all for five cents. He had a case full of penny candy. Bolsters were my favorite, but there were so many choices.

My first job was picking strawberries for Harold Haug. His roadside stand was a short distance down the street. Watermelons were one dollar. He would cut a plug so you could check out your melon before you bought it. I earned five cents a box picking berries. They sold for twenty-five cents. A dirt road ran beside the market to the fields and barn behind it. Our gray tiger cat, Oscar, had her kittens every other year in Mr. Haug's barn. He was always ready to keep them, as they were good mousers.

There were truck farms on both sides of the street: hay, corn, and strawberries on the lower end of Third Street. Hurrs had a milkshake-shaped ice cream store. They had the best ever chocolate frozen malts. The Will-mont Barbecue was right across the street. That was a nice walk on a Sunday afternoon. Mosteller's Dairy was across the street. They delivered milk in glass bottles with a cardboard lid that lifted when the milk froze. How good that dollop of frozen cream was!

I remember Pearl Harbor. Mom motioned for me to be quiet, and then took my hand and we sat in front of the radio to listen to the news. The radio stood taller than me and had a small crescent-shaped dial. Everything changed after that. My brother, George, along with several of his football buddies, joined the Navy. Betty joined the Marines. Ann married her Army husband. Mom put the star banners in the windows for George and Betty. I took change to school to buy war bonds. Phonographs were collected to make blackout paint. Rationing began. White "butter" came with a capsule to break and make it yellow. My dad was sent to Knoxville, Tennessee to work at the Oak Ridge Plant. Later that year, Mom closed up the house, and she and I moved to Knoxville to be with Dad. But that's another story.

Proud Drill Team Champion and Dad
By Ernest C. Pagano of Galeton,
Pennsylvania
Born 1926

My parents were born, raised, and were married in the province of Salerno, Italy. In 1900, they immigrated to the United States and had their first child in December of that year. My dad started work on the B&S Railroad, but he got sick and had to quit the railroad. A brother-in-law gave them backing to start a merchandise store near the car yards in Galeton. After that store burned, they purchased property on Union Street (where the Wonder Bar is) and they rebuilt a merchandise store and worked it until it burned down in 1920. Then they got financing and built a two story brick building housing a new business specializing in Italian imported goods.

I was born in Galeton, Pennsylvania on May 11, 1926, as the 12th child out of twelve children, to Pasquale and Grace Martucelli Pagano in their twenty-seventh year of marriage. They lived at 22 Union Street, attached to the "Wonder Bar".

Having been born and raised during the Great Depression was a whole different life style. I remember when the only lighting in our home was gas mantels on the walls and oil lamps on the tables. We didn't have electricity yet, no clothes washer, refrigerator, cook stove, or small appliances. In the early 30s, we had electricity installed, my parents bought our first radio, and we got our first telephone. I even remember that our phone number was 58.

In 1932, I was six years old. Roosevelt was president, and he ended prohibition and brought beer licensing back. My parents and an older brother applied for and received the first license in Potter County and one of the first in the state. I remember them remodeling the building by taking half of the store and eliminating the living quarters on the first floor. Then they added a two-story brick addition on the back of the building to make the bar bigger, and it also added living space on the second floor. My mother kept her little store, and my older brothers operated the bar. My mother also cooked for the restaurant.

About a year later, the CCCs invaded our area, and as a seven year old, I remember the first trainload of men pulling into Galeton. The train stopped at the corner of Union and Germania Streets by the Wonder Bar, and every person (all young guys) got off the train and spent what little money they had and cleaned out the candy counter and cookie shelf. I remember my mother giving to a lot of the boys who did not have any money. Those boys did not forget her kindness. After they got settled into their camps at Cherry Springs and Lyman Run, they spent what money they could spare and made the Wonder Bar their second home.

I recall some of my friends and some of the things we used to do growing up in Galeton. Some of my friends were Nick Basile, Floyd and Larry DelGrosso, Johnny and Mike Piquadio, Charlie and George Close, Eddie Esgrow, and Vince Caracciolo. We used to play a lot of street/stick ball, cowboys and Indians, cops and robbers, and at night, we would play hide and seek. One of our favorite things to play was street hockey. We used limbs from a tree and tin cans. We didn't have real equipment. In the summer time, the hillside was our favorite playground. We would build shacks to play in, and after a couple of weeks we would tear them down and build a different one somewhere else. We always played outside until about ten at night before we had to be home. Summer was also great for swimming, and we had swimming holes all around Galeton. Big Rocks, Little Rocks, and The Ash were all popular for us kids.

There was an old iron bridge they called the Wonder Bar Bridge and there was a big hole there and the water slowed down. In the winter when it would freeze, we would play on the ice. The older kids would chop a hole in the ice and fill it up with slush, and then one of us younger ones would fall in. That did happen to me, and I was lucky enough to come back up in the same spot I went down. I lived right across the street, so I ran home, peeled off those wet clothes, and stood by the wood fire, I think for the rest of the day before I got warm again.

I started school in 1932 and for the first five grades attended Southside Elementary, and then it was off to Northside Middle School for sixth, seventh, and eighth grades. Ninth through twelfth was at Galeton High School that was also on the north side at that time.

Galeton VFW Drill Team
1950

While in high school, I was quite active. I played the trumpet in the band but really didn't like it, so I went back to playing the accordion. I was in chorus and Glee Club. I received some honors in music and gymnastics and also earned two letters for basketball, plus I received a dancing award in my senior year. I had a lot of the same friends and some new ones like Paul Cimino and Bill Culver. We used to go crusin' around town. I was the only one with a license and a car, so I was kind of the leader of the pack.

I graduated from Galeton High in June of 1944 and in August of that same year went into the U.S. Army. In January 1945, I went overseas to the 759th FA Battalion stationed in Belgium and then Germany until the end of the war in May of 1945. After the war ended, I signed up for the Army of Occupation and was in Belgium for another year. After my service was over, I went to work tending bar at the Wonder Bar.

I started a music combo called the Melodiers, and I played the accordion. We played for round and square dances in Galeton and Coudersport. In May 1948, I met a girl named Trudy Bickford at one of the dances. We got engaged in December 1948, and on June 25, 1949, we were married. Trudy worked at the Coudersport Hospital as a Practical Nurse. I worked as a bartender and played in the band. Trudy didn't drive, so I drove her to work, a fifty-mile drive round trip. Then I would pick her up when she was done with work. I was doing that twice a day. After a couple of years it got to be too much, so we decide that she should quit her job and stay home. This made money a little tight, so I tried other jobs. I worked construction and then laid carpet and installed TV sets and antennas. In 1953, my brother who was managing the bar passed away, so I quit my job and went back to work for my mother, managing and tending bar again.

From 1948 to 1953, I spent some of the proudest years of my life as a member of the Galeton VFW National Champion Drill Team. I was one of the original six members. We started out as pallbearers for returning World War II bodies. We would arrive at the train station early to wait for the train to arrive. While waiting, a marine drill sergeant put us through marching maneuvers we had learned while we were in the service. In time, we recruited eighteen more vets and started a 24-man rifle drill team. We won our very first contest and every one after that in Pennsylvania and New York State for the next two years. In our second year, we won our first state contest in Harrisburg, PA. In the two years that followed, we won first place in state contests in Pittsburgh and Philadelphia and also were tops in a National Competition in Chicago. Continuing with our winning ways for the next two years, we won top honors in the National Competition in New York City and Los Angeles. After that, because of the many marriages and children, we disbanded and retired as undefeated National Champions.

In 1960, Trudy and I decided to try and adopt a child. We applied at St. Joseph's Orphanage in Erie with the help of our Parish priest and other parishioners. We were approved and adopted our son, John, in 1961. Two years later, we decided to try to adopt a girl. Again we were successful and in adopted our daughter, Lori. That was in 1963. Our new family was doing well, and we thought we were all set with the family we were at that time. In 1966, we got a call from the orphanage asking us if we would be interested in adopting another girl. We said we were, and headed to Erie as fast as we could. One look at Elizabeth, and we were hooked, so in 1967, we had our second daughter and a very happy family of five.

In 1965, I had been approached by Nationwide Insurance Company and asked to become a part-time agent. The following year, the Postmaster in Galeton offered me a part-time job at the Post Office delivering packages two hours a day and I accepted that because it fit into my schedule. Now I was working three jobs, plus playing in the band. I continued this pace for a couple of years, and then hired a part-time bartender but continued to manage the bar plus worked the insurance and post office jobs. Later on I had to choose between the insurance job and the post office job, and I decided on the insurance job.

In 1991, after working constantly for many years, I made the decision to retire in 1992. In

February of 1992, I retired. On the last day I would be in business, I locked the door at 5:00 pm for the last time. That same night I woke up at two in the morning and was having a heart attack. I was taken to the Coudersport Hospital and the next day, I was transferred to Guthrie Clinic in Sayre. Two days later, I had an operation and was given a triple by-pass. I am now 85 and still going strong. I still play the accordion in about four different bands, and I am usually playing somewhere four to five nights a week.

My living family of three older siblings, a brother 91 and two sister ages 89 and 93, three children, nine grandchildren, and seven great-grandchildren all support me in my new lifestyle and are happy that I try to stay young, happy, and healthy. Through the years I have stayed active in some organizations. I have been a member of the Galeton Moose since 1946 and was an officer years ago. I also belonged to the Galeton VFW Post since 1946 and was Commander for two to three years. I joined the Knights of Columbus in 1948, was Grand Knight for two to three years, and have been a member of the Galeton Rotary Club since 1965 and have served as its President for two to three years.

When World War II started in December of 1941, everything changed; our town, the people, our country, and the world. We went from being children to grownups overnight. The time has gone fast, from high school, graduating, entering the military, coming back home, and now you know the rest.

A Great Mom and a Jealous Sister
By Viola M. Barrett of Curwensville,
Pennsylvania
Born 1943

I was born at home, in Olanta, Clearfield County, on September 11, 1943, at 2:30 pm on a Saturday. I already had a sister who was two years old. A few days after I was born, my mother said she heard me crying really hard. She checked and found my sister's teeth marks on my big toe. Of course, my sister was jealous.

The house I was born in was across from the only church in Olanta. Then when I was three years old, we moved down the road to a much larger house. It was 1946, and we

Ernest and his first new car a 1948 Ford

Viola's mother, Adaline, and Viola 1947

had our first Christmas there. My maternal grandparents gave me a rocking chair. I still have that rocking chair. A month later, my maternal grandmother died at the age of forty-seven.

As days went by, before I entered school, my mother panicked one day when she couldn't find me. She said she looked everywhere. She said she decided to look behind the living room couch. There I was, sound asleep. She told me I did that quite often.

Growing up, I had some good times. One thing though, I never liked it when my birthday was on a Monday. I worried that I wouldn't get a cake because that was a busy day for Mother. She'd bake bread, do laundry, and fix a good supper. She never let me down. She seemed to find time to bake that cake.

When it was time to start school, I went to the only school in Olanta. It was a one-room school with eight grades. I had the same teacher for my first six years of school. The school did eliminate the seventh and eighth grades about two years after I started. In school, they had single and double desks. My sister and I had to share, so we had a double desk. If someone did or said something, I'd laugh aloud. Everything was funny to me. So the teacher stood me in the corner every day until lunch. This happened every day for the first six weeks. I also got punished at home, but I can't remember what kind of punishment.

We had forty-five minutes for lunch. Most of the time, my sister and I would walk home for lunch. During the winter, we took a packed lunch. We liked taking our lunch so we could sit around the potbelly stove. Our

teacher walked about five miles to our school. Sometimes she'd get a ride, but if not, she walked. She always had the school nice and warm for the students.

Once a month, the parents had a PTA meeting. Someone would invite the teacher to their house for supper. Then that family would see that the teacher got home after the meeting. The PTA always had a Christmas program.

I remember some of us girls had to sing a song and bring our doll babies. My mother stayed up until 3:00 am sewing matching dresses for me and my doll baby. My dress had a dark blue velvet top with a plaid taffeta bottom. My doll's dress had the taffeta top and a dark blue velvet bottom. My mother could sew anything.

Mother was a very good cook. She always said when we turned ten years old, we could learn to cook. The first thing we were allowed to make was a chocolate cake. We would have it as soon as it came out of the oven, with milk on it. I was a better cook than my sister. Even now, I love to cook and bake. I even make homemade bread from scratch.

Growing up, we didn't have much. My mother didn't work and my dad worked in the coalmines before learning to run a coal shovel, stripping coal and loading coal trucks. Back then, he usually worked six months and was off six months. I remember in 1956, my dad only got $30.00 a week in unemployment.

Jiggs 1950s

188

One thing, when my dad worked, he came home to good hot meals. Mother would even get up at 3:00 am to have the house warm by 5:00 am. She knew he had to work out in the cold, so he needed to be nice and warm. At night, when Dad came home from work, while eating supper, we all listened to how many loads of coal he stripped that day, plus what kind of coal it was.

We could put several different kinds of coal in front of Dad, and he would name everyone. He only went to the eighth grade, but he was very smart. His stories were always interesting. He knew everybody's car or truck licenses. Even though they were new every year, he'd remember them. He read newspapers a lot.

Another thing I remember is that Dad

Adaline and Viola in 1947

could tell who was at our house by the tire tracks. One time, my parents went on a day trip with my dad's bother and wife. Dad told my sister she was not to go anywhere with the car. She was seventeen and I was fifteen. Well, at the time, she liked this guy, whom she later married. She wanted to go for a ride to see if he was home. I told her that Dad would know. She didn't think so and we went. As soon as Dad hit the driveway, he knew she had the car out. Of course, she was grounded for two weeks.

During the 1950s, we had an ice storm. We didn't have power for a week, plus school was closed. We had to dip water out of the well for drinking. We did have a gas stove. So my mother was busy cooking for the neighbors in order for them to have one nice warm meal

each day.

My mother could sew anything. She never took lessons. She made a winter coat. She took a coat of hers, tore it apart, and made a pattern out of newspaper. She cut the coat to the pattern and sewed it, lining and all, in order for me to have a coat when there just wasn't money to buy one. In the 1950s, my paternal grandfather would get feed for his chickens at the local feed store. At that time, the feed came in very pretty feed sacks. He would always make sure to get two alike. He'd give them to Mother. She would wash and iron them, and then she would make dresses, jumpers, and even two-piece outfits for me. She would decorate them with lace or rickrack. I had school pictures taken wearing the nice outfits. I was so proud, and my granddad was proud, also.

Our family was about the last family to get a TV. We got one in 1956. So I'd go to my friend's house. I actually was like a family member. Before we got a TV, my mother and I would lay on the couch. She laid at one end and I at the other and we would listen to the radio. We'd listen to *Archie*, *The Lone Ranger*, *Roy Rogers*, etc. While listening to the radio, Mother would always tickle my feet, but I wasn't ticklish.

I was very close to my mother. She always said I was a very loving child. Mother would even wake me every morning when she came back to bed after my dad left for work, taking me to her bed. I'd sleep with her until time to get up again.

My friends, Linda Cathcart, Ruthy Beckman, and her sister, Caroline Beckman, and I had a girls' club. We had our club meetings in the upstairs of Linda's dad's garage. We met once a week and even had a secret pal. So when we had gifts or letters for our secret pal, we would take them to the Olanta Post Office. The lady, Pearl Witherow, would put our gifts or letters in the mailbox of the receiver. She never charged us any postage. You sure couldn't do that today! She was a very nice lady.

The post office was next to our house. It was a small one-room building. When my mother baked cookies, pie, or a cake, she would always take some to Mrs. Witherow. Mother would even give her a cup of coffee to go with the goodies.

By now, I haven't said too much about my sister. Everyone said we were different, like

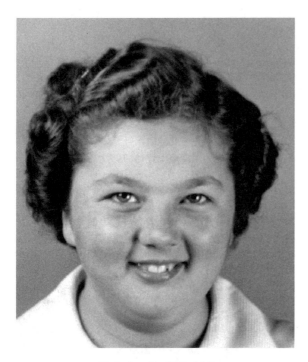

Viola Rawles 1953-1954

night and day. If she thought it was time to do the dishes or anything, she always had to go to the "john". Back then, it was outside. She never liked to get dirty.

So one day when I was about ten years old, my mother let me use the hatchet. She trusted me, and I wanted to chop some small limbs. My sister came to see what I was doing. She wanted the hatchet. It didn't matter what I had, she always wanted it. So on this day, I had had enough. I had the hatchet in my right hand. I put up my hand and drew it back to throw it at her. As I did, I didn't realize I had the hatchet aimed at my head. I had planned on throwing it, but when I went to throw it, I cut open the back of my head.

My parents rushed me to the doctor's office with towels soaked with blood. The doctor cleaned my head and stitched it. Then he put a big bandage over it, about the size of six inches across and two inches wide. I had to go to school like that. Not a pretty sight. Probably I would have killed my sister if the hatchet had been turned.

My sister and I never got along. She was very rude to our mother. She treated my dad a little better. She never had too many friends. I had a lot of friends. Now that our parents are gone, and she is seventy years old and I am sixty-eight years old, she is closer. She calls and talks to me every week.

I remember something my dad did for me. When I would get a splinter under my fingernail, he'd take some fat from bacon and put turpentine on it. Then he would place it over the end of my finger. He'd wrap it and leave that on for two or three days. Then he'd unwrap it, take tweezers, and get the splinter. That method was used a lot.

About a year ago, when my grandson, Austin was twelve years old, I asked him if he'd like to see a picture of our swimming pool when I was growing up. He got excited. I showed him a picture of my sister and me outside in a large, wooden, round tub. He started to laugh. I told him that was our pool. The only other place we went swimming was in the Olanta Creek.

We had a playhouse in the lilac bush. There were two bushes and they grew in a way that we could have a playhouse in the middle. We could always find something to do or play. When I was eleven or twelve, Dad made a pair of stilts for me. I just loved them. I would walk everywhere on my stilts.

During the summer, I attended Bible School at the only church in Olanta. It was a Lutheran Church. For years, I never missed Sunday school. When my mother passed away, I found my pins for perfect attendance. I was also a 4-H member. I always had fun.

Great-Grandfather's House
By Rachel (Sandra) McClintick of Bradford, Pennsylvania
Born 1940

I was born on October 30, 1940, around 5:30 pm, to Dan Malcolm and Alice Genevieve Murray Vreeland. I was born in the hospital at Degolia. This is where The Heritage Suites are located today.

Dan and Genevieve named me Sandra Yvonne and I weighed in at seven pounds, fourteen ounces and I was twenty-one inches long. My thick head of hair was a shiny copper color, and my eyes were brown with faint green flecks. Genevieve also had copper colored hair, but it was a darker copper and curly.

School Days
I began first grade at Lincoln School in September 1946. I remember the registration process for first grade in April or May of 1946. My first grade teacher was Mrs. Knapp.

190

The Superintendent of Schools was coming to school to note the progress of the pupils. Four students were chosen from our room to participate, and I was fortunate to be one of those chosen. We had to spell words and my word was yellow. I quickly learned my word, but I was so scared that I would goof up. Everything went well, however.

Mrs. Rupert was my second grade teacher. She was very stern and brooked no nonsense at all. We were all afraid of her. I know I surely was and was never intentionally disobedient. When anyone committed an infraction of her rules, she snatched them up, turned them over their desk, and paddled them with a paddle. What scared me so much was that she did the same thing to boys or girls. In those days, all girls wore skirts or dresses. The little girl's dignity went flying out the window as they were flipped over their desks and paddled.

One day, Mrs. Rupert had gone out of the room for a minute, and we were to

Sandra is the third child in front, Patty is the second child, and Sandra's mother, Genevieve is the third adult with a belt

look over our alphabet to review it. She came back in and said I was saying my alphabet out loud. I don't believe I was. I think I was moving my mouth but not saying anything. Needless to say, I was flipped and paddled. How embarrassing. Another time, we were on our way down to lunch and were standing in line. I accidently took the turn on the landing too wide and was grabbed and taken to the office, where I was paddled for my infraction.

My family and I lived in a small portion of Foster Township that was between the end of Bradford Township and the New York State line. We attended different schools than our neighbors closer to town. The year that I was to enter third grade, it was decided by the school board that our group would be attending Lee Driver School. This was a few more miles away than Lincoln School.

My third grade teacher was one of my three favorite ones. Mrs. McGee was a lovely person. She was stern when she had to be, but I remember her smile when I had done well. What a delight after the horror of my second grade year. Later, when I was in seventh grade, my girlfriend, Alberta (Bertie), and I got to go over to Mrs. McGee's room and correct papers and help students in her third grade. We had time because our bus was called last after school. I really enjoyed this.

In high school, when a senior, I had a teacher who worked with me and helped me feel good about myself. Miss Mottey was my English teacher and advisor for the school paper, *The Courant*. I belonged to the Courant Club. Miss Mottey made me business manager. I took requisitions down to the office for various reasons. At the Awards Assembly my senior year, I received an award for being business manager. I was tickled pink.

I had forgotten another English teacher in high school, Miss Mutter. She always had interesting classes. Years later, she still smiled when she met me downtown. What a difference good teachers make!

Each year that I attended school, my mother was the keeper of the "waiting room". This waiting room was a small structure, approximately eight by eight feet. My mother and I would walk a good half of a mile, against the wind, to unlock the waiting room for about a dozen children who lived on a steep hill. About five lived at the top and some six or so lived at various degrees of elevation. There were children who lived along the main road who were allowed to wait there also and use it as a refuge against the fierce winter storms. It had benches inside and provided more warmth than just standing singularly. Mother rode the bus back down to our stop and disembarked.

Dandra age 1

The school district reimbursed her for this job. I can still picture in my mind Mother walking in front of me to shield me from the north wind.

My sister, Patty, knew her first grade teacher, Mrs. Mortland, when she started at Lee Driver School. Mrs. Mortland and her husband lived in the apartment above my great-grandfather's house. His name was Daniel Vreeland, and when he lost his money when the banks failed in the Great Depression, my great-grandfather turned the second floor of his house into an apartment to help make ends meet.

Great-grandfather's House

Daniel had built his house on Seward Avenue around the turn on the Twentieth Century. It had been endowed with a full width front porch and gingerbread trim along the top of that same porch. The house was painted in a yellowish tan. On the southeastern side, a sidewalk extended the length of the house, beginning at the steps from the public sidewalk to the stairs the Mortlands used to access their apartment. The back or side door was reached via this sidewalk. A little entryway provided entrance; a wall on the right and a wall of windows on the left provided the setting for a delightful breakfast nook. From the entryway, one stepped into the kitchen. To the left was that delightful little nook with a square table and benches on three sides.

I remember Great-Grandpa giving my sister, Patty, and me a cooking lesson. He taught us to mash boiled potatoes with our fork, and then add some butter, milk, salt, and pepper, and voila, mashed potatoes. I never forgot this recipe.

There was a large root cellar off of the large kitchen. It was set back into the hill that ran along the back of the house. A bathroom, trimmed in oak, had a claw foot tub, a lavatory, and an oak bench with a lid for storage. I can remember having my diaper changed on that bench. Of course, there was also a toilet. The dining room was reached through a swinging door from the kitchen. From the time I was familiar with the house, this had been turned into a bedroom for my great-grandfather. My great-grandmother had died the year after I was born. Opposite the bedroom, also opening from the kitchen was the living room, a very large room with a large oak table in the corner. The oak staircase rose from this room, but of course it only went so far because it was closed in at the top for the apartment. There was also a grandfather clock and the large chair and stand where my great-grandfather held forth.

From the living room, a small room, evidently a parlor was also the entranceway for the front door. It had a prism window, which faced the sidewalk that ran alongside the house. I remember the dancing lights when the sun hit that window. As I remember, there was an old type sofa in the parlor, perhaps horsehair?

Opposite this room was an even smaller room reached through a heavy curtain. It appeared to be an office with a desk and a few bookshelves. Continuing on around, there was the dining room turned into a bedroom again, and on the left was the door to the basement.

My great-grandfather worked in the oil fields and did carpentry work in his younger days. He was born after the Civil War in 1862 and had two sons, Harry, the eldest, and my grandfather, Henry. After graduation, Harry moved to Salamanca and Olean to raise his family. My grandfather, Henry, was a member of the illustrious Bradford High School Football Team of 1908. He married my grandmother, Zelah Canfield in 1910, and they had eight children. He was also an oilfield worker. He had played football and been friends with a boy whose father had been an oil producer.

My father, Dan, also found work with Smith-Newton when he returned from his peacetime service with the U.S. Army in July of 1936. When he joined the Army again in June of 1943, my great-grandfather would walk up to our house to help my mother with the garden, etc. He spaded the large garden for her when he was in his seventies. I guess he did not have a vehicle at that time, although he did have two ribbons of cement on the sidewalk side of his house. They led to the two storied garage and wood workshop that he had. It was around this garage that he grew his roses.

Outhouse

My Aunt Lois and Uncle Ken Vreeland, my dad's brother and his wife, had an outhouse until the late forties or early fifties. I remember how scary it was to use it. My vivid imagination conjured up an "outhouse monster" coming up to bite my tush. The outhouse was located not far from the house and had stepping stones to get there. In the winter, it was very cold. Thoughts of the outhouse monster added to the shivers. Thinking back, my uncle did an excellent job of maintaining it, for the smell was not as bad as most. I barely knew it was there. When they built the inside bathroom, I can remember how excited everyone was when we visited for the first time since the abandonment of the outhouse.

This particular aunt and uncle had five children and two bedrooms. One was for them and the two younger children. The other was for the other three kids. Later, they put in a

Patty 1944

basement and had a bedroom there, which relieved the pressure of the one bedroom for the children and all the storage space they needed.

Family

My Aunt Lois was an excellent cook, and it was a treat to eat at her house. Canned venison, sour cream cookies, sour cream cakes, and homemade ice cream. These are the moments we treasure!

Many Fourth of Julys found the three families of my dad's older group of siblings at Aunt Lois and Uncle Ken's for a picnic, watermelon, and homemade ice cream.

Their oldest child, a boy, was born legally blind. Aunt Lois had German measles when she was pregnant with him. Although he was very intelligent and could play the piano by ear, he was never able to really overcome this disability. It was one of those "what might have been" situations.

Illnesses

I did not have any experiences with castor oil, but cod liver oil tasted pretty fishy. My sister and I would take it in the winter time when we were young. The use of penicillin was still not too widespread. When I had pneumonia when I was around ten, I may have been given some. I cannot remember. I know I didn't have to go to the hospital but stayed at home. The doctor would come to the house in those days if you were not able to get to him.

When my sister had an appendicitis attack at the age of nine, the neighbor took my mother and her to the hospital and another neighbor took me for the night. Patty's appendix ruptured and she was one sick little girl. I remember how happy I was to have her home again.

The Old Swimming Holes
By Ken Gerg of Emporium, Pennsylvania
Born 1936

Before the advent of community and private pools, there was high adventure, danger, no lifeguards, ice-cold water, and ghost stories around the warming fires as the sunset. In addition to questionable diving apparatuses and great work parties on the make shift dams always in an effort to increase the pool size or water levels.

The swimming holes were mostly bends in the stream that naturally dug deep holes that were never left uninhabited during the long hot summers. In those days, summer seemed to last forever. It was memorable. Life, however, can be compared to a roll of toilet paper; the closer it gets to the end the faster it seems to go, but I digress.

Holes and Dams that I recall were Bum Rock on Iron Run below the old Swacks Pond just over the hill from Berwind Heights. Bum Rock drew its swimmers from the heights as well as the Spruce, Maple, Chestnut, and South Saint Mary's street area. It was a bit further away than Silver Creek. Consequently, the Minnie Hole, Scout Dam, Bridge Dam, and the Big Hemlock Hole got more of our attention. Besides, you could hitch hike a ride to these holes much easier.

Probably the most famous was the Dam across Silver Creek just above the Route 255 Bridge. With the cooperation of West Penn Power and Corbett Cabinet there were huge used power line poles secured and put in place to form a breast works maybe forty to fifty feet across. Then, hemlock slabs from Corbett Cabinet were nailed to the poles rising up fifteen to sixteen feet from the stream floor on a forty-five degree angle. After the super structure was in place, hundreds of potato sacks were filled with sod/ground and stacked in place from the base to the top. The result was a dam approximately ten to twelve feet deep and backing up water for one to two acres.

The head water of Silver Creek were at the time the primary source of drinking water for Saint Mary's and the pumping station was about a half a mile upstream from the Dam. The water was always cold and offered some good trout fishing. The dam demanded constant maintenance and there were some accidents associated with the work like bruises, abrasions, teeth loosened, to nails amputated, and so on. This Dam saw its heyday from about 1948 to 1957. Doc Dornisch would be the storyteller on many summer evenings as we all stood around the fading fire and were consumed by the ever present swarm of mosquitos.

The first major dam on Silver Creek was the Scout Dam, which was down stream approximately one half mile from the above described impoundment. I believe it was initially started about 1939 but fell into

disrepair during World War II when most of the scouts were off shore, overseas, taking care of other things.

The Big Hemlock Hole was approximately three hundred or four yards upstream from the Bridge Dam and my recollection of it was primarily the large fire that was always started just prior to entering the icy water. The fire was such a ritual that from day to day it could be rekindled by just stirring the ashes as the fire was maintained by the hemlock needles that had built up under the tree for probably 100 years. A major injury occurred there as a young girl swimmer not being familiar with the fire pit stepped on the hot ashes and sunk virtually to her knees. Although she suffered some severe burns, we got her out of there and back to Saint Mary's for medical treatment and she recovered with no permanent injuries.

Minnie Hole was two hundred or three hundred yards below the Scout Dam and was the product of a bend in the stream. It wasn't much of a hole, but it had one redeeming feature; a very large stump on the bank right near the deepest end which made for a great jumping and diving platform. I'll always remember a female swimmer jumping off this stump somewhere around 1942 or 1943 shouting the question, "What did Hitler say when his wife had another baby, hotsy, totsy, I got another Natzie!"

Laurel Run Hole was another stream created hole that offered lots of swimming and no work, obviously on Laurel Run about five miles west of Saint Mary's. The favorite pastime at this location was to splash water on the high steep mud banks until the crystal clear hole was like chocolate, then play under water tag. You had to be under water to make the tag and you could not see through the clouded water to tag your opponent. We sure were not affluent enough to have goggles! The Laurel Run Hole is long gone covered by the Laurel Run Reservoir, which is presently the Saint Mary's, and surrounding area's water supply.

West Creek offered the Old School House hole. Another stream created natural hole and again with icy cold water. Too far for our gang to frequent very often, but my brother-in-law had the misfortune of loosening up or maybe losing some front teeth in a swimming or diving accident at this favored spot.

As noted earlier, all of these Holes were on relatively small streams and all near their headwater. All had very clear and very cold water as well. Therefore, all had a mandatory fire on the bank to warm up immediately after exiting the water. This warming procedure generated smoke, consequently we would get home smelling like smoked sausage and most of the time a nice tan caused not by the sun, but by a layer of mud! We never noticed it, but our parents sure did!

As time progressed Marshall's Swimming Pool came into being and for a quarter you could swim all day in chlorinated water in a large pool that wasn't near as cold as most of the streams. You could also enjoy maiming your body diving from a high and low board. I was visiting a chiropractor on a regular basis by the time I was thirteen, but it was fun and makes for great memories. One of the special stunts was to jump from the high board, land on the low board and catapult yourself into a one and a half before hitting the water. Think you could get away with something like that today? To the best of my knowledge, we never had a fatality. The old Holes were special to so many great memories!

Raised in Coal Town
By Diann Lenig Ferry of Shamokin,
Pennsylvania
Born 1945

I was born in the second story bedroom of a rented double home on Market Street in Trevorton, Pa. It was the normal thing to do if you could not afford to go to the hospital for the birth of a child. It was a snowy cold day in January 1945. The town doctor had two activities that day. His activities were the death of the wife of a prominent citizen and the birth of me. The doctor walked to both places as it was snowy day and the roads were slippery. My mom's friend and my dad stayed with my mom for the day Helen. Mom's friend made a big pot of homemade spaghetti for the family.

I remember lots of things while growing up in Trevorton. Trevorton was a coal town. Every dad had a job connected to either coal mining, the coal stripping operation, the coal washery, or they just had a small independent mine of their own. Coal royalties were paid to the school district and we had nice new buildings because of it. The class sizes were small coming from both the town of Trevorton

and the rural areas also. Classes were around 30 to 45. We knew everyone in our class and their family too.

We played outside all summer and felt comfortable in anyone's yard. All the moms were home so someone always knew where we were and what we were up to. Bathrooms or outside toilets were outside so we never gave it a second thought to use one where we were playing. I had an older sister who always made me go to the outside toilet with her at night. It was all the way up at the end of our lot. One night she dropped the flashlight down the hole, we were in trouble.

My dad and grandpap always had a beautiful vegetable garden. We helped dad carry water almost every evening to water it. One day he came home with a hose, boy were we happy! We helped my Gramma hoe weeds too. Stuff tasted so good coming from that garden.

Every family in our block was Catholic and my sister and I were the only Protestants. Our block was called little Italy. We didn't know anything about being prejudiced. We went to every wedding that was held in the Catholic Church. All the neighborhood kids would sit up in the balcony. When the wedding was over, we would walk quietly out the side door. We thought no one knew we were there, but now I can say were probably wrong.

In the winter, we went sleigh riding down two hills. We would post someone at the bottom at the intersection to stop cars or to yell for us not to go yet. I shudder now to think how dangerous it was! If you didn't have a sleigh, you could use cardboard or someone would share their sled. We all shared.

If it rained and a woman had wash on her line and she had to be away from home, she didn't have to worry because she knew one of her neighbors would take her wash in and put it on her porch. There was a family grocery store near our house. All week long, we went to the store and got stuff and they marked it the book. When my dad got paid, he went to go pay our bill. We didn't have a phone yet but we could use the one at the store for emergencies.

Our neighbor lady had a baby boy and we went to see them. She had it in a real wash basket; I can still see how he looked. I think that is my first memory of seeing a new baby. I was around six years old and I pestered my mom and dad to get us a baby. They didn't.

By today's standards, I think we would have been considered poor, but we were so blessed. We had a wonderful set of grandparents, a roof over our heads, food for the table, and two loving parents. I can still hear my dad rocking me and singing You Are My Sunshine to me. I must have been old to be rocked because I remember the whole song and my sister said we were big when he still rocked us. She is five years older than me so she would remember it better than me.

We always went to church and Sunday school. I can't remember a time in my life when I did not go to church. That was just what families did. Saturday night we would get our bath in the round tin tub in the front of the coal stove with the open door to keep us warm. Mom set our hair in pin curls and polished our shoes because they had to look nice for church. They tied our collection in the corner of our hankies, it was probably just a nickel but we wouldn't dare lose it.

I even remember the iceman coming on Market Street. My gramma did not have an electric refrigerator so she got ice from the iceman. We loved it when it was summer and he came around because he gave us chunks of ice to suck on.

My one friend Judy had a Black Oxhart Cherry tree in her yard. We loved those cherries. I never tasted cherries as sweet and as big as those. We used to climb on the garage roof and eat the cherries. Her mother would yell down the yard and ask if we were on the roof. She would always yell back no mother.

We knew everyone in town and felt safe. We talked to everyone. We all pitched in to help wherever there was a need, cut grass, shovel snow, and other things. My daughter married and moved to York, Pa. One week when they were visiting, it snowed. She lived in a double home. When they got home, she called me and she told me that I would never believe her so she took pictures.

Her neighbor that lived in the other half shoveled the walk but he only shoveled half width! What happened to being neighborly? What a shame thing had to change. When I was at home we never locked our door, now I have security cameras on at all times at my house. I was so disappointed when we were robbed. Not because things were taken but because people could do things like this. Give me the good old days back!

A Favorite Pastime
By Ellen Ann Verbjar Colegrove of Greeley, Colorado
Born 1939

Here is a poem that tells of one of my memories while growing up in Galeton, Pennsylvania. It was such a great place to grow up!

Bonnie and Jean 1956

A Favorite Pastime
"Let's meet at the bridge over Pine Creek,
And walk together around town."
Smell the lilacs, feel the breezes'
As we stroll tree-lined Elm and Sherman Streets,
And the curved sidewalk down Brewery Hill,
Schwarzenbach Brewery once loomed here,
Past the community building to the left,
Where we roller-skated Saturday night.
Turn left on Germania Street,
We'll follow the tracks,
Crossing the short Pine Creek Bridge.
West Hill Cemetery is high on the hill,
Where "they" once walked this way.
Past Lush's Furniture Store.
Owned by a most prominent family in town
"Lush is the word for the way you live" say they.
Here we are.
We have reached Main Street,
So narrow the lanes it is true.
There is barely room for two cars passing.
The stores that bustled during the week,
Are closed for the day of rest.
Except for Jenkins' Restaurant.
We sojourn for a while to sip on a soda.
Refreshed we continue the jaunt,
Past the library, the small jail behind,
Meandering Pine Creek Bridge,
Where the water flows and widens.
Waving at people, we know as they pass.

We succumb to Brewery Hill,
Reaching the top,
Breathless!

J.W.'s Big Scam
By Donald Lindsey of Hanover,
Pennsylvania
Born 1932

While working on a stream bank restoration on the Cowanesque River after the Agnes Flood of 1972, J.W. Burgess found a bottle with a note inside. The note asked the finder to let Sue, the writer (age nine years) know when and where the note was found. J.W. found it one day after it was put in the river.

The Cowanesque River flows east across Tioga County, north into New York state, and into the east branch of the Susquehanna River, which flows into the Chesapeake Bay and to the Atlantic Ocean.

J.W., whose home was in Mississippi, called his sister in Mississippi and had her write a letter to Sue, saying, "My boyfriend and I were sitting on the bank of the Mississippi River and noticed the bottle with a note in it". This letter was dated one week after the bottle and note were place in the Cowanesque River by Sue.

Sue wrote back to J.W.'s sister in Mississippi and said that her parents didn't think it could be her note, since the Mississippi River went to the Gulf of Mexico, and the bottle could not have traveled that far in one week.

In the meantime, J.W. had mailed the original note to his sister in Mississippi. So his sister wrote back to Sue and enclosed the original note from the bottle as proof that they had found it in the Mississippi River.

Sue and her parents were completely mystified as to how this could happen. Since the original note was returned from Mississippi, it had somehow gotten there in a week's time, a real mystery!

Several years later, Sue and her parents were sitting across from me at a dinner meeting. I asked Sue if she had ever put a note in a bottle. Her mother, hearing the question, almost choked on her dinner. She looked at me and said, "What do you know about

this"! I then told her the entire story. They said that they knew the note could not have gotten into the Mississippi River. However, when the original note was mailed back from Mississippi, they had to accept the fact that it had gotten there, even though it was impossible. Now a mystery was solved after several years.

I worked in Tioga County for twenty-four years with the Soil Conservation Service. After the 1972 Agnes Flood, we did repair work on most of the major streams and rivers, over one million dollars' worth of contracts. This is just one of the stories that I could tell.

My Expulsion from Eden
By John G. McEllhenney of Cornwall,
Pennsylvania
Born 1934

It was an Eden-like Sunday in Mifflinburg: Methodist Sunday school, followed by worship with a sermon by the Rev. Chester Warren Quimby. If only I could recall what he talked about, this preacher who had been the president of the American Academy of Religion and a professor of Bible in a number of colleges. Who now, probably because the Depression of the 1930s caused colleges to cut their faculties, was the pastor of a small town church – my pastor, the man who wore sweaters on weekdays instead of suit jackets. All I know with certainty is that he collared my imagination by using his collection of costumes, everyday objects, and models to connect the Bible, in his words, "solidly with this planet and this life".

After lunch on the Sunday I'm remembering, my father drove Mother and me out into the forested hills beyond Hairy Johns picnic area to cut a Christmas tree. We looked…and looked until, yes, this one will tower just right above the silver Lionel train in our Christmas village. Dad sawed it off, loaded it in the trunk, and turned the car toward home. As we pulled up in front of our house, Uncle Harry came dashing across Chestnut Street, shouting, "Have you heard the news," What news? We've been out in the woods picking a Christmas tree, "The Japanese bombed Pearl Harbor!" Suddenly, at age seven, I found myself east of Eden, and before long, I was pulling my wagon from neighbor to neighbor, collecting tin cans. For my other war work, I enlisted in the campaign of the ladies next door against Nazi rodents; they paid me five cents for each mouse I pried loose from their traps.

Poor Little Rich Girl
By Jean Cooke Redka of Williamsport,
Pennsylvania
Born 1923
Grew up on a farm in Frosty Valley,
Danville, PA

My father, Arthur Cooke, was a farmer. My mother, Rennay Kester, was a teacher in a one-room school on Frosty Valley Road before she married my father. I was the youngest of five children: Helen, my half-sister, was the oldest, followed by Charlie, Don, Betty, and me.

My older brothers were always pulling tricks on us (or trying to) such as finding a black snake, killing it, and cutting it into bite-sized pieces. Then they put the pieces in a bag that had previously held candy. When we reached into the bag, they loved hearing us scream. They also enjoyed setting a mousetrap and putting it in the dishpan. Ouch!

We were poor when it came to material possessions, but not when it came to love or caring. My mother taught me to read and learn poetry at age five and how to plant a garden, including flowers! We had no money, no

Jean's mother, Rennay Kester Cooke

running water, no electricity, and no tractors! We had food because we raised chickens, hogs, and cows. Horses were used to work the fields.

I attended two different one-room schools. The first was Styer's School on Columbia Hill Road. Starting in 5th grade, I went to Sheep's School on Jerseytown Road. The teachers came in early to start the fire, carry water from the neighbor's house, get the day's lessons organized, and do anything else that needed to be completed. I loved going to school where I not only learned the lessons for my grade but also listened to the lessons of the classes ahead of me so that I already knew a lot of the material by the time I got to that grade. I finished eight grades in seven years.

One of the most shocking days of my life happened when I was eleven. My mother packed our lunches and sent us over the hill to meet the horse and sleigh to take us to school at about 8 o'clock. At 9 o'clock, Uncle Alvin came to school and told the teacher he needed to take the Cooke children home. On the way home, he told us our mother had had a heart attack and died. She was buried the day before Christmas. My Aunt Maud came and stayed with us. Uncle Alvin and Aunt Lois lived on the next farm and also helped out.

After a period of time, my father remarried. His new wife, Barbie Fitzgerald, was good to us. She cooked, washed our clothes with a wringer washer, hung our clothes on a clothesline to dry or freeze, and ironed all of our clothes, even socks. She used "sad" irons to do all of the ironing.

Jean's father, Art Cooke

Betty and I wanted to go to high school, but there was no public transportation, and the school was seven miles from our farm. We were able to find a ride to school by paying a small amount to Frankie Wintersteen, an older agricultural student who was allowed to drive his dad's car. He often had other activities after school, however, and Betty and I had to walk home. Betty took the Commercial Course while I took the Academic Course, graduating after four years of high school at age 16.

When I was 13, we went to an evangelistic tent meeting with Bob Lancaster where Betty and I both came to know the Lord. That meeting changed my life. Life had been very difficult after my mother died, but suddenly the grass looked greener and the sky looked bluer. I now had a purpose for living. I never looked back!

In 1943, I married Wilson Redka, a wonderful man who served three and a half years in the United States Army Air Corps during World War II. When my dad decided to sell the farm in 1947, we bought it from him and raised our children there. Patti became a nurse; Jim became a doctor; and Joyce became a teacher.

This year we will celebrate our 69th wedding anniversary! Is that great or what? Rich beyond measure! Riches more precious than gold! God brought us full circle, turning our rags into riches that will last for eternity.

Jean Cooke (Redka)

A Rich Heritage
By Patricia Redka Souder of Montrose, Pennsylvania
Born 1947
Grew up on a farm in Frosty Valley, Danville, PA

My earliest memories involve riding on my daddy's back, playing hide and seek, rolling down grassy hills, chasing fireflies, taking Saturday night baths in a large round galvanized tub by the wood cook stove, telling my brother and sister stories, and pretending to be Indians under the apple tree where we

Pattie Redka 1949

found stones shaped like small dishes and a mortar and pestle.

So many memories rush through my mind when I think of growing up on our family farm . . .

Priming, pumping, and carrying water. Cuddling soft, fuzzy, Leghorn chicks when they arrived. Playing store with the piles of cardboard coins we amassed from punching out the circles used for ventilation in the boxes in which the peeps were shipped. Gathering, cleaning, and candling eggs. Petting the friendly chickens while trying to outsmart the nasty ones before they pecked or flopped us. Waking to the crowing of roosters that roamed and ruled. Searching for the nests where the hens sat on the fertilized eggs. Hoping to see the chicks peck their way through the eggshells, tumble out, and flap their tiny wet wings.

Churning butter. Untangling clothes in the wringer washer. Hanging them up to dry. Watching shirts and sheets blow freely against a blue sky on clear days. Feeling them freeze solid while still pinning them to the clothesline on frigid days. Hurrying to get them inside when a storm threatened. Draping them over drying racks to thaw and dry. Blowing on our fingers to restore circulation.

Huddling together in the kitchen to stay warm. Reading together. Singing together. Playing games together. Going to the outhouse. Reading the Sears catalog while sitting in the outhouse. Hating to get out of bed to go to the outhouse at night. Being grateful when the moon and stars were out and there were no snakes on the way to the outhouse.

Waiting for the burst of pussy willows, forsythias, crocuses,

The Redka family
Jim, Patti, Wilson, Joyce, and Jean in 1952

daffodils, violets, tulips, lilacs, peonies, larkspur, and irises, especially Mother's prize varieties. Planting marigolds and zinnias with seeds gathered and dried from the previous year. Weeding. Watering. Watching flowers grow, bud, and bloom.

Planting onion sets, spinach, carrots, peas, beans, corn, potatoes, squash, tomatoes, peppers, cabbage, broccoli, Brussels sprouts, kohlrabi, and whatever else seemed good in any given year. Hoeing and weeding. Picking off slugs and cutworms. Pulling onions and carrots, cutting spinach, digging potatoes, picking peas, beans, corn, tomatoes. Trucking vegetables to market. Shelling, slicing, snapping, scrubbing, blanching, cooking, canning, or freezing the rest.

Bringing in cows from the far end of the pasture. Ducking under the electric fence to avoid getting shocked. Milking cows. Trying to avoid being switched by their tails. Feeding pigs. Cleaning the pigpen. Chasing cows and pigs when they got out.

Riding on the fender of the tractor or on the seat of the rake. Ah! Nothing could be finer, except when thrown off the fender on a side hill or narrowly missing decapitation by a low branch. Nothing except being allowed to drive tractor yourself to help mow, rake, bale, and pick up bales of hay and straw. Or picking and husking corn after school in the fall.

But wait! I haven't mentioned climbing trees to pick cherries and apples and pears ... or just to hang from the branches. Nor have I mentioned playing under the grape arbor. Or the hours spent finding flocks of wooly sheep or great castles in the ever-changing clouds. Nor the richness of rainbows, sunrises, sunsets, star-studded nights, or moonlight magic. Nor carefree days running through the fields to go to the woods to pick spring beauties, arbutus, May apples, teaberries, wild strawberries, raspberries, and blackberries. Nor the sacred feel of the evergreen grove carpeted with spongy green moss and stumps that became pulpits where we sang and preached for our own church services.

Nor have I talked about my big orange Tiger Cat or the myriads of kittens and cats that meowed while we milked the cows and purred when we filled their bowls with warm milk, then snuggled or struggled as I kid-carried them all over.

Nor have I mentioned Tippy . . . a black-brown shepherd-collie-maybe-lab mix with a white chest and white paws who bounded toward me with happy brown eyes and a waggling white-tipped tail to kiss me profusely, play catch, listen to my childhood woes, defend me against spankings, and repeatedly bark and push me off sled and bike so often that I spent much of my childhood with skinned knees and elbows. Tippy was always sorry, barking and standing guard with super sympathetic eyes while I lay in the gravel howling with pain, but he never caught on that "his girl" needed to do some things on her own.

Cataloguing my memories gives only a fraction of all we did on that 80-acre all-purpose Frosty Valley farm where my mother, Jean Cooke, the youngest of five children, had grown up with her half-sister, Helen; brothers, Charlie and Don; and sister, Betty.

In October 1943, Jean left the farm to travel to Miami Beach to marry Wilson Redka, a handsome dark-haired GI who had been told he would be stationed in Florida. Before Christmas, however, his orders were changed and he was sent to England to repair airplanes in WWII. Jean stayed in Florida for several months, returning to Pennsylvania to work only after it became clear Wilson would not be returning. They wrote letters every day and were finally reunited when the Allies won the war in Europe in 1945.

I was born on February 16, 1947, just two days after my father was laid off from his job at the American Car & Foundry in Berwick. Tough economic times sent my parents back to the Cooke farm where Mother had grown up. When her father, Arthur Cooke, decided to sell the farm, they bought it.

Life on the farm remained much the same for me as it had been for my mother, except I never attended a one-room school, walked seven miles to get home from high school, or learned to ride horses because they had been replaced with a tractor. I also never achieved Mother's prowess in Latin and French, subjects she helped me with when I was in high school.

We never went hungry because we raised most of what we needed plus extra to sell.

Patti, Jim, and Joyce with their new bikes in 1957

We knew the realities of crop failures due to drought, massive thunderstorms, or hail and of losing livestock because of accidents or disease. Slaughter days were necessary, but I hated them so much that I often ran and hid under my bed because I couldn't stand to see even the mean chickens run around splattering blood after their heads were chopped off.

The farm consumed much of our life, but it didn't provide enough income, so my father had to work second shift at Thompson Ramo Wooldridge (TRW). That meant the rest of us had to take care of the evening chores most nights.

I started school when I was five and loved the new worlds it opened up. I discovered that most families had electricity, warm and cold running water, a telephone with an operator on a party line, and an indoor bathroom before we did, but I still felt sorry for the town kids as I rode past their postage-stamp-sized yards on the school bus. I was convinced we had a glorious wealth that surpassed their greater conveniences.

Amazingly, in addition to all of the previously listed activities, Mother also sewed most of our clothes (many of which were made from carefully selected feed bags) and baked bread, pies, cakes, and cream puffs for family, neighbors, and bake sales. As for her cream puffs . . . they seldom made it to the table on school bake sale days because the teachers snatched them up before anyone else had a chance!

Despite the endless responsibilities of farm, work, and a growing family, my parents provided music lessons for Jim, Joyce, and me, sometimes by bartering fresh eggs or vegetables for part of the cost of our lessons.

It was a wonderful gift we have used and enjoyed all our lives.

My parents recognized the importance of spiritual development and read Bible stories to us and took us to church every Sunday. We loved Sunday school with its action choruses, Bible memory verse games, fascinating flannel graph Bible and missionary stories. North Mountain Bible Conference (Red Rock) was a summer favorite where we could swing, slide, and ride the merry-go-round or go swimming as well as participate in meetings with lively singing and outstanding Bible teachers.

My father left TRW when he had an opportunity to become a rural letter carrier as this allowed him to be home in the evenings. However, because he had to be at work early in the morning six days a week regardless of weather conditions, my parents sold the farm in 1960. I wept many tears, for I loved the freedom and wide-open spaces we left behind.

Life on the farm required lots of hard work, but that gave us purpose and a healthy work ethic. We built happy memories as the jobs were coupled with word games, silly songs, and a treat such as going out for ice cream . . . or making it ourselves. We lived close to the earth . . . and close to God.

When I look back with adult eyes, I don't know how my parents managed. I graduated from Geisinger Medical Center and became an RN, after which I married Larry Souder, whose passion is radio, not farming. My brother Jim became a doctor who married Peggy Page, a nurse. My sister Joyce became a teacher who married Ken Miller, a minister. All raised our families in town as we pursued our various careers.

Our experience mirrors what is happening nationwide as multi-purpose family farms disappear at an alarming rate. I treasure my reservoir of rich memories and wish today's children had more opportunities to enjoy God's marvelous world and the shared responsibilities I knew as a child, but times have changed.

I've discovered I can survive (and even thrive!) in a town setting because the real essence of life is not found in where we live, monetary wealth, or technological conveniences but in the warmth of meaningful relationships with family, friends, and the God who created us. That's an eternally rich heritage worth cultivating no matter where we live!

The Stilt Racing Champion
By Melva Smith of Muncy, Pennsylvania
Born 1918

I was born on September 13, 1918. I was raised by my grandparents, William Oscar Confer and Ella Margaret Rupert Confer of Muncy. I was never told why I was raised by my grandparents. Their home was located at the upper end of South Main Street in Muncy, Pennsylvania and is still standing today. It is on the left hand side and is right across from the on ramp to 180 East.

When I was ten years old, my grandfather made me a pair of wooden stilts. To learn to walk on them, I leaned them up against the side of the barn and climbed on them. At first, I could only go a couple of steps before falling off, but I began to master the art of balancing myself and soon could go a good distance. An important technique that I learned helped me to walk faster. Instead of keeping the tops of the stilts behind my shoulder, I learned to walk with the stilts in front of my shoulders. Sometimes in gym class, we would have stilt races, and I always won. I can credit my winnings to my determination to master the stilts and to my enthusiastic response to competition.

Talking about gym class reminds me of the one piece blue gym suit and the ninety-eight cent high top sneakers we had to wear. I remember my grandfather being unhappy about having to buy sneakers for gym class.

Back then, Muncy, Montgomery, and Hughesville Schools had a track meet every spring. It was always held at Montgomery. As I recall, it was held at the ball field that was near where the present day Montgomery American Legion Post is located. Much like a track meet today, there were numerous events: mile race, relay race, 50-yard dash, long jump, shot put, javelin, high jump, and pole vault. The year when I was twelve, they featured the stilt race, not as one of the competitive events, but as a special intermission entertainment. There were maybe six of us who entered the stilt race. I remember feeling very confident, and it came as no surprise to me that I won. I had also come in third in the 50-yard dash. That was a special day for me, and a day that I will always remember.

As I was taking a walk down memory lane, I also remembered granddad's Model T Ford. There were vase holders on both sides of the back, and there was a sun shade in the back window. The button for the windshield wipers was located directly in front of and above the driver. That may not seem so unique until you realize the windshield wipers were manual. That's right! Manual. Every time the rain or snow needed to be cleaned off the windshield, the driver had to reach up and turn the knob back and forth. I felt pretty important when Granddad would let me run the wipers. Yes, I certainly have some special memories of my grandparents and the way we lived in the fore part of the 1900s.

Growing Up in South Renovo
By Alice Redis Hevner of North Bend,
Pennsylvania
Born 1933

Growing up in South Renovo in the 1930s and 1940s was a wonderful way of life for the Redis children. There were eight of us; six girls and two boys. We lived in upper South Renovo for eight years, where we had many nice neighbors and friends.

Across the street from us lived the Andy Fantaskey family, where we loved to go and play. We would slide down their hill in winter and gather eggs from the chicken coop in summer. A large toboggan sled was used on the road on Pennsylvania Avenue, and as it came by our house, we'd jump on it and have the ride of our lives down to the end of town.

We moved into a home built by my grandfather. It was a long walk to school from there to St. Joe's. There was no bus. When the river was frozen in the winter we would cross over, which made it a much shorter distance.

The only ones who had to walk further than my brothers and sisters were the Stellfox family. They had a farm in lower South Renovo that had a skating pond. We spent many a happy hour there, cracking the whip, unless you happened to be on the end! Mr. Stellfox sharpened our skates, and Mrs. Stellfox fixed hot chocolate for us. What a treat on a cold winter day!

Cheerleading, band, and orchestra were a big part of my life while attending St. Joseph's School. The nuns cracked the whip, so we were all well behaved kids, or so our parents thought. Being forbidden to go out to Cross Forks on a Saturday night made it very tempting. We'd catch a ride with some older kids and square dance until midnight. What fun, and we never got in trouble. Just lucky, I guess.

I remember the air raids when we had to turn out the lights and the tramps who stopped by and wanted a handout. One time my gram, who lived with us off and on, was soaking her feet in a basin of water by the kitchen door. There came a knock late at night, and Gram upset the basin of water as we all ran for the living room, which back then was called the parlor. Our Nannie, as we called her, filled our kitchen with the smell of fresh baked sticky buns on many an occasion.

Our house was surrounded by cherry trees, mulberry trees, and grape arbors. There were plenty of vegetables from the garden. A ripe tomato tasted so good right off the vine.

We had a ball field below our house where they played baseball games. I helped out selling pop and hot dogs, so I could earn a quarter to go to the movie that night.

Then when I turned sixteen, it was time to work at the five and dime store. That and babysitting for all the families up and down the block took up most of a person's time.

But we still had time for fun, and walking across town to buy an ice cream cone at Bert McGowan's store on 8th Street was a big deal when I was eleven or twelve. Bert always kidded us about the 8th Street Bridge going down and how were we going to get home. His wife would always say, "Bert, stop that".

There was a grocery store, a flower shop, an ice cream shop, and a photographer's studio in town. Now those are all gone, but we do have a new restaurant at the end of town, which is kept quite busy. Yes, it was and still is a nice little town.

The Spirit of being Born in the Mountains of North Central Pennsylvania
By Dawn R. Zetto of Houston, Texas
Born 1945

In the early 1900s my grandparents ventured into the forests of North Central Pennsylvania from western Lancaster County, Pennsylvania.

Of nine children born to Mary and Chris Heisey in eighteen years my mother was the middle. Born at Lucullas in 1918 a month before the Armistice of WWI, she was named for her mother Mary but was called Polly.

Mary (Polly) Heisey grew up on the family farm, attended one room rural school in the 1920s and went to high school "in town" from 1932-1936 in Jersey Shore, Lycoming County, Pennsylvania. After attending Lock Haven Normal School, she received a teaching certificate in 1938 and a teaching assignment to the Slate Run one-room school in Lycoming County. Slate Run was small lumbering town and outdoor sporting center along Pine Creek.

After two years in Slate Run, Polly taught at Piatt Township just east of Jersey Shore for two years. In her fifth year of teaching, she became the seventh and eighth grade teacher in the newly consolidated Porter Township School in Jersey Shore.

As a young teacher, Mary was active in the county chapter of the Pennsylvania Sunday School Association. At a summer camp at Camp Kanesatake in Juniata County, Pennsylvania, in 1942 she met Ray Singley whom she would marry in 1944 and remain with for over sixty-one years until his death on August

Raymond A. Singley and Mary Heisey

17, 2005. She lived until September 2, 2007, six weeks short of her eighty-ninth birthday.

It was the re-meeting Raymond on the mountain near the place of her birth that brought them together. Polly's older sister Barbara and husband, Clair Miller, were members of a hunting camp near the childhood home of the Heiseys. Within this rustic woods location, along the pike road was a Tidewater Oil Company booster pump station, which was manned during WWII by Raymond, and one or two other men working eight to twelve hour rotation shifts to increase the volume and speed of the crude oil over the mountain. Raymond had grown up as the oldest of four children of Ambrose Singley and Helen Harger at the Shumans Tidewater Oil Pump Station along the Catawissa

Creek between Bloomsburg and Hazelton, Pennsylvania. The Shumans station and the mountain station participated in pumping oil east from the fields of Western Pennsylvania.

A broken down car, the necessity of hitchhiking, and the recognition of a friend from camp who "came by" with an invitation to a camp meal was not taken lightly. Mary (Polly) was a native to this mountaintop, well acclimated to it and open to sharing its life with Raymond. Mary and Ray married June 8, 1944, at Epworth Methodist Episcopal Church, Jersey Shore, Lycoming County, Pennsylvania.

Housing for the newly married couple was a challenge but soon resolved by the help of the Pennsylvania Forest and Conservation Department. A Forest Ranger's lovely log cabin home, a few miles from the pump station, and from Mary's place of birth at Lucullas, was made available for rent. Mary and Raymond were in love with each other and with their pristine mountain life. With no phone and no car Mary was content to garden, write letters, entertain visitors, hike and observe the wildlife around the mountains she loved so much. Mary thrived and Raymond had company through the snowy winter of 1944/45.

On this mountain, my life as the first born to Mary and Raymond began. From here, I would learn that life never remains static; that life's work calls for flexibility and adaptation. The auxiliary pump station was never a permanent assignment. Periodically it was temporarily shut off when oil supplies slowed down. Such was the case in late 1945.

The new dad-to-be took a few weeks off in early December to relocate the mom-to-be to Jersey Shore with Barbara and Clair Miller. He reported to New Jersey to lay new pipeline into Tidewater's Bayonne Refinery. I, Dawn Rae Singley, arrived, in mid-December 1945,

Mary Heisey Singley with Dawn in 1946

at the small Jersey Shore Hospital, in the midst of a heavy snowstorm. Many visitors came to congratulate my parents and welcome me. Our wise family doctor allowed mother and me to remain in the hospital for two weeks, which included Christmas. Mother loved to tell how the nurses provided a Christmas tree. Upon leaving the hospital, Mother and I went to the Miller home where we were lovingly cared for as we awaited news from Daddy of available housing in New Jersey.

At this time in early 1946, many soldiers were returning from WWII. Housing was at a premium. Dad, along with other employees, had a room in his boss's home in Bound Brook, New Jersey. By March 1946, Raymond felt he had located a possibility for housing for mother and me. He brought us to New Jersey, where we were united as a family. The Schmidt home near Piscataway and then a bungalow in Neshanic Station, New Jersey became places of shelter for us.

After a little more than a year in New Jersey, the Coudersport Pike Pump Station opened again in the spring of 1947. In 1945, my Heisey Grandparents had retired from the family farm and moved to Allegheny Street, a main axis street in Jersey Shore, where they bought and managed an apartment building. The Singleys (we three and one on the way) returned to Jersey Shore, and located in a back apartment on Allegheny Street. Soon it was determined we could live on the second floor of an old brick farmhouse on the Susquehanna River farm that had been recently bought by mother's brothers. The farmhouse, more spacious and more private than the apartment, was positioned near the intersection of Pine Creek and the Susquehanna River. It was flooded on the first floor during the spring flood of 1947 and the furnace did not work, but

the second floor was adequate for occupation during the summer.

This is where my first early memories began. As a one and a half year old I enjoyed the summer sun, playing with dolls and kittens, and watching the farmers come and go up and down the lanes. I once again became part of my loving Aunt Barbara and Uncle Clair Miller's household when my sister, Jean Marie, was born in Jersey Shore Hospital in August 1947. When I became shy of Mother and Daddy, the grown-ups decided it was time to reintegrate me back into the Singley family unit. Aunt Barbara and Uncle Clair would always be my surrogate parents.

Housing was again a question because we could not stay in the farmhouse during the winter. The nearby village of Waterville held the solution. Daddy roomed with a family in Waterville before he and Mother were married. Waterville was the post office address of the pump station and fourteen miles closer to the pump station than Jersey Shore was. While the roads were steep and windy up the mountain from Waterville to the pump station our Dad knew them well. So we settled in Waterville in early winter of 1947.

Waterville was, and still is, a small village at the intersection of Little Pine Creek and Pine Creek at the west end of Lycoming County. The village is on a flat at the base of the mountains. Life was all about hunting, fishing and living by the creek-side. Several of Mother's childhood school classmates lived in Waterville. Mother and Daddy joined the village church across the creek. The pastor's family had young children, as did numerous other friends and neighbors. Older children of close friends were available for babysitting. Mother and Daddy were pleased

Raymond A. Singley with Dawn in 1946

to rent and live in the bungalow just below the railroad bridge where the giant black steam engines roared. I once fell under the railroad bridge while a steam engine passed over. Mother scooped me up while also carrying my baby sister and hurried us home. She sat me up on the wooden oak chair and poured burning meththylade onto my scraped up knee. OOOH, did it burn. She wrapped it in gauze, and held it in place with adhesive tape. For years, I carried the double lined scar embedded with cinders. A broken kneecap at age sixty replaced those scars with a singular line scar. I still have our little, then painted yellow, kitchen table at which I sat for my first "knee surgery". Today the Rails to Trails bike and hiking trail runs through the village instead of steam engines.

By spring of 1949, there was again a slow-down of the oil being pumped across the mountains and the extra push over the mountain was not needed. Dad went to work at the refinery in Bayonne, New Jersey. I know Mother did not really want to go back to New Jersey even though they had made some friends there. It wouldn't be like living in this village of her life-long friends, and nearby family. It would mean more change, more adaptation. Would her girls ever know a life of consistency, loyalty, and the fruits of seeds sown?

Dad got his first new car before we moved. It was a Pontiac with Chief Pontiac on the hood. He bought it from the Pontiac Dealer halfway up the hill on Allegheny Street. It was a light blue two-door coupe with the new pneumatic shifting to assist Mother in learning to drive. The windows in the rear only went half way down. Dad said it was a safety feature for us girls in the back seat.

The McCray family, former New Jersey neighbors, came to Waterville to help pack our belongings to move back to New Jersey. Mr. Schmidt helped Dad with the difficult job of finding housing. They found three rooms on the third floor of an old farmhouse near Camp Kilmer in Piscataway for us.

The farmhouse was full of young couples with children. One family that Mother and Dad befriended was originally from Indiana, but had come to New Jersey through the war. The men shared the ability to communicate by Morse Code. Our mothers with two girls each walked across the fields in search of eatable, non-poisonous mushrooms.

At the farmhouse on the third floor, Mother baked my fourth birthday cake in December in a small gas stove oven. The cake was covered with green icing just as I requested.

The small apartment of three rooms was not a permanent home. Mother was distraught at living this way. But she did take driving lessons and got her New Jersey driver's license while there.

Mother and Dad searched for an affordable permanent home. Mr. Schmidt knew a man building
three, four-room Cape Cod style homes in the town of Fanwood, just on the other side of Plainfield. The lots were sited next to the main Central New Jersey Utility right-of-way and the Jersey Central Railroad line. They were within walking distance to the railroad station for commutation for Dad to Bayonne. The schools were good, the neighborhood full of young families and there was a young church within the one-mile square borough.

Christmas 1949 presented us with the best Christmas present possible, a new home of our own. At age four, I had already lived in six temporary places. Although we carefully identified ourselves as native Pennsylvanians, we hoped this seventh "home" would be a place of rest and joy. I had in these few years learned to be an adventurer, a risk taker of sorts, in the spirit of my grandparents, along with my parents, for the sake of finding a place to work and grow. For me, this was and is the spirit of being born in the mountains of North Central Pennsylvania.

A Happy Life
By Barbara Danko of Osceola Mills, Pennsylvania
Born 1931

I grew up on a small farm in the Depression years, the youngest of twelve living children. My parents came from Russia, the area that is now known as Belarus, a small village called Samary. They were married in 1906, and then my father came to this country in 1907. He worked in the coalmines for three years to save enough money to bring my mother here in 1910. They worked on farms owned by landlords. My father was also in Czar Nicholas' army during the Russo-Manchurian War. The three years he served, he never

Barbara's family about 1937

received a letter from home.

Growing up, I had to weed the garden and tramp hay, both on the wagon and in the barn. I picked blueberries in a ten-quart bucket, which took all day. Sometimes my two older brothers would go into town and sell the berries for ten cents a quart. When I was in my teens, I had to milk three cows, as my father and brother would be "making hay" in the summer. Three of my brothers were in the service at that time, during World War II.

I went to a one room school for eight years and then to high school. There was no running water at the one room school. A neighbor would bring water every day for drinking. Everyone drank from the same tin cup. There was a big, round stove that heated the room. There were two outhouses in the back of the school. We carried our lunch.

Naturally, everyone walked to school no matter what the weather. It was at least a mile to the one room school and the same distance to the high school, which was in the opposite direction. I walked to school with two friends, who were sisters. We walked on a dirt road, through a field, across a small creek, and then on to a railroad track. When the water was high in the creek in the spring, we had to walk to school the whole way on the dirt road, which was longer in distance and usually muddy at that time. One time, the younger sister decided she was going to "pee" on the edge of the ice in the creek. Her sister tried to tell her it would melt and she would fall in. Needless to say, that is exactly what happened. She ended up with her rear in the icy cold water. When they

got home, the older sister was the one who got the "dickens".

We didn't get electricity until 1941. I was ten years old then. We did our homework by a kerosene lamp before we got electricity. We had an outhouse, and in the winter, we ran out in the cold in the morning to the outhouse. It sure got us awake in a hurry!

We had a windup record player, which seemed like such a luxury. What a treat it was when one of my older siblings had enough money to buy a new record.

We washed clothes on a washboard until several years after getting electricity. Then we got a wringer washer.

When we were a young age, we took Saturday night baths. Being the youngest, I was first and then my two older brothers. We carried water in buckets from a well and heated the water on a coal stove. Sometime later, we got a water pump hooked up in the kitchen.

There was never much money, but we

Barbara 10 years old

never felt like we were deprived. We had several cows, pigs, chickens, and a horse for the farm work. We usually had a large vegetable garden and an apple orchard, so there was always food. Living on a farm had its moments. Sometimes there would be a mean rooster who would attack us. One time, my father had to rescue me from such a rooster. Another time, one of my sisters was chased down our lane and out onto the main road by one.

Our first phone was a party line. If you were real careful, you could eavesdrop on someone's conversation. It was also frustrating if you needed to make a call, and the phone would be busy for quite a while.

My mother baked a lot of bread every week. Either one of my brothers or my father would go into town to buy the flour in fifty pound sacks with the horse and wagon. The cloth sacks were washed later and used for other purposes. Life was hard, but no one complained. It was also a happy life.

We walked everywhere, to work, church, school, or anywhere else. My oldest brother, who was nineteen years my senior bought a 1936 or 1937 Model T, which was the first car in the family. It had a rumble seat in the back. It was such a treat to ride in that seat.

Kids in a Little Green House
By Ivan W. Hunter, Jr. of Wellsboro, Pennsylvania
Born 1948

I was born in 1948, and have seen a lot of changes. I have lived in Pennsylvania my whole life. I came from a large family, of ten sisters and one brother with mom and dad that made 14 of us! We didn't all live at home simultaneously, due to the age differences. There were many times, however, when the house was full. We had good days and bad days like any siblings would. We didn't always agree, but for the most part, we all got along.

School was very different back then. We all rode on the same bus, and could even take our rifles along if we wanted to do a little hunting after school. I shouldn't say this, but sometimes we didn't make it to school! We packed our own lunches, and we often shared them! One day, my friend and I, decided we had a good plan. We ate some leeks on the way to school thinking, surely, they would send us home, and then we could hunt all day. Well, they kicked us out all right to the schoolyard for cleanup duty! We didn't try that again. Discipline was allowed in those days. There was more than one occasion, when mom swatted me with the broom. We thought long and hard before we did something bad, but that's not to say we were angels.

We lived in a little farmhouse in Whitneyville, which is in Tioga County. Our house is still there, but it's a radio station now. I remember our house very well. We had long hard winters, with snowdrifts halfway up the telephone poles. We would go days without power, being able to go to school, or grocery shopping. We dug tunnels to the barns, to feed the animals, and most importantly to the outhouse! We had an old kerosene heater in there, and had to use old catalogs! No Charmin back then! There were many nights when we would make a dash for the outhouse, and then run as fast as we could to get back in bed for the warmth. We had silk stones to warm the beds back then; not an electric blanket. We did have chamber pots for nighttime use though.

I remember when we had to wait for the state to plow a way to town. Friends helped each other back then. We got someone to make it to town in a truck, and get food for all the people who couldn't make it. Then we took toboggans and delivered their food to them. It was just the right thing to do. We did still have fun in the snow though. We would ride downhill on anything from shovels to car hoods; whatever we could find. We ice-skated and made fires by the pond. Those were good times.

Mom baked constantly. She was a good baker. She sold our extra baked goods to help out dad, who drove a bulldozer. We always had fresh cookies, cakes, pies, and bread. We often had friends and family at our table. Mom never turned anyone away, and everyone sat at our long kitchen table enjoying each other's company. We all had what we needed. We may not have had a lot, but we always took care of each other.

Christmas was hard for a family like ours, but we were happy with only getting a new tablet and a pencil. Homemade gifts were the best, because they were from the heart. I laugh when I see the movie about my BB gun. I got it for Christmas one year. It was the best Christmas ever, until one of my sisters shot the balls off the tree. I got blamed for it, of course, and my gun disappeared. I won't mention any names, but she knows who she is!

We really thought we were stepping up in the world when we got a phone, despite the fact it had a party line. The phone was entertainment for us. I'll explain it for those of you who don't know what a party line is. Two families shared the same phone. Each family had a different ring, to distinguish which line the call was for. That didn't stop us from picking up and listening though! Gossip was all we had sometimes. We had dances and gatherings as well. It was all just plain, good old-fashioned fun.

I won't say that we didn't get into trouble now and then; after all, we were kids. Once, my friend and I smelled one of those freshly baked pies cooling on the windowsill. We just couldn't resist taking that blueberry pie. I still remember my sister chasing us. We ran like jackrabbits and she never caught us. We dropped the pie though, and never did get a taste of it.

Sure, we pulled pranks, but they were never the kind that would hurt anyone. They were just good clean fun. Yes, those were the good old days; we just didn't know it then. I sure miss them. All of us grew up and went our separate ways. Most of us still keep in touch. We have a family reunion once a year at Hills Creek State Park. I find that it's wonderful to see how the family has expanded. Some of my sisters still live here in Tioga County, while others have moved away. This place will always be home to me, no matter what. That little green house in Whitneyville, Pennsylvania.

Vacuum Tube Transactions
By Darlene Hanley of Beech Creek,
Pennsylvania
Born 1946

I remember when I was a little girl my mom shopped in Lock Haven, PA. The one store she went to always amazed me. When she was done shopping, she would go to pay for the things she bought. She would give the money to the lady and she would send it upstairs in some kind of tube, the lady upstairs would send the change back down in the same tube. I believe the store was Montgomery Ward's or maybe Newberry's. I just know it was fun to watch all the action that was going on in that store.

Snowy Night, Swimming, and Swats
By Marsha Siple of Brookville, Pennsylvania
Born 1947

When I was about twelve years old, my older brother and several of his friends decided to take a toboggan down Shanghi Street (or North Pickering Street) in Brookville. They asked me to go, so there were six of us on a toboggan. Pickering Street is the highest hill in town. It goes practically straight up and down a hill. Down we went, passing six or seven streets, which ran horizontal to the Redbank Creek Bridge, going fast. Since it was three o'clock in the morning, two people blocked off Main Street, but back then no cars were out at that time. We then had a Jeep that went around the hill, pulling the toboggan in back and we did it again. That was back when we had a lot of snow.

The swimming hole in Brookville was called the Dam. All of us kids swam at the Dam in summer, and many still do. In the summer, it was a great place to meet friends. Once I was swimming from the falls ledge under the diving board to the stone ledge to get out of the water. When I got to the stone ledge to get out, there was a mud puppy. I almost drowned, because I was afraid of the mud puppy. Someone above the stone ledge saw me and chased the mud puppy away and grabbed me. This saved my life. I could have drowned.

In the old high school, which has burnt down since I went there, I had an eighth grade teacher named Phil Ruffner. He told me and Susan, the girl who sat in front of me to stop talking. We wanted to finish our idea in one sentence, so we naturally talked. He took us both to the hall, which was at the top of a wooden stairwell, which was three stories high. Everyone heard us get a loud swat. I was embarrassed to get a swat for just talking. I never told my parents that I got a swat at school.

Neighborhood Fun
By Charles T. Barnum of Renovo,
Pennsylvania
Born 1947

Kids today aren't getting together to play games outside like we did in the neighborhood. There was a kind of announcement that kids would all get together after supper at 6 PM. For some reason, Saturday and Sunday were not used as game days.

Some days we played; Three Stop Mickey, Kick the Can, Red Light-Green Light, Ghost, (but, our all-time favorite) was Hide and Go Seek. We set boundaries so everyone knew how far we could go. Sometimes we would set the boundary for half the town. The kids would go to the movie theatre, a comic book store, or play 8-ball at the pool hall. The guy that was "It" had the job of tracking everybody down. If you didn't get caught, we would return on the top of the hour.

In the winter we'd go sled riding in the street. They didn't put ashes down on the road. The cars would just ride on top of the snow and pack it down. The roads would get like ice and we would flop down on our sleds and try to catch a bumper of a car going down the street. People didn't see it as being dangerous, and sometimes the driver would let you tie a rope on the back bumper and we'd make a train of sleds, all going down the street. We had a lot of fun playing together, boys and girls, we all got along.

Fried Egg & Peanut Butter Sandwich
By A. K. Reitz of Mayport, Pennsylvania
Born 1930

Some of my most vivid memories are from the time I spent in a one-room school in the 1930s. I walked one mile and was hauled one mile in a neighbor's car, which the school board hired. Each morning all students repeated the Pledge of Allegiance to the Flag and prayed The Lord's Prayer. The school was heated by a coal stove in the center with a sheet metal shield except where the coal was put in. there was no artificial light, water was kept in a large crock with a spigot on the side, and water was obtained by walking to the neighbors and getting water from their well. If the well went dry, we got

Thomas School class of 1938

it from another neighbor's cowshed. There were two outdoor Privy's or outhouses. It was the teacher's responsibility to keep the room clean including windows, building fire in the coal stove, and being sure the coal buckets were full.

Discipline was maintained with a large paddle on the teacher's desk that they did not hesitate to use. Our outdoor playground equipment was a tree with branches. Most of the boys wore bib overalls. Everyone carried their lunch usually in a lunch bucket and some had a thermos. One vivid memory was the last day of school one year. The teacher built an outdoor fire and fried eggs. I put a fried egg in my peanut butter sandwich and I am still eating them.

Saturday Night Baths
By Pauline P. Myers of Smoke Run,
Pennsylvania
Born 1945

On Saturday night, it was time for everyone to get their bath. First, the water was heated on a coal stove in the kitchen and then the water was put into a round galvanized tub, which was our bathtub. All the doors to the other rooms were closed to keep the kitchen warm. We would use Lifebury soap and Halo shampoo. In the winter, my mother would wrap us up in a blanket to keep us warm. Then we would put on our pajamas and crawl under the covers so we would stay warm.

World War II Mission
By Eugene F. Bliskey of Lady Lake, Florida
Born 1925

I'm a World War II veteran and I'm going to relate a story about an experience aboard the USS Catskill LSV-1. While sitting on my General Quarters G2, the loud speaker announced, "Bogie, 80 mi., Bogie, 70 mi., Bogie, 60 mi." It was overheard and he released his torpedo at our ship, but the Captain outmaneuvered the Japanese plane, circled around, intending a suicide mission this time. Standing on the bridge by this time, he was driving straight toward me, so close I could see their face. One of our big guns hit the left wing, flipped the plane back on the fantail of the ship and bounced into the water, this saving all of our lives.

This experience haunts me to this day. My ship was in Leyte Gulf and the Japanese were approaching on both sides of the island planning on boxing us in. my brother Joe's ship, The Swanee, a baby carrier. All their planes were dispatched to stop the attack. Upon attempting a return to ship, the Japanese planes flew above Swanee planes, making it impossible to shoot. One enemy plane hit the forward elevator of the Swanee and blew out the sides of the ship, resulting in the death of my brother Joe, who was on the upper deck.

The Family Pet Groundhog
By Jane E. Lane of Coudersport,
Pennsylvania
Born 1920

My name is Jane Lane; I was born and raised in Galeton, Pennsylvania. I remember one afternoon we were digging up potatoes at my aunt and uncle's place in Germania when mom and dad came across a dead female groundhog along with its babies. All the babies but one were dead. It looked as though they had been run over by the farmers plow. Mom and dad decided that we would take the only survivor home and see if we could raise it. We started out bottle-feeding it and after a while, we just fed it whatever we ate. In the winter, it would hibernate in the old style abandoned icebox on the closed in porch. You know I just can't remember that little rascal's name, but boy I remember how he played with us kids just as a dog or a cat, chasing after us everywhere we went.

My father, Silas Finch, was the brakeman on the B & S Railroad in Galeton. I remember he would take us with him from time to time and we'd ride across the switchbacks to Cherry Springs, or we might take the train to Austin to visit with Dr. Page, our family doctor. I remember that times were tough all those years ago and you had to make do with what you had. Of course, there were hand me downs, but there were also aprons and cute little dresses made out of flour sacks. I don't remember all the details, but I remember a time when we had to have our hands stamped to get nation coupons.

The Last Time He Used the Outhouse
By Carolyn Eckert of Williamsport,
Pennsylvania
Born 1926

Before I was married, I lived with my parents, Edward and Ethel Hornberger. I had five sisters and two brothers on 144 H. farm on Hoagland's Run Road in Lycoming Twp., Lycoming County, Pennsylvania. My father ran a small dairy farm where he sold milk, veal, and eggs. This farm is still in existence today and is still in the family, owned by my youngest brother, Clyde, or as we call him Sandy. The farm was about four or five miles from Coal Mountain where soft coal was mined for many years. This was also another income for the family by boarding two coal miners for a while. Where 10 people in our little farmhouse stayed, I can't quite remember.

Then on March 12, 1945 at 8:00 p.m. William Eckert and I were married in the little country church, St. Michael's Lutheran in Quiggleville, this was also my 19th birthday. It was during the 2nd World War and they had to ration gas, so we didn't get too far on our honeymoon, Penn Yan, New York was as far as we could go. We started our married life in Quiggleville. A little old lady owned a store and a house. She sold us the house and she moved out taking only her clothes and leaving the rest for us to use and with rationing going on, she left us cans of flour, sugar, canned vegetables, antiques, and she had the only telephone for miles around. Many neighbors came to use it after we moved in. As we settled into our home, we made very few changes at first. There was no bathroom. We soon started having children and gradually started to remodel the old house. We put in a bathroom and so on. From 1945 to 1958, we had six wonderful children, three boys and three girls.

As our oldest son grew up he started working over the summer for my brother Sam on his farm, and this really got him interested in farming. So we started looking for a small farm. We found one in Bottle Run, just outside of Williamsport, Pennsylvania. Well, we left our newly remodeled house and moved. Of course the home being without a bathroom again. We managed without one for one year, I don't know how with six kids, but we managed. After a year, we figured we really needed a bathroom. Meanwhile we left the old out house stand for use when working outside. One day when the kids, some working, some playing, our youngest son had to go to the toilet, he was probably three or four years old at the time, so he went in by himself. Soon they heard him hollering and screaming. Two of the sisters ran to see what was wrong, he was stuck in the seat and couldn't and couldn't get out but they finally managed to free him. If I remember correctly, that was probably the last time he ever used the old outhouse. It stood there for a while until our oldest son wanted to tear it down, before he brought one of his girlfriend's house to meet the family.

The Siamese Twins
By Donna O. Pongrat of Montoursville,
Pennsylvania
Born 1937

My sister and I were always together when we were young and they called us the Siamese Twins. There is an 18-month difference in our ages. My sister was two years old and I was six months old when our father died of lumbar pneumonia, in January of 1938, and there was no penicillin and medicine like today.

Our mother took in two women boarders; they worked at the local Sylvania plant. They came after their work on Mondays and went to their prospective homes after work on Fridays. Mother got $5.00 a week from each lady. Mother gave them breakfast, packed noontime lunches, and a good balanced supper. We had three bedrooms. My mother's father, our grandpa, lived with us also. The ladies had one bedroom, grandpa had the second bedroom, and mother and the girls had the third bedroom.

Grandpa was 80 years old when he came to live with us and had broken his hip and was only hospitalized a short time then came home and neighbors made a frame over his bed so he could pull himself up and to help get in and out of bed. Mother would help him do exercises. Mother's two brothers gave her $10.00 each month for grandpa's care. He did not get social security. Also, our father was sickly off and on and did not have enough paid into social security for my mother to get any benefits. All she got was $68.00 lump sum, which was the portion our father paid in. She raised chickens, sold eggs, and dressed chickens to sell.

The feed mill was 1-½ blocks from us and she would pull my sister and I in the wagon to get chicken feed. She would pick out the bags that had the material that she liked to make my sister and I dresses. We had the prettiest dresses. She would get corresponding buttons to trim or lace and ribbon. She made ribbon bows for our hair to correspond with the dresses. We never felt poor. Our mother had so much faith. Wednesday nights we would go to Prayer meeting. We were taught to sit still and listen. There was no children's nursery. Our Christmas was not with gifts from the stores. Mother got a wagon in the dump that was minus a wheel and had a neighbor weld a wheel on it and she painted it and we would pull it up and down the street and sell eggs.

We were very blessed when I was nine and my sister was 10 ½. Mother met a Christian man who fell in love with our mother and accepted my sister and I as his own, in 1946. We were so happy to have a daddy. He did not have a lot but gave us a good life. He died in 1968 and mother died in 1985 at the age of 85. I would not trade my life with anyone. Mother was a strong individual and she installed it on my sister and I. we were truly blessed.

Donna and Doris Osler

212

Stamps and Bonds
By Donald Shirey of Sarver, Pennsylvania
Born 1934

I was born on a farm in the southern part of Jefferson County, Pennsylvania, near Punxsutawney on the 11th of July 1934. It was in the midst of the Great Depression and jobs were scarce. My father was 19 and working in a Government C.C.C. Camp planting trees. Following my birth, he secured a job with the Punxsy Beef house, a meat packing plant. He worked the night shift and slept during the day. I seldom saw him. With that new job, we moved into town to a little house in an alley.

My earliest memories were from this location. By now I had two younger brothers, born in 1935 and 1937. We shared the few toys we had. I recall a large tree near home with a patch of dirt near its trunk. We had several small hard rubber cars with wheels. Roads were laid out in the dirt with garage space to park. We played there until mother called us home for supper. About that time our grandparents surprised us with a red wagon. I think they were called Radio's. It had a wooden rack around it. I do remember seeing a picture of me standing in this wagon and urinating over the side. I don't remember doing it, but the picture is proof.

In the summer of 1939 things were still tough. My father moved our small family to his brother's little farm along Mahoning Creek just outside Punxsy. Probably doubled up to save money. Both worked at the Beef House less than a mile away. There were a few cows, a small barn, and a small pasture enclosed with an electric fence. One day after a rain shower Uncle Bob asked me to wipe the raindrops off the fence in my bare feet I complied and got a small jolt. Uncle got a good laugh. There was a railroad track about 200 feet from the house. It cut through an uprise which provided a nice overlook for three little boys to watch the train go by. We could hear the whistle blow a long way off so there was plenty of time to get to our lookout. Soon the coal burning steam engine came around the bend puffing smoke and pulling the cars heaped with coal to the delight of wide-eyed kids.

Soon we weren't satisfied with that and decided to engage in our first scientific experiment. We put a penny on a rail to see what it would look like after the train ran over it. It was flattened of course but a stupid idea.

Fortunately parents intervened and put a stop to it because the next step would have been to see if it could crush a rock and who knows what else.

In the fall of 1940 I started school entering 1st grade. There was no kindergarten. No school bus; we walked the half-mile to school. The safety of youngsters walking to and from school was no concern. There was no cafeteria, we carried our lunch from home. Also no playground so recess was a short walk outside two by two when weather permitted. My fondest memory from 1st grade was the traveling circus that passed through town. A big canvas tent was put up in a field. Two huge poles held up the tent, which enclosed the temporary seating. I got to go see it. I am sure it was a little two-bit operation, but in my six-year-old eyes, it was a Cecil B. DeMille spectacular.

By the summer of 1941 there were four adults and five children living in that small farmhouse. Space became a premium and I suspect that this was the reason my dad moved our family to Fairview, just outside the borough limits of Punxsy. The street was unpaved with lots of ruts. It had a living room, dining room, kitchen, and two bedrooms. A coal burning, potbellied stove stood in the corner of the dining room. It provided the only heat for the whole house. After getting out of bed on cold winter days, we boys would grab our clothes and scramble to gather around the only heat in the house and get dressed.

Every fall a truck came and filled the coal bin manually through a cellar window with a coal chute. As soon as I became of age, my chore was to keep the coal bucket filled. We did have city water in the kitchen, but the toilet was outside in a little building called an outhouse. We also had a chicken coop with a half dozen hens and a rooster. Everyone in the neighborhood had a garden in their backyard. We did also. All the gardens near us that I remember were spaded by hand with a shovel or a spading fork. We had no car and downtown Punxsy where the stores were was about ¾ of a mile away. Walking was the means of locomotion, for shopping, going to school, attending church, visiting friends, recreation, and everything else. Milk was delivered in heavy glass bottles sealed with a cardboard cap.

The fall of 1941 and the opening of school found brother Dick and I trudging off to the one room school that served the families residing in Fairview. The building was a classic model

213

for rural schools of that time period. A large open room with desks ranging in size from small to large, front to back, filled most of the space. A coal-burning furnace stood in the back corner to supply heat. The coal shed was outside but nearby. The bigger boys were assigned the duty of keeping the coal bucket filled. I could hardly wait till I was big enough to help with that task. A water cooler stood on a bench in the opposite corner. I had a water cup that was metal but collapsible to the size of a snuffbox. Two boys were assigned to walk to the nearest house to fetch water as needed. That was another task that I waited patiently to be big enough to take my turn. There were boys and girls outhouses on the grounds. Recess was a fun time when weather permitted us to be outside. Inside on inclement days some of the bigger boys Indian wrestled.

For art class we placed a clean sheet of paper over an outline of a bird, or any animal, then went to a window, placed the two sheets on the pane of the glass and traced the picture. Returning to our seat we went about coloring our masterpiece. For music we sang songs from a songbook without instrumental accompaniment. One song I liked was "My Grandfather's Clock". I can remember almost all the words to this day.

Back home on that day that lives in infamy, December 7, 1941, we had just returned home from church. I was lying on the floor reading the funny papers when the news came over the radio. We were at war. It didn't mean much to a seven year old, but as time went on, I found out that it changed everything. At school we began a scrap pile for the war effort. The boys began to scour the neighborhood for scrap metal to lug to school to add to our pile. We also collected milkweed pods, the insides of which were used to stuff lifejackets. We also began filling stamp books for the purchase of U.S. Savings Bonds. Stamps were $0.10 each and when filled for a total of $18.75, one received a bond worth $25.00 when mature. It was at this time that I began to build model airplanes out of parts cut from strips of balsa wood onto which stringers of balsa wood were glued and then covered with paper. The engine was a rubber band attached to a propeller. If built carefully, the propeller could be wound up and the plane could actually fly short distances. During the war I knew all the fighters and bombers in our arsenal as well as all the enemies. I made models of a half dozen of my

favorites. As the war dragged on, more and more of my relatives, including my dad, were called to serve. More and more stars on blue fields were showing up in the front windows of homes, white for serving and gold for killed in action. Ration books were needed to purchase many things. Gasoline, rubber tires, and sugar are three that are still in my memory. After my dad was called in the government paid my mother an allotment of $110.00 a month to pay the rent, purchase our food, clothe herself and her three boys, and pay the utilities. There was very little left over the discretionary spending. There was no money for entertainment, so we had to entertain ourselves. We had no car, but we did have cardboard boxes and lids from cooking pots and pans for steering wheels. So we did have cars. We didn't have horses to play Cowboys and Indians, but we had benches with legs to tie clotheslines to for harnesses. So we did have horses. We did have a big old radio to listen to our programs. During the day while we were at school mother listened to Ma Perkins and other soaps. After school we listened to Jack Armstrong, Tom Mix, Sky King, to name a few. In the evening it was the Lone Ranger, Inner Sanctum, The Shadow, and others. Saturday morning it was Buster Brown and Let's Pretend. Outside in the summer we played war games, dressing in homemade uniforms, camouflaged, with helmets, faces blackened with burnt cork, and carrying toy army rifles. In the winter the side roads were not salted and ashed as they are now. Covered with packed snow, they were perfect for sled riding. No traffic since gas was rationed and chains were needed to get about. We took our Lightning Guider sleds and had a great time. For skis we made our own by nailing straps to barrel staves. How else did we entertain ourselves? We made a crude racecar out of some boards and four wheels off a baby carriage. We pushed each other around in that. I dreamed of flying like Icarus and made a pair if wings of sticks and an old bed sheet. The wings were hinged so I could flap them. I climbed to the roof of the chicken coop and with a running start jumped off, flapping vigorously, but to no avail. I plummeted straight to the ground, but mercifully landed on my feet and was not hurt. If that trial flight had worked , my plan was to climb up onto the roof of my grandpap's barn and soar away from there. Flying was a dream. The local airport was about two miles away. Once a day the mail plane came in close to the ground, dropped the incoming mail in a bag, and picking up the outgoing mail with a hook on the end of a wire and fly away without ever landing. We picked blackberries and huckleberries and peddled them to neighbors for 50 cents a quart. Saturday afternoon was the double feature matinee at the Alpine Theater. Admission was 11 cents. If we didn't have enough money, we scavenged the junk piles at the back edge of people's properties for glass pop bottles which we could turn in for 2 cents each. Lawns were small. Mowers were manual reel type. Mowing with those, especially if they weren't sharp was daunting.

After the war, my dad became a Game Warden and his first assignment was in Smethport. We moved there in the summer of '47. Home then was an old farmhouse. No electricity, no telephone, no refrigerator, outside toilet, carried water in a bucket from a nearby spring. We walked a mile to get the school bus. The good old days! Loved 'em.

The Duck Pond 1958

Fence Mending
By Shirley Ostrander of Smethport, Pennsylvania
Born 1939

Around the time sap was running in March and April, dad would say it was time to mend our fences. The first time I was permitted to go with him I was eight years old. We hooked Prince and Tom, our horses, to a stone boat loaded with newly sharpened posts and post mall, wires, staples, and crowbars, and set off for the fence line. Mom had packed hot tea and sandwiches for our lunch. The horses would munch on the grass sticking up through the snow.

Each time we went "fence fixing" was an adventure. Woodpeckers, partridges, crows, ruffed grouse, rabbits, squirrels, deer, and sometimes even a fox would suddenly appear to brighten our day. If the sap was running dad would cut a notch in a maple so I could taste the sweet liquid right from Mother Nature! While we worked, I was allowed to drive the horses. What a thrill for me! As we passed along the edge of the forest dad would teach me the names of the trees and how their wood was used. One day he pointed out several Hemlocks that he planned to cut down to build a new chicken coop. While we loved

our horses dearly, as the farm grew in size the work became too much for them to handle. Dad said it was time to let them go to a new owner and buy a tractor. It was the saddest day of my young life.

In 1952, dad decided we needed a pond on our farm. He selected a depression between two fields just below a spring. From a neighbor he borrowed a slip scraper and we started the job. I drove the tractor and for several days we scooped out a hole about 4 ½ feet deep. The dirt was used to build the dam to hold back the water. When the pond was filled with water, it became home to frogs, dragonflies, and fish, including bass that the game commission supplied. The frogs, tadpoles, salamanders, newts, and fish were feasts for raccoons from the nearby woods. Our hen and drake also loved the pond and soon many ducks swam there.

My three sisters and I, along with our friends, spent many hours diving and

Betty, Shirley, Mary, Ellen in 1956

215

Shirley Ostrander in 1947

swimming in the pond. One of our favorite games was "Grab the Ducks' Feet", we would shallow dive and swim under water until we saw ducks' feet and grab hold of them. But soon the ducks got wise to our game and paid close attention to where we were. When we got too close to them, they would dive under the water to get away from us! So a new game had to be invented: "Dive for the Ducks"! Of course, they always managed to outwit us, but the fun we had was indescribable. I'm sure the ducks and the other pond dwellers were happy when school began in the fall and the pond once more became a place of peace.

Late August was the time to harvest the oats and barley we grew to feed our livestock. This was the season I loved the most. It meant that all the farmers in the valley would exchange and share in all the work. On opening day, ten men would meet at the first farm, bringing along either a team of horses and wagon or a tractor and wagon. At age eleven, it was my job to drive the horses and tractors so that all the men were free to load the shocks of grain onto the wagons. I had the

Shirley in 1965

great luck of driving two different teams of horses and eight different kinds of tractors. It was a merry time with all the men laughing and joking and playing tricks on each other.

When noon came, half of the men would go to the farmhouse for their meal. There was always a feast of plentiful food and the most delicious pies and cakes! Each farmer's wife would try to out-do all the other wives. Again, laughter and playfulness were enjoyed around the table. The work and fun would continue until we reached the last farm in the valley. Then we all left for home, happy, but knowing we would miss the camaraderie of days spent together in the fields.

Besides working with dad in the fields, there was also a lot to be done in the house. Mother saw to it that we all were well taught in cooking, ironing, cleaning, painting, wallpapering, and other household tasks. By the time I was 12, I could put a full meal on our table!

One of our favorite foods that mother prepared was baking powder biscuits. One day my sisters and I decided, we wanted to bake some, so we asked mom to tell us how. She told us what to do and then she left for town to sell the dozens of eggs that the hens had laid. When she was gone, we began baking. Soon we had the dough prepared and the stove heated. Into the oven the biscuits went and we watched anxiously as they browned. When they looked done we placed them on the counter to cool and waited. Taking them from the pan, they seemed awfully heavy. My sisters, Ellen and Mary, tried to bite one but they were unable to do so, the biscuits were too hard. We couldn't break them with our hands either. So we took a biscuit to the barn and hit it with a hammer. Again, no luck. What was wrong?

My sister Betty, who always seemed to know the answer to everything, asked me if we had put baking powder into the mixture. I looked inside the pantry and there stood the box of baking powder, unused. Our baking was a failure! What could we do with stone hard biscuits?

As farm kids we were accustomed to making up our own games. So we hung the biscuits from a board with pieces of wire and then hung the board onto a fence post. Then we loaded the 22 rifle our dad let us use and began firing at the biscuits. Success at last, the biscuits were breakable after all!

The Star System
By Thomas E. Gausman of St. Marys,
Pennsylvania
Born 1928

In contrast to the texting of today, the high-speed method of written communications in the days of World War II was the Telegram. Small towns like Ridgway, St. Marys, and Kane had their local Western Union Telegraph office. In Ridgway that office was located on North Broad Street just north of the Hyde Hotel, which stood on the corner of Main and North Broad Street. These buildings no longer exist. For three years during World War II while I was in high school I worked on a part time basis as a messenger boy at that office. Since the office was open from 8:00 a.m. to 5:00 p.m., overnight messages were accumulated at the dispatcher's office of the Pennsylvania Railroad station. So my job was to pick up those overnight messages and deliver them to the office before I went to school, then stop at the office at lunchtime to deliver any accumulated messages, then return to the office after school and deliver any messages until 5:00 p.m. On Saturdays it was an hour in the morning, one hour at noon and then two before closing. Sundays were 8:00 a.m. to 10:00 a.m.

Messages were sent and received over the same machine called a Simplex Printer, which had a typewriter keyboard for sending the message over the telegraph wires and ¼-inch wide paper tape with glue on one side that the text was printed on. For outgoing messages the paper tape was simply discarded. For incoming messages the tape was fed through a hand held device, which contained a water bottle and sponge to wet the glue so the tape could be glued to a telegram message paper. A razor blade type device was worn on the index finger of your left hand to cut the tape at the end of a word or sentence to make it fit on the page as pasting of the message progressed down the page. When sending a message if you made a mistake there was no way to back up or erase so you hit the equal sign several times and rewrote the word. Then when the message was taped on the page, the correct word was taped over the incorrect word and the equal signs.

The Elliot Company was the largest employer in Ridgway at that time and they were busy making motors and generators for the Navy. Resident Navy Inspectors in uniform would stop by almost daily to pick up or deliver messages. The volume of telegrams going to the Elliot Company was large enough that there was a separate printer and line dedicated to them.

The telegrams that were most important to the people of Ridgway were what I call the Good and Bad Telegrams of World War II. The good ones were those messages mostly from sons, but a few from daughters to their parents when they would tell them when they would be arriving home for furlough or leave, or to ask for money so they could come home. The bad ones were those from the government that started out, "We regret to inform you—".

Unlike today when the military sends a representative to inform the next of kin of the death of a serviceman, in World War II it was a message on a yellow piece of paper delivered by a messenger boy. And in the case of Ridgway, Pennsylvania the messenger boy was this 15, 16, or 17-year-old high school boy or the Murningham Taxi Service if the wait was too long for me to get out of school.

Western Union had a coding system for these bad telegrams. They used a rubber stamp with a star. Four stars meant Killed in Action, three stars meant Missing in Action or Prisoner of War, two stars meant Seriously Wounded in Action, and one start meant Slightly Wounded in Action. The instructions were to deliver the message to the house and then go next door to a neighbor to inform them of what had happened. These instructions were not always necessary in a small town. I remember one instance when the neighbor lady came running before I had even left the porch of the house where I had delivered a four star telegram. In another case with a one star telegram the mother had broken out in tears as soon as she saw me at the door. Fortunately this time the one star symbol helped me explain that the news was not really as bad as she was anticipating before she opened the telegram. This was the period of time after the Normandy invasion when the number of bad telegrams was increasing and my bicycle and I were well known around town. On one occasion kids shouted at me as I went by, "Who was killed this time?" My response was, "Santa Claus".

Delivering bad telegrams was not a pleasant task but there was another concern for me in that I had two brothers serving in the European Theatre at the time. The simplex printer had a bell on it, which the operator on the other end of the line would ring several times when one of the star messages was being sent. When that happened all in the office would go to the machine to see whom the message was for and I always had the thought that someday it might be about one of my brothers.

Another effect of the war on the telegram was the cancellation of all greeting, congratulatory, and singing telegrams since the wires were needed for the war effort. One day a young Priest, Fr. Hickey from St. Leo's Church came in and wrote out a congratulatory message to another Priest. I was at the counter and told him we couldn't accept it, and the office manager confirmed that. Fr. Hickey thought a minute, took another message blank and proceeded to write a message in Latin. The manager smiled and said to accept it. This same Priest enlisted as a Chaplin in the Army Air Force shortly after this incident and the next time we saw him was in News Reels standing at the end of a runway blessing bombers as they took off on bomb runs, which I think were in the Pacific Theatre. The newsreels would have been shown in the Strand Theater on Main Street in Ridgway, another building that no longer exists.

Hostilities with Japan ended in August 1945. I graduated from high school in June of 1946 and enlisted in the Army. I soon found myself serving with the Occupation Forces in Tokyo Japan for almost two years and remember sending my father a Father's Day greeting via telegram in 1947. I wonder who delivered that message?

Apple Butter Sandwiches
By Marion Wirth of Williamsport,
Pennsylvania
Born 1917

I was born in 1917 into a family of 10. I was the eldest of eight children, all who were born at home and raised on a farm in north central Pennsylvania. I'm 94 years old and had a stroke that affected my left side in May of 2011. Part of my therapy is typing this.

We had no refrigeration or electricity. We used the springhouse and cellar ground floor to keep perishables from spoiling.

Later on we had an iceman come through the neighborhood and one could buy a 50-pound cake of ice for an icebox we had. We used kerosene lamps for light and wood stoves for cooking and heat and a pipeless furnace that radiated up through the registers in the center of the house. Water was provided by a windmill that filled a 500-gallon tank that was in the attic of the house next door and then flowed by gravity for use by our home and the neighbors.

Our Saturday night bath was in the kitchen in a galvanized tub. The girls always bathed first. The outhouse was a busy place daily. There were two big round holes for adults and some small holes for children. During the night, we used the chamber pot. Then in the morning, someone in the family would empty it in one of the big holes. The silo pit was a secure location for the outhouse and nearer for outsiders. The Sears and Roebuck catalog with its many pages made for a handy ruffled toilet tissue. Later on one could afford a roll of prepared tissue. We slept in two beds, sometimes three of us in a bed in one room.

We had no car, so my dad walked two miles to and from work each day to help build a highway. It was dug by hand and he earned $30.00 a week, half of which was spent on groceries. Dad also did farm chores before and after work. Mom was a homemaker and did a lot of sewing. My aunt would occasionally send a box of clothes her kids outgrew and my mother would alter them to fit us. She canned vegetables from our garden that myself and my siblings weeded and apples and peaches from our trees that we picked. My mother made eight loaves of homemade bread weekly and apple butter when the fall apples and cider were ready. It was an all day job and so tasty. My folks always butchered a pig in the fall and smoked the butts, ham and bacon to give it a delicious flavor. We also raised chickens for their eggs and to have roasted or fried chickens, which we all loved. We always had for our supper our daily vegetables canned with the hot water method. You always had to check the top of the jars for any nicks or cracks to make sure they would seal.

We went to a one-room schoolhouse with six grades and one teacher. We had a potbellied stove to keep warm. Since we carried our homemade sandwiches for school, another pupil always wanted our homemade apple butter sandwiches. So we exchanged ours because we liked the store bought meat sandwiches. After we got home from school, we all had our daily chores. In early spring, several of us had to pick dandelion from our yard for our supper. We washed it thoroughly in water and cut it up. Then added pieces of bacon, chopped onion, and cooked potato chunks and made a hot dressing of water, vinegar, salt, pepper, and sugar to wilt the dandelion. All of which made for a delicious, nutritious, cheap supper vegetable. We carried wood each day for the kitchen stove and the pipeless furnace. My brothers milked the cows morning and night and stored the five-gallon milk cans in the springhouse in the cool water, then skimmed the cream from the top of the milk to make homemade butter and cottage cheese. We washed our clothes and scrubbed them on the washboard, rinsed them and hung them on a rope outside. Hopefully they would dry in the sun and the wind. The clothes smelled so good after fluffing outside. During the summer months, the ragman went through the neighborhood with his horse drawn wagon calling out in broken English, "Rage!" I was afraid of him until the age of seven because I couldn't understand him and was scared he would do us harm. Until I realized he was only there to gather rags and torn and dirty clothing. We used to take turns washing, rinsing, and drying dishes after supper. When dishes were done, we spent several hours studying schoolwork by kerosene lamps. Not as difficult as it might seem as I was on the honor roll quite frequently.

During the summer months I walked barefoot, however if I was lucky enough I'd dress up a bit, otherwise I'd go to Sunday church service barefoot. We walked to school and church. From the age of two and now, I've been taught to talk to the Lord in prayer daily to seek God's will and blessings and to obey the Ten Commandments. When I was around five or six years old I took the pledge to never drink alcohol or smoke. I took the pledge in Sunday school and I never broke it. No one in my family ever smoked, drank alcohol, or used drugs.

By the age of 12 I was an ardent hobby grower of African violets, cyclamens, ferns, and Christmas cacti. If I got too many of each I would donate them to my church rummage sale and they sold rapidly. During the summer I did housework for a couple and took care of their two-year-old daughter for $2.50 a week

with Wednesday afternoons off.

For my high school graduation from Williamsport Area High School in 1936 and my senior prom I had to wear one of my cousin's dresses altered by my mother to fit me. A senior fellow asked me to go as his date. He drove me in his father's car as I lived in the country. He and I had a good time. He drove me to the party and back home and on the way back he stopped and asked if I kissed! I said jokingly, "No" and he evidently took my answer for real, meaning it as we said goodbye and thank you! I didn't find my true love until sometime later. His name is Charlie and he was 23 and I was 24. We were married four years later and not long after he was drafted to serve our country in the Navy in the Pacific during World War II. When the war was over he came back to resume our life together. This past year we observed our 70th anniversary!

Farmer's Market
By Ruth E. Burns of Pendleton, South Carolina
Born 1923

Born at Montoursville, Pennsylvania in 1923, one of my earliest memories was sitting on the floor, wrapping my long underwear around my ankles so that I could put on my stockings. Another thing I remember was the Saturday night's bath. The bathtub was a tub my mother used, when she did her washing. It was placed on two chairs and the hot water was from the kitchen stove. Although we had a furnace, the kitchen was the warmest place in the house.

During the summer, my grandmother came to visit and she and my mother made clothes for my younger sister and me. Grandmother was very good on the Singer sewing machine. Her foot was heavy on the treadle. For school our clothes consisted of three dresses each and bloomers to match. We had a special outfit for Sunday.

Washday was an all day job for my mother. First, there was a large tub in which the dirtier clothes were soaked overnight. After wringing those out they were placed in the washer. The wringer was turned by hand and one of my brothers turned the wringer with a handle along the side. If there were still dirty spots on the clothes, you used the washboard

219

to remove them. Then they were put through the wringer again and went to the rinse water. They went through the wringer once more and then to the clothesline. The white clothes and lighter clothes were not soaked ahead of time but some of them after being washed were put in a tub of bluing. After the washing was done the water was used to scrub the kitchen floor and the back porch was also scrubbed in the summer time.

On the back porch we had an icebox. The iceman came a couple of times a week in the summer time. They had big chunks of ice, which they delivered, to your icebox. Sometimes they would chip a small sliver off and drop it on the ground and the kids in the neighborhood would grab it. What a treat.

We also had a victrola; it had a picture of a dog in front of a horn. The caption was, "His Master's Voice". You had to wind the machine up so it would play. The records were very heavy and you could not stack them so you played one at a time. I loved this record player and spent hours playing it. I don't remember if we had electricity from the beginning or if it was put in later, but I do remember getting a radio. The receiver was not incorporated with the radio but was a horn, which sat on top of the radio. Some of the programs we listened to were, *Edgar Bergen and Charley McCarty*, the original *Amateur Hour*, *Amos and Andy*, and *George Burns and Gracie Allen*.

Then there was the milkman. At that time, milk only came in bottles. We had no plastic cartons. In the wintertime the milk sometimes froze, pushing the cream up out of the top of the bottle. If you scooped the cream off the top and added a little sugar it was almost like having ice cream. When my sister had scarlet fever and we were quarantined the milkman poured our milk in jugs, which my mother had placed outside the night before. The milkman was not allowed to leave the bottles for us.

My dad and brothers were hunters, so we had dogs. One dog we had was very special. He was allowed into the house at night. He liked to sleep over the register, which he did except when my dad caught him. He was very well known in town. When he was not hunting, he used to meet a lady at the bust stop in the morning and she gave him a candy bar and he sometimes rode the sidecar on the town cop's motorcycle. But he was a good hunting dog.

I loved school. If you lived in the borough, you walked to school. It was quite a long walk for me. In the wintertime the long underwear felt good. Thanks to good teachers, reading was my favorite subject and I still read a lot. When I was in junior high, they started gym class for girls. The gym teacher for the first year was the school's football coach. The next year the librarian took over. We wore one-piece gym suits and the bottom was like a pair of bloomers. But summertime was special. I learned to swim before I went to school. Whenever my sisters, brothers, or my dad went swimming I went along. There were several swimming holes in the Loyalsock Creek and I knew them all.

We also played baseball. There was no Little League and we chose up sides and played in the fields near our home. Sometimes making our own rules and playing the way we did made future leaders. At night we would sit outside and sing. Sometimes the neighbors sang with us. Sometimes my dad would buy us ice cream cones at $0.05 each. Sometime in all of this the depression came. My dad, who was in partnership with another man, brought his tools and came home because there was not enough work for the two of them. He went in business for himself. His shop was at backyard of our home.

Then we got a telephone. It was the only one in the neighborhood. Neighbors came to use our phone, when they had an emergency. One day the lady next door came to call the doctor. Her husband had become ill, she wanted to call the doctor but a lady was on the party line and she refused to hang up. One of my sisters ran to the doctor's office. Doctors made home calls in those days. During the depression many people went hungry, but we were very fortunate. We had a huge backyard and my dad planted it all. We all helped pick the vegetables but I hated to pick string beans because of the yellow beetles on the vines. We had plenty of fresh vegetables in the summer and as soon as the vegetables started coming ripe, my grandmother came and she and my mother canned all summer long. We had a bin in our basement that was filled with potatoes and apples. My dad and brothers hunted and we had game for meat. I can remember having roast rabbit for thanksgiving dinner one year. What meat we bought came from the farmers market in Williamsport. At first each farmer had a cart but later the Grower's market was built. We also bought our butter from the farmers there. It would be in rolls and would be wrapped in paper that was the same as paper used for wrapping meat. Although there was an A&P in town, we bought what few groceries we needed from a local grocer. We charged it and when spring came my father would do whatever repair work was needed on his furnace, spouting or roof. Then they settled the bill between them. He also did the same with the doctor.

In 1936 there was a huge flood and later my father died and my life was completely changed. I went to live with my brother at Jersey Shore, Pennsylvania. At Jersey Shore they had a summer program in back of the YMCA. There was a baseball field and we played by the rules. They had many other programs set up. A friend of mine had an older brother and he used to take us swimming in his car, which had a rumble seat. I loved it. We went swimming up Lycoming Creek in a hole just above the Girl Scout Camp.

I did not go to school there very long, but the one thing I do remember was going to the auditorium for a showing of television. They took two of the senior girls into another room and then they showed them on a screen. The screen had a purplish color and really wasn't to clear but it was awesome to us. My brother was transferred to Williamsport and we moved to South Williamsport and I graduated from South Williamsport High School in 1941. I will always remember December 7th the Japanese bombed Pearl Harbor. I enlisted in the Coast Guard in 1944.

Baiting Bees
By Cy Anderson of Kane, Pennsylvania
Born 1925

When I was a young fellow, a favorite pastime on an early fall afternoon for me, my brothers and our neighbor, Red Kessler, was baiting bees. Why would we bait bees? To find a bee tree is why. What would we do when we found one? Well, occasionally we would fell it, take the honey, strain it and use it. But usually it was just for the satisfaction of finding the tree. Keep in mind this was the days before television.

The first thing you need baiting bees is a "bee box", which is simply a cigar box. The thin walled kind with the lid like is in the display case at the cigar counter (or at least they used to be). Then you need a small piece of old honeycomb, a shallow saucer like dish that will fit in about half of the box, a small bottle of sugar water (about 4:1 mix), a tiny bit of anise flavoring in a bottle, a little bottle of white paint, and a couple of Q-tips.

Now you pick a calm sunny afternoon after the first heavy frost, you go into the woods and find an opening in the trees maybe 40 to 50 feet across where there are lots of golden rods. An old well location is a good spot. Here is where you set up the bee box; it is best if you can find a stump or an old well casing sticking out of the ground to set it on. Set your dish in a box and the honeycomb in the dish. Fill the openings in the honeycomb with the sugar water. Add a drop of anise to the water in the dish. This will be enough to attract the bees, but not enough to harm them.

Sit back and watch. Sooner or later, hopefully sooner, a wild honeybee will find the box and start to "work it". He will fill up with sugar water and take off. Watch him closely. He will circle until he is just above the trees and then head straight for the bee tree/hive, hence the term "bee line". Soon he will return followed by the others. Observe them leaving also, now you know the direction of the tree. After a bit dab your Q-tip into the white paint, when one of the bees is filling up, touch his rear with a Q-tip leaving a tiny dot of white paint on him. Note the time when he takes off, watch for him to come back, and note the time. Do this a couple of times, if you want, you can time a different bee by painting him in a different place.

A bee will travel about ¼ mile a minute. Suppose the bee you timed is gone eight minutes that means he traveled about two miles, or a mile each way, probably a little less, allowing a half minute or so to make his deposit in the hive. Now you know not only the direction to the hive, but the approximate distance too.

Pick up your bee box and walk in the beeline direction for approximately the indicated distance (in this case one mile). Set up your bee box again and repeat the procedure. After the second or third set up you will be close enough to see the bees going in and out of the hive (probably a hole high up on a hallow tree) and hear the buzzing of the swarm. You are now on your own.

The Baseball Game

I have kept the following in my memory for over 70 years and have decided it's time to record it. I am probably the only person still living who was listening to the broadcast of the baseball game when Gabby Hartnett, in the September twilight of Wrigley Field and in the twilight of his career, hit the ninth inning homerun that dashed the pennant hopes of my beloved Pittsburgh Pirates, the year was 1938 and I was 12 years old.

I remember the Pirates lineup on that sad day, it was: First Base, Gus Suhr; Second Base, Pep Young; third Base, Lee Handley; Shortstop, Arky Vaughn; Left Field, Johnny Rizzo; Center Field, Lloyd Warner; Right Field, Paul Warner; Catcher, Al Todd; Pitcher, Mace Brown (in relief). Bill Brubaker and Heinie Manush may have played that day also, either pinch-hitting or as a defensive replacement.

Cy Anderson, Richard, and Patricia about 1937

Rosy Rosewell was doing the broadcast, I don't remember if it was a live broadcast or a ticker tape rebroadcast, which they sometimes did for the road games in those days. I do, however, remember the words of Rosy after the ball left the ballpark. Although he was heartbroken he said, "Well, you can't begrudge a fella in a hit like that."

The Pool Room

When the U.S. entered World War II in 1941, I was not quite old enough to enter the service, but was old enough to hang out in Berkwater's Pool Hall or as we called it, The Pool Room. At that time there was an elderly Italian couple living on the 600 block of Park Avenue in a house somewhat obscured by lilac bushes in front and with what appeared to be grape vines in the back. The talk among the young guys in the poolroom was that their son, who came from out of town to visit them on occasion, was a member of the Mafia. He would come tooling into town every couple of months in a big Cadillac bearing New York plates and he certainly looked the part of a Mafioso. He was big and slightly overweight with black wavy hair and a raspy voice. He would stay for a day or two and then head back out of town. We were told his name was Louie Nicolazzo, a.k.a. Jiggers Nicalazzo, a.k.a. Louie the Jigger. This was heady stuff for the poolroom gang. Some of the Italian guys from the west side claimed they knew him and if he spoke to them, they walked with a swagger for weeks.

I grew up and went to work for Uncle Sam for a while. Fast forward now to after the war: I am back in Kane and so is Jiggers. I am loafing, drinking, and chasing girls and he is hustling Clara Rose, a widow who owns the Colonial Inn. This was the old Colonial Inn located in an old house up on the hill in Wetmore. They had a bar and I think they also served meals. I would stop in for an occasional beer and Jiggers would be tending bar. Sometimes there would be no one else in the place and we had some interesting conversations. He told me that during the war he started a construction business up in Syracuse. The business did well for a while, but eventually went bankrupt, mostly because as company president, he was drawing a big salary and spending the winters in Florida.

Later he married the Inn's owner, who with his help was determined to drink herself to death. Shortly after they were married, the Colonial Inn burned down. The talk at the time was that it was a friction fire: the mortgage rubbing against the insurance policy. Later Clare died and Jiggers dropped out of sight for a while. After a while word was that he had married a wealthy widow from Bradford, but was not too happy. She put him to work tending wells on her oil property over there.

Old Swede

Then there was this old Swede. I guess he was somewhere between 60 and 70 years old. His named was Hildebrand Johnson and he and his son Rudy lived in an old rundown farmhouse at the end of the Greendale road on Claude Olson's farm, about four or five miles from town. Rudy wasn't exactly retarded, but he certainly was a little bit backward. One morning I was walking up town and I met Rudy coming down the sidewalk toward me. As we passed I said, "Good morning Rudy". He took about three steps past me, stopped, turned around and said, "Tank you."

Their house was on a knoll that they called Mockingbird Hill and I don't know why the Olson's allowed them to live there except they did a few odd jobs like cutting wood for them and stuff like that. Hildebrand and Rudy had some source of a little income, social security or relief, or maybe Claude Olson paid them a little bit. Pretty often, they would come to town and get roaring drunk, especially Hildebrand when he got his "sheck". He was usually dressed in a khaki coat and cap with khaki pants stuffed into rubber boots coming nearly to his knees. He would be clean shaven had a thin face and a long, thin nose. He walked bow legged and bent slightly forward at the hips and could really motor when headed for town and then taverns.

He would sometimes go up to the Eagles Club. Their rooms were on the 2nd floor of a building on Chase Street. My dad was a member and spent a lot of time there. He would ply Hildebrand with drinks and get him to sing "Nickolina" in Swedish. This annoyed the other members because they considered Hildebrand a nuisance. That tickled dad because he was somewhat of an agitator. When he got pretty well into his cups Hildebrand would announce, "I'm Hildebrand Yonson and I ain't no got damned fool for nobody, never was and allus will be." Once someone from the Salvation Army got hold of him and in a weak moment, he got the power and signed the pledge. It didn't last long though. He went to a meeting and got up and declared, "Since I found Yesus Christ I feel so yoyous I could yump right up and kick a hole in the got damned drum."

Kane had a taxi service back then and when he had blown his money he would stagger to the City Garage where the taxi stand was located and announce, "Take me out to Mockingbird Hill." Claude Olson will pay you. Claude Olson owes me $500.00. Sometimes they would take him and sometimes they wouldn't but they never got paid.

One time Marge and I, on a warm summer evening went out to visit Cork and Eleanor Olson. Marge and Eleanor were friends. Cork had an old four-wheel drive power wagon and decided to take us for a ride around the farm and down through the woods and maybe see some deer. He drove up on Mockingbird Hill. Hildebrand and Rudy were out in the yard drinking beer. Cork started chasing them around the place in the power wagon and they ran like crazy, whooping and waving their beers. I was afraid he was going to run over them but they always managed to dodge at just the right time. And they thought they were having fun.

Sometimes after a night of whooping it up in town, if they couldn't bum a ride, they would walk home via the Waterworks Road. It went up through the woods and ended right at Mockingbird Hill. On this particular night it was about 25 below zero or maybe even colder. When they got down past the Waterworks, Rudy sat down to rest and Hildebrand kept right on trucking for home. Rudy was still there next morning, frozen stiff as a statue. I never saw Hildebrand after that. I do know he didn't live long.

Little Italy
By Michael Marchese of Williamsport,
Pennsylvania
Born 1924

I was born in 1934 into a poor Italian family of 11, seven boys and four girls. I lived in what was called Little Italy. In 1939, there was a large convention in town and on the last day, a large parade was held. In the parade was the Governor of Penna and movie stars Alexis Smith and Erla Stone, who played Henry Aldrich on radio. It was a great parade.

We had an old wood stove and at night, us boys would be cutting wood with a two man cross cut saw. I remember sitting on the logs while my brothers cut the logs. I said to my father, "My leg is bleeding", so he said, "We will go to Flannigan's Drug Store". He asked my father what happened. Dad told him we were cutting logs and that I wasn't watching where I had my legs. Mr. Fannigan was like a country doctor, whenever someone was hurt they went to him. He patched them up at no charge and mom would send him homemade bread and rolls for his kindness.

Both my parents were from Italy, dad was from Sicily and mom from Calabria. All the Italians lived in Little Italy. It ran from Church Street on the north and south on Front Street. It went from Hepburn on the west of Market Street and east to Eastern Wood. In 1942, we moved to East Jefferson Street into a double house, which my great aunt owned and her husband, who were both from Italy. It was a nice neighborhood, besides Italians there was a Jewish family, two African American families, and a couple German families. My parents enrolled us into the public school. My twin and I were put in the 1st grade and our teacher was Miss Sherman. I remember her words "We have two sets of twins, both identical twins." Me I loved it when it snowed I would throw snowballs at people and cars one day one of the other teachers took us to the school principal and said, "Mr. Sanders, the Marchese boy was throwing snowballs." Mr. Sanders stated which one, the teacher stated, "I don't know since they're identical and dress alike." Mr. Sanders was like King Solomon because he had wisdom. He said to the teacher, "I will not paddle them because of the innocent one." He told her keep an eye on the twins. When we walked to our rooms I thought this was great, so every time we had a hard snow I was back throwing snowballs. Again we were taken to the principal's office. Mr. Sanders said to the teacher, "Which one?" she replied, "I do not know, but he is left handed." Mr. Sanders said to my twin and me, "Write your names on this paper." My twin brother wrote Harry using his right hand and I wrote Mike using my left hand. Mr. Sanders said to my twin, "Go back to your room." I said, "What about me?" Mr. Sanders said, "I have been waiting for you for six weeks." Which I was paddled three days in a row and when I went home after school I got paddled again. The next time it snowed I went to the teacher, stood by her and said, "I am Mike Marchese and I got both hands in my pockets." School was nice we went home for lunch hour, no so called snow days we would walk to school no matter how high the snow was and teachers had their meetings after school.

We had no outhouses but we knew where it was. Whenever it rained hard the backyard would fill up with water. We looked for a small whirlpool, and then we could use a large pipe to make the hole bigger. Water would be going in 10 minutes. On Saturday and Sunday nights we would sit on the floor listening to the *Lone Ranger* and *Shadow* to name a few and then we would go to bed after we took our bath. Mom would boil water on the cook stove and put it in a large washtub so we could take our baths.

Since we lived close to the river dad would take us fishing. Since we were poor and could not afford rods and reels we would use throw lines. After the line was thrown in the river, we would cut a tree branch and put it in the ground then tie the line to it. We would use the line for a teller. The only fish that was in the river was carp, catfish, and suckers. Our Jewish friends would buy them for $0.15 and the next day we would go to the movies for $0.12.

World War II we would collect any type of scrap metal and tires and take it to school and put it in the gym. Our teacher thanked us with a party. I remember everything we bought we had to have rations or food stamps, even for gas. When the war was over a friend of ours took his trailer and put a dummy of Hitler and hanged it from a gallows he made. He decorated the trailer and drove us kids all over town. Since my two older brothers were in the service during the Korean War my twin and I quit school to help our parents raise the rest of the family. We both worked for Western Union delivering telegrams. We were paid so much an hour and a penny an hour for our bikes. The only thing I did not like was delivering a telegram to a family that their son was killed in action.

We had a wringer washer, us kids would help mom wash clothes and the girls would hang the clothes on the line outside to dry. Mom made aprons out of flower bags she always wore one whether it was for baking, cooking, or doing housework. I remember coming home from school and a truck made a sharp turn and seven bags of flower fell off and busted the corner of the bags. I asked the driver if we could have the flower, he said okay. I had two of my brothers watch the flower the rest of us went home for a wagon and wheel barrel. We took it home and mom baked bread, sticky buns, and macaroni for spaghetti, and mom made more aprons out of the flower bags.

On Saturday I would work at the market

house shelling peas making $0.25 for four hours. When I was done working I would go back to the incinerator to get celery, peas, and tomatoes to take home so mom could make homemade vegetable soup. I would give her $0.13 and keep $0.12 for the movies. My favorite western star was Wild Bill Elliot. We would go in at 2:00 p.m. and still until 11:00 p.m. When they put Sunday movies on the ballot it was turned down and the second time it came up we decided to come up with signs saying, "Vote for Sunday movies" and it was approved by the state of Pennsylvania.

My favorite animal was my dog Rusty, he was a mongrel, but very smart. When I would go for a ride he would hop on the carrier on the back of the bike, put his front paws on my shoulders and we would ride all over town. We also raised pigeons whenever my father would get ready to cut wood with an electric saw that he made. The pigeon would fly to it and dance for my dad.

We made our own toys. We would take a 2x4 and nail roller skates on front and back, a wooden crate that oranges came in for a scooter. Or go up to the market house to the fish market for wooden crates that they got there fish in. We would make wooden Army tanks we would use those when we played Army. We would go to the local junkyard for Army helmets, also old headlights when we played rocket man. We also used carnation milk cans for cowboy's horse's hoofs; we made rifles out of broom handles. Our favorite swimming hole was the river under the bridge where we would use a rope to swing on or over to an island or the race to the old dam.

The Italians had gardens along the river before the dike was put in then lost them after. Each Italian had a large area with a mountain-stove building where buckets, shovels, and rakes were also used for shelter when it rained. In evenings us boys would help our father. We fired a sawdust boiler and pop rested while they work. Pop worked at the former sweet steel on Arch Street in Newberry. He would walk to work and home. When they chose, he worked at Ciminis Bakery cleaning up. My twin and I would do it for him and had the paycheck put in his name. Earlier he had another part time job at night from 11:00 p.m. to 7:00 a.m. on the weekends. My father, twin brother, and myself would go with him. I told pop you rest and we would fire the boiler all it burned was saw dust.

When we went to school mom would say to all, "Make sure you put on clean undershorts and socks in case you have an accident." After school walking home we would stop in #4 Firehouse if we had to use the rest room. They were great. Later in life my twin brother and I became city firemen. My father was very proud, he would say, "Five sons work for the city, three firemen and two police men." The other two had their own business. The oldest was a foreman for the gas company.

My first love was Jackie who went to the same school. I would walk her home and one evening she had a party. We played spin the bottle and after several times I finally kissed her. When we kissed, the rest of the kids clapped their hands.

We had a wooden ice box when the ice man would come bring our ice in the house he would go out to his truck, take a small chunk of ice and chip it and give a piece of ice to all the kids. My favorite was our milkman; his horse knew every house on the block. He would take his milk carrier walk down the street to different houses and his horse would follow him. Family time sitting on the back porch, working in the garden, playing games with father, and monopoly.

My oldest brother John, after the Korean War, bought my parents a silver tone floor model radio and phone. Later he bought a television. It was the first one on the block, it only had three channels, but it was great watching on Saturday nights when wrestling was on. We would invite some of the kids on the block to watch it. Mom would come in with her apron on carrying a big bowl of popcorn for all of us.

Saturdays were great, after morning chores we worked at the market house until noon. If we didn't get vegetables from the market house we walked around town. Mom always bought us high tops. They always came with a pocketknife. The best movie back then was Keystone. Saturday was double feature day, two westerns, three stooge cartoons, and movie serial coming attractions also some movie places that showed Roy Rogers films gave a 8x10 photo out to the kids. When Roy married Dale Evans I quit watching Roy movies they became musicals.

Can I Have Some "Wooder"?
By Shirley H. Evans of Citrus Springs,
Florida
Born 1934

My siblings and I were privileged kids! Oh, not privileged the way you might think. We didn't live in a big house with servants, have the finest store bought clothes, eat in fine restaurants, attend private schools, have our own bedrooms, or rub elbows with the elite society. No, we lived in a small house, wore hand me down clothes, never saw the inside of a restaurant, but ate what was put in front of us and liked it, attended neighborhood schools, slept three in a bed, went to Sunday school and church and played with the neighborhood kids who were just as poor as we were. But we were privileged to have a mom and dad who loved us more than anything in the world and grandparents who felt just the same.

When World War II approached, dad joined the throngs of others who had come out of the depression era, thankful for defense work. Dad found work in Baltimore with the Glenn L. Martin Aircraft Company and soon found a house for our family of six. We were so excited. The big city was a whole new world to us, leaving our comfort zone of Clearfield, Pennsylvania. Streetcars and big buses, who had ever seen such things? Big schools where we even had to wear gym suits, a subject new to us. And guess what? No spankings in the Baltimore Public Schools! Supermarkets with carts that people pushed around and filled with their groceries. Escalators in the big, downtown stores, and signs that we couldn't understand, "White only" above the restrooms and drinking fountains. Yes, a whole new world, a foreign world in many ways. Many of our friends spoke in strange accents, coming from other states near and far and even the natives of our new city "talked funny". They said "wooder" for water.

We missed the small neighborhood in Clearfield, and most of all missed being able to visit our grandparents. Dad's folks lived in town and mom's owned a farm where we could run and play, the next thing to heaven in our minds. I'm not sure what, or if all the factors played a part in the decision, but for the years following until each one of us graduated from high school, we spent the entire summer vacation back in Clearfield, mainly "on the farm". The four of us, then ages four to 10

packed our bags and had them waiting the day school was out in June, not to return until a day or so before school started. I can only imagine how empty our house was for mom and dad, who woefully, but willingly gave us their blessing.

By this time, the war had begun and Clearfield was slowly seeing its fine young men go off to places and names they had only seen in their geography books. Our uncles were gone, one to the Pacific and the other to Europe. The Clearfield Progress carried names of its native sons, and published the news from all fronts. Grandma had a globe that she used to show us where our uncles were as well as the others we knew. We learned the names of important military men: General Douglas MacArthur, General Dwight D. Eisenhower, General Omar Bradley, the list went on and places like New Guinea, Japan, China, Belgium, Germany, France, Holland, and Italy.

Life on the farm was care free with chores that were such fun we didn't realize that they were. Gathering eggs from the chicken coop every evening was certainly a learning experience. Sometimes there would be a mean old cluck that would peck at our hands when we tried to raise her up and steal the eggs. When the cows were in their stanchions and grandpa began the milking process, it was our job to hold the cow's tail to prevent it from hitting grandpa in the face. It was fascinating to watch the weathered hands gently squeeze the teats in a melodious rhythm. After milking, if there were any calves they would be released, each one going directly to his/her mother. One time I asked grandpa how in the world did they know which cow was its mother, they all looked alike, I thought. Grandpa looked directly at me and said, "Well, you know your mother don't you?" that made sense. When calves were being weaned from their mother, grandpa showed me how to stick my hand in a bucket of milk, let the calf smell and lick it, and then put a milky finger in its mouth, a substitute teat, I guess. Eventually they learned to drink from the pail. After milking, grandpa carried the heavy milk pails into the cool cellar where the milk was put through a separator. Rich yellow cream came out of one spout and that was put aside for churning into butter. Another spout filled the milk bottles that we would cap, watch the cream rise to the top and then carry upstairs and put in the refrigerator. Another spout provided the left over milk that would go to the weaning calves and pigs. For me, it was a mind-boggling process. The machinery had to be kept scrupulously clean and as a little girl I watched grandma many, many times accomplish that chore. At age 7, I decided that it was my goal in life to be able to clean the separator.

We all looked forward to "thrashing time". In the absence of our uncles and other neighboring farmers who usually helped due to the war, we all pitched in with our assigned duties. Grandpa always fed the wheat or oats into the big red, shaking machine, grain first. I sensed that it could be a dangerous job. He would grab a shuck of wheat or oats, cut the twine and feed it into the thresher. The straw was blown into a pile and the grain emerged from the side. It had to be measured and then put into gunnysacks for storage. By the time the last shuck was put through, we were all hot, sweaty, dirty, and tired, but satisfied with a job well done. What better reward then, but to go down to Blue Hole for a dip in the nice cool water. We took a bar of soap with us.

The farmhouse sat on a hillside with a panoramic view. During the day, we could watch the mail plane fly low in the valley and snatch the mail pouch from a pole and then soar up into the heavens. In the coolness of nighttime, we would watch the two beacon lights swoop across the sky guiding pilots as they made their way in the darkness. We counted the automobile lights descending on Carr Hill and listened to peaceful nocturnal sounds. We loved to sit around the big dining room table playing games with grandma. Monopoly was a favorite, as was Tiddley Winks. But we took our letter writing seriously, too penning faithfully to our parents and our two uncles in uniform. Special nights were when we tossed the inflated dried pig's bladder around the big kitchen like a balloon.

We loved berry picking at numerous places on the farm. There was a line of currant bushes out by the garden, just below the "privy" too tart to tempt the taste buds. And out along the lane were numerous raspberry and blackberry bushes that would be heavy with fruit. Of course, we filled our tummies, but the pails were heaping when we took them to the kitchen. Sometimes we would go out to the pasture and pick the bushes clean out there. One time little sister complained that,

she had never stood so long in all her life. This amused us since the surrounding ground was covered with tall, soft grass, perfect for sitting or stretching out, for that matter. When it was cherry picking time we rose to the challenge to climb as high as we could to reach the biggest and best fruit. What fun.

On the farm, Monday was washday, Tuesday was for ironing, Wednesday for mending, and so it went through the week. We usually dusted and cleaned on Fridays and grandma baked on Saturday morning. Now I wouldn't expect our younger generation to even begin to understand why in the world it took all day to wash clothes. The Maytag had to be rolled out from the corner, a bench brought in front of the porch to hold the rinse tubs and water heated in the big copper boiler on the coal stove. All the linens and clothes were strewn around on the kitchen floor in piles usually according to color and use. When the water was hot enough and poured into the Maytag the laundry process began. Sheets were always white back then, and the first to go into the steaming hot water. After they had agitated enough, grandma would take a wooden stick, pull up the end of the sheet and carefully feed it into the wringer. The sheets and all the laundry that followed would then fall into the first rinse tub with bluing, again through the wringer and the second rinse tub, through the wringer again and into the clothesbasket for hanging out on the clotheslines. Usually we would be finished by dinnertime and have a hearty gravy bread meal. The Maytag had to be emptied by means of a hose and bucket, we used that nice warm water for scrubbing the kitchen floor and the porches. We used the water from the rinse tubs to water the rose bushes and gladiolas in the garden, nothing was ever wasted. As soon as the clothes were dry they were brought to the kitchen table, sprinkled with water, rolled and put in the ironing basket for the next day. Grandma allowed us girls to practice learning to iron on handkerchiefs, pillowcases and flat things like that. We were so proud when we graduated to grandpas work shirts.

Is there anything better smelling in the entire world than bread baking in the oven on a Saturday morning? Grandma would tilt the tins and loaves of golden brown crust would fall onto the cloth. She'd quickly cover them and then we'd put freshly churned butter on thick slices, close our eyes agree that grandma made the best bread in Clearfield. It was a perfect prelude to the biggest night of the week.

With aching arms, we took turns churning butter and could hardly wait till the thick cream turned into chunks of yellow butter. Grandma would use her wooden paddle and pull away the butter, forming it into rolls. The left over milk was absolutely the best tasting buttermilk in the word. Little bits of butter floated around, just a dash of salt and pepper, yum!

Yes, the good ole days. They will never be forgotten. At 78, I constantly pass some of these memories on to my children and grandchildren. I cherish them and hopefully they will too.

No Sleeping In
By Carol Leathem of Brookville, Pennsylvania
Born 1951

Saturdays were not for sleeping in til eleven or twelve o'clock. You were up before 8:00 a.m. and then before any playing, there was work to do. My three brothers did garden and yard work. My dad always had a beautiful garden, 50 feet long and about 25 feet wide. The boys had to use a hoe to do between the rows and then pulled weeds in between the plants. The yard was mowed and the trimming (weed eating) was not done by a machine. We used hand clippers and usually had blisters when finished.

My sister and I had the laundry and housework. Washing—strip beds (five),

Carol's dad in the garden

gather up everyone's clothes, and take to the basement. We used a wringer washer, which you changed the washer water at least three times, rinse water twice. To dry the clothes, you carried the baskets outside and hung them up. Later in the day, you ironed. My dad had to have his handkerchiefs ironed and no wrinkles. Cleaning: wiping down cupboards, counters, refrigerator, stove, etc. The house got dusted and swept. Scrubbing floors was done on your knees because the corners got cleaned that way. You moved couches and beds so to get the dust bunnies.

If during the week my dad found a dirty cup or plate, someone got to wash a whole bunch of plates. My dad despised two things at the kitchen table—a dirty dish or a hair in his food.

We had a good life, but we learned life wasn't for goofing off all the time.

My First Kiss
By Kathleen A. Coy of Bradford, Pennsylvania
Born 1944

LeRoy was my brother's best friend. I had seen him before, but I really didn't give him much thought until that day. It was my 13th birthday. I was in the kitchen getting some cups when LeRoy came in and said. "Happy Birthday." Before I could say anything, he took me into his arms and gave me the sweetest kiss. It's been 55 year and I still remember my first kiss.

The Bully Bull
By Nellie Harlan of Cogan Station, Pennsylvania
Born 1920

This is a true story. It happened when I was six or seven years old. I am now 91 years old, but I still remember this scary time.

We had to walk about a mile to school. It was a one-room schoolhouse with grade first through eighth. No snow days then! We buckled our four-button boots and headed out—rain, snow, or sleet!

One spring day as we were walking home from school we noticed our neighbor's bull was out. All at once, it started pawing the ground and snorting! When we saw that, we started running. I made it to the porch of the neighbor's house, but my brothers and sisters were behind me. The bull was coming fast! My, there was no place for them to go but up a haystack close to the barn. That bull snorted and hay flew—in every direction!

The farmer's son came out of the house and grabbed a pitchfork and finally got the bull back in the barn.

It wasn't long before that farmer sold the bull!

Thank You Dorothy
By Mary E. Nelson of St. Marys,
Pennsylvania
Born 1920

My mother and father separated when I was about nine years old and my father got custody of the children. We lived in the country in an old house. No screens and drafty. Heated by a coal stove. My father worked in a coal mine.

After my mother left, we had to fend for ourselves. My older sister had to quit school to take care of the younger children. The youngest was about 18 months old. One about three, four, six, seven, and nine. Names were Dorothy, Elsie, Mary, Francis, Margaret, Edward, and Betty.

Dorothy had to bake bread every day. She washed clothes on a scrub board after carrying the water from a spring and heating it in a boiler on the stove. Ironed with a flat iron, heated on the kitchen stove.

The neighbor kids waited at our house for the school bus, which was a horse-drawn wagon.

We had an outhouse with two holes and an opening on the outside with a trough with a handle on it, which my father used to pull it out to empty it in the field and then put it back in again. It used to get rats in it. Our toilet paper was catalogues and magazines, which came in handy to read while sitting there.

On payday, Pop would get an order from the grocery store, which had to last until the next payday. We looked forward to a bag of candy that sometimes was in it. We got mostly staples such as 25 pounds of flour, sugar, macaroni, spaghetti, peanut butter for our lunch sandwiches, also potted meat, a slab of bacon, salt pork, tomato paste, canned milk, and oleo, which we had to color to look like butter.

Our clothes were mostly hand-me-downs. Dorothy was good at sewing with the treadle sewing machine. She even made a snowsuit for the youngest girl from an old coat.

Dorothy was bright in school and it hurt her to have to quit but she did get her GED in later life. I really appreciated all she did for us.

I used to play in the water of a beaver dam with some friends and learned to swim a little there. It's a wonder that we didn't drown with no supervision.

There are only two of us left from a family of ten, the youngest and me. I am 91 years old and not in the best of health.

Sledding Scofield
By Joseph Shaw of Curwensville,
Pennsylvania
Born 1930

One of my favorite memories is sled riding/bobsledding on Scofield Street in Curwensville, Pennsylvania in the late 1930s and early 1940s. We would start at the top of Scofield Extension. We had to take turns as "watchman" at the intersection of Scofield Street and Susquehanna Avenue. If the watchman gave us the all clear we flew across Susquehanna Avenue (as most often happened), sparks flying off the sled runners, and coasted down Scofield to near the old covered bridge across Anderson Creek (between today's Lezzer Lumber and the VFW).

If the watchman waved us off and yelled, "Gas buggy," we all dragged our feet to get stopped. That didn't happen very often. There were very few cars 70 years ago. If the roads were good for sled riding the cars wore tire chains as there was very little ashing the roads then. What little traffic there was on Scofield Street was about 3:30 p.m. when the tannery workday ended.

If the roads were slick, negotiating the first turn at the bottom of Scofield Extension was a real challenge. We were really flying. More than one of the neighbors' shrubs became a victim of a bobsled crash. But somehow, we survived the "Good Ole Days."

Ethics, Today and Yesterday
By Robert M. Rinn of Munsy, Pennsylvania
Born 1924

As more fishing traffic appears, on fewer streams, the problem of manners becomes a matter often discussed when anglers review their experiences. We seem to feel that streamside encounters are becoming worse with each passing season.

Visions of fishing 80 years ago should show gentlemen with attitudes reflecting pleasure in giving fellow fishermen a pleasant experience—NOT SO when some of the poaching secrets of that period are reviewed. Sometimes the trout population in the smaller brooks would be all but eliminated by an avid poacher. We no longer encounter the use of "links," using the vertical members of a trotline as single lines tied to roots and branches over trout pools. Baited hooks were attached in the late hours of the day, sometimes involving a mile of stream. The catch was harvested next morning.

Another successful endeavor was termed "The Lithuanian Flyrod," a nine-foot rod strung with two fine wires attached to a blasting cap dropping a distance from the tip. The opposite wire ends are touched to a battery, under the poacher's belt, after the blasting cap is drifted into trout cover.

And "tickling," a favorite of many poachers in years past, is probably used today. A hand reaching down under a rock may yield a fish or a water snake.

We have encountered all of these illegal ideas: Clorox, carbide in mason jars, jigging, nets, carbide spotlights, chumming, and wire lassoes. There are amazing ways of violating the code of good sportsmanship. There were many individuals guilty of destroying the other fellow's fishing 80 years ago. Today we find less evidence of these schemes along our favorite streams.

Mother Drove the School Bus
By Marian Slawson Feness of Depew, New York
Born 1924

In 1929, I was five years old. My name is Marian Feness, my maiden name was Slawson, my parents were Harold and

A friend, Pete with Mom's bus

Beatrice Slawson. We lived on the Gold Road about five miles from Genesee, Pennsylvania. My father was a tenant farmer and worked for his father, Lewis Slawson. My mother decided she'd like to bid for the job of driving the school bus. The town was taking bids for the job and my mother won the bid, so she bought a 1929 Chevy truck secondhand, and had a wooden bus built on the back of the truck. It seated about ten students. They were all children of farmers who also lived in the same area we did. That bus lasted about five or six years and, when the bids came up again, my mother bought a larger, big, orange bus. That one seated about 20 or 30 students, and since that was the only bus at that time she had two routes—one on the Gold Road to Rag Hill Corner and the other one was to Andrew

Marian Slawson age 18

230

Settlement to the McGinnis Farm and Cabot Town. She drove a bus for 26 years and retired. She had at least two other buses in those 26 years and we moved downtown to Genesee, Pennsylvania, where my sister Virginia and I finished school. There was one other bus at the time and the driver was Halsey Graham of Ellisburg, Pennsylvania and he had a route to Ellisburg, Pennsylvania.

When I reached high school there was a basketball team and we would go to other towns close by like Caudersport Pennsylvania, Galeton Pennsylvania, and even Wellsville New York, and Allentown Pennsylvania. My mother was hired to transport the boys' team, teachers, and cheerleaders; we were four girls and one boy. These students were Leitha Mae Jackson, Anne Huges, Claribel Hunt, Tom Button, and me, Marian Slawson. All of us girls made our cheerleader outfits. They were red corduroy full skirts and Eisenhour jackets lined in black satin. We really looked great. This lasted til 1940 and my mother continued to drive the bus til 1952 and retired and moved to Buffalo, New York, to be with my sister and me. Both my sister and my mother are deceased, however I still live in the Buffalo area of Depew, New York, and will be 88 years old this year in April 2012.

Marian Slawson Feness

Sears Roebuck or Corncobs
By Dick Sheltis of Montoursville,
Pennsylvania
Born 1926

I was born October 30, 1926 in a small, soft coal mining town names Rossiter in Western Pennsylvania, Indiana County. We lived in a company house with four rooms and bath. Mother had three boys; they were all born at home. My aunt was the midwife. We bought everything at the company store. Dad bought a 1927 Whippet car, food, and furniture from the company store. They took from my Dad's paycheck every payday for rent and the bill from the company store. In 1938, we moved to a little town called Amity. It was not a company home but we still bought out of the company store.

The house had five rooms downstairs and two bedrooms upstairs, no electric, no inside plumbing, and no water on the property. We had a coal and wood stove, an outhouse, coal shed, and wood shed. The outhouse was better known as the "shithouse." In the summer when it got too hot, the bees got in the outhouse. In the winter it was so cold we didn't sit in there too long. We used Sears Roebuck catalogues for toilet paper. The farmers used dry corncobs as toilet paper. We had to carry drinking water and cooking water cooking food and for washing water. We used the leftover water to scrub the shithouse and porch every week.

We had five chickens for our eggs and once in a while, we had chicken for Sunday dinner. We had a male and female rabbit for baby rabbits. We would breed the young rabbits and then eat rabbit for Sunday dinner. I went to school at six years old. I got punished at school and then when I got home, I got punished again. We had a chamber pot. We called it a piss pot in the hallway that we used at night. We emptied it every morning and then rinsed it out. Dad would cut three heads of hair; we could not afford 15 cents for each haircut. We called them piss pot haircut. There was no shape to them and they were cut all round. Took a bath once a week in a small tub on the floor in front of the stove with the oven door open to keep warm. On Saturday night, we had to carry wood and coal for the two stoves, one in the kitchen stove for heat and the other for cooking, washday, baking bread, etc. We did not have a refrigerator or icebox. I

231

went to the Korean War in 1950-1952. At 15, I worked on a farm from 4:30 to 5:30 for 50 cents a day. I got my first job when I finished school for $20 a week. I had to drive four miles each way.

Summer with Grandma on the Farm
By Judy Walker Bush of Austin,
Pennsylvania
Born 1947

My grandparents, Harry and Gladys Brooks, lived on a small, family farm about one mile up the East Fork from Wharton, Pennsylvania. Grandma ran the farm because Grandpa worked for the B&O Railroad in DuBois. Every summer my brother and I couldn't wait for school to be out because then we went to help grandma on the farm. Every child should experience this. The fishing, the swimming in the creek not caring about how cold the water was, just head for the swimming hole. Cold, but refreshing.

Monday was always workday. Get out the wringer wash machine. No small children because Grandma was afraid of little fingers getting into the wringer. You start the day with feeding the chickens and always watching out for the rooster. While the chickens come out to eat you collect the eggs and, if there are any chickens still on the nest, be careful or you'll get pecked when you go to get the egg from under her and she'll make a fuss, then the rooster is back and both are coming for you. The rooster tries to spur you and the hen tries to peck. My brother was better than me with putting his foot up to protect himself from the rooster. I had a hard time standing on one foot. Eggs collected, chickens fed, now back to the house for breakfast—eggs, bacon, and toast covered with Grandma's jam. After this, the leftovers went to the pigs' slop barrel to feed the pigs. Now all leftovers and extra go in a barrel with water to ferment. What a stink. Dip the pail pour in the pig trough. Splash, splash. Now to the clothesline, grab your towel and off to the swimming hole. Back to the chickens, time to clean the coop. Get hayfork, remove hay and poop and put in wheelbarrow, take to garden. Dump! This is tilled in for fertilizer to grow vegetables. When finished lay down more hay on floor and in nest. Oh the dust and stink. Back for your towel and a trip to the creek. In for lunch,

NOT McDonalds but better. It was Grandma's homemade hamburger patties and fry them one by one. Lunch was a burger with canned vegetables or peaches. Now to the morning milking. We kids were not allowed near the stall when Grandma was milking. The one time we did was not good. The barn cats were always there for a squirt of milk. We tried to be helpful and were giving the cow some new hay. I backed up because you have to watch their whippy tails. I stepped on a cat and feet were flying, cats, cow, and Grandma off her three-legged stool. Kids banned from cow stall. Now pail of milk goes to house to be cooled. Cooling makes milk go down and cream to top. Now cream goes to churn. Now we take turns churning. Long time and them butter gets slapped into wooden bowl Slapped over and over. This takes water out of butter. Add salt to taste and then into mold. Remove from mold, wrap in wax paper. Now, the best part. Grandma made homemade bread. Fresh baked bread and butter, that makes all the churning worthwhile. But you work up a sweat so grab your towel and back to the creek. Now about snakes, every year one black and one yellow rattlesnake tried to make it across the farm. But you can smell them. They smell like musty cucumbers. No snake could make it past my brother. Get the shovel and we are all safe. "Hello, Mom. What do you mean school is starting in a week? We have blackberries to pick and a garden to harvest." Grandma canned everything but her favorite was peaches. Did you ever eat warm tomatoes fresh from the garden or berries from the bush? We may not have learned from a book in the summertime but we had more valuable lessons.

Dill Hill Memories
By Christine Wolfe of Johnsonburg,
Pennsylvania
Born 1924

My oldest memory is of a one-room schoolhouse built on Dill Hill, Ridgway Township in Elk County, Johnsonburg, Pennsylvania 15845. My older siblings went to this school. It's been long gone. It was located across the road from the Herman Tillack Farm. That was a little farther back from my family homestead, which was right at the top of Dill Hill.

When I was close to six years old, a green

The dairy's milk cap

Then in July 1942 when the terrible cloud burst flood happened, I remember my mother and I walking down Dill Hill a ways to witness the horrible sight of seeing the bottom of the hill, "the Flats" or Grant Street, all rushing water with trees, a house roof and other articles being swept away. My husband's family lived on Clarion Avenue and lost property because of the water. He also lost an uncle, the only death as a result of the flood.

I also remember how much we kids looked forward to threshing time. Only one farmer could afford a threshing machine. So, when others had grain, like oats, to harvest, that farmer would bring the machine to the farm where the oats were ready. Then, our family, when our turn came, worked hard to provide lots of good food for all the workers. All of our playmates came too. It was a grand, enjoyable holiday for us youngsters.

In those days there was also an "icehouse" and an iceman to deliver blocks of ice to the customers.

Back then, we delivered our milk in quart, pint, and half-pint glass bottles. It was done by horse and buggy until my brother became the age of 16 and had a pick-up truck to do the delivering. I still have a bottle cap with our dairy name on it.

One time, when I was riding one of the horses bareback "down to water" at the farm pond, some neighbor boys nearby shouted, "Sic'em Pal," and the dog chased and bit the

truck with black curtains from the roof served as our school bus. It took us to the A&P Store in town, where we were allowed to wait until the school bus from Daguscahonda arrived. Daguscahonda was below the town of Ridgway. That better bus took us to Rolfe School because that school was in Ridgway Township too.

Our Dill Hill was a dirt road until many years later. In those days, we just called it Dill Hill. Later our address was Dill Hill Road. Later, my husband built a house on the lower part of the road called Blaine Avenue because it was in the borough of Johnsonburg.

The borough of Johnsonburg also had a school building on the avenues. That is no longer there either.

When our dairy business became too large and we had too many cows, my father purchased the Roy Straessely farm located at the very end of Dill Hill. This provided more level acreage to plant hay to feed the cattle. The skyline over Dill Hill is so beautiful and when riding from there on the hay wagon around sunset, we enjoyed the beauty of the changing colors in the sky.

When my brother first flew the airplane he built, he had to take it from our homestead farm to the level fields of the "Straessely Farm" in order to have the level space to take off from. That was November 1941, then Pearl Harbor happened and he went to the Air Force. He built a "lean to" behind the barn on the homestead to shelter his plane.

Edward Frank Amacher in 1941

233

The plane built by Edward Frank Amacher in 1941

hind legs of the horse. The horse jumped into a gallop, which knocked me off. I landed on my knees in sharp cinders. The doctor said it would be impossible to remove all the cinders, but he did a pretty good job.

Growing up, we youngsters used to get together evenings, build a fire to roast apples, corn, hot dogs or whatever we had at the time. Also, we walked to wherever we wanted to go. I remember walking to the other end of town to attend twice weekly confirmation classes for church membership.

Or, we walked, just to take walks. In strawberry season we walked down to the B&O Railroad tracks to pick strawberries because there were so many of them there.

Chop Sack Fashion
By Betty L. Hicks of Philipsburg,
Pennsylvania
Born 1937

Let me begin by saying I was number nine out of a family of eleven. There were six girls and five boys. We were all born at home. We lived on a farm. We produced almost all our food. We had cows, pigs, sheep, chickens, and horses. We didn't have indoor plumbing. We had an "outhouse." We got running water and a bathroom in the house when I was in seventh grade. At night, we used chambers, which had to be emptied and cleaned each morning. We walked over half a mile to go to school. Our schools consisted of two buildings. The first one was called the "little room" as it held grades one to four. The other one was called the "big room" and it held grades five through eight. Each school had one teacher who taught all subjects and she did all the grades. The first two rows were first grade, the second two rows second grade, and so on. We also had a cloakroom and furnace at the back of the

school, which the teacher was also responsible for. We also had an "outhouse." The teachers were allowed to spank if necessary although I don't remember anyone getting spanked. The teacher did take a ruler and would smack your finger if you didn't hold your pencil correctly.

On Friday afternoons, the "little room" went over to the "big room" and we learned songs and sang. It was fun! We learned poems and had to stand up in front of the class and recite them.

At our house, we had to take buckets and walk 500 feet to get to the spring for drinking and cooking water. We had to draw water from the cistern to wash dishes and do the laundry. Our mother used to heat the water on the coal stove then put it in the wringer washer and the two rinse tubs, then after the laundry was done, she had to empty the water.

On Saturday night, our mother heated water on the stove and filled the two rinse tubs with water. Since we didn't have a bathroom, our kitchen served as our bathroom. Our mother divided the kitchen with a large wooden clothes rack and draped a sheet over it. The girls bathed on one side and the boys on the other side. At least we were clean!

Since we had cows, we had our own milk. Our father milked the cows every morning and evening. After the milk cooled, the cream came to the top. Our mother would take off the heavy cream and after she had enough, she'd make the butter. We had a wooden churn. It took a long time to get the cream to turn into butter. From that process, she also got buttermilk and for the fresh butter she had a wooden mold, which measured a full pound of butter. She also made homemade bread, cinnamon rolls, and plain rolls.

We had what we called the "Bread Man." He delivered bread, cupcakes, and sweet rolls which we used for our lunches for school.

We lived over a mile from town so we didn't get there often except for church and school. Our father used to take us to the next nearest town, which was six miles away to get us our clothes and shoes.

Since we lived on a farm our dad had to buy feed for the livestock and the feed came in beautiful, printed chop sacks. After my dad emptied the chop, our mother would wash the chop sacks and make clothes out of them. When I was dating (now my husband of 52 years), one night I said to him, "I didn't know what to wear." And he said, "You'd look good in a chop sack." I just laughed, as that is what I had on. My mother had made me a top and skirt out of chop sacks!

My mother came over from Germany and she remembered the war so when World War II was going on in the 40s she made us pull down the blinds, turn off the lights, and made us be quiet. She was afraid we'd get bombed. We also had to kneel down and say the rosary.

We had electric lights but no phone until much later.

Memory Lane
By Norman L. Davis of Galeton, Pennsylvania
Born 1932

My growing up years were mostly in Hector Township, Potter County. They all started in what had been a one-room schoolhouse, situated along a dusty, country road. Wood stoves were used for heat and cooking. When I could walk well, sometimes I would help carry in some wood.

Kerosene lamps provided lighting, chamber pots and the outhouse served our needs, and washings were done by hand.

I enjoyed riding on the wooden wheelbarrow with the big iron wheel, which my father had made. He sometimes took me out the corduroy road, which bisected the large swamp behind the house. This road led to his parents' and grandparents' homesteads. They were subsistence farmers, growing most everything they needed. Great- granddad had his own blacksmith shop where many items were made and repaired.

These were the Depression years and most people used horse and buggies or wagons for transportation. Many folks just walked to where they needed to go, even the nine or so miles to town. They often carried butter or eggs to barter for things like salt and sugar. It also was a transition time when automobiles, trucks, and tractors were just coming into use. I remember watching, in awe, as a Farmall tractor came chugging down our road, punching holes in the sunbaked earth. Model A's and Chevrolets would occasionally fly by the house, sending a cloud of dust across the yard and sifting into the house. There was the big milk truck with the wooden stake body that made its rounds picking up milk. At one

Norman L. Davis in 1935

time, my grandfather had a Model T Ford and I was given a ride in that and I thought that was exciting.

Our water supply was a spring-fed, shallow well back from the edge of the swamp. Across it lay a plank. One day I went there with my mother to get a pail of water. I liked to look for frogs that lived around the swamp so I went out on the plank. As I leaned over to look more closely at one I saw, I lost my balance and fell in. Quickly my mother fished me out, coughing and choking. For a long time afterwards, I avoided water of any depth. But I still looked for frogs.

Tadpoles were intriguing, especially when they started to get legs. Mother sometimes caught some in a glass jar for me to look at and then took them back and let them go.

The spring before I turned five we moved up a hollow to the homestead of mother's grandparents, who were no longer alive. Now we had a two-story house with an ell to live in. Later on, I had a bedroom that faced west. It had a window that opened sideways on heavy, leather hinges and fastened shut with a wooden "button". I enjoyed looking out of it at sunsets or to listen to toads trilling on a late spring evening as they sat in the overflow of the spring where we got our water. The spring was in the side of the hill and the water flowed through an iron pipe to where we could catch it in a pail. From there it flowed down a wooden trough to an old, moss-covered, hollowed out log, which was the watering trough for the livestock.

Sometimes on winter nights when the wind was bringing a storm from the west, I could hear the mournful wail of a locomotive whistle.

When it was time to start school, I was taken to the doctor for my smallpox vaccination. That was no fun, but it was soon over. I was too small yet to walk to school, which was nearly a mile away, so we had to spend winters closer for several years. When I became older, I walked down our road then cut across a field and followed a path through a brush lot, across the creek to school. I enjoyed seeing the different birds and animals each day to and from school.

Although we didn't farm the land, it was often leased out to other farmers. However, I had chores to do. Summers there was working in the garden and helping pick berries. As we burned wood there was wood to cut and stack so as to be somewhat dry for winter use. In the meantime, I had to get wood enough from our wood lot and cut kindling to start fires in the kitchen stove. Usually, dead limbs were easy to get for what we needed for summer fires. We had chickens so I had to feed them and gather eggs. Sometimes I'd find a hen in a nest box that wanted to "set" and she would peck me as I tried to gather the eggs beneath her. We had some nice roosters over the years. Dad had a nice, big Buff Orpington for several years. Then there was the mean rooster that loved to chase me and flog me with his wings. He ended up on the table and mother let me eat his heart. Sweet revenge!

Washdays were busy and there were no washers and dryers. I had to carry many pails of water to fill the big copper boiler and the two big tubs. When it was time to wring the clothes, I turned the crank on the wringer and after a while even both arms were lame. I wonder how my poor mother did it all herself before I became big enough to help.

When grass needed to be cut, it was done with a scythe. Under dad's watchful eye, I learned to make a clean, close cut. That became yet another job for a few years.

There was no ice delivery so no need for an icebox. Off the kitchen was the pantry where foodstuffs were stored. It was relatively cool on the hottest summer days. The one window was covered with an ivy vine almost completely and helped keep the room cool. Shelves and cupboards held the necessary cooking and baking utensils as well as providing storage space for other things.

Back then, we had wind-up phonographs, powered by a powerful spring and sound came out of a horn, either concealed or on the side. We had two, both made by Edison. One was tall and in a cabinet and played large, thick Edison records. The other one was a small, portable Amberola that played the cylindrical records.

Dad sometimes played his grandmother's old, pump organ. I liked to pretend to play it and could sometimes make a tune come out of it.

We had a battery-operated radio for several years. Dad put up a long, outdoor antenna so we could get better reception and in the winter, we could listen to country music from Wheeling, West Virginia. We could get Lowell Thomas and Gabriel Heater for news as well as other programs. I liked the Lone

Red-tailed Hawk

Ranger among others.

One year I raised a red-tailed hawk and released it. It sure ate a lot! Two weeks later, I found it perched on the back of an old buggy on the barn floor. It whistled at me as I approached so I dared pick it up and it didn't resist me. I carried it out to show mother before I released it once again. It had been successful at catching food recently as there was a splash of blood on the feathers of one

236

leg. For a few years, there was a redtail that seemed more tame than normal that flew over the place from time to time. I often wondered if it was "my" hawk.

By the time I was twelve, a .22 rifle was given to me to keep the rabbits and woodchucks out of our garden. I also trapped woodchucks for the same purpose. Dad taught me to kill cleanly and quickly as animals have feelings too. Traps were checked morning and night.

I grew up with firearms that were always loaded. If they were not, they were useless if needed in a hurry. Responsibility was instilled in me early. That included using matches, never as playthings, but only when a useful fire was needed. How times have changed.

For a while, I worked off and on doing farm work. I started with horses, learning to harness and hitch and ended up with tractors. I pitched and loaded hay by hand and ended with bales. It would seem that my life transitioned from the old ways to the ultra-modern.

The Wood Yard
By Barbara Long Glover of Pittsburgh, Pennsylvania
Born 1944

During the 1950s, at the age of seven or eight, my family lived in Johnsonburg, Pennsylvania, "The Paper Mill Town." On summer nights the older boys would play kick the can and other street games while sounds of the drum corps playing, "Cherry Pink and Apple Blossom White" filled the warm air.

I was youngest in a small group of West End children who cooled off at the Wood Yard swimming hole. A stream was diked and a diving board affixed to the dirt hillside. We entered via the opposite hill where our private playground consisted of the cool passageways between rows of stacked wood. The split wood was piled high and neat with snow remaining often into early summer. We would climb the piles; look through the openings created by the woven wood to spot friends or just to hide something. Splinters were a pain that we had to hide; they were a give-away of our daring play. Who needed swings or fancy equipment, if we got bored the boxcars offered another play area before our swim.

I was the only one who couldn't swim, but that didn't stop me from jumping off the diving board. Garnet Jones had lots of patience and she could tread water, also she was always there to catch me when I came up. Once she had a secure hold on me she would guide me to where I could stand in shallow water. I can still remember the thrill of it, until the day I jumped without calling out to her first. She didn't see me while she and the others swam upstream unaware I was there. They say when a person is drowning they come up three times. I experienced more times than that…enough times for Leslie Granlund who was sunning himself on the dike to save me. I'm here to tell this story because of his speed and actions to rescue me. Leslie's arms were bruised from my grip, but he was strong and grew up to be a State Policeman. I will always remember him with the kindest thoughts, and best wishes. Thank you, Leslie.

Memories of Proctor
By Genevieve Snell of Horseheads, New York
Born 1935

Hello, my name is Genevieve Snell. I was born and raised in Proctor, Pennsylvania in 1935. My dad raised six daughters because our mother was in a home; she was mentally sick. He was a good dad. We had an organ that he would play and we girls would sing country music songs. My dad would walk to work; he worked at a sawmill. We girls would walk to the country store to get groceries and the owner of the store would take us back home then help us unload the groceries.

For recreation, we would jump rope, playhouse, play tag, hopscotch, and play cards with neighbors. When they had movies at the community hall, we would walk quite a way to see the movie. It would cost us ten or fifteen cents to see it. When I was thirteen or fourteen, they would have square dances on Saturday nights that we would go to. I don't remember how much it cost to get in the dance. That's where we learned to square dance. I will be seventy-seven in April and I am still square dancing.

I can remember my Aunt and Uncle had a cow; it got loose one time, we had clothes hanging on the line and the cow would pull our clothes off the line and chew them.

We had a battery operated radio. My dad would listen to the Lone Ranger and on Saturday nights, we would listen to country music programs. In those days, we didn't have a phone. No running water, we had to pump our water. We had kerosene lamps and a wind-up record player that played records. We would heat a tub of water on the stove and take turns taking a bath. We walked quite a distance to go swimming. By the time we walked back home, we would be hot all over again. We had a dog and a cat or two. We had a wringer washer. It was run by gasoline motor. I remember half the time it wouldn't run and it would make us mad. We girls would get in fights, not real bad. I remember we had an ice box and the guy we bought ice from was Loren Emick. It was fifty cents for a block.

Our cousin Pearl lived near us and we played together along with a couple friends that lived up the road from us. To this day I always like going back to Proctor where I lived growing up. Two of my sisters still live in Proctor. We always get together for a reunion. Our oldest sister passed away when she was thirty-two. Five of us are still alive.

We had an outhouse. At night time when we had to go to it, my dad would light a lantern for us girls. We usually didn't go out alone; two of us would go together. Those were good old days.

My Memories of the Rural Two-Room School
By Darell D. Harris of Oswayo, Pennsylvania
Born 1928

All students of the school walked to and from school, some coming from their homes up to two miles away. We all carried our lunches. The school bell rang at 9 am to commence our day and we were dismissed at 4 pm. Recesses mid-morning and mid-afternoon, also lunch hour from noon until 1 pm were enjoyed by all. When it was raining, we were allowed to stay inside, but all were expected to play outside in dry weather.

There was no water to be had on school property; therefore, the teacher selected two boys to carry drinking water from a nearby home, using the pump on the porch of that home. If no one was at home at the time, water had to be carried from a spring that was further away. That water was poured into a large crock, which had a spigot and was caught in small paper cups. This crock held three to five gallons. One day, two of my friends went to the spring for water, where they spotted a ten or twelve inch trout. They worked hard to catch it, putting it into the pail. Secretly, they emptied the pail into the crock, causing some splashing noise. This, of course, attracted the attention of the teacher! This discovery led to such a scolding, as we had never heard. One of the boys told me, years later, that this scolding caused him so much nervousness that he quit school. He stayed home and worked on the family farm. In those days, the teacher "ran and owned" the schoolroom.

If you needed to go to the "outhouse", permission was granted if you held high one or two fingers. Two "outhouses" stood in the backyard of the school, one for boys and one for girls. One finger indicated a urinary need, and two fingers indicated a bowel need. I never understood why the teacher needed to know which the need was! The teacher simply nodded to you for permission.

In those fearful days, it was not uncommon to see a boy get his ear pulled, hair pulled, or a slap on the face for misbehaving. I do not recall that girls were punished in any way except a scolding. A most "vicious" punishment was given by a whipping with a ruler.

On the last day of school, certificates were presented to those who had not been late, nor were absent the whole year. After five perfect years, a student received a large certificate. Several students were awarded certificates at that time, with many parents and grandparents in attendance for the honors.

We studied reading, writing, English, spelling, arithmetic, health, geography, and history. During your class time, you went to the front of the room to sit at the "recitation bench." Each class time was about fifteen minutes long.

The highlight of the school year was when the teacher announced that, "Tomorrow morning, all the 7th and 8th grade boys should come prepared to search for and cut the Christmas tree." The next morning all the 7th and 8th grade boys came dressed warmly, carrying a sack lunch and their father's axe, saw, or rope, all excited about the day off from school, when they could run and play in the woods all day! However, before we could leave, we had to attend chapel. Every morning, the teacher read from the Bible, and then we stood to pray the Lord's Prayer and to recite the Pledge of Allegiance to the Flag. Finally, we sang a few simple songs. All this lasted about fifteen minutes. Immediately, the boys charged out the door, being followed by the teacher's word, "Be sure to be back in time to help with the milking."

We would be gone all day roaming all over the hills looking for just the right tree to put into the little Methodist Church, where the school Christmas program was always held. Our delightful day was spent on roaming over any and all hills and valleys with no thought of trespassing. In those days, no one was posting their land and everyone traveled freely over the area. Often, we spotted a hemlock tree, climbed up into it a bit, and cut the top off. Then, as we looked it over, decided it wasn't good enough. Then we set out again, over the hill or up the valley, sometimes cutting as many as four trees before we found the right one. Usually, we pulled the tree to the top of the hill near the school, and then spent the rest of the day in the snow and great beauty of the outdoors. Somehow, we always managed to return to school in time for the four o'clock closing.

The days I spent in this little two-room school were some of the best and happier day of my eighty-four years. Before I close, I wish to note that the grades 1-8 had no water except what we carried to drink. Yet these children were very healthy, even though they went all day without washing their hands. Now, when you are away from home, it is commonly thought you must wash your hands after touching doorknobs or an elevator button. Yet schoolchildren today do not have as good attendance records as they did seventy-five to eighty years ago!

Growing Up in a Coal Mining Town
By Larry Bunk of Clearfield, Pennsylvania
Born 1946

I was born in 1946 in the small coal-mining town of Mine 40, Pennsylvania. We had a "company" store, a hotel, and the biggest boney pile around. The creek behind our house was polluted with sulfur from a mine a few miles upstream. We lived in a company house, two-story double house. They were all either green, gray, or yellow. We did most of our shopping at the "company" store. Most people used a coupon book instead of cash. Of course, when payday came the money was taken out of their checks. The boney pile was always on fire at the base. With hot coals glowing, it was really a beautiful site at night, if you didn't mind the smell of sulfur. There was a pond between the rock dump and the creek that froze over in the winter. We used to ice skate on it and used hot coals from the boney pile to keep us warm.

I can never remember being bored for lack of something to do. As kids, we played outdoors all the time. We built cabins in the woods; we built a dam for a swimming hole just upstream from where the sulfur was being dumped in. We no sooner got it done when the company men would destroy it. We played football and baseball in an open field that a farmer used to grow hay. He would chase us away and we would come right back. At night, we would gather around the street light and play games like kick the can, hide and seek, or just run around and play tag. Big thrill for a hot summer night was to sleep out on the porch.

I can't remember sitting home in the house because we were always outside doing something. We used to take a pencil and paper and write down the house numbers of every house on our street. It took us a while but someone figured out the system. If my house was 1256 the next one on this side of the street would be 1258. It took longer to figure out that the other side would be 1257 or 1259... I mean how smart do you think the kids were that went to Scalp Level Elementary School? Some of my best friends spent the best ten or twelve years of their life there. One kid quit in the sixth grade because they wouldn't let him drive his car to school.

My neighbor, "Old Lady Glad", had one of the first TV's in town. She claimed it was a color TV before they had color TVs. The trick was to put a piece of green, red, yellow, or blue plastic over the screen. My favorite was blue. I liked to watch the Lone Ranger, Roy Rogers, and the Cisco Kid. The only time cartoons were on was Saturday mornings. She was also on our "Party Line" for the phone. Long and a short, long and a short was our ring. Hers was two shorts and it never failed she would answer our ring and then listen in on our conversation. My friend Dodo once took a peach seed and planted it under her front porch in hopes it would grow up through her porch. He would craw under there every night the entire summer to water it. Nothing ever happen with it, guess he got some bad seeds. She had a clothesline attached to her house and a pole in the yard. Dodo liked to drive her crazy by banging her clotheslines. It seemed like the whole house would shake and the noise was something else.

We had a milkman who would come in the morning, walk right in the kitchen, and set the milk down on the table. Nobody ever locked their doors. Wouldn't matter if we did we all had the same skeleton key. We didn't have an icebox, didn't really need one. We had a big pot we kept in the back part of the cellar. With its dirt floor it keep things pretty cool. All we had to do was make a daily run to the 40 Store to buy what we needed for that day. In the front part of the cellar there was room enough for the toilet and of course for a bath tub that we would sit in the middle of the floor and fill up with a hose from the sink.

Lefty was the baker who came every day with his station wagon loaded with fresh bread and baked goods. My mom would buy us one donut apiece once a week for our treat.

The company sold the houses in the fifties. We bought our half of the house for $1200. I used to have to take $20 a month to the company office in Windber every month until it was paid off. That was when the fun began. Everyone wanted to fix up their new house. Thing was that owning only half a house made for some strange looking houses. Some painted their half one color while the neighbor painted their half another color, or one side would be painted and the other side shingled.

I got a job setting pins in a bowling alley when I was eleven years old. I worked there until I graduated from high school. My best night I would make $1.80. Of course I would have to take out for a candy bar or soda so I didn't actually have that much to take home.

Ever see a snuff can ring in the back pocket of jeans? Well everyone I knew chewed Copenhagen snuff, except me. I was considered a weirdo. I mean who didn't chew snuff? Teachers just about gave up catching kids in class. They would swallow it and denied chewing. One time a nine year old girl asked me for a chew. I told her that I didn't chew. She kicked me in the shin and called me something a nine year old should not know.

Now the mines are closed, the bowling alley closed because they couldn't find kids to work, Copenhagen is no longer king, and the Lone Ranger ran out of silver bullets.

Pardee Remembered
By Martha M. Coval Kashtock of
Philipsburg, Pennsylvania
Born 1932

I was born October 12, 1932, a Columbus Day baby, in a small village namely Pardee, Pennsylvania in Clearfield County four miles from Philipsburg, PA. People were mostly of the Slovakian decent. I learned to speak it very well being among all the neighbors. My parents were strict in raising five siblings. We had our daily chores to do every day, morning and night, before and after school. Church was another priority. We walked to and from church every Sunday; snow or rain, it didn't matter.

I went to a one-room schoolhouse; I walked the distance, not too far from home. I had a male teacher. He was very good with all of the children. I was very impressed with him. Bullying and fighting was not common then. I completed four grades at the Pardee School then it was closed. I then had to be transported by bus to another small town

Grandma Anna, Martha, Edward, and Mildred

240

Martha M. Kashtock in 1945

story that's not as exciting as growing up as a child. I reminisce a lot about the good old days and would like to turn back the hands of time. The memories never die, they remain with me forever.

Martha M. Kashtock in 1947

namely Munson, Pennsylvania. I completed the remaining grades. I had a female teacher, which was in a way of saying not too friendly although I got along with her the best I knew how. There was a small grocery store in Pardee, which served its purpose for whatever was needed. I spent a lot of pennies there before I would board the bus to school. It was located near the bus stop.

My parents were farmers. They planted a huge garden. We had two cows, ducks, rabbits, chickens, and oh yes, we had a dog too. Each morning, I delivered two quarts of milk to an elderly couple before school that resided not far from my home. They rewarded me with cookies or monetary gifts and it was well accepted. I was a great help to my mother during the planting season. Summer vacation was another chore, making hay when the sunshine was bright and hot. Monday was washday; we had no modern conveniences in those days to help with the rinsing and starching the clothes. Harvest time approached fast and that meant a lot of canning and picking vegetables from the garden. Yes, I learned a lot from my mother, which I am glad for. Yes, I had spare time to enjoy myself with my best friend, Betty. We played hopscotch, took walks, went to the movies twice a week, and had a wiener roast before school began again. I had my favorite radio shows, Lux Radio Theater every Monday, Wednesday was Arthur Godfrey, and oh yeah, Hit Parade on Saturday night. I then entered high school, but that is another

Living with My Aunt and Uncle
By Mary Smith of Bradford, Pennsylvania
Born 1917

On March 19, 2012, I will be 95 years young. I have lived a good life, considering at age seventeen while walking home from school one day, I began to hemorrhage and later was diagnosed with TB. I was a senior in high school at that time and there were no antibiotics. My mother died when I was two years old and I was told that she gave me the "bug." My dad was alone and thought it best that I stay with my aunt and uncle, my father's sister and her husband. They owned a grocery store in Lewis Run, Pennsylvania. They had the funds, so they put me in a private institution for a year. They took good care of me and I loved them very much.

Across the street lived my grandparents. They had a dairy farm. I remember a time when I had to go get the cows from the field and bring them to the barnyard; I was afraid because they were not in the barn yet and I had to walk across the field.

We didn't have our milk delivered, as our grandpa would do the delivering; we didn't go to the store and buy it. He would carry eight cartons in each hand and deliver them to the neighbors.

My father was a conductor. He ran the street car, which ran from Bradford to Lewis

Run.

I remember one day my grandmother was down at the well getting water when out of the woods came an Indian. He asked her for a drink of water. So she gave him a drink from a tin cup.

I'm sure some of you have heard of the hobos or bums. They would ride the trains, hop off, knock on your front door, and ask you for something to eat and drink. If you were to give them something, they would somehow mark the house or property as friendly, or not friendly if you didn't so the next group of hobos would know where to stop on their way through.

Back in the good ol' days, I use to listen to Amos and Andy and also Jack Armstrong, the All-American Boy on the radio. An actual radio, not an ipod, walkman, or digital device with ear buds. My grandmother and I would listen to Gabriel Heather; he was the evening news man and let's not forget the Lone Ranger.

When the TV came into existence, it was black and white. Not like today, the screen was small, but we loved to watch the Little Rascals, Howdy Doody, Kooka Fran and Ollie, the Ed Sullivan Show, and let's not forget the test pattern and static. We only got two channels, how exciting was that was.

The telephone, now that's a different story. Not like today's cordless, cell, and smart phones. No sir-ree, we had a five family party line. There was this one busy body that always had to listen to everyone's conversations, and if you wanted to make a call, you got the operator. She would ask, "Number please?"

No computers, no CD players, no records or record players were around yet. We had a wind-up player. There was one song I never wanted my aunt to play; it was "When you are Gone I Won't Forget You." It made me sad because I had lost my mom and I did not want to lose my aunt and uncle.

I had to walk three miles to school and back, no buses. Although, sometimes in bad weather my uncle would take me to school in his delivery truck. School was sure different then. I asked my teacher one day if I could change my seat. She said, "No", but I did it anyways. When you were bad in school, you used to get paddled. That made you think twice about being bad again because when your folks found out, you would get another spanking when you got home. Today

there is no respect for teachers or bus drivers because children now know that they are NOT ALLOWED to correct them. NO RESPECT.

I used to have a lot of fun swimming in the creek in Lewis Run and Browntown. We went on a lot of picnics, played baseball, croquet, hide and seek, and roller skating. We use to go to the fair and amusement park.

People had to work hard back in the day. Until the refrigerator came out, we used an icebox. We had a wringer washer with a wash tub and good ol' solar dryer. I am sure you have still seen them, you know, a clothes line and clothes pins. We couldn't heat food in the microwave; we actually had to make food from scratch. We peeled potatoes, snap the peas, and cooked meat on the stove. After dinner when it was time to do dishes, you actually had to wash them by hand; no dishwashers, what slave work was that??

I played with lots of paper dolls and read a lot of books, but my favorite toy was the Bylo porcelain doll.

I worked for two doctors, Dr. Price and Dr. Ryan, who at the time was also Mayer of Bradford. While I was working there, I met my husband, Galen. He happened to be the bellhop. One day as I was leaving work, Galen asked me if I'd like to go swimming. I said no, but that I would go somewhere else. So we went to the movies, which cost twenty-five cents. Our courtship lasted about three weeks. We met in August of 1940 and got married August 22, 1940. Talk about a short courtship, or love at first sight??

After we got married, I had my own radio program, "What's Cooking." One of the commercials was about SK. Tates Furs and Fashionland.

We adopted a beautiful little girl, Gail Ann, then another beautiful little girl, Shelly. They have both brought us much joy.

I took piano lessons and one day my little cousin came to visit. She loved to bang on the piano. So one day I got her a beginner's book and I taught her how to play. She became the church organist until she retired.

Gail Ann was never interest in piano, but can she bake. She makes the best wedding cakes around.

Shelly learned to play and went to college. She majored in music and went on to become a music teacher.

My beloved Galen, an insurance salesman, passed away two years ago this May. We were married nearly seventy years.

To this day I do not take any prescriptions or medications, how cool is that? Why have I lived so long? Well let me tell you, I give all the praise and glory to my Father in Heaven and I believe everyone should know HIM.

We need God in our homes, back in schools, and certainly in our Government. Ahhh, the good ol' days! May God bless you all.

Growing Up in Rural Pennsylvania
By Armilda Miller of Brisbin, Pennsylvania
Born 1929

Many happy memories come to mind as I write. I was born on a farm in the Kishaquillas Valley; try spelling that when you are a little kid. I was third born of six kids. If we were poor, we didn't know it. We always had food and our clothes came from the Sears Roebuck catalog or mother made them. From a young age, I realized that I hated doing dishes and dusting. I would do anything, even hiding, to get out of these chores, instead I went to the barn and milked cows by hand, worked in the hayfield, and in the fall, I husked corn. At that time, there were neither corn pickers nor tractors. We walked through the cornrows and pitched the corn ears into a wagon drawn by horses. The horses were both gray named Fred and Tony. Tony had a brown face and Roman nose, that's what we called his "different" nose.

In my teens, I worked at a canning factory in the summer. Dad raised peas for the cannery and what a job that was. The peas were mowed with a hay mower, but they grew so close to the ground that we had to walk behind the mower with a rake so that they didn't choke up the mower.

We didn't have electricity or a bathroom. We went outside to the toilet. We always had running water, a spigot, in the kitchen. I had never been in a bathtub until one time I went to Aunt Maybelle's in Lewistown to stay the night and had my first bathtub experience. I didn't know how much water to put into the tub and I certainly was not going to ask Aunt Maybelle. Then I didn't know what to do when I got out of the tub, but somehow I got that accomplished.

Dad dealt in Shetland ponies so we always had ponies to ride. Ned was the first pony that we had and Ned sired most of the mares in the valley. We had a swimming hole so we did a lot of swimming. One time we had company who wanted to go swimming with us. Shinny, our company, wore a wig and we all knew it. We wondered what he would do when he got into the water. A bunch of farm kids gawked at him and what do you think he did? He only got into the water up to his knees. We also had an ice pond that was perfect for ice-skating and probably the best sled-riding hill in the valley.

We lived a mile from the main highway and the school bus stop. We got a lot of snow and dad had to take us to the bus stop in a bobsled pulled by Fred and Tony. Our neighbors lived further back than we did so they also rode in the bobsled. One time on the way to the bus, our neighbor, Frances, was bundled up for the cold weather. With that entire bundle she couldn't move and she rolled off of the bobsled then she had to be lifted back on. When it wasn't snowing, we all walked to the bus stop. We had to walk past a thicket and there was a bush that we passed. The bush had tempting berries on it, but we were afraid to eat them. We asked Frances to eat some. We watched her for a couple of days and when she didn't die, we ate some too.

Dad butchered hogs on the Tuesday before Thanksgiving every year. I remember cutting lard on a make shift table. This was the excess fat cut from the big pieces of meat. The lard was cooked in big black kettles over an open fire. When it was cooked it was rendered in a lard press. This lard is what mother cooked with. The remains of the rendered lard were cracklings, which we ate for a snack. The black kettles were also used to make PonHos, scrapple. We cut up off fallings that were left after the big pieces were trimmed. These parts were ham, shoulders, ribs, bacon, backbone, tenderloin, heart, tongue, stomach, and sometimes the brains were preserved by sugar cure and smoking, canning, frying, boiling, or pickling.

Off fallings from leaner pieces were made into sausage. Mother made the sausage casings from the hog's intestines. I remember mother and Mrs. Houser scraping the intestines, turning them inside out and putting them in salt water. The meat was ground and put into a sausage stuffer. The casings were worked onto a metal tube on the side of the stuffer.

243

This operation took two people; one person turned the handle to force the meat into the metal tube. The second person worked the meat into the casings.

More off fallings including heart, tongue, and liver were put into the black kettles. This was boiled until the meat was cooked. This broth was thickened with corn meal to make the Pon Hos. This mixture would stick to the sides and the bottom of the kettles. The person stirring this had to be on his toes so that it didn't burn. This was not a job for the helpers who made too many trips to the milk house for "refreshment."

Our family celebrated Goose Day for as long as I remember. If my recollections of Goose Day are not exactly correct I'm sure my brother, Frank, will let me know.

Goose Day, St. Michaelmus Day, is celebrated every year on September 29th. This is the season when the crops were harvested and the time for the tenant farmers to "settle up" with their landlords. The farmers gave the landlord a goose as a token of good health. This tradition started in England. My family has always celebrated Goose Day with roast goose and all the trimmings including scalloped oysters. After mother died, my brother Frank and his wife Barbara hosted Goose Day for forty-three years until it go too large to have in their home. We still celebrate on September 29th, but we go to a restaurant and eat goose together.

At school, I was definitely the "farm kid." We got on the school bus in the morning, got back on after school and we seldom went back to town. There was no cafeteria at school so we carried our lunches. My lunch was usually country ham sandwiches on homemade bread and chocolate cake or cinnamon buns. I used to trade my sandwiches with Mae Goss. She had bologna sandwiches on store bought bread. What a treat!!!

I'm not sure of the date of this "event", but there was an outbreak of small pox in the valley. We were all quarantined from Mill Creek to Reedsville and couldn't leave. This area was policed to enforce this restriction. We had to be revaccinated before we could go back to school.

Most of the farmers in Big Valley, AKA Kishacoquillas Valley, were Amish and Mennonites. I can remember only one other farm family who were English like us who lived in the Valley at the time.

My Friend
By Clair E. Slawson of Clifton Forge, Virginia
Born 1941

He was a hulk of a man, burly, one would say, on the ugly side. Some were offended by the way he looked. These were the ones who did not take the time to know the real man inside.

He was handicapped, his mind was slow. There was a limit to what he was able to learn. He was bullied at school because he was different. Some of the students often pushed him down in the cold snow. However, Bud never whimpered, never even shed a tear, even though sadness was on his face. They laughed at him, mocked him, and called him names. He would get up from the ground, board the bus, and go on to school. You had to give him credit; he never showed any sign of giving up.

He stayed in Special Ed as long as he could at school until he got too old; no one even thought that he would have much in life. He fooled them all even got a good job. He faithfully worked on the Highway Crew in the blazing sun, again Bud didn't give up.

He found a wife; they had a child. He rented some places that were not so good, but finally he and Jean had their dream house. They were so proud and I was proud of them; when I came they always put the coffee pot on, even shared some sweets. Friendship and hospitality, it was shared so beautifully.

Bud earned the respect of his peers. They could see he was the man who never gave up. He even worked to a state retirement. He made his mark on the world.

Bud was always there for me. He listened to those accounts of my tough times because he was "just there" meant a whole lot to me. I can hear him say, "I don't know what to tell you Clair, but it will work out right in the end…" the amazing thing, it did.

Bud lived to fish and man he was good. He landed some trophy trout, had one big one mounted for his wall and that was only one of many.

He love to hunt as well; he was a better fisherman, but he loved the forest wild.

There is a great man missing from the mountain streams, Bud retired his pole; his weary legs just wouldn't make it out there anymore. His gun cabinet is empty, no guns there anymore. I am sure he has a lot of good memories. He loves the land and the land was good to him.

I write this special tribute to a man who showed me what it was to be a friend. He and his wife Jean, they were simple mountain people filled with kindness, gladness, and a special knack to make you feel good. They will forever live in the memories of my heart. Bud, thanks old buddy for just being you!

Old Timer's Stories

The "Old Timers" is an expression you hear less now; they were the seniors of another time. We, that were younger then, still remember their tales. Some tales were spun just for that punch line joke at the end. One might spend five minutes building up to a fanciful story just to lead you to that punch line at the end. This created a hilarious round of laughter. Some of these guys were good. You would hear this laughter a block away coming from the gas station, feed mill, or at a small café.

Some of the tales took serious notes. They spoke of the hardship of the Depression. They spoke of hard labor at tough low paying jobs. Yes, those old timers had bragging rights. Some of the fascinating stories were about Native Americans, always called then Indians then. Different stories were told. The Indians past through the Genesee Valley, then traveled to the Allegany and southward to meet up with more of their clans in the Alleganys.

Grandpa and grandma always showed hospitality, as well as other farm folk in the area. It was told the Indians stopped by at a farmer's place. The farmer had run out of salt, which was an important commodity in those days. An Indian said he could help. He left and later returned with a fair sized bag of dug up salt from the earth. It was clean and quite useable. No one knew where it was found, but a farmer in the area claims he filled in a salty area with stones. It was drawing a lot of deer, this endangered his crops. The old legend is still told of a location the Indians knew of, of a deposit of lead it could be taken right out of the ground it was said and others said it was a mine. There still is an area off the Ellisburg Road where a hollow begins and it is called Leadville. Is there a connection, we probably will never know. Off Kenny Road area, there is an area called the Ore Bed, could it be a connection too?

Grandpa said Genesee was a camping ground for the Indians. It was a resting area as they passed on going north or south along the Genesee River. There was a support to this claim. My buddies and I would dig worms for fishing by the old manure pile back by Grandpa's barn. We found an arrowhead there and pieces of flint. We found what looked like a scrapping tool. Our neighbor, Mr. Smith, told us he had found a number of flint pieces as he worked his garden. His land joined our property in Genesee on School Street. Grandpa said there was flint over by the state line where Cyder Creek joins the Genesee. My buddies and I searched extensively to find this cache… we never found it. This was an area that had a lot of flooding, so the evidence of lore maybe under the river Loam deeply hidden by time.

Another interesting story was told by the old timers. This was a grave that was found. This was said to have occurred off Dog Town Road near Ellisburg, Pennsylvania. It is told that a couple hunters grew tired and sat down for break and noticed something particular about where they were seated. It was a mound edged by hand laid stones; they immediately thought it to be a grave, so they agreed to come back for digging. They dug up the mound and found skeletal remains of a large man. They said the skull was huge and the frame appeared to be around seven feet tall. They then reburied the remains respectfully. They were mystified as to what kind of ancestry the person had. It was thought Indian, but Indians were not normally large in stature. Some thought it might been a Viking from another land. I tried to find this mound, but to no success.

So the stories still live on in the minds of these who heard them. These were Good stories told in the little villages of the North Pennsylvania Mountains, told by the Old Timers who had ripened their lives with the experiences of life itself. Thanks guys for the memories that you have made.

My Father's Stories
By Lorrie Crawford Hartman of Watsontown, Pennsylvania

My father's name is Harold R. Crawford. He was eighty years old when he passed away on March 5, 2011. These stories took place in Dewart and Watsontown in Northumberland

The Crawford Boys
Don, Jim, and Harold (Lorrie's father)

County in Pennsylvania. I see these stories as a way of honoring a great man's memory. These stories are told through his eyes as he grew into adulthood.

He writes… I remember the spring of 1936 when the roads were drifted shut; a gang of men with shovels opened the road. They did it in three steps. The people on the ground put the snow up to the people on the second step and they would then put it up to the people on the top who had to throw all the snow out of the way. It was around that time of the year when Jim, my younger brother, and I were sled riding on the hill across from the house. He went down to the bottom of the hill and got off his sled. I yelled down at him and told him to get out of the way. I started down and he got out of the way, but left his sled set. I went down and ran into the front of the sled. It put a big gash above my eye and put a dent in my skull. When you're only that old, you can't guide a sled too good. My dad took me to the doctor at Watsontown.

We had a battery powered radio and around 1936 on Saturday nights, my dad listened to the Grand Ole Opry. It was on until one o'clock in the morning. About this time, I wanted to stay up and listen to it with him. Jim and Don, my younger brothers, wouldn't go to bed unless I went along, so my dad would whisper to me, "You go along and lay down with them and when they go to sleep you come back down." A few times I didn't make it back down as I also went to sleep.

In 1944, dad got me, Jim, and Don a work permit for thirty days to go up to Henry Lark's and help dig potatoes. He had acres of them. Don carried water to the pickers. We got forty cents an hour. A lot of the pickers were students from Montgomery High School, they used to get to singing, "Roll me over in the clover, if there is no clover, the potato patch will do."

In the spring of 1946, we got a whole lot of snow. The road from Rt. 54 up to our place was drifted shut for six weeks. Dad left his car down at the end of the road and had to carry groceries for six weeks a mile up the road. One morning when we got down to Route 54 there were two Massey Harris tractors hooked together with a V plow on the front one. They started to open the road and that night they hadn't got a half a mile all day. The next night Bob Callenberger brought a big bulldozer and he went right through it.

In the fall of 1946, I was a sophomore in high school. I took the Industrial Course and took up electricity at Williamsport Technical Institute. We were up there for two weeks and the down at Watsontown for two weeks, they also started football back up at Watsontown that fall. I was on the first string. We won three games, tied one, and lost one. My youngest sister Janet was born on March 16th of that year. I was sixteen in January of 1947.

Harold Crawford

I got my learner's permit sometime after that. It was in the summer that Uncle Wash came down to take me for my driver's test. He had Bill Crawford's 1940 Plymouth car down and it had the gear shift on the steering column and I never had driven a car like that before that day. I drove it to Williamsport to the place where you took the test and didn't have any problems. When the cop went with me for the driver's part of the test, he told me to turn around in the middle of the street and you could only back up three times to get turned around. Well I did all right until I backed it up the third time. That time I put the car in high gear instead of low. I went to let the clutch out and give it some gas, but it didn't want to go. I finally stalled the car. The cop said, "If you put it in low, it may work." Like a jackass, I told him that this was the first day I ever drove a car with the gear shift on the steering wheel. He said, "Then what the hell are you doing up here today?"

Lorrie's grandfather, Gerald Ray Crawford

Audrae's Story
By Audrae Ruby of Williamsport,
Pennsylvania
Born 1932

Ours was a large family living on a large farm with hundreds of acres just a couple miles north of Galeton, Pennsylvania, where its name to claim was that it had the only theatre in the world where you went downstairs to get upstairs in the balcony.

Life on the Farm

How safe and happy we felt as children living in those beautiful rolling hills on a country farm with our parents, four girls and two boys. Unfortunately, for a farmer, the boys came along as bookends to the string of girls in the middle seemingly almost a curse to a farmer. It didn't make any difference in the long run, since we girls worked just as hard as the boys. One sister lived with my Aunt in another town, so we didn't see her often. My oldest sister was ill for many years and never actually lived with the family.

During the Depression and war era, things were hard for many families including ours; however, I don't remember anyone saying we were poor. My Mother worked at the Sylvania Plant in Galeton, a defense plant, which made radio tubes for the war. Everyone helped with the war effort: war stamps and savings bonds. We even saved tinfoil from our gum wrappers to make balls of it and picked milkweed pods that were used to make parachutes.

My Dad was very strict, what we later described as being an authoritative, British disciplinarian. Everyone worked. Having a handicap didn't exempt me from my share of the workload. I have to say that I believe that is why I am so strong today at seventy-eight years old. We milked cows, pitched insulate out of forty foot silos (we had to cut the corn stalks down with sickles to load onto the wagon, later ground and blown into the huge silos for silage to feed the cattle in winter), feed chickens, cleaned pens, pitched hay down an opening from the upper part of the barn to fodder the cows while they were being milked, and helped lime the barns from time to time.

In the summer, we planted a huge garden with everything you can imagine. We had to can and freeze as much stuff as possible to help support our family. It pains me today to recall planting a bushel of onion sets. Try that for fun!

We helped "hay it." This was always a challenge since that part of Pennsylvania had rattlesnakes. We would pile the hay in mounds, but sometimes we had to leave them out overnight if it got too late and it was time to go after the cows and do the milking. Cows were milked twice a day, once in the morning and once in the evening. The next day after the sun came up we went out with the tractor and wagon to pick up these piles of hay. At times rattlesnakes went under them. Someone had to stomp the hay as it was pitched onto the wagon. We had to be very careful not to throw hay onto the wagon until we were sure no snakes were in it. A few times I remember Dad shouting, "Get off the wagon. I saw a snake in the hay that I just pitched up there." You learned to move real fast.

Summers were when I had a cast on my leg and Dad let me drive the John Deere tractor. That was fun, especially since we had very little playtime growing up. Sometimes at night, we would play hide and seek or play with our paper dolls. We didn't own a TV for many years and the radio was mostly for adult listening in the evening. We did listen to a few programs with our parents. For other entertainment, we had card games, checkers, Monopoly, and other games. Cereal boxes had cutout houses to color and put together to make a village and we all loved the coloring books that you painted with water. It was sort of magical to see the color appear on the page.

In those days, communication was far different than today. We didn't have computers with e-mail and no iPods or cell phones. I remember our first telephone, a big square box on the wall. There were four or five people on the line. Our ring was one long and one short ring. Unlike today, this new modern convenience was not for us to talk on for hours with our friends. We could talk, but only for five minutes. I'd talk to my future husband about when he was coming to take me to the movies.

We were not allowed to go on a date alone. The boy who was to be my future husband was originally supposed to go out with my sister, Wanda, who was snowed in up in Buffalo, so Mom made me go out with him along with my sister, Kay, who was going to the movies with her boyfriend. This blind date turned into the marriage to my husband now for sixty-one years and still going! We were married on August 13, 1950 when I was seventeen.

Speaking of movies, it only cost thirty cents after 8:30 pm, the popcorn was free. We had to go right home after the movie even when we were sixteen years old! Sometimes Dad would forget to pick us up from school or the movies so we had to walk the two miles back home.

Our clothes were made by our Mother who was a seamstress by trade, before moving to the farm as a result of the Depression. Many of our dresses, skirts, and blouses were made from feedbag material, which in those days was very pretty. Mom was off to the Sylvania Plant early, so we had to get breakfast and help the younger kids get ready for school. The youngest and oldest were boys, but there was no respecter of persons when the division of work was divided up. With so few boys, it was inevitable that a few girls had to work at the barn and the others worked in the house. We learned to cook, sew, and clean early on in our lives. A little side note: it seems odd now, but we put corn meal on the rug to cut down on dust. We didn't have a sweeper.

I worked in the house and made pancakes *every morning*. I made them from scratch; the bowl was put in the refrigerator and I would save a little for the next morning. It made the most delicious pancakes. We always had bacon so put a liberal amount of hot bacon grease and sugar on our pancakes. We even used mustard for a tasty spread at times. Since we raised chickens, we had eggs at times, but with eight people to feed, there wasn't enough for everyone to have as many as they wanted.

We packed lunches of sandwiches and apples and then were off to catch the bus for school. I remember a few times when the lunches weren't made and Mom would send hot biscuits with butter and honey to school. This was always a treat.

School Days

We attended a two-room schoolhouse in West Pike, Pennsylvania, which was only a mile or two from our farm. The first floor was for first grade through fourth and the top floor was for fifth grade through eighth. When students finished these grades, they attended high school in downtown Galeton where classrooms and the ball field were spread all over the town. It was up one hill and down the other; it seems like nothing in Galeton was built on the level.

Our teachers were very strict. Each morning we were read from the Bible and stood while reciting the Pledge of Allegiance with our hands over our hearts and facing the American flag. We also said the Lord's Prayer. Each class was called up front to a long bench where we sat when it was our turn for the teacher to teach our lessons and give out homework.

There was a large coal stove, which heated both floors. There wasn't any plumbing in the building so we had to carry water from the milk house of a neighboring farm next to the school, which just happened to be my cousin's place.

All students had chores assigned which were rotated from time to time like getting the water and bringing coal and wood in from the shed in back of the school. We had to clap erasers out on the fire escape, which I hated. I was very afraid of heights since I was born with a clubfoot and had to wear special shoes with high tops and thick soles. That made me unsteady on uneven surfaces. We also washed the blackboards, dusted desks, and clean the floors. Can you imagine students being required to do that today?

There was no warm and decorative bathroom. Ours was an outhouse at the top of a fairly steep slope; a challenge when you had to make a trip up there in the winter, but severed double duty as a great place for winter sledding.

My first grade class had five students. We played baseball with one ball and one bat; we also played hide and go seek at recess too. I remember putting a small Christmas play and the props were bed sheets for curtains. We learned poems and recited them. Spelling bees were fun. All the students lined each side of the room and as they failed to spell a word correctly, they took their seats.

We went to and from school on a bus. One afternoon on the way home, a small gas truck hit the back of the bus and I flew out the backdoor onto the concrete pavement. I still remember lying on the road in a cloud of dust. I only had a bump on my head, no 911 or hospitals. I was taken by my parents to a local doctor in Galeton. It made the news and I still have a clipping of that story.

So many memories at a time when life seemed much simpler than today. One wonders if we have moved forward or backwards in our overall quality of life.

Grover, My Hometown
By Linda L. Earle Marriner of Arnot,
Pennsylvania
Born 1949

Grover, Pennsylvania, a small town located in the southwest corner of Bradford County, Pennsylvania; this is my hometown, surrounded on all sides by beautiful mountains

Linda L. Earle and Sam Williams in 1953

and many memories of growing up from birth until I graduated from high school in 1967, married and moved to Tioga County, Pennsylvania.

Grover is located three miles south of Canton Pennsylvania off Route 14 and sits in a valley with a creek running on both sides of town. Grover has one main road going through town with three side streets. I lived on Water Street. There were four houses on this street.

Not too far down the road on Rt. 14, the three counties of Bradford, Tioga, and Lycoming meet. It was always said a tall man could stand with one foot in Bradford County, the other foot in Tioga County and bend over and touch Lycoming County.

I came from a family of four. My father, Charles R. Earle worked at the Grover Farms Milk Plant. My mother, Rachel E. Dean Earle was a housewife until around 1965-1966 when she began working in Canton. The factory she worked at was named Glamorize and they made brassieres. She would bring home sample cups and my sister and I could wear them for hats because they were so big. My sister Barbara R. Earle Brokaw is six years younger than me. She grew up in Grover and still lives there.

My neighbors were all wonderful people. On the right side of our house lived the McCauley's. They had two sons, Janford and Lindy. Their father, Bill, worked at Swayzc Folding Box Company in Canton. I remember when he came home from work he had a very distinct smell from his workplace.

On the left side of our house lived the Alfred Rusk family. They had eight children. Bill was the oldest and I remember he delivered the newspaper on his bicycle. Pat was the next oldest, then JoAnn, Jim, Tom, Marilyn, Mary Jo, and Ted. Growing up so close, we played together and went to school together and they were like brothers and sisters. They lived in a five-room house with no inside plumbing for as long as I remember. They had a pitcher pump in the kitchen and would heat the water on the stove for washing dishes, doing the laundry, and bathing. Laundry was done in a wringer washer and was an all day affair. The outhouse was located in the back yard by the chicken coop. The chamber pots or thunder mugs, as we called them, were used at night and in the winter. It would be difficult to raise children these days with those living conditions, but those children all grew up happy and loved by two parents and are all now married with families of their own.

Grover has two churches located at the east end of town. There is a small creek running between them. On one side of the creek is the Church of Christ and the other side of the creek is the E.U.B., Evangelical United Brethren Church. I attended both on

Grover Farms Milk Plant
Richard Franklin (Boss), Floyd Vermilya,
and Charles Earle

and off going to Sunday school and church services.

At the west end of town was the Post Office. This building reminded me of a western movie prop. The mail mistress, named Ester Griswold, would walk to work every day. We not only would get our mail, but she sold ice cream cones, some dry goods, soda pop, and potato chips. There was a candy counter, bread and cupcake rack, all occasion cards, pens, pencils, notebooks, writing paper, and a small library in the corner. I remember the mail truck being an army green color and would bring the mail very early in the morning and again in the afternoon. When I was old enough I would mow the lawn for Ester and she would always give me a free soda pop and fifty cents for mowing. I also got a free sunburn. She was a very sweet lady and respected by all.

Across the creek beside the Post Office was Grover Farms Milk Plant. This was where my father worked along with other men from Grover. Early every morning the farmers would arrive with their trucks full of milk cans. They placed them on a conveyor as they traveled into the milk plant, where emptied, rinsed out, and returned on the other side of the conveyor. The sound of milk cans banging together was like a musical tune. How I missed that sound when I moved away.

My dad was our personal milkman. He carried a gallon milk pail to work and would bring home raw milk for my mother to pasteurize. After it had cooled in the refrigerator, she would put the milk into milk bottles. I very much disliked skimming off the cream particles from my milk glass. Dad also had a cream bucket and we had the best whipped cream ever made. It was scrumptious on our Sunday pies.

Alongside the milk plant was the railroad tracks. The railroad lights would come on if the train was coming to stop the cars from crossing the tracks and, of course, the train whistle would blow very loud. The tracks ran in front of my house so the neighbor kids and I would sit on my front porch and count the train cars. In the 1950s, there were only flat cars, box cars, and coal cars on the train. At one time passenger cars would stop daily and also the train delivered the mail. The train depot was still in town when I was very small, but was torn down and used to build a cabin.

My uncle told me during the Depression,

250

my grandfather, Walter Earle Sr., worked for Mr. Paul Griswold who owned a three story building beside the railroad tracks. This building at that time stood where the milk plant was built. The bottom floor was a general store. My grandfather made the sauerkraut in barrels and in the winter he would take a sleigh pulled by a team of horses up the mountain to Lake Nepahwin for ice. After filling the ice boxes in Grover, he traveled to Canton to sell more. The ice was stored in an ice house next to the depot. The walls where built three feet thick of sawdust. The ice would keep until the following winter freeze.

In the middle of town was our general store. It was owned by Gerald D. Avery. He sold just about everything. There were all kinds of groceries, clothes, jewelry, wallets, ice cream, and a candy counter filled with lots of goodies for a penny, nickel, or dime. Gerald sold tires, tire chains, car batteries, oil, and at one time tractors. There was a bubble gum machine on the counter. Behind the counter were cigarettes, cigars, and pipe tobacco. I remember calling the store to ask if they had Prince Albert in a can and Gerald would answer yes, so we told him to let him out. He also had a meat counter

Walter Earle, Jr. on bicycle and Charles Earle going back to work

with fresh meat and a greenhouse attached to the rear of the store. In the front of the store were the gas pumps and a big Texaco sign that lit up at night. Soda pop cost seven cents and when the bottle was empty we returned it for the two cent deposit. I remember a heating stove beside the counter where we would stand and get warm in the wintertime.

Gerald Avery was one of my most memorable people. As I got old enough to hang out at the store, about age twelve, Gerald and I would play checkers, tic tac toe, hangman, or just tell stories. He was always happy and laughing. He was my bus driver when the Grover school closed and

we had to go to Canton school. He always looked out for me. After I married and left home, the store was struck by lightning and burned to the ground in 1970. Gerald set up a temporary store until a new one was built out of cinderblocks. It just wasn't the same and now the store is no more.

Next to the store lived a very special gentleman in my life. His name was Samuel Williams. We called him Sam for short. Sam's house at one time was a meat market. He raised pigs and butchered them. His property line and ours touched. His house was so neat to me. He had no inside plumbing, so there was a pitcher pump in the kitchen with a dry sink and a mirror hanging on the wall so he could see to shave and comb his hair. On the wall was a cupboard with few dishes and the opposite wall had two windows facing the store. The kitchen table and two chairs were placed there. Behind Sam's chair was a pantry. I remember he kept milk and buttermilk in there. The best part of Sam's kitchen was the big ole cook stove with a wood box on one side and his rocking chair with his spittoon on the other. He made the best ever pancakes on that cook stove. Out the backdoor was another water pump and his woodshed. It was a short walk to the outhouse and the pig pens. His living room had a gas heater with another rocking chair and spittoon beside it. There was a day bed underneath a large window for napping and a television in the corner. By the front door was an old Victrola that played cylinders. We spent a lot of time listening to old music and he let me do the cranking, sometimes. I also enjoyed looking at his viewfinder with very old pictures. His bedroom had a double bed, one dresser, a straight back chair and a chamber pot with dark green pull down shades in the windows.

At the other end of town beside the Church

251

of Christ was our two story school house. On the bottom floor was first, second, and third grades and our teacher was Mrs. Brann. I remember falling asleep at my desk in third grade and one day at recess I was getting ready to go down the slide and my underwear got caught and almost ripped off of me. This was one of my most embarrassing moments. Upstairs was fourth, fifth, and sixth grades. Our teacher, Mrs. Lida S. Lund, was the best teacher I ever had. She was tall with red hair, caring, compassionate, yet stern. There were four children in my fourth grade class. I remember one time three were absent, so I was the only one in class and got all the attention that day. Our mornings in school started out with pledging allegiance to the flag, saying the Lord's Prayer, and taking turns reading scriptures from the Bible. When it came to my turn, I always chose Psalms 100 because it was short. Mrs. Lund would then walk up and down each aisle and inspect each child for clean fingernails, combed hair, and a clean handkerchief or tissues at the top corner of our desks. We carried our lunches either in a lunch box or paper bag. We had drinking cups hung on nails for water and a milk truck would deliver small glass jugs of milk for lunch. On Friday we could buy chocolate milk.

When driving through Grover now, it's not a very pleasant place to look at. The houses that are left are mostly run down and dumpy. The old milk plant is a disgrace to see. The oldest person living that I knew as a child is a sweet lady named Jessie Herman. She celebrated her 94th birthday February 11, 2012. She now lives in Canton. I am very glad to have grown up in Grover as a child and I will never forget the people I knew and the memories of my childhood in my hometown.

Diehard German
By James Schlimm of Yardley, Pennsylvania
Born 1929

I was born and raised in St. Marys, Pennsylvania, a small town in Elk County, located in north central Pennsylvania.

Sometimes it is hard to remember all the things you did growing up that now make you laugh. Times were really different raised with 11 other brothers and sisters; much of what we did or didn't do was always thrashed over, and will stay in our memory forever. Six boys

and six girls, one set of twin brothers and a set of sisters, born on my birthday, always provided instances and incidents that had me to wondering what life was all about.

Living with us was my grandfather, George Nissel. He was the custodian of the local cemetery and on many Saturdays, I would spend my school day off helping him do whatever had to be done. Mowing lots, cleaning areas that needed it, and when the situation called for it, I helped "dig" a grave for the recently departed.

My grandfather was a diehard German and there was only one-way to do things, his way! One of the things he used to measure when he thought the grave was deep enough was a shovel he had that he said was official depth size. I remember one occasion I said I didn't think the grave was deep enough. He replied that in all the years that he was a custodian he never remembered anyone getting up and walking away. For a young helper, I took it as the truth and kept my mouth shut until I told my mother and her reply was to just do what I was told.

Streak of Greased Lightning
By Candy Detwiler of Viola, Delaware
Born 1933

Ah, the days of no electronics. My ancestors liked to talk. My dad, uncles, and grandfather would gather around the pot-bellied stove in winter and swap yarns. Since I shadowed my dad, I was right there. They rolled their own cigarettes, took out the papers, the little cloth bags, and shook the tobacco from the bag to the paper, rolled it and licked the edge to seal it, and the room, tiny as it was, turned blue with smoke and stories started. Hard to tell what stories they told later, but the ones they told when I was there, after dark, were always ghost stories. I would sit there bug eyed and then my mother called from two houses up to come home. Can you imagine how many trees and bushes those ghosts had to hide behind before I got home? Don't think they would have seen anything but a streak of greased lightning as I passed.

For a while, I thought my name was, "go out and play". Seemed like as soon as my mother set eyes on me that was the first thing out of her mouth. Who could afford toys? You went out and improvised. Hopscotch was drawn with a stick and stones were markers. If it was kick hopscotch, you searched for a block of wood to kick. If you got hot, you went over to the outside hand pump and pumped water in the tin cup hanging on a nail, or cupped your hand over the end of the pump and slurped. Easier to watch the catfish swim in the half wooden tub of water underneath. Grandpap had caught his supper and left it there

Stomach Pump
By Pauline B. Bell of Ginter, Pennsylvania
Born 1925

I was born in 1925. My dad went for my mom's mom, but I came before they both got back. There were eight of us kids. We had no electricity and no indoor bathroom. We all used one chamber pot which mom emptied every morning and we had no toilet paper so we used the Sears and Roebucks catalog. We cut paper dolls out of the colored pages. We had to dress for bed before dark or take turns using the kerosene lamp to see by. We had no toothbrushes until we went to school. The first oranges we ever had were from our teachers who brought us a big mesh bag full one Christmas. We had a springhouse where we kept our milk, butter, cream, and eggs. My school had eight grades, all the kids walked to and from school. We filled our mattress with straw and carried it to our house. It made rustling noises when we moved, and yes, we had bedbugs which mom killed with kerosene. One year when I was two, I drank some kerosene, passed out and dad carried me to a neighbor's house to take me to a doctor to have my stomach pumped because we had no vehicle. We slept three girls in a bed and since I was the youngest, I got to sleep in the middle. Mom carried water up from the spring and heated it on a coal stove. She boiled the print out of feed sacks and made our bloomers and slips from them. I have a picture of me in black bloomers, but I don't know where she got that material. For toys, we cut sticks and made our own cars with them. I never had a doll until I was 12 years old. We used a wringer washer. Six years ago when my husband died and I moved into a senior apartment. I'm living with my daughter and son-in-law now. One year our road, which was a dirt road, was covered with lots of snow in the spring and fall, it drifted shut and the men shoveled it out. One crew threw the snow up about four feet and another crew threw it up another three feet. It is the Deer Creek Road now.

Service
By Shirley Mills of West Decatur,
Pennsylvania
Born 1926

I have, in my possession, the Valedictorian speech, delivered at the Bigler Township High School in Madera, Pennsylvania on April 16, 1914 by my mother. Her subject was "Service", a small word but gigantic in content. She spoke of service children owe their parents in return for the service parents have rendered to their children. She also speaks of service rendered to society by men such as Horace Mann and Thomas Edison.

In 1914, electricity was just beginning to impact our society. One of my earliest memories of childhood was a task performed before we owned an electric washer. I remember summer days on the back porch about 18 years after my mother's Valedictorian speech.

Washdays for me as a child consisted of operating the handle on the wooden tub washer filled with hot water, which was heated in a copper boiler on the top of a coal stove in the kitchen. The gyrator in the wooden washer consisted of a wooden disc with three or four perpendicular spindles that swished the clothes. The operator pushed and pulled the wooden pole in the outside of the washer. Then the clothes were put through the hand operated wooden wringer into a tub of cold rinse water. The clothes were then doused up and down, several times, then put back through the wringer. The clothes were then shook and hung out on the wire clothesline in the backyard for the "Solar Dryer" if the sun was shining, otherwise they slowly air dried in the breeze.

For clothes that needed an extra touch there was the washboard in a tub of water on the porch floor. The operator stood or kneeled on the first step down and vigorously rubbed up and down over the washboard. Then rung out the clothes by hand and rinsed before hanging out. For me that was the first opportunity to render service.

Round about that time we were among or maybe the first in the little community to own a radio. My father rendered his service by building a shelf on the front porch. There he placed the table model radio. It was for Friday or Saturday evenings that the young fellows from the community could gather on the green below our home and listen to the boxing matches.

Crank it like a Motorcycle
By Carol Songer of Limestone, New York
Born 1937

I'm 73 years old. I was born and raised in Clermont, Pennsylvania. I was born at home and I was the last of six children. My father got hurt in the oil fields and couldn't walk very well. My mom had to be with him all the time.

We lived on a farm where we raised chickens and rabbits. At holidays, we would kill and sell chickens. We had a big round table and my mother would boil water on our old wood stove and we all would sit around the table, each one of us having a job to do.

We didn't have electricity or running water or inside bathrooms. When we took our baths, we had a big round bathtub and would have to carry all our water from across the road. We all took a bath in the same water.

We went to school in a one-room schoolhouse, with an outside outhouse. That was fun in the winter, you didn't stay any longer then you had to.

In the summer, you had to work in the garden, no matter how old you were. The little ones would pick off the potatoes leaves and put them in a bucket of gas to bill them. I remember a lot of our meals were pancakes and bacon grease; it kept us from being hungry.

In the winter, my mother wanted heat bricks on our wood and coal stove and wrap in blankets and put in our beds to keep warm. We had a unique washer with a motor on it that you had to start like you do a motorcycle. If it was cold, you pumped a long time to get it to start. We had a car you had to crank to get started and mother heated brick in the winter so we had heat in the car. At Christmas we never got new toys, we got toys that were repainted and someone made new cloth for our dolls.

My mother made our dresses out of feedbags and we were proud of them. My father got hurt in an old rig he couldn't walk so we had to move to the city. My father was bed ridden for 17 years and my mother stayed home and cared for him, day and night. My sisters and I would take a wagon and my mother would write a grocery list and we would go shopping for her to get our food. We were happy and loved each other. Now there is only two of us left and talk nearly every day.

A "Me" World
By Audrey Meyer of St. Marys, Pennsylvania
Born 1942

I was born in 1942 in St. Marys, Pennsylvania and I know that era was probably the best there was for children. I remember we had no television; we had to use our imagination to entertain us. There were no cell phones or private lines, we had party lines and now I feel shame because I used to love to listen in on our neighbor's conversations. I have to say some were pretty juicy.

I always felt in awe with my dad, he was the one who washed our clothes in a wringer washer and hung them on lines in the basement to dry. No such things as a clothes dryer back then. Wonder how many young folks know what a wringer washer is? It was a washer with a round tub that would agitate and when you thought the clothes were clean enough you put them through the wringer into the rinse water and back into the wringer then you could hang the clothes up. How easy life is today with automatic washers.

As I grew older a memory of my older sister pulling the refrigerator down on her emerged, I could never figure out how she did this, refrigerators are heavy and it had to be impossible for this little girl to do this and she didn't get hurt! She managed this because we had an icebox with no motor in it. I remember mom yelling, "The ice man is here, catch him, we need ice." We would run and stop the man in a wagon pulled by the horses to get a block of ice for the icebox to keep the food cold. The milkman delivered milk in glass bottles on the doorstep.

I was 12 years old when I left the house to live at another home to babysit four children; I did the wash, cleaned the house and started supper for her. She paid me $20 every two weeks. I wonder how many 12 year olds could or would do this today. This job was a summer job because I had to go to school. School was so different back then, if you got in trouble at school, you got a paddling at school and when you got home, you got another spanking.

Back then, we were taught respect, no such thing as I'll have you arrested for hitting my child. Snow days did not exist, there could have been six feet of snow and we went to school. If roads were slippery, they would put chains on the tires so we could get to school. I often wonder why they don't do this today; do people even know what chains are?

We had very little money but we shared what we had. We lived a half of mile from the railroad tracks and the bums, and I mean bums jumped off the boxcars. They carried a stick and at the end of the stick was a red hankie rolled in a ball carrying their meager belongings. They would knock at the door for food and mom, God bless her soul, would give them something to eat. They would thank her and go on their way. Even with the bums roaming around our doors were never locked, there was no need to. In those days, we had no serial killers, no drug problems, and no home invasions. We were fortunate because we lived in a safe world.

We had hard times in the good old days but as I recall my memories and compare them to how we live today, I would surely return to the good old days where neighbors took care of each other, serial killers were not heard of, child molesters did not exist, children respected their elders, and we did not live in a "me" world. We lived in a world loving each other. Yes, I would love to live in that world again.

Baby in a Bag
By Ruth Rupprecht of Saint Marys,
Pennsylvania
Born 1927

I was in a two-room schoolhouse, which had been two doors from my home. There were no snow days unless the water froze at the school. We had homemade clothes and we stood in line for shoes and clothes. My mother helped me make some of my clothes.

We had an icebox and you put a card in the window when you needed more ice. My father was off work for a long time, but when he was called back to work, he bought us a refrigerator and a car. We went to a farm to buy milk. My mother and I were sitting at the kitchen table when a ball of fire went by the window, we didn't know where it came from. My sisters and her boyfriend were parked out front and they saw it also.

I had two brothers in World War II in the Air Force. One brother was a prisoner of war in Germany for 16 months. One brother made it back to England in an airplane with holes in it. Two of my brothers were in the Korean War.

My mother died in 1945 and the snow was so deep they couldn't bury her. When we walked to school, we had to walk on the street. My godparents and their family were very good to me for my birthday, Christmas, and Easter. When my mother had a baby, we were told the doctor brought the baby in his bag.

My favorite teacher was Mrs. Gregory. When she had my deaf son, she called me to help her to know how to teach him. I told her to make sure he could always see her lips. My mother and I rode the last trip on the Shawmutt Loddleburg.

When my mother died I had taken over to help raise my two brothers, they were eight and 11. Even though I got married, I stayed home until they were raised.

Ruth Finfinger Rupprecht in 1945

Old Iron
By James Gotshall Sr. of Port Allegany,
Pennsylvania
Born 1933

In our town of Port Allegany, there is a Main Street. The number two street is Arnold Avenue. It runs from the bank on Main Street to our park. Left of Arnold is Broad Street. Broad runs past our house, up a grade, and at the top, turns, and becomes Oak Street. Oak runs down a hill, crosses Little Bridge Creek, then crosses Arnold Avenue, and continues on. There was a big iron bridge over this creek. You went over this bridge and at Arnold, you would turn to the left and there was our park. A turn to the right and in a short distance you crossed another newer bridge.

The summer of 1942, July 18th, we received our greatest flood of the century. I was eight years old and my brother Bill was 17. Our property and house sat lower than the street. The water was rising; mom and Bill were putting anything and everything in our attic, trying to salvage what they could. I was sitting on the kitchen table.

Ernie Mangold, our neighbor, came wading in. He carried me up the street to his house. Mrs. Mangold fixed me a bed on their couch. She said I looked tired and needed a nap. I was and I did. It finally quit raining, but the creek was still rising. In the afternoon, they shook me awake. "Jimmy, wake up, hurry! We're going up to the end of the street, the bridge is washing out." The bridge sat on huge stonewalls and we hurried up the street. The water was flowing under, through, and over the bridge. "Old Iron" creaked and groaned, swung around to its right and floated down Arnold Avenue. It washed over where the other bridge had been, went a short way further, and stopped. They replaced the newer bridge on Arnold Avenue, put a curve in Oak Street and the old bridge I played on and under was gone, forever.

No one ever refers to "My old iron". I haven't found any pictures either. It was not referred to in our sesquicentennial or quasquicentennial booklets. I guess it will remain, "My Old Iron".

A new bridge over Route 6 coming into Port was opened July 17, 1942. It washed out the next day, though, and had to be built again. Dad was operating a pump station in Guffy, over on Route 219, just out of Bradford, and

heard the water coming down the valley. He ran to his car, drove at an angle up a bank, got out; and, he was not able to get home for five days. My brother and I knew of a spring on "Old Baldy". We went up there for water for several days.

My brother's name is William Gotshall, Bill for short. He will be 87 in March 2012. I will talk about Bill and his tour of duty in Germany in 1945 and 1946. I could never describe his hunger, pain, and loneliness, but I will try and describe the anguish our parents and I went through. Bill graduated early summer 1943. He worked several jobs around Port Allegany, Pennsylvania. Most of his friends began enlisting in the service. Our country had a war in Europe and Asia. He tried several times to enlist but was turned down each time because of his feet. He tormented the recruiters so much that they finally took him in the service in early 1945.

After his basic training, he shipped out and soon found himself in Germany. All too soon, we got a notification he was missing in action. In our minds, he might be gone forever. I was 12 years old at this time. We all cried, a lot, but we still had hope. The time I spent with mom was so painful. I could do absolutely nothing. It seemed he was gone forever.

Sometime later in 1945 a letter came from the Red Cross. It was at the post office. We knew it had to be good news. Mom and I were so excited! She sent me to the post office, but my bicycle had a flat back tire. Anyone ever ride a bicycle with a flat back tire? You can't, but I did. Seven blocks that way, seven blocks home, the tears would not stop. We opened the letter. The Red Cross had located Bill in a prison camp in southern Germany. This time, we all cried with relief, but immediately began to worry about Bill's health and safety. We learned we could send a letter now and then.

I remember dad reading a letter pertaining to Thanksgiving. It was coming up; Bill described in detail every kind of food ever eaten at our table at Thanksgiving. Dad was working at Pittsburgh Corning in Port. They manufactured foam glass. He took a large piece, hollowed it out to fit a bottle. I assumed Old Kentucky or a wine, boxed it up, mailed it through the Red Cross to Bill; we couldn't send food. Older Germans were guarding Bill and another man who spoke German. All others were in their army fighting their war.

Time passed, the allies were coming one way, the Russians the other way. The Germans moved the prisoners. A guard helped Bill and his fellow prisoner to escape. The three of them made their way to the allied lines. Their last obstacle to freedom was a river. They crossed it by crawling over remains of a steel bridge left from bombings. Bill was shipped to England and then to the states.

He was sent to a hospital in Virginia. They finally let him come home for a week and then he had to go back to the hospital. I cannot describe his homecoming, we celebrated with the greatest Thanksgiving dinner imaginable and, lots of old fashioned plum pudding. It was nowhere near Thanksgiving. The box and bottle, unopened, came home a year or so later.

Mom and dad are gone now. Only memories remain. Bill lives in east Aurora, New York, about 70 miles away.

Homemade Pies
By Deloris M. Mertz of St. Marys,
Pennsylvania
Born 1930

The first 14 years of my life, I lived on South St. Marys Street, which was known as Million Dollar Highway. The street got its name because that's what they said it took to construct it. It was a two-lane highway, but it is now a four-lane highway.

We didn't have a bathroom in our house until I was about 10, so I remember the outhouse and pot and taking a bath in a washtub in the kitchen. Mom made our clothes for school. I remember a winter coat she made for me; it was a very pretty blue. Someone gave her the coat and she took it apart and made a coat for me. It had five big white buttons down the front and a flared skirt and was nice and warm. I remember party phones but my parents didn't have a phone until I was a junior in high school.

Across the road was a pond, called Zwack's pond. Before my time it was used for water for a sawmill. I don't know much about that. This pond had a wood blocking to hold the water. People from town used to come out in summer on Sundays and holidays to go boating in the rowboats. They also held picnics and get togethers in the grove below the dam.

It was called Zwack's Grove; it had a stand of evergreen trees where there was a building with shutters for windows that held dances here sometimes. There were picnic tables and a small building where they cooked. There was some kind of picnic several times a week in summer. Church picnics, choir, firemen, girl scouts, family reunions, and company picnics were some of the picnics held here. There was also a large field to play ball or other games.

There was a path that led from the grove to a bend in the creek and a huge rock. Kids from town could also come down State Street and come up a dirt road on the other side of the rock to swim. We had a lot of fun swimming at the base of the rock, and then lying in the sun on top of the rock called Bum's Rock. I don't know if any bums ever used it, but that was the story the kids told.

In winter, we used to ice skate on the pond and when the ice got thick enough, they cut ice blocks down by the blocking. I don't remember the size of the blocks but they were large. They used saws to cut the ice, and then they were pulled with big tongs onto a board runway and slid down to a building and stored in the basement, covered with sawdust so they didn't melt. They kept well into the summer this way. There was a truck that used to go around town selling ice to people who had iceboxes. I was still too young to know how these things worked. Kids liked to follow the ice truck around the neighborhood to get the ice chips that fell when they cut the blocks to what size the people needed. Sometime ago the blocking washed out when we had high water. It was never repaired. Now there is only a stream running through the middle of it.

As kids, we didn't have television, computers, and all the gadgets the kids have today. We made our own fun and I don't think too many got into trouble back then. We went sled riding down Knights Hill, West Theresia Road, there was not much traffic back then. It probably took us about 10 minutes to pull our sleds up to the top of the hill. We did this once and then started about half way up. Kids from town came out on Sunday afternoon and we would have 30 to 40 kids riding. The best part was, I don't think anyone ever got hurt other than a minor scrape or bruise.

When the weather was nice, mom, dad, and my sister and I spent a lot of time in the woods. I remember one fall, dad parked the car and we walked in the woods and came to some apple trees that my grandfather had planted years before. The property had been sold and grew wild again. There were no roads anymore. We found a couple of trees that had some pretty nice apples (Northern Spies) on them. Dad put as many in his hunting jacket as would fit. We then took my snow pants and tied the legs shut and filled them with apples. The snow pants had straps and dad carried them on his back. We still had to walk back to the car, which was about two miles away. It was a tiresome trip, but we had nearly a bushel of apples and mom made pies and applesauce, mmmmgood!

Milk Can 133
By Linda Schall Austin of Wellsville, New York
Born 1943

North Fork, Pennsylvania is located in Potter County, a bit north of Westfield, which is in Tioga County. In 1946, my father returned from World War II. My parents, Clarence and Winifred Simmons Schall, purchased the family farm from my grandparents, Adolf and Louise Knoll Schall. He became the third generation to own this 188-acre dairy farm. The farm was located on a dirt road just north of the village very close to the New York state line. In fact, the property was in New York, but the address was Westfield, Pennsylvania as was the village of North Fork, Pennsylvania. North Fork had no post office, although there were 13 houses, a Grange hall, a Methodist church, and a grocery store/gas station at the end of Benny and Grace Truax's home.

The dirt roads leading out from this village were where dairy farms were located. This was the main employment for the area at the time my parents began farming in 1946. The income was generated by the sale of the milk to a Westfield milk plant. Thomas Snyder was the "milk hauler" at that time. When Thomas decided to retire from this daily job, my father became the "milk hauler". He purchased a green 1953 Chevrolet truck with a flat bed. He built a rack that was higher near the cab and had "gates" on each side. This was painted green to match the truck. Straps were added to go across that would stabilize the milk cans. This was especially important on the higher section where cans would be piled two high. He had to cut and make the bigger doors for a portion of the shed at the north end of the barn so the truck would fit. Even then, the side mirrors got bent or broken a few times driving into this shed.

The job was added to his daily farming duties to bring added income to our household. Each farmer's fee was based on the weight of the milk taken to the plant each day. We lived for those "milk hauling" checks. Each morning my father would get up about 4:30 a.m. to milk our cows, about 20 or 25 of them, and to do the chores. Then after breakfast, which was about 7:10 a.m. he loaded our 10-gallon milk cans onto his Chevy truck and headed down the road to pick up the cans from many farmers between our farm and Westfield. His destination was the M.H. Renken Dairy Company, the Renken Milk Plant.

Milk at this time was strained into cans as each cow was milked on the farms. Full cans were lowered into a vat of cold spring water, which remained at 40 degrees year round. These vats were located in a small separate building from the barn called a milk house. The milk house was usually located up near the road and had a concrete stoop or step outside where the full cans were placed each morning for the milk hauler to pick up. Some farmers were able to purchase electric milk coolers that resembled large two door

The milk truck that Linda's dad drove

258

refrigerators to chill their milk.

My dad was very "rugged" since he was just returning from being a soldier. These full milk cans were heavy, weighing about 100 pounds. When dairy cows were producing generously, he would have about 130 cans on the truck as he arrived at the milk plant. He unloaded them onto a roller style conveyor and the cans rolled into the plant. Inside the milk was tested for butterfat content and weighed in each can. The farmers got credit for their daily delivery based on their milk can number. Our number was 133. The milk was dumped into a common tank, the cans were steam washed and sent out another conveyor for dad to reload onto the truck. In the meantime, other haulers were unloading the full cans they had collected on their routes. He then reversed his trip and dropped off the clean, empty cans to each of the farmers. This routine was seven days a week and 365 days a year! Yes, even Christmas morning we waited for that green truck to reappear coming up the road because we knew we could now have Christmas. Those mornings he would commit to less visiting with his good friends, the farmers, and would be home the exact time he said! At that time my older sister, Barbara, was married and lived in Westfield. They knew this committed time and would be right behind him as he came up the road on Christmas morning. This is a very emotional family memory!

Sometimes the milk plant would have a supply of buttermilk to give away and dad would leave the plant with one of our cans full. As he returned to the farmers, he would give some to them if they came out with a container. My dad loved that real buttermilk.

My grandparents moved to West Main Street in Westfield when we bought the farm. Therefore, dad drove by their home every day. On many summer mornings, I would ride the route with him and he would drop me off to spend a few days with them. They watched for him each day and many times, he would stop for a quick visit and morning coffee.

One winter, about 1958, we had a big snowfall and then the wind started blowing. Since we already had snow ridges on each side of the road from previous plowing, the wind blew the snow into these tunnels and we were "snowed in"! That meant the milk truck was stranded about two miles from the cleared hard top road. Well, as communities operated in the 50s, the farmers walked through fields, up to our farm with shovels and they shoveled a short distance. Dad drove the truck that distance and that continued until the truck was down to North Fork. Our neighbors, Logan and Nina Metcalf, had horses and a sleigh and that's how the three farmers on our road got their milk down to North Fork for several days. The township actually later cleared a "road" in a field next to the road so we could drive out. We were "snowed in" for 10 days! Other winters it was very common for my dad to get up several times in the night and plow our road with his 1946 John Deere A and the plow he had made using a metal field roller and his welding ability. He was a devoted milk hauler and he did not want any of his farmers to have to dump their milk. Farmers would run out of cooler space for the milk cans after about two milkings and they would then have to dump the oldest milk until the milk hauler could arrive.

I want to tell you a bit more about our neighbors Logan and Nina Metcalf. They had a 100-acre dairy farm and were somewhat older than my parents. Logan wanted to retire and move to Ulysses, Pennsylvania. They approached dad about buying this acreage and buildings. This was going to be a great tenant house for a farmhand and his family. The only catch was their home had no electricity and the only running water was a pitcher pump on the kitchen sink! Our farm became 288 acres and the house was updated!

In the mid-1950s, the Renkin Milk Plant in Westfield burned and dad had to take his load of milk on down Route 49 to the town of Osceola, Pennsylvania. My younger sister, Lorraine, wasn't in school yet so she rode with him many times. She couldn't pronounce Osceola and called it "oseelinlow". She left the house with her breakfast of a peanut butter and jelly sandwich that she ate when they got to Cleland Hall's farm!

As times changed farmers began putting in bulk tanks for their milk and large tank trucks came to the farms on alternating days. These bulk tanks came in various sizes and farmers purchased the size appropriate for their dairy size. This progress also caused farmers to have to build larger milk houses that were usually attached to the barn. In 1959, my father began the building of a cement block addition to the southwest corner of the barn for the eventual bulk tank.

The new milk house in 1959

The milk inspector, Merle Eaton, was the enforcer of the health regulations relating to these buildings. The wash station for the milkers and temperature of the hot water were just two of these regulations! One day when dad was going over his plans for this new milk house he told Mr. Eaton the toilet was going to be in a certain corner. Dad enjoyed telling the story of Mr. Eaton's response of, "You can't have a toilet in the milk house!" I think he believed dad because of how he told it right along with the location of outlets and water lines. For some time we had a milk cooler in that new milk house but eventually he got a bulk tank and sold the milk truck. He used that bulk tank until he sold the dairy in his later years. Another farmer actually bought it and moved it to his farm.

Dad's milk truck served many purposes over the years in addition to hauling milk for area farmers. He designed and built another door for the one side with a grain shoot. This was used when the oats or wheat were harvested in the fall as a collection container. When he had a load he would drive the truck down to the grainery and shovel the grain onto an elevator to go into the grain bins for winter storage and feed grinding ingredients. This truck was also a moving van on several occasions. When Lorraine began going to horse shows to compete this truck became a horse trailer with the addition of a ramp. The milk truck was a big part of our farming history for several years. Dairy farming has changed so much since the 1950s!

The Snake in a Pine Tree
By Marian Webster of Cogan Station,
Pennsylvania
Born 1923

We were raised on a farm that our dad and mother purchased from his parents after returning from World War I. They raised two boys and six girls.

A stream ran through the property, and through the woods. There was an old dam down in the woods they used to cut ice on for use in the summer months, and stored in an icehouse. We older ones would walk to the dam in summertime to fix the old dam up and swim.

One hot summer day we went to the dam to swim. There was a picnic table right under a big pine tree. People were playing cards and chatting. We stopped to talk to them. They wondered what was dropping from the tree right where they were playing cards. We looked up in the tree, and right above where they were sitting was a big black snake laying there on a limb. Boy, did we all get out of there in a hurry!

I don't remember if we went home or went on to swim.

Tom Mix and the Horse
By Ron McGonigal of Jobstown, New Jersey

I grew up in Johnsonburg, Pennsylvania, which is located in Elk County. As a young schoolboy in the 1940s, I wanted a horse of my own. When I was almost twelve years old, I went to the nearest dairy farm on the road where I lived with my family. Mr. Wally Shaffer, who owned the big Shaffer Dairy Farm on State Road in Johnsonburg, needed a helper, so he hired me. That made me so happy, because after school every day, I could work for Wally and earn some money to buy the horse I always wanted.

My dear mother told me that I was taking after a very old, famous relative from her side of the family. I was so surprised when she told me it was Tom Mix! He was a cowboy TV star who was born in Driftwood, Pennsylvania and Driftwood was also the birthplace of my mother.

I was a very happy boy the day I bought my horse, and knowing also that we were related to Tom Mix. To this day, I still have horses.

260

The Narrow Slop Jar Escape
By Eva B. Gouldthread of Grampian,
Pennsylvania
Born 1926

One Halloween, four of us girls decided to dress up and go out Halloweening. We had gone to a number of houses when we came to Aunt Tillie and Uncle Perry's house. That is what the whole town called them. They were in their fifties, no children, and not very nice. We finally decided we would be nice and go into their house.

We were no more in the house when Aunt Tillie tried to take off my sister's mask. She was pulling at the mask and her hair and face. We left in a hurry.

After taking off our costumes, we decided to get even. We got some soap and set out to soup their windows. It was a two-story house. Two stayed to watch for them, while myself and another girl went to soap windows. Suddenly, they yelled, "Run!" We took off, but could hear water splashing behind us. Uncle Perry was upstairs and had opened a window and emptied a slop jar on us.

After a while, we went back to see what he had thrown at us. Sure enough, there was urine and bowel movement where we had been standing. Needless to say, we never went near them again.

When it is November, I once again think of our close call. God was with us.

The Top Man on the Saw
By Clair F. Burns of Brookville,
Pennsylvania
Born 1928

My father bought this farm in the early 1900s and raised four children: two girls and two boys. I came around in 1928. My mother passed away when I was four-and-a-half years old. That didn't stop my father from farming.

Everywhere my father went, I had to go also. I rode the farm tractor on my dad's lap, or sitting on the fender. Sometimes, that old Fordson tractor had a mind of its own and would not start.

To make a long story short, Dad built an icehouse. In those days, ice was a rare item. The icehouse was probably 25 feet square. I'm thinking Dad hauled sawdust from a sawmill in our woods, that Dad owned. Anyway, every winter, my dad would put new spike shoes on the team to haul ice cut from a pond on the Country Club golf course. The ice would be fifteen to eighteen inches thick. My dad would chop a hole in the ice, take one handle off a two-man crosscut saw, and start cutting squares of ice blocks out. Dad would pick out the cakes of ice and load them on a bobsled for the icehouse.

One day, a neighbor stopped to ask what he was doing. The neighbor told Dad that he had never seen a one-man crosscut saw. Dad said, "Not a problem. The man on the other end is down in the pond and is pushing up." Dad never told him any different, and the neighbor left.

The icehouse was big enough to hold eight to ten wagonloads of ice. We didn't have a refrigerator, so we used ice from the icehouse all summer long. First, Dad put in about two feet of sawdust, then covered the ice with more sawdust, then more ice until full. There wasn't a roof on the icehouse, but the ice would keep all summer long.

I remember my one aunt would call: if we brought the ice to their house, we could make ice cream and chocolate cake. Who could turn that down after doing my own cooking? So away, we would go in Dad's 1923 Model T Ford with the ice that Dad and I put up for summer use.

Semper Fi Soap Opera
By Freda Foster of Rochester Mills,
Pennsylvania

When I was young, in the 1940s and 1950s, my parents were very fussy about my playmates. As I became a teenager, it was worse. I couldn't date anyone: "This boy's grandfather stole horses!" "This boy's mother smokes!" "This one's parents don't go to church!" By the time I graduated, I knew that I would end up an old maid, like my sister. So, I decided to join the Marine Corps, just to get away from home, and to have a job, food, clothing and a home.

My dad wouldn't sign the papers at first. He said it was no place for a lady. I said that I could be a lady anywhere.

I did join, and spent boot camp at Paris Island, South Carolina. Then my next duty station was at Camp Lejeune, North Carolina.

Since I had not dated, I kept to myself, and worked diligently at my job as a sign painter.

After work, we girls took turns at barracks duty: two-hour shifts from four P.M. to six A.M. We sat at a desk by the door and logged everyone who came in or went out the door, other than those living there, unless on a date, then both names were logged down.

This nice looking Marine came by, and said he was looking for a girl. I asked just who was he looking for. He said that he did not know, just a girl. I said it did not work that way! He had to know just who he wanted to date. He told me that he had been in a seminary studying to be a priest, and realized that he did not want to be a priest all his life, and dropped out and joined the Marine Corps. He said that he had not been out of boot camp very long. He had gotten out about the same time I did. He was from Jackson, Mississippi and I was from Pennsylvania.

The next day we had our first date. Three months later, we were married.

His mother later told me that she had worried about him as he would not date girls and his younger brother was, and even tried to set up dates for him, and he would take the 'coon dog and go out in the woods hunting 'coon. Then he wanted to be a priest! He told me he was bashful and did not like girls chasing him.

I was his first date and he was mine! This could go on like a soap opera, but I'll end it here.

Snakes and a Short Italian Boy
By Mary L. Shenk of Denver, Pennsylvania
Born 1939

My first six [school] years were in three classrooms: one for first and second grades, one for third and fourth and one for fifth and sixth. It was in Nelson, and my very first teacher was Mrs. Dorothy Gleason. She was a wonderful lady and I kept in touch with her for years until she passed.

Then comes castor oil! How I hated it. I was in the hospital at age seven and they told me they had some orange juice for me. Well, it tasted horrible and it was later I learned that it had castor oil in it.

I also remember getting baths in the back room in a round metal tub. I remember that back room also for the wringer washer and doing the laundry.

My mother was quite a runaround, so I spent a lot of time with my dear grandmother and grandpa. They spoiled me a lot. She used to make me a lot of pretty clothes and I remember standing in her sewing room so she could measure me. Such wonderful memories.

Then we got a telephone and were on a party line. Had to check if anyone else was on the line, then dial an operator and she would put your call through. Then when I was a teenager, I was on that phone and lightning struck it and it threw me across the room onto my stepfather's lap. How scary!

I was at my grandma's house playing outside. I came by the chimney and there was a rattlesnake curled in the corner. I didn't move and called Grandpa and he came out and killed it. I often saw grass snakes slithering around, but not rattlers. To this day, I do not like any snakes.

Well, my first love was a short Italian boy at school. Used to meet and go to movies together.

I graduated from Elkland High School in 1957. They have torn down that school. I still keep in touch with classmates, and enjoy remembering. We usually had sock hops on Friday nights, and was that ever great. Everyone came to those and we all had a great time. If we could only turn back the clock and enjoy this all again. But we must thank God that we have these wonderful memories.

As for memorable people in my life, there are two: my grandmother and Mrs. Dorothy Gleason. Those two women were wonderful Christian people. Grandma played organ in church for fifty years and took me to church with her. Mrs. Gleason took me to church also in Nelson and I joined MYF and also was baptized there. They were both great ladies and I still miss them.

So the last thing is family time. I have two older brothers and we did not have much family time. As I said, my mother was a runaround and was not home a lot. So me and my brothers came home from school to an empty house, and we fended for ourselves to eat, etc. The family times we did have were at Grandma's house, and we kids loved it. I will always hold these times in my mind and heart as long as I live.

I was born in Blossburg Hospital in Tioga County in 1939, and spent my younger years there. I moved away in 1958 and returned in 1985. I lost my husband in 2002, and stayed in Tioga until January 31, 2011, and now I have moved down here to be near my three sons, as I'm getting older, too.

The Woodshed Tarpaper Experiment
By Richard Bova of Port Allegany,
Pennsylvania
Born 1932

I was born and raised in the tiny town of Duke Center, Pennsylvania. More specifically, on Oil Valley Road. Duke Center is in the middle of the Bradford oil field, which at one time was the source of the highest quality crude oil in the entire world. My dad worked as a pumper/roustabout on leases that adjoined our property. This story, however, is not about oil production or my dad's job. It's about a four-year-old who learned a whole lot in just one afternoon. The year is 1937.

I was the "baby" in our family. I had a sister, Bernice, who was married at the time of this caper. My oldest brother was Bernard, who worked as a tooldresser on a drilling rig. Then I had a brother, Don, who was about four years older than me.

It was late September or early October and Don and the other guys in the neighborhood were in school. Must be my buddy, Jim Harvey, wasn't allowed out that day, because I was all alone, looking for something to do. The State highway workers were busy pouring hot tar in the cracks in the concrete road. I watched them a while, then a question arose in my inquisitive mind. I wondered if the tar on the tarpaper on the woodshed would melt. Yep. We had an outbuilding that Dad called the woodshed, although we didn't burn wood in the furnace—we used coal. It was mostly a place where Dad kept things that he probably would never use.

Tarpaper was used a great deal in those days as an exterior covering for buildings. It had a rather heavy coating of tar on both sides and served its purpose very well.

I needed a match in order to perform my experiment. Mom was in the living room crocheting, so it was pretty easy to sneak a wooden match from the matchbox in the kitchen. I went to the rear of the woodshed, which was surrounded by dry grass about a

Dick with his big brother, Don Dova

foot deep. Since this was long before the days of power mowers, at least in Oil Valley, high grass was common and neatly mowed lawns were rare. No one mowed any more grass than they absolutely had to, so high grass around outbuildings was the norm.

I struck the match on a stone and carefully held it to the bottom edge of that tarpaper. Sure enough! That tar melted quickly and dripped to the ground!

Although most of this event is etched deeply in my memory, I truly do not remember if I put the match out or if it fell to the ground, still burning when it got too short to hold any longer. At any rate, a short time later, as I was messing around in the yard, smoke began rising at the rear of the woodshed.

I rushed into the house and headed to the living room where Mom was, but somehow, I couldn't find the words to tell her. She must have sensed something wrong—the way mothers can. Looking at me, she asked, "Why are you so white?"

"I washed my face," was my reply.

Now she knew for sure something wasn't right. "What is it?" she insisted.

"The woodshed is on fire," I whimpered.

Out the door we hurried, but there was

nothing we could do. We had no garden hose, nor a faucet to attach it to if we did have one. We also had no telephone to call for help.

Mrs. Higley, our neighbor, came running around the house, and after Mom assured her that no one was in the woodshed, she said, "I'll call Johnny!"

About that time, a young man came running up through our yard and asked Mom if he could help. She told him there was a 55-gallon drum of fuel oil in the shed. He entered the shed, tipped the drum on edge, rolled it to the door, and let it fall to the ground, where it rolled down a bank safely into the yard. Anyone who has never tried to tip a 55-gallon drum full of fluid on edge and roll it cannot appreciate the strength and skill

Dick and his dog

that man possessed. I heard people saying later that he was foolish to do what he did, but to me he was a hero. I'm sure Dad and Mom appreciated it too, because it probably saved our house from destruction.

Back to Mrs. Higley: she was referring to Johnny Boylan, a man who owned a really nice garage and service station in Duke Center. Johnny had a fire truck. That's right—the town fire truck belonged to an individual. We didn't have a volunteer fire company nor a warning siren to summon help in case of an emergency. Johnny was the only one allowed to drive the truck, and was usually the only one responding to a fire.

I think this truck was a Reo and probably

eight or ten years old. It was bright red with no cab and no windshield. The hose was probably an inch in diameter and there was a small tank full of water. Years later, when we did get a volunteer company, they used to display the truck at parades all around McKean County.

I guess my dad was there by the time the fire truck arrived, because as I said before, he worked right close to home and probably saw the black smoke.

The woodshed was determined to be a lost cause, so they let it burn while Mr. Boylan used the hose and pump on his truck to douse the burning grass. I'd never seen so much water come out of a hose, but I wasn't enjoying it. The only thing I could think of was the much deserved whippin' I was going to get when things got settled down.

As I recall, Dad did ask me what happened, and I had to own up to everything. I was verbally reminded that I had been warned many times about playing with matches, as had every kid in the neighborhood, and this is what can happen!

Later that day, when my big brother Bernard came home from work, he wanted to give me a good lickin', but Dad intervened on my behalf and I was spared the pain.

The lessons I learned that day stuck with me throughout my life. Don't fool around with things you don't understand, and sometimes formal punishment is not necessary. Living with the mistakes you make can be more effective than any other form of punishment. The pain of spanking is soon gone, but the memory of the act and the love of a parent is never forgotten.

By the way, Don, and all the other big guys in the neighborhood, were disappointed that they missed the fire and the fire truck.

Flat Stones and Watered Beer
By Irene Morton of McElhattan,
Pennsylvania
Born 1946

In the 1950s, the small town I was born and raised in, Jersey Shore, Pennsylvania, had little organized entertainment for children. The block we lived on had about fifty kids, so there was always someone around to play with.

Our favorite thing was hopscotch, drawn on the sidewalk with chalk. One could see hopscotch boards at several homes. The trick was finding a flat stone that would lay where it was thrown. And if you were not well-balanced, like me, it was hard hopping on one foot. The other kids liked to play that with me because they knew they would probably win.

You could also find round circles drawn on some of the walks where we played marbles. We sometimes played "for keeps," which meant any marble you shot outside the circle (and the shooter stayed inside the circle) you could keep. We all had tin cans that we kept our marbles in; sometimes they got quite full, but other times, they were quite empty.

My fondest and most memorable times were in the summer when we would spend time with our grandparents in the small town of Cammal, Pennsylvania, about a 45 minute drive from home. In the summer, on nice days, we would walk to Pine Creek and keep ourselves cool in the clear water. The creek is full of stones, so it was quite a challenge just getting out deep enough without falling down. There were two swimming holes, and one had a large rock called "Minky" which everyone used as a diving board because the deepest hole was there. Only problem for me was that it was on the opposite side of the creek, and you had to be a pretty good swimmer to get to it. I panicked when the water was over my head, as I never conquered the talent of overhand swimming. I was an underwater swimmer, but when I went up for air, my feet would have to be able to touch bottom. It took several years, but I finally made it over to Minky; the creek was down and I found a water path to it. When we tired of swimming, we would skip stones on the water. We had to search for thin, flat stones to make them work. Dad was one who was very good at it, and although he gave us instructions, we never mastered it like he did.

We loved walking the railroad tracks that ran in front of Gram and Pap's house. We would walk from one end of town to the other. There was a crossing at both ends, so we always knew when a train was coming, as they would blow their whistle before getting to them. Gram always warned us to get a good distance back from the track. She could have saved her breath, because if you were too close, those metal wheels on the metal tracks really smelled! I liked the sound of them at night when we got into bed. Once you got used to them, they lulled you to sleep. The railroads at that time were used quite a bit, so they went by frequently.

Grams's brother and his wife lived on the mountain above Cammal. If you had a good car, you could take it part way up to their house, but we always loved walking from Gram's house. We would take buckets and pick blackberries and raspberries that grew wild along the road. Of course, when we got there, most of them were already consumed. I remember one day my sister, Gram, Aunt Naomi and I were going up the mountain, and we girls were walking ahead. Gram didn't like us getting too far ahead, but we were having a great time being ahead, but not out of sight. Gram hollered for us to stop and turn around…we both had stepped over a blacksnake that was stretched across the road, sunning himself. We were used to seeing snakes now and then, but never got that close. He never moved, but on inspection, when we touched him with a LONG stick, we found he was alive. For a time after that, we kept our eyes pointed down!

There was plenty of wildlife there, and I, for one, loved it. There were lots of white-tailed deer, raccoons, rabbits, squirrels, and of course, skunks and snakes. The skunks, when they had babies, would come down the hill with their little ones following them, and it looked like they were marching in step. We always stayed in the house or on the porch when they paraded by. We rarely saw a bear, but often saw the destruction they caused, such as raided garbage cans, etc.

One thing we liked to do on the mountain was gather eggs from the henhouse. They didn't all make it to the house without cracks, but it was really neat putting your hand under the hens, because it was so warm in the nests. There were a few of those hens that were not very friendly, and we often got pecked. We liked to feed them, too, but then it was safe to say you were definitely going to get pecked.

Gram's house had running water in the house from a well in the yard. However, water was sometimes scarce. So at night, we would wash in a basin, and Gram would heat the water on the wood stove that she cooked on in the kitchen. On Saturday night, we could take baths in the tub. But we had to take them together. We were not allowed to use the toilet, only at nights, so we had to use the outhouse. My sister especially hated it, as it had a nasty odor, and the seats were wood. Being older than me, she often picked on me, so one day I saw my chance for a little revenge, and when she went in, I turned the lock on the outside just as a train was going by. When she couldn't get out, no one could hear her yelling. At the time, we were playing with some other kids, and although I let her out after the train passed, she never knew until much later who locked her in. Needless to say, she was upset with all of us.

There were lots of chipmunks—"chippies," as we called them—around the house. We often saw them run into the downspouts on the house. So we got the idea to put a box at the end of the downspout, then while one of us held the box, the other one would knock on the downspout at the elbow where it connected to the house. It was nearly foolproof that we could catch one. Of course, we couldn't handle them, and we were fortunate that we never were bitten. But to us, it was fun, and quite exciting.

Pap built us an area in the yard for what would now be a sandbox. But instead of sand, he put sawdust in it from a sawmill up the road, and we had the best time playing in there. We used old dishes and spoons and whatever else we could find to build or play house in that box. The aroma from the sawdust was wonderful. Of course, sometimes at night cats and other creatures thought it quite appealing to use for their outhouse, so if it wasn't covered, it had to be emptied and new sawdust put in. When he emptied it, he would put it in his garden, as it made good mulch. We spent many hours in that sawdust box, and as we had to take off our shoes and socks to play in it, it was not hard to brush off; so we didn't drag too much in the house.

We liked helping Gram with the laundry, as she had an old tub with the wringer on top. When it was time to rinse, one of us would start a piece of clothing on one side, and the other would catch it as it came through. Then we would take them outside and hang them on lines that were low enough for us to reach. Gram was only four feet, ten inches tall, so they were down that low for her. Then we would get props Pap made from tree limbs to push up the lines so the clothes didn't touch the ground. We liked doing the wash, but hanging it was not one of our favorite things.

On Christmas one year, Mom and Dad surprised Gram with an electric washer. It took her quite a while to get used to it, but as she got older, she appreciated it. On another Christmas, they got her an electric stove, but as I remember, she always seemed to prefer the wood stove, especially in the winter. It was what they used mostly for heating the house, also, so it was always hot (no need to heat up the electric), and when it got really cold, we would close the doors to the dining and living room, and just stay in the kitchen, as it was plenty big enough. There was no heat in the upstairs, but Pap had put an open register from the kitchen into the bathroom upstairs; it was a big help at night to keep our bottoms from freezing to the toilet seat. We slept up there, and piled on the blankets at night. When we woke in the morning, it was so cold getting out of bed, but once we got down to the kitchen, it was great! That heat felt so good from that old stove.

On occasion, we had to stay at Gram's house during the week on school days. There were buses that took us to school, but the roads then were not in the greatest shape, so the ride back and forth to Jersey Shore was a long one, In the winter when we got on the bus in the morning, it was still dark out. And when we got back after school, it was also dark out. I didn't like going there on school days. It was depressing. I don't know how those kids that lived there managed those days. Of course, it wasn't too long before the times when we stayed there, that they used the one-room schoolhouse there. Gram had been a teacher when she was younger, so we walked to that schoolhouse one day so she could show us what it was like. It was still in good shape, the desks with the inkwells, etc. My mother had gone there. It schooled grades one through eight. When she got to the ninth grade, she went to Williamsport for high school, staying there in a room through the week, and then going home for the weekends. She was an only child, so it must have been quite lonely during the week. But it was where she met my dad, so it was a good thing.

Pap was quite a country style musician. He played a fiddle and a banjo. My sister and I both played piano, so he would get one of his instruments going, and one of us would chord with him on the piano. He loved to sing while he played, and often, he would make up his own lyrics to tunes we knew that would make us laugh. He'd get his foot tapping pretty good when we got going. He really loved doing that, and we did, too. Sometimes, a couple of the neighbors would come over in the summer when the windows were open and enjoy the music. There was lots of foot-stomping then! It was a player piano, and there were plenty of scrolls, so when Pap wasn't there, we really got that old piano rockin'. It was so much fun, pumping that piano and all that wonderful music came out. You had to pump it at a steady pace, as the speed would go up and down if you didn't, but it was lots of fun making it go slower, then faster.

Gram and Pap took in hunters every November, about four or five of them, from down state, from the Philadelphia area. She was a great cook, so she cooked them the best breakfasts and dinners, and even packed lunches for them to take. Since school was closed for Thanksgiving and a couple of days of hunting season, I always stayed with them to help her. One of the hunters, a butcher from Philly, was especially fond of the Cammal area, so one summer; he brought up his wife and son for a vacation. And it became a yearly ritual for several years after, until he became ill, long after the hunters stopped coming. Again, I stayed there when they came, and they took me anywhere they went, calling me their adopted daughter. He and Pap would sit on the front porch towards evening, each with a bottle of beer, just enjoying life. He was quite a prankster, so one day, his son and I decided to pay him back a little, and put water in an empty beer bottle and gave it to him. The shocked look on his face was priceless! And the four of us couldn't stop laughing.

These are but a few of the fond memories I have of those years. How fortunate that we experienced them!

Memories of the Early Years
By Marian B. Hutchinson of Williamsport,
Pennsylvania
Born 1933

Born a country girl, I do cherish the good old days.

This little farm girl was very shy and always felt intimidated by the town kids.

I went to school in a one-room schoolhouse in Lairdsville, Pennsylvania for eight years, September 1940 to June 1948. I had four different teachers: first grade, Mr. Frank Birch; second and third grades, Miss Pearl Houseknecht; fourth, fifth, sixth and seventh grades, Mrs. Edith Houseknecht; and eighth

Marian's mother, Edna Swisher Arthur

grade, Mrs. Lena Diltz.

In second grade, I had to stand in the corner for chewing gum, the worst punishment I ever got in school. I was a very good student. I'm sure I shed a few tears, even for that minor infraction.

Being so shy, I never wanted to do anything I could get in trouble for. Most of the time, other kids called me teacher's pet. I was just so shy and quiet, they didn't understand me. My mama had taught me to always be pleasant and use proper manners.

The one-room schoolhouse had a big old coal furnace in one corner. In winter, some of us would bring a potato to put on the ledge inside the stove door to bake for our lunch. Yes, we had to carry our lunch in a lunch pail. I still have my little lunch pail that I carried the whole eight years. Some of the kids who lived in the village went home for lunch.

The one-room schoolhouse had two outhouses, one for girls and one for boys—no inside plumbing the whole eight years. We got our drinking water from a well. We would pump the water into a pail to put in the old fashioned crock fountain.

One-room school with eight grades. The day started with the Lord's Prayer and the Pledge of Allegiance to the flag.

In the front of the room was the teacher's desk, facing the students. There were two long benches on each side of the center aisle called the recitation bench. Each class from each grade would come to the front and sit there, and a lesson would be presented, be it history, English, arithmetic, geography or spelling. There was a big chalkboard on the front wall, also big pull down maps to study geography.

I did not start school until I was eight years old, because I was a skinny, frail little girl. I had to walk two miles each way to school. It was not so hard going to school; it was all downhill. Coming home was a different story, all up hill and with a load of books for homework. Even though I was late starting school, my mother had taught me my numbers and alphabet, how to print my name, and write the numbers to 100.

Imagine walking two miles to school in the wintertime. Many a time it would be snowing and the wind blowing, making big snow drifts. I never missed any school because of bad weather—rain, snow or ice. I walked to school.

My parents warned me to walk in the fields so I wouldn't get covered up by a snow drift. I'd be dressed warm in snow pants, a scarf covering my face, mittens and warm boots.

My favorite teachers were Mr. Frank Birch in first grade and Mrs. Edith Houseknect in grades four through seven. In high school, Mrs. Martha Starr, who taught me typing, shorthand and bookkeeping, and Mr. James Ritter, my music teacher. I sang in the school choir.

We did not have modern conveniences on the farm. I did my homework by light from kerosene lamps. We had bare necessities in the house; no electricity and no telephone.

We had cold running water coming into the kitchen sink, from a spring, by gravity. We had a wood fired cooking range, where water was heated in a tank in the end of the stove.

Yes, Saturday night was bath time. Hot water was put in a washtub, water from that hot water tank in the stove.

Marian Arthur with her dog in 1939

There was a wood/coal heatrola in the living. Only downstairs had heat. All the bedrooms were upstairs and very cold in winter. We had flannel sheets and lots of heavy quilts to keep warm. The quilts were handmade by my mother, Edna Arthur and other family members, aunts, Aunt Martha, Aunt Mary and grandma, Bessi Swisher.

We had no bathroom; it was an outhouse. For use during the night, there was a chamber pot under the bed. Imagine going to the outhouse in the wintertime! We did that.

We did not get electricity until 1943, after the Depression and during World War II. I was ten years old then. It was many more years before we had a bathroom, and even longer before we had a telephone, not until about 1962. It was then that my family and I came home for a brief stay between jobs for my husband, and he needed phone service. My parents, Kenneth and Edna Arthur then had a phone installed. It was not a party line, however. One grandparent, Jason and Bessie Swisher had a party line much earlier. We lived several miles from it.

Even with electricity, it was some time before we could get a refrigerator. It was wartime and we were put on a waiting list. We did not have a place to keep things cold, only in a water gully in the springhouse. One grandparent had an icebox on the back porch.

Every winter, chunks of ice were cut from a neighbor's pond and put in an icehouse. The ice being put in sawdust. That ice would last till mid-summer.

We had no icebox. Everything was canned, fruits, vegetables and even meats. We butchered pigs and a beef every winter. We could keep the meats frozen for a while. Mother canned pork sausage, pork loins, and beef of all kinds. We smoked the hams. I'm sure the current generation cannot comprehend a lot of this.

Here is where I'll mention castor oil. My mother was a good cook, and very conscious of making healthy foods. One thing she made was a grated raw beet salad. I hated it. Maybe I was six or seven years old. I was made to sit at the table and I was given a choice: eat the beet salad or take a tablespoon of castor oil. You got it: I forced it down—the beet salad. Today, I like it.

Our laundry was done in the old wringer washer. It had a gasoline motor. Then, when we got electricity, Mom got a new wringer washer with an electric motor. She used that

Marian and her mother, Edna

wringer washer her entire life till about year 2000. It was then my sister-in-law did her wash. However, Mother still washed a lot of things out by hand. She lived to be 94.

We had lots of homemade clothes. Mother made all my clothes. I had no store-bought dresses till my freshman year in high school (September 1948). Even after that she made many of my dresses. Mother was a great seamstress.

For entertainment, we had a radio (powered by batteries) and a wind up portable record player. We had lots of family time. We went to church every Sunday. Mom and Dad were very active in church. Mother played piano for Sunday school and church. After church, we had family dinner at a grandparents' house. Everyone got together—maternal and paternal relatives. The children played games: tag, hide and seek, ring around the rosie and drop the hanky. In winter and rainy Sundays, the inside games were the board games, Uncle Wiggly, dominoes, Chinese checkers and Old Maid, the only card game we were allowed to play. In the summertime, there were lots of Sunday picnics, and the country churches had Saturday night ice cream festivals.

There were lots of farm chores. The cows were milked by hand. The pigs and chickens had to be fed. I liked to help gather the eggs. We had a nasty rooster that would chase me.

We went two miles to the village of Lairdsville once a week, just for a few things like sliced cold meat and American cheese. I'd be given a choice of a five cent Popsicle or a red cream soda, which I loved. We were not allowed a lot of soda. Mother made orange and lemonades. Maybe I'd be allowed to get five cents worth of penny candy. Our major shopping for staples like sugar and flour, bought in 25 pound bags, we went to the mill in Hughesville.

Living on a farm, of course, we would have an encounter with a snake occasionally. We even had blacksnakes in our dirt cellar. There were deer, bear, fox, groundhogs, skunks, squirrels and rabbits. There were porcupines and our dog would get quilled. Dad would have to pull them out. Of course, we had rats and mice. The barn cats were good at keeping those at a minimum.

I cherish all of my childhood memories. They were happy years. I've written how it was in those early years. Just a few things from those years.

No Outhouse! Boy, What a Mess!
By Shirley Rifle of Montrose, Pennsylvania
Born 1936

For several years, my parents lived in a lease house on the property where my dad worked as an oil pumper. I don't remember much about the house, because I was probably four or five when we moved to the farm.

Dad loved the oil fields; Mom loved the farm. So, after they bought the big old house and a hundred acres of land at an auction, Dad still went to his pumping job every night for several years. He farmed by days and caught catnaps when he could. He must have been exhausted.

The thing I remember was that our bathroom was a two-seater outhouse not too far from the big house.

Saturday night baths were accomplished with one kid after another climbing into the same bath water in the galvanized tub supported by two chairs.

My oldest brother, now probably sixteen, had, had enough of that outhouse and the slop pail. So, knowing that the bathroom fixtures that had been removed from my grandfather's house were sitting in the barn just waiting to be installed, he and his buddy pushed over the outhouse on Halloween night.

Well, Rome wasn't built in a day, nor was the plumbing accomplished in a day. So, we now found ourselves running out to a spot under a portion of the barn whenever the urge grabbed us during the day. At night, there was the slop pail. Needless to say, outfitting the bathroom became a priority. We became one of the first families on our country road with a real bathroom.

Now 70+, I think about those days often when I luxuriate in my claw-foot bathtub, and a trip to the bathroom at night involves only nine steps. Yep, I counted them!

Memories of Growing Up in Central Pennsylvania
By Elizabeth "Betty" Sustrik Reese of Houtzdale, Pennsylvania
Born 1938

I remember very well those Saturday nights. That was the only night in the week the stores stayed open. Main Street in our little town was crowded. People were shopping, visiting, greeting each other and exchanging well wishes and stories.

We had a "Peanut Shop" on the main street. There was a peanut roaster in front of the store. You could smell the heavenly smell of peanuts roasting for blocks and blocks away. People would buy a bag, stand out front, shell and eat those peanuts, and leave the shells on the sidewalk. No one complained, including the manager and owner. It was all part of the routine. After closing, one of the clerks would sweep up the shells...and I might add... Happily.

McCrory's Five and Dime store was where I worked. At that time, the hourly rate was about fifty cents per hour. I thought I was rich (even after income tax and social security was taken off). This was a big paycheck for a kid in high school. I was a salesclerk in the yard goods; men's, women's, children sox, oil cloth, and curtain department. When I saw a beautiful piece of material that I especially liked, I would buy a yard and a half, take it home and on my supper hour, sew up a new skirt and wear it back to work that evening. Store hours were from 9:00 in the morning until 9:00 at night. After the store closed, my friend and I would go across the street to one of two movie theatres in town.

After the show, we would go next door to the Pero, which was a soda-fountain shop. We would sit in a booth, drink Cherry Cokes, eat a bag of potato chips and play the jukebox. Then, we would walk home. We didn't need a car. We were all in walking distance (even if the distance extended for a mile or so).

Iceman, Milkman, Bread man, <u>No More</u> Street Parade
By Patricia A. Vincent of Williamsport, Pennsylvania
Born 1931

I'm glad I was born where I was—growing up in the 30s made for a perfect childhood, at least if you were lucky enough to live in a small town (So. Williamsport) and have other kids in your age group on the same block.

Hardly anyone had a car, so we were free to play in the street and alley—caddy-on-the-bounce or hide & seek or roller-skate on the sidewalks (skates strapped to your shoes).

In winter after an ice storm, we could ice-skate in the street, (yes, ice-skates also strapped to your shoes).

Speaking of ice, the main event of the week was the iceman coming up the street—some people still had iceboxes, and when the iceman carried a block of ice into the house, all the kids would swarm to the back of his wagon, scrounging for loose ice chips.

The milkman came up the street so early, you didn't always see him, but you could hear the clip-clop of the horse pulling the wagon. When the horse barn burned down, Hurr's Dairy switched to van delivery.

The bread man was vital to the street "parade". I don't remember how often, but he drove a van that opened up to display his wares.

Even the dry-cleaners picked up and delivered in those days, but the most interesting of all was the "ragman". He had an open cart and you could hear him coming from a block away, yelling, "Raw eggs, raw eggs!"

By the late 40s and early 50s, the only truck driving up and down was Charles Chips, with chips and pretzels and wonderful cookies.

Now, you can't go into an antique shop without seeing a Hurr's Dairy front porch milk box or a Charles Chips can.

I recently saw an ad for a workshop on how to make a rain barrel—"going green" is such a good idea—after all, back in the 30s and 40s almost everybody had a rain barrel. People were naturally "green". It makes me hopeful that other things "old fashioned" might soon be considered "new-fashioned".

Wilfred
By Grace L. Butler of Philipsburg,
Pennsylvania
Born 1928

"Wilfred" arrived about two months ago; he was an uninvited guest. Since we were not notified of his visit, we were completely unaware of his presence, until our attention was called to his terrible deeds. He had no compunction or conscience for his evil acts, and nothing was too debase for his character.

One day, after making some cookies, I placed the remainder of some pecans on the top shelf of my closet. I thought they would be safe there from the busy fingers of my two hungry youngsters, but I didn't know about Wilfred then. However, he was soon to make his presence known.

Sometime later I needed some pecans for my fruitcake, and to my amazement, they were gone! I immediately blamed my two children. They protested that they didn't even know the pecans had been placed in the closet in the first place. An investigation was launched immediately. We had a thief in our home! After a through probe, we discovered the culprit. Wilfred was no longer a houseguest, he was a thief. We made many unsuccessful attempts to rid our home of this nuisance, but all our efforts seemed to fail miserably.

For some time, we heard nothing from this pest, and we thought perhaps he had gone to greener pastures. Our hopes soon fell when he struck again. This time he stole a slice of bread, potatoes and beans. Wilfred was no longer a petty-theft; he was a hardened criminal, a second offender and must be destroyed. The time had come to take drastic action.

We began to try various schemes to annihilate this pest. Friends and relatives offered numerous suggestions and sure remedies, but nothing seemed to bring about the desired results. We have set several traps, which he adroitly evades. Gumdrops, cheese and bacon are just a few of the many things we have used for bait, but he doesn't even take a nibble. His escapades at night have caused loss of sleep and jittery nerves. When all was dark last night, I heard this stealthy creature sneak into the closet. I quickly turned on the light, but he had vanished completely. Wilfred had returned.

You see, Wilfred is a rat, but he's no ordinary rat. He has a character, a very bad character. He has no respect for other people's property. He's very destructive and he makes no apologies. We have decided he is quite intelligent. He seems to sense danger; he has stumped the experts. Since we never see him during the daylight hours, we have thought perhaps he accompanies me on my trip to the Pennsylvania State University every day. Could he be taking a course in trap detection? His uncanny shrewdness is incredible.

I believe that Wilfred intends to stay. Our efforts are exhausted. How can we rid our trailer of this naughty rodent? I hope we find a solution soon. If you see Wilfred, please tell him he is not welcome. Tell him to run away as fast as he can, because sooner or later we will catch that rodent.

Never Saw Bought Bread Until I left Home
By Mary Jane Baker of Roulette,
Pennsylvania
Born 1920

I was born in Austin, Pennsylvania, 2-27-1920, daughter of Lena Williams and Ward Casbeer, 4th of 12 children. Mom went to Austin hospital 15 miles by horse and sleigh on a very cold night, where I was born. I lived most of my life in Potter County.

I went to school 3 miles by horse and buggy in a one-room school at Conrad. Twenty-four children attended all eight grades. On very cold mornings, there was just a big wood stove in the corner. We were lucky. We had chemical toilets. We had a water jug and a dipper and we all drank out of the same dipper.

At noon, we all went out and played Annie-Annie over the wood shed and we also played dodge ball with a big ball. When it was nice we took our lunch and ate on the bank behind the school house

On Sundays, we went to Sunday school. In the schoolhouse, we sang and prayed. Lena and Ward were my parents and Ivy and Ernie Hunsinger were our teachers.

On Friday nights, we had prayer meetings in our homes where four or five families got together, read the Bible, sang and prayed; about the only place we ever went.

My favorite teachers were Doris Boyd from Coudersport, Pennsylvania and Edythe Goodsell from Germania, Pennsylvania.

Dad had an old Atwater-Kent radio. We listened to Amos & Andy and KDKA. It was run by battery.

Lena Casbeer (Mary Jane's mother), Jane Williams (grandmother), and Albert Williams (uncle) in 1936

Mary Jane's parents, Ward Casbeer and Lena Williams Casbeer

We had kerosene lights and sat by the table at night. Dad taught me my times-table and how to tell time. Mom was sewing, and made all of our clothes. We all went to the outhouse before we went to bed at 8 o'clock.

Six of us slept in the same room with three in a bed.

We all had a bath Saturday night in the old washtub. We carried the water ¼ of a mile and heated it on a wood stove.

We had a wonderful home life. Our grandmother lived with us. It was her home. Jane and Zebeth Williams, Grandpa and Grandma, built the house and it still stands on East Fork Road. The road use was dirt, but now it's blacktop.

We had a wringer washer. When we were old enough, we helped with the wash, cleaning and milked cows, washed dishes, churned butter, made cottage cheese and it was real good.

We all helped with the haying. We had 3 cows, 2 horses, 3 pigs, and chickens.

Dad worked on the railroad and it was a very hard job.

Grandma did most of the garden. I helped her some one day and pulled her carrots instead of weeds. She was a good grandma and she taught me carrots from weeds.

We canned loads of vegetables and had a fruit cellar across the road, under the ground. We raised all our potatoes and canned chicken, beef and pork.

In the summer, we all picked berries and canned 80 quarts of blackberries, strawberries and raspberries. We canned 100 quarts of corn every year and we never went hungry.

Mom made all her bread, 14 loaves at a time, and I never saw bought bread until I left home at 16.

I went to work at Lindy Cottages at Coudersport and saw my first movie then.

I married a neighbor boy, Arnold Wykoff, at 19 and had four children. I lost him to cancer after 25 years. I then, married Ronald Baker and lost him after 41 years. They were two very good marriages. I still live in Potter County and I am 92 years old.

Hometown Memories from the "Good Old Days"
By Warren M. Garrison of Williamsport, Pennsylvania
Born 1941

I was born on a Monday, December 15, 1941 to Warren and Violet Garrison. We lived at 508 Mulberry Street in Williamsport that is now Lycoming College property. Our phone number was 5258 that's it, just four digits back then.

We lived across the street from the Gas Company. It was loud, because now and then, the valves or whatever they were would pop off and make a lot of noise, day and night, but it's just something everyone got used to.

I can remember the railroad tracks and the many trains that came thru each day and night, because we only lived three houses up from the tracks. This is now Little League Boulevard. When the trains came through, a gate man who worked for the railroad would lower the gates so traffic would stop. We used to count the train cars as they passed, with many of them loaded with coal. I used to run errands for these men, for coffee or sandwiches and they would give me a nickel or a dime. In those days, for a kid that was a lot of money. The railroad had crossing guards at Mulberry St, Market St. and Campbell and I'm sure many more crossings in town, but these are the ones I remember.

During the flood of 1946, I can remember people going up and down the overflowing river in boats at Campbell St. and East Third St. There were underpasses at Campbell St. and also on E. Third St. that would flood many times during heavy rains, too.

I remember the Karlton and State and the Rialto theatres in town, as well as the Capitol theatre. We used to go see Roy Rogers and Trigger and Dale Evans and Gene Autry on Saturday mornings. Westerns were very popular back then. In February 1950, the city added an amusement tax of 10% to theatre tickets, which made the price of a movie ticket; go from fifteen to twenty cents.

Back then, you could buy a coke for a nickel. The Sun Gazette cost six cents and it was three cents for a lunch bar.

For a kid, you had to figure out ways to make money, because these were hard times for everyone. Besides running errands for the railroad crossing guards, I also collected pop bottles, which were glass back then, and were turned in and reused by the companies. There was no such thing as throwaway bottles. I got two cents for a small bottle and a nickel for quarts.

The milkman delivered milk to our door and put it in an insulated box that was put on the front porch. Milk bottles were glass and had to be returned to the milkman too. Bread was also delivered door to door.

I remember the Williamsport Growers Market or, commonly called the Market House. It was just off the Market St. Bridge. There, you could buy fresh fish, clams, baked clams, fruit, vegetables, delicatessen foods, fresh meats at the butcher shops, freshly baked breads, pies, cakes, and cookies. There were many other foods too, at descent prices. Just walking in the door gave you a good feeling, because you could smell all the good aromas that made people feel welcome. As a kid, it was a fun place to visit.

Grocery stores in the area were, the A&P, Churchoes, Weis Markets, and I remember Walton Meats. As I recall, his father had a stand at the Market House, and there was Fry Brother's, which was about the middle of one of the many rows we had to shop at. The new outdoor markets of today will never match the Market House of yesteryears.

I miss the Five & Ten Cent Store and Kresge's and Woolworth's. Oh, and don't forget Grant's over on W. Fourth St. I remember you could get those sugar wafers for 39 cents a pound. Glick Shoes was just up the street. The West Branch National Bank was on the corner of Fourth and Pine. It is still there, but I think it is vacant now.

Trolleys carried many people from place

to place before busses. There are still tracks that were covered in later years with brick. I especially remember the ones on Hepburn St.

In 1957, the Lycoming county Tuberculosis society had a TB Clinic in downtown. You could also take your kids to get a free Polio vaccine, which was a sugar cube with the vaccine on it. It was a red liquid, I think.

Dice Drug Company was on the corner of Mulberry and E. Third St, which was across the street from the bus terminal. Down the street from Dice's was the Coney Island and Paul's Lunch. You could get a baked hamburger that fit on a hotdog bun. They would put mustard, relish, onions and catsup on it, if you wanted.

Dickey Grugan's was a hardware store on the corner of E. Third and Market St, where you could get about anything in the hardware line that you needed. I remember how the wooden floors creaked when you walked on them from the many floods that they had seen.

I also remember a place called the Uptown Café' on W. Fourth St, Community Restaurant, Wilson's Army and Navy Store, and next door was Milo's Sub Shop. They put subs in plastic bags. They cut the middle out of the bun to make meatball subs, which meant less for the customer.

Lycoming College is in the same place and has bought up a lot of homes, including our home and expanded to include a wide range of buildings and parking lots. All the older boys back then could be crossing guards. They were there before and after school to help kids cross the street safely.

Curtain Jr. High was 7th thru 9th grades, but is now a middle school. The Williamsport Sr. High School, as we knew it then, on W. Third is now Penn College. They also had a Williamsport Tech, so that they could teach students many different trades.

The old Court House is still there on Pine St., but houses many different offices now. LL Stern's and the Carrol House, Sears and Sears Farm Store and many others are gone and only the older generations remember them.

At the place where McDonald's is, use to be Mountain Beach. They had a pool and they had bumper cars to ride. They also had wild animals in that area too.

The new Market Street Bridge was built in 1951. Since then, the bridge has been rebuilt several times. Across the river in S. Williamsport was a Hurr's Dairy Store where you could buy all kinds of cones, sundaes and banana splits, as well as milk products to take along home with you. As kids, our aunt would buy Dixie cups and take them into school on our birthdays. They were kept cold with dry ice, and there were little wooden spoons to eat the ice cream with. The Hurr's Dairy sign is still on the building

I remember Frey's Tire Shop, Carpenter's Hardware Store, Stroehmann's Bakery and Clark and Hoag Tire Shop.

Radio shows that were listened to; were Fibber Magee and Molly, My Little Margie, Amos and Andy and others I can't remember.

The Yellow Cabs were behind Stroehmann's Bakery on Washington Blvd. waiting for the next customer.

The one mayor I can remember is Leo C. Williamson. He had a big Christmas party for all the kids in town and it was held at the Capitol theatre. They showed movies and handed out small boxes of hard candy to all the kids afterwards. It was a happy time to look forward to.

Brandon Park was another place the kids spent many hours during the summer. They had crafts to make and take home with you. I remember making gimp key chains and I made a belt that lasted a long time. There were days when we made Plaster Paris things from molds, and then painted them at a later time. We also could pack a lunch one day a week and ride the bus to go swimming out to the Sportsman's Club, out Rt. 87. That was really a fun time for many kids in the area. There were many shows in the bandstand, too.

Back in those days, if you were lucky enough to have a phone, it was a party line with two or three other families on the same line. Sometimes when you picked up the phone to make a call, someone else was on the line. You could hear both parties talking and would politely hang up and hope they wouldn't tie the phone line up for long.

I'm 70 years old, and if I had the time, I could tell you lot's more stories of my younger days. It was a fun time, no one locked their doors and kids could run and play safely, because everyone watched out for everyone else and it was sure a better time then, than it is these days.

The "Good Old Days" were tough, but they were the "Good Old Days".

Us Girls Had to Help on the Farm Too
By Pearl E. Smith of Danville, Pennsylvania
Born 1940

I think to begin my memories would be to explain that being from a large family living in the country, we had to improvise for "toys". Our home was right along the road and on the other side was a bank. I had a sister 1 ½ years older than I, and also another sister 3 years older than I. We often played on the bank, and what we intended to use rocks for, I don't remember, but we were throwing them in the road and my sister, 1` ½ year older, decided she would go down and start carrying them away. The next stone I threw down, hit her right on the forehead. It immediately raised up a gooney egg and her screams brought our mother out of the house. When she seen what happened, she told whoever

Pearl Ellen, Kathryn Anne, and Mary Jayne

was guilty to come down from the bank. This wasn't the first time I disobeyed.

Being born on my brother's 4th birthday also brought me my first math lesson at the age of four. He explained to me that, him being eight and I being four; he was twice my age and that this would never happen again.

One Christmas, another disaster happened. I was the recipient this time. My sister and I had gotten new doll-baby buggies and when my aunt, uncle, and family came to visit, my cousin decided he would see how fast he could push it around the dining room table. Our table was quite large, being we had 10 children plus our parents to place around it. My cousin had a good start until he got to the corner, which had square ends. My buggy

ended up with a tear in the hood.

I also had a sister 14 years my senior. One summer during haymaking, she fell out of the haymow and broke her ankle, badly. With my mother pregnant, my aunt decided to take my sister and I to her home to relieve my mother of extra work. I soon made fast friends with my aunt's neighbor boys. I needed new shoes and was determined to have high-top shoes liked the boys. This is what I got. I think it was when we were going shopping for the same that my aunt had me ready to go, and found me out playing in sand with the boys. It required another bath, and my aunt was so "upset" she threatened to wash me, till I turned pink.

I got another brother and always said I was my parent's biggest disappointment. They wanted boys to help with farming, and I had been the third girl in a row. Of course, us girls had to help on the farm, which I'll relate later.

I was only four years old when we moved. It was only ¼ mile further up the road, but it was like a mansion. We had running water in the house and barn. At the first house, all water was carried. The pump was below the house and all water was carried up steps and all water to the barn had to be carried. No wonder Dad and Mom wanted boys!

Back to moving day: my younger brother, being a baby, was placed in the back of my uncle's panel truck in his crib and given a bottle. My mom said, with the bottle and ride to the new house, he'd be asleep. Daddy had a workshop in the basement and he backed the horse and wagon up in the yard and told us three girls to load it from his workshop. He said, "Stay away from the horses". We made fast work of throwing everything in the wagon. It was soon loaded over the sideboards. I can still see my dad jump on the wagon, and rearranging many items to the front of the wagon.

So, now we are at the new home on moving day and my grandmother is wallpapering the bedroom that was to be for my sisters and I. We had three brothers, next up the line and they started telling us girls, if Grammie didn't get finished with the wallpapering, we would have to sleep at the old house all alone. Of course, that brought us to tears and weeping, and Grammie soon set them straight. She told them and us, if the job wasn't finished, we'd stay at her house, not alone.

This Grammie was a lifesaver many times. She was an excellent seamstress and during the 2nd World War, the adults old coats were remade for us children. Every time we visited her, she had new clothes for us to try. Usually, we had matching panties to go with our dresses. Other spare material went into quilt squares for each grandchild.

I was only five, when we had to face her death from cancer, but before her death my mom had a new sister for us and Grammie was there to make dinner for silo fillers. Grammie sent me down to get potatoes from the basement. There was no inside way to the cellar and when I got to the doorway into the basement there was a large snake lying across the step. I made a fast retreat up around the house and back into the kitchen. When Grammie seen the empty pan and heard my story, she took me by the hand and we went down to get the potatoes. The snake was gone, but this was only the first of my encounters with snakes. I was happy when we built a piece on the house, and that we had inside basement steps added.

My two oldest sisters were canning corn and we were warned to get out of the kitchen when they got it out of the canner. The stair-steps went up from the kitchen and I wanted to watch after the warning of danger, so I stood in the stairway with the door open. Behind the door was a pantry, and a cool breeze was coming in the open window. One of the hot jars blew up and with the door open and me leaning out; the hot corn hit me on the neck. With my screaming, my mom was soon on the scene. I was holding the skirt of my dress up to my cheek, which only made the burn worse. I got a lesson in survival this time. Mom said

if I ever encountered such an incident again, to get my clothes off immediately.

I had often sat on the porch swing waiting for my sisters and brothers to return from school. Then, it was time for me to go on the ½-mile hike to and from the bus stop. The first and second farmland joined up over the top of the fields. The cow pasture came right over to meet the old pasture, which made it very convenient for the cattle to get water. The old farm had a very nice pond. It was also a great help during the school year, as us kids could bring the livestock home when we came from school. During the summer we got our exercise, as we had to go down to get the cattle in the evening. In the winter, we had an agreement, if we fell before we got halfway to the bus stop, we went home.

Speaking of the cattle, and as I said before, I'd say something about the girls helping on the farm. Daddy would take the boys and the combine to other farms to harvest crops. That meant that the girls had the job of milking the cows in the evening. We had a very large cow that was a favorite of mine to milk until one night when a fly bothered her, she tried to kick it off and her foot came down in the bucket. I was not big enough to hold the bucket between my knees and just propped it against my foot. Well, with the cow's foot in the bucket, the top of my foot was skinned. I told my sister I would never milk another cow, and I have not. That evening I carried all the milk out and poured it in the strainer and milk can, and my sister milked over 20 cows and ended up with blisters on her fingers.

This sister was the farmer and a true country girl. At Halloween we would not go to the neighbors unless we all had a hold on her.

In the summer we had our own baseball team and spent many Sundays up behind the barn playing ball.

In the winter we had many good places to ride our sleds. Another memory from the snow was when the bread delivery truck slid off the road. In all our excitement, I went out without my boots. I guess I didn't even tie my shoes, and when the tow-truck came, Mom made us all get on the bank. Of course, I lost a shoe in the snow and my brother found it for me. It didn't take me long to retreat to the house.

The bread delivery truck only brought bread for lunch packing. Mom made 11 loaves of bread 3 times a week. If something was prepared for mealtime that we didn't like, we were just offered homemade jelly bread.

We also had a large garden, because it was customary to can 100 quarts of each vegetable and fruit. Of course, TV dinners and such was unheard of as well as no microwave.

Boy, I sure didn't like when nature called and we had to practically disrobe in the outhouse. Like I said, my Grammie had died shortly after we had moved. I am told she wallpapered the outhouse to keep out the cold. Ours was not wallpapered.

When the gooney egg hit my sister, I don't remember getting a spanking, but Mom had one rule. If anyone came in and tattled on a brother or sister, the one that tattled got the tree branch on the backside first.

One other time when I disobeyed and wore a new spring coat to school, I got the yardstick used on me. I was afraid to come home and stayed with a neighbor till it was getting dark. I still hid in the corner of the porch. Mom said then, she only punished me, because I got cobwebs on my coat.

I also got the paddle at school once when I disobeyed and took my baton. The teacher had said not to bring it, because one year she had a student hurt seriously with one. I had my neighbor girl keep it in her room and played with it at recess, but my mom had initialed it and someone told on me. The teacher kept it till the last day of school.

A Little Daredevil, "A Fracture to My Jawbone and a Concussion"
By Nancy W. Eichenlaub of Williamsport, Pennsylvania
Born 1942

My name is Nancy Wright Eichenlaub, and I grew up at 341 Hastings Street, in South Williamsport, Pennsylvania with my parents, Charles and Edith Wright and my brother who was 5 years older than me. His name was John. We lived in my grandparent's home, Mame and George Morrison while we were in South Williamsport. When I was born, my daddy worked with the federal prison system and we lived in Praireton Indiana on the prison's land. My mother's house was my grandmother's house. Mame Middleton

Nancy's dad, Charles Wright in 1940

Morrison and her parents, Mr. and Mrs. Harry Bruce Landon Hunt, lived next door at 339 Hastings St. When my grandmother married George Morrison, they moved into the house next door to 339 Hastings St, 341 Hastings St.

When my mother married my father, Charles Gerald Wright, they lived in the Hastings St. house for a while, but my dad got a job with the prison system and then they lived in Punxsutawney when they had my brother and then were sent to Praireton, Indiana for the prison system. When I came along 4 years later, my mother came home to 341 Hastings St. to have me, and when I was old enough to travel, they took me out to Prairieton, Ind. With them and my brother and we went to school out in Prairieton. When I was two, they were transferred to Lewisburg Penitentiary and Dad and Mom moved in with my grandparents at 341 Hastings St., S. Williamsport, Pa.

My dad's brother, Leslie Wright, married Claire Huffnagle who lived at 351 Hastings St. and she was my mother's best friend since they were young children. Aunt Claire had a brother, Mac Huffnagle, who was one of the coaches and teachers at S. Williamsport, Pa. School. My cousins were, Margie, Jane and Leslie Wright who lived at 351 Hastings St. There was a little girl next door to them at 353 Hastings St, Norma Maggs, and she and Leslie and I played together every day. We had a very carefree life playing dolls and dress ups, cowboys and Indians and swimming and playing in the creek, Hoaglands Branch, which came from the Mountain Beach Lake. We were taken to Mountain Beach to play and swim when we were old enough to go and play there. It was a great place to swim and play in the sand and they used to say there were snakes in the parts of the pool area that was roped off, and we had to stay out of that area.

The creek that ran behind our Hastings St. house came from Mountain Beach and it was called Hoagland's Run. It ran between Main St. and Hastings St. My cousin Leslie's Uncle George Huffnagle was a lifeguard at Mountain Beach. My brother and his friends who lived on Hastings St. and Main St., S. Williamsport, got together and dammed up the creek behind our houses and we could swim in that creek. The creek bed was kind of dangerous though, because people dumped their ashes in the creek from their furnaces and there was glass and tin can lids and other things to get hurt on. My brother John, and his friends tied a rope to an old garage that over-hung the creek and would swing from the rope and jump into the dammed up creek. My brother's friends were Larry Stabler and John Manzitti. They played ball and went bike riding down along Sylvan Dell Road, and also played ball in the street on Hastings and Main Street.

When I was three, I had to have my tonsils removed and my father insisted that he would stay with me in the hospital all night, and he did. I was really scared, and I can remember this, and I have always felt that God gave me the ability to remember so much from my childhood because of losing my father at such a young age.

When I was three years old, my mom had a man come and knock on the door while she was upstairs cleaning and I let the man in the house and he told my mother something that made her scream and cry. I was afraid, but then the man left and I really didn't know what was happening, but when I was older, I found out that man told my mother that my daddy had died while working at Lewisburg Penitentiary.

Later on, my mom got a job teaching in Montoursville School district and I had to go to a nursery school, which was the Lycoming Day Care Center for working parents to take their children too. I was really unhappy here, because I didn't understand where my daddy was and why I had to go to this strange place with strangers and eat lunch there and take a nap there and then my mommy would come and pick me up every day and take me home.

My mom taught penmanship and Pa. History. Later in her teaching career, she started Jr. Historians at Montoursville School and had quite a few students interested in Pennsylvania history. She did some fun things with the club and made history interesting to these students and made it come to life for them. At one point in her teaching career, she got the Students interested in refurbishing an old one-room schoolhouse between Montoursville and Muncy, Pa.

Mother also directed school plays for Montoursville in the Junior-Senior classes. She really enjoyed doing this and she often took me with her, because she had no one to watch me at home. She didn't want to ask my brother to watch me, because we would just get to fighting since I didn't want him telling me what to do. She also helped direct some of the musicals they put on at school, and one was "Oklahoma" with Helen Kay Raehorn as Ado Annie. Some of her students had fathers that were doctors, teachers and businessmen and all the families were so nice and helpful and took an interest in their children.

I really had a great family surrounding me, though. My grandmother and my Aunt Clair and Uncle Leslie Wright, and their three girls, Margie, Jane and Leslie helped my mother cope with her situation. The whole neighborhood was there to help each other and watch over each other's children.

Norma Maggs and my cousin Leslie and I played all summer long, swinging in each other's back yards and climbing trees and playing hide & seek with other friends on the block, and

Nancy with her family and friends

hopscotch and racing each other and roller skating and playing with dolls. Norma and I played cowboys and Indians with the boys on the street and would let them tie us up to trees and tell them the ropes were too tight, and then walk out of them when the boys would walk away.

My cousin Leslie moved away to Lewisburg when we were about five. Norma and I were allowed to walk across the Market Street Bridge to the movies when we were about nine, and it was the old Market Bridge. We walked across the bridge to the movies on Saturday afternoons and then, would walk back across the bridge to S. Williamsport. One time we looked down at the boxcars in the railroad yard next to the bridge and there was a naked man inside the boxcar waving to us. We were so scared; we ran all the way home across the bridge to S. Williamsport. We told our mothers and they called the police.

When Norma and I were in about fourth grade we got a pack of my mother's cigarettes and smoked them in the basement of my home and would hide the cigarettes in an orange crate where we kept our dress-up clothes. The cigarettes happened to be Camels (no filters), Yuck! We stuck the stubs in the cement wall of the basement and my mother and brother found them when she was house cleaning the basement and she gave me a spanking and Norma's mom gave her a spanking.

We also use to ride our bikes down Sylvan Dell Road. We rode our bikes all over South Williamsport; stopped at the store on Hastings Street going to and from school, and played on the playground at Mountain Avenue School.

We also did a lot of roller skating and I used to skate on the curb down along the corner where the corner would turn. I was really a daredevil and luckily did not get hurt very often, except one time when I put chains around the spokes of my tricycle and the trike wouldn't go up over a little bump in the sidewalk and I tried to force it and I went flying over the handlebars. I got a fracture to my jawbone and a concussion. In those days, the doctor came to the house and then, Mom had to take me to his office to have him put stiches in my chin.

I remember when I was very young, we had a coal stove in our kitchen and they had holes in the floor upstairs for the heat from the stove to go upstairs to heat the upstairs. We also had a Heatrola stove in the middle room

Nancy at Rickett's Glen in 1951

of our downstairs.

When I was about five, I was allowed to walk to the A&P store on the corner of Market St. and Southern Avenue to get things for my mother, like coffee, cigarettes, milk and bread. We also had a Hurr's Store down Market St. near the Market St. Bridge, and we were allowed to walk down there to buy ice-cream cones.

I remember one night we heard fire alarms and found out that Hurr's Store and Creamery was on fire and there were horses in the back in the barn, and we went down to see if we could rescue them. They got some out, but some died. It was sad.

Other things I remember from those old days was the rag man coming down our street yelling rags, rags, and the women would run out and sell him their old clothes, or maybe some of them bought clothes from him. We also had an iceman come with big chunks of ice for our icebox, which was on our back porch, and it was the way people kept things cold. It was a wooden box with a door on it, and the ice went into a holding metal tray under the box and the inside walls were metal. The people kept food in there to keep it cold and not spoil. The iceman would always hack off pieces of ice for the kids in the neighborhood standing outside his wagon. The wagon was pulled by horses. Also, the milkman came and delivered milk to the neighborhood and his truck had horses pulling it too. And there was a bread man who came to the neighborhood and he sold bread and sweets like cakes and cookies.

I also remember when I was very little, before my father died. He would plow a field up on Main St. in S. Williamsport, between Central and Mountain Avenue for the neighbors to grow things for the war effort and also for themselves. I guess the land was given to the people to grow vegetables and keep them for themselves, but maybe they gave some to whoever fed the soldiers.

I always felt I was given a gift of remembering because my father died when I was so young and I have a lot of memories of him even though he died when I was three. One memory was when we went picking chestnuts from trees in a special place in the woods and I can remember him carrying me on his shoulders to go see things away from where my mommy was picking chestnuts. My brother was there too, and then he brought me back to where they were and I was on his shoulders. I looked down in the hollow at my mom and brother. I can still picture being on his shoulders.

After my father died and my mother had to go to work, she also had to hire someone to take care of my grandmother who got crippling arthritis and was unable to get around on her own. She needed someone with her just to help her to the bathroom and help her get into bed for a nap. The first lady helper we had was Mrs. Hester Meek, and she had two children, Lucille and Richard. She used to make lunch for my brother when he came home from school at Mountain Avenue Grade School. Lucille was a year older than John and Richard was about 3 years older than John. The Meeks were the nicest people you would ever meet. My grandmother died when I was in 4th grade.

I also had a cousin named Evelyn Hunt. She was the first person I knew to have a television set and I used to go over and watch the Mickey-Mouse Club. My friend Norma Maggs also had a Television and the screen was so tiny I couldn't understand why anybody would want this, and her father only watched boxing and wrestling on it, so it wasn't any fun to watch anyway.

Norma and I used to entertain ourselves with cereal boxes that had opera stories on them. We could act them out with cutouts off the cereal boxes. We used to pretend we were the actors on the soap opera story. Also, we played with cereal boxes that had cutout paper dolls on them.

Mom got the idea one summer when I was about 10, for me to hold a doll contest for all my friends to bring their dolls; all sizes,

shapes and all kinds of dress and have judges decide which doll was the pretties, biggest, smallest, and oldest, and give prizes to the girls who won. She had some of the neighbor ladies do the judging and no one knew whose doll was whose, so it would be fair. One of the girls brought a doll that was very old and won the prize for the oldest. One had the very smallest, which was a teeny-tiny doll that sat in a tiny high chair from a dollhouse, and there was the prettiest and the funniest and the best dressed and the girls got prizes for their dolls that won.

Life was really fun and exciting and wondrous back in the old days of the 40s.

First Generation Italian
By Rita Kittka of Williamsport, Pennsylvania
Born 1933

In this small town of Williamsport, Pennsylvania in the 1940s, so many great memories were created. Going to a small private school with a lot of tradition made things really great, one being the St. Patrick's Day plays, which were held each year. The whole school was enrolled, from 1st grade through 12th grade. One time, a 4th grade boy had on his knee a 4th grade girl. He sang his heart out to her. "Did your mother come from Ireland, cause there is something in you Irish." This little girl was of first generation Italian and was so proud. There was a lot of Irish songs and dancing truly a wonderful time!

The Flood
By Richard H. Allison of Ocala, Florida
Born 1935

I was born in Williamsport, Pennsylvania in 1935. My father had a grocery store behind the house that was very successful and had loyal customers. In the 1946 flood, as the water was rising in the lot behind the store my brothers and my father were busy moving the items from the lower shelves up higher to avoid the water when it came into the store. We decided that if we moved everything up five shelves that it would be high enough to avoid the rising water. We were wrong however as the water rose almost to the ceiling. We also moved what we could carry upstairs in the house, and had to live there for four or five days. The water raised about seven steps leading to the upstairs bedrooms. When the water went back down, we went downstairs and started cleaning the mess that it left.

We sold certain items to our customers from our living room until the store was repaired and cleaned. The floodwater came up to the clothesline in the backyard that ran from the porch roof to the store roof, much higher than we expected. Living in the second floor was inconvenient but we had three bedrooms and a single bathroom (toilet only). But we survived.

The Peddler Man
By Kathleen Horchen of Wilcox,
Pennsylvania
Born 1935

In all kinds of weather, rain or shine, Sammy the peddler man walked the rural roads of Elk County. He started in the 1930s, but I remember him from the 1940s and 1950s stopping by our house to sell his wares. My first memory of his visits started when I was about eight. He was near 50 then. He lived in Olean, New York, and travelled south to reach my hometown of Wilcox. He would arrive around four in the afternoon. We shared supper with him. He ate whatever was offered with a slice of bread. He enjoyed dessert after dinner, especially pies and cakes. Travelling like he did, he didn't always get treated to cooked meals. I once saw him eat raw hamburger.

My mother often let him sleep on our couch. In the morning, we would fix him an egg and toast. One time I made the toast and he gave my mother a new pair of cotton underpants for me. Sammy was a pack peddler. He carried and sold items such as tablecloths, socks, shoestrings, underpants, petticoats, brassieres, sewing needles, and thread. Most items were not breakable.

Sammy Nahara was well known and very friendly. He had emigrated from the suburbs of Beirut, Lebanon. His wife and two sons stayed overseas. He kept up his route selling well into his senior years. He did not like to have his picture taken. Even though I have no photos of Sammy, I still have many memories of his visits.

The Radio
By Elizabeth Madeira of Williamsport,
Pennsylvania
Born 1929

Ah, "the good old days", not all so "good", no air conditioning, no central heating, no television, or many other modern conveniences. But there was the radio. When it came into the home and there was only one model-table or floor-it attained a shrine like status, especially in the evenings when the family gathered around for whatever program was offered. Never before was news reported as it happened; entertainment took all forms-music, comedy, quiz shows, and contests. Remember *Major Bowes Amateur Hour*, when some unfortunate contestant failed to deliver as expected and a gong sounded ending the performance. There were also mysteries, *Only the Shadow Knows*, or the squeaking door introducing *Suspense*.

Imagination knew no bounds. What young boy could not thrill to "It's a bird! It's a plane! It's a man!" and envision himself flying off with "Superman". Or the sound of horse hoofs accompanied "Hi ho, Silver" as the *Lone Ranger* and his sidekick, "Tonto" took off for another escapade. For adults, women listened to the daytime soaps like *Stella Dallas*, *As the World Turns*, and *One Mans Family*. In the evenings, the family gathered around for the witty comedians such as Jack Benny and Rochester, Fred and Gracie Allen, and who couldn't dread with Molly when Fibber McGee opened that closet door and we heard all the contents pour out. We laughed along with the high jinks of ventriloquist Edgar Bergen and Charlie McCarthy, as well as comedian Red Skelton as Klem Kadiddilehopper. The male population sat attentive to the latest baseball games, never mind that the plays were being read off a ticker tape as received by the announcer. Boxing was an attraction to all, when Joe Louis kayoed one opponent after another.

Advertising too was memorable. One could picture Johnnie in his red suit and hat as he voiced his call for Philip Morris cigarette ad, or the sound of the plodding of the 20-mule team with their wagonload of Borax soap powder. Washdays were promised sparkling results "Rinso Bright, Rinso White, happy little washday might." Serious moments occurred when news commentators such as

H.V. Kaltenborne announced, "Ah, there's good or bad news tonight." The fireside chats of President Franklin Roosevelt attempted to give hope to the nation when he stated, "The only thing we have to fear is fear itself." Of course, today the radio has evolved into many different forms, but it still retains some of the magic of yesterday and recollections of the good old days.

The Animals of the Farm
By Sylvia Daniels of Williamsport,
Pennsylvania
Born 1927

A farmhouse seemed the best option for my parents during the depression years to move with their four children. Daddy was born in town and left school to work in a wood-planeing mill. When World War I came, he enlisted in the Army and fought in France and Germany. Upon returning home, he again worked in the planeing mill until he lost his job and his new house. Mother was raised on a farm and had some experience with country living. The move was very difficult for my parents, but to a five year old, it was a new adventure. One day my seven-year-old brother introduced me to a cow pie and persuaded me to step in it with my bare feet! Ugh! Mother was furious with my brother.

As time went on, we attended a one-room school. It had two outhouses, one on each side to separate the girls from the boys. To get to school, we walked more than a mile up hill, through cornfields, mud, barbed wire fences, small streams, and snow sometimes nearby knee deep. It was scary to get caught in the rain or a thunderstorm. Besides our schooling, we learned how baby chicks hatch, how cows are milked, grain harvested and threshed, corn shucked, and a lot more country experiences. Our chores included feeding cows, horses, pigs, chickens, turkeys, ducks, rabbits, and any others we had. My brother had rabbits a few years and I had to help care for them. I really hated to clean out those rabbit pens!

There was a duck pond where we went wading on some especially hot days. Later on, we found some frogspawn at the pond's edge. The following days and weeks, we watched the eggs hatch into tadpoles and then develop into frogs. A very protective and trusting pet dog lived with us. He was a German shepherd mix and our best buddy. Mother worked hard for her family. Since there was no electricity or plumbing, she used a hand churn to make butter and a hand crank washer and washboard. She baked all of the bread and cooked and canned all of our food. Water was carried in buckets from a spring about 100 feet away from the house. It was heated on top of the old iron stove, which also warmed the house. Saturday was bath time in an old wooden tub. The outhouse was very scary after dark so we carried a lantern to go and come back. It was so frigid during cold weather.

Without any radio or television, we made our own entertainment including checkers and card games, especially Pinochle and Rummy. In the summer, we played outside with clay and built playhouses under three pine trees and also in a brush row. We built chairs and tables with large flat stones and arranged them to our liking. A few days we took sandwiches and ate lunch there. After my sister and I graduated from the one-room school, we entered high school in the city. I was always very reluctant to talk about the country to avoid some criticism but they are many of my most treasured memories.

Mama's Chicken Stew
By Jennie Knorr of Millheim, Pennsylvania
Born 1945

I was too young to remember the days after the war, or even which war—may have been a combination of World War II and the Korean War that drove the solitary wanderers to walk the US highways. All I'm sure of is it was the summer of 1953, Eisenhower, better known to us as "Ike", was President and our nation was on the upswing. I recall images of hobos, tired, dusty, and hungry men who stopped by our Nittany, Pennsylvania farmhouse in hopes of finding a meal. They usually sat alone next to the Sears Kenmore wringer-washer on our wrap-around porch with the aroma of chicken stew filling the air.

I can still feel the warmth of the summer sun, hear the buzzing sound of the cicada, and smell the aromas from the old coal-burning cook stove in my Mama's kitchen. Every time I smell chicken soup, I see my young mother, dressed in her faded blue cotton dress and floral apron, stirring the contents of a mouthwatering chicken stew—chicken, potatoes, carrots, peas, and corn, aromatically simmering in the rich broth. Standing in front of the old stove stirring the stew, flames licking the sides of the pot, Mama added whatever vegetables were ready for picking from her side garden—a garden as large as a football field—the chicken hand-raised and slaughtered by Mama.

The weary wayfarer sat on the steps of the front porch, sipping a tall glass of ice water through sun-parched lips. His clothes were tattered; his shoes were dusty and worn. Beside him lay a small cloth bag holding all of his worldly possessions. He stared out across the cornfield as he related his experiences in the war. He told us his heart was heavy, burdened by the loss of his best buddy during his last battle—in which country I don't remember. He had shed no tears since it happened, six long months and hundreds of miles ago. Plodding onward with blistered and battered feet, he barely noticed the beauty of the country he had traversed while the vision of the battlefield played over and over inside his head.

As Mama continued to stir the stewpot, she thought about the story the traveler had just revealed. She had never gone farther than Colorado where she had attended the University. Her knowledge of the world was from reading books and she read a lot. She must have tried hard to imagine what it had been like for the stranger sitting alone on the porch. Mama was sheltered by the beauty and peacefulness of Nittany Valley.

Mama ladled steaming stew into a large bowl and carried it out to the man. She always added a chunk of her homemade bread and butter to go along with the meal. She left the man to dine alone while she went back inside and said a silent prayer for his soul. After he finished eating he thanked Mama and continued off to who knew where-not even he knew.

Dad referred to these wanderers as "shell-shocked", although they weren't all as pitiful as that one. There were at least 10 hobos who stopped by the farm during that summer for a taste of Mama's home cooking. They would offer to do a chore in payment for the food. Many of them played a musical instrument and would entertain us while they waited on the porch. Some told us about riding in boxcars on trains and of their plans to make it to California where they hoped to find work. We weren't suspicious or afraid during the hobos visit—in fact; we welcomed them and secretly envied their freedom.

Principal Dad
By Karen Dietrich of North Huntingdon, Pennsylvania
Born 1944

I was sitting at my desk in homeroom looking out the window. The late bell hadn't rung yet and I was wondering if the boy running up the lane would make it on time. He did this every day. I thought and hoped he would be late just this one time. His name would be announced to go to the office. I was in complete shock when the principal called my name instead. Everyone looked at me and I was very embarrassed. The teacher told me to go and I did. Very slowly, I went not knowing what to expect. I kept thinking about what I could have done wrong to get me in trouble. The hallway to the office seemed very long.

I walked into the office and the staff all looked at me and quickly went back to work. The secretary told me to go into the principal's office that he was waiting for me. I went in and he told me to sit down. He said, "Now young lady, I understand you forgot something today." I thought for a few seconds and could not think of anything. He then handed me an

Karen's graduation in 1962 with her father, I. B. Nolan

283

envelope with my name on it. I looked inside and it had my lunch money in it. I said, "Oh! Thanks dad!"

The principal was my dad. Sometimes he would stand in the hallway when we were changing classes if I would see him. I would never know to say hello as to a principal or "Hi dad!" As I would get closer, he would give me a big wink. I loved those winks so I always said, "Hi dad!" Many teachers, students, and classmates would tell me years later they remember my dad for his sayings. The one they all remember was the one he always ended our assemblies in the auditorium with. He would always leave us with "You're the best in the county, the state, and the nation." This was the motto most remembered by everyone many years later.

I. B. Nolan
The Principal of BEN

The Country Store
By Eleanor M. Taylor of Allenwood,
Pennsylvania
Born 1929

I was 10 years old when World War II started there was five kids, two boys and three girls in our family. Our home was adjacent to a country store. My dad and mother owned and operated this store for 40 some years. My dad was also the postmaster for the village of Elimsport in Lycoming County until it was closed in the early 1950s. The government closed many fourth class post offices at

this time. Our addresses were changed to Allenwood, Pennsylvania. We were assigned road names and a zip code later.

The post office was confined to a back corner of the store. We were taught as children this was "Uncle Sam's" property. We were never allowed to play there or disturb anything associated with the postal service. I was always afraid Uncle Sam would arrive to check out his office anytime, so it was demanded to stay out of that area. Our parents always had a hired helper to clerk in the store and was sworn in and bonded to work in the post office also.

I can recall some unique things of our store during the war days. During this time, a lot of items were handled in bulk quantities. In order to resell those items they were bagged, weighed, and priced. There were different sizes of bins under the counter. Items such as sugar, dried beans, rice, tea, coffee, spaghetti, and macaroni were stored there. These had to be scooped out, put in paper bags, weighed and tied by string. This is before scotch tape was invented. The string was hanging from the ceiling on a spool. It had to be cut the size needed. The scales that were used were large, gold in color, and very attractive with numbers easy to read.

Rationing was started at this time. Everyone was given a ration book. After Japan bombed Hawaii, pineapple and sugar became very difficult to get. The ration book was used for gas, groceries, and shoes. These are some that I can recall. Our shoes never lasted as long as they did before the war. The soles seemed to be made of paper instead of leather. Newborns were given ration books. We girls were so thrilled when our baby brother was born in 1943. We could use his stamps for shoes, as he didn't need any until he started to walk. You could buy almost anything at our country store. Some of the items were men's shoes, boots, shells, batteries, pencils, writing tablets, yarn, thread, needles, first aid supplies, cereal, bread, milk, cigars, cigarettes, gas, kerosene, and fresh fruit in season and even farm machinery parts.

Our store was open from 6:00 a.m. to 10:00 p.m. or later, six days a week. War was a scary time for us kids. When the alerts were sounded and sirens blared, we'd get our dog and get under the kitchen table. Having the only siren in the valley, dad would get the call from the authorities to turn on the siren.

We never knew if it was just a test or that we were going to be attacked. We lived just three miles from the Susquehanna Ordnance that is where they stored TNT for the war. We were sure Japan would bomb us. This is before television was invented. To get any news, it had to come by radio or newspapers.

Another thing I remember about our store is that dad would give credit to people who didn't have food or money. This is before food stamps or welfare checks. Dad had enough faith that most people would pay when they got the money. A few moved from the area or died before paying their debt. Rearing five kids was no easy chore with living quarters next to a store. The candy, ice cream, soft drinks, and other goodies were at our fingertips as we passed through the store to go to school or out to play. We all survived, some over 80 years. We loved every minute.

Listen to the Call
By Jean Lent of Coudersport, Pennsylvania
Born 1930

It has been a long and spiraling road that brought jean Lent to Coudersport, Potter County, Pennsylvania. Jean lived in Tulsa, Oklahoma for her first seven years. By 1938, her parents had parted ways and her grandparents decided to take their family to California, as so many did during those difficult dust bowl years. Her grandfather had an old Ford car, Jean remembers, and he built a wooden trailer to hook on behind it. The trip took them, she says, through some very lonely and difficult country. At night, the kids slept in that wooden trailer and the adults slept on the ground. Her grandfather, a carpenter by trade, soon found work once in California.

About the time that Jean turned 16, her mother, a very religious woman, felt a call to go back east to do mission work. She left Jean with a cousin, who was red-haired and had the temper to go with it. That situation did not work out and Jean climbed out a window one night and called an aunt for help. The aunt financed Jean's trip east to find her mother. All of this time, Jean was rebelling against her mother's beliefs, but began to feel "under conviction". While waiting at a ticket window

in Grand Central Station in New York City, Jean heard her name excitedly called and there was her mother!

In time, Jean entered the Zion Bible School, in Providence, Rhode Island. After three years there, she went to Long Island to do mission work. There she met her husband to be, Al Lent. Over the years, the couple became the parents of four children, three girls and a boy.

As the children grew up, the Lents realized that the bad influences of the city were not good for the girls. So, they determined to move and decided to make their home in Coudersport since they had been friends with the Reverend David Minor and his family for years. Jean had met the Minors while attending the Zion Bible School and knew them well when they had a church on Long Island. The move took place in 1969. In Potter County, Mr. Lent found work with Pure Carbon.

In the meantime, Jean's mother had felt a call to go to Europe and spent several years in mission work there. In 1974, Jean received a phone call telling her that her mother was very ill, quite possibly near death, and needed her daughter. Pastor Minor helped Jean get a passport; her sister bought her ticket and Jean traveled to Germany to see her mother. In time her mother recovered, and took the opportunity to take Jean to Switzerland and Israel. "I fell in love with Israel", Jean says.

Now it was time for Jean to feel the call. She made several trips back to Israel doing mission work. She could only spend three months on her visa, but as many apparently did, she sometimes made a trip to Cyprus, spent a week or two, and then could go back to Israel for another three months. She took classes in Hebrew and Arabic and also volunteered to help in a home for mentally challenged and disabled people. She made the trip to Israel about every two years.

The children were grown. Now on her own, Jean lived many places, in Tucson, Arizona, back in California and finally with her daughter in Chicago. However, since various health problems were plaguing Jean by this time, her daughter did not feel that her mother should be on her own.

Then one night, it occurred to Jean's daughter that maybe her mother would like to go back to Coudersport and live in Sweden Valley Manor, where several old friends would be nearby. Jean thought about it for a couple of days, she says, and then agreed that even though there were some very painful memories associated with Potter County, she would like to go back.

Jean has been residing at Sweden Valley Manor for eight months now, and is very content. There are family members in the area who visit her from time to time and several old friends come to visit her. "My life has made a big circle," Jean said with a smile.

Mama (Jean's mother) and Jean around 1995

Everyday Life
By Jane S. Naugle of Montoursville, Pennsylvania
Born 1930

During the Korean War, my husband and I got married. While on our honeymoon, his draft notice arrived at his parent's house, so his brother took our marriage license to the draft board and they were not taking married men. That was 61 years ago. My mom used a wringer-washer for many years. She also hung the wash outside until it was too cold and her fingers would crack and bleed. When she was unable to go outside, she would carry baskets full of wet clothes three flights of stairs from the basement to the attic. The clothes would still freeze on the line. What a day it was when the automatic washer and dryer arrived at our house.

A friend of mine would get on the city bus about a mile from me and I would get on in front of my house. We would then ride to Williamsport. It would cost $0.15 one-way and $0.50 for the movie. After the movie, we would wander into the stores to see what was new. Then we would have an ice cream "sundie" or a coke, get on the bus and head home.

Being born in 1930, I was too young to know a lot. We were very conservative. Parents did not dwell on it. As children, I heard some people lost their homes, but did not know what it meant. Men sold door-to-door bread that their wives baked. In the warmer months, men would knock on our outside kitchen door and ask for something to eat. My mom would always give them a good home cooked meal and coffee. This would happen about once a month. She thought our house was marked. I didn't tell before that we lived in the only funeral in town, which would have stuck out like a sore thumb.

We had an icebox until World War II broke out. Every time the iceman came, my mother would lay newspapers on the floor so we had no drips on the clean kitchen floor. We would put a sign in a front window for a nickel, a dime, or a quarter a piece of ice the iceman would bring into the kitchen. If we kids would stand by his truck on a hot day, he would chip off a small piece of ice for us to suck on. My father, shortly after the war started, went to our local hardware store to buy an electric refrigerator. They had a small one left, so my dad bought it. The only place we had for it was in the dining room. A little unhandy, but that was the end of appliances till the end of the war.

The milkman came every morning, except Sundays, very early. If it was very cold weather, we had to bring it in before it froze. If we didn't, the bottle broke and glass and chunks of milk were on the porch floor. The paperboy would put the paper on the front porch every evening and would collect once a month.

The school was built in 1905. My mother and father both graduated on the third floor from high school. The third floor was the high school, the second floor was the 4th, 5th, and 6th grades, and the first floor was for the 1st, 2nd, and 3rd grades. The basement had restrooms (left side for the boys and right side for the girls), plus a huge coal furnace. The janitor went to school at 4:30 in the morning to get the fire ready for school. We had fire escapes on both sides of the building and twice a year we would have a practice. The principal was tough. The boys that didn't behave, he would grab them by the back of the neck and take them from the third floor to the second floor, where his office was and their feet never touched the steps. In 1930, a high school was built two blocks away.

Kids missed a lot of school because of measles, mumps, chicken pox, and scarlet fever. A man would put signs on your house so no one would come inside, it could be 10 to 15 days. Boys wore knickers, long cotton underwear in the winter. Girls wore cotton dresses, long tan stockings that pinned to their cotton underwear. School started at 8:45 in the morning, lunch was at noon and at 3:45 we walked home. Country kids carried their lunch to school and there were no buses.

We used outhouses at Girl Scout camps. I did not like them. I visited a friend's old farmhouse and used a chamber pot. It was not easy to do. My great aunt and friend were Chamber Maids in the summer time at a fancy summer hotel that well to do people form the Philadelphia area came by rail to visit. Guess what they did?

My grandfather listened to *The Lone Ranger*. My aunt listened to soap operas such as, *As the World Turns* and I listened to the *Hit Parade* with Frank Sinatra on Saturday nights. My youngest brother and girlfriend drove drag cars until his best friend forgot to put oil in the engine and that ended drag racing. My dad owned a Packard Clipper, which we could drive to run errands. After I graduated and worked one year my dad allowed me to drive his Packard Convertible and take three girlfriends to Cape Cod for a week.

We called them Victrolas. There was one in our attic, which my brothers and friends would wind it and put on some records and listen to crazy music and laugh our heads off. Wish I had them now. During World War II, I had two cousins, one in England heard lots of bombings the other was in Africa and went up through Italy. Quite rough.

We had peddlers walking in the street pulling wooden carts with big wheels once a month in the spring and summer. One man would yell Huckleberries and another would call out rags. People tried every way to make money. We even had a fish man come by every Thursday.

At school, kids played baseball, but girls and boys separated. Boys played marbles, and wore out pant knees and had very dirty fingers. Girls jumped rope and played boys chase the girls and girls chase the boys. Where my home was located we had lots of room to play many things. The town park was right beside us. We played Capture the Flag, lots of baseball, and basketball. We roller-skated all over town, wore skates that fit on our shoes and we all had a skate key to keep our skates tight on our shoes. Most of us had access to a bike. We would ride out in country go to the grocery store for our mothers. In the winter we went ice-skating anywhere there was ice. There was a large ice pond five miles away and during World War II, the owner would pick us at the west end of town with his two horses and a wagon and we would all pile in. After a couple of hours he would bring us back and we would walk home. We have an active creek on the west side of town and many kids would swim in it from the first warm days to when school started in the fall. I did once in a while, of but that was not my "cup of tea".

My father's parents moved to Montoursville from a small town about 30 miles south of our town. My great grandfather was a funeral director in New Berlin, so my grandfather decided to leave and be on his own. There were lots of furniture factories in the area and he was a wood turner. This gave him a job to hold him and his family together between funerals. As time went by he was able to buy a bigger home to have funerals in. At this time most funerals were held in the family's home. As more time went by my father was born, went to local school, embalming school, married, and had four children. So more time went by and they put more additions on to the house, which gave our grandparents an apartment. Then we needed more space for our family so we had our kitchen and dining room on the first floor and our living room and bedrooms on the second floor. The rest of the house was the funeral home. We had tons of driveways and the town park was beside us and tons of kids used to play with us between funerals, we were lucky kids. It took lots of hard work, sacrifice, and foresight to do what they accomplished. My grandparents died in the 40s and 50s. My parents died in the 80s and 90s. My oldest brother took over the business and now his son has it.

287

Have You No Respect?
By Linda J. Brungard of Mill Hall,
Pennsylvania
Born 1948

I am the daughter of Joseph and LoveLean (Weaver) Falls. I have four brothers and three sisters. I had a happy childhood. Being from a large family, we learned how to share and love. We were poor but we always had enough to eat, warm clothes, and a warm home. Our home wasn't fancy, but it was always clean and comfortable. My mother used to say, "It's no sin to be poor, but it is a sin to be dirty."

I grew up in the Marsh Creek area in a little place called Polecat Hallow. We had three bicycles for eight children. One day it was my turn to go for a ride on the gravel road in front of our home. I was so excited so I started pedaling past my Uncle Boyd and Aunt Betty Falls house and a chicken ran across the road. The front wheel of the bike hit the chicken and I went flying head first out over the handlebars and skidded down the gravel road on my stomach. The darn chicken was fine, but I wasn't. I wore gauze from my armpits to my waist. My mother picked stones out of me for weeks.

My father worked at Cerro Metal Products (formerly Titan Metal) in Bellefonte, Pennsylvania. He also cut paper wood to supplement the income to raise a large family. My mother was a "stay at home mom". She

Linda (Falls) Brungard 2 years old

Lovelean (Weaver) Falls holding Steve Falls (the youngest of 8 children) beside her is Linda (Falls) Brungard 1950

and the kids helped peel the bark off the logs. If we got a truckload done, Balser Weber of Howard, Pennsylvania, picked it up. Then we could go to a festival in Blanchard, Beech Creek, or Howard on Saturday night. Each child got a dollar for the festival. Hot dogs were a dime, hamburgers were $0.15, and a bottle of soda was a dime.

We planted a big garden and we canned our own fruits and vegetables. Every spring we bought 50 chickens, 25 turkeys, a beef cow, and four pigs. In the fall, all the animals were butchered and put in the freezer for the family to eat through the winter. The butchering of the pigs was always on Thanksgiving Day because no one had to work that day. The big meal consisted of fresh pork tenderloins, spare ribs, and all the trimmings. It was a hard job, but also a lot of fun. Uncle Harold and Aunt Maria Weaver and their family came to help. Also, Uncle Earl and Aunt Betty Thompson and their family helped. Homemade pies and cakes were the desserts for the meal. Dill pickles were a must according to my mother, "Dill pickles help cut the grease from the pork."

Christmas was a very special time for a family of eight children. It was the only time we got fresh fruit. Mom and the children would sit and cut up fruit for fresh fruit salad. She made a five-gallon crock full and it was so delicious. Each child got five gifts. One year I got socks, a doll, new pajamas, and coloring books. My mother went seven years without a new dress, so that dad and us children would look presentable when we went to school and work.

Before I started school the huckster, the ice cream man, the bread man, and the

288

milkman came. Dick Wolf on Howard was the huckster. He had a school bus with shelves. On the shelves were canned goods. In the front were apples and oranges. We usually didn't buy much because we canned and froze a lot of food. The milkman was Doc Shady from Blanchard, Pennsylvania and the bread man was Kelsey Lomison from Orviston, Pennsylvania.

There was no kindergarten then, so I started to Blanchard Elementary School and later attended Lock Haven High where I graduated in 1966. My favorite grade school teachers were Mildred Kerstetter and Marion Hottel. Our family carried cheese whiz sandwiches and homemade cookies in our lunch. Cheese whiz was $0.79 a jar. One year over Christmas vacation, I left my cheese whiz sandwich in my desk. When we came back, a darn mouse had built a nest in my desk. I had to clean out the nest and the mouse droppings. Yuck!

When I was in 3rd grade, I received my first Bible. A group of people came into our class. If you could learn John 3:16, you got a Bible. Each day was started with the Pledge of Allegiance and the Lord's Prayer. Marion Hottel taught grades five and six. She would stand in front of the class and shake her fist and say, "We have got to beat the Russians!" We had penmanship once a week. At the end of the year, I received an award from the William Peterson Company for nice penmanship. Not too bad for a left-handed person.

There were no such things as "snow days". If the bus came, you went to school and if it didn't you stayed home. In junior high we got on the bus in the dark and we arrived back home in the dark in the winter. My strongest memory of high school was when I was in 10th grade, in bookkeeping class. J. Arlington Painter was the teacher. The news came across the intercom that John. F. Kennedy had been killed. A couple of students in the back of the room were laughing and behaving badly. Mr. Painter took off his glasses, wiped the tears away and said, "Have you no respect? Our president is dead!" This was the first time I saw a man cry.

I always enjoyed listening to my mother talk about her childhood. When she was nine years old, she stood on a chair and learned how to make bread. She carried bacon grease on homemade bread to school for lunch.

On Mondays mom used a wringer washer to do laundry. I was terrified because my parents knew a woman who got her breast caught in the wringer. I didn't have any breasts yet, but I wasn't taking any chances. On Tuesdays mom ironed. On Wednesdays, she baked bread and cookies. On Thursdays, she did laundry and on Friday, she ironed. There was always a hot meal prepared when we got home. On Saturday, the four girls did the cleaning and mom would bake as many as 15 pies. Aunts and uncles and cousins would come to visit and by Monday morning the pies were gone and it was time to start all over again. My mother was 14 years old when she married my father. They had eight children in 10 years. My parents were married for 35 years until my dad died. Who says "young marriages" don't work? They taught me that, "Anything in life is what you make it".

Mr. and Mr. Joe Falls

Berry Picking
By Wanita Lane of Turtle Point,
Pennsylvania
Born 1931

I was born October 2, 1931 on 2nd Street in Coudersport, Pennsylvania. My mother had moved from Johnstown after being divorced from her first husband, James Miller. I had two sisters. After moving into the house, mother took in boarders and did washing and ironing to support our family.

We lived near a junkyard. It was prohibition times and mother made the best home brew.

She met my father there because he worked at the junkyard. Because of the coming war in Europe, junk was paying good prices. When they got married, they moved to a farm east of Coudersport on Ayers Hill. My grandparents owned a farm not far from them.

Everyone liked my mother. She loved to sing and dance. After marrying my father, they started having parties on Saturday nights. Mom invited all the right people and it became a favorite place. I loved the parties. I would sing at the parties. My father was very jealous of all the attention my mother received, so it wasn't long before she packed us girls up and moved a couple of miles away to a house her brother owned. I was two and a half years old. Mom was married to my father for seven years.

My stepfather entered our lives after becoming involved with my father at the junkyard. He had returned from being in prison down near Pittsburgh. He had returned

Wanita's step-dad, Roy Palmatier

to Potter County after serving three years for taking a piece of junk from a farmer's land that had been there for years. The farmer had seen him and had him arrested.

When he returned from prison, he discovered his wife had divorced him and married someone else. He discovered his children were gone, his two young sons had died from pneumonia and his three older daughters had a new father. Having no place to live, he moved in with his parents and being able to resume his job picking up junk. When he started dating our mom, he moved in with

us. We moved to Olean, New York. Junk had become even more lucrative because Japan was purchasing it to turn into war articles such as tanks and machine guns. Stepfather had no idea why junk prices had risen so much.

I recall going with him during the day and helping to pick up junk that had been thrown away. Because my mother worked at a diner as a cook, he had to take me with him. Emporium was a good place to look for junk because of the amount of railroad iron being abandoned. I remember a gas station below Emporium, I believe a place called Rich Valley, and he would treat us to a bottle of pop and a candy bar. Mother had always packed us a lunch. That summer was very hot. While Roy was picking up junk, I would take a nap in the truck. Because the rattlesnakes lived in that area, I couldn't just nap under a tree. That fall Roy got a job hauling logs. We had moved from Olean to a small place called Gardeau. My older sister went to high school in Emporium. Being no bus transportation available, she rode with a neighbor who left for work in Emporium at 5:00 a.m. I started 1st grade that year at Keating Summit. My sister Rose went there also and we rode the bus. Rose was in 6th grade.

My stepfather had a wood job on the hill in the back of our house. A creek ran behind the camp and to get to the wood job he had to cross a bridge with a gate. We along with the neighbor kids would watch for the trucks coming off the hill and rush to open the bridge gate and close it after the trucks went through. The lucky kids would always get a dime for being helpful. A filling station with a small store was available where the dime went.

The Friday before Easter in 1938, our camp burnt down. We lost everything. Mother was lighting the wood in the big old iron cook stove, the kerosene she added turned out to be white gas they had given Roy the day before in Emporium. I was dressing for school in the room next to the kitchen. I walked to the door and when the stove exploded, I turned and ran out the front door and across the road to the neighbor. Dad was getting dressed and ran out to move his wood truck parked next to the kitchen. Mom had gone to the water pump outside the kitchen door, but had to run to the creek to get water to prime the pump. I watched the camp go up in flames. It had been a woodcutter's camp so it didn't take long to disappear. After the embers cooled, we

Wanita in the 12th grade

walked around the ashes. I found my marbles. Marbles was a great game back in those days. They were melted together and misshaped.

A lady who had the store about a mile from the house let us move into it because it no longer was being used as a store. I couldn't attend school for the next six weeks until mom's brother brought us clothes. They had brought each of us an outfit, which had to be washed and ironed each night so we had something to wear the next day.

When school was out, my stepdad outfitted his log truck so we could live in it and headed west looking for work. He could pick up a day or two of work at farmers and garages working as a mechanic. The Salvation Army always would help us. One place we stopped they gave us money and a pair of sidewalk roller skates for me. Work was supposed to be plentiful in the west. I don't know how far they had planned on going. My sisters Louise and Rose stayed in Erie.

In Nebraska, a hailstorm met us just after we had crossed the line. That night we stopped at a school and they decided to return to Pennsylvania the next day. A fireplace outside the school was where we cooked our supper. When we arrived back in Pennsylvania no house was available. While at Wilson's Fruit Market in Portville, New York, Mr. Wilson told us about the huge blueberries and how they were plentiful on the Armenia Mountains near a camping area. He told Roy he would buy all we could pick. We camped there for six weeks. We picked berries and sold some in the nearby town. The last 1,600 quarts my family picked went back to Wilson's Fruit

Market. I was given a small tin cup to pick with and was told to add mine to my sister's buckets. I wasn't very helpful to them because they tasted so good, I would eat them. Mother would put me down for a nap while the rest of the family worked. My sister had to keep an eye on me while they picked.

Coming back to the Portville with Mr. Wilson's blueberries was a lasting memory for me. While in the town near the blueberries, Roy had bought a car that had been in the flood earlier that year. He had worked for the garage to earn the money to pay for the car and got it running. My mother drove the truck back to Portville and Roy drove the car in case it would break down. Roy's brother Leonard had been with us. After delivering the berries to Mr. Wilson's Roy and mom took me to their favorite bar on a back street in Portville called Ethel's. They had some money and had to celebrate. My sister had stayed with Roy's mom and dad in Betula when we returned from picking.

Wanita Lane

Hunting at Seven Years Old
By James Coulson Laws of Phillipsburg,
Pennsylvania
Born 1918

My name is Jim Laws, James Coulson Laws. I was born December 25, 1918 in Phillipsburg, Pennsylvania to Laura Schiele Laws and James Marshall Laws. I had one sister, Myrtle, two years younger. The part of Phillipsburg I grew up in was known as "Slabtown" because of the way the houses were sided, mostly out of "slab" wood.

My father, James Marshall was a "market hunter". But as I remember it, he supported our family, mostly by odd jobs he and his brother-in-law, William C. Schiele could get working for the borough and he hunted, mostly small game (grouse, squirrels, and rabbits) because the deer were pretty much gone from Pennsylvania by the early 1900s. We actually have a newspaper article with the headline that reads, "Local hunter sees deer track just outside of town." My father Marshall was born in Wales and immigrated to this country with his brothers and a cousin to mine coal in the late 1800s. However, Marshall but soon found that he could make more money selling his game harvests to local families to supplement his income and soon was Market hunting. Marshall hunted with a Damascus steel side-by-side hammer gun that is still a cherished possession in the family gun cabinet.

I spent all of my early life in Phillipsburg. In the 1920s, most of the roads around our mountain top town were of the corduroy type, paved by laying logs over the road bedside by side, which made for a very bumpy ride, especially in our first car, a 1923 Ford Model A. So people walked, a lot, and most of the town was served by trolley by the mid-20s. For most of the winter, which was generally pretty harsh, what local roads existed would be impassable after the first deep snow and hard freeze. The winters were cold, much colder than now. By mid-January the dam was generally frozen over and it was a source of ice for the local icehouse, run by the Mays family until the late 1950s they would cut blocks of ice for the lake and store them in the insulated icehouse for delivery as far into summer as they would last, first by wagon, then by truck to homes equipped with ice chest refrigerators. Often the kids could talk the deliveryman into chipping of a hand-sized chunk of ice as he made his five to 10 cent per block deliveries down the side streets of "slabtown" on summer mornings or evenings. Midday deliveries were unusual because the ice melted too fast even though it was covered with sawdust to help keep it solid.

My dad and I fished mostly the mountain streams around Phillipsburg. Six Mile Run and Black Moshannon were all day trips; the old stage route over the Rattlesnake Mountain was rarely passable much before May. We would walk to Cold Stream and Black Bear Creeks on half-day excursions and the Big Fill and Flat Rock creeks were also frequented. Most of the fishing then was with bait, but my dad was a very good wet-fly fisherman and taught me a lot about the ways of the Brook trout that inhabited the local creeks. Stocked fish were pretty much unheard of on these mountain streams until after the war, but once you got away from the roads a mile or so, there was usually no competition for fishing space. The CCC camp along Six Mile Run opened up the Wolf Rocks section of that stream in the early 1930s under the leadership of Captain McMullan. I never knew him, but his name would be significant, as my son and his would become best friends in the early 50s and remain so to this day. The Black Moshannon forests had mostly been harvested for their Hemlock and Oaks by then and the CCC boys spent a lot of time replanting the forests of the region. This made for pretty good grouse habitat across most of the area and my dad got very good at shooting a brace or two or three, which he sold a quarter a brace he fed us and many of the neighbors almost every time he walked a covert. Thus began my love of the outdoors.

I hunted and fished with my dad almost as soon as I could follow along. I got to carry a game bag by the time I was seven and was allowed to shoot my first squirrel about that time. Usually I was pretty tired by the end of the day, but only once did I let dad and his friends know. I wasn't invited along the day after I told them I was plumb tuckered at the end of a day's hunt. I learned quickly that nope was the right answer when asked if I was tuckered. I didn't make that mistake again. The bird hunting would diminish as the forests matured. It would all change again as the strip mining of the 50s and 60s laid waste to the hillside coverts around town. It would gradually get better again into the early 80s, but I had no idea what was happening at the time, most of that perspective is in retrospect.

I graduated from Phillipsburg High School in 1935, having skipped the 5th grade. The high school was on 9th street then and that building would eventually become the elementary school my kids would attend in the 50s, which are now closed but still standing. Even back then, 16 was a tough age to be looking for work. There were still lots of "old folks" out of work as the depression had hit the coal mining towns hard in the 30s.

My first job after graduation was in Stewart's Bakery where I stoked the ovens at 4:00 a.m. along with my good friend Joe

Fitzgibbon to get them ready for the days baking. It wasn't a hard job, and at 25 cents an hour, it kept me in gas money for the Model A we had. I could use it when dad didn't need it, which wasn't often. I worked at each of the three bakeries in town, stoking ovens and learning a bit about baking. When I turned 18, I got a job at the local Power Plant, still stocking furnaces, but now with coal. My dad died in my arms that year of the black lung he'd acquired working in the coalmines of his homeland and around town. He'd quit mining years before, but not before the damage had been done to his lungs. My work at this time was to help generate the steam that flowed beneath the streets of town and heated most of the homes and businesses in the communities.

There were trolleys that ran through about half of the streets in town and out to the surrounding communities of Hawk Run, Chester Hill, Morrisdale, and Osceola. Most of these would be gone by the early 50s. About that time, I met my future wife, Peggy Dugan, who was then a nursing student at the Phillipsburg State Hospital, just up the hill from the power plant along Cold Stream Creek, in North Phillipsburg. Id sees her walking to town with her friends as they passed the power plant. We dated a couple of times, but didn't really hit it off.

The Big Band sound was the music of the day. We would travel as far as Altoona or Johnstown to hear and dance to the likes of Tommy Dorsey and Glenn Miller. Gas was 20 cents a gallon. Our pocket change could get us over the mountain to Tyrone or Port Matilda and beyond to State College in spite of the depression, we seemed to be able to find ways to entertain ourselves. There always seemed to be somewhere to go or something to do. In the summers, you could hitch a ride with the loggers or the dam builders out to the lake. There was always a stream to fish or game to hunt. Phillipsburg had a great baseball league and there were games just about every spring and summer night at the powerhouse grounds in "Slabtown". Growing up I worked most summer afternoons and a lot of evenings in my Uncle Bill's garden, tending two to three acres of his beloved gladiola's and vegetables, the latter which my mother would spend countless hours canning come fall. We also raised a pig or two and always had chickens in the coop behind the house on Clay Street. I also raised and raced homing pigeons as a

teen along with my Uncle Bill. I don't ever remember wanting for something to do, but in my spare time I loved to hunt and fish and I am proud to say that that legacy lives on in my son and his friend TG.

I was not quite 23 when the Japanese bombed Pearl Harbor. I still remember President Roosevelt's address to the country December 8, 1941. In February of 1942, I was on my way to Washington State to train with the 29th infantry armored. By early 1944, I was on my way to England where I would train for and participate in the D-Day invasion as a staff sergeant in the field artillery. We spent the next year fighting our way across Europe. Thankfully, I was home for Christmas in 1945.

When WWII ended, I came back to Phillipsburg and worked for another year at the power plant. Then I took a civil service job at the Post Office in town. I tried commuting to Lock Haven, which was 57 miles over back roads to get a college degree in teaching on the GI Bill, but by the that time I had remit Peggy Dugan. We were married in August of 1946. Our son Jeff was born in December of 1948. Our daughter Jenifer followed in February of 1950. Try as I might, college was not in the cards. I needed a paycheck. We rented a couple of years from my best friend's mother, Aggie Ammerman and finally scraped together the down payment on a $1,500 bungalow a couple of houses down from my mother's home on Clay Street, back in "Slabtown". We got our first television that year. The screen was about 5x8 inches. My sister, Myrtle, bought it as a Christmas present for the kids. I pretty much settled into my post office job and worked at it until 1962 when I took on the new rural carrier route delivering to the rural mail section just outside of town. In 1955, my wife and I bought a two-story house at the corner of 11th and Locust and began a 10-year remodeling project that would see the cellar dug out mostly by hand and completely finished along with every room in the house. Most of the work my wife and I did ourselves. In 1968, we moved our present home on Windy Hill above the old state hospital.

After the war, I still hunted and fished whenever I could. Throughout the mid-50s and on into the 70s my son and his good friend T.G. McMullan were my constant companions as we traipsed the hills and valleys around town. The hunting, especially the deer hunting seemed to get better each year from the 50s into the 70s. But the fishing got a lot more competitive than I remember it as a kid growing up. Over the years, my son and his pal became better fisherman than I would ever be. They hunt and fish together still. My days of that are over, but fishing and hunting have kept the three of us pretty close since those days back in the 50s. Together we spent a lot of time as my dad Marshall would say, traipsing about, I have enjoyed every minute and I don't think I'd change much, even if I could.

Tire Chains and Window Ice
By Arlene Yonker Klinczar of Bradford,
Pennsylvania
Born 1937

Something most memorable to me is waking up on a winter's morning to the clink-clink-clink of the chains. The chains were used on tires of cars and pickup trucks in the wintertime so people could navigate the snowy roads in my hometown of Wilcox, Pennsylvania. This was back in the mid-1940s. Then I would run to the window to look out to see how much snow had fallen and to watch the cars slowly making their way down the street. If it were cold enough outside, maybe the inside of our windows would have ice forming on them and of course, I always had to run my tongue over the ice!

Our town road crew would have a pickup truck with cinders in the bed and two guys would stand in the back of the truck and take turns shoveling the cinders on the road so motor vehicles would have traction. How cold that must have been for the guys doing that job! Close to 70 years later, I still remember and that brings a smile to my face. Oh the good old days! But to a kid, it was exactly that.

The Swimming Pool Pond
By Elmer Ferragine of Johnsonburg,
Pennsylvania
Born 1929

In the winter of 1940, we were ice-skating in the Paper Mill Dam or Lagoon as it was referred to at the time. The dam is located along the Clarion River about a mile downstream from the Grant Street Bridge. The dam is made up of earthen walls. The dam is located between the river and the B & O Railroad.

We found a 50-gallon barrel buried in a hillside on the banks of the railroad. Inside the barrel there was a wood box, which was about half full with dynamite probably left by the people who built the dam. We built a fire on the side of the dam wall and we got the fire going real good. We then threw the box with the dynamite into the fire and ran to the railroad about 50 yards away and waited for an explosion, which never came. All we got from the box with dynamite was a big orange flame. If the detonators had been in the box, we may have had an explosion. Thank God for that. Kark, Tom, Rudy, Buckskin and me there could have been others that were skating that day, but I don't know.

There was a cement pond located about a third of a mile downstream from the Grant Street Bridge close to the Clarion River. Due to the moss and algae that covered the bottom, we thought Greenie Pond was an appropriate name for it and the pool itself was a cement pond that was intended for Johnsonburg's first sewage plant that was never used to my knowledge. It was around 1939 or early 1940 that a group of kids from Clarion Height decided to clean the pond and make a swimming pool out of it. It was closer to home then the pool that was in Decker Town at Powers Run to fill the pool we had to pipe water from a pipe that flowed under the B & O tracks. This pipe was about 100 to 125 yards away from the cement pond. We used any kind of pipe that we could get our hands on that would get water to the pond.

Ralph and Dick had the idea to nail two boards together to form a V to carry the water after we ran out of any other pipes, with the help of some other kids who were a little younger. We got the job done. The water was finally flowing into the pond. It didn't take too long before we were swimming in it. The flood of 1942 really filled the pool to over flowing. We still swam in the pool even though it was filled with floodwater. The cement pond is still there the last time I looked.

History Repeats Itself
By Mary Wetmore of Knoxville,
Pennsylvania
Born 1929

Certainly history does repeat itself. I've observed this happening so many times in my lifetime. Many times the "now generation" will hit upon a supposedly new way of doing things or re-discover something of value that has been put in the background for a few years, only to regain prominence again. Then it is heralded as a new step forward while some of us oldsters greet the idea with a smile, and try to refrain from saying we had that a long time ago, and wonder why it was ever discarded anyway. Usually these things or ideas were replaced in the name of progress and then revived in the same name.

Antiques are a prime example. Old furniture items were often discarded many years ago in favor of newer pieces, but are now being sought after like crazy, refinished and sold at fantastic prices. Likewise all types of antiques, tools, machinery, automobiles, you name it. Antiques are, for the most part, now considered as luxury or show piece items and not necessary to life.

However, we are also seeing many old-time ideas, ways and practices being revived for very practical purposes. Consider wood burning stoves and furnaces. I can remember in my earliest childhood when most folks in our area used them. But as time went on, most households around gave up wood heat, switching to other fuels, which were more efficient, more convenient, more uniform, and relatively cheap. Then came the "oil crisis", with all types of heating fuel raising considerably in price and guess what? Back came the wood stoves, furnaces, fireplaces, woodsheds, and woodpiles! Now many people in our area use them, the well to do folks along with the not so well to do folks!

In recent farm papers and magazines, we are reading about Lisa. What is this Lisa all about? It's just a new name for old-fashioned farming. Now it's called Low Input Sustainable Agriculture, using few, if any, chemicals, back to cow manure, minimum tillage, and I'm wondering eventually to cultivating instead of weed killers. For a while hormone implants for beef cattle were advised for faster growth. Now we're hearing that hormone implants are not so popular. There is more and more demand for organically grown foods, raised without chemicals. Then of course there are clothing fashions and shoes, and even hairstyles that seem to be revived every few years. Yes, history does repeat itself in these and many more ways!

In recent months or years, we have been hearing that maybe the old-time shortenings such as butter and lard are not as bad for our health as some researchers and medical "experts" would have us believe. I get very confused when I hear various medical opinions, just as we get confused when listening to politicians expound on their various ideas. Ill leave the subject of healthy or unhealthy to the experts, but will continue to use some animal fats in my diet in contrast to hydrogenated fats.

As I write this, I am also taking time to occasionally stir two big kettles of ground pig fat melting down into lard. For my daughter, who is in this project with me, it is a new experience. For me it is a renewal of a common experience some 30 or more years ago. For both of us, it is enjoyable and rewarding, but it does take time and patience. Our old-fashioned method takes several hours, but we can work in some other jobs between the stirring. Some people may prefer "trying out" the lard in the oven. I prefer the top-of-the-stove method used by my mother, my mentor, in my childhood. I also made lard in my early years of being a farm wife, but before Ellen remembers it well.

Many of the older farms had lard presses, but I never used one. We strain ours after cooking with a large strainer lined with two layers of cheesecloth, similar to straining fruit in jelly making. We have a large canner that we strain the melted lard into. We also press the fat globules with a large spoon down into the strainer. When cool enough, we gather the cheesecloth bag up and squeeze it to expel more of the liquid lard. When cool, we pour or spoon it into freezer containers to freeze, reserving some to refrigerate for use within two or three weeks. The lard is almost white when firm and ready for use in piecrusts, cookies, cakes, or any baking recipe.

Soda and Beer Bottle Admission
By James Fulmer of Clearfield, Pennsylvania
Born 1942

My name is James W. Fulmer; I was born on August 20, 1942 on a farm in the area known as Wolf Run. The farm was rented by my parents, Charles and Mary, and sat next to the West Branch of the Susquehanna River. I had two brothers, Robert and David, both deceased and one sister Alice.

I remember my two brothers and I sitting on the back porch watching the coal trains going to and from Clearfield. We moved to 105 High Street Clearfield also known as Hillsdale in 1946 in a house built by my grandfather. I now live at 103 High Street in my grandparent's home. In the 1950s, all the kids I ran with would pick blueberries and blackberries and would sell them at 20 cents a quart to earn money to go to the Clearfield County Fair. To us the fair was a really big deal. My best friend, Tom Anderson, and I would ride our bikes 14 to 15 miles to Parker Dam State Park to fish or swim all day in the summer.

When I was 13 or 14 I set pins at the local bowling alley for 10 cents a frame. I enjoyed watching the pins fly around and making sure none hit my head. I earned $3 to $6 a night. To earn the money to go to the movies I gathered soda and beer bottles and sold them to the local's taverns for two cents each, admission was 14 cents. I saw a movie every Friday and Saturday. There were two theaters, the Roxie and the Lyric. They sat across from each other on the same street.

My favorite movies were ones with these actors, Gene Autry, Roy Rogers, Abbott and Castillo, Bowery Boys. My very favorite was the Tarzan movies with Johnny Wisemiller. My favorite cartoon was Popeye. One of my neighbors had an icebox. When the iceman came to fill the icebox, he chipped the ice and all the neighborhood kids would gather up the chips and eat the chips.

At this time my first love was a girl, a tomboy named Rosie Myers whose nickname was Pudgie. The favorite game in our neighborhood was kick the can. There were at times 20 of us kids playing. My friend and I made rubber guns out of old car inner tubes. We cut the rubber into strips, stretched over a long stick, and added a trigger and relief handle. The rubber flew pretty well. I shoveled snow all over town for $2 to $4 a day, about 50 cents to 75 cents a sidewalk.

In March of 1957 my whole life changed, as I was target shooting with a friend and was shot in the back and became paralyzed from the chest down. That was 55 years ago, but I never gave up. After rehab in the 1960s I organized and managed a baseball team, the Hillsdale Hawks. We played in the country and mountain league we didn't win a lot of games, but had a lot of fun.

In the 70s I met my partner Mary Yetter, also paralyzed and we have been together since 1974. In the 80s I shot 8-ball pool for the Clearfield Eagles Club. I also shot 22 silhouettes and won some trophies. In 1995 I started working as a people greeter at our Clearfield Wal-Mart. I have been doing this for 17 years and hope to keep working as long as I am able.

Highway Kiln
By Evelyn F. Gehr of Montoursville,
Pennsylvania
Born 1920

I am a 91-year-old resident of beautiful central Pennsylvania in a town five miles east of Williamsport (home of Little League Baseball) in the valley with the Susquehanna River flowing east and south to Chesapeake Bay.

The valley north of the river has a range of hills north and a main beltway highway to Harrisburg, Pennsylvania. My hometown is five miles east of the city. These hills have over the years produced lime from pockets of limestone slag, blasted and refined in huge stone kilns carved from the stone. These are huge furnace type construction not unlike house chimneys. Some are as large as a small house. The heat during summer months from these fires is intense as it burns day and night for days. As it burns it sifts down into a well where workers haul it by wheelbarrow to storage containers. Deep blasting had been used to acquire stone chunks.

About six or seven of these burners were at

Lime Kiln

one time using these features later only three were in operation. Unfortunately all of this procedure has disappeared on the interstate. The highway now runs along this territory where one beautiful kiln was preserved by the state and rests along the highway. Some limestones have been braced by heavy wires to keep it from erosion. Weather and the ravages of times past. Young people seeing this limekiln have asked what it might be, its past and its use. I am always more than welcome to inform anyone interested at this great part of settlers' life.

Washday and Loafs of Bread
By Geraldine Milliron of Scranton, Pennsylvania

I am 83 years young. We washed clothes with Maytag wringer washers. When washers broke down, we washed clothes with rubbing boards and attached wringers to tubs so we could wring them out, or wrung them out by hand. In winter, we hung the clothes on lines in the living room by a big old coal stove. We had a well by the house, but when it would go dry, we had to carry water from a spring in backfields. It never went dry. All the neighbors used it. I hated washday. I always had to stay home from school to help. It was my job to wash all the diapers.

We never had lunches in school, we would go home from school we had blueberries, blackberries, or dewberries, which we canned. We would have dogers or dumplings made from dough from homemade bread. We fried dogers or put dough in boiling water and cooked them. I would mix up the bread in the morning before school. My stepmother would form them in loafs and bake them. Our school was a two-room school. The big old furnace in the corner of the room would keep it warm. The older boys would carry coal from the basement and the teacher would take care of the fire. We also had backhouses, one for boys and one for girls with a half-moon in door. We would use Sears's catalogues for the toilet paper or old newspapers, which we would rough up to make it softer. The teachers had wooden paddles and if you were misbehaving, they were not afraid to swat you.

Back to washing. When clothes were ready we would roll the clothes up let them set in the basket then we would iron them. If our lights were cut off they would put a seal on our meter box that was in the living room. I would have to put iron on stove to heat it put wooden handle on it and iron. It was like lifting a brick every time you lifted it. I would iron all the little ruffled dresses of my sisters.

The only time we had ice cream is when my dad would give us $1.00 and the bottom of his lunch bucket. It was aluminum, there were two parts to it, and the top was for sandwiches. Mrs. Fuge would put ice cream for five cents a dip. Till we would get home it would be soft. My dad dug house coal. We would walk back a tunnel; there were tracks for coal cars. We would sometimes ride back in coal cars but most always walked. Dad had shot the coal toss with dynamite, and then we would loose the coal in the car. We had two donkeys that pulled the car out to be loaded in trucks.

We also had dried up water well. My dad would go down in it and dig coal. He would fill a bucket and I would bring it up like I was bringing up a bucket of water. He would go house to house and sell it for $2.00 a ton. When we would back in tunnel for coal we wore a cloth miner's hat, that you hung a lamp on front. It was fueled by carbide; you spit on carbide to start gases turn it on and light it with a match. That was our light to see and mine.

When I married we lived with my in-laws who had running water in the kitchen. You would pump it with a hand pump. My in-laws had a cow and chickens there were a lot of feed sacks. I made my maternity tops and addresses out of flowered, plaid sacks. I made wrap around dresses, kitchen curtains, and crib sheets. Some women would make nighties and bras out of the flour or feed sacks. Flour came in 25-pound bags. You could make dishtowels and pillowcases out of flour sacks also quilt patches on peddle singer sewing machines.

Mom would put our shoes over iron shaped like your foot; they would nail leather ones the sole if it had a hole in it, or put new heels on made out of rubber. They also had rubber soles you could live on. You never wore shoes in summer, and if by time school time came if last year's shoes were tight, you still wore them.

In winter we had chamber buckets we used at night in the morning you took it out to the outhouse. Some people had a chamber shaped like a big cup they would slide it under their bed. I was at a neighbors and I heard a loud crack. I said, "What was that?" Oh Charlie just knocked the pot down stairs. You had to be there to appreciate it.

When we had a cough or colds we would melt real lard mix turpentine with it and rub it on our chest and back or caramelize onions and use syrup for coughs.

Railroad House
By Mary L. Shaffer of Montgomery,
Pennsylvania
Born 1934

I would like to share my memories of growing up, in a house next to railroad tracks, in a family of 15. There were nine girls and four boys, plus our mother and father, John and Edna Metzger Woodling. I was the ultimate middle child, there were six older and six younger than me. We lived in a house owned by the Pennsylvania Railroad, between Muncy and Montgomery. Our dad was employed by the railroad in the Maintenance of Way Department.

We lived so close to the tracks, that when a train passed by, it seemed to shake the house. In fact, we would tell people that when a train was due, we had to open the front and back doors of the house to let it pass through and the train whistle was so loud, it would echo for a long time. We would play in empty

The Railroad house
The home to 15

boxcars and in the train station, when it was empty. Sometimes we would see circus trains go past and men going off to war and even a presidential candidate. We also saw hobos, but were discouraged from feeding them because dad told us that they would mark our house so others would stop, but we would sneak them a sandwich or something.

After they had 12 children, someone asked my dad if he was going to try for a baker's dozen, so there was number 13. We were all born at home, except the last one. We were

told babies came in the doctor's little black bag and we believed it because every time the doctor showed up with his black bag, there was another baby.

Our dinner table was so long, it buckled in the middle and dad would tell us to eat everything on our plates, because there were starving people in the world. To this day, I usually finish most all of my food. But I must confess, when I was growing up, I did not like the crust on my bread, so I stuck them under the corners of our table.

I remember when our five cousins, the Harding kids would come to visit, we would sleep crosswise in the beds, instead of lengthwise. We had so many old railroad blankets on the beds that you could hardly turn over and it took real courage to get out from under them to get dressed. When we needed a haircut, our dad would get Dick Stahl, a barber from Montgomery to come and give us all haircuts. He would tell him to cut it just as our ear tips showed. So we all looked alike, boys and girls.

I remember picking strawberries at Blessings Farm and Detassling Hybrid corn at Sherwood's farm in the summer, when we were in our teens. I remember taking a pound or so of Hamburg or a can of salmon and putting enough filler in it to feed us all and our turkeys at Thanksgiving and Christmas were so big that it took two of us to get them in and out of the oven, especially with stuffing in them.

Our mother made some of our clothes and they were passed down from oldest to youngest, until they were worn out and we looked as good as anybody else. Some of us attended or joined the St. John's Lutheran Church and sang in the choir and attended youth meetings and sometimes we would walk to Muncy to see a movie. Neither one of our parents drove, so we mostly stayed at home and amused ourselves.

There were hard times, but also good times. I give my mother and father a lot of credit for raising 13 kids without too many mishaps. They celebrated 50 plus years of marriage. Our mother was Pennsylvania Dutch and she had some funny sayings that I still use today. For example, "Give things a lick and a promise." When dusting or cleaning and my dad was so proud of his name that he would spell it out, so people would get it right, especially the last part. Once I bought something in a store and said my last name was Wood(ling) spelling out Ling. When I looked at my bill, it was Mary Ling, so that didn't work!

We all rode the school bus to the Montgomery-Clinton school, where nine of us graduated. There was one of us in about every other grade and the poor teachers would go down the list of Woodlings until they got the right one. After graduating, a lot of us were offered jobs at Sprout-Waldron Company in Muncy. There were so many of us employed there at one time, that they teased us that they were going to call the company, Sprout-Waldron and Woodling.

I did not stray too far from the same railroad tracks, when I left home. Only about five miles to Montgomery, where I married James Shaffer, who was in the same graduating class as me. We have two sons and guess what? We are only about two tenths of a mile from the same railroad tracks that run through the center of town. We can still hear the train whistle, but at least the trains don't shake our house!

Vogt's Ice Cream
By Gordon L. Vogt of Rocklin, California
Born 1933

In the summer of 1924, my father Gordon A. Vogt, established a business for producing 75 gallons of ice cream a day in Emporium, Pennsylvania. Imagine that! My dad made ice cream for a living! By the time I came along, nine years later, his business was already established. Vogt's Ice Cream kept soda fountains, restaurants, gas stations, post offices, lawn socials, and individuals supplied with their ice cream needs in 1, 2.5 and 5.0 gallon sizes. Vogt's offered the standard flavors, vanilla, chocolate, strawberry, maple-walnut, and our specialty, Whitehouse, which is essentially vanilla ice cream with cherries.

As an added inducement, gallons were also available in half and half flavors as well as my favorite, fudge ripple.

What an experience! I remember the popular phrase, originator unknown that summed it all up: "I scream, you scream, we all scream for ice cream." As a youngster, I often found myself inviting my pals to head into the factory with me while my dad was making ice cream. He would look up from his standing position at the mixer and see a handful of kids moving toward him holding out container lids in preparation for some freebies. He obliged by drawing out a sample of the softest, sweetest textured ice cream I ever tasted; it was like a Dairy Queen blizzard without the add-ons. I made a lot of buddies in those days. Commercial customers purchased the larger sizes while individuals bought the gallon size for $1.25 each before WWII. When that event drove up the price of most ingredients, the gallon price also got bumped up, to $1.35. Noteworthy is the fact that after the war, dad restored the price to $1.25.

The variety of flavors appealed to a wide band of consumers. However many preferred the chocolate and believed that a "secret recipe" was used in its manufacture that kept customers returning, many from nearby towns to buy the ice cream. Years of successful business perpetuated the legend but the truth of the matter is, dad simply used extra butterfat in his basic mix and everyone enjoyed the result. In the early days, our rural commercial customers needed only a refrigerated cabinet to be in the retail business. Once acquired, the sale of ice cream cones would follow, along with hand packed quarts of ice cream. This led to most unusual spots for such treats; a post office in Cameron, a gas station in Driftwood and a restaurant in Sinnemahoning, about 20 miles from home. Making that delivery was a wonderful mixture of business and pleasure driving in those beautiful, rolling mountains of north central Pennsylvania, where gas was only $.19 a gallon.

Delivery to businesses became quite an adventure. Most ordered the five-gallon size, which was a steel cylindrical can, 21" high and 9" in diameter or the 2.5-gallon can, half that size. The usual practice was to remove the outgoing can from the refrigerated cabinet at the place of business and replace it with the incoming one. Any remaining ice cream in the outgoing can was placed on the top of the ice cream in the incoming can. Much of the time there would still be a small amount left in the can and the enterprising neighborhood youth, familiar with the process, waited by the delivery truck for their chance to make a final cleansing swipe in the cans. Our drivers were popular with these kids.

Other frequent customers were the sponsors of summertime lawn socials who offered cake and ice cream served up on portable tables situated on the grassy lawns of area churches. Insulated canvas jackets kept the ice cream in the large size cans firm enough for the duration of the social. These affairs were quite popular and attended in large numbers, with no television at home to distract the folks.

The ice cream factory included a walk-in cold room to keep ingredients refrigerated prior to use. Among other things, 20-gallon containers of ice cream mix and assorted additives were kept chilled in the cold room until needed. This space was not always fully utilized. Accordingly, my father provided a side benefit to area hunters during hunting seasons. The word got around that field dressed deer and bear taken in season could be stored short term in the cold room at the factory. As a result, as many as a half dozen dressed carcasses, tongues extended, could be seen hanging on the walk in walls at any one time. Unfortunately, for me, my 8-year old curiosity led me to inspect these trophies, whereupon my older brother, John caught me looking, slammed the door, turned off the light and gleefully listened to me yell for help.

The ice cream market changed after WWII. Gradually major ice cream manufacturers introduced the half-gallon size to grocery stores. The consumer didn't have to store as much ice cream and only paid half the price. Our sales of the gallon size dropped and our commercial customers sold fewer hand packed quarts. In 1956 dad sold the business to my brother, Jim, and retired. A few years later Jim ceased the manufacture of ice cream and delivered pre-packaged ice cream for Sealtest.

No more making Vogt's ice cream for a host of satisfied customers. No more kids cleaning out cans or delivering homemade ice cream to church socials on warm summer evenings or rural customers in the endless mountains. They became and remain very fond memories of the good old days.

The Town of Strawbridge
By Joan Fox of Hughesville, Pennsylvania
Born 1950

This is the story of the town of Strawbridge. Strawbridge got its name from founder Thomas Strawbridge. Strawbridge was of Irish decent; he was born on May 23, 1800 and died in 1879. He migrated to Pennsylvania seeking work in the lumber business. Strawbridge and his wife had four children. Strawbridge was buried in a cemetery on a hill overlooking the town.

The town of Strawbridge consisted of approximately eight houses, a sawmill, general store, schoolhouse, church, and a gristmill located at the lower end of town. After the passing of Thomas Strawbridge, the mill was sold to James Myers and his wife. Myers operated the mill for several years then sold it to his son Leon Myers Sr. the mill then went to Leon Myers Jr. who sold it to Jack McClintock.

The sawmill was operated by a steam engine, which was fueled by sawdust. There was a steam whistle blown every morning, noon, and quitting time. The logs were washed down with steam then carried into the mill by a hand railroad car. Horse and wagon would haul logs in then in later years by truck. The original sawmill burned down and a new building was erected which is now a stone crushing business.

Muncy Creek runs along the north side of Strawbridge. At the west end of town was an

Mable Myers McClintock

300

Ezra

old covered bridge. Many a horse and buggies crossed over the bridge going from Penn twp. to upper Shrewsbury twp. The bridge had seats on both ends for resting places. The men would eat their lunches there to get in out of the heat and rest. The children from the school would go over on the bridge to play on rainy days during recess. Women used the bridge to carry their eggs and butter to the grocery store to exchange for goods. When the bridge was torn down, it was knocked into the creek then cleaned up.

In 1884, construction was started on the WWB Railroad to run from Hughesville to Sonestown and branches off for Satterfield and Eagles Mere. The track was a "standard gauge" track; it took three years to reach Nordmont. The cost of the track was $30,000 a mile. In 1937, it was the last year the train ran. The track was 44 miles long and was known as the "picturesque passenger route". Todd Simmons was one of the engineers. At one point in time, there were nine engines. There was a train stop at every town along the track. At Strawbridge two of the men, Hurl Fenstermacher and Herman (Dump) Stackhouse would go into the store to purchase snacks and items for their lunches, using the pump cart while working on the railroad. The railroad ticket office was located in the grocery store owned by James Myers. James' daughter Mabel worked at the store taking care of the ticket office. The train's engines were fueled

by coal. Launderer Michael Maylet was the driving force behind the establishment of the railroad. The railroad hauled logs, coal, and passengers. There was a Pullman car for the rich people.

The house of James and Jane Myers housed the first telephone exchange. There was a post office in the original general store, also the railroad ticker office. The mail was received and dispatched by rail. In 1924, Ezra McClintock and his wife Mabel Myers McClintock built a new store. The store sold candy, 5 and 10 cents a piece. Sugar, coffee, tea, rice, butter, and many other items came in bulk and had to be weighed and repackaged. Lard was purchased in 50-pound cans and repackaged. Farmer's wives for trade brought in eggs and home churned butter. Ice cream sold for five cents a cone.

The men who worked at James Myers Mill would go to the store at noon hour to listen to the radio in the back of the store to get the farm and home report from Chicago which aired 12:00 – 1:00 p.m., it gave the farm and weather reports.

In 1946, the store was sold to Ezra's daughter and son-in-law, Marie and Leonard Stackhouse. The Stackhouse's purchased the store upon Leonard's return from service in WWII. The Stackhouse's had a full line of goods from groceries, feed, clothing, shoes, nails, gas, and oil. Fresh meat was their specialty. Candy was sold loose out of a large glass candy case and jars. Gulf was the brand of gas that sold for six gallons for $1.00. The store was sold in 1965 to the Chamberlain's, in 1972 the store was sold again and today the general store of yesteryear is now a gift store.

On the west end of town was the schoolhouse and church. A one-room schoolhouse was built and later closed in 1944. The school was named Muncy Creek School, in Penn twp. The school was one room with eight grades. The building was 24'x36' with a potbelly stove for heat. The teacher was responsible for keeping fire and all other janitorial duties. School started at 9:00 and left out at 4:00 with a lunch break and 15-minute recess. Every morning was started with bible reading, prayer, and the pledge of allegiance. Reading, writing, arithmetic, geography, spelling, civic, art, and music were the courses. Lots of lunches were heated up on the potbelly stove. Edna Sones was the last teacher.

Kedron United Methodist Church was built in 1874 and is still in use for Sunday services. The Kedron name comes from a ravine near Jerusalem, formerly a stream that flowed into the Dead Sea. The church was built on land owned by George Edkin and was built by Dave Myers and Ellis Swank for a total of $2,200.00. The bell that rings every Sunday morning came from the schoolhouse when it was torn down. Leon Myers was responsible for the moving. C.W. Burnley was the first pastor his salary was $378.00 a year. He was the pastor from March 1874-1875.

In the early 1950s the church was jacked up and Ted Houseknecht dug a basement with the help of his bulldozer. In 1985 a two-story addition, kitchen, and storage area, were built on. A lot of volunteers and hand labor over the years has made the church what it is today. The women's society of the church was organized in 1939. The first car in Strawbridge was in 1916 owned by James Myers.

James Myers' car

My Biggest Mistake Was Leaving Home
By William James Stiffler, Jr. of Gladys, Virginia
Born 1946

Clearfield, Pennsylvania is my hometown and Alma Mater. How great it was. We lived across from E.M. Browns on Mountain Joy Road in a little old house we rented for $17.00 a month from Ralph Fetzer who owned the store next door. There was my sister Dawn, mom, dad, grandma, Pap Becton, and I. I remember well the old house, now long gone.

The house had no insulation and broken windows and no indoor bathroom. We nearly froze in winter and anything left out would freeze at night. The sink in the kitchen would have an icicle from the spigot, which always leaked, which extended to the drain. We had rats, which got in somehow and grandma was always setting traps for them. Meals were cooked on a kerosene cook stove, which was always kept lit to help warm the house. Food was kept cold in an old icebox until our Aunt Mable and Uncle John gave us a Leonard Refrigerator. The bottom panel was missing and I remember watching the wheel go around whenever it was running. There was a big stove in the living room, which was always loaded up with coal.

Dad and Pap Becton were coal miners and worked long hours to keep food on the table. They both worked for E.M. Brown, D.C. Penoyer and Ben Lingle coal companies at one time or another. I started 1st grade at Hillsdale School with Mrs. Harrier, my 1st grade teacher. We had moved to east end in a section called Weaverhurst. Both dad and grandpap worked at Robison Clay, which everyone called the sewer pipe. I remember watching the clay buckets in along a cable to the mine from the plant strung on tall steel towers.

We moved into one house in Plymptonville next to the one I was born in. There I started 2nd grade at the school there. School lunches used to cost 25 cents and were very tasty. Our cafeteria director, Miss Tyler, always made sure everything was good, tasty and properly prepared. All kids had a choice to eat at school or go home for lunch. I usually went home until the school changed its policy that all students had to eat at school. It was great living next to a grocery store there. Our milk was delivered by Miller Dairy and put in an insulated box on the porch. If you left the milk in the box too long, the cream would pop off the top.

When we moved back to Plymptonville, I met the Kelly boys. They would become lifelong friends. Their mother Peg became my second mother and I ate many meals at their house. None of us were well off financially but we had good friendships and great families. The Kelly boys and I had great times together getting into a lot of mischief. Halloween was spent soaping windows and throwing cans. If we were mad at a neighbor, we would throw gravel and use wax and not soap. We would spend a lot of time, in the summer, playing in the woods that were near our house. We played Tarzan by swinging from the many vines that grew there. We built several tree houses and forts and played cowboys and Indians. We did several things we never told our parents about. We went skinny dipping in the streams and open pit mine ponds. One of the most dangerous things we did was to play in the old coalmines that went far inside the mountains. Our favorite mine was above John Jury's coal yard on Ginea Hill. There was a long line of old mine cars that ran on tracks inside the opening. We took turns pushing each other back into the darkness in the cars. The possibility of the mine caving in on us never occurred to us. I remember that the mine had rotten beams holding up the ceiling, but as kids having fun, we were not concerned.

Everyone in Clearfield will remember the mine cave in Morgan Run where two boys died inside. They were Wesley Lowe and Larry Husted. Many days were spent trying to dig into the cave in to rescue the boys, but they had died in the cave in. Soon after that, all old mines in the Clearfield and surrounding counties were bulldozed shut to keep everyone out. Saturdays were spent at the old skating rink at the park skating. State rentals were 25 cents and you could skate all day. Many people will remember Francis Thompson. He was always at the rink skating and would always be the one to lead a train of skaters. I was greatly saddened when they tore down the old rink, which we called Exposition Hall.

A yearly event that everyone looked forward to was the Clearfield County Fair. The fair literally put Clearfield on the map. People came from miles around and still go to the fair. James E. Strates shows owned the fair. Folks would gather to watch the fair come in on a train across from the A and P super market. There would be a steady stream of tractors back and forth from the park moving the fair from the train. The cars were orange with blue lettering proclaiming "James E. Strates Shows" a "50 All Steel Railroad Car Show". We kids would beg or gather pop bottles to make money to go to the park. Bowman's French fries, Motter's old-fashioned milkshakes, Barret's fudge, and Sutter's salt-water taffy were some of the many attractions there. Many celebrities came and put on a grandstand performance. There was always a thrill show of Jack Kochman's world famous hell drivers. Later Joey Chitwood replaced Jack. A packed grandstand watched in on some of the most clever dangerous drivers rolling around the racetrack. I remember seeing drivers take a car, balanced on two wheels completely around the racetrack and then make another ½ time around without losing balance. What a sight. I still try to get to Clearfield every year but it will never be the same. Only fond memories remain of yesteryear.

I well remember the Saturday movie features at the Lyric Theater on 3rd Street. You could sometimes get in for six Pepsi Cola caps as an admission fee. The Lyric was policed by a no nonsense lady by the name of Marie but we all called her Duffy. You had better behave or asked to leave. Popcorn was 10 cents and a dime drink plus 20-cent hot dogs. Oh how times changed. Many will remember sock hops and street dances, which were usually held on Market Street between 2nd and 3rd. stocking feet with Bobbie socks were the dress for the dance. Later on dances were held at the YMCA with parents volunteering as chaperones. I could go on and on about growing up in Clearfield. I have so many fond and precious memories. I never miss seeing see my music teacher from grade school, Miss Beverly A. Owens. She was and still is a grand lady to learn from. She is the reason I am such a music lover today. I graduated from Clearfield high School in 1964 and went into the U.S. Navy two weeks later. Boot camp, Vietnam, and seeing the world followed. I really never lived in Clearfield after my Navy time was over. I try to get back to my high school reunions as much as possible.

It's sort of sad to see your old hometown and remember how things used to be and will never be again. So much has changed. I think I am a very rich person having the privilege to have been born, grew up and to live in Clearfield. There is no place sweeter to me then there. I have lived in Virginia for 43 years now and still miss Clearfield. I often think my biggest mistake was leaving my home there in the first place. I hope everyone who was born and have lived in Clearfield will have so many fond and priceless memories as I have. I have seen much of the world and many places, but my alma mater remains foremost in my mind. I'm looking for this summer for the County Fair. Again and I hope I can be there. Many years have passed and times have changed. When my earthly trials have ended and my time here has slipped away, I hope to have no greater joy then to rest beneath the kindred soil of the mountain Joy Methodist Church cemetery. That is the church I attended as a small child with holds so many memories I will truly be home there again both in body and spirit.

Our Ancestors Settled in Bloomberg Grove
By Betty Johnston of Cogan Station, Pennsylvania
Born 1923

Mother told us kids the story of our ancestors coming over from Germany. They were the second group of immigrants from Moehringen, Germany who settled in the Bloomberg Grove area north of Williamsport. Arriving in the fall, they spent the winter in Germantown. In the spring, they left to join the first group already established in Bloomberg Grove. One gentleman, (Mother never said his name) borrowed a wheelbarrow from someone in Germantown, put his belongings in it and pushed it the many miles to Blooming Grove. He followed the Indian trails, which ran along the Susquehanna River to Blooming Grove. The man then took the wheelbarrow back to the people he borrowed it from in Germantown, and walked back to Blooming Grove.

The Dunkard Meeting House was built in 1828, and still stands. A museum has been built to house many of the household and farm items used by the early settlers. The museum is open with free admission on Sundays from the beginning of June through the end of September, from 2:00 to 5:00 PM, or by appointment.

Mules and Manure
By Lola Jane Houchins of Clearfield, Pennsylvania
Born 1928

My name is Lola Jane (Rowles) Houchins. I was born July 1928 in Mineral Springs, Pennsylvania, a small village near Clearfield, Pennsylvania. My parents were Charles and Susie "Peters" Rowles. My parents had 10 children—two died as infants, I was number 9.

When I was 5 ½ years old a brother was born. I told my parents to give him to Mrs. Snyder, she likes kids. Low and behold, Mom kept him! I started school the next year.

My father worked in the clay and coalmines. The Depression years were hard times for many families with no jobs, no help; many families worked hard to care for one another. They were days of larger families.

My parents raised chickens, and had big gardens. Pigs and cows were kept at my grandmother's house. I started school the year after my brother was born.

We lived near a brickyard. Clay was mined across the road. Mules were used to bring the clay from the mine. They pulled hoppers full of clay from the mine and it was dumped in the brickyard.

The mules were kept in a barn across the road from the brickyard. The manure was kept in a closure next to the barn. There was a concrete wall around to contain the manure. The highlight of the day was to visit the mules and walk the wall. At times, someone would fall from the wall. The wall was not very high. The smell was not very pleasant. I don't think children can smell. When you went home, no one seemed happy to see you, especially my mother.

At the end of my first grade, we moved to Clearfield, a town about 6 miles from Woodland. My dad got a job in Clearfield.

There was 7 children at home. No more mules and barn!! No more stinky manure and animals. Moving was slow. Someone always had the chicken pox until it went through the family. We couldn't move until I was over the chicken pox. That yellow sign was on our house for quite a while.

Growing up in a big family was memorable and time went by very fast. In no time, children grew up and left home. My dad expired at 74 and my mother at 74. She was 5 years younger than my dad.

I will be 84 years old on July 21, 2012. I am the last member of my family.

Hang On Boys for the Church Hill Buggy Ride
By James Stebbins of Sabinsville, Pennsylvania
Born 1940

The year was 1950-51. The place was Sabinsville, a small town in north central Pennsylvania. The event was a fast and furious ride down a hill on a road called Church Hill.

304

My name is James Stebbins, better known to local folks as "Jimmy".

At the time of this event, I was about 10-11 years old. There was about four or five boys my age in on the ride. We scrounged an old buggy or wagon frame, which consisted of four wooden spoke wheels approximately 48 inches in diameter with a steel band around the perimeter. The two front wheels were mounted on a solid axel with a pivot in the center for steering; the tongue was missing. This fixture was mounted on a 2"X 4" and 8 foot by 10 foot long. The rear wheels were mounted on a fixed axle.

The steering mechanism was a loop of rope hooked to each side of the front axle. One person sat in front with their feet on the front axle and holding the rope. To turn left, you had to pull the left side rope and at the same time, you had to push the right side of the front axle with your foot. To turn right, you had to do just the opposite.

After we got the steering rigged, we took turns riding and pushing. We traded off so everybody got a ride. This was a lot of fun, but after a while, it got to be old hat.

Now, Sabinsville had a nice hill that went past our church. It was quite a steep hill, but we were all fearless, so we decided we would take our buggy to the top of the hill and ride it down. Oh, Boy!!

The hill was a dirt road that ended at an intersection in front of the church. To the right was a street called Locust Street. Straight ahead was a secondary road that curved by the Church Hill Road and Locust Street. The road then went on past a street called Maple Street and on to an intersection of Main Street.

At that time, there was not much auto traffic, so up the hill we pushed the buggy to the top of the hill, approximately ½ mile long.

After we rested, we all piled on. As near as I can recall, there was five boys, total. They gave me the job of steering, so off we went. The farther down the hill we went, the faster we were going, and at about the halfway point it was getting a little scary. The buggy had no brakes, so we could not slow down. It also had no shock absorbers, so every little bump we hit sent us a little bit air-born. We were going too fast to jump off, so we had to ride it out.

After we passed the church and the first intersection (Locust Street), we were approaching the second intersection (Maple Street), when an automobile had just pulled out of the intersection (Maple Street) just ahead of us. We were flying low with no brakes, so I had to steer the buggy around and pass him. The driver of the auto was shocked and stunned when we passed him. He veered off the road, crossed a sidewalk and drove onto the Memorial lot lawn and stopped. We continued en-route to and then past the next intersection by making a right hand turn and continuing down Main Street for approximately another ½ mile before coming to a stop.

As I recall, everybody seemed to be kind of quiet for a time, almost like in our thoughts, we were all thanking the Lord for a safe journey.

As we pushed the buggy back into town, we were back to normal, but as we all departed for our respective homes, I seem to remember some of them were walking kind of funny.

That buggy and crew made two trips down that hill that day. THE FIRST AND LAST.

My Friend, Muff a True Hero
By Rocky Holland of Kane, Pennsylvania
Born 1946

Growing up in a small town in the late 50s was something that I'll never forget. There were no cell phones, computers, and very few of us even had a TV. We spent most of our days outdoors playing baseball, or football, and couldn't wait until dark when we could play "kick the can".

Turning 13 in 1959, I started noticing the older guys and their "hot cars". The "older guys" were also teenagers, but all old enough to drive and have their own cars, something I dreamt about every night before I fell asleep. In the evenings, while walking home, we would stand under the streetlight at the corner near our homes and hope someone would come to the stop sign with a hot car. We would then try to get them to burn a little rubber, or in our words, "get a wheel". Most nights were successful in getting a "peel out" or two, and that would make our whole evening complete.

As we got a little older, I guess 14 or 15, we would wander a bit farther from home, or as we would say, near the action. The action, as I remember, was a couple blocks up the street from our neighborhood, at a small local gas station. Yes, they would pump your gas, clean your windshield and always check your oil. It was the true meaning of "full service". The owner of the station was a well-known and very popular racecar driver. He became a hero to the local hot rodders, who would visit his station almost daily.

In those days, changing transmissions was almost a daily occurrence, and spark plugs were changed faster than light bulbs. The older guys would use the garage almost daily, working the pumps, and helping out, in exchange for some garage time. Our group would hang out there for hours, watching every car and every interaction the drivers had with their "hot" cars.

The older guys mostly ignored our little group of wide eyed, curious bystanders that occasionally got in their way. We had no idea what they were doing, but with every sound we heard, and the roar of the souped up engines, our eyes got wider and the grins got bigger. In all this creative madness there was always that one special person that actually did take notice of the young group of wide-eyed kids hanging out in the corner. I remember him well. His nickname was "Muff". I do believe at that time, all the older guys had those great nicknames. Muff would always come over and ask how we were doing and joke around with us. We even go to hand him a wrench once in a while. To actually get a ride with one of these guys was like being reborn again. A thrill, like you wouldn't believe. I know if our mother ever found out we were in a car with one of these guys, we would be grounded for life.

Through the years we grew up with Muff and other "older" guys, eventually having our own cars, and going off to bigger and better things. The gas station is now long gone, replaced by a convenience store with self-service pumps. I kept in touch with our little group through the years, and also with the "older" guys. They all became lifelong friends. Many are not with us anymore, but the memories will always be there. I will always remember my friend Muff, who was my "hero" with the hot car when I was growing up. He took the time to be a friend to everyone. It was the time in your life you wish you could just stay in forever.

Potatoes and How I Met a Friend
By Lynn V. Kemp of Shinglehouse, Pennsylvania
Born 1920

Potatoes was the cash crop in Oswayo and Sharon Township in the early 1920s. To plant them, rows were made by a three-row marker drawn by a horse. A small boy could ride on the marker. The seed potatoes were cut and dropped by hand in the row, then covered with a hiller. They were cultivated with a one-horse cultivator with loving care.

After the vines died down in the fall, then came "potato digging" that consisted of a potato hook and a strong back, picked up in bushel crates. Then, they were carried to the cellar and stored on a dirt floor. At that time, they were sold for as low as 27 cents for a 60-pound bushel.

Bert Dunshie and Ora Kemp went from farm to farm with a potato sorter. The sorter graded the potatoes and separated out the small ones and put the good ones in a bag, one hundred pounds per bag. Bert and Ora would call for a railroad car to be set at the Millport siding. That was the New York and Pennsylvania Railroad. Also called "The Nip" it ran from Ceres, New York to Canisteo, New York. The names on the bags were Litchard Sheltice and Johnson. Horses and wagons hauled the potatoes from the farms to the depot. At times, a small boy rode on the wagon with his dad, hauling potatoes. They passed a house between Nickles Store and the depot where Lew and Edith Blauvelt lived. They had a son named, Doug. Doug would run away and come to the Depot to play with Ora's boy. After Edith came and took him home a few times, she asked Ora if his boy could come to her house to play with Doug.

The NY & P ended about 1937. The houses

Millport, PA Depot

306

Millport Depot with "Old Baldy" in the background

and wagons are gone, but "old Baldy" still looks over the Potter County Fair Grounds. That friendship that started more than eighty years ago, remains.

Doug grew up and bought the farm on Herrington Road that included "Old Baldy". The small boy was riding on the potato marker in the spring of 1927 and saw the first deer that Ora ever saw in Oswayo Township!

For Years, I Hated Oranges
By Jeanne Hawkins of Coudersport,
Pennsylvania
Born 1918

I was born on in a small town in Pennsylvania, on August 23, 1918, the fifth girl in the family. A few years later another girl and later, a boy arrived.

We lived just outside of town with forty acres of land in a large house my grandfather had built in the 1870s. We had cows, pigs, two horses and a few dozen chickens, also an apple orchard and a large vegetable garden.

The school was in the center of town, about eight blocks from our house. Hours were nine to four with an hour for lunch. No matter what the weather was, we walked to school every day. It could be pouring rain, or 10 degrees below zero! As there was no such thing as a cafeteria, we walked home for lunch.

I remember one day when I was in eighth grade it was 30 below zero. We went to school as usual, but despite his best efforts, the janitor couldn't get the coal furnace to put out enough heat, so we were excused and walked back home.

We played outside in winter and summer. The hill behind our house was perfect for sledding and skiing. I still have a pair of skis we used. There is a leather strap you slipped your foot through—down the hill you went, then back up the hill and started all over again.

In summer we played a game we called "red light" (like hide & seek), tossed a ball over the two-story wood shed, played "school" on the front steps, climbed trees and took hikes through the woods.

We had an outhouse, which we were encouraged to use if we were outside playing. It was a nice steady building with siding just like the house.

If we didn't feel well, we were given a dose of castor oil, which was a sure cure for everything. My mother would give us a piece of an orange to take the horrible taste away. For years, I hated oranges.

Our phone was a two party line—number 206-J, with one ring. Of course, our neighbors were always listening in!

When we finally got a radio, it was wonderful if you could get a clear station by tuning the dial ever so carefully. We enjoyed the Lone Ranger, Amos & Andy, and Fibber McGee & Molly.

My sister and I enjoyed dancing to the records we played on the old record player in the parlor.

My mom caught the middle finger on her right hand in the wringer of the washing machine and it bothered her for the rest of her life.

We used to get much more snow back then. Sometimes after a big storm, we would take a bowl of fresh snow and sprinkle it with cocoa and sugar, really good; and a great substitute for ice cream.

There was never any money, but we always had plenty of food. With no electricity, of course, there were no freezers, so my mother was an expert at canning fruits, vegetables, jams, jellies, pickles, relish and even venison after hunting season.

My younger sister and I never had new clothes, as everything we wore was a hand-me down. If it didn't fit, my mother made it over, so it did.

Clothes were washed on a scrub board in a large galvanized tub, wrung out by hand and hung on the clothesline. Everything had to be ironed. The irons were heavy iron—they must have weighed five pounds or more. They had to be heated on the stove every few minutes.

We had a bath every Saturday night in the same tub used for the laundry—the water heated on the stove.

Spring cleaning was a real chore. Mattresses were taken out in the lawn to air and placed on wooden saw horses. Rugs were hung on the clothesline and beaten with a rug beater. Lace curtains were measured, then washed and put on curtain stretchers and set on the front porch. It was a wooden frame with tiny nails set an inch apart and it took quite a while to place the edge of the curtain on the little nails, but when dry, they were the same size as before.

There were seven children, my parents, grandparents, an occasional uncle and a cousin who spent summers with us. I often wonder how Mother ever accomplished so much work and prepared three meals a day for all those years. We always had breakfast, dinner, at noon and supper in the evening.

School Days—From Student to Teacher
By Twila Grimm of Emporium, Pennsylvania
Born 1928

I walked about a mile to school every day. It was a one-room schoolhouse and accepted grades from one through eighth. The name of the school was Bryan Hill School. There were three schools on the mountain then. They were named after the men who had cut the virgin timber up there. The schools were named, Moore, Bryan, and Whittimore,

Twila with Brownie

Miss Twila Lyon and Christie Close

and two of them still stand today. One is a granary, and the other is a church.

Some of the games we played at school were, Annie-Annie Over, which took two teams with one team on one side of the school, the other on the other side of the school. When one school threw the ball over the top, then yelled, "Annie-Annie Over," if the other side caught the ball they would yell "Caught" then, everyone would run around the school and try to tag the person with the ball. The other team would then throw the ball and do the same, until one team tagged the other team all out, and there were no players left.

The other game we played was quite unique. My uncle owned the property around the school. Every spring he would burn the field so the green grass would grow better. Then, on a moonlit night, we would get a white ball on the black burnt field and play our own version of soccer.

My grandfather's family worked the logging camps in West Virginia for a while. He had a pet bear he kept chained up. The pigs were left to run around the yard free. They would get close to the bear and he would scratch their backs to get them relaxed, and then he would swat them with his paw just to hear them squeal. He would get loose sometimes, too; the women would run in the house till Grandpa got home. The bear would go to the food storage area and have a ball, until Grandpa came home, that is. It was hard to keep a camp full of supplies way out in the boonies.

One of the chores for the kids to do around the farm was picking up stones out of the field after it had been plowed. My dad made a "stone boat", as it was called. It was a big wooden sled with a box on it to throw the stones in. It was a rough and bumpy ride. My brother used to say, "Hang on to your gizzard Sis" as he would move along. I asked him, "what's a gizzard", and he said, anything that doesn't have teeth has a gizzard" and I would tell him, "I guess Grandpa must have a gizzard, then."

I had always loved horses, but my favorite pet was a little dog named Brownie. I decided to make her a little harness so she could pull my little wagon for me. She learned all the commands, just like a horse would. Whoa, gee, haw and get-up; she did them all. One day we went to get the mail and she got bitten by a rattlesnake. The next morning we found her dead, laying on a piece of my clothing. It was a sad day I will always remember.

When I was little, the telephone was a big box that hung on the wall, with a separate speaker that went with it. It was a party line, and each neighbor had a different ring. Everyone would hear the phone ring, but would only pick up their specific rings. Our ring was used as a family signal too; two long rings followed by two short rings. It was my job to bring the cows from the woods where they were pastured. Sometimes I wouldn't find them as I looked around, I would hear the family signal, two longs and two honks on the car horn, and I knew they went home by themselves. Even now, when I mark library books I read, I put two long marks and two short marks on them. Our family signal is still in use today.

Before the time of combines and such, the farmers had to depend on each other to thresh the grain. One farmer owned the machine and would take it from farm to farm. They all helped each other do the threshing. It took seven men to man this machine, which was full of pulleys and belts. A tractor powered it. One man would cut the twine and feed the machine. It would travel through the machine and head the grain, which would travel down a trough, and caught by two men who were waiting to bag it. Then, the straw would be carried to a mow, and sent up a big, long elevator. When the monster was running in full power, it shook and groaned so much, that to a small child, it reminded her of a big dinosaur.

The wife was expected to cook a good meal for the workers, so, on the day of the threshing Dad would clean the soot from under the oven. Then, he would throw the soot out below the house. I used to find it and play in it. Mom had to clean me up, and then, cook a dinner; she wasn't very happy that day.

I must say, my favorite teacher came later in life, after I had become a fledging teacher myself. Her name was Christ Close. She was my mentor. She not only had lots of wisdom and experience to share with a new teacher, she was a powerhouse full of new ideas and approaches for making the school year a memorable experience for the students. One idea she had was to have a "hat parade" at Easter time. All the fourth graders would design their own hats. The teacher would march them around the gym to be judged, the ugliest, the prettiest, the most original and the most personal.

I will always be grateful to her for her willingness to help me, and for being the best friend.

Easter Hat parade
Clarice, Twila, and Christie

Tannery Town, a Little Place Where Some Wishes Did Come True
By James Lucas of Downey, California
Born 1927

I was born in October 1927, in the small town of Ralston, Northern Lycoming County, Pennsylvania. Ralston had been quite a lively place at one time. There were coalmines on the mountains on both sides of the valley of Lycoming Creek, which bisected the town into uptown and downtown, or more commonly known as Tannery Town, which—you guessed it—was where the tannery was located. The north end of the town contained the remains of a brick factory that made use of the fire clay, which is sometimes found with a vein of coal. Across the road from the brick factory was a large coal tipple that had received the coal mined up on the mountain in the town of Red Burn, and brought down the mountain on an inclined plane that operated by the weight of the loaded coal cars going down, and pulling the empty cars back up. These things had all ceased by the time I was able to see them.

The Pennsylvania Railroad also did an even better job of bisecting the town on its nearly straight line through Ralston. It crossed Lycoming Creek just south of town, again almost in the center of town, and a third time as it left on the north side. The Pennsylvania Railroad had a small rail yard at the north end of Ralston with a water tank and coaling facility for their locomotives, and also a sand tank for the locomotives, as they often needed a large quantity of sand to assist them on the steep grade going north toward Elmira, New York. Additionally, there was a wye (as it was called) that was used to turn a locomotive around.

I believe one of the old tannery buildings is still being used by a local lumber company. I worked in the same building as a teenager before joining the Army. It was then used by the American Fork & Hoe Company, now True Temper Corporation. They made wooden handles, of white ash, for tools.

At one time, there had been seven hotels in Ralston; I only ever saw four of them, and watched one—the Connelly House—being torn down for the wood.

My dad worked for the Pennsylvania Railroad as a freight train brakeman until the Great Depression came along; he was laid off with thousands of other people. The house we were living in at the time belonged to a Mrs. Smith. She had a son working at Kodak Company in Rochester, New York. He also lost his job, and needed a place to live. We were evicted and moved up the road to the last house in a row of tannery houses. These were houses that had been built by the tannery

company for use by their employees, and basically were all built alike. While we lived there, the houses were owned by Harry Jones who also owned the Ford dealership—the only one in Ralston. The rent, at the time, was five dollars a month if you had it. I don't think Mr. Jones got very wealthy from the rent he collected. Some of the other houses had no electricity, although ours did. In both the kitchen and dining room there were bare-bulb ceiling lights with a pull chain. In the front room—it wasn't a parlor or a living room—there was also a wall receptacle where the radio was plugged in, and where our eight-bulb strand of Christmas tree lights were plugged in. Behind the front room was Mom and Dad's bedroom; upstairs were two bedrooms that each had a ceiling light. In the tiny cellar there was a light operated by a long string from just inside the cellar door, unless the string broke, and then you had to feel your way down the steps and grope around in the dark to find the broken string to light the light. Even so, this was all much better than some folks who had to depend on kerosene lamps and lanterns for light. We had a large heating stove in the dining room and, of course, the cook stove in the kitchen.

Of course, all the tannery houses were equipped with an outhouse, which brings back some memories. I guess we didn't mind it so much then, as this is all we knew. Never a pleasant place—always stinky! They were hot in the summer and bitter cold in the winter. I remember being afraid of those huge spiders that lived in there. I didn't realize they weren't after me, but only trying to control the fly population in there.

Not all the houses in Tannery Town were built or owned by the tannery. There were perhaps twenty other homes that were privately owned. They had nice clapboard siding on them. The one we had been evicted from had running water in the kitchen, but that's all. Not all our neighbors were so lucky; some of them had a pump outside, and some carried water from nearby springs. All the others had bathrooms, I guess, because I don't recall outhouses behind any of them. And then, there was the "BIG HOUSE" which was where the superintendent of the tannery had lived. It was the greatest house in Ralston!

There was an old millpond, a few hundred feet up in the woods from our house that had once supplied a sawmill at that location;

however, it had not been in use for many years. A bunch of us kids repaired the washed out portion and had a super ice skating pond. At that time, we usually had ice to skate on at Thanksgiving time and then all winter long. Nearly every night there would be a few of us skating. Of course, we had to have a fire to see by, and Shorty Hannon always had a huge pile of firewood within a few feet of the ice. I never knew of Shorty Hannon to do anything except cut firewood for his own use. Pete Hannon, his son, was one of the best ice skaters in town. That was in the days of clamp-on-skates; shoe skates were unheard of.

One thing I will always remember about those days has to do with my life-long love of ice cream. I don't recall ever having much of it at home. Mom made it a few times with a borrowed ice cream freezer, but during the Depression, there was never any money for ice cream. Occasionally, my Aunt Ollie and Uncle Ski from Galeton would come to visit on Sunday. Uncle Ski had a liking for alcoholic beverages and he knew that it was available on Sundays at a certain entrance to Hackets Hotel. He would take my brother, Lyell and I for ice cream. We would drive up town to a gas station where he would buy a carton of twenty-four ice cream suckers. Uncle Ski would then drive over to the Hackets Hotel and go in for his drinks, while brother, Lyell and I sat eating the ice cream before it had a chance to melt. In each box of ice cream suckers, there was always one that had "free" painted on the stick. Whichever one of us got it would run back over to the gas station to claim the free one.

We didn't go up town very often except to go to school and to go to the store, where both of them were. I did have a favorite schoolteacher, Miss Selma Peterson, who taught first and second grades there for many years. I also had some teachers who were not so favorite.

Money was almost non-existent during the Depression years. What little money not spent on food was usually spent in one of the mail-order catalogues that came Spring & Summer and Fall & Winter from Sears-Roebuck & Company, Montgomery Ward, and Spiegel May Sterns—a smaller one than the other two giants. It was always a red-letter day when the Fall & Winter editions arrived. I could then start wishing for a new pair of high-top shoes for the winter, and especially a pair with a jack knife in a little pocket on the upper part of one shoe. Sometimes they even had a two-bladed knife. However, usually it was all just wishing which is how those books got the name, "wish-books." At nearly three dollars a pair, unless it was absolutely necessary, there would be no high-tops.

Dad was always quite proficient at repairing shoes, and could make them last for quite a while. I remember wondering how they would deliver a team of horses through the mail, not realizing they were only selling the harnesses that the horses were modeling. Upon the arrival of the new wish-books, the old ones could then be relegated to the outhouse where they played a more important role. I guess that was one of the earliest forms of recycling.

Monday morning was always washday for my mother; no matter what the weather, it was washday. In the coldest days of the winter, she would hang the clothes on the line in the backyard, and before they were all hung up, they were frozen stiff. She would later bring them inside and they would stand up against the walls, and eventually dry on the lines she had strung up in the dining room. She scrubbed the "dirtiest" clothes on a scrub board in one of the galvanized tin tubs; she rinsed them in the other tub and ran them through a hand-cranked wringer mounted on the side of the tub. Mom, also had an old wooden washing machine that originally had a handle on top, which operated what looked like a three-legged stool that hung on the underside of the lid and agitated the clothes in the wooden tub. The handle on top had been replaced by an electric motor that did the hard work.

Tuesday was always Mom's ironing day, and it seems that everything had to be ironed in those days. She had a set of three irons, which always sat on the back of the cook stove. There was one handle that adapted to all three irons. Of course, on ironing days the irons were on the hottest part of the stove all day.

We had a hand-cranked floor model RCA Victor phonograph that got a lot of use, especially on rainy days. Many of the records were scratched, and some would repeat over and over. A couple of them that I remember were, "The Wreck of the Old Ninety-Seven" and "Letter Edged in Black."

The tin wash tubs Mom used every Monday were also, at least the bigger of the two, used as bathtubs on Saturday nights—whether you needed it or not. In the summer months, we spent enough time in the water swimming that we didn't stink too badly, but in the winter, I imagine we really did stink. How it hurts me today, just to think about me folding my body up and getting into one of those tubs. Fortunately, I now have a little more convenient bath facility.

After ironing all day Tuesdays, Mom spent all day Wednesdays sewing, patching holes and darning socks, and making clothes for my two sisters and my brother and me. I can't recall when I got some store-bought clothes, but I do remember my first pair of long pants. Mom made them, and how proud I was to finally have some long pants; not wearing those long stockings with my pantywaist garters to hold them up. How badly I felt when I fell at school while out at recess, running. The playground was covered with cinders. I tore a big hole in the knee of my new pants and was deathly afraid to go home with that report.

We never had many toys to play with. We had some building blocks with alphabet letters on them, a set of tinker toys that got lots of use on rainy days, and an erector set that was quite time consuming. Outside, nearly every kid had an old worn out tire that we would roll along ahead of us as we ran all over the neighborhood. For fun, we would sometimes stuff my baby brother, Cliff, inside the tire. We would roll him down a small hill aiming for the little creek, but he always managed to fall out before getting to the creek. My older brother had done the same thing to me.

I did get a new sled for Christmas one year, but never got a chance to use it. You guessed it! My older brother Lyell and his friend, Bob Weigle took it over on the rough and tumble where they broke my sled before I ever got to ride on it.

It was my duty to see that the wood box by the kitchen stove was always full, and that there was always dry kindling wood for Mom to start the fires in the mornings. Even with the biggest chunks of wood in the stove at night, it was usually burned out by morning. At times, when there was no dry kindling wood available, I had to put it in the oven at night after supper so it would be dry by morning. At that time, we ate dinner at noon

and the evening meal was supper. I don't recall ever having pancakes for breakfast, but Mom would often make them for supper. I never understood how she could stand there making pancakes for all the rest of us until we were all full, and then she would sit down and eat one herself. I didn't realize it at the time, but in later years have come to the conclusion that mothers are a truly special breed. Where would we be without them?

Another of my chores was pulling weeds out of the garden. We always had a large garden planted in every available bit of ground. The weeds grew ten times faster than the vegetable plants, and how I hated them.

My dad was an avid trout fisherman and thought I should be too. He sometimes took me with him. Usually, I would fall in the creek first thing, getting all wet and then had to suffer along until Dad had caught a limit of ten trout. I would take the fish and run home; he would stay and catch another bunch of them. I did enjoy eating them though.

Dad took me hunting as soon as I was big enough to carry a small shotgun, and I've never enjoyed anything more than hunting. This is something I have not done since moving to California, thirty-three years ago.

Living off the Land
By Marie A. Wilcox of Morris, Pennsylvania
Born 1932

I, Marie Mast, was born May 12, 1932, youngest of ten children. There were 6-boys and 4- girls. My parents were, William and Millie Mast. I was the only one born in a hospital at Blossburg, Pennsylvania. The others were all born at home. Two of my brothers died young, before I was born.

I started school at Oregon Hill; this school had two floors, first through fourth grades down stairs, and fifth through eighth upstairs. There was just me and two other neighbor kids in my grade. A car use to comer to the end of our driveway and pick us up to go about three miles to school. In the winter when the snow was deep, a team of white horses would pick us up with an enclosed wagon that had a wooden bench on each side, and a door on the back with a small window in it.

My favorite teacher was Miss Thomas. She always seemed to have time to do things

Grandma Mast

that made school more interesting. One that stands out in my mind was pictures of birds, and on the back of them was their habitat, and we would use them for flash cards to learn to identify them. We would do that during recess when the weather was bad. I could pass this on to my children when they would ask, "What kind of bird is that?"

She kept a coal fire in the huge stove and the bigger boys would bring the coal in and take the ashes out for her.

We would take 5 cents a week to school and on Monday, Wednesday and Friday the teacher would warm up soup and on Tuesday and Thursday, we had hot chocolate and marshmallows in it to go along with our lunch we took from home. I was the only one that attended high school because they put a big school bus on to take kids from Pine Township, to Wellsboro, Pennsylvania, which was more than 30 miles. I graduated from there in 1950. I had at least 3 miles to go meet the bus.

We didn't get electricity here until I was in 11th grade.

Saturday night baths was taken in a wash tub in front of the wood stove in cold weather, and of course, we all had our turns going to the outhouse where each was trying to be first to use the index pages of an old Sears & Roebuck catalogue that was always there. At night, we could use a large chamber pot with a lid. Back then, we called it a "slop jar", don't know if that was the right name.

I remember Monday's wash was done with a gasoline powered wringer washer with

the exhaust pipe out a propped up window so the fumes would go outdoors.

Printed chicken feed bags that worked, were for making blouses and skirts.

Our battery powered radio, which had a long wire hooked to the back of it and ran out the window and very high on a hill, would bring in the far away stations real clear. Everybody listened to the "Grand Ole Opry" on Saturday nights. I can remember my dad listening to the news of Walter Winchell, Lowell Thomas, etc. and the morning the news came over "Japanese Attack Pearl Harbor", which at that time, I didn't realize how many ways that would affect our close-knit family. I was 11 years old and the next thing was, the draft called my brother and "Bill" left to go in the Army, February 3, 1943. My brother Bill was 20 years old at the time. He had been away at CC-Camp in Schenectady N.Y. He was stationed in Camp Croft, S.C., and knew he was going to be sent overseas and never getting home. He tried to see us by coming to Wellsboro, Pa. on a Greyhound bus. The family packed in a car and sat over night during a "blackout". When the bus came in, he wasn't there. His pass was too short. The MP's took him back to camp. He was sent to North Africa and later was killed in action at Anzio Beach Battle in Italy, February 4, 1944. We were shocked and heart broken. We never got to see him. Among the things my mother saved, is the little V-mail letters that was sent back and forth during the war, and as I'm writing this, I wonder if there is very many people alive that remembers them.

Thinking of all the things that we had we could enjoy even without electricity I recall a big stand-up wind-up record player. It played really old thick Edison records. In shopping in Sears Catalogue, we found that they sold an arm that would hold a different kind of needle

Making apple butter with Grandma Mast, Aunt Mary Thomas, and Marie

313

*Marie's Dad and Mother
with Oline, Betty, Kenneth, and Marie*

that would play 78 records, and we sent and got it along with the records. They sold "Gene Autry" and we listened to them.

I remember a lot about things from catalogues, because that was our main source of a way to get anything, as we did not have a car.

My dad's first car was a 39 Plymouth with a rumble seat. I remember the kids making fun and saying, "Pa's new Plymy".

We kids didn't have as much or was able to go anywhere like the other kids in school. I remember attaching shoe stamps on order blanks to get our shoes. So many things were rationed during the war. I remember the telephone on the wall. Our ring was a long and two short rings. If you turned the crank to ring a short ring, you got the operator. Everyone had a party line and my aunt use to tell about hanging the receiver down on her pillow on the couch for an afternoon nap, and if anyone started a conversation, she would listen.

We lived back far enough that we didn't see too many people. Our nearest neighbor was a mile away. Our mailbox was also a mile away.

My grandmother, Mast, use to get a Sunday "Grit" in the mail, which was read by all of us.

My grandmother, which was my dad's mother, used to tell us about coming from Germany in to Philadelphia and settling here in the 1800s. She and an uncle and an aunt lived in one house and my dad, mother, and kids lived in the other house real close to us.

All of my family has passed away, but one

sister lives in Willsboro.

We do not get the big snow storms that use to keep us snowed in for days at a time and now that 911 upgraded addresses, we have a mailbox at our driveway and a snowplow comes to our driveway.

In remembering farm chores, we had chickens to feed and gathering eggs. My uncle had milk cows and used metal milk cans to keep milk cooled in a trough of spring water in the milk house, and a truck came and picked them up from scales they sat on at the end of our driveway.

The old saying like you use to hear people say, "Living off the land", fit us to a T. We had our own meat, beef, pork and stream with trout that ran by our house. Chicken was a Sunday dinner many times. We had a big garden cellar that my mother kept well stocked with canned vegetables and a lot of wild fruit.

A yearly thing was making apple butter out in the yard in a big kettle over a fire. My grandfather had two orchards planted and some trees had more than one kind of apples, as he grafted trees.

My mother had one cow she milked two times a day and saved milk and us kids run it through a cream separator and she made homemade butter and sold it for 50 cents a pound. We didn't have to mow grass; the cows did a good job to keep that under control.

As far as getting into mischief, I can remember a few things about my brothers who use to go up on our house roof and smoke cigarettes and my mom would go outdoors and say, "I can smell cigarette smoke", but we never told on them.

Back in the 40s my grandfather, Henry Breed; my mother's father lived with us. He used to take a cushion and put it on a chair in the front yard under an upstairs window and we use to get a clothes sprinkler and sprinkle a little on him. He would come in saying, "Millie, I think we are going to get a little shower." We would just laugh to ourselves and never tell what we did.

We use to spend lots of time walking in our woods and got to know a lot about nature. We use to, each have a favorite spot. We each had our own we could go to when things didn't seem to go right, and that's where we went to have our time alone.

As us three youngest ones were home after the older ones left to go out and stay with some aunts and uncles to find some jobs, we passed time with inside things like puzzles, jacks and other games that passed away some time.

Outdoors it was hopscotch, Dodge black ball, softball and a lot of walking.

We also self-taught ourselves with music instruments that my aunt brought us. She was a secretary in a music store in Elmira, New York. I played guitar and piano, which I worked at playing in a band after I got married and still do today. I got married in 1951, and raised 5 girls and one boy and never moved more than 40 miles from here, and now that I am a widow it is bitter-sweet to live back here with my son that has special needs.

Writing about my life in a "down home story" about the good old days has been very easy, because I am here to relive them every day. I have pictures and it is the original home. "How many people get to do this, I wonder?"

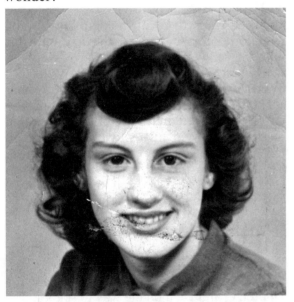

Marie Mast Wilcox in 1950

Life's Opportunities, All it takes is, "Caring & Sharing"
By Harold M. Ingram of Williamsport, Pennsylvania
Born 1931

What ever happened to those days when we made our own fun and exciting times with natural God given things that cost nothing, but your own ingenuity.

We are lucky in Lycoming County with the mountains, rivers and creeks. Here we have mountain roads from the lumber era, when lumber filled our mountains and rivers. As a child growing up, this was the world, and I thought everyone enjoyed the same thing.

I was born in 1931 and I can remember from four years old. We lived next to the YMCA on Neece Street. I remember the metal fence around the YMCA, where we climbed over and collected worms for fishing in the river. I do remember my dad taking me to the Market Street Bridge and fishing off the pier for catfish.

I also remember Wong's Chinese Laundry on the corner of Neece and Fourth Street.

The flood of 1936 forced us to move due to water all around us. I remember seeing washtubs and benches floating all around our house.

My older brother went to Washington School only one year, and I thought it was the greatest thing to bring books home from school. After the flood the next year, we moved to East Jefferson Street.

Not many people had family cars in those days, so we used our red wagons to move things. We didn't have a car until 1940, as I remember my dad walking there blocks every day to be picked up for work by a buddy of his boss. On Jefferson Street, we lived next to the railroad tracks and the "dinky tracks" right next to the river. Yes! The dinky tracks were neat. They were the spurs that serviced the factories up and down Williamsport along Jefferson and Canal Streets. I remember how the railroad men and those who rode the rails would throw hunks of coal off the cars, then we would go out after the trains pulled out and gather the coal by the buckets full.

I recall that every time we had a hard rain, Jefferson Street would flood and the kids would run up and down the streets in water up to their hips.

In those days, we always had food on the table and patches on our pants, but they were clean patches.

Childhood diseases like chicken pox, mumps, and measles were almost always posted on someone's home. This frightened our mothers to no end, since the whole neighborhood played together or went to Jefferson School where someone was always quarantined.

We always walked to school (2 miles) we didn't have school buses like today, but we did have school festivals and large Parent Teachers Meetings, attended by both parents.

I remember walking to school down thru the Wood Pipe Co., past the city dump, the Gummo Laundry and the Candy Factory, then, cross Railway Street at the fire station, turn right to the Reading RR underpass, or go straight ahead to the Eureka Paper Box. Co. and Jefferson School. There weren't many cars, so it wasn't a problem. We did have patrol boys at all street crossings. I remember when I was in 6th grade I was captain of the Patrol Boys. I had a badge and was very proud to assign the crossing guards, and direct the students out the correct doors.

I remember the vagrants coming in our back yard looking for a meal for which they would clean your yard, cut wood or most anything for food. Sometimes my mom would even wash their shirts. These men would reward us by throwing coal off the rail cars in appreciation. These guys always knew when bake day or washday was. Every neighborhood seemed to have their own day for washing clothes, baking pies or cakes, ironing or house cleaning.

People sat on their porch at night and the kids played in the streets (no cars). Games like kick-the-can, softball, catty –on-the-bounce, and hide & seek were popular. What fun "Team tag" was!!

With no cars, we had our bread and milk delivered by horse-drawn trucks and these trucks would bring ice for iceboxes; remember there were no refrigerators back then!

People back then, would save their scrap iron, rags, and paper boxes and sell them to the junk man. Joe Wise, the junk man lived across the street from us. It was the last home on East Jefferson Street and he had a horse and wagon on his property and a homemade barn to keep the horse. He went all over the area, even South Side collecting junk. I went along with him once when I was 10 years old and I remember his horse bucked trying to cross the hump at the Market Street bridge railroad tracks. I only went with him once, but I often went to the barn to feed his horse a carrot.

We had a neighborhood grocery store: Sammy Raes. What a blessing, he constantly filled grocery lists on credit. It was surely a nice place for ice cream. I remember when you got a Popsicle; the stick may have the letters free, and you could get another treat.

One time I chewed the end of my stick and you could barely see the word, FREE, but Sammy gave me a free-bee anyhow.

At Easter time, they had monster real egg hunts at Mountain Beach in South Side. A thousand kids and parents went up the mountainside and cleaned out thousands of eggs. Of course, at Mountain Beach was the place families went to swim on hot days, rather than the dirty river. We kids swam in the river on the Williamsport side. Now, I want to tell you that we had fun just swishing away the feces. Remember there were no sanitary sewer facilities—the sewer emptied into the river about 30 yards from shore. The sewer pipes coming from town were tall enough to walk in. There were sewer rats as big as small dogs all over the city at night. There were even several men who would root thru the sewage at the end of these large pipes and find money and all kinds of diamond rings and necklaces. Needless to say, we swam at the Hepburn Street Dam when we wanted to cool off. The Fire Company also came in the neighborhood and opened the hydrants for kids.

Remember the Wood Pipe (Now Eastern Wood) and the fun we had on the large lumber stacks that they used for the pipes and the barrels of hard tar and wood chips that coated the pipes, to give them a long life to withstand the in-ground moisture and vigorous use. We snuck into the Valmont Planing Mill on weekends and played with the dollies that were on the rail tracks where someone always got hurt—wheels would run over fingers and we would go to Mostellers Drug Store to get stiches and he would bandage us up all for free. When we had a few cents between us, we stopped at Mostellers and got a one cents big pretzel and ate it on the way to school. We always fought over who got the knot.

These were the days when doctors came to your house to treat you if you got sick or broke a bone, but we were all pretty active and not much sickness. I always got a perfect attendance certificate. We paid the doctor with homemade produce. Every family had a garden. Why not? They were fertilized along the river!

There was always something to do like climbing onto a boxcar sitting empty on the Dinky tracks, making kites and flying them all over town, or making sling-shots and shooting rats at the city dump. We also made scooters from old pairs of skates.

When the Moose Club burned down, they dumped all the trash, even slot machines at the city dump and we had a ball breaking them open and rooting for coins and whatever, and sold a lot of stuff to junk dealer, Joe Wise.

The school had "Grey Y Clubs" that would compete against one another in basketball and baseball and we got to swim at the YMCA. This was an experience, because you weren't allowed to wear suits. Yes! We all swam naked at the "Y" in those days, men and boys alike, and we didn't give it a second thought.

I remember going to Anderson's Lumber Yard down in the woods behind C.A. Reeds and playing around all the logs with my friend Eric Anderson, and the occasional encounter with a couple of vagrants who spent the night in the woods. These guys would always have a bottle of booze in a brown paper sack.

I remember the Dickenson Seminary and the Army men training there and at Brandon Park. They were very disciplined and it was real Army. This was around 1942 or there about.

Around 1946 the powers-to-be, thought we should have a dyke after the flood of 1946 along with a new sewer system. This all changed the area I grew up in. My street, East Jefferson, is long gone, but we will always have the memories of the river, the Market House, large political parades, street lights and music in town at Christmas time, the Keystone Theatre, and don't forget the magnified Santa and work shop at Sears.

We grew up without the need for many resources, but it is with pride that we had the opportunity of growing with the likes of P. D. Mitchell, Clem Ladd and Leo Willamson. These men, along with our parents made those years of Depression something special for you and me, and it didn't cost a nickel. All it takes is "caring and sharing" our short lives!

Becketts Run School, Forward Township, Ella Hollow, Alleghany County, Pennsylvania

By Howard E. McDonald of Emporium,
Pennsylvania
Born 1929

The year was 1935, and I was six years old. This meant I was to embark on my way through the Pennsylvania public school system and Becketts Run, a two-room schoolhouse, would be where I would go for the next seven years. They had six grades there, first through third in one room and fourth through sixth in the second room. I had to repeat first grade, because I didn't have enough complete days to move to the next grade. I had five bouts with pneumonia and a tussle with diphtheria that kept me from class. Miss Coulter, the first love of my life, and my first grade teacher, came a couple of times a week to tutor me, but I still didn't make it, because of the number of days that I missed. Money was tight and times were hard. There weren't many fancy things in the old schools. We had no running water, but we did have a two-room outhouse, or I should say a one-room outhouse that had a wooden partition inside of it.

In those days, every boy carried a pocketknife and a hole was cut into the partition so we could peek into the girl's side. The girls had complained to the teacher who was the head honcho, and she staked out the girl's side; low and behold, she saw this big blue eye glued to the peephole. Glen Morris was the peeper and he had one blue eye and one brown eye. Old Elsie rubbed a little snuff on her breaks, so she spit snuff juice right in old Glenn's blue eye. For the next few weeks, we called him "Red Eye". We carried our drinking water from across the highway and stored it in a blue crock, which had a tap on the side. Everyone brought a tin cup to drink their water out of, and we stored the cups on a shelf above the crock. Mr. Hepner, the caretaker of the school, furnished the water and he always kept an eye on us kids.

The teachers ran a roster of who carried the water; on my day, it was very cold. Becketts Run passed under the highway and the bridge had iron pipe railings. The railings were coated with frost and I decided to taste this natural substitute for ice cream. In a microsecond, my tongue was "welded" to that pipe. Mr. Hepner had seen the whole thing take place and he screamed at me to not move. In a flash, he was there with a glass of water and saved the day. With the water, he got me unglued and saved the skin on my ice cream licker. Fridays we got out of school an hour early. Friday was also the day that the outhouse was scrubbed down with lye water and it was a chore that every boy wanted to do. This job meant that you got out of class earlier than the rest of the school.

We always planned the finish of this task so that we would be done a couple of minutes before the final bell. When the scrubbing was completed and the dirty water emptied, the scrub buckets were then placed atop the broom and mop; you marched past the school windows to show that you were finished. This act always got a loud uproar from the kids. This was the signal that another exciting week at Becketts Run School was at an end.

Important Information is Disappearing
By William J. Brooks of Bradford,
Pennsylvania
Born 1961

I am a native of Bradford, having been born at Bradford Hospital, graduated from BAHS, and majored in College Prep for Petroleum Production – Pennsylvania grade at Smethport Area High School, a member of Future Farmers of America, majored in Bee Keeping, kept 12 colonies of Italian bees, studied land judging, and was awarded 2nd place Penn State Finals from Instructor Lt. Col. Willis Conable.

I served in the military, USAF in San Antonio, Texas, Chenoa, Illinois, and Myrtle Beach, South Carolina. I was an honor graduate at Canute HFB in Illinois. For duty I was stationed at Myrtle Beach AFB, South

William J. Brooks
Bear Hunt 1990

Carolina flew A10 Warthogs, a Jet mechanic engine test. At the test facility, I flew 100,000 times under Bob Callahan, Chief Master Sgt. and Base Commander Col. Shultz. I tested 65 engines with secret clearance.

I remember the good old days when in elementary school I walked ¾ mile and the police crossed us on the highways. Now Amreica is fat and lazy and nobody walks, the school buses stop every 25 feet to load and unload. The roads are terrible, the Federal government is corrupt, the State government is corrupt, and the local and county government is corrupt. Important books are disappearing from the Bradford Library. God please help us help ourselves to go get back to the good old days.

William J. Brooks
Basic Training 1980

"Cow Foam" on the Creek
By Cheryl Dunlap of Carlisle, Pennsylvania
Born 1947

Summer was always special for our family. With our friends and relatives, we headed to the creek, our favorite place.

My aunt and uncle had a cabin by the creek. It was called "Sel-Dom-In." We would cook our lunch and supper on the open flame; all eat together and then head out to play in the creek. We had inner tubes and a homemade surfboard. Cows were always on the other side or in a field, and some would even come in the creek.

One Saturday evening my dad, cousin, and uncle decided to make a wooden raft with barrels for us to use on Sunday. They finished

318

it around midnight Saturday. After church Sunday, we headed out to the creek once again. We would jump off the raft, get in our inner tubes, and float down the creek. Cows were still in the creek and floating beside us down the creek was "cow foam."

Later in the day, my uncle got his boat, the "Chip-a-wa Chief" out, we all piled in and then went for rides up and down the creek. For the kids not in the boat, he would go fast and make a fast turn so they had little waves to play in with the inner tubes.

The days went fast during summer, all giving us wonderful memories of our favorite spot, the creek.

Halloween Memories
By Mary Lou DiNardo of Johnsonburg, Pennsylvania
Born 1932

The night before "Trick or Treat", my dad made a "Tick Tack". He took a large empty thread spool and cut a V shape around both round ends. Then he tied a cord to the spool and wound it around tightly. We put a large nail or pencil in the hole, put the spool up against a window and pulled the chord. Wow! Loud enough to see people jump out of their lounge chair. (Now, Run as fast as you can, re-roll the chord and on to the next house.)

Every time I eat a meat spread sandwich (ground bologna, pickles and mayonnaise) I think of holiday church parties, especially the Church Basement Halloween party. First, the Halloween costumes-- I would go through the family cedar chest. I find a blue and yellow "flapper dress", dance shoes, a huge gold and white fringed shawl and a red paper rose. (I am a Spanish Dancer!)

No "store-bought" costumes, but lots of white sheet ghost, red underwear clad devils and moonshiners! The only thing we would buy at the 5 &10 store was our half-masks.

We bobbed for apples, and in the darkened basement, listened to a horror story as we passed around "body parts" grapes for eyeballs, ketchup blood and spaghetti "innards." (UNDER MY MASK, THE SMELLS SURROUND ME: MOTH BALLS, POWDERED SUGAR DOUGHNUTS, APPLE CIDER, EGG SALAD, AND AS I RUN ALONG HOME, GOBLINS CHASE ME!)

Remember When....
By Georganna Doran of Knoxville, Pennsylvania
Born 1938

It used to be, no one had a television. That's right boys and girls! We gathered around a box like device with knobs we turned to get the sound to come in, and listened. If you had an imagination, you could "see" in your head the villain or the good guys. As the story unfolded, you slid closer to the edge of your chair, not wanting to miss a word. "Listen, were those footsteps the guilty one? maybe it was the good guy coming."

Finally—there was the answer, the music swelled, the mystery was solved and all was well for another week. Then, we could tune in this RADIO for another exiting adventure happening behind the "squeaky" door!

Time moved on, and then there appeared an even more exciting box in the living room. This "box" showed black & white moving pictures of real people moving around talking, and most excitingly, WRESTLING, Yes!...Television had arrived! You could see Gorgeous George or maybe Argentina Rocca in an exciting match. Oh, look! He picked him up and threw him over his shoulder!

But, know what? These exciting scenes weren't nearly as interesting as those sounds coming out of that box we used earlier. Imagination provided it all. Could that be why a book still draws me in like those boxes never did? I could use my private mind's eye to "see" it all happening, as I would prefer it to appear.

Try it! Turn off the set and read a book!

My Dad, the Real "Bread" Winner
By Nina J. Dymeck of Williamsport, Pennsylvania
Born 1928

This is my story from the good old days. I was born in Erie, Pennsylvania, in 1928. We moved to Renovo, Pennsylvania in 1931.

My father was a baker by trade and opened a bakery in Renovo. When the Depression hit, he lost the bakery. To have some money coming in, my father baked at home and Mother went door to door selling the baked goods.

We left Renovo in 1933 and my dad got a job at Leo Williamson Bakery on W. 4th Street. At one time, he also worked at the 20th Century Bakery on Court Street.

There was no TV at that time, but we had a Zenith floor model radio and listened to some good radio shows.

We lived in Newberry and to get to school, we walked, and to get to high school we took the city bus. We had to pay our own way. We had a friend who had a car with a "rumble seat" and he would pick up my sister and I to take us to school once in a while.

Our activities included swimming in Lycoming Creek at 4th Street in Newberry and up at Sunset Park, which is now the location of Weis Market. We also went roller-skating at the rink in Memorial Park, Sunset Park, and there was a rink up over the old Park Theatre. Also, there was a pond at Memorial Park where we went Ice Skating in the winter.

In the summer, we would be outside playing baseball, hopscotch, and marbles, etc., not just sitting in the house playing video games, etc. Of course, they did not exist!

The First Jet-propelled Plane (My Rocket Booster Piper Cub)
By Joe Venderi of Johnsonburg, Pennsylvania
Born 1924

In 1937, our local New Stand brought "MEGOWS" Model Airplane Kits to our village. They were rubber propelled Balsa wood and Japanese tissue kits, complete with plans.

In June, I had already made two planes the smaller 10-cent models. With the Fourth of July around the corner, I bought the usual firecrackers, torpedoes, and "Penny Sky Rockets" also known as "Bottle Rockets", as they could be placed in a Coke bottle and fired. These rockets gave me the bright idea of gluing a rocket under each wing of a small lower wing "Aeronca". My buddy Fred helped me with the "TAKE OFF". I held the wound-up propeller in check while Fred lit the rocket fuses. The plane flew almost straight up and then burst into flames. I knew immediately, the highly flammable "doped" Japanese tissue covering the plane made the perfect combustion for the rocket's sparks.

Back to the drawing board!

I wasn't about to give up! I felt that a meeting with my science teacher might provide a solution (I hoped!) He suggested that I Make-up a mixture of water and Borax. When applied to the Japanese Tissue, the tissue would shrink as usual on the wings, fuselage and tail sections. The Borax would leave a film, making the plane somewhat fireproof!!!

I bought a larger model "Piper Cub", assembled it putting a tiny raised platform in the middle of the wing/fuselage. It was there that we glued the Penny rockets. This time we used a steep road to launch our "JET". IT WORKED!!! The plane sailed into the air about 30 feet and headed toward the river valley below. Here it picked up an updraft, which also created a turn so that the plane glided gracefully following the course of the river where it finally landed and quickly became waterlogged, and as we watched in anguish, it sank!!!

EPILOGUE

As there were no "Penny Rockets" available, it was a case of wait till next year. 1938 rolled around and June found us on a camping trip at the newly opened State Park, "Twin Lakes". After seeing all those pretty girls in swimsuits, my love for aviation was replaced with the "rapture" of the feminine "Mystic". The rocket plane brainstorm became a memory!!

Oh, Those Nightshirts!
By Bill Thompson of Ridgway, Pennsylvania
Born 1949

One of my most memorable family times was when I was between 8 and 10 years old. My two younger brothers and I shared a Saturday night each, at our grandparent' house, which was every third Saturday for me. I would help clean my parent's house on Saturday morning after breakfast, then, it was cartoons for a while, then playing.

Sometime in the afternoon, I would get ready to go to my grandparent's house, where I would bring them up to speed on all that had happened since my last overnight stay. Somewhere along the line, I would go to the closet and get out my favorite toy, which was a set of Lincoln logs. I would play for hours while my grandmother would start making dinner. It always tasted so good!! Nothing could beat Grandma's cooking!

While they did the dishes after supper, I would play for a while. We would relax for a bit, and then it was off to the movie theater to see a movie. We never had to worry at that time, as the only movies that were played at the theatre were good clean movies, (Western, comedies, etc.)

When the movie was over, we would go home and get ready for bed. I looked forward to bedtime at Grandma's, as she had a nightshirt and nightcap and slippers for me to wear. Then, off to the oversized bed for some wonderful dreams!

Sunday morning after breakfast, it was off to church. We came home and Grandma would start lunch, which was always so much for a guy my size. After lunch, it was on the floor to play with my logs and listen to the ball game on the radio, in the summer. While we listened to the game, they would read the Sunday paper. Around 5 o'clock, it was off to my house to start a new week.

I really miss those "good old days"! When I got older and got married, I was telling my wife how much I missed those nightshirts. That Christmas, I found a couple of them under the tree. I am 62 years young today and I still wear the nightshirts!!

Double Rescues, But Years Apart
By Harold E. Jones of Osceola Mills, Pennsylvania

When I was growing up my family was going through hard times, and being a small child, I didn't know.

For a time out, my mother would pack a real big lunch. We would stay all day and swim at the old stripping cuts. The one time we went, my brother started going under and pulled me under with him. My dad was real quick to get us, but if I hadn't been there, he would have drowned. What a good memory to remember.

Years later, I met my (not knowing), wife-to-be. I took her and my sister-n-law to be to a swimming place that was an old stripping cut and they were swimming and her younger sister started going under and she grabbed my wife-to-be and pulled her under. I had to rescue them. Weird!!!!

Now, years later, (it's been 40 years) and we have 3 children, 5 grandsons, and 5 granddaughters.

I remember when I was a little boy. My brother and I was playing tag, and I was chasing my brother so I could tag him before he tagged me. We were going in one door and out another door. I jumped to tag him and at the same time, he slammed the door shut and my fist went through the door window. Needless to say, we called it "Hospital Tag" all the time from that day on, because I ended up being taken to Philipsburg Hospital for stiches. They said I wouldn't be able to use that hand, but I'm so thankful it healed and I was able to use my hand. I ended up becoming an equipment operator and had to use both hands for work.

Another story I remember, growing up in Osceola was that my birthday is on the Fourth, and I thought everyone was celebrating my birthday on the Fourth. After the parade one day, my cousin and me went to the carnival and went on the Dive-Bomber and the chain broke while we were on it. Seemed forever that we were up in the air and we kept rocking the ride to make it go around. Eventually we were off of the ride and it was so much fun for me and my cousin.

Very Bad Boys at School
By Edward Raybuck of West Windsor, New Jersey
Born 1955

My name is Edward Raybuck. I am writing on the behalf of Mary Raybuck on the suggestion of Ron McGonigal.

I would like to write about my dad and his family and things that I remember from growing up.

Dad was born in 1921 by Pansy, a little village near Brookville, PA. He was one of seven children, four boys and three girls. There are only two sisters and one brother living now.

His father's name was Jacob Raybuck and his mother's name was Ella Hetrick.

They had a farm in the Pansy Hollow, which was farmed with horses. There is a spring on the side of the hill. The water comes in the house without a pump. As I was growing up Grandma had a woodstove, which the cooking was done on. Then there came bottle gas for a stove.

There was no bathroom so you had to use the outside outhouse. It wasn't too much later on in years after taking a bath in a small washtub that a bathroom was put in and a furnace of hot air only for the down stairs. The upstairs was very cold in the winter. Dad would tell about how they put warm bricks in the bed at your feet to keep warm.

Dad and others had to walk to school over a mile down a dirt road, which is still there today to a one-room schoolhouse still in Pansy today.

Dad, Uncle Wilbert, and Cousin Bill were very bad boys in school. They would make pop guns out of elderberry, hollowing it out, and making spit balls to shoot at the kids. One day the teacher got it so all the pop guns went into the stove, which was in the center of the room.

When the skunk cabbage was growing Dad would fill his pockets up and sit by the stove in the classroom until the whole room smelled like a skunk, so no more class for anyone.

Everybody played baseball. They had a field near the farm. Uncle John would come to see Dad play, to see a heavyset guy run so fast.

One day while we were at the farm Dad made me a toy. A hoop from a barrel and a piece of wire to push it along.

A little about Uncle John. He lived on a farm down a dirt lane far off the road. His first wife died so he asked Grandma's sister Amara if she would marry him. She was a great cook. When we were there we would eat Sunday dinner there.

They had a dog who would sit up at the table and eat like we would. Aunt Anna had a loom, which you made rag rugs on so I have a few family rugs.

Uncle John's farm was farmed with by horse until he could not farm anymore

There was an outhouse there too. Also a picture pump for water. So I had fun pumping water.

Uncle Wilbert, the oldest, served in the Army. He went in on D-Day during the war. It was very bad, he told me. Once that was over, he would tell me how he loved to get milk and potatoes, which they found along the way.

Grandma and Dad's sister would make homemade quilts so I have a collection of them.

Dad worked in a coalmine near home. The next day when he came back it was caved in where he was working so he decided to move on. His dad didn't like it, but he moved to Newtown, PA, to work on a farm there. Later on he worked at Walker Gorden Farms in Plainsboro.

Thank you, these are a few items I remember from Dad. We would go back every summer to the farm, which is still there as a camp house because the barn fell down. I sure miss going there. It was peaceful.

Woolworths, a Variety of Fond Memories
By Bonnie Springman of Williamsport,
Pennsylvania
Born 1949

I was an employee of FW Woolworths 5&10 Department Store right in downtown Williamsport, and enjoyed coming to work every day to be there for my customers. The courthouse was right across the street and I loved to see families come into the Woolworths to have ice cream. We had a "SPECIAL", Pick a Balloon—where customers could win a banana split for just 1 cent! Wow! We also made several sandwiches too.

There was even a Hot-dog Stand out in front of the store where employees and friends came and lined up for a Hot-Dog and chips for lunch, then they would find a bench to relax

Bonnie Springman
In the front of Woolworth Store

and enjoy watching people walking by.

Every year the city put on the "Heritage Days", where many vendors would set-up and sell all kinds of food and treats, with craft tables too.

Employees who worked in the shops around town would dress up in old fashioned long dresses and hats and go outside on their breaks and mingle, and shop around too. What a great time for everyone, there was music, dancing, face painting, and all kinds of activities for all of us to remember.

Woolworths was a Variety Store and we had a little bit of everything, even pets. We would decorate for all the holidays and have good sales and specials. It was sad to see it close, but sure was a lot of good memories for all of us.

Bonnie Springman

Memories of a Prayer
By Georgeanne Freeburg of Johnsonburg, Pennsylvania
Born 1933

Large banks of piled snow glistened in bright winter sun touching the mounds outside our elementary school in Johnsonburg, Elk County, Pennsylvania. Boot imprints in the shoveled path for students and teachers led into the old red brick two story building.

It was 1944. Talks of the war in Europe and a place they called "The South Pacific" were discussed at home, or we caught the News Reel at the local theatre, Saturday matinee. But, on that sunny, wintry afternoon, we were snug at our wooden desks, with the warm radiator pipes lining the sidewall under the blackboard.

Our little paper mill town's elementary school was comprised of grades 1 through 6. Our sixth grade "homeroom" also served as our mathematics classroom. It was ruled by a tiny lady, Miss Garrity, handicapped by childhood polio, but who was always teaching by moving from desk to desk, to the blackboard and back to us. And believe me, we were diligent students under those stern eyes. But, during that afternoon of memory, Miss G was called out of the room. Most of us continued to be busy with the assigned work…with the exception of the other "ruler" of us 36 students (in Miss G's absence, of course): **The Bully!**

He was **Big!!** A couple of years older than most of us, and he was **Mean!!** Why, he even had stubbles of black whiskers starting to shadow his chin! And there were whispers about his waiting outside the school after dismissal at 4 o'clock and then chasing screaming girls (and some boys) with ice crusted snowballs. We also knew there were days when he was "kept after class" for numerous classroom violations.

As the octagon wall clock ticked and no Miss G, **Big Bully** lumbered up to her desk, propped his feet up on the edge, picked up the "grade book", opened it, and before our horrified eyes, plunked out a big wad of spit into its center and slammed it shut! He leaned forward and was leering at us, when that tiny, limping figure suddenly returned: **He was caught in the act!!** We were glued to our seats, and so was he, as she stood sternly beside him, crossed her arms, fixed him with **the eyes**, and then pointed to his seat in the center of the back row.

The only sound was him stomping back, plopping down and glaring at me to his left, then a blonde, Mary Lou, to his right. To top off his performance, he crossed his eyes at each of us, stuck out his huge tongue and put his head down on his desktop.

Now ML and I were gigglers of the first degree…and this was all just too much. We caved, tried to stifle our snickers, but too late. Miss G stood rigidly in front of our seats. The dreaded "**STAY AFTER SCHOOL**" for us **three** was mandated.

After 45 minutes of writing "I will not laugh, or disrupt class" about 100 times which felt like forever, time was up and ML and I pulled on our winter coats and boots and started down the snowy path home. No sign of BIG B…He must have left ahead of us while we were putting on our wraps. Now our biggest worry was what to tell at home, about why we were late!!

So, when the looming figure jumped out at us from behind a snow bank, we froze! BIG B yelled, "On your knees!" We dropped. "Start praying!" he yelled. (Hey, this wasn't very funny!)

"What—what—should we p-pray?" I stuttered. ML for once, was totally silent and wide-eyed, but I saw she had both mitten hands up in proper prayer form! I followed suit. "Pray THE HAIL MARY!" he shouted, waving his big arms in his brown wool jacket. ML gulped and said bravely that she didn't know it. Then, I caught a kick on my knee from the toe of one of his big galoshes: "YOU DO IT! TEACH HER!"

There we were, ML and I, all pigtails and mittens, and kneeling in the snow while I led "Hail Mary…" (ML would repeat)…"Full of Grace" (ML repeat). And then, when it was finished in our quacking voices, he grinned and said, (almost **NORMAL-LIKE** to our astonishment) "OK. You can go!" We did our best to run, but we were a little wobbly…one thing for sure, neither of us looked back.

Funny thing, the rest of the year, BIG B waited outside the school, but this time, he simply "walked" ML and me down the hill towards our homes. And NO One dared heave snowballs at us.

And the prayer? After all these many years, ML, a non-Catholic, can say the "Hail Mary" perfectly. All from that snowy day with BIG BULLY.

Got Wet Coon Huntin' and It Wasn't Rainin'!
By Francis T. Ayers of Austin, Pennsylvania
Born 1930

I will start off by introducing myself. I am Francis T. Ayers, "alias" "The Prouty Prowler." As of August 22, 2011, I turned 81. My dad was a Forest Ranger for 44 years, so I growed up in the mountains of Pennsylvania and I am still there. I could write a hundred stories or more, but I will write one about two of my sons, Dennis and Kenny. By the way, I have 4 sons and 3 daughters, 23 grandchildren, and 34 great-grandchildren, so I guess the Ayers name will carry on for a while yet. My wife and I have been married for 63 years.

Okay, now back to my story. One night Dennis and Ken came home and said, "Dad, will you come along and help us to get some raccoons? We need some spending money." I said, "Sure", because I thought it would last only a night or two. Well, it turned into two weeks of one of the most exciting times of my life that I will never forget, and no one else will that my boys talk too.

We got three big coons the first night and that was all it took to keep going night after night. We didn't take no small or medium coons, only large or bigger. We would go to all the apple orchards and spot their eyes shining in the trees. Armed with ball-bat and a 7-cell flashlight the boys would run to the tree and keep the coon up the tree until we planned our next move.

It was Dennis that did most of the climbing and shaking the coon loose. I would hold the light on the coon until he fell to the ground, and that was when Ken would have to swing into action with the ball-bat. By the way, he was pretty good, not many got away from him.

One moonlight night the boys came over and said, "It sure looks like it will be a good night for coon tonight." We didn't go very far before we scared a big coon out of a corn-patch, and up a tree with Dennis right behind him. I was holding the light on the coon and Ken was all-ready with the bat. I hollered up to Dennis to shake a little faster and harder, because it is starting to rain. Ken said, "I am standing right beside you and I don't feel no rain. After a couple of seconds, I realized he was right, it wasn't rain. My eyes started burning and I got the worst sickening bitter taste in my mouth. I dropped my light and started vomiting; I thought I would die for sure.

Dennis almost fell out of the tree from laughing, and Ken heard the coon hit the ground and took a swing with the bat, but connected with my leg. Needless to say, that coon lived to see another day.

Going home that night, I said, "boys; we have been hunting for over two weeks and almost got 50 coons. I have been going to work with my eyes half open, a few black and blue marks, and urinated on by a coon."

I wouldn't take a million dollars for them memories that will last while I am on this earth.

We took our furs to a Fur buyer, Bill Schroll who was in business for many years. He said it was the nicest bunch of hides he ever bought. We averaged $20 a hide.

Francis and Dennis in early 80s
Kenny took the picture

Ninety-Four and Still Have my Facilities
By Everett Saulter of Coudersport,
Pennsylvania
Born 1917

I noticed today, your request for information about life in Potter County in the Good Old Days. I am 94 years old and still have use of my facilities, whatever they are. I was #1 in a family of 10 children and got to wear the new clothing first. The remainder of the family got hand-me-downs. Nothing of any value was ever wasted.

We lived in a rural area 3 miles from school. The school season was in summer time only. Many roads closed all winter. The teachers lived at students homes near the school. I have been told that their wages sometimes were $10 per week. They were all very good teachers too.

This is an item I will never forget. A couple with a large family moved into the area. It was summertime. It was also noticed that all the students had for lunch was an old fashion pancake. The food, if you call it that, was covered with meat fat and was cold, with nothing to drink. It was also noticed that they all had some kind of itch trouble. The teacher

checked, and it was head lice, and a lot of them. The next day the whole school lined up and everyone got a head wash. Regular students got plain water. The new ones got louse killer. No one was offended.

As mentioned previously in 1920-1930 all county roads were made of plain dirt and some stone. Many were not passible in the springtime. Governor Pinchot of Pennsylvania started the WPA, Work Progress Program Administration of Pennsylvania. People in need of work could get, so called, "bean orders" for food and necessities and also help improve the roads with stone and gravel. They called it, "getting people out of the mud and dirt roads." It was very successful!

I was in high school at this time, about 14 years old, but they allowed me to work out the families, bean order or grocery allowance. I could not smash stone, but I could carry drinking water to the workers. Eventually, all main roads were improved and anyone who wanted work could work there---School records.

As mentioned previously, summer time was school time. It was most impossible in rural areas in wintertime. Also, school activities were difficult.

The family got a pony and carriage for summer use to get to school. One day during recess, the students moved the carriage to the top of a small hill, turned it around and most of them got in. Down the hill they went, the further they went, the faster they traveled. About half way down the hill, the people who were steering and controlling the buggy fell down and the buggy tipped over. There were students all over the hillside with a lot of bruises, but no injuries.

At the same school, but at a different time on the same location the teacher let a group of students out of school to mow the lawn. They had an old push type mower. They took the mower to the top of the hill, attached a rope to it for one of them to pull, and two others were to control the mower. The farther they traveled, the faster they went. The person pulling the mower fell down. The teacher heard him cry with pain. His big toe had a cut and was bleeding. The pony and buggy was a short distance away. We went to get them to take the student home. When we turned the corner to the schoolhouse, going too fast, the buggy tipped over. No one was hurt! At this time, the teacher took the injured student home after all the previous problems were solved and the story went on and on.

NOTE: I could write a book of the "Good Old Days". They were simple compared with what we have today.

The Village Barn Theater
By Catherine C. Straub of St. Marys, Pennsylvania
Born 1940

These are facts never thought of by the author while growing up.

My dad was born a New Yorker—from Manhattan, New York City. He remained that station, all his life. He was raised there and never forgot the entertainment part of New York City. He met our mother working in the area for a medical doctor. They married, existing in a Manhattan apartment for two years with a boy coming first and girl second. Mother talked him into going back home (where she came from) to country living.

It was the land of four-seasons somewhat like the city, but the snow seemed mountains high, when you were young and free. We all wished for another season: getting sick of summer, fall, or winter, and then longing for spring after a harsh winter snowed us in, at times. Plows were not a famous word back then.

Harry Conroy in younger years

Harry with his wife Genevieve

Coming of school age, we one way or another made the trek to the school bus stop (that picked the kids up) down on the main road (Washington Street Extension) to town and the grade schools.

There was a pond on either side of the dirt road leading to the house and back property. We loved listening to the pollywogs sing at night. They hadn't yet turned into frogs.

We had to wait to the end of January to ice skate on the frozen ponds. Our parents wanted to make sure the ice was set to avoid any hazardous accidents.

In summer time, we walked to town and saw movies at the local movie theater with friends or younger kin. We watched our elder brother play knothole baseball rooting for his team. The baseball team involved the elder sister's future husband, as a young kid.

Mother had gained the home and property from her dying stepmother. The two children were at the toddler age and into more things in the city apartment. She found it hard living in the big city with no yard space for the youngsters.

Dad was a polka writer and devoted to certain music. His daughter writing these memories is a fiction and nonfiction writer going by her abbreviated initials: C. C. Straub.

Getting back to the optimistic-move to St. Mary's, PA That is; Dad and Mother and the two elder children who were toddlers at the time, arrived in nice weather: at the old homestead. There our parents raised four more kids.

The country home had an old barn down from the house. Dad built a stage in the barn, and called it (written on the front) "The Village Barn Theater." He had bands come to play on the weekend. This was the amusing atmosphere the two elder kids recall.

Dad brought the entertainment capital of the world to a small town in the PA Wilds Area. At the time, the PA Wilds must have been known as the middle part of the state with less population.

Dad was not a hunter and none of the male children turned out taking up that sport. He would rather have his bands (at his barn) playing on Saturday night.

Taking the bus to school for first grade, there was no kindergarten or a half-day thing called kindergarten. The drivers were like the pony riders delivering the mail in the Wild West, no matter how ruthless the weather, the mail had to go through. Nowadays the kids have snow days and stay home from school, but make the missed days up prior to the school ending for the yearly term.

Life was different with the long skirts and blouses with bobby socks. There were more decent females and males at that time and going back further in history.

With so many Carbon Plants in the area, it was known as the "Carbon Center of the World."

Later on, when Dad wrote his polkas, he went to area dances to hear his polkas played.

By that time, the eldest girl had met and married her dancing husband.

Say the family never inherited the property; there would not be a full story here.

Harry Conroy

From Fox-Holes, To Farming
By Ronald S. Worden of Shinglehouse,
Pennsylvania
Born 1923

I was born in 1923 on a backwoods farm. My father had to go pick up the doctor with a horse and buggy when I was born. It was 20 mile round trip. Then he had to take the doctor back after delivery. We lived in an old farmhouse heated with wood. My mother was a very good cook. There was no electric back then. She had a wood cook stove. On it she could bake wonderful bread and a lot of other stuff. We were very poor money wise, but always had plenty to eat.

Each year we would have a large garden from which my mother canned many quarts of vegetables. We grew potatoes and had a big orchard. Each fall we would have a bin of apples and one of potatoes in our cellar, also a barrel of cider that we would drink all year round. It would get very strong (hard cider), but we all liked it. We had cows, pigs, chickens and horses.

The depression years were hard years to raise a family. I had two sisters and one brother. We all worked doing farm chores, milking cows, and driving horses, etc. Our farmhouse had running water from a never-failing spring. We heated water on the wood stove.

We did have a battery radio. Each night we would listen to "Lowell Thomas" with the news, then later to "Amos and Andy". On Saturday nights, we would listen to 'The Grand Ole Opry" from Nashville.

My father had a nice team of horses that he worked skidding logs in the oil fields, or anywhere there was work. Some men could find work for $1.25 a day at different jobs, mostly cutting logs and firewood. Once on a log job, a worker was killed by a falling tree. They wrapped his body in a horse blanket and my father hauled him out on a log boat.

My mother and I would go to town once a week shopping for groceries. We bought sugar, salt, flour, cornmeal and buckwheat flour for pancakes. In the summer, we would use our horse and buggy. After it snowed, we would use a one-horse sleigh. It was fun to ride in one, but we could get very cold. Once in the summer time, we had a new horse. He was young and a high stepper. We had a very steep hill to go down; it was 300 yards to the bottom. The buggy bumped the back end of the horse and it ran away, all the way down the hill. At the bottom, it turned into a barnyard. The buggy rolled over and came loose from the horse. We weren't hurt much, but I still have a scar on my head from the wreck. We had eggs and butter that we would trade for groceries at the store. They were all ruined; the buggy was a total wreck.

I went to school in a one-room schoolhouse the first 8 years of schooling. It was heated with a large wood stove. We carried water in a tin pale from a nearby spring. The bucket was set on a bench in a corner of the schoolhouse. A tin dipper hung on a nail beside it. We would get a dipper full, take a drink and pour the rest back in the bucket. It was a 2-mile walk to school. It had a large outhouse with a partition in the center, with boys on one side, and girls on the other side. When we succeeded, we could hear screaming from the other side. It was hilarious. A few students went on to high school. That was a 6-mile walk, and I did graduate from high school in 1940. After high school, I worked on a drilling rig in the oil field near our farm, then, I was drafted into the Army.

The Depression days were fading and my father bought a Model-A Ford car. It was much better transportation than the horse and buggy. I learned to drive it at 14 years of age and got a driver's license at 16 years.

After I went in the Army and I wound up in the Airborne Infantry, I was trained in gliders and paratroopers. Once I came on furlough and broke up with my girlfriend. Later she married someone else. Our 17th Airborne Division was shipped to Europe. We saw combat action in France, Belgium, Luxemburg, and Germany. In the "Belgium Bulge", I was blown out of a foxhole by an enemy artillery shell and lost the hearing in my left ear. I served as a rifle squad leader S/ SGT. My squad had 12 men. Our Company had about 200 men at first. When the war ended, we had 80 of the original ones left. I was discharged on Thanksgiving Day, in 1945. Shortly after I was home, I met a wonderful girl and we were married six months later. We had three children. We were married 48 years and she passed away from a stroke. Later I looked up my old girlfriend (her husband had passed away). A short time later, we were married. Seven years later, she too, passed away.

All of those years since World War II, I have been a dairy farmer. I bought a large run down farm in a remote area. For the first two years, I farmed with horses, as tractors were just coming into use. Later, the work was much easier after I got a tractor. It took a few years to get the farm up in good producing condition and I bought a second farm. It was a lot of work, but I enjoyed it.

I always hunted deer, and for several years had a coon dog or two. Sometimes I hunted coon until 3 a.m. I didn't think anything of staying out most all night in the woods hunting. My wonderful wife didn't think much of it, either.

Now I'm retired, but still live on the farm. I keep a few beef cows and put up round bales of hay each summer. Somewhere I heard this song; "if I had to do it all over again, I'd do it all over again"….

Jar Rubbers Held Our Stockings Up
By Emily Cary of Westfield, Pennsylvania
Born 1938

The first snowstorm I remember was 1941-42. My dad was in the Wellsville Hospital with TB. It was by the Northern Potter School. The snow was so deep it took 4 or 5 days to open the road.

My grandparents used to play music for the dances they had. Grandma played the organ and Grandpa the violin. She was Pa. Dutch and he was an Englishman. People took their kids also.

We got one pair of shoes a year. If we got a hole in them, we put in cardboard on the bottom.

I remember the old bathtub for our Saturday night baths. It was behind the kitchen stove. It was nice and warm there.

My mom made all of my dresses, made from the flowered feedbags that they got feed in. And then, we had those old brown long stockings we wore with jar rubbers to hold them up.

One place we lived, the neighbors had a Billy goat and it would come and chase us, so we couldn't get in the house. We had a pile of wood by the granary we would get behind it and try to get out one end and it would come and chase us back the other way.

I helped with splitting the kindling and

carry in wood to fill the wood boxes.

Those old out-houses we had for all the years that I was at home, and the old Sears & Roebuck catalogue for paper and my brothers would try to tip it over when I was in there. Tell you, we didn't stay in there long in the winter!

I helped Mom with the washing. I would turn the crank on the wringer and pull the clothes through. We had to pump our water from the well and put it in pans on the stove to get it hot.

We also had a wind-up Victrola we played records on. The first radio we had, Dad would bring in a battery and hook it up so we could hear the "Grand Ole Opry" on Saturday nights.

We had kerosene lamps to see with. One had a mantle and it was nice and bright. We would heat up those old flat irons and wrap a towel around them and put in our bed to keep our feet warm. It was always cold upstairs.

My dad died in 1946, so my mom raised us kids. We lived on a farm where an old man had a dairy and we had to do the milking. My mom got sick, so my brothers and myself had to do the milking. That is when I learned how to milk. While we lived there, my oldest brother put a clothesline on an old buggy and we would pull it up to the top of the hill in the road and ride it down. There was a sharp bend at the bottom, but we made it. There wasn't much traffic back then.

We had to walk out to catch the bus a few times when it snowed too much. It was about 1 ½ miles. We would ride down the hill in the winter, no matter how cold it was.

I remember my grandma's house smelling like sweetbreads as she made them in a steamer pan on top of the stove. It smelled so good!

I had a big dog named Touser. She was a lot like Lassie. She died with cancer on her belly. I also had a puppy once, but don't know what happened to that one.

My grandpa lived with us for a while after my grandma died, until he died the same year.

There was an old Hobo that would walk up the road. He would stop for a drink and Mom would fix him a sandwich.

We finally moved to a house that had electric. We got a radio and Mom would let us listen to "Stella Dallas, Just Plain Bill, Green Hornet, The Lone Ranger" and other programs.

My mom had a horse and buggy for years. She would trade horses with Howard White every few years. I guess it was like trading cars today. She still had one when I got married in 1954. She finally, did get her license and a car when she was in her late 60s.

I helped Mom in the garden pulling weeds and I was always singing, "You are my Sunshine." Our neighbor had a garage and laughed that he knew what I was doing.

We would get to go to Westfield to the movies on Saturday nights if someone would stop and pick us up.

My brothers and myself would play softball. They always batted first and I had to chase the ball. When it was my turn, they would quit.

I learned to cook at age 13. Out of six of us kids, there are now two of us left. Thank you for the memories!

School of Hard Knocks
By Barbara Hepler of Kane, Pennsylvania
Born 1947

I have fond memories of the old Central Elementary School in Kane, Pennsylvania. We could walk to school and come home for lunch in those days. In the winter, we dried our hats and our mittens on the old radiators in the hallways. It was really cool when they came on, thumping and hissing, especially when we were being very quiet during a test. We always stopped at one of the corner grocery stores before or after school if we had some money for penny candy, or my favorite, cinnamon toothpicks.

I also have memories of Mt. Jewett Elementary School. Walking to school in those days was a little scary, as we had some bullies back then. There was one boy in particular who was so tough and mean, he would hide out front and try to beat us kids. I was so scared, that I would take the long way home. I can remember one boy in class who really got beat up by a teacher, (Now deceased). I was so afraid for him, even though he was really bad. Now, a teacher would surely be in trouble for that sort of thing.

And then, the bus rides to Kane—some of the more well to do kids would save certain seats and you didn't dare to sit there—you just knew not to. I always ended up on the wheel seat, which was pretty uncomfortable with a load of books on your lap. Some of the older kids would get pretty bad. They would throw things at the bus driver. Sometimes they would hang out the emergency door. Riding the bus was quite an experience!

The best thing was after school going to the corner Drug Store for Penny candy, or the New Stand for a cherry coke or a chocolate root beer. That is, if you were lucky enough to get a booth that wasn't reserved.

I can remember (with fear) page 88 in math class. The teacher who is now deceased I believe. It was only one page of math problems, but you had to get them all correct, or by the end of the week, you would have to go to the front of the class by the desk where she had a big paddle, and you would get one painful smack with it. Well, every day I only missed one or two problems, but try as I might, the last faithful day I missed one problem and sure enough I had to go up front for my smack with the paddle, Boy! Was I embarrassed!

We had a really nice movie theatre back then, and my friend and I, (if we had enough allowance money), went on Friday nights. When the original Frankenstein movie came out, my friend and I just had to sit in the front row. Wow! When old Frankenstein came out on the screen, we screamed our heads off. To this day, I am still fearful that Frankenstein lives. Then, after the movies, we went to Pete's Candy Kitchen for a soda or Sundae. That store had heavenly treats and most of the ice cream was homemade.

On Sundays on the way to my grandmother's house in Wilcox, we sometimes stopped for a treat called a "Mexican Mountain"-delicious! If only that store was still there!

We sometimes would wade in the creek below the Kinzua Bridge. One day we went for quite a ways, when all of a sudden my friend was screaming for help. There she was sinking in sand up to her knees. It looked harmless there, the water was clear and deep, and there was an area of white sand at the bottom. I guess it was Quicksand. I tried to pull her out without being another victim. She got out, but lost her shoes in the quicksand. That was the first time we ever encountered anything like it. I wonder if anyone else ever came upon it.

We used to ice skate on a frozen puddle in the park, which in later years they made into a skating rink. It actually was an old swamp,

not too deep, but if you fell through your feet got pretty soaked. I don't know if it is still there, but we had some fun times there.

My grandmother had one of the old outhouses. It had three different size holes, I guess for what "might fit" best! There was a shelf in the corner with old newspapers and a Sears catalog. There was a calendar on the wall. I am sure it was pretty scary to go in there at night. I guess every year my grandfather moved it to a new location, for obvious reasons!

My grandmother told me about the Saturday night baths. She would heat the water on the wood stove and bring the old tub out in the kitchen. I guess the whole family then, got turns taking their baths.

A Cheesy Story
By John Lewis Guiswite of Jersey Shore, Pennsylvania
Born 1935

My grandfather, John L, owned and ran the Loganton Creamery from 1915 until the early 1940s. He closed it down when his boys and hired help were drafted into WWII.

His main product was sharp cheddar cheese but he also made butter and buttermilk. His son Lester was in charge of the buttermilk process and therefore acquired the nickname "Buttermilk".

Mazie, John L. Guiswite, Ora Sue Guiswite, and Paul Guiswite in the late 1930s

330

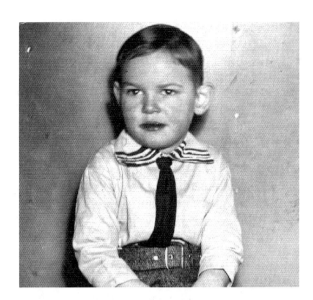

John Lewis Guiswite in 1939

The cheese making process began when his two trucks picked up the milk from local farmers. Each farm had two sets of milk cans that had a number on them. When the cans filled with milk was picked up, empty ones were left in their place. When they arrived at the creamery, the milk was dumped into the processing vat, which was elevated about 18 inches from the floor. Steam pipes were underneath the vat to heat the milk to the correct temperature. The vat was 10 feet wide and 26 feet long.

After the milk was measured to be of the correct warmth, a certain amount of rennet was added. After a time the curd or solid part of the milk separated from the water or whey, as it was called. The curd was then raked with a long toothed wooden rake to hasten the process. The whey was drained off and stored in a concrete pit. Farmers would pick up the whey as needed to mix with chop to "slop the hogs".

The curd was scooped into carts and then put into a form lined with cheesecloth. The correct amount of pressure was applied to eliminate any further whey. These finished cakes of wrapped cheese were dipped into wax to seal out air. Each "cheese" or round weighed between 35-40 pounds. It took a little more than a gallon of milk to make a pound of cheese. Each batch made 30-50 cheese rounds.

The cheese was stored in a large walk-in cooler at a temperature of 40-42 degrees. The temperature was controlled with ice from the icehouse that was attached to the rear of the cooler. Blocks of ice were rolled in on rollers night and day to maintain the temperature. The cheese was stored 3-4 months to age or "ripen" before being sold.

The ice was cut in the winter from farm ponds when it was about 20 inches thick. It was hauled to the icehouse with horses and sled. The ice was covered thick with sawdust to keep it frozen until the next winter. It was year around hard work but all seemed to enjoy their jobs and we kids loved to watch.

The Loganton Creamery was noted for its very sharp cheeses. Some was shipped as far as Wisconsin, which was "the cheese capital of the US" at the time. I have one of the original cheese boxes that were handmade by my aunt. Yes, the girls in the family also helped with the process. It was a family business. My box is identified as having contained a 35-pound cheese that was shipped to a S.L. Gephart in Rebersburg, PA.

I have explained the process to my family at a reunion, also made a cheese press and two kinds of cheese so they knew it could really be done this way. They liked the cheddar best but said it didn't taste like the cheese they buy today. They gave me a cheese hat to wear.

One of my memories of the creamery occurred in the late 1930s when I was four years old. A traveling photographer was scheduled to come take my picture one morning. My mother had bought me a new sailor suit for the occasion. The photographer was late and I became impatient so I told Mom I was going to the creamery to watch. She told me not to get dirty. Well, I was watching and being careful to stay clean when the man raking the curd bumped me with his arm or the rake and I fell backward into a large bucket of sour whey. I was not only dirty but smelly as well.

The top of the original cheese box from John's grandfather's creamery

331

I went to the house expecting a whipping but my mother just redressed me in a pair of shorts and long stockings. I got the licking after the picture was taken. I still have the pictures and my children get a kick out of seeing them. Many good memories of the 30s and early 40s when food processing was done without all the additives and government regulations required today. Grandfather's cheese was the best!

Kane & Ludlow, a Time of Warmth and Security
By Mary Ann Fees Johnson of Bradford, Pennsylvania
Born 1912

This story was submitted by May Ann's daughter, Rosanne Conaway

In most lives, there must remain a deep gulf forever fixed between the present and the past-a gulf across which a person may look back on youth only to meet the eyes of a stranger with a stranger's mannerisms, but a stranger who bares his own name. Even though I know, I will be the person I am now for the rest of my life, that girl I used to be is not willing to be banished. The secret things she and I share seem to be written on a scroll that rolls back, back, back, in time.

Some say the past is a fascinating place to journey, but a dangerous place to settle down, and others claim that memory can be a terror destroying their best moments. I have found that my memories that take me back to my growing up days are mostly good. I think to have a happy childhood means more than anything except faith in God and that He will take care of us. Good memories ease present pains and fears and they strengthen us to face what lies ahead.

I am confident that my days in Kane and on the farm and in Ludlow will not be spoiled by a "now" examination. I so want to share (not necessarily compare or evaluate) pasts with you three as we cope with the present and contemplate times to come. I am thankful that every stage of life offered me an opportunity to grow. Even though the pace and the stress shifted from time to time, the strength to deal with each remained steadfast, due, I believe, to the values learned

in those two towns. They and their people set me very straight about capabilities, goals, education and decency. They encouraged me to face head-on weaknesses and defeats. At the same time, they were allowing me to dream my dreams; they were telling me not to look past realities. Most of all, they were saying to me during those formative years that I must be a survivor as so many of the women in our family had been. True, my remembrance of our foremothers does not go back to pioneer days when women learned to stock wood sheds before the snows came, or to use guns to keep coyotes at bay, but they did lose loved ones; they learned to leave secure surroundings, to care for and utilize the homes their men provided, to pay taxes, to balance budgets, to write checks for education and to be sure the money was there to back them and to secure loans if it wasn't. They did prepare themselves like soldiers to do battle for their own when necessary; they did at times sweep the cobwebs off the dream castles. They even dug moats to protect those castles when necessary. At long last, they got to sit down at quiet times to write scenarios for their future.

In the fifty odd years since I left home, I have come to know that there is much to be said in favor of living in small towns in which I spent my early years. I often long to return to Kane and Ludlow whose warmth and security I so well remember. Their people had roots deep in the past, roots linked deep to each other through several generations. Those people lived their lives the way I think their Creator intended.

When Thoreau talked about Walden Pond and "simplifying", he could have been reminiscing about the two modest villages I've so long loved –they were so uncomplicated, so comfortable—my leaving them meant losing a very special and good way of life. I never return to them without a feeling of "coming home." I never leave them without nostalgia and, heart tugs that hurt, even as they warm my heart.

In the years away, however, I have had to face facts—although familiar streets may point the way home, the essence of any homecoming is in family and friends. I don't have to drive hundreds of miles to and from any one place to discover that memories reside not only in places—memories live, too, in the heart of the rememberer. Too, I hope I've learned that any great happiness can be duplicated. I have to shut doors on the past properly.

In our part of the glorious state of Pennsylvania, it has ever been the hills that brought me a full realization of the eternal goodness of life. Here there were hills aplenty, stark white and black when winter stalked through. Someone has said that winter shows the bare bones of a countryside, and those bones form a well-nigh perfect structure in our hill country. In the spring, they are bud-laden and soft green, in the summer warm and full of sun. Flamed-colored and breathtaking they become when summer leaves.

In the fall it was that the leaves, down from all those trees, made pleasant sounds when we scuffed through them. Their vibrant colors were a sight to behold and their burning scent heavenward a scent of their own, which still can make me homesick. My friends and I jumped in great piles of them that we raked up in October just before Kane became a place of frozen ponds, snow, bare trees and plummeting temperatures.

Winter memories remain the clearest and dearest to me. I so enjoyed winter sports, whether I was skiing on the great natural slope in back of Gusty's Inn, ice skating on the Park Pond across from the high school, or tobogganing from the Kane Manor down, down Ethan Frome fashion through the woods. It was such a long trail that we could only make one run an evening. Then, there was the long walk back with Bill dragging the toboggan all the way home to hot cocoa, cookies and visiting by the fire. There were basketball games in the gym with sometimes an all-school dance later—memories are made of this.

The walk to and from high school was a long one for the sometimes 30-degree-below-normal temperature. My mother kept the large kitchen stove going all night to warm the kitchen to which we all came early in the morning. She baked potatoes through the night, and many a sub-zero morning (the air cut like a knife and made it hard to breathe) saw Fred and me with a hot potato pressed into our mittened hands. We held them up to our faces until we got to school where they were placed on the school's furnace, retrieved at noon for the journey home for lunch—no buses, no cafeterias, no snow suits.

Mother's kitchen range (which I later brought to my own kitchen in Bradford) had a bowl of buckwheat batter at the back of its top. A new batch was always started from the last bit of batter in the bowl—all winter the same bowl. Part of the secret was not starting a new bowl. Too, on many cold days Mother baked big Bermuda onions for lunch in their skins like potatoes. We broke them open and popped in butter. I can still remember how good they smelled and tasted. Mother's stove also did duty baking her wonderful, so tall angel-food cakes known all over town, as well as her brownies, an almost daily after school treat.

I had a red chinchilla coat. It had been Mother's. Grandfather Cox brought such treasures from England. He traveled across the ocean to England, his homeland, quite often. (Recently one of the ladies in Book Club had a list of passengers on one of the liners in the late 1800s. There was Cox listed. (I wonder if her grandfather and mine traveled together way back then.) Mother wore her coat all through boarding school, and years later, it was mine. Even now, I don't feel right if winter comes and I don't have a red coat.

Then there were the holidays, Thanksgiving and Christmas in Kane. Even yet, although I consider my thinking reasonably modern, I go back to seek my Christmas in what is everlasting. My Christmas bell will always chime for Mr. Dickens and for his "God Bless us everyone." My heart will ever be touched by the birth of the dear Babe in Bethlehem. Then, at home and ever since, there is a candle burning on the doorstep all through the night so that He will not lose the way. Even though my candle may cast a very small light, it is beautiful to see, and it warms my heart.

Someone has said that the year does not have four seasons. There is a fifth—the season of Christmas. It lasts from Thanksgiving (when the town's decorations go up and the lights come on) until Twelfth Night when we make bonfires of the trees—if we follow our customs. At home, we were promised and received the things we wanted most. Mother, my grandmother and the aunts prepared for the season generally all year long and specifically for weeks ahead. Our beautiful simple faith was much on our minds; our church was an ever so meaningful part of the holidays. There, too were joyous reunions with family and friends, festive meals, afternoon teas in homes, and evening musicals. There was always a magnificent natural tree cut from the farm and stretching up to the high ceiling in the library. We made strings of popcorn, sometimes of cranberries and got out our treasured ornaments, some of them Mother's when she was a little girl. The tree smelled like a Christmas tree should and blended with the fireplace's pungent scent and the turkey cooking. Christmas was so good to believe in once long ago—so good to be remembered still.

Ours was a home full of music and lights and people and love, and outside the snow fell softly and silently. I still like snow—it seems like a blanket covering plants and grass so they can rest until it's time to stir in the spring. For many years, I grew sad as Christmas came on. After 1934, my mother's name was never going to be on my list again—it had always been first. Through the early Bradford years, I had to try so hard not to show my sadness. I just wanted to be back home. I hope someday you'll be writing to your children and grandchildren about our Christmases together.

The summer memories are mostly of Ludlow—they were long, easy and unstructured. Not for me and my friends rounds of lessons and hectic scheduling. We swam and we played tennis; later there was golf at our tiny very hospitable Country Club, we had picnics, hay rides and we rode the horses with Joe, Monty and Frau (German shepherds and so bright) as our constant companions. We went bike riding in the evenings, to the movies at times, especially "to meet boys" and later to congregate at Mike's, the local soda fountain. We cooked hot dogs in Evergreen Park and sat around the fire and sang, and at times, our get-togethers were at people's camps. Ours was outside Ludlow on a beautiful natural stream (great fishing). On the weekends as we grew up, we danced to the jukebox at Clear's Cows and drank Brown Cows at the Limberlost. As we grew older and came home from college, we headed toward Celeron and sometimes big band music.

"Deep in December it's nice to remember" the abundance of flowers in our town in the summer time. They were in old-fashioned gardens where, it seemed to me, where flowers belong. Like Topsy, they just grew. If they were gathered and brought into the house, they were allowed to bend gracefully in simple vase arrangements. (I think the wiring of flowers and jamming them into foam contraptions is one more of the failures of the twentieth century to appreciate natural beauty.). Then, flowers clustered in porch boxes on the verandas people had. There were rocking chairs, fans and lemonade, where now there are almost sterile, hot, plastic –filled cement patios. People sat on their verandas after dinner and watched the stars come out.

I could go into the garden out back and chew on parsley or a sprig of mint—there was a bed of each on either side of the back steps. I could eat a sun-warmed tomato out of my hand or take the tiny crisp cucumbers into the house to make a sandwich on homemade bread. I could get a handful of chips out of the icebox after the iceman had chipped the fifty-pound block to get it in—the tiny pieces were as clear as diamonds, and the drink I could take out of the garden hose was never a threat as to purity.

Long before the house and farm in Ludlow belonged to us, it had been the Curtis Luther Company's boarding house. It was run by a lively lady, Mrs. Allie Johnson, a widow with a son, George, Fred's age. (She would, upon closing the boarding house, come to live in Kate with us.) By that time, my grandmother was very ill in the hospital in Philadelphia for months at a time. George and Fred went to Allegheny. Mother was with her mother, so Mrs. Johnson and I kept the home fires burning. I loved to visit with her in Ludlow after riding early in the morning, and I often visited Uncle Walt at the office. He was the purchasing agent for the leather company, and he let me smell the samples of the fine leather they produced there.

In the woods around Ludlow, there were wooded trails cleared by Boy Scouts under Mr. Olmsted's supervision. They were used by campers, hikers, and horseback riders. Tis imaginative scoutmaster had signs posted on the winding paths bearing the names of New York's famous streets. In the midst of all that natural beauty, I would suddenly find myself in Times Square!

I wonder at times, if I imagined those golden days in Kane at home when "no one wept except the willows." To reassure myself when I idolize my town and my state, I call to mind what others have said about Pennsylvania's natural grandeur.

Sayings from My Grandmother
By Florence Bailey of Millerton,
Pennsylvania
Born 1935

I was born in 1935 and spent a lot of time with my grandmother on Jackson Center Road, Millerton, PA, in Tioga County.

There was no electric and used wood heat. We put a boiler on the stove to heat our water for dishes, washing, and taking baths. Our bath was usually on Sat. night in a round washtub in the kitchen. Afterwards we took a kerosene lamp to light our way upstairs to bed. There was no heat up there and you could see your breath in the winter. A soapstone that had been on the stove all day was wrapped in newspaper and a towel and put in the foot of the bed. We would use that to warm our feet and body. We slept on goose feather pillows and under sheep wool quilts made by my grandmother. We would use a chamber pot in the night and in the daytime an outhouse. The outhouse was a small building out back of the house with three holes: A big one, medium one, and small one for children. Where was no toilet paper; you used a page out of a Sears catalog.

Florence's Grandfather Everitt's house

Wash day was usually on Monday if nice. We would fill two tubs with hot water from the boiler on the stove, place our clothes in to get wet, and then we took a bar of Fels Napa soap and scrubbed our clothes on a scrub board until clean, rinsed, and hung on a line. Men's overalls were hung on a line in back of the stove. Ironing was done by irons heated on a stove then with a handle clipped on it. You would iron until cooled and go exchange for a hot one.

We made our own butter, bread, cakes, cookies, and pies by hand. No box mixes. We grew our own vegetables and canned them in the fall. Jelly and jams were made from apples, grapes, and crab apples. We grew cabbage and made sauerkraut by putting it in a brine in a big crock. Everything was put in the cellar. We had no freezers or refrigerators. There were a few iceboxes around.

We did our own butchering. Pigs were stabbed and lowered into a barrel of boiling water. Then a metal scraper was used to take the hair off. We would smoke our hams and hang them in the cellar. Some meat was cooked and placed in crocks. We killed our own cows, geese, and chickens.

We made our own ice cream by placing the mixture in a can, then put snow and salt in a tub and crank until hardened. Of course, there were always kids around waiting to clean off the ladle when done.

Thanksgiving was a big dinner with aunts, uncles, and cousins. Christmas we cut a small hemlock tree and placed it in the living room. We popped popcorn and strung it in a chain for decorations. We even cut paper and made a chain. We had some pinecones as decorations.

My clothes were handmade. Material was sometimes feed bags with nice designs. I can remember my grandmother making me a skirt. It was red with white daisies. It had a saying, "He loves me – He loves me not."

We did have a battery operated radio, a phonograph with 78-speed records. When I was 12 or 13, my great uncle gave me the first Edison record player with a big Morning Glory horn. It played a round disc. Everyone enjoyed listening to it. The telephone was on the wall. There were all different rings. A long continuous ring was an emergency. If there was a fire, men took off with pails and shovels to help.

Some of the programs I remember listening to on the radio was WLS Barn Dance – Chicago, the Grand Ole Opry, Lone Ranger, and The Shadow.

If you had a cold, a piece of flannel with lard, flax seed, or onion was put on your chest. Sometimes you were given tea made of herbs. Also whisky, lemon, and lots of sugar, and put to bed. You would sweat and usually broke a fever in 2 or 3 hours.

Funerals were held in family homes. Doctors made house calls. Midwives delivered the babies if doctor didn't make it. There was an Old Rawleigh man who peddled medicines. Cuts were treated with a paste of brown sugar, Fels Napa soap, and water.

Chores were done by lantern light, cows were milked by hand. Milk was weighed, night and morning, and recorded to each cow with a name. Milk

1936 Essex and a friend by the barn

was strained through a cloth into cans. Cans were placed into tubs of cold water, then a man would pick them up and take them to a plant. You were paid once a month.

All work was done by horses. Crops were planted by hand with a sack over your shoulder with a handle turning a wheel to plant.

The first car my grandmother had was a 1936 Essex.

We took lambs in by the stove when their mothers wouldn't own them. We fed them by bottle. If an eyelid wouldn't open, you took a needle and thread and sewed it open. Then a drop of milk was put in it. Guess it helped preventing it from going blind.

I remember reading a book of clippings about a murder that happened in a barn at the end of Jackson Center Road. A migrant worked killed her and got away on a train.

They know he got to Binghamton where he purchased a change of clothes. He was never apprehended. Everyone was shocked. Things like that just couldn't happen as everyone was so close to everyone.

I can also remember my grandmother telling these tales or sayings:

You never cut your fingernails on Friday or do important matters as Friday is it was considered an unlucky day.

You don't sew on Sunday that would bring you bad luck.

An owl hooting at night is a sign of a death in a family.

A white spot in your fingernail means money is coming to you.

You always place your right boot on the floor when you get out of bed. When you enter a house, use the right foot first. If not, your day will be unlucky.

If your nose itches, company is coming. I was also told you were going to kiss a fool.

In July on the 15th, grandmother would tell me if it rains on St. Swithin's day, it would rain for 40 days and nights. If it was nice and fair, it will rain no more.

Two spoons in a cup or saucer, you'd be married before the year-ends.

If you drop a knife, a man with a sharp tongue was coming. A fork was a woman. A spoon was a fool.

A red sky in the morning, sailors beware. A red sky at night, sailor's delight.

Thunder in the fall, no winter at all. Thunder in the winter; freeze the hair on the dog.

The length of an icicle hanging from the roof was a sign of the depth of snow.

If you pick up a penny, you'll have good luck.

My mind has gone blank but I know I sure enjoyed my life back then. No TV, no cell phones, and all the modern ways of life now. You didn't feel rushed and pushed. There weren't cars riding on your bumper, you could enjoy the country.

Four Sisters on a Farm, Not an Easy Task
By Thelma Walker of Montoursville,
Pennsylvania
Born 1930

I was born in 1930 in Lycoming Co., Pennsylvania. I had three sisters. My grandfather lived with us until he died.

As a young child, I had asthma. My father would stand me against the wall, and drill a hole into the wall. He would cut some of my hair and stuff it into the hole. This was done to heal me. Maybe it worked, as I eventually got over it. He would blow pipe smoke in our ear if we had an earache. If we had a cold, Mom would make mustard plasters and put on our chest at night.

We went to a one-room school called Frenchtown School. There were about 20 students each year with grades 1 through 8.

Two teachers from Williamsport, Pa. got jobs as teachers in our country school. School was from 8:30 to 4:00. The teachers boarded at a farmhouse about 2 and ½ miles away. They had to walk, and many mornings would oversleep! The boys would climb up the flagpole and ring the bell. Other times we all would walk to their house and wake them up. Then, we all would walk back to the schoolhouse and start our day. The boys had to carry wood inside to heat the room. There was a well for water and they also carried water in buckets for us to drink.

At recess time, we played baseball using a piece of wood for the bat. One day while playing ball, a small plane flew over and lost its propeller. We ran to where it landed, got it and ran 2-3 miles to where the plane came down in a field.

No such day as a "snow day" or a snow plow. Dad would go ahead of us, and with a scoop shovel, clear a path. There was a high bank and snow would drift 8-10 feet high. Of course, everyone walked one-half to two miles every day.

Holidays would be one day. The school year was from September 1st. to mid-April. Once a year we had a "play" with a "box social." Dad always auctioned the boxes.

Usually the same two or three boys got a spanking. They leaned over a chair and the teacher used a wooden paddle to spank them. One summer one of those boys drowned.

The schoolhouse was at the top of the hill. At recess time, some of the kids would go over the hill and smoke a pipe filled with "corn silk", as tobacco. Sometimes they would smoke cigar stubs they found along the road.

At school and at home we had to use the "outhouse." We used Sear's catalogues or old paper to wipe.

Living on a farm with three sisters (no boys) was not an easy task. We had to "doodle" hay, shock wheat and oats, and pick corn. We fed chickens, cows, horses and picked eggs. After school, we would pick corn in baskets after Mom, Dad, and Granddad husked corn all day. Old rooster would "flop" us every day.

We always had a large garden. My granddad would tie a rope around my waist and I had to pull a cultivator while he guided it to "work the garden." Mom would give him heck for making me a horse.

Mom always canned everything from the garden. It was not unusual for her to can, 200 quarts each of peaches, pears, etc. Also, in winter we would can beef and pork, as there were no freezers. She would separate cream from milk and make butter in a wooden butter bowl. Every week she also made cottage cheese. We called it "smear case." She baked 6-8 loaves of bread and 3-4 large pans of rolls. She would also make 5-6 pies and a cake.

She did the wash in a wringer washer and a tub of rinse water. She would hang clothes outside in winter and summer. In winter, they would freeze as hard as a board! We heated water in large kettles on the wood stove. We also heated water this way for baths. We had a bathtub later but no running water.

In the fall, my aunt and uncle would come at night and we would peel apples. The next morning at 6 AM, Dad would start a fire under the large black kettle to make apple butter. This was an all day job. Later, Mom canned the apple butter and Dad made hard cider from the left over apples.

There was a small stream on our land, and our neighbor's kids (3 of them) and 3 of us would go to the stream and kill crabs with stones and catch five or 6 fish. We would go to their home and the boys would clean them. Then, we would fry them and eat them.

An older lady lived down the road from us and my younger sister and I would go visit her. She'd be baking bread and had it "rising" on a bench. I'd either punch holes in it or try to sit on them. She called my sister "black eyed pickle pie" and me "little devil." My sister couldn't pronounce my name, so she called me "Ottie."

Dad and my uncle would go "coon" hunting at night. Us kids had to play Chinese checkers, regular checkers, or cards with Mom for entertainment. One night, close to midnight, a man that lived down the road (he lived with an old woman) came home drunk. Not having a car, someone dropped him off at our house. He stumbled down the road and finally fell into a ditch. He laid there and called, "Sadie, Sadie!" Finally, she came up the road with a lantern and helped him home.

We had a "wall" phone. We would ring it just to hear the operator ask, "What number you wanted?" There would 8 or 10 "parties" on your line and to call them you would ring "short" or "long" rings.

In the summer if a thunderstorm came, Mom would get us up and dressed in case lightning struck. One night it did strike an old barn that was empty. Not having fire companies, the men carried and hauled water, but it did burn to the ground.

Before the farmhouse and barn were built, there was a bank on the grounds. We would find old coins, but one day my granddad found a dollar gold coin. He gave it to my sister. He would give us 5 or 10 cents to spend if we went someplace. We thought we were rich!

During the Depression, we always had enough food to eat. As sugar and gas were rationed, we had coupons to buy those items with. I still have some of those coupons. My relatives from Bloomsburg, would come over once and a while for gas. Dad had a gas pump, so he would give them extra gas for their cars.

We never had a "vacation." Once in a while on a rainy summer day, we'd go to Williamsport shopping. Some Sundays we'd go on a picnic or just for a sightseeing ride.

Besides all the housework and working in the fields in the summer time, Mom would make us winter hats, gloves, and coats. She would use patches from "old" coats or where ever she could find them. We always wore "long johns" or black stockings. When we needed new shoes, they would go to the store and buy us a new pair without us trying them on.

We had a wood burning stove to heat the whole house. The only heat to reach the upstairs bedroom was by registers cut in the wooden floors. We would slice potatoes and lay the slices on the stove for French fries! To pop popcorn, we would take the lids off the stove and put a wire basket popper on the hot coals.

We had an icebox. The "ice man" would bring us a 50 lb. piece of ice, maybe once a month. I remember when refrigerators came on the market and Mom and Dad bought one. Dad called it the "White Horse."

About once a month the "fish man" came. They would buy two or three fish that weighed 8-10 pounds.

In winter when a crust was on the snow, Dad would take us sled riding. Sometimes if we didn't have enough sleds, Dad would wax a scoop shovel with paraffin and that would be our sled. We would use the handle of the shovel as a steering wheel. Often times we did this on moonlight nights.

In the summertime, the neighbor's kids and us would make paths in the woods and make "huts" from branches to play hide-and-seek. If we got bored, we would tie a string to an empty wallet and lay it on a bridge. When a car came, we would pull it off the bridge. They would stop to get the wallet, and there would be no wallet!

There was a turn in the road above our house and two or 3 times cars would miss the turn and come crashing through our yard. They would hit our front porch, go down through a field, and land in a stream. This happened at nighttime. The State Police would come to investigate and they'd wait until daylight to begin. They would stay for breakfast. Mom would fix ham, eggs, pancakes, and sausage. After that, every time those police were in the area, they'd always stop in to eat with us. In one of the accidents, a man died.

I would tease my younger sister by lying on the sofa with my head hanging over the side. I'd tell her the blood was going to run to my head and I'd die. Then, she would cry and cry. Other times, I had a scab I'd pick at it, and again tell her I'd die, and again she would cry!

We always went to Sunday school and church at night. One night after a "young Peoples" meeting, the preacher took the older kids to a deep hole in the creek for a swim. When parents found this out, they went to the preacher and really told him off and never to do it again because it was pitch dark and the only light they had were the car lights. Most of the kids couldn't swim.

Once at a Bible School meeting, one of the girls swallowed a nickel. They grabbed her by the head, turned her upside down and shook her. The nickel came flying out!

Granddad always smoked a corncob pipe while Dad smoked cigars and a pipe.

Granddad would take the two horses and a plow to work in the fields about ½ to ¾ mile from the house. He would never wear a pocket watch, so at dinnertime one of us girls would walk to the field to tell him it was time to eat. The neighbor's fields were always covered with wild yellow mustard weeds. The seeds would blow over on our fields and Granddad would take me and one of my sisters to pull the weeds from our fields. We never understood why, because the next year they always grew back.

One Halloween Mom and Dad and my sister and I dressed up. Our neighbors also dressed up and we all went to another neighbor's house. They wouldn't answer the door, so we went to more friends and as we parked behind the barn the woman called to her husband who was inside the barn that the other neighbors called and said Halloweeners were on the way, and with that she fired the shotgun out the door! With that, we got back in the car and went home.

My Uncle Charlie was a carpenter. He made me a little cupboard with three shelves. I was 3 years old when he made it. I still have it and keep my little antique dishes in it that belonged to my mother-in-law. He made my sister a table and two chairs. She had them until her daughter got married and she took them, but they have now disappeared.

Another Uncle Chet hunted groundhogs in the summer. He would skin them and my aunt would cook them for him. He'd sit at the table and eat them while the grease ran down both sides of his mouth!

In the winter, my family and this aunt and uncle would get together at nighttime and make two eight-quart freezers of ice cream. My uncle could eat three or four big bowls.

Every Sunday Mom cooked an extra special dinner. She always invited someone to eat with us, even the preacher and his wife.

During WWII, a young man who lived about two miles up the road was in the Air Force. One day he and his crew flew a B-25 bomber over his parent's house and the surrounding area. Mom and my sisters stood out and waved to them, but I ran in the house and hid under the kitchen table scared to death!

There were two hobos that would stop by once in a while. If we saw them coming down the road, Mom would lock the doors and we would hide somewhere in the house. Once in a while Mom would pack a lunch and give it to them.

When I was a junior in high school, they sold the farm. My granddad had died and Mom had surgery. My two older sisters had married by this time, so Dad decided to have an auction and sell the farm. There was a small house down the road from us for sale. They bought it and added on to it and moved there. That ended my fond memories of living on a farm.

Eight "Good" Girls
By Mary Prince of Jersey Shore,
Pennsylvania
Born 1925

I am one of the eight "Good Girls." My name is Mary Good and back in 1931, I went to first grade in a one-room schoolhouse in Vilas Park, Jersey Shore, Pennsylvania. Our first privilege every day was to stand up and salute and pledge allegiance to the American flag, then we repeated the Lord's Prayer. I ask this question, "Where is this privilege today?" The school then stood near the current Thomas Street exit and was torn down to make way for Route 220 when it was built. I remember we carried drinking water from my parent's home, which was just across the field from the school, for all the student's washing and drinking needs.

Our teacher always had a favorite "pet" who would be the truant officer and the janitor who attended the stove to keep it burning. It was also the person's duty to raise the flag every morning and take it in after school. His name was Rudy Prince. When a student was absent from school, the teacher would send Rudy to the persons home to make sure she or he was really sick. So, Rudy got out of a lot of classes. We called him the teacher's pet, and he liked it. In the school, one would pass by the coal room to get to class. If a student was really bad, the teacher would send him out to the coal bin for 10 minutes. In those days, most kids listened. No one wanted to stand in the dark coal bin (that was too scary) it was pitch-black. When a student had to go there, all the other kids were motionless, and never whispered until his time was up. One day a student, Cally Whitton was sent there, but ran home instead. Rudy had to check on him and you could hear a pin drop until Rudy got back, because everyone wanted to know what happened to Cally.

A school nurse would come once a month and each child would have to march up front and take a tablespoon full of castor oil, this was to keep us healthy and it was torture.

For bathroom facilities, we had two-seaters outhouses located behind the school, which would get cleaned by an unruly student. Vaccinations were required to be given in the arm before starting school, which would often become sore and get infected and look ugly sometimes taking about 3 weeks to heal.

We had individual classes 1 thru 8th grade. Each day would start with first grade. They had to "march" up front in a straight line and sit on two large benches and have their lessons. If it was arithmetic class, we would go to the blackboard and do math work. As each student finished the problem, the teacher would OK it and she would go back to her desk. If one couldn't do the problem and had a friend who was finished, the friend could help by raising his hand and signaling the correct answer with the use of his fingers. Of course, we were not supposed to do this. If you didn't have a friend to help you, you had to stand there one hour and finally the teacher would say, "Oh, go sit down!" This meant you got "0" instead of A, B, or C for your grade.

We had two recesses, twenty minutes in the morning and twenty minutes in the afternoon. No matter how cold it was or how deep the snow, we all had to bundle up and go outside. We had a ball field where we older children played baseball. One day in my eighth grade, I got hit on the forehead with an out-of-control ball bat. The batter threw the bat while running to first base. I had a big goose egg on my head and two black eyes. In the winter when recess was over the teacher would have a student ring the bell and everyone had to run in and huddle around the pot-bellied stove to get warm. Then, the teacher would just tinkle the bell, which meant get back to your seats for school was in session.

In those days, we had lots of snow and sometimes we had to wade through snow up to our knees. Some students walked miles to school. The Heisey kids were brought to school by a horse and sleigh. I can still hear those sleigh bells ringing.

As a child growing up with seven sisters (thus the Good girls) we had a pot-bellied stove in the living room which was our only source of heat, a cook stove in the kitchen, a primer pump on the back porch was our only source of water, a wringer washer machine, an outhouse and chamber pots.

Saturday nights were bath nights in a big washtub that my mother used to do the laundry in. Of course, the water had to be heated on the cook stove.

Every two days the milkman would bring us milk. We did not have a vehicle, so my father had to walk 5 miles each day to work to the Avis Railroad Station, and he did this for approximately 30 years. Sometimes a friend would see him walking and would pick him up and give him a ride. He also was a barber and had a shop on Allegheny Street in Jersey Shore and the house still stands today. Haircuts were fifteen cents and a shave cost ten cents. His sign read B.A. Good, and "Love" the Barber. Mr. Love, also a barber helped my dad cut hair sometimes.

Speaking of cars, do you remember what fender skirts were on curb fenders, steering knobs or suicide knobs, or maybe necker knobs? Continental kits were rear bumper extenders and held a covered spare tire. These tires were supposed to make the cars as great looking as a Lincoln Continental. Rudy's first car was a Model-T Ford, which he purchased for $50.00, and he thought he was the hit of the town!

In those days, kids often had head lice and if someone in school got lice, my dad would go to school, take those kids outside and shave all their hair off. Some kids who did not have lice were jealous and wanted their heads shaved too, so Daddy would shave their heads and the parents did not have anything to say in this matter.

340

My father was also a good carpenter. He made most of our Christmas toys by hand. I remember the little red wagons, table and chair sets, high chairs for our dolls, and even tricycles with peddles and all. When my father became sick and could not work, my mother had to go on W.P.A. assistance or so called relief. This organization supplied all of us girls with dresses and we felt that we were the best dressed kids in school! Saddle shoes and penny loafers were the fad at the time.

We had a wooden icebox for our refrigerator. When the iceman came, the kids in the neighborhood would run out and ask for ice and he always gave us a handful of ice chips.

We had an ice-cream man, Finny Maggs, who came with his horse and buggy, ringing his bell. The cost of a cone was five cents and a large dish of ice cream was twenty cents, but we never had money for ice cream. Every holiday, or Birthday and every Saturday night, my father would make delicious homemade ice cream in a hand cranked ice-cream freezer. We kids would take turns turning the crank. My favorite flavor was strawberry.

After I graduated from common school (grade school), I had to walk one mile to the high school, which was on Allegheny Street. Now that building is Lingles Grocery Store. One morning I had wet my hair to make a wave in my bangs, and by the time I got to school my hair was frozen. Soon afterwards, my hair thawed out and dripped all over my desk. I never wet my hair after that. Anyway, that style is the style of today, straight, parted, or bangs.

Years later (in the 1960s), I moved to Ramsey Village up Pine Creek in Pennsylvania and took care of the three Ramsey girls who were school teachers. Their grandfather, Mr. Thomas Ramsey, settled in this area in the 1790 circa and was also the Wagon Master for George Washington's Continental Army. The Ramsey family had a hired hand named Bailey who just wandered in one day looking for work. Baily's chores consisted of taking care of the cattle, plowing fields, and doing odd jobs. He grew potatoes, and I remember he said it was difficult for him to sell a bushel of potatoes for fifty cents, because people just didn't have the money back then. For protection, the Ramsey's had a beautiful large, longhaired collie dog named Sarge, who would accompany Baily by walking behind the plow.

In those days, we had very little, but we were happy and contented. In the end, I married my childhood sweetheart, the love of my life, who was the janitor and truant officer, Rudy Prince, and together we raised three lovely daughters and celebrated 59 wonderful long years together. I would never exchange those days for today!

Grade 7th and 8th
Mary is in the front row (first person on the right)

School Days and Our Shopping Escapades with Momma
By Jane V. Major of Trout Run, Pennsylvania
Born 1952

It was postwar 1958, and my mother was still caught up in a wave of patriotism. Every Saturday she'd gather me and brother and three sisters into the '55 Chevy and head down the mountain to spend the old man's money, sure that she was doing her part to rebuild the economy. Minnie Agnes was a patriot, all right! She'd sing along with Elvis all the way down Steam Valley Mountain, proud that the boy had served his country, loved his Momma, and had a good healthy appetite. She didn't slow down for anybody, or anything. Once that check was in her hand, she was on a mission.

341

Daddy said he got his idea to get rich selling lumber while lying in the battlefields of Italy waiting for the medics to haul him off. Minnie was determined to pump every dollar he made off that brilliant little scheme right back into the American market, thinking that Eisenhower was going to send her a Purple Heart too!

I suppose the thing that set this Saturday apart from any other, was that I had turned six and was starting school the following Monday. I turned out the usual "Love Me Tender", "Jailhouse Rock", and "Hound Dog" dreaming about the new shoes I was going to get for the first grade. When Minnie tucked me in the night before, she had promised me three pairs. She understood my passion for shoes, and said I got it from the Wizard of Oz, how I went on for days about those red shoes of Dorothy's. Besides, she was determined to spend every cent Daddy had dished out, knowing full well that the following Saturday, a fatter check would be waiting for her and Eisenhower. When she kissed my cheek, she told me I could get a set of those new little cotton underpants that had the different days of the week embroidered on them, too!

I was daydreaming about Mary Jane's, saddle shoes, and black patent leathers, when I heard a thump. "Get out and see what the heck I hit this time," she yelled to my brother, Gary Lee.

Now Gary was a whole other story in himself. He was thirteen and still running around with a coonskin cap ready to shoot anything that he took a liking to. He made us four girls be Indians every chance he could, delighting in scalping us or taking us captive so he could practice his barbaric forms of torture and degradation. We thought he had a few "screws loose".

Gary Lee jumped out of the car, and immediately held up the dead rabbit to see if Minnie wanted to stick it in the big old stainless steel cooler we kept in the trunk of the '55 for some of our finer road-kills. 'Too much blood, Leave it", she shrieked, I'm hungry for squirrel!" Disappointed, Gary Lee stuck it right up to the back window, trying to get my two baby sisters to cry.

You know the trouble with most folks these days…" Minnie started on one of her little escapades about how people didn't appreciate Elvis any more. My two baby sisters gave in, started whining, convinced that Peter Cottontail had met an early demise.

By now, my sister, Kathy Rae had her fill of the whole shooting match. "Could we, like, get to Williamsport any time soon? You know I want a poodle skirt and they'll be picked over if we don't get going. I wish once, just once, we could go to town without dragging all the brats along."

It's got to be hard for a twelve year old girl to head down the mountain with a delusional Davy Crockett, two whining babies, and a snot-nosed six year-old with a budding shoe fetish.

I woke up Monday morning with a smile on my face. I jumped out of bed, slipped the Monday panties up over my scrawny little butt, hoping I had enough to hold them up, tied up my saddle shoes, and pulled a new plaid dress down over my head. We stood side by side, Kathy swirling her poodle skirt, me in my new shiny shoes, and Gary Lee in the mangy coonskin cap waiting for that big yellow bus to take us off.

I guess old Gary thought I was adjusting too well and decided to give me something to think about. He was feeling kind of cocky anyway, knowing he would be going to the big school up at Liberty, and I was stuck at a one-room schoolhouse for the next three years. "You know what they have waiting for you, Janey? Big rats, outhouses, and a witch just like the one you cry about in the Wizard of Oz. Your teacher is a witch, and when you go outside to the outhouse, she has rats that fly just like the monkeys. Janey's afraid of monkeys, Jane's afraid of monkeys". So I got on that bus speechless.

Sure enough, the first thing I spied when we pulled into the schoolyard was two outhouses and a big rat scurrying off into an adjacent cornfield. My fears pushed themselves aside at my first glimpse of what would become the center of my learning for the next three years. In my mind, I was Laura Ingalls Wilder, going to her first day of school, just like in the books Minnie Agnes read to us each night. I suppose I fell in love with the ambiance, the feel of wooden steps, and I almost tripped over someone's foot.

"Watch what you're doing." It was a scruffy little boy. I looked up into the two biggest blue eyes I had ever seen, and for some reason my panties suddenly fit better. He smiled at me, and I knew I had my first boyfriend.

Mary Miller was a witch, all right! But, not like old Gary Lee had conjured up for me. She was like Glenda the Good Witch and I couldn't get enough of her. I was fascinated with everything about her. The way she combed her hair, the things she had in her lunch box, the way she taught, custodian, nurse, disciplinarian, and her passion for funny poems.

That first week went by so fast, I got my days of the week panties all mixed up and by Friday, I had on Sunday's underwear. This had Minnie in a stew. Kathy Rae couldn't wait to tell old Gary, and he started on me immediately. "Janey's got her panties all mixed up." Once again, old Gary had me in tears, and they splashed on my patent leather shoes.

1959 came, and we moved into what seemed like a palace to me. Daddy figured it was time to use some of his timber to build a new house for Minnie Agnes. He hoped it would keep her out of the stores. Actually, quite the reverse happened, and she started dragging us down that mountain twice a week. Now she had a real battle to fight! She was determined to have the best of everything in her new showplace. 1960 was only months away, and we drug home turquois chairs, cans of pink paint, a big colored TV, and every Elvis record she could get her hands on. One consolation to all of us was that old Gary had quit making the trips. A new era was upon us, and my two baby sisters quickly became the thorn in my side.

Denise Louise and Mona Dale had been conditioned to see which one could whine the loudest. Sibling rivalry took on a whole new meaning, and I became the center of their obsessions. "Daddy likes her best." "Why can't we take piano lessons?" "Look at all those shoes." "Daddy likes her best.

We never were quite sure what got Denise to chewing, but old Doc Buckley said she was lacking something in her system. Some type of vitamin deficiency or something crazy like that. As soon as she got tall enough to reach the windowsills, she started. She chewed every windowsill in Minnie's new palace. Old Gary said she was part beaver, and the whole family was relieved when she fell over the Electrolux and knocked her two front teeth out. Especially, the Electrolux salesman! Daddy bought a newer compact model and Minnie was in her glory. Pretty

soon, word got around of Minnie Agnes's devotion to economics, and every salesman in a two-hundred mile radius was knockin' at the palace. We got encyclopedias, fire alarms, every brush the Fuller Brush Co. ever invented, and Daddy got so exasperated that he started staying in the woods longer, and longer.

1964 came and went along with our fascination for the British invasion. We suddenly realized that Mona Dale had sat in front of the TV for two days without moving! She was the true product of the new generation. She sampled every kind of TV dinner, soft drink, junk food, and every new toy that modern times could produce. She'd see it on the tube and Minnie would take her down the mountain so she could experience the various sensations the new times had to offer. Pretty soon, it was obvious that we had another "shop-till-you-drop" dame on our hands. Whining took on a whole new meaning and Mona's bedroom full of Sixties mementos grew the louder and longer she'd go.

By now, I had moved up to the big school at Liberty. I know it is hard to believe, but I didn't like that fancy school with its indoor plumbing, big cafeteria, and stage where the PTA presented every type of new-fangled educational idea that came down the road. I longed to return to the simplicity, the romance, the uniqueness of that one-room schoolhouse. I wanted Mary Miller to teach me forever.

Kathy Rae and Gary Lee were in senior high now, and they became too involved with their social responsibilities that I substituted the connections I had with them and the Fifties, with my more upbeat Sixties sisters.

Denise was going to the orthodontist what seemed like every week to be fitted properly for her two little false teeth that jutted from her tiny new partial. Minnie saw it as a status symbol, and all of a sudden, we headed down the mountain, not on shopping trips, but to every type of specialist the Sixties invented. We had dermatologists, ophthalmologists, pediatricians, dentists, and every one of them kept Minnie happy buying eyeglasses, braces, lotions, and potions. A new war was on the horizon and Minnie was in a frenzy of economic patriotism.

It's funny when you look back on your life and see just how little really changed in the thirty-nine years since I took the first bus ride to that little one-room school house. Daddy is still in the woods. Minnie Agnes is spending it, and the economy is thriving. Old Gary is fifty-one and just got back from another hunting trip to Maine. The old coonskin cap is long gone, replaced by hunter's trophies and we still think he has a few screws loose. Kathy Rae and her family are running the sawmill and my two baby sister's still whine.

When the school district merged with Mansfield and Blossburg, the old one-room schoolhouse and its entire contents were sold. Daddy bought me the blackboards, the pull-down maps and twelve of the little wooden desks and fashioned me my own little Laura Ingalls Wilder school house right in the basement of Minnie's big new house. Parts of the school house were donated to The Lycoming County Historical Museum, and I cringe knowing that on the day I wore my wrong day-of-the-week panties all of those years ago, it was because I was so darn scared of that outhouse, that I peed in Thursday's pair and stuck them in the back of one of the shelves that they told me hangs as a reminder of the olden days when the poor kids in Lycoming County had to endure many hardships to get a decent education.

Rose Hill Street, So Full of Charm
By Patricia Butler of Westfield, Pennsylvania
Born 1937

This is about Catherine and Patricia who lived in Philadelphia on Rose Hill Street. It was so beautiful there with flowers in the front garden, big trees to shade your sidewalks so you could play jump-rope, hop-scotch, and Mother-may-I, and the fresh smell in the morning or afternoon. Mom, Catherine Bauer had our front porch so clean and pretty with wicker chairs and big pillows so soft to sit on while we colored in our coloring books. Philadelphia was so full of charm and pretty back in 1945.

Dad, Marty Bauer had a Barber Shop with three men working for him. They would have card games in the back room at nights. There was a big calendar, a girl without clothing on, so, this dear lady made a bathing-suit and they put it on her cause Friday nights or sometimes Saturdays, Mom would take my sister Catherine and I on the trolley to the Barber Shop. We would come home with Dad. That

Patricia and Catherine

was so fun to us.

Well anyway, this man, John O'Hagon had a big garage across the street from the Barber Shop. He won the Irish Sweep Stake and of course, up in the Center Square was a Hotel/ Café & Summer House for sale. He talked Dad into moving and being a partner. They did it and Dad and Mom borrowed $6000 from Grand-pop Brown. What a special man he was! He had a Bakery and saved his money, then bought houses in the Depression somehow. He used to work 16 hours a day, so Grand-mom always said when each of his four daughters got married he gave them all a house with everything in them. Grand-mom did the inside, dishes, towels, sheets, just like their own. Grand-pop fixed things, so they only had to move in, of course. We had our beautiful home that Mom and Dad took so good care of too. Dear Mom gave it up so we could move to Center Square in the County.

They fixed the Hotel up along with the Café and Summer House. My grandparents did so much work. The plumbing was a big wooden barrel in one room on the 3rd floor for bathrooms. They had a well for drinking water. Grand-pop changed all that. He really worked so hard. Dear Mom giving up the dream house with those orangey curtains. Sweetness of home did wonders to the hotel. It was like a dollhouse with big stairs going up the front as you walked in the double doors. There were also stairs down the back to the small family dining room and the big kitchen.

We used the back stairs to our bedrooms. They were two extra-large rooms connected. There were three floors and each room had a look of Hollywood with beautiful marble top dressers, big cherry wood beds big shiny mirrors and windows so big and bright. What a look when you would look out.

There were two men who came with the hotel, Old John and Willie. Old John helped Mom inside and Willie worked outside. We had clambakes, weddings and floorshows with dancing on Saturday nights. Real nice people from Philadelphia, Blue Bell and Norristown came and it was like a movie. Catherine and I were only 10 & 12 years old, but we knew how to work.

Mom had Kline Laundry Service to do our sheets, bed stuff, and towels and all were so white and stiff with starch, I guess. Mom always went into the rooms first and took off the sheets and picked up the towels. We went in, made the beds and would dust and run the sweeper. We got so busy that Dad got this young couple to live on the third floor. Millie helped with cleaning and cooking meals. Her husband was a truck driver. They were really nice.

We had a special dining room to eat in. Old John and Willie had a table in the big kitchen for themselves and had just what we had to eat. Mom made sure of that! Millie would eat with us lots of times if Johnny was out trucking. She had a kitchen of her own.

Mom made dinner for the pipeline men too at a certain time. They were really nice men, careful with their big boots and shoes. They really took them off to go up the big pretty stairs to go to their rooms. The stairs were all wood with just a little carpet in the middle. The rails and banisters were so shiny and pretty polished and dust free. Like a movie, there was a young fellow with his dad, guess he was 18 or 19 years old, I'm not sure, but Mom took a shine to him. He would sit outside after dinner and dishes on this big swing and ask me my spelling words and do homework too. Catherine was so funny. She wanted him to look at her. She fixed her hair, walked like a model and say, "Hi Charles." It was so darn funny. Mom knew all this. She would come out and say, "Charlie, do you want some pudding or ice-cream?" We always said yes! He was like a big brother.

The other men would go to the bar that was in the hotel and watch TV with a black & white 10-inch screen. Wrestling was a big thing back then, but they didn't stay real late cause they had to get up early in the morning. They had a few big trucks and off they went to work. They went home Friday night and came back Sunday night for work on Monday.

On Saturday nights, there was a live band in the Café floorshow and dancing. People really liked it. Dad would have me sing sometimes. The song; "Now is the hour" and other songs. They called me "The Song Bird of Montgomery County". It was neat! We didn't stay over the Café for long. We went to our room in the hotel to stay.

Willie was parking cars with a real big flash light. Catherine and I would holler out to Willie, "Can you tell Mom we want a Club sandwich, chips, pickle and soda?" He said

Catherine and Patricia

after I got done, "Stay in your room," He was like our guard. When we had to go to the bathroom one of us would stand by the door with this big pink bottle of bubble bath, so if anyone tried to get us, we would hit them on the head.

So, we thought that Sunday morning Catherine and I would walk to church, about one mile or more.

Helen and John O'Hagon and Catherine Bauer

Never did we wake Dad or Mom cause they worked so late Saturday night. Sometimes on Sunday, we went to visit grandparents if there were no weddings or parties.

Willie lived in the summerhouse all year. Old John had a room in the hotel. Sunday morning was busy with cleaning the Café up, tablecloths all off, chairs all up, so the floors could be washed and polished, and ashtrays all cleaned.

Willie would get the Sunday paper and a bottle of whiskey and go to his room. We wouldn't see him till Monday. He never had dinner. Mom would just say, "Leave him alone." Old John was so sweet, Willie too.

Our very first Christmas, Catherine and I were so excited we wouldn't open our presents till they came, then they had to go first. I can still remember how they looked. Old John had tears running down his face. They both were full of surprise. Mom got them pants, socks, shoes, a hanky, and a big flashlight for Willie. It was something to see and I'll always remember. I don't think they knew about Christmas. They had no family. We loved them though.

Old John died in mom's arms. We heard him coughing and called Mom. The doctor came; Mom cleaned him up while we peeked in the crack of the door. When Mom was in there, Dad buried him in a suit and tie with a white shirt. No one came, only us.

Rest in peace, Old John, Mom couldn't get over it. Grand-pop passed on too. Mom was really sad.

Grand-mom wanted the $6000. John O'Hagon and Helen wanted out of the partnership. They never did much, but had the most money in it. When Old John passed and Grand-pop, that was really hard times. It was too much for Mom. She just couldn't hold on.

Saturday nights were a big thing. Dad had four bar tenders and six waiters. Mom stayed in the kitchen with this other lady. Old John made club sandwiches and steamed clams, and really big ham and cheese sandwiches. There were baskets of chips and pretzels. In the winter time there was a coat check lady and she would get tips. The women had beautiful fur coats. In summer, we had clambakes baseball games, volleyball, a game like bowling; it was bocce, an Italian game. It was so cool and pretty under the trees. People just loved it outside.

I could write more on all of that, but for sure, life did change for all of us. Memories of those yesterdays will always be with us now. Catherine and I have our times together as family to make good times for our families now. Catherine is 77 now and I will be 75 years old in April.

A Spirit of Togetherness
By Myra Liddic of Williamsport,
Pennsylvania
Born 1935

I remember the serious looks on my parents and grandparents faces as they listened to the radio before supper in December 1941, when President Roosevelt made his famous speech about the "Day of Infamy" and told about the bombing of Pearl Harbor. I was only six years old at the time and had no idea as to how much this country would be affected by the declaration of war. Some of the biggest changes occurred in my own family.

My grandfather had been the owner and professor of the Williamsport Commercial College, where he and others taught shorthand, typing, and other business courses to young men and women. My father had several salesmen's jobs, but most of the family income came from grandfather. As the young men were drafted into the service, fewer students attended the school. Some young ladies came to the house after the school had to close so they could finish their classes.

Now the family had a hard decision to make. In 1942, it was decided that since some men from other areas came to work in the factories that supplied war materials and need a place to stay, we would make several rooms in the house available for roomers. My grandparents turned the dining room into their bedroom, my parents moved from their back bedroom to a front bedroom on the second floor, opening up two rooms for rent. My father also started to work in a local steel plant and my mother worked part time for an insurance company. Now several strangers became part of the family. How we all managed with only one bathroom is something I never figured out. There was a small powder room under the second floor steps with a toilet and small corner sink. Grandma would go in there and open the small window to smoke her cigarettes. Grandpa did not think smoking was ladylike so she went in there or out on the back porch. It was hard to hide the odor of tobacco if you used that little room after she had been in there.

Other changes occurred all over the country, most of which was the rationing of so many products of everyday use. Sugar, butter, meats, eggs, gasoline, items made of rubber, soap, and other things became hard to get. People of all ages had ration books with stamps that were used to buy necessities. Stickers were issued for people to buy gas. Emergency vehicles were able to get the most gas while lesser gas was given for everyday use.

Because it was feared that the Germans might bomb this country, heavy blinds were required on the windows at night to block out the light. Men who were too old for the service served as air raid wardens and patrolled the streets to make sure everyone complied. There was also a curfew so people were not out on the street at night. People trained as airplane spotters and would watch the skies for enemy planes. My mother worked at an air raid warning station. There people would answer the phones and sound a siren if planes were spotted. There were air raid drills as well at school. When an alarm was sounded, the teachers closed the blinds on the windows and everyone went out into the hallways and sat on the floor away from doors and windows. The music teacher led us in singing rounds to keep us calm until the all clear was sounded. I remember I wore a type of dog tag with my name, address, birth date, parent's names, and phone number and I think maybe blood type inside it. Schoolchildren bought books of savings stamps, which were then used to buy War Bonds used for the purchase of war materials. Scrap metal drives were big occasions with children from different area schools competing to see who could bring in the most metal reused for the war.

People found new ways to make do without the everyday items. One new product that came out of the war was oleomargarine. It came in a plastic bag, was white, and had a red food color capsule enclosed that when the bag was kneaded and the capsule broken, would turn it into a substitute for butter. The bag was then opened and the contents squeezed out onto a plate for use. Mixing it was a lot of fun! We were also able to get several dozen eggs from a local farmer. Those that were not used right away were put in a large crock of some smelly liquid that kept them fresh. When you needed them, they were removed with a slotted spoon and washed off in cold water.

Other ways were found to help the war effort. My mother and grandmother went to the Church Surgical Dressing League and made up different kinds of bandages to be used to treat wounded service men. When a trainload of soldiers or sailors would stop at the local train station, ladies would be there to welcome them with drinks and baked goods. Shoemakers repaired shoes, clothes were patched or re-made, the newspapers were thoroughly read to keep up with events, and radio broadcasts were listened to nightly. My grandfather had a large wall map of the world and after the news, would mark where the battles had been.

This was a different way of life, but all worked together for the good of the country.

I can only wish that if something like this were to happen again, that there would again be a spirit of togetherness.

Almost Giving Bob Orris a Heart Attack
By Luci Ross of Sigel, Pennsylvania
Born 1949

When I think back to when I was small I realize what a sheltered time and place I lived in. Also, what a wonderful time despite what we did without.

I went to a small country school where six grades were crowded into five rooms. In second grade, I had a wonderful teacher named Miss Hazel Wallace.

For Christmas, we exchanged names with everyone in the room, boy or girl. The night before my Christmas party in second grade, we had a major snowstorm. We lived a mile off the main road which was Route 36 and the roads were not plowed or maintained very well back then. My parents started to the nearest store which was another two miles once you got on the main road, only to have the car end up in a ditch. Mom and Dad walked to the store and back just to get me a cap gun for my exchange gift. The day of the party, I couldn't get out my road to go to school so missed the party anyway! On my return in January, I took my gift in for the boy whose name I had gotten and was told that the gift for me had been given to him so all the children would have a present. I gave him the gift anyway and when I left school that day I had a large can of the best peanut butter filled hard tack I had ever eaten, given to me by Miss Wallace!

We were not allowed to chew gum in school. If we got caught, we had to put it on the end of our nose and leave it there until the teacher said we could remove it. One of my classmates couldn't resist and popped in a stick of gum, had it chewed to the juicy stage and got caught! He had to sit there with it on his nose and the goo running down his face while the rest of us choked on laughter!

I missed quite a bit of school in the winter because of the road. There was a row of electric poles the whole way and when I complained, my sister would keep me going by saying, "come on, walk a pole, run a pole"! So I would walk to one and then run to the next. The running helped warm us up and also got me moving so we reached the bus on time!

Being a mile from the main road, we didn't have a telephone until I was fourteen! When we did finally get one, it was a party line with five other families on it. I think ours was three long rings and one short. For a teenager who had waited all her life for a phone you can imagine how I tried to hog it. I know my father got complaints from the neighbors and I got into trouble for tying the line up too.

At home we didn't have an inside bathroom when I was little. I guess most people did but we lived in what they called the "boonies". We had an outhouse and my mom had a chamber pot in one corner of her bedroom for us kids for late night visits. Most times we had toilet paper, when we ran out we had the Sears Roebuck catalog pages. People would think I was crazy today if I admitted that but when they are crumpled enough they do soften up!

We didn't have a bathtub or shower either. We "washed up" at the sink and went to the cellar where it was warm and private to take a sponge bath. Neither did we have an automatic washer or dryer. My mom used an old wringer washer that sat on our porch.

We did our grocery shopping at the little store in Sigel. There was an old pop machine in front of the window. Not a big glass one like now but a small red metal one with rounded corners and three black oblong lids on top that opened from each end. You could get your pop, mostly Coke or orange and grape Knee-Hi from one side, and ice cream bars from the other side, especially Nutty Buddies, my favorite. They also sold six pack bottles of Coke and RC Cola (Royal Crown) which you paid a deposit on. When we returned the empty bottles, we got two cents for each bottle we returned and on "dollar a car night" at the Moon-lite Drive-in; we would scour the area searching for enough pop bottles to pay for our way into the drive-in. They used to give us a small paper, like a mini catalog of coming attractions that we saved so we'd know for weeks ahead what would be playing and could save our money and pop bottles for the next great time.

Cartoons were only on TV. on Saturdays and it was a long week as I waited for Saturday morning and prayed the channels would come in clear enough to watch Roy Rogers, my favorite, and Sergeant Preston of the Yukon and his dog King, Rin Tin Tin, and The Gabby Hays Show. I was a tomboy and liked westerns. Sunday mornings were for religious shows like Oral Roberts and The Guiding Light, I liked the stories told on this one, but the highlight was waiting for 7:00 and Lassie followed by The Wonderful World of Disney where I could watch Davy Crockett and Daniel Boone. My dad was a man big on ice cream and a lot of happy Sunday evenings were spent with a bowl of ice cream in front of the television as we watched Lassie.

Winter was fun as long as our hill wasn't "ashed" and we could sled ride or make snow angels. I remember putting bread bags over our shoes if we didn't have boots, as we sometimes didn't back then. But summer nights were the best! They were warm and there were fireflies everywhere. We'd stay out late playing Hide and Seek, in a circle with our fists in the center going "one potato two potato three potato four...." and Red Rover Red Rover or Simon Says until my mom would make us go to bed. Daytime was for baseball, and in the woods by our house were long grape vines to swing on, pretending we were Tarzan and Jane, or finding a nice chunk of wood and hacking our way through the wilderness like Davy Crockett.

We, the neighbor boys and I, also liked to hunt for snakes. For some reason I never was afraid of them and despite all the horrible fates my mom predicted would happen I never did get bitten by any of them. Most were plain old garden snakes and my dad had a lot of lumber piles, which was a haven for them. Sometimes I would just catch one nice long one to chase my sister with. I thought she was a sissy, she thought I was horrible!

I remember once I had a very big garter snake and I lay in wait along the pathway in some weeds as our neighbor, Bob Orris, came along. I waited until he was almost even with me and let the snake go. Of course, it slithered out right in front of him. He screamed and jumped like a crazy man as I jumped up laughing like it was the best joke in the world. Mom and Dad came running to see what was going on and all I could say was "I got you good this time!" Well, Bob was a good sport and said, "Yeah, you got me good." I never told him but boy did I "get it good" later! I had no idea a grown man could be terrified of snakes until then! Mom just kept saying, "You could have given him a heart attack!"

A lot of our summer days were spent picking wild strawberries or blueberries that grew in the fields around us, sweet and juicy. We had a large collection of movie magazines also, like Movie Mirror, Modern Screen, Silver Screen, and Photo Play, full of Roy Rogers and Dale Evans, Clark Gable, Rock Hudson, Kim Novak, and too many to count. We would spend rainy days or evenings cutting out the stars and pasting them into a large scrapbook.

My mom made some of our clothes. I have a picture of my sister and I with skirts on that she made. My best memory though is of some slips she made for me when I was seven or eight. Mom got some heavy soft flannel and made me two slips from it. They were the warmest things I ever wore. We had to wear dresses to school even in the winter so I was very glad to have those slips my mother made!

We had a lot of animals also. One special dog, named Lassie, was red and kind of like an Irish setter. Once, a mother cat died suddenly after giving birth to some kittens and Mom found Lassie in the box trying to nurse them. We tried also but they didn't make it. Lassie carried each kitten out beside the house and dug a hole and buried them one by one. It was the saddest thing to watch. I remember giving her a big hug because she looked so sad. She was a very special dog.

I liked my mom and dad's stories about Christmas the best. My mom's father had died

Luci Ross and her sister, Louise Crawford in 1958

349

when she was only six months old and she was raised by her widowed mother. She said she and her siblings always got something small but best of all they got a big orange every Christmas and looked forward to it as it was the only time they got one. And my dad would tell me how his father always made the pies for the holidays. His mom did the rest but he said his dad made the best pies ever.

Christmas was and is still my favorite holiday. My dad was like a kid and we had to have a bowl of fruit, a bowl of nuts, and a dish of hardtack candy, especially ribbon candy! We always seemed to get enough presents. I don't know how my parents did it as my dad was out of work a lot when we were small but I always had the doll I wanted and one year a pogo stick, one year an Uncle Wiggly Game and always, every year a Little Miss Christmas coloring book (which I still buy online!). But one year was different. We were older then, old enough to understand how rough things were and my mom forewarned us not to be asking for things because there just wasn't any money that year. Now my dad was a wheeler and dealer, and it happened someone had traded him a beautiful rifle for something they needed. It had been my dad's original plan to give the gun to my brother for Christmas but when he knew he couldn't get us girls anything he decided to sell it for our presents. I remember it had a beautiful stock with three marble diamond shaped chips in it. When we learned what he was going to do we begged him not to sell it, but to give it to our brother as he'd planned, telling him there wasn't anything we really wanted anyway. I know Dad knew better but we really didn't want him to get rid of that beautiful gun. Knowing my dad as I did, I knew it had to be harder on him than us that year. The hard times always stick with us more than the easy ones.

But I sure was fortunate to live in the good old days!

The War Changed Everything
By Robert Logue of Blossburg, Pennsylvania
Born 1931

Our teacher, Miss Smith, was a spinster when she started teaching; since no teacher was allowed to be married, (This law was changed in the 20s). Most teachers boarded at a home near the school, so not to walk too far to school. The home provided her with a room, supper, breakfast, and lunch. Lunch consisted of a sandwich and an apple. Miss Smith owned her own home two miles from school and she walked the two miles every day regardless of the weather. Since teachers operated under contract, they were moved from one district to another at the end of each year. Miss Smith had taught at this school for at least three generations. It was thought because she owned her own house and didn't have to board that had something to do with the decision made to leave her there. She may have started to teach so long ago she was probably grandfathered in.

Recesses were from 10:15 to 10:30 and 2:15 to 2:30 with no supervision. Lunches were from 12:00 to 1:00. Lunches consisted of whatever the parents sent for their children to eat.

School was not only educational but also social. Parties were held around the holidays, and the monthly PTA meetings were always crowded. Sometimes a speaker from out of town was asked to attend, such as the local politician. The ladies of the area used this as an opportunity to trade recipes. Some even hand printed pages in a book with their favorite recipes. Everything was canned. I can remember my mother making catsup, cottage cheese (called smearcase), sauerkraut, and anything else, which was required to feed a family.

A government program called the "Civilian Conservation Corp", or "CCC", was established in order to give employable men a job and a place to live. They were paid $25 a month, half of which was sent to their families. They were fed three meals a day, but had restricted leaving. One of my cousins was in the camp at Masten and I went with the family to visit. The place was so neat and orderly. The majority of men were between the ages of 20 and 40 and were in good health. There was another camp at Grays Run.

Another program the government established was the Works Project Administration, better known as the WPA. (We called it the We Poke Along). They maintained state roads, and one can still see the walls they built in order to protect the highways.

Bodines was a tannery town with a population approximating 200. Almost everything in town was owned by the tannery company. That house rent was deducted from the pay, along with what was purchased at the company store. There were a few houses that were individually owned, since they were there before the tannery moved in and built more houses. When the tannery company put in a generator to supply power for the tannery, they ran electric wires through the houses, and charged inhabitants for electricity used. This worked out fine until the tannery moved out and took its generator with them. Back to kerosene lamps! It was another 30 years before the town had electricity again.

When the tannery moved out, an individual purchased the company houses and store. He sold the store to another enterprising individual, who proceeded to operate it as a general store. The houses were either sold to individuals on a per month basis rate or were rented. The rental price before World War II was $5 per month.

The major method of transportation was the train. All the villages had the name station as their names, such as Cogan Station, Field Station, etc. As the train went by a crossing, the mailman on the train kicked a bag of mail out the door and reached out with a hook to pull the outbound mailbag off a stanchion. While the train proceeded, the mail was sorted.

During 1936, there was the St. Patrick's Day flood. A couple of homes were flooded out, but it was much more serious in the larger cities like Williamsport. The one family who was flooded seemed to be flooded every year so it was something they were used to.

Employment increased in the late 30s. Electric wires were installed to each home. The general store now had a gas pump. Cars became popular. Radios were plugged in rather than run by batteries. A multitude of programs were now listened to included Tom Mix (Ralston cereal), Terry and the Pirates, the Lone Ranger, Orphan Annie (Ovaltine), and many others. Then the nighttime programs, The Shadow, Gang Busters, Sherlock Homes, I Love a Mystery, Bulldog Drummond, Green Hornet, etc.

Now came Pearl Harbor! Two brothers from the area enlisted in the Navy the day after Pearl Harbor. The son of the general store manager was already in training as a Marine pilot. Later a local farmer's son enlisted in the Marines. Two brothers were drafted into the Army, later to serve with Patton's third army.

A cousin of mine who lived in town enlisted in the Navy as soon as he graduated from high school. War affected everything, including our radio programs. The Green Hornet's Japanese houseboy named Kato was immediately changed to a Philippine houseboy named Kato. A Hawaiian guitar player who was on the radio Sunday afternoon was found to be sending coded signals to Japanese spies.

All comic books were drafted into fighting the war. We heard on the radio about "Juke Joints" and "Jitterbugging" but the only social meeting we had was in front of the local general store and there wasn't any music there to dance to. We could hear modern music on the radio, but the only record music we could hear was from a Victrola, you had to wind up between each record.

"Big Little Books" were amount to the majority reading material. These were about 4 inches square and 3 inches thick, and contained such characters as Buck Rogers, Flash Gordon, Tailspin Tommy, Orphan Annie, Apple Mary, and several other characters.

Patriotic songs filled the airways, e.g., "A wing and a prayer" and Kate Smith's "God Bless America", and "Praise the Lord and Pass the Ammunition". Movies came out with the war theme, such as Guadalcanal Diary and 30 seconds over Tokyo and many more.

Cigarette manufacturers also converted. Lucky Strike green has gone to war! Cigarette packages named Wings came out with airplane cards on them with each pack. The Chesterfield show went on USO tours. Saving stamps sold for 10 cents, and you could fill a book and turn it in for a $25 savings bond. Schools gathered milkweed, the fiber to be used in life jackets.

Almost everything was rationed. Gasoline, tires, meat, coffee, sugar, and butter (an imitation butter made from lard and a food coloring capsule). Ration stamps came in a book, red stamps for meat, blue stamps for butter, etc. Most of these country people, because of the Depression, had been rationing themselves due to necessity. They got their butter from local farmers, their groceries from the garden, meat from chickens and rabbits, sugar from syrup from those people who tapped trees. They did miss their coffee. A.B.C. stickers on the right side of the vehicles indicated how many gallons of gasoline one could get depending upon his occupation. Farmers had a high availability to gasoline due to the necessity to feed people. Tires and inner tubes were not available.

Air raid wardens were appointed in each town to spot airplanes and to make sure the town was dark during blackouts. It seemed to me it was rather stupid to black out our little town until it was explained by the teacher that the planes could use our town as a method of telling where they were in relation to their target. Each air warden was issued a whistle, an armband signifying that the wearer was an air warden, a white helmet, and a flashlight, and he patrolled the streets at night looking for violators of the blackout.

Boys made model airplanes out of balsa wood. The box they came in said they would fly, but they really did a lousy job of flying, although they did a good job of crashing. Piper Aircraft sent out a cardboard model which, after you put it together. You could pull the stick and the elevator would move, causing the plane to dive.

The European War was over. Although there were celebrations in the larger cities, of which our local paper showed pictures, our people just looked forward to our boys who were over there to come home and not have to go to the Pacific. The boys started coming home except for the grocery store owner's son. He was killed in the Pacific. Some of them went to college under the G.I. Bill, and others joined the 52-20 club, which was 20 dollars a week for 52 weeks, sort of a GI bill unemployment compensation.

Popular Science and Popular Mechanics magazines were full of what the future would bring. One atom pill in your gas tank would run your car the rest of the car's life. Mom would take a small helicopter to the grocery store. Dad would drive the car onto the runway, put its wings out, and fly to his office, no matter how far it was.

My mother was a schoolteacher who didn't pass the freshman class in high school. She dropped out her freshman year and instead went to Muncy Normal School, and learned to teach. When she was twenty years old, she taught school at Grey's Run logging camp, which was about 12 miles off the nearest paved road. She would ride the log trains in on Monday morning, board locally at a home in the village, and ride a log train out Friday, catch the Susquehanna and New York train to Fields Station, and ride the Pennsylvania train home. She taught from Pennsdale to Hoppistown and a lot of places in between.

The area I was raised in was settled by Irish farmers whose families had migrated to Cascade Township from Philadelphia and settled in Cascade Township. At its most heavily populated time during the late 1800s, approximately 600 Catholic families lived in the township. It had a large church, what was known as a "mission church", because the priest was assigned to a nearby church in Ralston. Any masses other than Sunday morning were said in Ralston, because the local church had no lights. For five years, I was an altar boy at the Cascade church, and sometimes, because the Ralston church was near the high school, I would be assigned to a midweek wedding at that church. I liked that because the altar boys always got paid.

During the 1860s, the two churches initiated an annual festival known as The Cascade Picnic in order to raise money to support the churches. It was a one day festivity with games, dinner, and with square dancing at the end of the day. During the early days, an extra train from Williamsport was employed to bring people to and from the picnic. Of course, after the invention of the automobile the train was discontinued. On one occasion, the local doctor who resided in Ralston was on his way to the picnic in his buggy and was robbed. These festivities were discontinued in the 1990s due to the closing of the Cascade church.

The population of the township was nearly eliminated due to the influenza epidemic of 1918. Many families were totally wiped out. There were so many deaths occurring so quickly that a trench was dug on the eastern side of the church, between the church and the cemetery, and bodies were brought in wagons and buried in the trench. Names were not taken so no one knows who is buried there.

Trips to Town
By Nancy A. Toles of South Williamsport, Pennsylvania

My twin sister Bonnie and I would take the bus trips into town on Fridays and sit at the counter in Woolworth's five and ten store. We would order their fish dinners. They were our favorite meal there.

We would go shopping in all the stores: LL Sterns, the Carol House, Kreasgies, and

Revco drug store. Our favorite time was at Christmas, with the store fronts all decorated for the holidays. People were all over, lots of families in town. Kids were lined up to see Santa in his little house set up in the area. Also, there was the Christmas show at the Capital Theater that was really exciting then.

We enjoyed all the hustle and bustle of the holidays. Going to town was always a big deal to us. We looked forward to our many trips. Summer was great, too, always something going on and things to see and do.

Downtown with Grandma
By Felicia Gelnett of Williamsport, Pennsylvania
Born 1968

Remembering back more than twenty years ago, I was not even a teenager then.

Downtown Williamsport was so exciting. Going downtown with my grandmother, my brother and I on our birthdays, and holidays, was so looked forward to. J. C. Penney's, Sears, Roebuck, L.L. Stearns & Sons Five and Ten, Krims Toy Store, Neyhart's Places to eat, stores to shop, always so much fun stopping in at Twentieth Century Bakery for sticky buns. Going to see Christmas lights up, or shopping at Lucasi for cards or walking the streets.

Looking back now, it was like living in a big city. Remembering downtown with my grandmother are memories I will have for a lifetime.

Felicia, Grandma, and brother, Garth

The Planing Mill Fire
By Vivian I. Johnson of Williamsport, Pennsylvania
Born 1929

I wonder how many people remember the old planing mill in the 800 block on First Street in Williamsport? On New Year's 1940, when I was only ten years old, it burned down to the ground. When the turpentine barrels exploded, the flames went across the street and set fire to six homes. They couldn't be saved. Where I lived was one of them.

My father, Herbert Grugan was at home alone because my mother, brother, and I had gone to Renovo visiting friends for Christmas. My father had to jump over the banister to the first floor. He grabbed our dog, Skippy, and took her out in the garage. He got dressed in the backyard. He went back to the kitchen and dining room door to get our floor model radio because it wasn't paid for yet. He just made it outside when the whole house fell to the ground. Thank God, he made it out.

We got back to town New Year's night and found out about our home and others. The officials weren't going to let us walk up the street, but my mother insisted, so they said all right. All that was left of our house was the bathtub, held in the air by the pipes.

We started asking people if they knew where my father was. Finally, one of them said he had gone to my grandmother's in Montgomery. Thank God, he was all right except for singed hair and eyebrows.

Thank God, no lives were lost. It was a terrible memory, which I will never forget. I am now 82 years old.

Floods and Footlongs
By Patricia Brady Malone of Potomac, Maryland
Born 1930

I grew up in Johnsonburg, Pennsylvania in the 1940s. I remember being able to walk to Fulton's Confectionary Store in the West End of Johnsonburg to get a five cent ice cream sucker. I always hoped to find the word "free" on the stick when the ice cream was gone. If I found a "free" stick, I would get a replacement. They also had penny candy. Mrs. Thelma Fulton was very patient with each child as they were selecting their penny candy.

I remember having potato roasts at small fires in the evenings. I would go home to get a potato, and throw it in the fire. It would come out all black, but we would peel it and eat it. We children played Kick the Can and Red Light, Green Light.

In July of 1942, there was a flash flood in Johnsonburg. Our house and all the furnishings were damaged in the flood. Water came up to the window ledge on the first floor. Mother had made donuts, and after swimming around in the water, they lay much larger in size on the carpet. All the carpets and the living room couch and chairs had to be taken to the dry cleaners to be refurbished. Our neighbors on the higher streets were very generous at feeding us and giving us a place to sleep for a night or two.

During my high school years of 1945 to 1948, I walked to school each day and home again for lunch. My friends and I would walk to the East End Deckers Memorial Fountain on Sunday afternoons to take pictures. After school, we would go to Phelps for Cherry Cokes or to Weister's Pharmacy for peanut butter fudge sundaes. After the school dances, we would stop at Weirich's for hot dogs. We also liked to go to Kane, Pennsylvania for footlong hot dogs. One summer, I went camping with a group of girls at Twin Lakes Park for a week.

The Helpful Telephone Operator
By Gwen Klus of Laporte, Pennsylvania
Born 1939

I grew up in the small town of Eagles Mere, Pennsylvania. According to the census, the population in 1960 was 130. Everyone knew everyone in town. My fondest memories of the summer resort town of Eagles Mere are in the 1950s. As a teenager in that decade, I did a lot of babysitting, both in the summer and winter.

The "downtown" area consisted mainly of one large building, which housed the post office, a grocery store, a general store, and an office for the town realtor, all on the first floor. The second floor housed the telephone exchange and an apartment for Florence, the town telephone operator. Because it was in

the center of town, the telephone operator could look out her window in the front of the building and watch everything going on below.

This arrangement made it possible for the operator to keep track as people came for the mail at 10:00 in the morning. It was also helpful in several ways. I remember once trying to make a call to Bert Feaster when Florence said, "You'd better wait five minutes. He just left the post office"!

I remember another way the arrangement was useful. If I was babysitting in the evening, I would let Florence know where I could be reached. If anyone called me, she would put the person through to me, no matter where I was. I'm sure she did the same for everyone else in town.

The telephones at that time were hung on the wall and each had a crank used to contact the operator. I am sure more populous towns had more modern telephones. Of course, these were party lines with four families per line. Our phone number at home was 125R3, translated as line 125, ring 3 shorts. The rings varied and sounded on all the phones on the line according to the code listed in your number. Since there was not a lot to do in the winter, some people would relieve their boredom by listening in. You could always tell, because you could hear them pick up the receiver.

The Four F Club
By C. Dean Sharpless of Philipsburg,
Pennsylvania
Born 1929

In the village of Sandy Ridge, Pennsylvania, in the early 40s, lived a man by the name of Nig Umholtz. Nig made sure the youth of Sandy Ridge stayed out of serious trouble. He bought us a clubhouse where he told stories and showed pictures. One in particular was in 1936 when the snow was very deep. The picture showed deer going around in a circle until each died of starvation.

We called the club the Four F Club, Fish, Forest, Fun and Food. We had a lot of fellowship in those years.

It was common to see Mr. Umholtz going somewhere with a pickup full of the kids. Nig had his own camp near the Sandy Ridge fire tower that was open to the public all year long, so we spent many weekends in the camp.

He wanted to show us where a herder was buried on the road between Tryone and Houtzdale.

We carried food he provided with a big black kettle to cook hobo stew. The trip was about four miles from the camp, so we made shelters to stay overnight. One of the boys poured water on each of our lean-tos, so Nig said, "Pack up, boys, we are going back to camp, four miles, in the dark."

He had us build barriers of railroad ties and big pipes in the big fill run to protect the fish. We got permission to shoot kingfishers who were taking the fish. He also made a dam where all the kids in Sandy Ridge could fish and he awarded prizes for the biggest fish, as well as who caught the most.

I am now over 30,000 days old, but the memories of Nig Umholtz are very vivid to this day.

School Troubles
By Clarence McHenry, Jr., of Hughesville,
Pennsylvania
Born 1950

I would like to give you two stories of my childhood. My name is Clarence McHenry, Jr. I was born in Bloomsburg hospital in August 1950 to a great set of parents. I went to and graduated from Benton High School and finished in 1970, which should have been 1968. I liked school so much I repeated 1st and 4th grades. If you believe that, I'll tell you another (yea).

My dad told me if I got a spanking at school, I would also get one at home. My cousin and I would tussle each other. My other cousin thought we were fighting so one time we faked like we were about to get into it again. Our other cousin ran and told on us and when the teacher found out she took us to the basement and we got our rears warmed. Recently our cousin Linda passed on.

This storm we had in the late 1960s was bad, we didn't have the forecasts then we have now. I was in high school so after Health class on a Wednesday we had homework the next week. I have always been a person to put things off so I figured I could get my book Monday the next week and study enough to pass the test. That weekend it started to snow and snow into Sunday night. Monday when

school closed, I wasn't too worried because there was Tuesday. When Tuesday morning came and school was closed, I got concerned because there was not nearly enough time to study or even time to look over the material. So when Wednesday morning came my ear was glued to the radio. Finally, our school was added to the list of closings. That storm was equal or worse than the March 1993 storm.

Houtzdale, A Great Place to Grow Up
By Joseph Zeigler of Houtzdale,
Pennsylvania
Born 1949

In the years before all of the electrical gadgets, I remember growing up in Houtzdale. Every day I woke up, it was a new adventure. I never knew what my street friends and I were going to do. Build a cabin, play baseball, football, or basketball, pick berries, ride bikes, make go-carts, etc. We never played in the house unless it was raining! We were always outside until it was time to eat or go to bed.

Sometimes there would be snowfalls overnight of up to two feet. We would make igloos at the football field, where the drifts were over our heads. We'd go sled riding down the streets of Houtzdale. The streets were blocked off by the borough at Main Street. Ashes were placed at the intersections, and barricades were placed so we could not go onto Main Street.

Friday, Saturday, and Sunday nights were set aside for watching our favorite television shows. I'd lie on the floor with the best pal that I had, Spike the beagle dog. We'd watch *Chiller Theater*, *Walt Disney*, *Outer Limits*, *The Screeching Door*, cartoons, *Lassie*, *Howdy Doody*, *The Ed Sullivan Show*, *The Lone Ranger*, *The Cisco Kid*, *Gunsmoke*, and more.

My friends and I would go to the Houtzdale movie theater. We could get in for bottle caps from Pepsi and Coke. Fifty cents would get us a lot of good candy and other things.

We couldn't wait to look for pop bottles, so we could cash them in for money to get candy and ice cream. We would steal the wheels off of the girls' baby carriages in the neighborhood. Then we would make go-carts and take them down the streets as fast as they would go.

Houtzdale had as many bars as it did churches. I believe there was seven of each. There were so many stores to choose from. We did not need to go out of town for anything. There were restaurants and ice cream shops with jukeboxes. We would groove to the music on Saturday nights. There was a pool hall, where most of us got our education. Houtzdale was surely a great place to grow up back in the fifties and sixties. I sure do miss those days.

Robert Brown, U.S. Veteran
By Connie T. Brown of Wellsboro,
Pennsylvania
Born 1922

The first time I, Connie T. Tarszowicz (Brown) saw my husband to be, Robert L. Brown, was when my mom, Mary Tarszowicz, and I went to shop in Wellsboro, PA and stopped at Hawk's Gasoline Station to get gasoline. Robert came out and waited on us. My mom knew who he was and told me his name as I asked her who he was. When he went back into the garage to work, he asked someone inside who I was. He called me and we went out on a date. We later got engaged and married in Jan. 1942 and moved to Buffalo, NY, although Wellsboro, PA was always his hometown.

Connie T. Brown and Barbara Ann Brown (Johnson)

World War II had already started and he was one that received an early draft notice. He did not want to go into the U.S. Army so he enlisted in the U.S. Navy. He had been working in the Chevrolet Plant in Kenmore, NY prior to enlisting in the U.S. Navy. He was called in February 1942 to go into training. I moved back to Antrim, PA with my mother and after his training, he came home. He was then sent to California, then to Pearl Harbor, and eventually to the Pacific Area. He never came home until the war was over, that was the first time he got to meet his 3 year old daughter Barbara Anne.

He was honorably discharged as Machinist's Mate Second Class U.S. Naval Personnel from Separation Center, Bainbridge, MD in September 1945. We had a wonderfully happy marriage for 45 years and three additional children: Marla Jean, Robert John and Gina Marie. Robert L. Brown passed away on November 11, 1987, Veteran's Day.

Robert L. and Connie T. Brown in 1942

The Name Game
By Tammy Breighner of Abbottstown,
Pennsylvania
Born 1961

What does *that* mean?
Recently on a trip to Potter County, Pennsylvania, I asked my husband that

question. We had set out on an evening ride in search of wildlife when we came across a cabin with an odd name: Moncharglen. We had quite a discussion about the possible meaning, and before we knew it, we were searching for different cabin names with the same excitement as searching for deer or bear.

In 2000, my husband and I were blessed with the opportunity to purchase a cabin of our own. It took us weeks to come up with the name for our cabin. Just like the story behind the name we finally chose, we found that there is a story behind every name. Some are short and to the point, while others originated in events and people years and years ago. Some cabins are named for their surroundings, while others bear the name of the owner. Some choices were obvious, while others were not.

We talked to cabin owners in Potter County and other counties in central and northern Pennsylvania. They were proud to tell us their stories. They expressed themselves as if they were talking about a member of their family. We discovered that no matter how big, little or primitive the cabin may be, the name and the story behind that name are true reflections of the people who own it.

Take, for instance, The Preacher's Dream. We imagined an older, maybe white-haired man who had spent his whole life in service to God. This cabin was his getaway when the strains of fulfilling that duty got to be a bit much. The story we were told was not even close to that. The only similarity, if fact, was the white-haired man.

As I stood in the living room that was decorated with family pictures and a small spattering of antiques, my question was

Ervin and Martha Jacobs

answered with a big belly laugh and a look that said I had taken him back to days gone by.

"Well now, you have to remember that this was years ago, back in the fifties when I was a drinking man. My buddies and I were sitting in a bar. The Yankees had just lost the game that we were all watching on TV. A man at the bar who was a big Yankees fan was so upset by the loss that he started swearing. He was using every word in the book and even made some new ones up. One of his buddies jokingly yelled out, 'Yeah, mister, you might want to watch your mouth. There is a man of the cloth sitting at this table.' He was pointing at me.

"It got so quiet you could have heard a pin drop, and all eyes had turned to look at me. The only thing I could think to do, to let them know that I really wasn't a preacher, was to let fly a line of curse words."

"The place erupted in laughter. From then on, I was known as The Preacher. You wouldn't believe how many young couples have asked me to marry them."

"In 1975 when we bought this place, I asked my wife what we were going to name it. She instantly said, 'That's easy: The Preacher's Dream.'"

He might not be a preacher, but it is obvious that he and his wife are living their dream.

We saw far too many places to name individually that are named for their location. But if you sit back and close your eyes, it wouldn't take your mind long to conjure up a picture of these cabins and their surroundings from their names: Hemlock Hideaway; Aspen Acre; The Slippery Slope.

Also, many places are named for the owner. There is Fay's Haven, Ed's Mountain, and Ruth's Roost. The list goes on and on. In many of these cases, the owner said it was a quick and easy name.

Along this same thought, we have R Place. The owner's last name starts with the letter R. Then there is Triangle B. Three family members own this place. Their last name starts with the letter B.

The owners of Loggers Lodge own and operate a sawmill where they live. The name 200 Mile Camp was given because that is the distance between home and cabin.

There are cabins whose owners tried to be clever. Pot Luck is decorated with a toilet seat. Missembuckem is painted on a target

9 Point Lodge

with arrows coming out of it, and none of them are in the bulls eye. And then there is Quityourbellyachin, Hazaname, and Porky Pine.

Potter County is a popular hunting area, and cabin names are a reflection of the owner's love of the sport. For example, there is Little Buck, Big Buck Camp, Antlers, White Deer, 9 Point Lodge, Back Rub, Running Buck Camp, and the Rocky Buck Camp.

We found that there is a very special story behind 9 Point Lodge. This story dates back to the late 1930s or early 1940s. No one knows for sure. Ervin Jacobs was a young man with a family to feed. He would come to Potter County with a couple of his buddies and hunt for a week during deer season.

Potter County also has long been known for its timber value. Back in the late 1800s and early 1900s, northern Pennsylvania was a Mecca in the logging business, and there were camps for the lumberjacks set up everywhere. As the logging business came to an end, these settlements were abandoned.

Ervin and his friends found one of these abandoned buildings near Lyman Run. This horse stable became their camp while they hunted. But the next year when they arrived at the stable, there were already two men using it. They worked out an agreement and they all stayed together, but it was at this time that they decided that they would like to get something permanent, something that was theirs.

It would take until 1948 for their dream to come true. They wanted to purchase land at Plummer's Rest, but the owner would not sell it to them. But he did agree to sell them a plot of land about a mile down the road. They bought one acre of land for a hundred

dollars, and built a small cabin. They had an agreement that whoever shot the biggest buck, point-wise, in one year, would get the honor of having the cabin named after that buck. Ervin shot a nine-point buck during that year. Hence, the name 9 Point Lodge. But the story doesn't end there.

Ervin had nine children who gave him many grandchildren. Even though the cabin had been built onto several times, the family kept growing and outgrew the cabin. After much thought and deliberation, the family decided to sell the cabin. Most of Ervin's children decided to branch out and get places of their own. After some time, even these places have gotten too small. Some of the grandchildren have now gotten places of their own.

One of Ervin's grandsons bought a couple of acres of land with a small white house on it. He put hours of work into it, making it his home away from home. When he was done, he called his uncles together for a meeting. He wanted to name his cabin and thought that they could help. He told them that after much thought, there was only one name that he could think of to name his cabin. He asked them for their permission and blessing to name his cabin 9 Point Lodge.

Ervin had a deep love for this area of Pennsylvania. He also treated the land and the wildlife with respect. It is obvious from the story above that he passed this down to several generations. He has been gone for 24 years, but his memory lives on in the family members that continue to visit these beautiful mountains and in the name of the cabin.

There is a cabin named The Flying Dutchman. Not only is it near our cabin, but we know the owners. We thought that finding the meaning of this cabin's name would be easy. Boy, were we wrong.

Two of the present-day owners are second generation, and when I asked them about the name, they didn't have a clue. The other owner, who is in his late sixties, scratched his head and said, "I think we found the sign somewhere, nailed it up and thought, "That looks good." He wasn't sure that his recollection was correct, so we went to the widow of one of the original owners. She couldn't remember; in fact, she said she doesn't think she ever knew. She suggested that we ask her brother, who had also been one of the original owners.

When asked, Clair, who is a no-nonsense

358

kind of man, got right to the point. He said, "It's named for me. I would fly up from home in Adams County and fly back home again."

I realized that he didn't mean it literally. He had a lead foot and would drive so fast that he practically flew up and flew back. Then he added in a matter-of-fact tone, "When I was young, I spoke a lot of Pennsylvania Dutch. So we named the cabin The Flying Dutchman."

This story left me with a feeling of melancholy. Here is a cabin that has a name and only person knows why it is called by that name. There are many places that are passed from generation to generation. Sadly, family stories, traditions, and even something as simple as the meaning of a name are getting lost and forgotten with the passing of time.

Back in 2000, when we bought our cabin, giving it a name was quite a big deal. Just like some of the other owners, I had been very clever, and thought that I had come up with the perfect name. I wanted to name the cabin The Hunting B's. Let me explain:

My husband and three sons all hunt wild game. While I don't hunt for animals, I do hunt for bargains. The guys all spin their tales of hunting and I tell stories of the best buy I ever got. The letter B is the initial of our last name. Perfect, right? They didn't think so either.

Since we live in a democracy, and due also to the fact that I was outnumbered four to one, the name didn't get voted in. Being the only female in a house of five, I am used to being outnumbered and out-voted, but rarely ever outsmarted. So I challenged them to come up with something cleverer than that. I was confident that my feminine smarts would outdo their male brains.

Very reluctantly, I must admit that my

The Flying Dutchman

son got me. He said, "When someone asks you where you are going this weekend, you never say, 'I'm going to Hemlock Hideaway or to The Flying Dutchman.' You always say, 'I'm going to the cabin.'" It is because of this reasoning that there is a wood sign hanging from the roof eave of our cabin that reads "The Cabin." Chalk one up for the male brain.

In 1947, six men, who, interestingly enough, were not all acquainted, came together and formed a "surviving partnership" hunting camp and association. The association legally dictates that shares can only be sold to surviving members at the original investment value, plus any additional money required for maintenance. These six men came from three towns in the Pittsburgh area. Martin Perecko, Joe and Steve Bartek and Vic Bindi all came from Monongahela. Bob Hoehl came from Charleroi, and Bob Ortmiller came from Glenshaw. By using parts of these three town names, the camp was given the name Moncharglen.

The original six founding members have all passed, allowing the next generation to acquire equity in the camp and association. This young generation feel that they have been given a legacy that they are proud and grateful to accept. They are eager to pass on the traditions and love of nature that they enjoyed in their childhood.

No matter what these places are named, or if they are called lodge, cabin, or hunting camp, they all have one thing in common: they all provide shelter from the cold, rest for the weary, and a place to get away from everyday life. They are places for friends and families to gather for hunting stories to grow into tall tales.

Potter County has an abundance of seasonal lodges. In our township alone, almost sixty percent of all dwellings are cabins. Every one of these cabins has a history, whether short or long, and a story that it could tell. Some have been passed down from older generations, while others are just now becoming the fulfillment of life long dreams.

Every cabin name has a story behind it, as well. No matter what that story may be, it is a reflection of the love the people have for this area of Pennsylvania and for the cabins that provide sanctuary under their roofs.

Home in the Country
By Harry Wanamaker of Williamsport,
Pennsylvania
Born 1948

Growing up in Williamsport was a lot of fun. I had the opportunity of meeting a lot of different people, because we were always moving due to my parents getting evicted from our homes.

I can remember going to first grade at Washington School. When the bell rang for recess, I thought it was time to go home, so I walked all the way home.

I remember all of us kids taking a bath. There were ten of us, and we had to use the same bath water to save electricity. Sometimes getting up in the morning, we would all stand in the kitchen in front of the oven because we were out of oil or coal, and there was no heat in the house. A lot of times there was no cereal for breakfast, so we would break up some bread and put milk and sugar on it.

As time went on, things got better. We always enjoyed our mother singing us Christmas carols. When we went to bed on Christmas Eve, we would peek down through the register holes and try to see what gifts we got. I remember one year we three boys got bicycles all alike. They had streamers and saddlebags. We really felt like we were rich.

Then my parents rented a house out in the country. It had four ponds and lots of wooded areas. Living out there was the best time of my life. I would go to my friend's house, and we would ride on the tractor and do things around the farm. One year we made maple syrup. That was a lot of fun. At night, I would sit up and watch out my bedroom window. I would watch the animals running around outside. Then my parents moved back to town. That broke my heart. I loved the country.

Now we were older and met new friends. After school, we would come home and change our clothes and grab our single shot shotguns or our .22s and walk to the edge of the city. We would go squirrel hunting, or we would go over to the dump, which was in the middle of the city and shoot rats. We had a lot of fun, and the police never bothered us.

In all, we all grew up to be good people. One thing we did learn through all of this was to be responsible and not to waste and to conserve energy.

The Turkey Stole the Show
By Olivia Hartman of Kane, Pennsylvania

When we were kids, we jammed the toes of our snow boots under the leather straps on our 1938-style skis and headed down the hill. Fortunately, most of us fell before reaching the bottom where the Conococheague Creek still runs. Most of the winter, it's without ice strong enough to support a human body. Today, those old-style skis form a big X on the wall of our camp, and they remind me of the days in Southern Pennsylvania, before I married and moved to Northwestern Pennsylvania.

When my boys were ready to ski, we went to the local ski hill called Big Gusty. The boys buckled the slim-grooved skis around their World War II Army surplus ski boots, and down the hill they went. The tricky part of Big Gusty was avoiding the trees in the woods at the bottom of the hill.

If you stopped safely, the next challenge was to get back up to the top using the homemade rope-tow. It was pulled by a discarded 1946 Oldsmobile engine. Unique as it was, rigged with wheel rims at the top and bottom of the hill, it could pull one person at a time but not two. At the top, there was a safety man by the exit bar. He helped the kids let go of the rope before their jackets, gloves, or arms could get caught between the rope and the tire rim as the rope turned around the rim to start down again.

For those of us who did not ski or no longer skied, there was a warming hut with a big, brick fireplace, where we could wait in relative comfort. Although we knew our ski slope was not of Olympic quality, we had many races and competitions, and much family fun at Kane's Big Gusty.

Kane Players was a new organization in our town, and we were presenting our first production of *Scrooge*. Our actors and stage crew were relatively inexperienced.

The curtain opened on Act Two, as Ebenezer Scrooge was about to knock on Bob Cratchit's door to deliver a roasted turkey for their Christmas dinner. Suddenly, the prop man realized that Scrooge did not have the turkey. It was on the wrong side of the stage. In an inspired moment, the prop man grabbed the paper mache bird and slid it out onto the stage, where it skidded to a stop right at the dining room table just as Scrooge entered. Bob grabbed the bird, jumped up and excitedly exclaimed, "The turkey has arrived!" The audience roared with laughter.

This was the funniest moment of the show, and one of the many memorable moments we had over the years with our hometown theater group.

Natural Air Conditioning
By Eva M. Shutt of Genesee, Pennsylvania
Born 1946

Living on a farm in a family of ten was very challenging. Chores were done before play, and if ignored, we were spanked and no dessert for supper.

Farming, caring for the animals, gardening and washings were done without plumbing. Water supply was carried from a spring or a nearby creek. Oil lamps provided the light, and wood stoves were for heat and cooking because there wasn't electric or natural gas.

Clothing was cut from patterns and hand sewn, or we received a few donations from the church. We walked ten miles for groceries and carried them home. Occasionally, we were offered a ride, but one was never accepted from a stranger.

A peddler arrived once a month and the folks purchased soaps, shampoos, wool blankets and other household products. Sometimes, we were treated with cheese, oranges and gum.

The outhouse was down a well beaten path to the edge of the woods. During the night, if I had to go, I teased for company. Doing the "duty" was very quick with natural air conditioning and a visit from the wild creatures. The softest tissue that I recall was a well crumbled page of Sears and Roebeck catalog, or a week old newspaper.

If we fought in school, on the bus, or walking from the bus stop, we were disciplined. If you were punished in school, there was another waiting when you arrived at home. I tried to hide, but was warned, if found, it'd be harder. A lesson learned, take the consequences, sweetie, it's easier on the seatie.

Our Saturday night special was a nasty dose of castor oil and a hot bath in a galvanized tub. A reservoir on the wood stove supplied hot water. And there was little left when it came my turn. I was usually the fifth or sixth

child for a bath.

There was always church on Sunday and death would be the only excuse for not attending. Your offering was whatever you wished, and mine was a dime.

We never had a family vacation, but went to Grandma's for a week during the summer. It wasn't leisure time, because there were chores before play.

Family entertainment was sitting on the front porch, singing and picking guitars. On Saturday nights, we listened to the Grand Old Opry on a hand-me-down radio, or danced to foxtrots played on a wind-up phonograph.

During the summer months, we also enjoyed the swimming hole, which was our spa bath as the water rushed over the rocks. In the winter months, we entertained with board games, cards and reading. We slid down hills, built forts and made snow angels. Later, we warmed ourselves by the potbellied stove. Everyone gathered for a tale to tell.

Our folks had real hard times, compared to ours. The memories from my childhood will never be forgotten, as time has passed into a prosperous future.

3 Dollars a Day at 14 Years Old
By Edson Snell of Williamsport,
Pennsylvania
Born 1930

I was born in 1930. My mother was up warming my bottle and she caught on fire and died. I was raised by my grandmother. When I was 6 or 7 years old, I helped my grandfather pick stones and helped in the garden. I helped feed the cows and milked them. I went to school until I was 14 years old and I quit school. I got my working papers and went to work at a farm. I earned $3 a day. I was there for 2 years. I drove a tractor and plow, and harrowed and helped make hay and hauled out manure.

When I was about 15 years old I bought a 1930 model A Sedan. I paid $85. After two weeks, I traded it with another guy for a 1931 Model A Coupe. I came back to my grandparents'. My grandfather wasn't real well. I helped him take care of the cows.

When I was 16 years old, I worked for the PA Game Commission. It was a turkey farm. I built fences. They bought a new bulldozer and they had me run it. The first thing I did was dig a cellar and they built a house.

After that job, I drove a truck for Lence and Guinter. They moved out of the states and then I drove a truck for Blair Lumber Company for a long time. Then I began cutting logs in the woods. During that time, I bought my own log truck and contracted to haul logs for him.

Later I hauled logs for Lewis Lumber Co. I worked for them until I was 55 years old. I got hit with a tree and became paralyzed. After I was in the hospital for three months, with lots of exercise and therapy, I got so I could walk again. After I came home, my wife gave me therapy on the living room floor. I just turned 82 years old last month.

I always lived in my grandparent's house. I purchased it after they passed away. It burned down in 1968. Within a year, we built another house here. I had lots of help building it, friends and family. We moved in it before the inside was completed. We got it finished as we could afford it. We still live here.

Cure for Tetanus
By Barbara A. Smith of Loganton,
Pennsylvania
Born 1939

In the early forties, Lock Haven, Pennsylvania was a bustling town, especially on Saturday evenings. Main Street was busy with traffic and shoppers. Stores, such as J.C. Penney, Woolworth's, Montgomery Ward, Luria's Dress Shop, Grossman's (a ladies' shop), and Grants were all open. Woolworth's had a soda fountain and booths where they served food. Three movie theaters, The Roxy, Garden, and Martin, were open for business. What fun it was to come to town and see the bright lights, fancy hats, beautiful shoes, and the hustle of the town. Now, only The Roxy Theater exists. Very few stores are downtown, as all have closed or moved to the mall about thirty miles away. Even The Smart Shop, a nice local shop for many years is now gone. I miss the excitement of coming to town and to the movies. Except I didn't like movies then, so I would sit in the lobby and color in coloring books while my grandmother, mother, and aunt went to see a movie. This was wartime; the men were away.

My grandmother had a gas-operated

Barbara's mother, Clara E. Andrews Muthler about 1943

wringer washer, but she had no running water in the house. We kids helped carry water inside to heat on the old cook stove, then she would carry the water back outside. I remember the noise the washer made and how I was to be careful around it because of my long hair. I did not have curly hair, so my hair would be twisted around rags somehow, and then it would curl.

My mother also had a wringer washer, but by then we had electricity. The washer was in our cellar, and we always used very hot water for the whites. Then we rinsed them in bluing that was put in the cold rinse water. By that time, I had pigtails, so I still had long hair. I still was told to be careful around the washer. Our cellar had a drain, so if we couldn't use the rinse water elsewhere in the yard or scrub the porch and sidewalks, then we could drain the soapy water. Then again, we would carry water to be used where it was needed. Now we don't reuse our water – what a waste!

In 1946, I was in second grade, and we moved to Sugar Valley, to a farm. We had a bathroom in the house, the only one on our road at that time. I walked about ¾ of a mile to a one-room country schoolhouse. There were two students to a desk, usually an older one and a younger one. That way the older one helped keep the younger one in the seat. We had eight grades, one through eight with no kindergarten. We learned from the older kids as they recited the times tables, states and capitals, and read stories. There was a potbellied stove in the center of the room. If you sat close to the stove, you were always too warm. We carried water from a neighboring house, maybe five hundred feet away from the school. This was our drinking water. It was exciting to miss school to carry water, but you had to be so big to do that. We had outside toilets for boys and girls. When the boys chased the girls, we always ran for the toilets.

At Christmas time, we had a day when we each learned a poem to recite before the school. Then we had snacks and a gift exchange. Our teacher always had a gift for us, usually a book.

Recess was fun, with snowball battles, softball games, tag, jump rope, and building forts in the woods close by. This is where I tried to jump the barbed wire fence and didn't make it. The school nurse happened to show up that day, and she sent a note to my mother that I needed a tetanus shot. Instead, my mother and stepfather put pure alcohol on the open wound. I was probably heard screaming in the next county.

Once, the whole school walked to another one-room school two or three miles away to play softball. We thought this was really fun because there was no school that day.

Finally, the big day came for me to start high school in Loganton. We even had school

Barbara A. Smith
with rag curls in 1944

buses to transport us. I was so happy to have a school library, because I loved books.

Reflecting the Summer of 42
By Charles S. Hughes of Hughesville,
Pennsylvania
Born 1935

Probably my fondest childhood memory was our annual visit to my grandparent's farm, via the Pennsylvania Railroad from Hughesville in North Central PA (about 15 miles east of Williamsport) to Warren, PA in Northwest PA, about 200 miles apart.

These took place from the time I was about 6 months old, till I was 12. I will describe the 1942 trip. My dad would take us from our home on Broadway Street to the "Pensy" station at Muncy in our 31 Chevy. He wouldn't wait for the train, but said our good byes as he had to return to work.

The train was late as usual in those busy years of World War II. We would board the train with the help of the conductor and his footstool. Once on board, there was standing room only because of all the service men. Always one of the young men would give up his seat for my mother. This inconvenience lasted only to the first stop in Williamsport. Enough people would vacate the coach so we could have a seat to ourselves. This was the longest stop - about an hour.

Next would come Jersey Shore and Lock Haven. After a very scenic view of the winding Susquehanna River we would reach Renovo with its huge railroad yard and then Emporium where we had to change trains to the Erie train, leaving our modern "art deco" style car to the rather ancient car on the Erie train. Emporium was a long stop also. There was a USO stand there with coffee and donuts for the service men. I was impressed by the service men, soldiers and sailors alike. Everyone was very patriotic in those war years, all anxious to help the war effort. Being only 7 years old in 1942, I was proud of all those guys. How couldn't we win the war?

Up to Emporium the R.R. followed the Susquehanna River, but then turned northeast and followed the Senamohing Creek. Saint Mary's was next then Ridgeway where they connected to another engine to pull up the mountains to Johnsonburg and Kane. The railroad people call this "Double Heading". The pull up to Kane made those engines really work. On long curves, you could see the fire belching out the stacks. I would have my face up tight to the window, which resulted in a black nose and face, as the coal fire trains were always "sooty".

Reaching Kane, we waited for the train crew to remove the extra engine. During this wait, a black man with sandwiches, coffee, and ice cream would come aboard to sell his wares. He had a white jacket, a shiny black head, and booming voice that you could hear from the car before to the car after. Mom would get a small sandwich and coffee. I would get a Dixie cup of ice cream and a little wooden paddle to eat it with.

Next came Ludlow and finally Clarendon - the last stop before Warren. Mom always pointed out the little house she was born in when passing through Stonham. Finally, at last Warren. We could get off the train, collect our baggage, and sometimes wait for my uncle to pick us up to go to the "farm." It would be early dark now. The train trip took all day to cover the 200 miles.

Once my uncle picked us up, greeting over with, we would leave the city of Warren for the 4-mile trip to the farmstead. There were only two other farms to pass before we turned down the private lane to ours.

It would be full dark now. Grandma would meet us at the door with a kerosene lamp. Even though the R.E.A. program, a federal program to electrify Rural America in the 30s was underway then, it did not reach that area until the 50s.

Mom would get me washed up and to bed with the kerosene lamp turned low while she had lots to visit about with Grandma, Grandpa, and Uncle Jake. Those stark shadows cast by the lamp were spooky. But, I was soon asleep with the help of a whippoorwill.

Morning brought new sounds: the cattle, chickens, rooster crowing, and voices in the big kitchen. I would dress and go down to a big breakfast of sourdough pancakes, gravy, ham and eggs. Breakfast was as big a meal as dinner. Supper was the smallest. The men would have already milked the 10-12 cows, cleaned the barn, and separated the cream from the skim milk. The cream was sold weekly and kept in a water trough in the springhouse. The men would start their workday after breakfast mowing hay, cultivating corn, etc. This was done with two-horse power, a huge pair of Belgians named Dick and Bess.

There were just Grandma, Grandpa, and Uncle Jake - the oldest son, unmarried out of the eight offspring. Grandma and Grandpa were up in years, so most of the work fell to Uncle Jake. Needless to say, they were always glad for all the help they could get. Mom would help Grandma clean house, which was the object of the visit. I was old enough in the summer of 42 to help with making hay, barn chores, feeding chickens, gathering eggs, and "slopping" the hogs. The biggest chore and the most boring was cutting wood. Wood was the only source of heat, and two room stoves and the huge kitchen range with its attached water tank took a mountain of cut and split pole wood for the year.

Jake would have a small mountain of poles. The chestnuts had died in the 30s and were comparatively easy to get and made excellent firewood. My job was to "tale" these poles to the saw. The saw was run by a 5 hp Galaway gasoline engine mounted on a wagon-like frame that was pulled by the horses. Jake would pick up one end of the pole and I the other (smaller and lighter) and walk it to the saw. Jake would push the pole through the saw 16" at a time until the 15 to 20 foot pole was gone. Grandpa took away and threw what he could into the woodshed. This might go on for 2 or 3 days. I was glad when it was over.

After evening chores, milking etc. and supper, it was getting dark and everyone was off to bed. I slept well.

The best days were weekends, Saturday was market day, and eggs, and dressed poultry were taken to Warren in our neighbor's 29 Chevy 4 door sedan. The back seat was missing so the produce could be hauled. Sunday's were best. All Mom's brothers and sisters would come to visit and all my cousins. We had a glorious time that is still one of my fondest memories. Too soon would come the day to go back to Hughesville, the train trip again, and once started I would be anxious to get home to my dad, my friends, and neighbors.

Nowadays, the "Pensy" is gone. No passenger service; only occasional freights. All of those bright young men in uniform have either passed on or are in old age, as my family is also. The farm is remarkably the same. New owners, but yet untouched by urban sprawl. I could almost hear Dick and Bess whinny when I visited not long ago. A few of my cousins and I still meet once in a while and the Susquehanna and Senamohing still wander through the Alleghenys to the sea, as if to reflect my memories of the summer of 42.

1953 on First Avenue
By Fred L. Adams of Erie, Pennsylvania
Born 1943

I grew up in the small town of Johnsonburg, Pennsylvania, nestled in a valley in Elk County. Looking back, it seems it was the best of times and the best of places for a kid in the 1950s. I had two older brothers, two older sisters, and one younger sister. My older siblings were teenagers when I was a kid, so I was closest to my sister, Joanna who was just five years younger. She followed me everywhere, which I hated when I was with my buddies, but when we were home, she was my best friend. We had a large attic in our house where we would play games that we made up. They usually involved the use of the play money from the Monopoly game. I was usually the banker or casino owner. Other than that, I don't remember much of the rules.

I always considered 1953 as the best year of my life. I was ten years old and life was good, as least at that time, I certainly thought it was.

I had a group of close friends who lived in the neighborhood, and we did things together every day. My closest circle of friends were Joe, Jim, Roger, Mike, John, Rich, and a few others from school who might wander into the neighborhood because their parents were visiting someone nearby. We spent a lot of time together, but my closest friend was Joe. We spent so much time together that some people thought we were brothers, and some would call me Joe and him Fred. We are still best of friends today, even though he lives in Arizona now.

My friends and I would build camp houses like the one the Sluggo had in the *Little Lulu* comics, with a sign that said, "No girls allowed". Parents would tear them down not long after we got them just the way we wanted them, but we would just build another in some other location. Days had us at the community

center playground, where we would play pick up ball games, such as spud or fly and first bounce, and yes, someone always had to be chosen last for the team games. It was often me.

There were woods all around us and it was just a short walk up the hill past First, Second, Third, and Fourth Avenues to the place we call the "airport", because it actually was an airport in the twenties. We had a ball field there, and a shooting range, and apple trees, blackberries and teaberries, and spring water to wash them down. If you didn't mind a bit of a hike, there were the "Big Rocks", which were some mighty large rocks, laid down by the Ice Age. These rocks had some caves to explore and were just fantasy playgrounds for boys of ten or so.

Nights had us on First Avenue, playing hide and seek or kick the can. In the summer months, we could stay out until the mill whistle blew. That was at ten o'clock. Sometimes we would just hang out on the wall on the corner of First Avenue and Bridge Street, just chatting about the happenings of the day and what we might do tomorrow. We certainly couldn't go home yet, the whistle hadn't blown.

On the corner opposite that wall was Haser's Store, a corner grocery/meat market. In those days, there were numerous little neighborhood stores like that and no one had to walk very far for a loaf of bread or a quart of milk. My mother would often send me there for a forty-nine cent pound of hamburger that Mr. Haser would grind for me while I looked at the penny candy to spend that last cent out of the half buck Mom had given me. So many choices: Tootsie Rolls, Root Beer Barrels, licorice pipes, banana marshmallows (my favorite), Double Bubble, or Bazooka Joe, and many others. For years, I thought the store was called Pazers, because Mom would always say, "go up Hasers" for milk or bread. In the hot summer months, we could buy our favorite flavor of Popsicle (banana) for a nickel, and if I was rich some days, I could splurge on my personal favorite, the triangle-shaped Eskimo Pie. Something must have been done differently back then, because those treats just don't taste the same today.

While many kids had paper routes at that time, I earned my spending money doing yard work or shoveling snow. We did not have a power mower or snow blower, but it never seemed so hard at the time. I also delivered

Fred, Sam (nephew), and Joanna (sister) in 1953

a new little magazine called *TV Guide*, off which I could earn four cents a copy. Some of the things I was able to spend my money on were Saturday morning 17 cartoon shows or cowboy serials. Roy Rogers was my favorite, while Joe preferred Gene Autry. The movie was fourteen cents to get in, a nickel for popcorn and six cents for a Coke, which would blow a whole quarter.

Then there were the comic books. *Superman* was the best, but I also enjoyed *Superboy, Supergirl*, Jimmy Olsen, Lois Lane, *Batman and Robin*, Detective, Action, *Aquaman, Captain America, Flash, Green Hornet*, and *Justice League of America*. They were ten cents each, except for the occasional Big Issue for a quarter. A Superman comic had to be accompanied by a Fifth Avenue candy bar for another nickel. The Newsstand was my choice for the comics and candy, and it was conveniently located across the street from the Strand Theater, just three blocks down the hill from my house.

It seems almost everything I enjoyed was an easy walk from home. We had so much available to us in that small town. The main street had the school, the community center, a playground, two soda shops, a five and dime, a bowling alley, and Western Auto. Within just a few blocks of that were another bowling alley, two poolrooms (which were off limits), two more restaurants, three barbershops, and many other establishments that the adults would frequent.

The community center was great. It was a building that was given to the town by the largest industry, the paper mill. The basement had a swimming pool and two bowling alleys. The first floor was a gymnasium with a running track in a balcony above it. The second floor was a library, poolroom, and social hall. We had our gym classes and swimming there and frequented the library often, but the poolroom and bowling alley were for those fourteen and older. Turning fourteen was great. We must have spent every evening in the poolroom. Pool was five cents for a half hour and bowling was five cents a game, affordable for a teen.

One of my fondest memories from 1953 was of that fall day when I was walking up the hill from Holy Rosary Catholic School with some classmates. Our house was a few blocks up the hill on the opposite side of the street. As I passed the church and crossed Penn Street, I noticed some activity on the roof of our house. Someone was installing a TV antenna. I ran home as fast as I could and found that it was true. We were actually getting a television. I would be able to watch *Howdy Doody* at five-thirty, and even better, *Superman* at seven!

Then there was that Christmas. I still refer to it as the best Christmas ever. It certainly was the most memorable. We didn't usually get many gifts at Christmas. Even our stockings were filled with stuff we didn't really care much about, like apples and walnuts, and maybe some hard candy. But THAT Christmas was special. My sister Joanna got her cowgirl outfit, complete with fringe, hat, boots, and six shooters, a guitar, a huge doll that cried, and games and coloring books. I got the roll-top desk and typewriter that I wanted to keep the books on my *TV Guide* business, and most of all, I got the proverbial Daisy Red Ryder BB gun. I never knew until many years later why we got so many gifts that year, and the TV as well. It was because Mom won a large sum of money at the Knights of Columbus Bingo game.

That little town was so special in those days. There was just so much there that we didn't appreciate at the time, but looking back has caused me to realize its value. Everyone had a father or brother who worked at the paper mill, and the mothers and sisters worked at the Stackpole Carbon Company. The town was doing well with other industries and businesses, too. The businesses supported the town and contributed resources to many local events, theme parades, and sports. We even had professional wrestling come to town. I remember helping set up the rink for them and the colorful Don Eagle with his Mohawk haircut. The King and his Court softball team came every summer and put on a nice display, similar to what the Globetrotters do with basketball.

I left Johnsonburg after high school, but I return often to meet with old friends and relatives, and we reminisce about those times. The town is not the same. The paper mill remains but most other industries are gone, as are many businesses. No more corner groceries, no movie theater, bowling allies, poolrooms, even the long-standing Newsstand closed its door recently. For a brief period there was no grocery store. The community center is still there, but it is not as active as it was. An effort is being made to restore it to its past glory, with some success. Now there is a nice Senior Center, which is good for the people to have a place to socialize, and the Volunteer Firemen have done an outstanding job of building a large fire hall that is used often for social events, including an annual reunion. I am sure the kids growing up there today will have fond memories, too. But I don't see how they could ever match those of people who spent their childhood in the fifties in a small town where everyone knew your name. In my case, it was 1953 on First Avenue.

My Brother Howard
By Charles E. Sharpless of Phillipsburg,
Pennsylvania
Born 1909

As I recall, I was born May 31, 1909. I was a great big red-faced baby boy. My dad always bragged about it, so I stayed this way, even when I grew up and knew better. My parents had ten children: five boys and five

Charles (dad) and Howard

girls, which one died at the age of sixteen days, so that left four girls.

As I grew up, Mother had a piano. I was little sitting on her lap, and she used to play with one finger and sing. I recall those days. I'll always love my mother. This is something for my grandchildren or anybody: honor thy mother and thy father. You will never find anything sweeter than your mother and father, plus years later, you will understand what I mean. It's the greatest thing for love, the things she did for me. As I grew older, my dad made me a little wheel barrel, and I prized that and the things that happened.

My brother Howard, I always followed him and what he did I tried to do. He showed me different things, how to play so you make your own enjoyment. So one day he took me out in the woods and he had a saw, an ax, and a brace and bit. I didn't know what he was going to do. I discovered when he cut this tree down. He cut it in blocks about four inches long and three to four inches across. He got me to hold the block while he put a hole in it. I then realized he was going to make a hammer. Well, he made me one. I thought that was the greatest thing, making a hammer.

I followed Howard every place he went. I was with heart and he was older. He had other things to do. As I came up through life around him, he was a great, great kid. So as my brother got older, I started watching him. He was 15 years old in school and didn't graduate. We didn't have money to send anyone to college. That was just out of the question. So he got a job in the brickyard, and he was doing the man's work. That's what they call the magnesite. It was heavy stuff. It was shipped in from

367

Austria, to New York, and then shipped to Sandy Ridge in 300-pound bags. Fellows had to unload them, put them on two wheels, like you move fridges today with. Then take them out of the car and down into the brickyard, cut the bags open. Those little pebbles, they were just like marbles, that's how they made for lining steel furnaces. This pile, it was dumped from the boxcar to the second floor man. Then he would load the wheel barrel up then run up a steep plank. He was only fifteen. Well, on payday, he always gave his pay to Mother. It was helping Dad, plus taking some of the burden off of him, so I still had that one in mind.

Howard got the flu, and Freddy Vaughn across the street did, too. Howard's doctor was Dr. Eaton. He was given pills. It was hot. We had the windows all down, hotter than a dickens. Dad said, "Well, he can't go on. I'm going to change doctors". So he paid Dr. Eaton and Dr. Amerse from Philipsburg. He said, "Will you come up and look at my boy"?

Charles and his mother, Emma

So he came over and looked at him. He said, "Oh, my God". He jumped up and took them windows out on both sides, covered him up. I was still beside his bedside. I recall it very well. He said Howard was going to die. Well, we were all downhearted. He was still my prize brother. So the doctor said, "I am going to give you until midnight tonight. Mr. Sharpless, you son is going to die, or he is going to get better". Everybody was sitting with their head down, my sisters, Mother. Dad, who was still out of work, stayed right there with him while I couldn't stay up that late. About 9:00 I had to go to bed but wasn't asleep. At midnight, Howard's fever broke. When the doctor came up in the morning, he said he was tickled. He said, "Your boy is going to get better, but it's going to take a lot of time to get his strength back". Well, Dad took care of him like a baby, but my job was to empty the urine pan. Well, he got up, got his strength back, and went back to work.

Howard needed lots of water. Lots of water, no shortage of water in those days. But while he was in bed craven for water, I went over to Timbler in the deep snow and got a bucket of water, and then took it home. He knew it had come from the spring. Peace of mind, I suppose. He said, "That's the sweetest water there is". I made two or three trips over there. So to compensate me, Howard bought me a BB gun, and he took me fishing. This BB gun meant a lot to my life.

Howard took me fishing down at Mini Run. Man, how that was a long ways down in there. Mother packed me a lunch and my molasses bucket. Howard had to have a little bigger bucket. I didn't know how to fish, but he was showing me how to bait the hook. I would sit there and he was a good fisherman. I recall the first fish I got out of there. A storm would come up, a thunderstorm. In a while the water would rise, he would go down there and fill a three pound molasses bucket up with fish, brook trout. Man, was they pretty things.

When Howard got a job, why I was handed his chores after school. Well, that was to get the wood in. My dad made a wagon, too. He made a bigger wheel barrel for me to play with. But I had to go in the woods, it was down by the brickyard or Sunny Moores' and cut this wood have it in, stack it for winter. My job was to take that wood and bring it in the house every night. I was to build the fire in the morning, and I made sure the wood was in then. It had to be dry. If it was wet outside, I had to put it in the oven to dry so it would be there for morning.

So Howard's job was to turn the washer. Oh man, that thing was a man killer. It had a long handle on it. So he got over it and started to work. So now, that was my job every Monday morning, to go back and turn the washer. I look back; it should have been a pleasure to do that for my mother. I gave it a jerk one day when it had some heavy carpets in it. I ripped the handle off. I thought that was the end of that washer and I would not have to turn it again. Well, it was made out of a light metal. So Dad took it down to the blacksmith. He put a welling splice on each side of it and riveted it together. It worked good then, as strong as it ever did. But that job still wasn't an easy job. I still had to turn it. I really didn't mean to break it. Then they finally got a washing machine. It was an easy electric one. They paid $99.50 for it. There was a great big brass tub on it.

So, Dad was a great gardener. He would plant that with veggies. I had to help weed, and I had to pick them potato bugs. Wow man, that was a hard job, I thought. They had to be done every day. He discovered I didn't know about turning the leaf upside down to find the eggs. So I found out what to do. Pick them over again, there dare not be a bug. There was no money for picking potato bugs off, but it was. Every night, that was my job.

Then Saturday come, or afternoon in the summer, while I go swimming. Well, the swimming hole we had was 3 ½ miles away at Blue Hole. We would run down what they call Mini Run, go back to Berry's, across Reservoir Road, down to Tiddle Wink, down over the hill to the Blue Hole. I thought that was an awful long way, but we would run that, a bunch of us. We would swim for about 1 ½ to 2 hours, and then we would put our clothes on, up over the hill, up the train road. Then again we would get home we was raining like we sweat.

If we would put anything on our plates, it had to be cleaned up. There was to be nothing wasted. My dad would make strict rules on what you would take, you must eat. Mother was a great cook. I don't know how she ever did it. She used to make the poor man's pie. Well, what that was, vegetables, meat, and it had a crust on it. Now today that meal is rich man's meal.

Looking back at the things we did, them days of the childhood. It was pitiful; there was nothing to do as a coal miner. Sometimes Dad would get a job at the brickyard for the summer, anything he would try to get just to keep this family shoed and clothed. It was just a great hardship. I didn't realize this. He worked seven days a week. He would go to work in the dark and come home in the dark.

Charles E. Sharpless in 1987 with a miner's bucket

Now those hardships that he enjoyed it, he enjoyed his family.

Dad had an awful temper and was a very hard man. I recall one time our middle room had a big stove in it. Dad was putting the ceiling on it, and Howard was out playing. Man, oh, man! I was sent for him to help him. He had a room. He would put one strip on, it would come down, and his temper was getting greater and greater. He had to pick on somebody, so he would see me, "Go get your brother". Well, I stayed a little longer and we both got a lickin'. Finally, after about three hours, they got the ceiling on. I couldn't figure out why he was so mean. His nerves were to a breaking point. I went through this. I said, "Women have it hard. They have it just as hard as us men. If he don't bring anything in, how can she cook"?

I was always taught to go to Sunday school. I have a great memory of the first day I went. My sister, Elizabeth took me. So they took me to school. When they hollered "recess time", I thought it was time to go home, so I ran out the gate and ran straight home. Then I found out what school was. I understood then.

Charles E. Sharpless was a U.S. Navy veteran.

Picking Stones
By Pauline M. Steinbacher of Jersey Shore, Pennsylvania

As a child, I had made a few trips to the old homestead that had been graced by my grandparents' presence, and provided a home for their large family. I did not have the joy of knowing them, but I did see pictures of their fiftieth wedding celebration.

My visits to the homestead on Coldwatertown Road were to see my Grandfather Steppe. John Thomas was his name, but most people called him Jack.

My grandmother, a most gentle woman, according to those who knew her, died at age fifty-two. Her name was Helena.

My mother often told how difficult it was to raise crops on the stony ground. Even after many stones were picked, and they were planting beans, they had to remove a stone to put in a bean.

It was a great place to raise berries, which was a source of income for the family when they went to the Williamsport street market to sell their produce.

One Saturday as they returned from market, on Route 654 near Nisbet, their horse was frightened by a train along the Susquehanna River, and panicked and balked. The new screen door flew off the buckboard and crashed, and Grandfather's hat went with it.

As for the stones, there are many stone rows and many stones. We always teased that they must reproduce. We've been picking them for over forty years.

After Grandfather raised his family of nine, he sold the wonderful old house, but I was able to purchase it some years later, and my husband and I raised four children in the farmhouse.

Grandfather was one of the best butchers in Nippenose Valley. Often, as a prank, he would pin the pigtail on us. He did local butcherings and also traveled to the surrounding area. He did some animal curing for people who had a sick cow, horse or pig. He was like an old time vet without a license.

Grandfather had a great sense of humor. He told his young sisters that if they carried water from the spring and poured it in the living room, they could go swimming. They carried the buckets of water up the hill, poured it in the living room, and it quickly went through the planks to the cellar. Even later, when he became a father, he continued his tricks. On Easter, when his children rushed up the stairs to show their Easter eggs, they lost an egg on every step as the eggs fell through the hole in the old hat that he had exchanged from a good hat. Those were the poor old days—no Easter baskets.

As was the custom years ago, and still is in many cellars in Nippenose Valley, Grandfather kept a barrel of hard cider, and sharing with folks during the long winter months.

My grandfather was a good neighbor, and once shared a deer with a struggling neighbor. Well, the game warden also offered a deer to the same family. They turned it down, saying their wonderful neighbor, Jack, just gave them some. Well, Grandfather had to pay a fine for giving deer meat away.

Speaking of deer, my uncle tells how he was about to shoot a trophy buck through an opening in the barn. Just then, his father (my grandfather) yelled "Supper!" and the buck took off through the field and into the woods.

Hunters always did well in Nippenose Valley.

Another story my Uncle Lewis tells is that when he was about ten, his father, who was a widower, started dating again. When Grandfather was leaving on his date, Lewis would jump in the car, too. No way was Grandfather taking him, so he would give him a dollar to stay with his aunt down the road in Ecktown. Uncle Lewis played the game and was soon getting two dollars to stay home.

My grandfather's aunt and uncle lived on the property next to him. They had a large barn that witnessed many Saturday night square dances. With a few ciders under their belt, they swung their partners to "Deep in the Heart of Texas," and they also went "Marching to Georgia," two of their favorite square dance tunes. The music was provided by family and friends who never had a lesson. They played the instruments by ear.

Many winter nights, the families played cards like Geigle, Hassie and Setback. The first two are German games. The Geigle deck is made in Germany, but can be purchased at Plankenhorns in Williamsport, Pennsylvania.

My mother, Martha Steppe Eck, learned to make sugar cookies from her great Aunt Lizzie in the house next to her. Her great aunt made them with vanilla flavoring, and my grandmother used nutmeg to flavor them. I've eaten both and they are great.

Most, if not all, of Grandfather's children walked over the mountain, through the woods to the Morgan Valley one room schoolhouse. My oldest uncle could speak only Pennsylvania Dutch his first year of school, and he was teased by the other children who spoke at least some English.

Some of our relatives lived in Morgan Valley. There were Deiberts, Kellers, Bennetts,

Freidricks, Semans, etc. All of the Deiberts were called to serve in the Civil War except Ulrich. A man offered him three hundred dollars to serve for him. Ulrich accepted and before he was in the thick of it, the war ended. The guy asked for the three hundred back, but Ulrich Deibert kept the money. That was a big sum in those days.

We are still on the property, and in the same old wonderful house with all its great memories, and we wouldn't want to live anywhere else on earth, picking all those stones.

School Lunch at the Tearoom
By Helen T. Spade of Woodland,
Pennsylvania
Born 1931

I went to the Woodland School. I only went to the eighth grade. My first grade teacher was Mrs. Henderson, second grade teacher was Mr. Berry, my third grade teacher was Mr. Miller, and the fourth and fifth grade was Mrs. Varner. Sixth was Mr. Varnor. I can't remember the rest of the teachers. At lunch time we went to a store called the tearoom at Woodland. I got an ice cream cone when things were better.

Dad worked in the coalmines. I was a coal miner's daughter. Mom worked in a restaurant. We had to go to an outside outhouse. We listened to the radio.

On Sunday, we had to go to church and then we would go on a Sunday afternoon ride. Dad had a big garden. Mom canned everything she could can. Monday was washday and baking bread. Tuesday was ironing day. We had to heat the iron on the coal stove. I was raised in a Christian home.

Mom made all my clothes out of flour sacks that were flowered and printed. Mom had the wringer washer. We got to go to movies on Friday and Saturday. Then we got to go shopping in a town called Clearfield, PA. We shopped at Grand's and McMurray's and Mc Corey's. We got milk from the milkman. We picked blackberries so Mom could make jelly. We had grapevines to make jelly.

The school bus picked us up in front of the house. I have a brother and sister. My grandmother took me shopping sometimes that was my dad's mother. My brother was in the Korean War. There was one teacher I didn't like, that was Mr. Berry. He was mean. I got in trouble because I was out having fun and was supposed to be down home before 11 o'clock and was half an hour late.

Helen T. Spade with a toddler

Playing in the Wood Stacks up Silver Creek
By Herb Dubler of Connellsville,
Pennsylvania
Born 1934

This is my story of life in the 1940s, during World War II, in Johnsonburg, (Elk County) PA.

Helen's homestead

Johnsonburg had a big paper mill as the focus for workers. The paper mill sat right in the middle of town while the main highway, US Route 219, ran through it. The primary raw material in the making of paper was wood and the wood utilized by the papermaking men and machinery came from hundreds of miles around Johnsonburg and included wood trucked in from Canada or brought in by the Pennsy and the B & O Railroads. This wood was cut into five to six foot logs and was already debarked and stored in big piles west of town, in what was called Silver Creek. The railroad box cars would be parked along tracks laid down so that the unloading would be done by able-bodied young men who threw the logs onto a chain driven hoist that ran some 75 feet up a steep incline, then the logs would drop and pile up until there would be a stack of logs up to 75 feet tall and shaped like a pyramid. Then picture these stacks of wood along a half-mile long track, and some three or four deep, with tracks laid between the stacks of wood.

I was 9 or 10 years old at the time. Along with several others, we all lived in either Johnsonburg or Rolfe, and at times, we played among the stacks of wood. Two vivid memories stand out.

In the middle of the summer when the temperature would be humid and in the 80s and 90s around town and in the entire region, the temperature amid the huge wood stacks would be quite cool. The temperature in and between the stacks would be in the upper 30s, and snow could be seen where we were able to look into the stacks. Brrrr! But what a delight! In the middle of a hot and humid summer day!

Also, behind of the last row of stacks of wood, back against "teaberry hill," where teaberries were picked for an afternoon delight, was a little stream known as Silver Creek. The source of this creek was the water that served the communities of Johnsonburg and Rolfe as drinking water. The creek was big enough for 10 year olds to dam up, and make a fine little pond for wading, in bare feet, and at times even splashing around and getting good and wet. Sometimes, after playing hard, we simply lay down in the creek and enjoyed the cool water for a while, in the heat of the day.

Johnsonburg and Rolfe were safe and fine communities in which to grow up, with lots to do for young boys on lazy summer days.

Moving Around Jaysburg
By Shirley Paulhamus of Williamsport,
Pennsylvania
Born 1936

I was born in Jaysburg, a small part of Williamsport, and my family—Mom, Pauline Labuski Dad, Fred Labuski, Sr. and 3 brothers (Fred, Don, and Stanley)—first lived on Mosser Ave. I will always remember the huge tree in front of our house, because every Easter it was plastered with egg yolks. My two older brothers would always throw their yolks at the tree.

We moved to Boyd St. from there and I

Pauline Labuski (mother), Stanley (brother), Fred (father), and Don (brother)

remember in the evenings all the kids in the neighborhood would gather under the arc light and play kick the can.

From Boyd St. we moved to Queen St. down by the river, where all the kids including my brothers and I went swimming.

On Queen St. We had an outhouse for a while until our landlord put in indoor plumbing. My brothers and I had to take turns emptying the pots we used at night in the morning.

Since we did not have a tub for a while, every Friday night was bath night for us 4 kids. My mom would warm water in pots and put it in a washtub. We would bathe in this tub in the kitchen by the coal stove. Thank God, I was the only girl. I went first, then my brothers would follow in the same water; my mom just kept adding warm water.

My dad always had a large garden in the backyard and Mom always canned everything. The best food in town.

Shirley (Labuski) Paulhamus with an old plow

My girlfriends and I had pajama parties out on the front porches and the milkman used to wake us up.

We did not have a TV set until I was 13. At night, we would listen to the radio: Amos and Andy, Fibber McGee and Molly, The Green Hornet.

We never locked our doors at night.

Those were the Good Ole Days.

Clearfield County Fair in the 50s
By Julie Hunsinger of Clearfield,
Pennsylvania
Born 1948

You could not have grown up in Clearfield County and somehow not be exposed to the annual Clearfield County Fair. The fair dates back to the 1800s and should be recognized as a piece of Clearfield history.

Growing up in the very rural area of Spring Valley, I was one of ten children who came from a poor family. Privileges were few. One event I did have the wonderful opportunity to attend was the Clearfield County Fair. Excitement escalated as the James E. Strates traveling carnival train pulled into our town. My trips to town were limited and I considered this a privilege in its own to gaze at the mile long, shiny, silver train in hopes of getting a free peek at carnival characters.

The fair offered a day for children at a reduced rate. My mother was employed at a local sewing factory and would always work a half day and then take the younger children to the fair. It seems silly today, but I remember wearing a fancy dress.

Looking back, a million dollars could not begin to make me feel like I did as a child anticipating the thrilling rides, cotton candy, twenty-five cent grab bags and kewpie dolls attached to a stick.

In order to attend the fair as a teenager, I picked blueberries and sold them for fifty cents a quart. The most exciting thing about the fair then was to walk the midway over and over looking for family and friends. My one and only adventurous time was when a friend sneaked my cousin and I in to what was then known as the "HOUCHIE KOUCHIES." What an embarrassment to a very naive backwoods girl.

Time goes by and ones needs change. Life took me out of my hometown many times. Wherever I was, when that annual date for the fair arrived, memories always flooded my mind to the times when I was so innocent and life was simple.

Today, highway transportation has replaced that silver, shiny train, side shows are few and less exciting, twenty-five cent grab bags and kewpie dolls long forgotten.

I am sixty-three years old and still love that fair, every year, the sights and sounds of the approaching fair revive my heart and mind of my childhood days at the fair.

Memories are one thing that can't change or be taken from you.

Fudge Under the Bed
By Mary Ann Swoope of Woodland,
Pennsylvania
Born 1946

At thirteen, my first cigarette was out of toilet paper. I lit it and it went up in flames. It got out of control and fire went up the wall. I got it out, but I had to clean the smoke stains off the wall. I was scared stiff. I never told my mom, but I think she knew, somehow.

In 1964, my mother and I were cleaning the attic. I went downstairs to get a drink. The TV was on and I heard them say John F. Kennedy was assassinated. I ran up and told Mom. She looked at me and we both ran down to watch. It was like the world almost came to an end. Mom had tears in her eyes. It was a very sad time for America.

I did some drag racing at the Black Mashannon Airport (which is not there anymore) with some of my friends at night with the lights out. No one got hurt. There was always someone chickening out.

Saturday nights were a family get together. Mom would make homemade ice cream or popcorn, and we would sit and watch *Gunsmoke*, and when that was over, we all went to bed at nine sharp. Sometime during the day, we would watch *Love of Life* and *Search for Tomorrow* and *As the World Turns*.

I lived on a farm, so I had plenty to do, lots of chores to do. We kids had names for all our cows. I fed chickens, slopped the hogs.

When it was hay time, I got to drive the tractor. One time, I was bringing a load of hay to the barn. I had to go up a hill and down the other side. At the hill, I was to make a sharp right, which I did. I cut the tractor too sharp and I went down through the yard. Mom had clothes hanging out. Well, I took the clothes and clothesline all to the barn with me. I was scared. I still do not know why that happened. Mom kept yelling at me to turn the wheel, but my hands froze on the wheel. I never drove the tractor again after that because Dad wouldn't let me.

We had a wringer washer and a rinse tub. We did our clothes all in the same water. That wouldn't happen these days, not in America. Then whatever water was left over, we would scrub our two porches with it.

I never got a spanking at school, but I will tell the time I went to school drunk over a boy. I was too shy to tell him when I was sober. Well, I had to go to the blackboard to do some math, and guess what? There he was. I stood beside him. I felt my face get hot and I passed out. Well, they took me to the office. They got me awake, then they made me cross my legs and hit my knee to see if I had a reflex. I didn't and they said, "My God, she's drunk!" They called my mom and she came and got me. She didn't yell or anything at me. She just made sure I didn't get into her whiskey. I remember Mom called me a name, but I won't say here what she called me. And they didn't kick me out of school over it.

My mom had to tell us a tale of a headless horseman in her running around days where she lived. It would stir up the other horses. She said her parents would go out and whip the fence post seven times to break the spell. I still think it's a tall tales out of school.

We had neighbors near us and they had two girls. We played a lot, cowboys and Indians and jump rope and played house. Sometimes we would get a can of Campbells beans and go to a patch of woods near us and have a little picnic. I'd like to see kids do this today.

One time, my sister and I made homemade fudge. Well, it didn't turn out right and we hid the fudge under our bed and we ate it till it was gone.

Friday nights were town nights. We didn't need much; we lived on the farm, so it was coffee, sugar and things we did not grow. Afterwards, we'd go to the Passmore in Philipsburg for a drink or two. The Passmore is no longer there.

I hung out at the Little Resrent. I had my first real cigarette, a Winston, and got sicker than a dog my first time. The Little Resrent is still there.

Remembering Osceola Mills
By Nancy Brown of Houtzdale, Pennsylvania
Born 1940

I grew up in a small town called Osceola Mills, Pennsylvania. My dad worked at the Osceola Brickyard, which still stands, but out of business.

We lived across from the Osceola School. All twelve grades were in the school. My favorite teacher was Miss Sarah Jane Mattern. She was the home economics teacher, and if we were making something, and we needed an ingredient, she would send me over to my house to get it.

Nancy Brown and her siblings

374

Nancy Frantz Brown age 13

For recess, we took hot chocolate in a jar wrapped in foil, and would sit it on the windowsill till recess.

Joe West was the hangout in town. It's no longer there, but everyone met at Joe's and played the jukebox and ate fries. When Joe closed because of his health, we all sat in the beautiful park and talked.

My mother had her hands full with six girls and one boy. At Christmastime, we always had. We would have to go to bed early Christmas Eve so the tree could be decorated. Dad never decorated it until we were all asleep. Christmas morning, we would have to wait till Dad went downstairs and turned the tree lights on. Then, Mom would tell us which pile of gifts were each one's. They were never wrapped, but stacked with love.

We had one two-wheeled bicycle, and we took turns riding it on the school ground. Each one of us got to ride for half an hour, then it was the next one's turn.

The Fourth of July was very special. The bands would start coming in the middle of the night, and we'd wake up and hurry to get dressed so we could go on the porch and watch. Our house was open to band members wanting water, or to change clothes. After the long parade, my dad would cook outside, and he'd invite anyone going by to come and have a burger.

We were a large family, but we survived. I am proud to say I am from Osceola Mills.

Answering the Coffee Pot
By June B. Edwards of Muncy, Pennsylvania
Born 1932

In 1951, I became an exchange operator at West Branch Bell Telephone Company in Muncy, Pennsylvania. We later had the name changed to West Branch Telephone Company, and dropped the "Bell" name as we *were not part* of the Bell Telephone Company.

At that time, we would wait for someone to ring in for "operator" and answer the call. These were numbers with drops on which would drop when a caller called in. We would then place the cord into the caller's number and continue to call the number the person requested.

There were five other positions at the time—Muncy exchange was LI Lincoln with at least ten people on the line. We would all work at a different time. When there was a fire, we had a button to push to sound the alarm. On the windowsill, we had a large empty thread spool with a tablet attached to a string wound around the spool. We would write the location of the fire on the tablet and throw it out the window to the alley below. The firemen, first one on the scene, would get the location of the fire and off they would go. Of course, we would get pretty busy, as everyone would call in to see where the fire was.

Our supervisor was Ruth App, who would write up the schedules. We all worked at different times of the day, and there was one night operator from midnight to seven A.M. This was Mrs. Fairchilds.

There was a couch that we could catch a few winks, and, of course, a loud bell to wake us up with if we got a call. Sometimes, we would even get a call for the police, and if no answer, we would lean out the front window, and if we would happen to see Chief Grenoble on the street, call to him and tell him he had a telephone call.

I remember one time when we had a terrible storm, knocking out our power. We, of course, could crank phones by hand to call numbers, but the fire company brought huge lights up and set them up for us to be able to see what we were doing.

We were always appreciated by the police and firemen. Each Christmas, we received large batches of cookies and candy from them.

Our telephone company also billed our

The Exchange Operators of West Branch Telephone Company in 1954

customers from the office, and made up a bill with their called numbers on. We collected payments at our office, too. In fact, sometimes we were not busy, and there was a Bingo game on the radio that we could join in on.

There was a huge machine that would print names and addresses on a metal bar, which we used to bill our loud [illegible] customers. These could be fitted into an automatic machine and print info onto paper. Very fun to run.

There were five working in the office at the time I started there: Ruth App, Miram Shaffer, Catherine Heincelman-Kilgus, Alice Sheridan, Elizabeth Hartman, Bob Rishel, who later became president, and Ralph Decker, Vice President. I replaced Charlotte Youtz in 1951 and later, Cheryl (Fuller) Rupert joined us. Otto Kilgus was plant manager, Clyde Hofer was head of C.O. or Central Office. We had a great bunch of people working together. Doris Fritz joined our staff later, and helped to bill and collect payment.

We also had pay stations at that time, and the I and R (installers, repair) men would go around and collect the money. We would then count it at the office and deposit it at the bank.

We would, of course, have our daily snacks from Hurr's, or the Chere Restaurant next door.

We had a small switchboard upstairs that was operated for the telephone business office by Ruth App and Elizabeth Hartman. We, of course, were on the upstairs floor and were not bothered by anyone, but once in a while, during the night, the men leaving the bars would stop at our building and urinate on the wall of the building in the alley. One night, the night operator was tired of it, so she dumped a

pan of water on the man's head. But of course, it would happen again. I guess they thought it was in an alley and no one was around. They soon found out different.

We had a wonderful bunch of ladies working with us. We all got along fine. Some of the operators were Jean Reuther (Pooler), Rita Dugan, Ruth App, June Bennett (Edwards), Millie Foust, Janice Martin, Barbara Frantz, and Frances Long. I know I have missed some of them and I apologize for this.

I remember the story about one of our operators, at home, plugged in her coffee pot and said "Operator." This was funny.

This is what is so wonderful to remember—the GOOD TIMES! But they are buried in my memory and can never be removed.

I retired in 1993 as secretary in the engineering department. A great bunch of guys to work with and some are still there.

Oh, for the GOOD OLE DAYS!

Downhill in a Suitcase Sled
By Patrick O'Brien of Meridian, Idaho
Born 1944

I never realized what a wonderful childhood I had. I drank water from a garden hose, from the stream where I hiked and from the soda bottle of my buddy. I rode a bicycle without a helmet, turned my pant leg up to keep it out of the sprocket, and parked it without locking it up. I never had a house key because we had no reason to lock our home. I entered my best friend's house without knocking and never got shot at. Our grocer delivered food after we had gone to bed and put it away, with no one there to watch him. I walked to school and never saw a predator. I took rides home with people who were friends of my parents, without knowing them. I hitchhiked six miles to go swimming at Marshall's pool and never thought a thing about it. During the summer, I left the house in the morning and came home close to dark with no cell phone, pager, or GPS to let my parents know where I was. I endured a lifetime of hearing, "I knew your brothers. You should be like them".

I crossed little fingers and said, "Double dare ya", and cut my thumb to be blood brothers with Chuck Fox. I fell in love with the first girl I kissed and the second. I prayed like crazy when my dad was dying, knowing we were all going to lose a good man. I rode my sled down the street in front of my house in the winter without giving a thought about traffic. My brother Gene put me in a suitcase and sent me down the street on the same sled. I carried a pocketknife and never got frisked. I never got spanked but was in mortal fear of offending my parents. I learned respect from the priests and nuns who taught me, and yes, I spent time kneeling on the wooden floor for my indiscretions. I hiked and went shooting a .22 without ever getting any instructions. The first *The Thing* movie kept me awake for a week. I went Christmas caroling with a group that couldn't carry a tune in English or German, but no one cared and they still applauded and invited us in for hot drinks.

I delighted in the smell of burning leaves in the fall and the roar of Friday night football games. Deer season came as close to being sacrament as anything I can remember. Our scoutmaster was a dwarf who taught us about dealing with adversity and life's challenges. My brother, Tom was the best fighter pilot in the world. I camped out in the backyard with my buddies and chased fireflies. Viewing my town from the back seat of a Piper Cub was one of the greatest thrills of my life. One dollar meant a movie, snacks, and some change left over. One good friend meant a summer of hanging around. Twenty-five cents bought a bag of the best French fries in North America. Saturday afternoons meant hours spent with Gene, Roy, Dale, Trigger, and lots of bad guys wearing black hats. Captain Video was the cutting edge of high tech special effects. Weeks of talk and anticipation always preceded a trip to Pittsburgh for a baseball game.

I never really did without. I lived in a safe place in a safe time in an age that seems improbable now. I'm getting older and these memories are gems in my mind. I really miss St. Mary's.

A Lifelong Friendship
By Harold Wicks of Litchfield, Connecticut
Born 1924

I registered to attend the Altoona branch of Penn State in the fall of 1946 and met Glenn Johnson in the Student Lounge. This was the beginning of a friendship that lasted four years, until graduation and still continues.

We roomed together at Penn State. Our recreation comprised trout fishing on Spring Creek, Ping-Pong matches in the recreation hall, and oh yes, one good education that helped us get good jobs!

State College, Penn 1949

Anna Lee and Glenn
State College, Penn.

377

Fond Memories of Williamsport
By Connie Stein Egli of Riverside,
Pennsylvania
Born 1929

It is so nice to bring back memories of my Williamsport days by going down memory lane.

Early in my life, I became aware of the ragman, who lived in a small old house in the alley behind our garage. He had an old horse than pulled an old cart to collect rags. After the horse died, he pushed the cart. I've always wondered what happened to him.

Transeau Elementary School was a pleasant experience when we played dodge ball nearly every recess on the playground. My girlfriend, Esther looked on as she stood by with the help of crutches. Her accident happened when she tried to get a ball from under a train car on the siding that suddenly moved. I still can picture that leg amputation miserably, as I was with her when it occurred.

Watching a circus parade was a highlight as it passed the YWCA on Fourth Street on its way to the big, empty lot on Maynard Street.

Various swimming holes were favorites, such as under the Third and Fourth Street Bridges. A more daring location was in the river, near the then Canoe Club.

Ice skating spots were at the Kramer Pond and the South Williamsport Lake at the end of Market Street. A special even was to go to Eaglesmere for the toboggan run. That may still exist.

Bowman Field was a vital part of our lives. At the seventh inning stretch, we were allowed and rushed to get a ten-cent box of Cracker Jacks. I still know to take warm clothes for the late evenings there, even if it might only happen. Sadly, the in ground ball box behind the umpire has been removed.

We Love Our Pigeon Holes
By Linda Stein of Muncy, Pennsylvania
Born 1944

It was the 1950s in Muncy, Pennsylvania. There was a man in Muncy who was the town drunk. As a girl, I accepted this characterization as gospel. His name was David Egli. They called him "Crocket Egli" after the then-popular song lyrics "Davey, Davey Crocket, king of the wild frontier".

His fantastic backyard on North Main Street would excite any child. Wide-eyed, I saw strange displays along the path to the back alley. Tools arranged as totem poles, a wigwam, scary faces drawn on things, and animal bones arranged in patterns. What I didn't know was the contents of the old shed.

The secret world of the shed was not known until many years later, when granddaughter Bonnie told her story. Inside and under the shed was a DEEP TRENCH.

As a little girl, Bonnie didn't care that Papap was the town drunk. She was his special little girl. When they played, he would go into the trench and reach up for Bonnie to jump into his arms. They played in their rug-lined secret trench. The rest of the family knew nothing of this. During these years, Crocket Egli was only known as the town drunk.

Decades later, another discovery was made by another of Papap's grandchildren, Dane Egli. Dane was a military officer taking an academic class at the War College in Washington, D.C. Dane happened to have inherited a military photo of Papap, who had served in World War I. The photo showed Papap on his warhorse. Dane shared this photo of soldier Egli on the horse with the professor, and together they discovered writing on the back of the photo. The writing indicated that Papap Egli had participated in every major battle in Europe during World War I. The professor was astounded that any one soldier could have survived such a listing of battles.

The people of Muncy have had a profound and rude awakening. Yes. We still remember the town drunk, but now we know the whole story.

Fresh Manure Warmed My Feet!
By Milton I. Beacker of Gaines,
Pennsylvania
Born 1930

I was born December 4, 1930 at the family farm in Carter Camp, the youngest of five children. I had one sister and three brothers and was delivered by Dr. Meikle of Galeton.

Mom said Dad paced the floor as it was deer season, and he was going to a hunting camp in Black Forest, near Jersey Shore, PA, as there were no deer in their area then. They named me Milton (which I hated and became

Granpa Beacker, Grandma Margaret, and Grandpa Carl

"Bake") after Milton Braun, who had taught school in Coudersport for years and owned the store in Germania. My parents were worried, because I didn't start talking until I was nearly two.

My brother, Vernon and I went to a one-room schoolhouse in Carter Camp, grades one through eight, taught by Miss Leanore Karhan. I credit her for most of my learning, although I graduated from Galeton High School and joined the Marines during the Korean War. Vernon and I walked up and down two steep hills to get to school. In the winter, we rode a Flexible Flyer hand sled downhill to school, Brother on the bottom and me on top.

One day, Miss Karhan was lying on a bench with a towel on her head. She had been hit in the eye by a piece of wood she was splitting.

Dad wondered why we walked the road home, because it was further. We stopped at the Carter Camp Store, as Mrs. Schribner would give us a free sucker whenever we had a penny, which bought three. A penny was like gold!

After seven and a half years, we went to Germania School. We walked to Carter Camp Store, which was four miles, and got picked up by a team of horses. In wintertime, it was a sleigh, and we covered up with a heavy horse blanket.

I remember having to wear corduroy knickers, which I hated. I had to save my shoes for school, so I went barefoot all summer. On a white, frosty morning, going to get the cows, I'd jump into fresh manure to warm my feet. It was messy, but it felt good.

We had a fair-sized farm, but we also worked my aunt's farm on the road to Cherry Springs. When I was five or six, Dad picked the big potatoes and left the little ones for me. I hated that job, but if I pick good, he took me to Carter Camp Store for a Mr. Goodbar, which was five cents then. If I didn't pick good, I got something that wasn't good.

I hurried home to do my chores so I could listen to *The Lone Ranger* on a radio that ran on a car battery, which had to be taken to town to be recharged.

There were two brothers, a neighbor boy, and myself who were like the four musketeers. In winter, we made Yankee Jumpers, which were old barrel staves with a seat, with bees' wax on the runners. Each of us tried to have the fastest one.

One buddy on a nearby farm and I used to go in his dad's barn and tie the cats' tails together, and then put them over a beam in the haymow. Their old dog, Fido, hated cats, so after the cats finished fighting, he chased them. We thought this was great fun, but one of us always kept an eye on the house for his dad! Our fun times would have been over.

One afternoon, the four of us got off school to get a Christmas tree for the school. We went far to get more time out of school. One of the brothers climbed up to cut the top from a bigger tree with an old dull handsaw. He was sawing and holding on to the top of the tree. Down he came. Luckily, he didn't get hurt too bad!

We all got along good most of the time. Once, the brothers ganged up on me. I waited for the one I liked the least at the schoolhouse corner and popped him in the nose. After that,

Milton's father, Carl Beacker, Sr.

Milton by the farm truck

they left me alone. Then we got to be buddies.

We worked together, planting potatoes or trees for seventy-five cents a day. They had an old car with just a seat and a platform we used to haul potatoes or whatever for a day's work. Gas was twenty-five cents a gallon. Once they had a flat tire, and we didn't have money for a new one. Their father was a great blacksmith, so he made a clamp and put two tires together. You could hear us wherever we went as it clopped.

My brothers and I got along really well, except for the one next to me. From age six, I had a cow to milk night and morning, as he did. He gave me a quarter to milk his. Then he would go to town and play pool for money. One night I got tired of that and popped him in the nose, ran up the silo, and put the silage down on him. But he came up, and I got a good thrashing!

I can remember Dad going to town to get flour, sugar, salt, and coffee. We had our own potatoes, beef, pork, chickens, etc.

Another job I had, and my worst one, was when we butchered pigs. Dad caught the blood for bloodworst. My job was to sit in the snow and stir it until it got cold.

Those were tough times. Mom and Dad did many things to make a living. He had two teams he farmed with and hauled logs to a sawmill about three miles away. We kept hunters, they took up a birthday collection when I was very young until I was about nine, with which my parents bought war bonds that I had for many years.

One hunter, a big man, was deaf and speechless. Because he got a deer, they celebrated. He wasn't a drinker and got sick. He went outside and lost his false teeth in the snow. No one knew where he had been. I found the teeth in the spring, frozen in ice. I ran in the house and told my mom I had found two funny looking horseshoes. We sent them to him and every year, he brought me a big bag of candy.

My grandfather lived with us, also. He had pure white hair, a mustache, and walked with a cane. He fed the chickens and gathered the eggs. He kept telling my dad that rats were getting the eggs. One day, he caught the two rats – my two brothers coming out of the small hole the chickens used. They were sneaking in, punching a hole in each end of the shell, sucking the egg out, and putting the empty shell back in the nest. He took his cane to them! They called them the Katzenjammer Kids, always picking on Grandpa.

Mom always told about my sister coming up missing! She could hear her yelling for help but didn't know where she was. Finally, she found her in the outhouse, a two-hole building out by the barn. She had stuck her head down the small hole and couldn't get out!

Dad, my brother, and I went weekly to Renovo to peddle potatoes, apples, eggs, and sometimes dressed chickens. I got to go up the

Grandpa Beacker and Milton

steps to the houses, knock on the doors, and ask, "Do you care for any apples, potatoes, or a dressed chicken"? I guess the people thought I was real cute, because I sold a lot, sometimes as much as my dad and brother.

Farming Wasn't That Bad
By Louise M. Frankenberger of Loganton, Pennsylvania
Born 1928

Our father had bought a farm but he lost it during the Depression. He had always farmed, so he rented a farm in 1936. The family grew. Our family was large, twelve girls and five boys. We are all living today. The oldest is eighty-three and the youngest is sixty. I am one of twins. We all had the same mother and father.

We worked in the fields the old-fashioned way, with none of the modern farm machinery they have today. We milked cows by hand, and we never complained. Father would take wheat and corn to the mill to be ground. Mother baked bread and cinnamon rolls.

We only had mules and a wagon to go anywhere. We never knew what it was like to go to a store. Dad would go to the store maybe once a month for sugar and salt. We never knew what it was like to go anywhere. We could walk to Grandma's and Grandpa's house, down a lane and through the woods. We had to wade across a small creek.

We did not have toys to play with. So we made things with what we had to entertain ourselves.

In the winter, we went sled riding. Dad usually went with us. The snow seemed to be deeper then. They did not have the equipment they have today.

The women would gather at homes and have wool parties. The home that had the wool washed it and dried it. Then it had to be pulled, and any dirt left in it had to be picked out. They would make blankets for the winter.

Christmas was a good time. We kids would each set a dinner plate under the Christmas tree. In the morning, it would be filled with candy, nuts, and an orange. Maybe there would be a little something else for each of us. I remember one time I received a ten-cent play wristwatch. I was happier then than kids are these days with a room full of toys.

I went to school in a one-room school.

Back then, the teacher could spank the children. I never got a spanking in school. We had to go get water at the nearest neighbor's house for the school. The teacher would let two of us go at a time.

We had kerosene lamps and lanterns at night in the hallway. Upstairs was a lantern and a chamber pot to use if you had to get up. There was no running water in the house. We had a watering trough with water running all the time. We had an old cook stove in the kitchen with a water tank at the side to heat water. It always had to be filled.

Mother had a wash boiler to heat water to wash. She washed with a scrub board. I can still see her washing. She also made her own soap. She never had anything easy.

We always got a lot of company, living on the farm. They always made it for a meal.

I never wanted to farm, so I made sure I did not marry a farmer. When I look back, it wasn't so bad after all.

Behind the Mystery Door
By V.J. Vane of Trout Run, Pennsylvania
Born 1952

Every Saturday morning from 1959 until 1965, I would make the trip to Grandma's house to labor what seemed an eternity for fifty cents. My instincts told me she lay awake into the wee hours, inventing small tasks to add to my ever-growing list of chores.

I remember vividly the little salt and pepper shakers sitting side by side, row after row calling out to be dusted, how much fun it was to stick the freshly laundered clothes just close enough for the tight wringer on her whirling washer to suck in, and how she sat the bread plate on the same corner of the kitchen table where I would claim my midday reward, a warm lunch of sizzling ham, home fries, and a vegetable of her choosing. But nothing sticks to me as clearly as the adventure of climbing the steep, narrow stairs to do the weekly cleaning of the bedrooms.

For then I would catch a glimpse of that black, wooden door at the end of the hallway. For months, the anticipation of getting a look inside that dark walnut grained door consumed me as I helped Grandma to dust, sweep, and change the soiled linens. As the months and years passed, my weekly chores became more and more mundane and the curiosity of that barrier more obsessive. I found myself exorbitantly volunteering for any chore that would get me up those stairs to see if that door might be ajar.

Gradually, my girlish intimidations blossomed into full pre-adolescent boldness, and one Saturday morning, I awoke knowing this was the day I would relinquish my pent-up curiosities. That door would be opened at any cost!

I ate my steaming oatmeal rapidly, dressed with a speed I am sure amazed my mother, and after a quick goodbye kiss, found myself hurrying up the broken sidewalk to the familiar structure that housed that door.

As I clambered up the well-worn porch steps, my anticipation came to an abrupt halt, for there was Grandma, sporting a new straw hat, rusted watering can and soiled gloves in hand. Oh no, this could not be happening; it couldn't be, it was impossible! Suddenly a warm breeze awoke my senses, and I knew Grandma was indeed about to fulfill her springtime ritual, the planting of her sweat peas. Sheer disappointment filled me as I realized I would not be ascending the stairs that day.

As we dug the tiny, narrow rows in the moist, spring ground, my mind churned relentlessly, devising a scheme that would enable me to ascend those stairs to that long-anticipated revelation.

Soon, the compounding curiosity forced me to utter in my most innocent voice that I was thirsty and wouldn't she too like a glass of water. At her surprised but pleased response, I ran as fast as I could past the garden, through the back door, right by the sink, and straight up those stairs, until I was face-to-face with that door.

A hurried peek through the window curtain confirmed Grandma was still busy hoeing; never guessing her sweet granddaughter could have an ulterior motive for quenching her thirst.

Then it happened. The doorknob called to me and as I turned that cold, hard, metal the door slowly creaked open. The first thing to envelope me was the stillness of that room. The tattered shade, half pulled, allowed streams of sunlight in, revealing the treasures strewn about. An instant passion for antiques filled me as I saw an old Victrola sitting stately by a pile of unspun records. Ornate picture frames,

oil lamps, weathered baskets, old advertising tins, forgotten volumes of long-ago read books lay discarded and dust covered.

Through the decades, Grandma's outdated household items had sat quietly behind that closed door, developing into a collection any seasoned antique dealer would envy. I knew this hoard of valuables would be mine!

To this day, I cannot remember what clever words I used or how I possibly flattered her or if I ever got her that glass of water, but I do know that as I sit here writing this, that old Victrola stares back at me. Those weathered baskets, ornate frames, and advertising tins adorn my home and at any given time, I can gaze at them and in my mind, I am right back in Grandma's house, dust rag in my hand.

The Loss of a Beloved Uncle
By Jane Snyder of Loganton, Pennsylvania
Born 1932

I am now seventy-nine years old, but my story happened back during World War II. In 1944, I was eleven years old. My mom, dad, little sister, and I lived on a small farm way out in the country in central Pennsylvania. My dad farmed during the day and worked at Piper Aircraft from three until eleven, making planes for the war.

This story is really not my story but my Uncle Sam's story. He married my mom's sister, Aunt Siv. Uncle Sam was my very favorite uncle. He talked with me, played with me (especially rummy), teased me, and braided my long hair into pigtails. We would sing silly songs together and laugh.

I'll never forget the Christmas he dressed up as Santa Claus and came to our house. I knew it was him the moment I saw his twinkling blue eyes above the white beard. He handed me a box, which held the very cowgirl outfit I had asked Santa for.

When Uncle Sam went to war, Aunt Siv moved in with our family. He landed at Normandy in 1944. A few days later, the mailman came down our lane and handed Aunt Siv a telegram. It said Uncle Sam had been wounded at St. Lo, France. We were all very scared and worried.

Since Dad worked evenings, it was my job to go out over the hill to the pasture and bring the cows in to be milked. On a hot August late

Uncle Sam, Mom, Woody, Grandpa, Dad, Nancy, Jane, and Grandma

afternoon, Mom sent me to fetch the cows. The mean old bull decided he did not want me in the pasture that day. He chased me, and I ran as fast as I could and climbed a big old tree.

I was high enough in the tree that I could see our house, front yard and the lane down over the hill as my story unfolded before my eyes, like a movie. The first car held Uncle Sam's parents, sister, and brother, Dick. In the second car was our mailman.

Mom, Aunt Siv, and my sister came out into the front yard. The mailman handed Aunt Siv a telegram. This time it said Uncle Sam had died August 3, 1944 at Marigny, France.

Everyone began to cry and scream. Aunt Siv ran back and forth in the yard. After everything quieted down, someone asked, "Where's Jane"?

Mom remembered then that she had sent

Aunt Siv, Jane, and Nancy (sister)

me to fetch the cows. Dick came out for me. He helped me out of the tree as the bull pawed the ground and snorted.

I was devastated. On hard days, I would go out the path to the outhouse to sit and cry and talk to God. I think I mostly asked, "Why"? I couldn't believe I would never see Uncle Sam again. For many, many months, every time I would hear a car coming down the lane, I would run to see if it was Uncle Sam coming home to me.

A Tribute to Amos E. Hunter
By Lauren Shumbat of Williamsport, Pennsylvania
Born 1951

My paternal grandfather, Elmer Hunter was employed as a rougher with a finishing mill in Lebanon, Pennsylvania. My father told me that Elmer did not drink, but he would take the other workers to a nearby pub on Fridays for drinks.

Elmer's wife, Harriet, was born in September of 1869. They had four children my father told me during their time together. Elmer passed away at a young age.

One of their children, Amos Ellsworth Hunter, was my father. He was born June 27, 1896. He quit school at the age of fourteen to go to work, because of his father dying. His mother needed help to feed and care for the other children.

Amos was a private with the First F.A. Regiment Company, Battery D during the short Mexican Emergency in 1916. Amos received the Mexican Service Medal for his service.

Amos married Clara E. Applegate, and they were divorced in 1948. They had five children before separating, Charles, William, Betty, Robert, and Lois. To my knowledge, they had fourteen grandchildren.

After the divorce, Amos married Lorrin A. Ayers on May 21, 1948. They had two children, Lauren Amy (me), born January 30, 1951, and Amos Edsall (Ed), born December 15, 1951. Lauren has two children, and Amos Ed has four children. Lauren's children are Stacey Lorraine and Larry Ray. Ed's children are Amos Edgar, Aaron Elliot, Marjorie, and Alexis. Lauren has five grandchildren as well.

Amos worked for fifty-two years with the former Penn-Central Railroad and was

Amy, Roxanna, Eddie, and Amos

a member of the Brotherhood of Railway Firemen and Engineers for forty-five and three-fourths years when he retired. He worked in the yard and around the station until he was able to make Engine Fireman and finally advanced to Engineer. Amos read every railroad manual and through his knowledge of Union matters, he could recite any section of railroad laws and requirements.

Amos assisted many railroad personnel when there was a court or pending Brotherhood matter. With little formal education, Amos was very knowledgeable and able to tackle many situations as a Railroad representative. He was not a college-educated attorney, but many knew of his knowledge, so they would ask him to represent them. Of course, without a license he never asked for a wage to represent them.

As a child, I can remember my father as a very good gardener, and we always had a large garden where he cared tirelessly for the plants until it was time to harvest them. My mother would clean and cook the vegetables. We lived on his planting expertise through the winter until the next crop was ready.

Dad also taught me how to fly fish. We would go out many days and stay until it got late in the morning. I must say fishing was never my forte, but I was rarely corrected about not wanting to fish or any mischief I got into. He would take me through the woods, and we talked about animals or the flora. I can vividly remember him helping any stray dog or cat, and we always had pets around our home.

One episode has remained a part of life with my father. While working as an engineer, Amos saw a large crow either hit by a vehicle or grazed by flying into the train. I was quite young, six or seven, although I was old enough to follow his directions. Dad and I cared for the black, noisy crow as it regained strength. We put the crow in a birdcage we had used for parakeets. After it was able to fly, we opened the cage door and chased the crow out. It did not fly away immediately, but after encouragement, the crow flew into a tree and squawked back at us. Although that crow was a wild bird, it would always come back to get the feed my father and I put out.

Although this loving, caring man was the father I admired, he chose to drink heavily, which led him to abuse his wives and become an alcoholic. Amos never abused me, but his wives dealt with his rage. I think Amos went through some experiences that altered his life. This may have caused him to do some unkind things, but I do not think it truly changed or soiled him.

Do any of us know about his previous life? If you have any proof or documentation of any family members, please make us aware so the history can be updated. Thank you and my God bless all of you. I offer Shalom and welcome to everyone in the Amos Ellsworth Hunter Family.

Amy and Shirley

384

Make It on a Cake of Ice and Set It in the Sun
By Theresa B. Esposit of Williamsport, Pennsylvania
Born 1931

I grew up in the small town of Renovo, Pennsylvania, about sixty miles west of Williamsport.

I went to St. Joseph's School, which was a mile from home. We walked four miles a day, because we came home for lunch. We never missed school or had delays because of snow, and we had snow from October to March. The only time school was cancelled was the 1936 flood.

We had an outhouse up about twenty steps from the house. We had the biggest tomatoes in a plot next to the outhouse. My sister and I would go up to the outhouse before bed, carrying a candle. We would *play* with the melted wax, pouring it between our fingers and then pulling them apart. It's a wonder we didn't burn the outhouse down. We had a big wooden rocking horse in the outhouse that we would sit on. We would look through the *Sears Catalog*, tearing out the colored pages. They did not work well to wipe with. We also had a chamber pot to use at night.

We had a party line phone on the wall. If someone was on it, we would hang up and try again, sometimes for a half hour or more. Then the operator would come on and say, "Number, please" and we would give her the number we wanted to call.

We had to make our own entertainment.

Mary, Theresa, and Eddie

We only had one radio, and Dad got to listen to what he wanted to. That was always the news.

We lived along a state road. We would put each other in a tire and roll down the hill. Oh, what fun! Roller skating was fun, too. We had keys to tighten our skates on our shoes. Dad would always say, "Don't make them too tight or you'll pull the soles off your shoes".

A mountain was behind our house. We would climb it a lot. We picked blueberries (huckleberries) and blackberries. Mom always made sure we had a stick to put in the bushes first to make sure there were no snakes in them. We would climb to the top of the mountain where there was a small stream and drink out of our hands. Gram always said, "If it ran over seven stones, it is pure". Oh, what faith.

We had a coal stove in the kitchen and a heater also in the room. There was no heat upstairs, only a small round register. We took turns dressing and undressing over it.

Saturdays were bath days. They fired up the stove and put water on to heat. Then the tub was put down by the stove, and chairs were put around it and covered by towels. We took turns, two or three in the same water.

Sunday nights, Mom and Gram filled tubs of water to heat for Monday's washing. We had a wringer washer. I loved to put the clothes through it.

Tuesdays were ironing day. Mom would put the flat irons on the stove to heat. When they got hot, we would take the handle and put it on the iron. When it got cold, we would exchange it for a hot one. I got to iron the pillowcases and hankies. We didn't have Kleenex back then.

Gram baked at least twice a week, always on Saturday so we could have fried dough for breakfast. Gram fired up the stove to bake. The pipes would get really hot. She would wet cloths and put them on the pipes. I can't believe we never had a fire.

We used a lot of flour, which came in twenty-five pound and fifty-pound cloth sacks. Some of them had flowers and some were plain. Mom made our dresses out of them, and even made bloomers to match.

We swam in the Susquehanna River. We had to cross about four or five sets of tracks to get there. We would have to crawl under the cars to get to the river. Mom would stand on the porch and tell us when to go, as she could see a long way from the porch. Swimming was fun except when we had to dodge the turds floating down the river.

We had an icebox. The iceman came twice a week. We could get a ten-cent or a twenty-five cent chunk of ice. We laugh now because Mom told us never to put anything hot in the icebox or it would spoil. Now we know it would melt the ice. We always had homemade ice cream in the winter so we could use icicles and not have to buy ice.

We never shopped for groceries. Mom called Dwyer's Store and ordered over the phone. They delivered them at no charge. If they forgot something, they would bring it back. We always had homemade soup, except for tomato. One day, Mom asked us to go to the A&P and get a can of Campbell's tomato soup. When we got home, we had a can of mushroom soup, because we thought Campbell's only made tomato soup.

I remember hobos coming for food. My Gram never refused them.

One of the best memories I have is of borrowing from neighbors. We borrowed eggs, flour, sugar, or whatever we needed. No one went to the store every day. When the neighbor would borrow something, she would say when her husband went to the store, she would pay it back. Mom or Gram would say, "Make it on a cake of ice and set it in the sun". I love this saying. I think they made it up themselves, because no one has heard it before.

Index A
By Hometown

Virginia Bell Lesher	Coalport	Pennsylvania	171
Linda "Hock" Avery	Cogan Station	Pennsylvania	104
Marybeth Carpenter	Cogan Station	Pennsylvania	144
Jay B. Decker	Cogan Station	Pennsylvania	46
Nellie Harlan	Cogan Station	Pennsylvania	228
Betty Johnston	Cogan Station	Pennsylvania	304
Jean Shink	Cogan Station	Pennsylvania	133
Marian Webster	Cogan Station	Pennsylvania	260
Herb Dubler	Connellsville	Pennsylvania	371
John G. McEllhenney	Cornwall	Pennsylvania	197
Jeanne Hawkins	Coudersport	Pennsylvania	307
Jane E. Lane	Coudersport	Pennsylvania	211
Jean Lent	Coudersport	Pennsylvania	285
Everett Saulter	Coudersport	Pennsylvania	325
Jane Kropinak	Covode	Pennsylvania	19
Viola M. Barrett	Curwensville	Pennsylvania	187
Fred J. Guarino	Curwensville	Pennsylvania	128
Ida E. Norris	Curwensville	Pennsylvania	45
Dorothy A. Phillips	Curwensville	Pennsylvania	30
Joseph Shaw	Curwensville	Pennsylvania	229
George A. Shearer	Curwensville	Pennsylvania	21
Pearl E. Smith	Danville	Pennsylvania	275
Mary L. Shenk	Denver	Pennsylvania	262
Marian Slawson Feness	Depew	New York	230
James Lucas	Downey	California	309
Elke Burrows	Eldred	Pennsylvania	156
Leon E. Hillyard	Eldred	Pennsylvania	54
Michael L. Myers	Elizabethtown	Pennsylvania	79
Ernest C. Butler	Emporium	Pennsylvania	39
Ken Gerg	Emporium	Pennsylvania	193
Twila Grimm	Emporium	Pennsylvania	308
Howard E. McDonald	Emporium	Pennsylvania	317
Ken Ostrum	Emporium	Pennsylvania	23
Martha T. Ryan	Emporium	Pennsylvania	169
Marcia A. Hoffman	Endicott	New York	59
Fred L. Adams	Erie	Pennsylvania	365
Audrey Zilker	Fillmore	New York	119
Jean Cooke Redka	Frosty Valley	Pennsylvania	198
Patricia Redka Sounder	Frosty Valley	Pennsylvania	199
Milton I. Beacker	Gaines	Pennsylvania	378
Norman L. Davis	Galeton	Pennsylvania	235
William M. Morey	Galeton	Pennsylvania	108
Ernest C. Pagano	Galeton	Pennsylvania	185
Eva M. Shutt	Genesee	Pennsylvania	361
Pauline B. Bell	Ginter	Pennsylvania	253
William James Stiffler, Jr.	Gladys	Virginia	302
James K. Williams	Goudersport	Pennsylvania	118
Eva B. Gouldthread	Grampian	Pennsylvania	261
Ellen AnnVerbjar	Colegrove Greeley	Colorado	196
D. LaVerne Zilcosky Sober	Greensburg	Pennsylvania	118
Donald Lindsey	Hanover	Pennsylvania	197
Jeanne Sherman	Harrison Valley	Pennsylvania	84

Evelyn M. Gibson	Hinckley	Ohio	164
Genevieve Snell	Horseheads	New York	237
Carol Confer	Houston	Texas	68
Dawn R. Zetto	Houston	Texas	203
Nancy Brown	Houtzdale	Pennsylvania	374
Shirley L. Johnson	Houtzdale	Pennsylvania	40
Elizabeth "Betty" Sustrik Reese	Houtzdale	Pennsylvania	270
Joseph Zeigler	Houtzdale	Pennsylvania	355
Joan Fox	Hughesville	Pennsylvania	300
Charles S. Hughes	Hughesville	Pennsylvania	363
Jack R. Jones	Hughesville	Pennsylvania	78
Clarence McHenry, Jr.	Hughesville	Pennsylvania	355
John H. Phillips	Hughesville	Pennsylvania	134
Barbara Leavy Spotts	Hughesville	Pennsylvania	119
Norma L. Flook	Jersey Shore	Pennsylvania	159
Alice H. Fox	Jersey Shore	Pennsylvania	88
John Lewis Guiswite	Jersey Shore	Pennsylvania	330
Sally A. Guiswite	Jersey Shore	Pennsylvania	15
Mary Prince	Jersey Shore	Pennsylvania	339
Mary Heisey Singley	Jersey Shore	Pennsylvania	147
Geraldine Starr	Jersey Shore	Pennsylvania	97
Pauline M. Steinbacher	Jersey Shore	Pennsylvania	369
Ron McGonigal	Jobstown	New Jersey	260
Mary Lou DiNardo	Johnsonburg	Pennsylvania	319
Elmer Ferragine	Johnsonburg	Pennsylvania	294
Georgeanne Freeburg	Johnsonburg	Pennsylvania	323
Kathy Fowler Alaskey Rickard	Johnsonburg	Pennsylvania	21
Joe Venderi	Johnsonburg	Pennsylvania	320
Christine Wolfe	Johnsonburg	Pennsylvania	232
Cy Anderson	Kane	Pennsylvania	221
Peg Coulter	Kane	Pennsylvania	175
Olivia Hartman	Kane	Pennsylvania	360
Barbara Hepler	Kane	Pennsylvania	329
Rocky Holland	Kane	Pennsylvania	305
Judith E. Hudson	Kane	Pennsylvania	177
Mary Ann Fees Johnston	Kane	Pennsylvania	123
Myles E. Casey Jones	Kane	Pennsylvania	163
Mary Jane Wright	Kersey	Pennsylvania	58
Winifred A. Doan	Knoxville	Pennsylvania	106
Georganna Doran	Knoxville	Pennsylvania	319
Mary Wetmore	Knoxville	Pennsylvania	294
Eugene F. Bliskey	Lady Lake	Florida	210
Shirley Wiggins	Lancaster	Pennsylvania	70
Ellen Trebik Wiker	Lancaster	Pennsylvania	45
Gwen Klus	Laporte	Pennsylvania	354
Christine Taft	Lawrenceville	Pennsylvania	117
Mathilda Jane Smith	Lewis Run	Pennsylvania	16
Carol Songer	Linestone	New York	254
Harold Wicks	Litchfield	Pennsylvania	31
Ida M. Condon	Lock Haven	Pennsylvania	97
June O. Naval	Lock Haven	Pennsylvania	130
Ruth Berry	Loganton	Pennsylvania	141

Louise M. Frankenberger	Loganton	Pennsylvania	381
Barbara A. Smith	Loganton	Pennsylvania	362
Jane Snyder	Loganton	Pennsylvania	382
Bob Johnston	Lutherville	Maryland	137
Glenn C. Johnson	Madera	Pennsylvania	42
Ernest T. McKay	Mansfield	Pennsylvania	97
Helen McKay	Mansfield	Pennsylvania	102
Imogene Winnie	Mansfield	Pennsylvania	180
A. K. Reitz	Mayport	Pennsylvania	210
Carolyn A. Hanna	McElhattan	Pennsylvania	103
Irene Morton	McElhattan	Pennsylvania	264
Patrick O'Brien	Meridian	Idaho	376
Linda J. Brungard	Mill Hall	Pennsylvania	288
Glenn Owen Confer	Mill Hall	Pennsylvania	95
Vivian P. Miller	Mill Hall	Pennsylvania	57
Alice L. Wheeler	Mill Hall	Pennsylvania	26
Florence Bailey	Millerton	Pennsylvania	335
Jennie Knorr	Millheim	Pennsylvania	282
Mary L. Shaffer	Montgomery	Pennsylvania	298
Raymond L. Allison	Montoursville	Pennsylvania	57
Frank H. Freezer	Montoursville	Pennsylvania	62
Evelyn F. Gehr	Montoursville	Pennsylvania	296
Mary Lee Harris	Montoursville	Pennsylvania	76
Betty McKinney Koser	Montoursville	Pennsylvania	28
Rosemary McKinney	Montoursville	Pennsylvania	117
Jane S. Naugle	Montoursville	Pennsylvania	286
Donna O. Pongrat	Montoursville	Pennsylvania	212
Dick Sheltis	Montoursville	Pennsylvania	231
Meda E. Stroble	Montoursville	Pennsylvania	105
Thelma Walker	Montoursville	Pennsylvania	337
Shirley Rifle	Montrose	Pennsylvania	270
Marie A. Wilcox	Morris	Pennsylvania	312
Shirley A. Carey	Morris Run	Pennsylvania	134
Edna M. Burge	Morrisdale	Pennsylvania	83
Linda Kopchik	Morrisdale	Pennsylvania	98
Jean L. Booth	Muncy	Pennsylvania	151
Sarah Hays Bubb Bruch	Muncy	Pennsylvania	75
Ronald F. Calkins	Muncy	Pennsylvania	50
June B. Edwards	Muncy	Pennsylvania	375
Linford Frey, Jr.	Muncy	Pennsylvania	136
Nancy Hess	Muncy	Pennsylvania	176
June Elaine Woodling Houseknecht	Muncy	Pennsylvania	13
Iva McCoy	Muncy	Pennsylvania	100
Margaret Plotts	Muncy	Pennsylvania	102
Robert M. Rinn	Muncy	Pennsylvania	230
Melva Smith	Muncy	Pennsylvania	202
Linda Stein	Muncy	Pennsylvania	378
Barbara L. Faque Sterling Wood	Muncy	Pennsylvania	49
Alice Redis Hevner	North Bend	Pennsylvania	203
Karen Dietrich	North Huntingdon	Pennsylvania	283
Richard H. Allison	Ocala	Florida	280
Barbara Danko	Osceola Mills	Pennsylvania	206

Harold E. Jones	Osceola Mills	Pennsylvania	321
Melvin D. Woodring	Osceola Mills	Pennsylvania	52
Darrell D. Harris	Oswayo	Pennsylvania	238
Elaine F. Harris	Oswayo	Pennsylvania	26
Rosanne Conaway	Oswego	New York	332
Ruth E. Burns	Pendleton	South Carolina	219
Grace L. Butler	Philipsburg	Pennsylvania	271
Darlene Dutton	Philipsburg	Pennsylvania	141
Betty L. Hicks	Philipsburg	Pennsylvania	234
Martha M. Coval Kashtock	Philipsburg	Pennsylvania	240
James Coulson Laws	Philipsburg	Pennsylvania	291
Shirley Melius	Philipsburg	Pennsylvania	63
C. Dean Sharpless	Philipsburg	Pennsylvania	354
Charles E. Sharpless	Philipsburg	Pennsylvania	367
Barbara Long Glover	Pittsburgh	Pennsylvania	237
Richard Bova	Port Allegany	Pennsylvania	263
James Gotshall	Port Allegany	Pennsylvania	256
Clyde R. Johnson	Port Allegany	Pennsylvania	36
Judy Niles	Port Allegany	Pennsylvania	150
Betty Plotts	Port Allegany	Pennsylvania	38
Patricia Brady Malone	Potomac	Maryland	353
Donna J. Jones	Pottstown	Pennsylvania	29
Mary Arnold	Renovo	Pennsylvania	17
Charles T. Barnum	Renovo	Pennsylvania	209
Ralph E. Crouse	Renovo	Pennsylvania	80
Lois E. Romanak	Renovo	Pennsylvania	145
Doreen Jo Cherry	Ridgway	Pennsylvania	129
Donald Speaker	Ridgway	Pennsylvania	133
Bill Thompson	Ridgway	Pennsylvania	320
Mary Skiba Siders	Riverside	California	77
Connie Stein Egli	Riverside	Pennsylvania	378
Leon Tillotson	Roaring Branch	Pennsylvania	151
Freda Foster	Rochester Mills	Pennsylvania	261
Gordon L. Vogt	Rocklin	California	299
Mary Jane Baker	Roulette	Pennsylvania	272
James Stebbins	Sabinsville	Pennsylvania	304
Floyd G. Jovenitti	Saint Marys	Pennsylvania	152
Mary E. Nelson	Saint Marys	Pennsylvania	229
Donald Shirley	Sarver	Pennsylvania	213
Geraldine Milliron	Scranton	Pennsylvania	297
Diann Lenig Ferry	Shamokin	Pennsylvania	195
Lynn V. Kemp	Shinglehouse	Pennsylvania	306
Ronald S. Worden	Shinglehouse	Pennsylvania	327
Luci Ross	Sigel	Pennsylvania	348
Marie Yoas	Sigel	Pennsylvania	110
Dorothy J. Britton	Smethport	Pennsylvania	86
David Johnson	Smethport	Pennsylvania	98
Shirley Ostrander	Smethport	Pennsylvania	215
Pauline P. Myers	Smoke Run	Pennsylvania	210
Arlene Eck	South Williamsport	Pennsylvania	152
Tom Woodring	South Williamsport	Pennsylvania	99
Thomas E. Gausman	St. Marys	Pennsylvania	217

Joyce S. Kuntz	St. Marys	Pennsylvania	43
Deloris M. Mertz	St. Marys	Pennsylvania	257
Audrey Meyer	St. Marys	Pennsylvania	254
Ruth Rupprecht	St. Marys	Pennsylvania	255
Catherine C. Straub	St. Marys	Pennsylvania	326
Kathleen J. Comilla	State College	Pennsylvania	123
Barbara J. Natalie	State College	Pennsylvania	122
Pete Bennett	Stevensville	Ontario	146
David L. C. Albert	Trout Run	Pennsylvania	182
Virginia M. Houseknecht	Trout Run	Pennsylvania	144
Jane V. Major	Trout Run	Pennsylvania	341
V.J. Vane	Trout Run	Pennsylvania	381
June Rovenolt Kline	Turbotville	Pennsylvania	160
Wanita Lane	Turtle Point	Pennsylvania	289
Donna Erway McCaslin	Ulysses	Pennsylvania	117
Candy Detwiler	Viola	Delaware	252
Lorrie Crawford Hartman	Watsontown	Pennsylvania	245
Robert (Buzz) Reynolds	Watsontown	Pennsylvania	167
Connie T. Brown	Wellsboro	Pennsylvania	356
Ivan W. Hunter, Jr.	Wellsboro	Pennsylvania	208
Betty Mengee	Wellsboro	Pennsylvania	121
Linda Schall Austin	Wellsville	New York	258
Shirley Mills	West Decatur	Pennsylvania	253
Bruce Shaw	West Decatur	Pennsylvania	128
Edward Raybuck	West Windsor	New Jersey	321
Otto Bud Burrows	Westfield	Pennsylvania	157
Patricia Butler	Westfield	Pennsylvania	344
Emily Cary	Westfield	Pennsylvania	328
Gene O. Harland	White Pine	Pennsylvania	162
Kathleen Horchen	Wilcox	Pennsylvania	281
Anonymous	Williamsport	Pennsylvania	44
Lois Bamonte	Williamsport	Pennsylvania	27
Shirley J. Confer	Williamsport	Pennsylvania	113
Sylvia Daniels	Williamsport	Pennsylvania	282
Nina J. Dymeck	Williamsport	Pennsylvania	319
Vivian A. Steinbacher Eck	Williamsport	Pennsylvania	48
Carolyn Eckert	Williamsport	Pennsylvania	211
Nancy W. Eichenlaub	Williamsport	Pennsylvania	277
Theresa B. Esposit	Williamsport	Pennsylvania	385
Mary Fischer	Williamsport	Pennsylvania	175
Kathleen L. Fullmer	Williamsport	Pennsylvania	97
Warren M. Garrison	Williamsport	Pennsylvania	273
Felicia Gelnett	Williamsport	Pennsylvania	353
Clara M. Gerber	Williamsport	Pennsylvania	76
Joy M. Grafius	Williamsport	Pennsylvania	75
John Hammond	Williamsport	Pennsylvania	177
Betty J. Hazel	Williamsport	Pennsylvania	41
Marian B. Hutchinson	Williamsport	Pennsylvania	267
Harold M. Ingram	Williamsport	Pennsylvania	315
Vivian I. Johnson	Williamsport	Pennsylvania	353
Ruth Garvey King	Williamsport	Pennsylvania	64
Rita Kittka	Williamsport	Pennsylvania	280

Myra Liddic	Williamsport	Pennsylvania	346
Elizabeth Madeira	Williamsport	Pennsylvania	281
Michael Marchese	Williamsport	Pennsylvania	223
Dominick "Chiz" Mazzante	Williamsport	Pennsylvania	174
Joan M. Miller	Williamsport	Pennsylvania	65
Katherine Moore Nittinger	Williamsport	Pennsylvania	183
Shirley Paulhamus	Williamsport	Pennsylvania	372
Verna Paulhamus	Williamsport	Pennsylvania	136
J. Milton Rogers	Williamsport	Pennsylvania	140
Audrae Ruby	Williamsport	Pennsylvania	247
Lauren Shumbat	Williamsport	Pennsylvania	383
Edson Snell	Williamsport	Pennsylvania	361
Martha Snell	Williamsport	Pennsylvania	39
Bonnie Springman	Williamsport	Pennsylvania	322
Barbara Steinruck	Williamsport	Pennsylvania	101
Elizabeth A. Stine	Williamsport	Pennsylvania	18
James H. Surfield	Williamsport	Pennsylvania	166
Nancy A. Toles	Williamsport	Pennsylvania	352
Helen Tucker	Williamsport	Pennsylvania	78
Patricia A. Vincent	Williamsport	Pennsylvania	270
Harry Wanamaker	Williamsport	Pennsylvania	360
Marion Wirth	Williamsport	Pennsylvania	218
Helen T. Spade	Woodland	Pennsylvania	371
Mary Ann Swoope	Woodland	Pennsylvania	373
James Schlimm	Yardley	Pennsylvania	252

Index B
By Year of Birth

Harold Wicks	1924	377
Christine Wolfe	1924	232
Cy Anderson	1925	221
Pauline B. Bell	1925	253
Eugene F. Bliskey	1925	210
Sarah Hays Bubb Bruch	1925	75
Arlene Eck	1925	152
Floyd G. Jovenitti	1925	152
Donna Erway McCaslin	1925	117
Dorothy A. Phillips	1925	30
Mary Prince	1925	339
Lois Bamonte	1926	27
Carolyn Eckert	1926	211
Eva B. Gouldthread	1926	261
June Elaine Woodling Houseknecht	1926	13
Glenn C. Johnson	1926	42
Joyce S. Kuntz	1926	43
Shirley Mills	1926	253
Ernest C. Pagano	1926	185
Dick Sheltis	1926	231
Priscilla Barrett	1927	31
Ida M. Condon	1927	97
Sylvia Daniels	1927	282
Frank H. Freezer	1927	62
James Lucas	1927	309
Iva McCoy	1927	100
Ruth Rupprecht	1927	255
Imogene Winnie	1927	180
Raymond L. Allison	1928	57
Clair F. Burns	1928	261
Otto Bud Burrows	1928	157
Grace L. Butler	1928	271
Blanche Chamberlin	1928	154
Nina J. Dymeck	1928	319
Louise M. Frankenberger	1928	381
Thomas E. Gausman	1928	217
Twila Grimm	1928	308
Darrell D. Harris	1928	238
Lola Jane Houchins	1928	304
Betty McKinney Koser	1928	28
Betty Mengee	1928	121
Herbert A. Schueltz	1928	154
Mathilda Jane Smith	1928	16
Jean L. Booth	1929	151
Ronald F. Calkins	1929	50
Winifred A. Doan	1929	106
Connie Stein Egli	1929	378
Elmer Ferragine	1929	294
Elaine F. Harris	1929	26
Vivian I. Johnson	1929	353
Elizabeth Madeira	1929	281
Howard E. McDonald	1929	317

Armilda Miller	1929	243
James Schlimm	1929	252
C. Dean Sharpless	1929	354
Barbara Leavy Spotts	1929	119
Eleanor M. Taylor	1929	284
Mary Wetmore	1929	294
Francis T. Ayers	1930	324
Milton I. Beacker	1930	378
Edna M. Burge	1930	83
Jean Lent	1930	285
Patricia Brady Malone	1930	353
Deloris M. Mertz	1930	257
Jane S. Naugle	1930	286
A. K. Reitz	1930	210
Joseph Shaw	1930	229
Mary Skiba Siders	1930	77
Edson Snell	1930	361
Dolores P. (Amon) Taylor	1930	58
Thelma Walker	1930	337
Barbara Danko	1931	206
Theresa B. Esposit	1931	385
Harold M. Ingram	1931	315
Myles E. Casey Jones	1931	163
Wanita Lane	1931	289
Robert Logue	1931	350
D. LaVerne Zilcosky Sober	1931	118
Helen T. Spade	1931	371
Irene G. Turnbaugh	1931	99
Patricia P. Ulrich	1931	178
Patricia A. Vincent	1931	270
Shirley Wiggins	1931	70
Phillip Yothers	1931	155
Richard Bova	1932	263
Norman L. Davis	1932	235
Mary Lou DiNardo	1932	319
June B. Edwards	1932	375
Linford Frey, Jr.	1932	136
Jane F. Grassi	1932	151
Virginia M. Houseknecht	1932	144
Martha M. Coval Kashtock	1932	240
Donald Lindsey	1932	197
Ken Ostrum	1932	23
Audrae Ruby	1932	247
Jane Snyder	1932	382
Ellen Trebik Wiker	1932	45
Marie A. Wilcox	1932	312
Barbara L. Faque Sterling Wood	1932	49
Marie Yoas	1932	110
Audrey Zilker	1932	119
Carol Confer	1933	68
Candy Detwiler	1933	252
Georgeanne Freeburg	1933	323

James Gotshall	1933	256
Alice Redis Hevner	1933	203
Marian B. Hutchinson	1933	267
Rita Kittka	1933	280
Gordon L. Vogt	1933	299
Herb Dubler	1934	371
Shirley H. Evans	1934	226
Joy Strauser Spare Himes	1934	72
Grace Landes	1934	158
Mary Marvin	1934	82
John G. McEllhenney	1934	197
Betty Plotts	1934	38
Mary L. Shaffer	1934	298
Donald Shirley	1934	213
Martha Snell	1934	39
Donald Speaker	1934	133
Richard H. Allison	1935	280
Florence Bailey	1935	335
Vivian A. Steinbacher Eck	1935	48
John Lewis Guiswite	1935	330
Kathleen Horchen	1935	281
Charles S. Hughes	1935	363
Myra Liddic	1935	346
Katherine Moore Nittinger	1935	183
Genevieve Snell	1935	237
Elizabeth A. Stine	1935	18
Dorothy J. Britton	1936	86
Shirley A. Carey	1936	134
Shirley J. Confer	1936	113
Ken Gerg	1936	193
Bob Johnston	1936	137
Rosemary McKinney	1936	117
Joan M. Miller	1936	65
Shirley Paulhamus	1936	372
Robert (Buzz) Reynolds	1936	167
Shirley Rifle	1936	270
Mary Jane Wright	1936	58
Patricia Butler	1937	344
Ralph E. Crouse	1937	80
Carolina F. Edwards	1937	107
Virginia A. English	1937	90
Mary Fischer	1937	175
Sally A. Guiswite	1937	15
Betty L. Hicks	1937	234
Arlene Yonker Klinczar	1937	294
William M. Morey	1937	108
Donna O. Pongrat	1937	212
Carol Songer	1937	254
Emily Cary	1938	328
Georganna Doran	1938	319
Norma L. Flook	1938	159
Judith Garrison	1938	33

Evelyn M. Gibson	1938	164
Virginia Bell Lesher	1938	171
Elizabeth "Betty" Sustrik Reese	1938	270
J. Milton Rogers	1938	140
Pete Bennett	1939	146
Ernest C. Butler	1939	39
Ellen Ann Verbjar Colegrove	1939	196
John Hammond	1939	177
June Rovenolt Kline	1939	160
Gwen Klus	1939	354
Shirley Ostrander	1939	215
Margaret Plotts	1939	102
Mary L. Shenk	1939	262
Barbara A. Smith	1939	362
Nancy Brown	1940	374
Elke Burrows	1940	156
Jay B. Decker	1940	46
Clyde R. Johnson	1940	36
Rachel (Sandra) McClintick	1940	190
Pearl E. Smith	1940	275
James Stebbins	1940	304
Catherine C. Straub	1940	326
David L. C. Albert	1941	182
Patrick Buccolini	1941	132
Warren M. Garrison	1941	273
Barbara J. Natalie	1941	122
Jean Shink	1941	133
Clair E. Slawson	1941	244
Nancy W. Eichenlaub	1942	277
James Fulmer	1942	295
Audrey Meyer	1942	254
Bruce Shaw	1942	128
James K. Williams	1942	118
Fred L. Adams	1943	365
Linda Schall Austin	1943	258
Viola M. Barrett	1943	187
Judy M. Cain	1943	135
Carolyn A. Hanna	1943	103
Marcia A. Hoffman	1943	59
Shirley Melius	1943	63
Melvin D. Woodring	1943	52
Ruth Berry	1944	141
Kathleen A. Coy	1944	228
Karen Dietrich	1944	283
Barbara Long Glover	1944	237
Betty J. Hazel	1944	41
Leon E. Hillyard	1944	54
Ruth Garvey King	1944	64
Patrick O'Brien	1944	376
Linda Stein	1944	378
Linda "Hock" Avery	1945	104
Diann Lenig Ferry	1945	195

Mary Lee Harris	1945	76
Nancy Hess	1945	176
Jennie Knorr	1945	282
Pauline P. Myers	1945	210
Christine Taft	1945	117
Dawn R. Zetto	1945	203
Larry Bunk	1946	239
Darlene Hanley	1946	209
Rocky Holland	1946	305
Irene Morton	1946	264
John H. Phillips	1946	134
Eva M. Shutt	1946	361
William James Stiffler, Jr.	1946	302
James H. Surfield	1946	166
Mary Ann Swoope	1946	373
Anonymous	1947	44
Mary Arnold	1947	17
Charles T. Barnum	1947	209
Judy Walker Bush	1947	232
Cheryl Dunlap	1947	318
Barbara Hepler	1947	329
Linda Kopchik	1947	98
Harry R. Litz	1947	37
Michael L. Myers	1947	79
Marsha Siple	1947	209
Patricia Redka Sounder	1947	199
Barbara Steinruck	1947	101
Alice L. Wheeler	1947	26
Linda J. Brungard	1948	288
Julie Hunsinger	1948	373
Ivan W. Hunter, Jr.	1948	208
Donna J. Jones	1948	29
Harry Wanamaker	1948	360
Judith E. Hudson	1949	177
David Johnson	1949	98
Shirley L. Johnson	1949	40
Linda L. Earle Marriner	1949	249
Judy Niles	1949	150
Kathy Fowler Alaskey Rickard	1949	21
Luci Ross	1949	348
George A. Shearer	1949	21
Bonnie Springman	1949	322
Bill Thompson	1949	320
Tom Woodring	1949	99
Joseph Zeigler	1949	355
Joan Fox	1950	300
Clarence McHenry, Jr.	1950	355
Jeanne Sherman	1950	84
Gene O. Harland	1951	162
Carol Leathem	1951	228
Lauren Shumbat	1951	383
Doreen Jo Cherry	1952	129

Darlene Dutton	1952	141
Jane V. Major	1952	341
V.J. Vane	1952	381
Robert Ginter	1953	92
Marybeth Carpenter	1954	144
Edward Raybuck	1955	321
Glenn Owen Confer	1957	95
Tammy Breighner	1961	356
William J. Brooks	1961	318
Douglas Tressler	1962	38
Felicia Gelnett	1968	353
Stacey Turner	1987	149
Kathleen J. Comilla	Unknown	123
Rosanne Conaway	Unknown	332
Freda Foster	Unknown	261
Lorrie Crawford Hartman	Unknown	245
Olivia Hartman	Unknown	360
Harold E. Jones	Unknown	321
Jack R. Jones	Unknown	78
Ron McGonigal	Unknown	260
Geraldine Milliron	Unknown	297
Judy Schell	Unknown	79
Mary Heisey Singley	Unknown	147
Geraldine Starr	Unknown	97
Pauline M. Steinbacher	Unknown	369
Nancy A. Toles	Unknown	352